Musical Lives and Times Examined

The publisher and the University of California Press Foundation gratefully acknowledge the generous support of the Constance and William Withey Endowment Fund in History and Music.

Musical Lives and Times Examined

Keynotes and Clippings, 2006–2019

Richard Taruskin

UNIVERSITY OF CALIFORNIA PRESS

University of California Press
Oakland, California

© 2023 by The Taruskin 2007 Revocable Living Trust

Library of Congress Cataloging-in-Publication Data

Names: Taruskin, Richard, author.
Title: Musical lives and times examined : keynotes and clippings, 2006–2019 / Richard Taruskin.
Description: Oakland, California : University of California Press, [2023] | Includes bibliographical references and index.
Identifiers: LCCN 2022033651 | ISBN 9780520392007 (hardback) | ISBN 9780520392014 (paperback) | ISBN 9780520392021 (ebook)
Subjects: LCSH: Taruskin, Richard. | Music—History and criticism. | Speeches, addresses, etc. | LCGFT: Speeches.
Classification: LCC ML423.T185 A5 2023 | DDC 814/.6—dc24/eng/20220812
LC record available at https://lccn.loc.gov/2022033651

32 31 30 29 28 27 26 25 24 23
10 9 8 7 6 5 4 3 2 1

CONTENTS

In Lieu of Dedication: Fine Friends, Presiding Spirits—László Somfai, Lyudmila Kovnatskaya, Richard L. Crocker vii

1. The Many Dangers of Music 1

LACI RÉSZE (LACI'S PART)

2. Liszt and Bad Taste 37
3. Goldmark's Queen: On Signifiers 66
4. Why You Cannot Leave Bartók Out 97
5. Liszt's Problems, Bartók's Problems, My Problems 125
6. Kodály's Pitiful Lament—and Mine 143

МИЛИНА ЧАСТЬ (MILA'S PART)

7. Russian Responses to Bach 165
8. So Much More Than a Composer 192
9. Rimsky-Korsakov Catches Up 211
10. Prokofieff's Problems—and Ours 244
11. Коле посвящается (for Kolya) 276
12. In from the Cold 299

13.	Flesh and Blood Juke Box	309
14.	Tales of Push and Pull	319
15.	Was Shostakovich a Martyr, or Is That Just Fiction?	328
16.	How to Win a Stalin Prize: Shostakovich and His Quintet	335

PARS RICARDI PRIMI (RICARDUS PRIMUS'S PART)

17.	Shooting a White Elephant	363
18.	Is This a Thing?	383
19.	Exoticism and Authenticity	407
20.	Pathos Is Banned	447
21.	Everybody Gotta Be Someplace: On Context	472
22.	Alluring Failure, Exhilarating Defeat	502
23.	Envoi: All Was Foreseen; Nothing Was Foreseen	512

Acknowledgments 525
Index 527

FIGURE 0.1. Magyar Tudományos Akadémia Zenetudományi Intézet (Hungarian Academy of Sciences Research Center for Musicology), Táncsics Mihály utca 7, Budapest. Photo courtesy László Gombos.

"Immortal Beloved." (In the 1994 Bernard Rose movie of that name, she was played by Isabella Rossellini.)

My nexus with this house and its inhabitants is vitally overdetermined. One of my long-ago graduate advisees, David Schneider, secured a grant to work for a year at the *Archívum* on the way to his dissertation, "Expression in Time of Objectivity: Nationality and Modernity in Five Concertos by Béla Bartók" (1997).[3] He came back from his year in Budapest with dissertation drafts, and also with a wife, Klára Móricz, who is now the Joseph E. and Grace W. Valentine Professor of Music at Amherst College (where her husband is Andrew W. Mellon Professor). Klára had been Somfai's assistant at the *Archívum*, and became my Berkeley *Doktorkind* in her turn. Both spouses have gone on to stellar careers in American musicology, but even without that brilliant outcome to justify it, Klára's old *chef* managed with good grace to stomach my indirect liability for the loss of his assistant. Indeed, my association with David and Klára only tightened the bond between me and the Hungarian musicological community; and once I had been invited to my first Budapest conference and given my first Budapest paper (chapter 4 herein), I

---

3. It formed the nucleus of Schneider's first book, *Bartók, Hungary, and the Renewal of Tradition: Case Studies in the Intersection of Modernity and Nationality* (Berkeley and Los Angeles: University of California Press, 2006).

became a happy perennial, having formed friendships with practically the whole of the Institute staff, as well as with the musicology faculty at the Franz Liszt Academy, Hungary's premier conservatory: László Vikarius, Somfai's successor as *Archívum* director; Tibor Tallián, the former head of the Institute; Pál Richter, his successor; Balázs Mikusi, who headed the music division at the Széchényi National Library; Katalin Komlós of the Academy, Anna Dalos of the Institute, and a host of others, have all become my friends. The reasons for our spontaneous mutual recognition had no doubt to do with the traditional assumptions of Hungarian musicians (recognized in The Ox by the title of the chapter in volume 4 that deals most extensively with Bartók and his contemporaries: "Social Validation"), but also with less tangible, less articulable matters that created a fraternal bond between Somfai and me that has lasted now for nearly four decades, and which has made of me not only an unofficial affiliate of the Institute but also an actual corresponding member of the parent organization, the Hungarian Academy of Sciences, for which honor Somfai submitted the nomination and to which I was elected in 2016.[4]

Even before he paid me that colossal compliment, I felt I owed a great debt of gratitude to my friend Laci, and a need to express my admiration for his character and achievements; so when on his seventy-fifth birthday in 2009 the editors of the journal *Muzsika* asked me to write a tribute that they could print, I was only too

---

4. My membership, contrary to expectation, has not been altogether passive. I was elected at a troubled time for the Academy, and I was unsure at first whether I should accept the honor. My friends assured me that from the inside I could help them resist government encroachments on academic freedom, and that my election had coincided with that of a new Academy president, László Lovász, a mathematician whom I already knew both by reputation and from having met him at Institute functions, where he had served in ceremonial capacities, so I both accepted membership and, the next year, responded to the Academy's request for support from its international network by writing the following letter to President Lovász, which was widely circulated on Hungarian social media:

I write as an honorary member of the Hungarian Academy of Sciences, as a frequent visitor to the Musicological Institute in Budapest where I have participated in numerous international conferences, as a member of the editorial board of the edition of Béla Bartók's works of which the institute is co-sponsor with Henle Editions, as a fellow laureate of the Kyoto Prize, and as one who has had the pleasure of meeting you at Institute functions in the past, to declare my fervent solidarity with my fellow scholars and with the Academy as you strive to maintain your independence and resist encroachments on your freedom of inquiry by shortsighted politicians.

Hungary has a high international profile in the musicological community thanks to the efforts of an enlightened and very productive group of scholars who know the value of maintaining contacts and free exchange of information and ideas. The prominence of Hungarian scholars in my own discipline is quite disproportionate to the size of the country and its scholarly cohort. This is the result of activities and cooperative endeavors that are now under threat. I write to assure you that the wider world of scholarship is watching events in Hungary with great concern, and hope that this declaration of solidarity will be of some help in your current effort to demonstrate the value of our shared enterprises.

happy to comply. My piece was issued under the title "His Diamond Jubilee, Our Silver One"; I include just below the previously unpublished original English text as the first of my three titular accolades.[5] Since then, Laci has logged another decade: as I write, he is a furiously productive eighty-five-year-old, who just last year published a volume of Bartók's piano works in G. Henle Verlag's Complete Critical Edition, launched in 2015, which he, more than any other individual scholar, had made a reality by dint of decades of persistent effort and patient diplomacy.

. . .

The first time I ever wrote about László Somfai it was indirectly at his request, when I was asked to furnish a letter of recommendation for I forget what fellowship. This was shortly after he had spent the fall 1989 semester with us at Berkeley as the Ernest Bloch Professor (our university's most prestigious visiting chair in music), giving the lectures—seminal, in the correct and literal meaning of that often abused word—that were later published as Béla Bartók: Composition, Concepts, and Autograph Sources.[6] *I was astonished that he had listed me as a reference, for (as I put it in my letter) while I wouldn't mind thinking of myself as a good-sized barracuda, Professor Somfai was one of the true leviathans of our profession and an evaluation from me would be an impertinence. I went on, of course, to furnish the requested impertinence, but only because a properly respectful silence would have been, in that context, a disrespect. On the many occasions when I have been given the honor of introducing him to scholarly audiences (five times at Berkeley, as host of the Bloch lectures, and thrice in Budapest at Bartók and Haydn conferences) I was able to finesse the task by observing that actually to introduce such a figure to such an audience would be an insult to both.*

For his is a singular distinction. I don't think there is another Hungarian musicologist, educated entirely at home (which is true neither of his seniors nor of many of his juniors), who has achieved such international eminence. His five-year term as president of the International Musicological Society (1997–2002) speaks for itself on that account, as do his American guest professorships and his corresponding membership in both American and British honor societies. Rather than compound impertinence with insult, then, I would prefer on this occasion not to praise one who needs no praise from me, but instead to recall the day on which he became my friend Laci. For our friendship, now twenty-five years old, is also marking a significant anniversary this year.

In the fall of 1984 Prof. Somfai was doing his first stint as a guest professor in America, at the graduate center of the City University of New York. I was then an

---

5. R. Taruskin, "Neki gyémántjubileum, kettönknek ezüst," *Muzsika* 52, no. 8 (2009): 12–13.

6. László Somfai, *Béla Bartók: Composition, Concepts, and Autograph Sources* (Berkeley and Los Angeles: University of California Press, 1996).

associate professor at Columbia University a little further uptown. Like so many other American musicologists (and not only Americans—it had been true of Prof. Somfai, too), I was taking a great leap forward chronologically. I was just then finishing up a project editing the Latin-texted works of Antoine Busnoys and starting to put words on paper for what would become a huge undertaking on Stravinsky. Prof. Somfai came to the Columbia music department to give us a colloquium on Bartók—a composer toward whom no budding Stravinskian could possibly feel indifferent (even if Stravinsky pretended to). I went out of interest in the subject, to be sure, but out of an even greater interest in the speaker. It had been only a few years since I had finally decided to make musicology rather than early music performance my career. Having decided late, and feeling I had fallen behind, I made a point (to which I have never before confessed) of looking up the work-lists of musicologists I admired in the then recent first edition of the New Grove Dictionary of Music and Musicians and making little mental calculations of how long it might take me to catch up with their outputs. The only one that seemed utterly, hopelessly beyond reach was László Somfai's (and he has never let up the pace: in his seventieth-birthday festschrift the list of his writings and editions takes up nineteen closely printed pages).[7] I had to see what this—forgive me—musicological Stakhanovite looked like.

I quickly forgot all about quantity and about my competitive neurosis when I heard the paper. It was the one on peasant music in the finale of Bartók's piano sonata of 1926 that was published a few years later in Jan LaRue's festschrift.[8] It so closely paralleled the problems I was facing in dealing with Stravinsky's "Russian" period, and it offered a view of the relationship between folk and art music that was so fresh and so helpful to my own ruminations, that in retrospect I'm afraid I became a pest at the reception that followed, so full of questions had the paper left me. I'm sure I kept the speaker far later than he wished, but when we finally did say our goodbyes it turned out to our surprise (and at least my delight) that we were going to see each other again the next afternoon, when the two of us were scheduled to speak (I on Busnoys, he on Bartók) at the local chapter meeting of the American Musicological Society. His paper was dazzling for the glimpse it afforded, corroborated many times over at the Berkeley Bloch lectures, of Prof. Somfai's genius for graphic representations—pie charts, bar graphs, flow diagrams, you name it, all set out calligraphically (this was before computer generation!) in many colors.

At the end of that meeting I made bold to invite my co-performer home with me (via dinner—very bibulous and merry—at a Japanese restaurant near campus), for I

---

7. László Vikárius and Vera Lampert, eds., *Essays in Honor of László Somfai on His 70th Birthday: Studies in the Sources and the Interpretation of Music* (Lanham, MD: Scarecrow Press, 2005).

8. László Somfai, "The Influence of Peasant Music on the Finale of Bartók's Piano Sonata: An Assignment for Musicological Analysis," in *Studies in Musical Sources and Style: Essays in Honor of Jan LaRue*, ed. Eugene K. Wolf and Edward H. Roesner (Madison, WI: A-R Editions, 1990), 535–54.

needed his help. I had a recording (issued by Bartók Records, Peter Bartók's label) on which Aladár Rácz, the great cimbalomist, not only played but also reminisced in Hungarian on his fateful meeting with Stravinsky in a Geneva restaurant in 1914. I needed to know what he was saying, so I asked Prof. Somfai if he would come and listen and translate. I had expected to play him the whole three-minute extract and have him give me a rough summary, but he insisted on doing it right. My phonograph was set up in that apartment behind a sofa. I'll never forget the sight of the great László Somfai crouching on his knees on my sofa so that he could face the spinning turntable behind it. He reached out every few seconds to the cuing lever, lifted the tonearm, and translated the few words he'd just heard, which I'd then scribble down. Then he'd drop the needle again and dictate the next few. It took half an hour, but we were both very much engrossed; and in the end I had a text from which I could quote. We bonded over the effort, it seems, because the next time I called him Professor Somfai, he extended his hand and said, "Laci." And Laci it's been ever since.

Having Laci as a daily colleague at Berkeley brought joy to all—Daniel Heartz, Joseph Kerman, Madeline Duckles (all of whom join me in jubilee greetings) as well as me.[9] *That is when we met [his wife and daughter,] the sharp-tongued, warm-hearted Dorka and the silent, hilarious Anna. It was a momentous time: autumn 1989 (need I say more?). When I asked Laci whether he regretted being away from home when Hungary was going through such historic changes, he said it was nothing new: he'd missed 1956 as well, implying that his absence created an auspicious parallel. I felt keen reverberations long after his term of residence with us was up, because, owing in part to the highly specialized and technical nature of his lectures, the University of California Press asked me to serve as their final textual editor on the way to publication, so I was able to relive them all.*

Thereafter, owing more to Laci's wanderlust than my own (or at least to the far greater number of invitations he receives), we have had many occasions to meet. I was happy to show him the way to Manny's, the musicians' music store in Manhattan, during a break from the Lincoln Center bicentennial conference "Performing Mozart's Music" in 1991, so that he could buy a "Dr. Beat" (tapping) metronome to get exact readings on recorded tempi. He had learned of the device from an article of mine on "period" recordings of Beethoven,[10] *and I was proud indeed to be, for once (and only once), a step ahead of him technologically.*

Reminiscing with me about our first meeting while having lunch at the Esterházy Palace last May, Laci teased me by recalling something he says I said then: "We've

---

9. Madeline Duckles (1915–2013) was the widow of Vincent Duckles (1913–85), the great music bibliographer, who had served as the Berkeley music librarian from 1947 to 1980.

10. R. Taruskin, "Beethoven: The New Antiquity," *Opus* 3, no. 10 (October 1987): 31–41; rpt. in R. Taruskin, *Text and Act: Essays on Music and Performance* (New York: Oxford University Press, 1995), 202–34.

been talking for four hours now and we haven't yet come to blows." Not that the delight we take in exchanging views necessarily implies agreement. Laci has always been a stronger (or as I would prefer to put it, less critical) backer of period performance practice than I, and I am also a bit more skeptical of sketches and autographs as conduits of insight into meaning. I would never promise my pupils access through musicological methods to "the exact and complete message" of any work (to quote the quoted statement with which Prof. József Ujfalussy concluded his tribute to Laci in his 2005 festschrift)—and now that I've said these things, I'm sure Laci will have a few things to say to me the next time we meet. Here is another: one time at a meeting of the American Musicological Society, when we happened to be sitting side by side at a performance-plus-commentary on recent compositions by the late George Perle (his immediate predecessor as Bloch Professor at Berkeley and another close friend of mine), he brought me up short with his negative, even dismissive reaction to what we were hearing. I couldn't help wondering whether his impatience with Perle's analytical writings on Bartók (highly influential in America, much to Hungarian chagrin) had rubbed off on his hearing of the music—could it be because Perle's own music can at times actually sound a little like Bartók as analyzed by Perle?

But we didn't come to blows then, and I don't suppose we'll feel like starting now. Outweighing all difference of mere opinion is the gratitude and admiration any musicologist must feel at Laci's unswerving dedication to the highest, best, and most exacting traditions of our discipline, his wish to place musicology at the service of performers and, through them, audiences (my fondest wish as well, although I go about it differently), and his ineradicably enthusiastic, ever youthful love of music. After I had introduced him in Budapest last month and as usual played the comedian, Laci turned to me from the podium in mock reproof and said, "You are incurable." Well said, brother Laci, and I take the greatest pleasure in saying it back to you. What has united us for twenty-five years in what I fondly believe to be unbreakable bonds of affection is the simple fact that you and I are both forever incurable zenetudomaniacs.[11]

II

The year 2006 was doubly a watershed for me. In March came the first of those dozen appearances in Budapest, for which I am so heavily indebted to Laci Somfai. The paper I read on that occasion, No. 4 in this collection, has had a reverberation that merited an update here in the form of an extended postscript. My contribution to the Liszt commemoration in 2011, printed here as No. 2, also had a reception worthy of report. My title, "Liszt and Bad Taste," was mischievously ambiguous. It suggested that the paper might take its place in a time-honored and by now commonplace tradition of complaint, which actually suited more than a few of the con-

---

11. Forgive the monstrous wordplay: *zenetudomány* is Hungarian for musicology.

ference participants. Mária Eckhardt, the conference organizer and former director of the Liszt Museum and Research Center at the Franz Liszt Academy, scheduled my paper as the last in the final session, usually a graveyard turn, in hopes that it would generate enough curiosity as to minimize early departures. And sure enough, I became aware of a buzz, which mainly took the form of people approaching me to confide, *sotto voce,* that they secretly agreed with me, or to ask whether some performance at a conference concert or recital had given me ammunition. When my paper turned out nearly the opposite of what my teaser of a title had seemed to promise, everyone took it in good fun, and I believe it helped drive my point home. The combination my audience thus evinced of ethical concern, quick comprehension, ideological flexibility, and delight in humor—so characteristic, as I've found, of the Hungarian musicological temperament, collectively mirroring the virtues that have so endeared my friend Laci to me—account sufficiently, I think, for my long record of eager participation in the Institute's proceedings. That association has lately taken on a double aspect, now that my appearances there have been reciprocated by the incorporation of books by a couple of younger Hungarian scholars in my University of California Press series "California Studies in Twentieth-Century Music," and the promise of more on the way.[12]

But in October 2006 there was an occasion of even greater moment for me, and of even more decisive impact on the direction of my work. I went back to Russia after an absence of three and a half decades to read a paper on a subject I had sworn I would not touch that year. That subject was Shostakovich, whose centenary was being celebrated with conferences all over the world, to many of which I had already declined invitations. Shostakovich studies had been so polluted by invective and mendacity in the wake of Solomon Volkov's *Testimony* that it seemed to me an utterly unprofitable prospect for continued research or publication, and especially for conferences. I had said my final word on *Testimony,* and on Shostakovich, at a Glasgow conference in 2000,[13] and never thought I would return to that

---

12. These titles, both published in 2020, are *A Wayfaring Stranger: Ernst von Dohnányi's American Years, 1949–1960,* by Veronika Kusz, and *Zoltán Kodály's World of Music,* by Anna Dalos. The first books of both David Schneider (*Bartók, Hungary, and the Renewal of Tradition: Case Studies in the Intersection of Modernity and Nationality,* 2006) and Klára Móricz (*Jewish Identities: Nationalism, Racism, and Utopianism in Twentieth-Century Music,* 2008), based on their dissertations, are also series titles, and Klára has been a series recidivist, with a second title, *In Stravinsky's Orbit: Responses to Modernism in Russian Paris* (2020). Yet another book in the series, based on research carried out at the Institute, is Danielle Fosler-Lussier's *Music Divided: Bartók's Legacy in Cold War Culture* (2006).

13. The paper I gave there was officially listed as "The 2000 Cramb Lecture," being the latest in a series of annual events that had been instituted at the University of Glasgow in 1911. I actually titled it "Shostakovich and the Will to Believe," and it was wholly devoted to debunking *Testimony* and the arguments of its supporters. I have never reprinted it; it was published, once only, in the improbable and for the most part inhospitable pages of the *DSCH Journal* (no. 14 [2001]: 25–43), normally a Volkovian stronghold. The talk made me very unpopular in Glasgow.

tainted terrain. But an invitation to St. Petersburg was different, and irresistible. My research interests, though they often cleaved to Russian music, had, once I became involved with Stravinsky, veered away from actual, terrestrial Russia, as he himself had done. I had carried on Stravinsky research in New York, in Washington, D.C., in London, in Paris, in Frankfurt-am-Main, and in various Swiss locations, but I saw little need to do any in then-Soviet Russia, where access to source material was often denied to foreigners, and where Stravinsky had composed nothing of consequence after *Firebird*. By the time Russia had emerged from the Soviet deep freeze—and, as we often forget, there was a deeply optimistic decade for scholarship (roughly the nineties) before the refreeze set in—my scholarly activity had entered the Oxford History phase that presaged an end to my identity as a Russian-music specialist. I had resigned myself to never again visiting Russia in a professional capacity, and as the years went by and my command of spoken Russian atrophied, I gradually began to put Russia out of my scholarly mind.

But my Russian counterparts had other ideas. Even slightly before the Soviet collapse, when the name of the game was still *perestroika,* I began to receive communications from Russian scholars who had discovered my work and had begun—something previously unthinkable—to comment favorably on it in the Russian scholarly literature. The first such feeler came from Marina Pavlovna Rakhmanova, then of the Glinka Museum in Moscow, who sent me an article she had published on recent Western scholarship on Russian music (including some of mine) that showed me, to my amazement, that Russian scholars now not only could read English texts with full comprehension, but actually wished to do so. (During my student year in Moscow in the early seventies, I did not meet a single person who could do this, except for those who had lived abroad.) I had the pleasure of meeting Marina Pavlovna in 1990, the last Soviet year, at a conference in Dallas that had been convened as an appendage to a production of Borodin's *Prince Igor.* Next I heard from Svetlana Il'yinichna Savenko of the Moscow Conservatory, who actually proposed collaboration. She had an article of mine on Stravinsky translated for publication in *Muzïkal'naya akademiya,* the successor publication to *Sovetskaya muzïka,* the old organ of the Union of Soviet Composers, in 1992, Year One of the post-Soviet order.[14] I met Svetlana Il'yinichna in 2000 at a Russian music festival in Iowa City, of all places.[15] Seven years later she invited me to give a whole series of

---

14. R. Taruskin, "Стравинский. Загадки гения" [*Stravinskiy: Zagadki geniya*/Stravinsky: Riddles of a Genius], *Muzïkal'naya akademiya,* no. 4 (1992): 103–11; this was a translation of "Stravinsky and the Traditions: Why the Memory Hole?" *Opus* 3, no. 4 (April 1987): 10–17, which was, in turn, an adaptation of the introductory chapter to *Stravinsky and the Russian Traditions,* which would not be published by University of California Press for another ten years, by which time it had gone through many metamorphoses.

15. I wrote it up for the *New York Times* as a way of paying for the trip: "Where Is Russia's New Music? Iowa, That's Where," *New York Times,* 5 November 2000, Arts & Leisure sec.; rpt. in Taruskin, *On Russian Music* (Berkeley and Los Angeles: University of California Press, 2009), 380–85.

lectures at the Moscow Conservatory, which brought me back to that city for the first time since my year of living there in Brezhnev's day. It may have been the same city, but it was a different planet.

And yet the most fateful meeting with an ex-Soviet counterpart was my third, with Lyudmila Grigor'yevna Kovnatskaya, a specialist in Benjamin Britten and modern British music and the head of the department of "foreign music" at the St. Petersburg Conservatory, with whom I was chatting in front of a newsstand in Toronto when the issue of the *Times* containing my Iowa City write-up was delivered for sale. I described that meeting and its consequences in a little memoir I was asked to contribute to Lyudmila Grigor'yevna's festschrift in 2016, when she reached the same age Laci Somfai had clocked seven years earlier (and which I reached on my own last birthday, earlier this month as I write).[16] Let it serve here as my second titular tribute.

. . .

Never trust memoirs, I used to tell my pupils in seminar. The only reason anyone writes them is to tell lies. (I learned this from Stravinsky.) But even when the motivation comes from without, as in the case of the memoir I am writing now at the request of her colleagues, about my acquaintance with Lyudmila Grigor'yevna Kovnatskaya, memory is a treacherous guide. What you are about to read is the result of an honest effort to get things straight, but that they remain crooked I cannot doubt.

One of the reasons I have found it difficult to reconstruct the occasion of our first meeting is that by now I feel I have known Lyudmila Grigor'yevna all my life. But in fact our personal relationship seems to have begun in 1998, when LG was putting together her collection of essays on Shostakovich.[17] Through Laurel Fay she had learned of my essay "Shostakovich and Us," which I had first delivered at the University of Michigan in 1994, keynoting a conference structured around a Shostakovich quartet cycle by the Borodin Quartet.[18] (It was at the end of that cycle of performances that the newly constituted quartet had its reunion with its founding leader, Rostislav Dubinsky, who was then teaching at Indiana University and who had come

---

16. R. Taruskin, "Насколько я помню . . ." [*Naskol'ko ya pomnyu . . ./*As far as I remember . . .], trans. Anastasia Spiridonova and Vladimir Khavrov, in *Liber amicorum Lyudmile Kovnatskoy*, ed. Ol'ga Manulkina, Lidiya Ader, and Nina Drozdetskaya (St. Petersburg: BiblioRossika, 2016), 536–39.

17. Д. Д. Шостакович: Между мгновением и вечностью. Документы. Материалы. Статьи [D. D. Shostakovich: Between the Moment and Eternity—Documents, Resources, Articles] (St. Petersburg: Kompozitor, 2000).

18. This essay was first published under the title "Who Was Shostakovich?" in the *Atlantic*, February 1995, 63–72; later, under the original title, in R. Taruskin, *Defining Russia Musically* (Princeton: Princeton University Press, 1997), 468–97, and in Rosamund Bartlett, ed., *Shostakovich in Context* (New York: Oxford University Press, 2000), 1–29.

up to nearby Michigan to hear the final concert.) Mila gave my text to Olga Manulkina to translate, and that is how I met Olga, too.[19]

Mila and I met face to face in 2000, on two separate occasions—and two separate continents. In October there was a Shostakovich conference at the University of Glasgow, organized by the émigré cellist and scholar Alexander Ivashkin, at which I was asked to deliver the keynote address. I took the occasion to state the case for regarding Testimony, the so-called memoirs of Shostakovich as edited by Solomon Volkov, as a fraud. Volkov still had many supporters, especially in the United Kingdom, and my address was met with both hilarity (since I made sure to include a lot of jokes) and consternation, and I was treated very roughly in subsequent sessions. (Not that I have any right to complain: I had, after all, provoked it.) There were even some Russian scholars at the conference who (I had to assume) knew better, but still wanted to lend support to Volkov's deceit. From Mila, however, I received a big hug, and from then on we were both allies and friends. Not only did she see through Volkov's deceptions, she wanted to fight them on Russian soil. I have often reflected sorrowfully on the way that other—perhaps honorable—commitments can sometimes override scholarly skepticism, the obligation of scholars always to seek the truth, even when bitter, and regardless of the consequences. For Mila there has never been any higher commitment, and that is why I not only love her but admire her as well.

Our second meeting took place at the zoo—that is, the gigantic, chaotic joint meeting of all the North American musicological organizations that was held in Toronto in November 2000 to greet the millennium musicologically. Laurel Fay and Mila invited me to a dinner I will never forget. Seated at a tiny table in the midst of a crowded, noisy restaurant, they ceremoniously unveiled to my incredulous gaze something that had been withheld from all of us for years: namely, the original Testimony typescript (that is, a photocopy thereof that had been sent to Irina Antonovna Shostakovich, the composer's widow, who had then copied it again and sent it to Laurel), so that I could see DDS's signatures on the first pages of all the chapters—except the first, where to my utter amazement it was on the third page (which, like all the other signed pages, contained material previously published in the Soviet press). The first two pages, containing scandalous material, had been slotted in afterwards, making (as we had long suspected) Shostakovich himself the principal victim of Volkov's trickery.[20] Despite the shocking revelation, it was a merry occasion. Laurel and Mila did not tell me what they were showing me. They just let me look, and as the truth about the first chapter gradually dawned on me and my mouth fell open, they giggled

---

19. Olga Borisovna Manulkina (b. 1966), then a docent at the St. Petersburg Conservatory, is now the head of musicology at the University of St. Petersburg and the foremost Russian scholar of American music.

20. For full details see Laurel Fay, "Volkov's Testimony Reconsidered," in A Shostakovich Casebook, ed. Malcolm H. Brown (Bloomington: Indiana University Press, 2004), 22–68.

like schoolgirls awaiting my giggles in response. So that's another thing about Mila. She enjoys her work and radiates that enjoyment to everyone who comes in contact with her. She and I have laughed a lot together.

It was then, at that Toronto dinner, that Mila first broached the matter of my coming to St. Petersburg to lecture at the Conservatory. I was reluctant. As of 2000, it had been twenty-eight years since I'd been in Moscow as an exchange student. My research had taken me from nineteenth-century Russian opera to Stravinsky, who had lived most of his life outside of Russia. Working on him had not involved any further trips to Russian archives. I am not a native Russian speaker, having grown up in a family of Jewish emigrants from the Russian Empire (present-day Latvia and Ukraine rather than Russia proper), whose daily language had been Yiddish before it was English. I learned my Russian in school, had practiced it well during the year I was stationed at the Moscow Conservatory, but had not been practicing it for more than a quarter of a century, and felt I no longer spoke the language well enough to deliver a scholarly lecture to a demanding audience. Mila—characteristically—laughed off my objections and told me to expect an invitation. She can be hard to say no to. So I said OK, and waited.

And in 2006 the invitation came. It was to a conference at the St. Petersburg Conservatory devoted to the Shostakovich centennial. I had been refusing many invitations that year to speak on Shostakovich because he had become, as we say in America, such an obnoxious political football in the wake of Testimony. *But I knew that this occasion would be different, since Mila and Olga were involved. And it was my chance to revisit Russia for the first time in, by then, thirty-four years. So I accepted, then laboriously translated two talks—one on Shostakovich for Mila, and one on "Jewish songs by anti-Semites" to give at Boris Katz's invitation at the European University—and laboriously delivered them.*[21] *My facility with spoken Russian was just beginning to return when, six days later, I had to go home. But there have been quite a few trips back—to St. Petersburg and (thanks to Svetlana Savenko and the composer Vladimir Tarnopolsky) to Moscow as well—and I have begun once again to feel at home among friends in Russia, even as Russia and the United States have begun reverting, much to my dismay, to their old antagonistic ways.*

But there is more. On the same trip to St. Petersburg for the Shostakovich centennial, I met a member of a third generation of Russian musicologists, Olga Panteleeva, who (along with Lidia Ader, another delightful new friend) had been assigned by

---

21. "'Jewish' Songs by Anti-Semites" was first published in the *New York Times* as a record review (21 September 1997, Arts & Leisure, 23); much expanded, it appeared as "*Yevreyi* and *Zhidy*: A Memoir, a Survey, and a Plea" in Taruskin, *On Russian Music*, 190–201. Boris Aronovich Katz (b. 1947), one of the leading *kul'turologi* (practitioners of cultural studies) in Russia today, is the dean of the arts history faculty at the embattled European University of St. Petersburg. He mainly works on the cusp between music and literature, having published studies of music in the poetry of Anna Akhmatova and Osip Mandelstam, and having edited and annotated Boris Pasternak's musical compositions.

Mila *to keep me company during off hours. Olga P., imbued with the same enthusiasm and keenness to widen her own horizons and those of Russian musicology that motivated her teacher Olga M. and her grand-teacher Mila, later became my own pupil at the University of California, which joined our scholarly families and kept me in continual contact with the St. Petersburg community. But I don't have to go to Russia to see my dear St. Petersburg friends. Since 2006 I have seen Mila in the US and the UK as often as I have in Russia.*

What I have been recounting here, then, is more than a testimonial to what has become a warm and precious friendship. It is also an account of Lyudmila Kovnatskaya's huge significance for Russian musicology. At a cost in personal sacrifice and risk that I can only vaguely imagine, she has consistently pushed for international contact against the grain of traditional Russian isolationism, a tendency that was formerly backed by official Soviet xenophobia and the attendant threat of reprisal. In this she was certainly acting to some extent consciously in the footsteps of her mentor, Mikhail Semyonovich Druskin (1905–91), the great cosmopolitan of Soviet musicology, who kept a corner of St. Petersburg alive, to the lasting gratitude of his pupils, at the Leningrad Conservatory;[22] but she has achieved a singular status as Russia's musicological envoy—as an officer in the International Musicological Society, a member of the editorial board of Tempo, *and an organizer of, and participant in, many international conferences. Her service to our discipline has been incalculable— and her internationalist spirit was what finally got me to overcome my own reservations and renew my own contact with Russia and with Russian musicology, to my own lasting benefit. We all owe Mila an immeasurable debt of gratitude. To know that such a fine human being exists is a great consolation and a great inspiration.*

III

Of the clump of ten chapters (7–16) devoted to Russian subject matter, only chapter 9 was first aired in Russia. Thus these chapters do not owe their existence to Mila Kovnatskaya and to the way our friendship changed my life's affordances quite as directly as chapters 2–6 do with regard to László Somfai. Nevertheless, the sense of solidarity with counterparts in Russia has been as sustaining for me as, they have said, it has been for them. It has kept my interest in my oldest field of

---

22. Best known in the West for his late monograph on Stravinsky: M. S. Druskin, *Игорь Стравинский. Личность, творчество, взгляды. Исследование* (Leningrad: Sovetskiy kompozitor, 1974), translated into English by Martin Cooper as *Igor Stravinsky: His Personality, Works, and Views* (Cambridge: Cambridge University Press, 1983). As a young Soviet pianist Druskin studied with Artur Schnabel in Berlin, played Beethoven's Fourth Concerto under Hermann Scherchen, and, on 12 January 1932, performed Stravinsky's Concerto for Piano and Winds in the composer's presence.

research fresh, and put me in contact with younger generations of Russian scholars. I have recounted elsewhere my great disappointment at my inability to maintain contact with the many friends I made during my academic exchange in 1971–72.[23] Unlike the friends made by my American counterparts in other fields, my Moscow friends were mainly musicians, not scholars, and they all feared that being known for having friends abroad would limit their prospects for foreign tours. I was asked by each independently, and equally shamefacedly, not to write to them, and I did not. (As the years went by, more than a few of them popped back into my life as émigrés.) Thus, being contacted out of the blue in the wake of *glasnost'* was the biggest and most profitably catalyzing surprise that ever came my way, and Mila was its culmination. Without her, without her invitations, and without the relationships and collaborations that came in their wake, my path would have been far lonelier and less adventurous. If her impact has been less direct, it has been if anything more profound.

Profoundest of all has been the impact of guiding spirits whose legacy informed the air around me as I learned to practice my profession. I have paid tribute to my teachers many times over, most volubly in the acknowledgment pages that formed part of the front matter in the original hardbound edition of the Oxford History, but not repeated in the paperbound *separata*. There was one figure left over, to whom perhaps the greatest homage was due, but who did not fall into the traditional categories that demanded honorable mention at such times. I was therefore delighted when Judith Peraino told me that she was planning a festschrift to honor her academic mentor, Richard L. Crocker, and elated when she asked me, as a former colleague, to furnish an appreciation to preface the scholarly contributions.[24] I wrote it with ebullience, read it with emotion at a luncheon Judith arranged at the national meeting of the American Musicological Society in San Francisco in 2011 to present the festschrift to its honoree, and now take one last full measure of joy in reprinting it here as the third of my titular homages, to preside symbolically over the third and last clump of chapters (17–22). These address the sort of big issues to which my previous collection, *Cursed Questions,* was dedicated. Were their titles in suitably interrogative form, they might well have found a place in that book. Richard Crocker's shining example has always irradiated my engagement with big matters conceptual and methodological. Thus it is more than apt that I invoke him as *spiritus rector* to officiate over that third batch of chapters, the more so as one of them (chapter 19) makes direct and somewhat detailed reference to

---

23. R. Taruskin, "Of Mice and Mendelssohn," in *On Russian Music*, 357–65, at 358.

24. R. Taruskin, "Ricardus Primus: *Praeceptor et Familiaris*," in *Medieval Music in Practice: Studies in Honor of Richard Crocker*, ed. Judith A. Peraino (Middleton, WI: American Institute of Musicology, 2013), 15–22.

one of his exploits. To pay my respects up front gestures toward the settlement of a debt long standing. Alas, he will not see it; I learned to my great sorrow, after this book had gone into production, that Richard Crocker died, aged ninety-four, on September 7, 2021. So this last tribute unexpectedly and most regrettably must take the form of a memorial.

. . .

When I joined the Berkeley music department in 1987, there were already two Richards on the faculty. I don't think anything special had been made of the fact before, but with my arrival we immediately became Richard I, II, and III. (Richard II was the composer Richard Felciano; everybody seemed to agree that my age had vouchsafed me the right number.) Entre nous, *however, and I think (though I could be mistaken) at my instigation, we were Ricardus Primus (pronounced as Mr. Chips would have pronounced it, to rhyme with rhyme-us), Secundus (refund-us), and Tertius (cher-che-us). But it was not only among the Richards that Crocker was* primus inter pares. *By the time I came to know him personally I had long revered him as a scholar—the most visionary scholar in all of musicology, I thought, and the most creative (whether as opposed to* sterile *or to* destructive*). No one I have met or read since has outstripped him in my esteem, and there is no one to whom I am more indebted for whatever there is of good in me.*

How to characterize the debt? It is not a straightforward thing. I am not a medievalist, and I find that our usual ways of describing inheritance and transmission do not cover it. It is not even that Tertius has found in Primus a worthy role model. Nor is he just an admired senior colleague. Here is something that may help clarify. Time and again editors have tried to correct "my pupils" in things I've written to "my students." The words seem to have become all but synonymous in most writers' vocabularies, but I see a very significant difference between them, and it is at the heart of my relationship to Ricardus Primus—a lifelong relationship, professionally speaking. I have never been his pupil. I never enrolled in his courses or sat in his seminars; he never graded my papers, nor would he claim (or admit) to having trained me. But while I have never studied with him, I have been studying him ever since I learned musicologically to read, which makes me his enthusiastic and grateful student.

My most influential teacher in college, Joel Newman, the man who set me on the track I have followed ever since, was a Crocker fan, and paid his Barnard and Columbia undergraduate majors the great compliment of assuming we could digest Crocker at full strength. He assigned us "Discant, Counterpoint, and Harmony" when it was still hot from the oven. It was the hardest twenty pages I'd ever slogged through as of then, but it taught me what I have been teaching my pupils as long as I've been teaching them: namely, that the word scholar *is synonymous with the word* skeptic, *and that it is always time to take a fresh look at what one thinks one knows.*

The opening paragraph has been resounding between my ears now for nearly fifty years:

> How often one reads, in discussions of medieval music, remarks like this: "Here the voices sound a major triad—but, of course, the composer did not think of it that way." A commendable reservation; but one that raises the urgent question: how did he think of it?[25]

That last question, embarrassing as well as urgent, is pure Socrates. It utterly corrupted my youth. Decades later, when the author and I were colleagues sitting side by side at a prospective faculty composer's classroom Probe, devoted to the usual taxonomy by faux-nationality of augmented-sixth chords, he exuded a lingering echo of that big bang, whispering in my ear that augmented sixths are the last vestiges of discantus *in the common practice, since they seek their resolution by* occursus. Who else would have thought of that? It suddenly made brothers of Magister Lambertus and Scriabin.

Ricardus Primus's most celebrated fresh look, "The Troping Hypothesis,"[26] appeared during my first year of graduate study, when I was taking the obligatory introductory course in medieval notation and attendant antiquarian concerns—the very course whose abolition as a requirement Joseph Kerman would celebrate as "a first step in the liberation of musicology," as if ignorance were ever liberating.[27] What was liberating was Crocker's warning how easily a priori intellectual constructs (we weren't yet calling them ideologies) could blind the eye and enslave the mind. We went around entertaining each other with Crockerian in-jokes like "Tropes come in three flavors—oranges, elephants, and meteoric dust," as a sign that we were hip. But it went beyond hipness. Our eyes had been opened and we saw that we were naked, and were ashamed. Ever since, I have been acutely conscious (and I have been forcing the consciousness on my pupils) that what we think of as phenomena are likely to be hypotheses and interpretations; that it is possible to fight this tendency; and that fight it we must at all times and at all costs.

The revisionary potential of Crocker's demonstration (even revolutionary, to use a word everyone was throwing around in the late sixties) impelled the editors of Current Musicology, *the then-newborn journal of the Columbia graduate musicologists—which is to say, my somewhat older peers—to commission from him a sequel that took*

---

25. Richard L. Crocker, "Discant, Counterpoint, and Harmony," *Journal of the American Musicological Society* 15, no. 1 (Spring 1962): 1.

26. Richard L. Crocker, "The Troping Hypothesis," *Musical Quarterly* 52, no. 2 (April 1966): 183–203.

27. Joseph Kerman, *Contemplating Music: Challenges to Musicology* (Cambridge, MA: Harvard University Press, 1985), 46. Just how liberating that step was became clear to me the year after Kerman's book appeared, when I published an article on Busnoys and the *Homme armé* tradition, and a colleague of mine at Columbia—a Berkeley grad and a pupil of Kerman's—said, "Looks like a fascinating article, Richard; I wish I could read it."

in a much vaster (indeed, unlimited) territory. Asked whether one can count as "a piece of music" a trope consisting of three phrases to be interlarded respectively into the antiphon, the verse, and the doxology of an Introit, Ricardus Primus answered, with his wonted cunning,

> Without reflection, I think we agree that such a trope is not a piece. As we consider the reasons upon which our reaction is based, however, I think we may well begin to have doubts. For the reasons we produce so confidently at first, do not seem so universally applicable when we try them out on different repertories, especially on very recent repertories, and even the repertory that we—or perhaps more precisely our immediate forebears—call traditional.[28]

Instead of using mental constructs that originate in aesthetic theory ("we expect a piece to be continuous"; "we expect a piece to have a certain minimum substance"; "we ask that a piece be by one, and only one, composer")[29] to critique observed phenomena—the idealistic method in which most of us were trained without knowing it—Ricardus Primus counsels that we use our powers of observation and the experiential knowledge they bring us to critique aesthetic concepts. If this be positivism, make the most of it. What it really is, of course, is phenomenology, albeit without benefit of clergy. The editors of Current Musicology, possibly prompted by Edward Lippman, their faculty adviser, recognized the West Coast medievalist's lucubrations for what they were. Phenomenology was briefly in vogue at Columbia in those days, spurred by a dissertation then in progress, The Musical Object, by Patricia Carpenter. The journal ran Ricardus Primus's piece in counterpoint with Carpenter's introduction and solicited a wide range of responses. Nobody who wasn't there seems to remember that symposium, but it was and remains a fascinating teaser, pointing in directions musicology might have taken earlier, if only.

As things actually turned out, Ricardus Primus was a bit too optimistic in predicting change. I don't think I am reading utterly in the spirit of my own obsessions when I see in the paragraph quoted above a call to dig out from under the dead weight of German romanticism. Four decades later and counting, we're still digging. Crocker's early publications have always been among my main shovels, tools I make sure to put in the hands of my pupils. Thus they too—and there hasn't been a budding medievalist among them for many years—have been students of Crocker.

And well they know it. I take perpetually renewed delight, when supervising their work, to point them toward evidence that Crocker was there before them. Most recently it was a student from Germany who was grappling with unconscious survivals of Nazi thinking in postwar German scholarship, and who had decided to focus

---

28. Richard L. Crocker, "Some Reflections on the Shape of Music," Current Musicology 5 (1967): 51.
29. Ibid., 50–51.

her attention on the writings of Hans-Joachim Moser and their fate. I'll never forget her astonishment (which of course I'd predicted) when I showed her Crocker's wicked and hilarious JAMS review of Moser's Die Tonsprachen des Abendlandes.[30] About a quarter of a century ahead of schedule, the review mounted, fully formed, what are now called antiessentialist and antiuniversalist arguments, both of which were touted in the 1980s as attainments of the new musicology. It is one of Crocker's less famed utterances, so here's a sample:

> Moser lists several characteristics of German music. German music puts more emphasis on content than form; while not destroying forms, German musicians fill them with content, giving them new meaning. German music tends toward the irrational, as opposed to the French taste for program. This gift for speaking the unspeakable inclines the German musician toward instrumental rather than vocal music. The German musician tends also toward harmony as a means of expressing his inner self.... In addition to harmony, German music is characterized by polyphony, for example, a keen joy in voice crossings which, when found in Morales, might well be due to an inheritance from the West-Goths. German music is apt to be dark. This quality affords a transition from the foregoing stylistic features to the more philosophic ones: German music portrays humanity, is concerned with ideas, with religion ..., das Ewig-weibliche. All of these things are Ur-elements of the German spirit. The irrational depths of music are described in the 9th century by the "German" author of the Musica enchiriadis, to say nothing of Tinctoris and Schopenhauer.
>
> So what else is new? From this repetition of commonplaces we learn only how Moser arrives at his conclusions. He chooses one moment in history, in this case the mid-19th century, as the source of musical values, then projects these values forward and back along the whole course of history. But this procedure is the very opposite of history. Instead of showing how the perpetual procession of events takes on now this shape, now that, Moser's method imposes one shape on all. Traits that German music did indeed develop at a certain moment in history are converted by Moser into the traits characteristic of Germany from the time of Adam and Eve; eventually these traits are taken to be the eternal values of music itself. Yet through it all there is no real analysis of musical style, only of Volksgeist.

But Crocker's antiuniversalism targets only the pretense that one particular Stamm has the privilege (or the duty) of representing the universe. What Ricardus Primus is after is "a fruitful discussion of the Western common language" through empirical style criticism, rather than the a priori assumption of "national characteristics," which leads us only "to glare at each other across the border." Long before Celia Applegate or Pamela Potter, Ricardus Primus was aware that scholarly methods, even the dowdiest, most traditional (and in the hasty judgment of some, outmoded) ones,

---

30. Strangely enough, it appeared in the same issue as "Discant, Counterpoint, and Harmony" (see n. 24 above).

have political implications and repercussions along with ethical ones, and that they should be chosen and critiqued with that in mind. It is a lesson that remains valuable even to those of us who no longer place the same premium on style criticism or who no longer seek the distinctiveness of the West. And the deadly aim of "Tinctoris and Schopenhauer"! That dry Down East wit has ever been my joy and my hopeless aspiration, one of the many little aphoristic turns that pop up in the unlikeliest places and that made Richard Crocker (especially early Crocker) for me what, say, Ambrose Bierce has been for the multitudes. (Others include "Is there no joy in Brooklyn?"[31] *not to mention the biggest scream of all, the table of "chords" Ricardus Primus vertically sliced out of randomly selected works of Josquin in response to Edward Lowinsky's* Tonality and Atonality in Sixteenth-Century Music*.)*[32]

Still before I met him, Ricardus Primus had his great moment of glamour. As I noted once, years ago, when introducing him to a graduate colloquium at Berkeley, the only way most musicologists could ever hope to get their picture on the front page of the New York Times *would be by killing another musicologist. ("Don't laugh—it's happened," I said, thinking of Jean Beck and Pierre Aubry; but I haven't checked whether the* Times *reported it.) Richard Crocker did it, by contrast, in the normal practice of his profession, when he performed (to his own accompaniment on "the only known reproduction of the ancient Sumerian lyre") what the* Times *called "the oldest song in the word," transcribed from a cuneiform tablet by a team of Berkeley Assyriologists and musicologists.*[33] *Partly, I guess, it was a slow news day. But partly, too, it showed how seriously scholarly and artistic discoveries could be taken not very long ago. The* Times *even commissioned an "appraisal" of the Hurrian cultic song, also on the front page, by their chief music critic, Harold C. Schonberg. (The headline after the jump—"Song Puts the History of Music Back 1,000 Years"—contributed a perhaps unintended construal.) Here too, Ricardus Primus put a spin on things that took it well beyond what most observers would have remarked. "It isn't weird or strange," he told the* Times *reporter. "It's totally familiar to us because it is, after all, part of our own culture." He went on to take a little swipe at the over-othered performances of early music that were then fashionable. "The myth that so-called 'old music' has to sound nasal and whiney obviously isn't true," he said, echoing a record review that appeared in the* Musical Quarterly *a decade earlier and that I've never forgotten, where he railed hilariously at "recent trends towards a medieval French*

---

31. Richard L. Crocker, Review of *The Worcester Fragments: A Catalogue Raisonné and Transcription*, by Luther A. Dittmer, *Journal of the American Musicological Society* 22 (1959): 71–74, at 74 (the last sentence).

32. Reviewed in *Journal of Music Theory* 6 (1962): 142–53.

33. Lacey Fosburgh, "Oldest Song in the World Reportedly Deciphered," *New York Times*, 6 March 1974, 1.

gamelan" and signaled to closet Gilbert and Sullivan fans that he was of their (our) number ("Oh bother the drum!").[34]

But what his remarks were really doing went beyond an attempt to counteract the fetishization of difference that remains one of musicology's Romantic sins. In later decades he put it more boldly, positing the "diatonic pitch set" as something we have been carrying around in our heads since, well, "whenever."[35] It was perhaps the earliest hint of the challenge neo-Chomskian cognitive psychology would give the behaviorist epistemology that underwrote much of the discourse of late-twentieth-century modernism, the challenge associated in the minds of most music theorists today with Fred Lerdahl. Again, Ricardus Primus was decades ahead.

He and I finally met at the 1978 national meeting of the AMS—at the business session, to be precise, where we were both picking up awards. He was getting the top prize, the Kinkeldey, for his chef d'oeuvre, The Early Medieval Sequence; I was getting the bottom one, the just-instituted Greenberg. He probably doesn't remember. But the occasion looks to me in retrospect like a watershed in his career, initiating a change in his scholarly profile. Since the sequence study appeared, his work has been less restless in purview, more concentrated, and, ultimately, centrally authoritative, culminating in the "second edition" (as the publisher euphemistically put it—or rather, the replacement and repudiation it was forced to commission for the famously useless second volume) of the New Oxford History of Music, *which Ricardus Primus co-edited with David Hiley, and to which he contributed six wholly authored chapters amounting to some three hundred pages, nearly half of the total. With the publication of that monument, Ricardus Primus became the primary authority on the history of Gregorian (or, as he prefers, Roman) chant and its medieval outgrowths, and I can stop the detailed survey of his output in its tracks, because his work since the 1980s will be as familiar to every medievalist reader by virtue of its centrality to their concerns as his works of the 60s and 70s are to me because of my lived experience. Not that his subsequent work has been any the less significant to me, or any the less influential on my thinking. Anyone reading the first volume of* The Oxford History of Western Music *will surely realize the enormity of the obligation I owe my preceptor and familiar. He did not fail to notice it when I submitted the first draft of the early chapters for vetting some twenty years ago. They came back with a note that began, "Finally!" And ended, rather chillingly, "Of course I agree with much of what you write.* Ma non sempre!" *leaving me to live in fear.*

---

34. Richard L. Crocker, Review of Deller Consort and Concentus Musicus, Vienna, *Music of Medieval France, 1200–1300, Sacred and Secular* (Vanguard BG-656), *Musical Quarterly* 51 (1965): 571–75, at 573 and 574.

35. As he put it in that colloquium to which I had made the introduction.

But it has been a productive fear—fear of falling short of an exacting standard that lies within grasp, but only if one is willing to strain one's faculties to the utmost. What I am most thankful for when I think of Ricardus Primus is that spur—a spur I have made every effort to pass on. It is a gift that demands repayment. The best repayment is one's work, but I have long been conscious of a wish to make a public declaration of some kind. It is something long promised. Pleased with the colloquium introduction recalled above, Ricardus Primus asked me at the time whether I had written it out so that he could have it as a souvenir. As it happened, I had been winging it from a scrawl of notes, but I said I hoped to pay a proper tribute someday. And now I have. And this is it.

1

The Many Dangers of Music

Or, Music Moves

I

I thought I'd begin by telling you how I know that God exists and watches over me. (Have I got your attention now?) It's because whenever I am thinking deeply or obsessively about some topic or question, usually in preparation for an event such as this one, God sends me clippings. Things turn up in my reading, in my mail or email, in the news, in conversation or in everyday experience, that assist my thinking or even answer my questions. Doubtless you are rationalizing this. I am just reacting to my surroundings and experiences with heightened alertness at such times, you are thinking. No doubt. But there always seem to be coincidences that go beyond that explanation, serendipities that simply come to me from God knows where. And if God knows where, perhaps He is the one sending them.

I was invited to address you today because, according to the publicity that CUNY has been sending out, I am "America's public musicologist." Owing to fortunate friendships and God-granted situations, I have had many more opportunities than most academic musicians to write for general-interest magazines and newspapers, in particular for the *New Republic* when Leon Wieseltier was the literary editor there, and for the *New York Times* when James Oestreich served as classical music editor. I wrote a dozen or so pieces for Wieseltier and more than sixty for Oestreich. My career as a public commentator lasted about a quarter of a century, beginning in 1986. It still trickles along. My durability in public media was

---

Originally given at the Graduate Center of the City University of New York as the Lloyd Old and Constance Old Lecture in the series "Music in Twenty-First Century Society," 7 December 2016.

due, I suppose, to my interest in politics and, in particular, to my interest in the intersections between politics and the kind of music that I studied and wrote about—that is, classical music, which is reputed, along with the other arts and sciences, to be unrelated to politics and therefore exempt from political (or, come to that, moral) critique. Possibly owing to my upbringing and the social conscience with which it saddled me, I disagreed; and my disagreement was, as we so love to say in the academy, transgressive. It broke a taboo and attracted rebuke. I found I could take it; and as my skin thickened, my appetite for debate got stronger, because I truly believed that the debates in which I found myself embroiled were important.

I still do; and if my appearances as a public intellectual or public nuisance are rare now, it is not because debates are settled, or because I have won or lost them, but precisely because they continue. They will never be settled; but now that I am a battle-scarred veteran with an identifiable point of view to which others refer, I see no point in repeating myself. And yet it is important that they go on, lest music—and when I say music, I always mean classical music—lapse into utter cultural irrelevance, as it seems to be doing in today's world. That only makes the necessity of debate the more urgent, and I am still game. Since old debaters like me, with well-known positions, risk becoming predictable and thus easily discounted, I decided to rely for this talk as far as possible on the most recent clippings I have received from the Good Lord—like the one that arrived in the *New York Times* the other day, 15 November 2016 to be exact, under the headline "It's Official: Many Orchestras Are Now Charities."

The article, by Michael Cooper, the *Times*'s classical music reporter, documented a shift in the balance between ticket sales and subsidies from individual donors in the budgets of American symphony orchestras, decisively toward the latter. So what else is new, you may be thinking: classical music has always depended on patronage. That is actually one of its definitions. But since the early nineteenth century that patronage has been predominantly collective rather than individual. The fact that for the first time since then audience support no longer accounts for the lion's share of revenue for public musical performances—that, in effect, audiences no longer collectively support the orchestras they come to hear—is, to many, a grave portent, as Cooper writes, of what may happen "as classical music's footprint in the broader culture shrinks."[1]

I don't want to take that lying down. And my way of fighting it is to stir up trouble. Public debate is good for the so-called high arts, which if left too much alone can easily lapse into moral indifference and social irrelevance (we like to call it "autonomy"). So we need gadflies and contrarians, and if no one else is signing up, I'll do it. One should be willing to defend one's positions lest one fall into compla-

---

1. Michael Cooper, "It's Official: Many Orchestras Are Now Charities," *New York Times*, 15 November 2016, www.nytimes.com/2016/11/16/arts/music/its-official-many-orchestras-are-now-charities.html.

cency, which is just a Latinate way of saying "taking it lying down." Not to recognize that danger is to put music *in* danger. God seems to agree, or else why would He be sending me so many clippings?

He's been doing it since 1978. My first taste of public controversy involved disciplinary matters that, although they occasionally attracted the attention of music journalists, were not themselves journalistic forays. In 1978, when I was just starting on a project that would consume the next eighteen years of my life—the project that culminated in the publication of my book on Stravinsky's Russian-period music[2]—the editors of *Current Musicology*, the graduate-student-run journal put out by the Columbia University music department, where I was then employed (and where, only a few years earlier, I had been a graduate student myself), invited me to review Allen Forte's book-length analysis of *The Rite of Spring*, which I had planned to work my way through anyway.[3] As I read it, I realized that I was going to have to question not only the analysis as such, but also the premises on which it rested, which meant I would have to register a fundamental critique of the method the author had devised for analyzing atonal music—a method that had by then been widely adopted in American and British graduate curricula. I quailed at the prospect of taking on the method *qua* method, because I had not been trained in it, and I knew that as a historical musicologist—that is, an outsider to the subdiscipline of music theory—I would have to earn my cred by demonstrating mastery of the method, which was based on seemingly forbidding mathematical set theory. So God sent me a summons to jury duty, and I spent the next week sitting around in the jury room of the New York State Supreme Court on Foley Square in Manhattan with Forte's textbook, *The Structure of Atonal Music*.[4] Providentially, my name was never called, and so it was just one long, uninterrupted study hall for me, after which I was equipped to write a review that demanded, and elicited, a response. That response, when it came, was unexpectedly thunderous, as some may yet remember.[5] It sucked me into a long debate that went beyond the immediate occasion into a general dispute over the necessity of historical contextualization in musical analysis, with side trips into matters of intention and representation. It got

---

2. R. Taruskin, *Stravinsky and the Russian Traditions* (Berkeley and Los Angeles: University of California Press, 1996).

3. Allen Forte, *The Harmonic Organization of "The Rite of Spring"* (New Haven, CT: Yale University Press, 1978). My review appeared in *Current Musicology*, no. 28 (Fall 1979): 114–29.

4. Allen Forte, *The Structure of Atonal Music* (New Haven, CT: Yale University Press, 1974).

5. It came, far from immediately, in reply to a letter to the editor of the British Journal *Music Analysis*, in which I noted that an article by Forte, "Pitch-Class Set Analysis Today" (*Music Analysis* 4 [1985]: 29–58), had failed to take proper account of criticisms his method had received, not only from me, but from other writers as well, including several from within the domain of music theory (Richard Taruskin, Letter to the Editor, *Music Analysis* 5 [1986]: 313–20; Forte, "Making Stravinsky Soup and other Epistemusicological Pursuits: A Hymenopteran Response," *Music Analysis* 5 [1986]: 321–37).

so loud that the *New York Times* chief music critic heard it and reported it in a Sunday think piece.⁶ But that repercussion apart, it was not what you'd call public musicology. It was confined to the profession.

By then I was involved, again serendipitously (or, if you prefer, by grace of God), in another dispute. Having been active in the performance of early music in New York as a player of the viola da gamba and as a choral conductor (something I got into as a result of being as a graduate student peremptorily assigned by God, working through Jack Beeson, the then chairman of the music department, to run the Columbia University Collegium Musicum in the late sixties and early seventies), I was asked, by D. Kern Holoman of the University of California at Davis, to contribute to a session he was organizing at the 1981 national meeting of the American Musicological Society, which took place in Boston, on musicological prospects for the 1980s. He asked me to give a status report on musicology in performance, probably expecting an evaluation of progress toward the then widely accepted goal of reviving, through musicological research, what were then called authentic performance practices. As I've already mentioned, I was then just starting out on my Stravinsky project, and one of the areas I was investigating was early theories of modernism as they affected the arts, neoclassicism prominent among them. It meant reading philosophers like Ortega y Gasset and T. E. Hulme, and it became increasingly evident to me that the practices the early music movement was implementing, as well as its governing aesthetic, were far more indebted to that early modernist theorizing than they were to the historical evidence its practitioners were citing.

That Boston meeting was the first, rather modest, airing of that contention, which had only occurred to me, most unexpectedly, in the course of preparing my talk.⁷ But then God intervened again, working through my old—alas, now late—friend the harpsichordist Kenneth Cooper, who put me in touch with Jim Oestreich just as Jim was starting up a wonderful magazine called *Opus*, which briefly filled a gap in the periodical literature between the fanzines and record collectors' mags, on the one hand, and the musicological journals on the other. I had many chances, writing for *Opus* between 1984 and 1988, for practical demonstrations that so-called historical performance did not actually correspond to the facts of history even to the extent that we could know them, and that the project of revival was not as disinterested and empirical as we had thought, but was as ideologically driven as

---

6. Donal Henahan, "Should We Care Who Wrote It?" *New York Times*, 17 May 1987, Arts & Leisure sec., 29.

7. It was published under the title "The Musicologist and the Performer" in the proceedings of the Boston AMS plenary sessions (D. Kern Holoman and Claude V. Palisca, eds., *Musicology in the 1980s: Methods, Goals, Opportunities* [New York: Da Capo Press, 1982], 101–18) and under the title "On Letting the Music Speak for Itself" in the then-newborn *Journal of Musicology* (1 [1982]: 338–49); rpt. in R. Taruskin, *Text and Act: Essays on Music and Performance* (New York: Oxford University Press, 1995), 51–66.

human endeavors inevitably tend to be, especially when they involve matters of aesthetic preference.

This debate edged closer to the public sphere because it involved commercial recordings and took place not just in academic journals but in that liminal space which *Opus* then blessedly occupied. Eventually it exploded in the pages of the *New York Times,* because God, working in His mysterious way, had caused *Opus* to fold after only five years' existence, and had enabled Jim Oestreich, after two years in the wilderness (or rather in Cleveland, where he was writing program notes for that city's orchestra), to take over the Sunday Music page (still the Music page, not yet the "Classical" page) at the *Times,* and invite his old troops, as he liked to call us, back into action. But by then I had been sucked into politics and publicity in the way that has led, ultimately, to my appearance before you today.

II

The first piece of mine that elicited notice beyond the music profession and its devotees was an essay that I published in 1989 in the *New Republic*.[8] I had written it during the fall of 1987 for the program book of the San Francisco Opera, which was putting on a production of Shostakovich's *The Lady Macbeth of the Mtsensk District.* I was newly arrived in the Bay Area, having been hired as an associate professor by the University of California at Berkeley. I was thrilled to be asked for the piece. I had lived forty-two years in New York, and had been pursuing a scholarly career for nearly two decades on the faculty of Columbia University. I had published a book on Russian opera and a bunch of scholarly articles and reviews. But the local performing institutions, the Metropolitan and City operas, the New York Philharmonic, and all the rest, had taken absolutely no notice of me—nor did I expect them to do so. That was not the way in New York, where the academy and the public life of the arts rarely intersected.

That mutual isolation was considered normal, even desirable, in those days. Academics were strongly encouraged to stay within their cloister, and forays beyond, unless you were a very well established sage, were strongly deincentivized. Just at random, I recall the case of my near-contemporary Doris Kearns, whose tenure case at Harvard was upended precisely by the sensational success of her biography, *Lyndon Johnson and the American Dream* (1977), a bestseller, which the Government (that is, Political Science) faculty at Harvard deemed to have been tainted with public journalism, or at least with popularity (plus the fact that she had engaged a fiction editor to help her shape the book, and was suspected of collaborating with her future husband Richard Goodwin, a Johnson speechwriter at

---

8. R. Taruskin, "The Opera and the Dictator: The Peculiar Martyrdom of Dmitri Shostakovich," *New Republic,* 20 March 1989, 34–40.

the time of their meeting).⁹ As the author of a bestseller, she could afford to flip Harvard the bird, but those of us who saw the academy as our inevitable source of livelihood took a cautionary message from her experience.

We were of course also counseled from within to ignore the wider world. Who doesn't remember Milton Babbitt's prodigiously overquoted exhortation that "the composer would do himself and his music an immediate and eventual service by total, resolute, and voluntary withdrawal from this public world to one of private performance and electronic media, with its very real possibility of complete elimination of the public and social aspects of musical composition"?¹⁰ That was, and remains, a controversial thing to say about composers, but it was the opposite of controversial to say such a thing about scholarship. It was a truism with regard to scholarship; indeed, Babbitt's whole argument was predicated on his belief that, to paraphrase a famous old aesthete, academic musical composition should aspire to the condition of scholarship.

But now, in the Bay Area, the public media were tempting me. During my first week at Berkeley, my office phone rang repeatedly with requests for contributions both written and oral from the San Francisco Opera and the San Francisco Symphony, and it was one of the things that most convincingly assured me that I had made an advantageous move. I craved a public voice, possibly because I had given up a career as a performer in moving across the continent. And so I gave in to blandishment, and accepted the Opera's dual invitation to write a program essay and also provide a round of preview lectures for the Opera Guild. I had no idea that this gig would lead me so far beyond opera and beyond music into the wider world, but then I started doing my homework. I made a close comparison between Shostakovich's opera and its literary source, a novella of the same name by the nineteenth-century author Nikolai Leskov. Leskov's Lady Macbeth (like her Shakespearean namesake) was a monstrous serial killer, whereas Shostakovich had sought through his music to create sympathy for the title character and justify her murderous deeds. He did this in various ways, partly by somewhat mitigating the heinousness of her crimes (in particular, eliminating the murder of an innocent boy, "which," as Shostakovich put it in a program note, "always makes a bad impression") and partly by borrowing a bit of action from Ostrovsky's famous drama *The*

---

9. See, for example, Gail Jennes, "The L.B.J. Book, Tenure, Her First Child: Doris Kearns Plays a Tranquil Waiting Game," *People* 6, no. 1 (5 July 1976), people.com/archive/the-l-b-j-book-tenure-her-first-child-doris-kearns-plays-a-tranquil-waiting-game-vol-6-no-1.

10. It comes from the peroration to "The Composer as Specialist," a talk Babbitt gave (originally titled "Off the Cuff") at Tanglewood in 1957, published under the incendiary and now celebrated title "Who Cares If You Listen?" in *High Fidelity* 8, no. 2 (February 1958): 38–40, 126–27, and endlessly anthologized thereafter, including in my own anthology, co-edited with Piero Weiss, *Music in the Western World: A History in Documents*, 2nd ed. (Belmont, CA: Thomson/Schirmer, 2008), where the quoted sentence can be found on p. 484.

Storm, which sympathetically portrays another unhappy, adulterous merchant wife, also named Katerina (who, however, commits no violent crimes, unless you count her suicide as a crime). Mainly, however, Shostakovich used his gifts of musical characterization to manipulate the audience's attitude. The title character's music is beautifully romantic and humanizing; all the other characters, and in particular her victims, are set out in ugly, lifeless style.

It's an amazing musical achievement, and I was quite astonished to see how clearly its earliest audiences, both at home and abroad, saw it for what it was. *Time* magazine, whose critic saw the opera in a production mounted in Cleveland and conducted by Artur Rodzinski in 1935, reported to its readers that "in the respectable quiet of East Side Cleveland one night last week an old man ate poisoned mushrooms, died in wriggling agony. A merchant was smothered with a bed pillow and his corpse dragged into a cellar. A prostitute let out a blood-chilling scream as she was pushed to her death in an icy black lake." And yet "by sheer vitality and shrewd orchestration Composer Shostakovich accomplishes exactly what he sets out to do: He makes the audience sympathize with Katerina Izmailova," the perpetrator in all these crimes, never with her victims. Admittedly, "[s]uch a heroine as Katerina seemed ludicrously impossible" in prospect, and yet the curtain rose to show her sitting by the window

> quietly, miserably restless as strings droned and woodwinds sighed. The audience instantly caught her mood and hated the old father-in-law, introduced by strident horns and a mocking xylophone. The husband first piped in a silly high tenor while the orchestra beat out a double-quick waltz in which even a piccolo sneered. . . . Katerina thereafter has lovely lyrical music, played by tender strings.[11]

All of which amounted to what seemed to me not only a questionable, dehumanizing moral inversion, but one that was all too closely analogous to the rationalizations that were given in Stalin's Russia for the suspension of bourgeois morality in the name of the class struggle. I had not expected to come to this conclusion. It surprised and dismayed me as much as my eventual essay surprised and dismayed many of its readers, because Shostakovich's opera is famous in the annals of twentieth-century music, even among those who have never seen it, for having suffered a fate no one foresaw when *Time* magazine reviewed it in Cleveland. It was condemned and banned in 1936 in what now appears to be the signal act of Soviet arts censorship.[12] That outcome had cast Shostakovich as a historic victim of Soviet power, and victimhood implies innocence.

---

11. E. Armstrong, "The Murders of Mzensk," *Time* 25, no. 6 (11 February 1935): 15.

12. The unsigned editorial in *Pravda*, "Muddle Instead of Music" (*Sumbur vmesto muzïki*), that appeared on 28 January 1936 and initiated the reversal is given in translation (together with a photo of the original text) in Weiss and Taruskin (eds.), *Music in the Western World*, 2nd ed., 422–24. It is now known to have been written by a staff writer named David Iosifovich Zaslavsky (1880–1965), who was frequently summoned as an attack dog in matters relating to the performing arts and literature.

The composer's status as innocent victim had, about a decade before I wrote about it, received an enormous boost with the publication of a book called *Testimony*, which bore a subtitle identifying it as "The Memoirs of Dmitri Shostakovich, as Related to and Edited by Solomon Volkov."[13] You may recall that the book's first-person narrative presented its hero as an embittered dissident, righteously aggrieved after a lifetime of mistreatment by the Soviet regime. And here I was, writing of the work that marked his first collision with Soviet power: "So ineluctably has the opera come to symbolize pertinacity in the face of despotism that it is almost impossible to see it clearly now as an embodiment of that very despotism."

That was the beginning of the original essay's concluding paragraph. I'm happy to say that the San Francisco Opera went ahead and printed it in the program book. Their very canny program editor in those days, a Croatian woman named Koraljka Lockhart, joked to me that people reading it would have already bought their tickets, so I could say whatever I liked. I had by then written exactly once for the *New Republic* at the recommendation of Simon Karlinsky, a Slavist on the Berkeley faculty, who had been asked to review a book based on a dissertation he had supervised and so passed it along to me, who had no such conflict of interest. Leon Wieseltier, the literary editor, had written me a nice note after my review had been published and invited me to submit more work; so I sent them this piece, and I added another paragraph to give it a more topical spin. The *fatwa* against Salman Rushdie over *The Satanic Verses* was in the news early in 1989, when the article ran, so I connected it to the matter I was addressing this way:

> In the liberal West, as we have been proudly reminded in recent weeks, we do not believe in banning works of art. If it is because we believe that they cannot threaten life and morals, then we are more vulnerable than we imagine to the dehumanizing message of this great opera. If it is because we believe that ethics has no bearing on aesthetics, then the process of dehumanization has already begun. If, for its inspired music and its dramatic power, *The Lady Macbeth of the Mtsensk District* is to hold the stage today, it should be seen and heard with an awareness of history, with open eyes and ears, and with hearts on guard.[14]

Need I even tell you that the mail in response to this piece ran very heavily, and very abusively, against me, or that writer after writer compared me with Ayatollah Khomeini, and even, given the immediate subject, with Stalin? Solomon Volkov's defenders seized upon my observation that Shostakovich's defense of his heroine resembled the defense of Stalinist repressions and blew it up into a claim that "the opera was intended as an endorsement of Stalin's genocidal campaign against the kulaks in 1930."[15]

13. Solomon Volkov, ed., *Testimony* (New York: Harper & Row, 1979).
14. Taruskin, "The Opera and the Dictator," 40.
15. www.siue.edu/~aho/musov/macb/ladymacbethfn.html.

None of this surprised me, even though the new final paragraph very plainly opposed censorship, because I had already noticed many times over that artists and art lovers in the West had a hard time distinguishing criticism from censorship—or even understanding the meaning of the word *if*. What surprised me was my reaction to the reaction. I was exhilarated. What elated me was not—or not just—the notoriety it brought me, but the fact that I had elicited an excited reaction from a nonprofessional audience with a serious discussion of a serious work of art, and that achievement had become a rarity. The isolation of serious art from the sphere of public and especially political discourse, which (as I have tried to show, and which many others by now have also shown) was an artifact and a consequence of the Cold War in the West, was killing off interest in it. If stirring political debate could revive interest in serious art and prolong its life in our distracted society—well, deal me in.

So I have actually sought opportunities to pit ethics against aesthetics—not because the one is right and the other wrong, but precisely because both are right. Both are genuine values, but they are independent variables. Good art can do evil. And of course bad art can do good. I once amused myself in a piece for the *New York Times* by listing a bunch of recent compositions that were "musically excruciating but politically attractive," by Joseph Schwantner, John Harbison, Aaron Jay Kernis, Ellen Taaffe Zwillich, and Philip Glass, most of them entrants in a prize competition in which God had arranged for me to be a member of the jury.[16] Ethics and aesthetics go hand in hand only fortuitously.

III

My other major skirmish along these lines involved an opera I do not rate nearly as highly as I do Shostakovich's, namely *The Death of Klinghoffer*, an opera I prefer to attribute to Peter Sellars, its mastermind and original director, rather than to John Adams, the composer, or Alice Goodman, the librettist, who joined the project after its conception.[17] I never thought to subject so mediocre a work to an aesthetic critique. My published remarks were addressed solely to its ethical dimension, and only in passing. Nevertheless, in the wake of the terrorist attacks of

---

16. R. Taruskin, "Orff's Musical and Moral Failings," *New York Times*, 6 May 2001, Arts & Leisure sec.; reprinted under the title I originally submitted before the *Times* editors went to work on it—"Can We Give Poor Orff a Pass at Last?"—and with an update, in Taruskin, *The Danger of Music and Other Anti-Utopian Essays* (Berkeley and Los Angeles: University of California Press, 2008), 161–67. Orff's famous composition was of course precisely the converse of the competition pieces: musically attractive but politically excruciating.

17. R. Taruskin, "Music's Dangers and the Case for Control," *New York Times*, 9 December 2001, Arts & Leisure sec.; reprinted, with an update, under the title "The Danger of Music and the Case for Control" in Taruskin, *The Danger of Music*, 168–80.

11 September 2001, this "review"—which wasn't even a review—has always been the piece the opera's promoters have been at pains to refute. Rather than a review, my discussion of *Klinghoffer* was merely one example among others offered in a general consideration of the applicability of ethical standards to the judgment of artworks. Because of its recent date and its freshness in memory, the opera became, you might say, Exhibit A, the prime test of my case for independent variability.

What established the connection between *The Death of Klinghoffer* and the events of 9/11 was the decision of the Boston Symphony Orchestra to cancel a performance of choral excerpts from the opera out of consideration for the feelings of the recently bereaved. I voiced approval of the move, and that brought forth charges of abetting, and in this case even practicing, censorship. The title of my talk today is a paraphrase of the title the *Times* editors put atop that piece when it ran: "Music's Dangers and the Case for Control." I did not write that headline, but I do not disavow it, and today I want to amplify its premises, and even, to some extent, attempt to explain what creates the danger that can inhere in art, even (or especially) in great art, and specifically in music.

Two years ago, in 2014, when *Klinghoffer* finally came to the Metropolitan Opera, attended by the usual clamor, I was interpellated by various reviewers and bloggers who demanded that I comment on the new production. Where in 2001 my defense of the Boston Symphony Orchestra led to my being lumped, by John Adams and a number of British journalists, with John Ashcroft and Donald Rumsfeld, this time, without even opening my mouth, I found myself lumped with Rudy Giuliani. If those demanding a word from me had sent airfare and tickets, I would have gladly complied, but I never saw the Met production and could not fairly offer a take. I would nevertheless observe that three times now producers of the opera have made adjustments to it in response to ethical critiques (specifically, to critiques of its claim to "evenhandedness" in the portrayal of the Palestinian hijackers and their Jewish victim) even as they have consistently rejected the premise that a work of high art can properly be subjected to an ethical critique (*that* being the attitude of theirs to which I have objected).

The first time, it was the original creative team who responded, after the first American performances at the Brooklyn Academy of Music in 1991, by removing a comic scene that juxtaposed a pop-music characterization of the Jewish characters with the opening chorus, which had portrayed the Palestinians in exalted tones inspired by the choruses of J. S. Bach's passion settings. The second, it was Penny Woolcock, the director of the first movie version of the opera, who responded by putting a couple of silent Israeli Jews (identifiable by their tattoos as holocaust survivors) on board the hijacked ship as extras, to balance the Palestinians better than American Jewish tourists, who had no legitimate claim to the disputed land. And the third time, it was Tom Morris, the director of the Met production, who responded by showing the actual murder on stage rather than mitigating it by hiding it behind the scenes. I am not claiming these concessions as vindications of my own or anyone's specific criticisms; but they are acknowledgments, albeit tacit ones, that ethical critique deserves a response from serious artists as well as from purveyors of popular culture (which everyone agrees is properly subject to ethical scrutiny). All I have ever attacked has been the claim of privilege.

I do think that the position I have espoused over the years has gained ground since the end of the European Cold War, which knocked the strongest prop out from beneath the wishful old German romantic cliché that, in Schopenhauer's words, the history of art and philosophy runs parallel to the rest of human history, and is therefore "guiltless and unstained by blood" (*schuldlos und nicht blutbefleckt*).[18] But even now I am brought up short on occasion by renewed resistance to ethical critique, sometimes quite unexpected, and I do not at all take it for granted that you, my present audience, are with me on any of this.

My most recent reminder was the clipping from God that furnished me with my gambit tonight. While writing this piece I was engaging in negotiations with the Bavarian State Opera, which was mounting a new production of *Lady Macbeth* by Harry Kupfer, the veteran, formerly East German, opera director. The program editor wrote me for permission to reprint my old San Francisco program essay, specifically in the form it took when published in the *New Republic* (and I must say I was surprised and actually impressed that they had scared that version up). They wanted it in that form precisely because of the new opening I had appended to the piece when submitting it, in which I summed up the case against the authenticity of Volkov's purported book of Shostakovich memoirs. The book has been discredited in the United States (by no means primarily through my efforts; the chief exposers of Volkov's fraud were Simon Karlinsky and Laurel Fay);[19] no one in this country, certainly no serious writer or scholar, would quote from it without serious disclaimers. In Germany, however, I am informed by my Munich correspondent, the book still has currency, and so they particularly wanted to reprint what he called "the great Volkov part" of my essay, especially since the conductor of their production, Kirill Petrenko, "coming from Russia himself, has always had his doubts about Volkov."

So far so good! But, the editor went on, "there's one big question, though":

> Your take on the opera is quite harsh. I have been discussing this with my colleagues intensively, and while we all agree that your perspective is as original as it has its merits and is certainly worth hearing for a larger audience (I, for one, was thrilled to read a

---

18. Arthur Schopenhauer, *Parerga und Paralipomena: Kleine philosophische Schriften* (1851), in idem, *Sämmtliche Werke*, vol. 5 (Leipzig: Brockhaus, 1874), 75.

19. Simon Karlinsky, "Our Destinies Are Bad," *The Nation*, 24 November 1979, 535; and Laurel Fay, "Shostakovich versus Volkov: Whose *Testimony*?" *Russian Review* 39 (1980): 484–93, rpt. in Malcolm H. Brown, ed., *A Shostakovich Casebook* (Bloomington: Indiana University Press, 2005), 11–21.

> "dissenting opinion" at last), it sort of differs from our stage director's interpretation—naturally, and not really a problem—, but for us as an opera house it's still rather a stretch to say in print that we play an opera that endorses mass murder.[20]

That is not quite what I said, but I won't get into that because the man from Munich did not really disagree with me, only expressed qualms about the impression my essay would make on the audience to whom he had to sell the opera. I have heard this sort of thing so often: *What Taruskin says may be true, but I just wish he wouldn't say it.* (And it made me even more grateful in long retrospect to Kory Lockhart for her jovial assurances in 1987.) You might be thinking that this example only points up the difference between scholarly and commercial pursuits, we scholars being the virtuously disinterested party. I will show you, though, that I have met with very similar, and at times even more intransigent resistance from my own corner. The Munich editor, evidently a perceptive and subtle man, did not ask me to suppress my opinion. He only asked that I

> add one last paragraph that discusses the value of a performance of this piece today. Why is it important to keep it on stage and ask ourselves the questions it poses? It seems to me that you do think this opera, as horrifying as it is, still has some greatness to it.

But of course I do. And that is precisely why the ethical issues are worth discussing. A potent ethical challenge to what I see as destructive complacency about aesthetics requires that the object in view have unquestioned or even unquestionable aesthetic value. Denunciations of blackface minstrelsy, or of religious and ethnic caricatures in movie soundtracks or Tin Pan Alley songs, so commonplace in the recent musicological literature, raise no one's temperature because no one's cultural capital is invested in such repertoires.[21] Susan McClary's stroke of genius was to aim her feminist guns at Beethoven's Ninth Symphony, the icon of all classical-music icons. No one could be indifferent to her onslaught. Unless you were a misogynist, and proud of it, your aesthetic and ethical commitments were placed in conflict. To attempt a refutation meant arguing on her ground, which is why most of those who engaged with her did not actually try to deny that the first movement of the symphony contained "one of the most horrifyingly violent episodes in the history of music," as McClary put it (let alone that it evoked "the murderous rage of a rapist incapable of attaining release"), but merely denounced her

---

20. Email, Malte Krasting to RT, 21 October 2016.
21. See, for example, Judy Tsou, "Gendering Race: Stereotypes of Chinese Americans in Popular Sheet Music," *repercussions* 6, no. 2 (Fall 2001): 25–62; W. Anthony Sheppard, "An Exotic Enemy: Anti-Japanese Musical Propaganda in World War II Hollywood," *Journal of the American Musicological Society* 54 (2001): 303–57.

for saying such a thing.²² Nobody objected when Donald Francis Tovey called that very spot "the heavens on fire" (as Scott Burnham reminded us in a recent plenary address to the Society for Music Theory).²³ That was just a metaphor. Well, guess what? McClary's interpretation was also a metaphor. That's all we've got when we talk about music (as Scott was reminding us). Scott gracefully, if tacitly, acknowledged McClary's version when he wrote of the "sense of sublime catastrophe in those bars [of Beethoven's], sometimes heard as a forceful collision, sometimes as transgressive violence, always as supremely unsettling."²⁴ Is there nothing to choose between them, then? Scott certainly meant to imply no such thing, nor do I. Which metaphor we choose makes a huge difference; and I mean to redeem this moment with something bigger and much more basic in conclusion.

In my most recent email to the Munich program editor I gave him leave to write the requested paragraph himself (since I could not write it well enough in German), prescribing that it distinguish carefully between description, critique, and censorship. Putting our hearts on guard (the metaphor I used in conclusion) means recognizing that there is a difference between arguing for mitigation of a crime, the way any decent defense attorney would do, and regarding a crime as virtuous, as totalitarian legal systems often do. The music associated with the title character in Shostakovich's opera does very powerfully convey moral worthiness and even innocence. "The part about 'hearts on guard,'" I wrote to my Munich correspondent, "is a comment on the unique persuasive powers that music, especially operatic music, has always exerted on listeners (only masked, never diminished, by the formalist postures so common in the twentieth century). . . . Music makes great propaganda."²⁵

And then God, working through Google Alerts, sent me, the very day I was drafting the foregoing paragraph (30 November, one week before delivery date), a clipping from the *Neue Musikzeitung,* which bills itself modestly as "Deutschlands größte Musikfachzeitung" (the greatest German newspaper for the musical profession, or something like that) containing a review of the new production. My correspondent had not even told me yet (although I got an email about it a few hours later), but they had indeed reprinted my article in the program book with an added

---

22. Susan McClary, "Getting Down Off the Beanstalk: The Presence of a Woman's Voice in Janika Vandervelde's *Genesis II.*" The version implicating rape appeared only in the January 1987 issue of the tiny *Minnesota Composers Forum Newsletter* (archived online at https://web.archive.org/web/20150419111253 /https://composersforum.org/sites/composersforum.org/files/jan_1987.pdf); when McClary reprinted the piece in her collection *Feminine Endings: Music, Gender, and Sexuality* (Minneapolis: University of Minnesota Press, 1991), she cooled the characterization down to "constant violent self-assertion" (128).

23. Donald Francis Tovey, *Essays in Musical Analysis,* vol. 1: *Symphonies* (Oxford: Oxford University Press, 1935), 18.

24. Scott Burnham, "Words and Music," SMT keynote address, Vancouver, BC, 5 November 2016.

25. RT to Malte Krasting, 22 October 2016.

paragraph drafted according to my specifications; and indeed, it contradicted Harry Kupfer's take on the action glaringly enough to warrant comment from the reviewer, Juan Martin Koch, who noted that Shostakovich, through his "empathizing music," makes sure that "we don't take offense at the mutation" of Leskov's malicious killer into a virtuous victim; that Shostakovich's Lady, unlike Leskov's, "deserves absolution"; and that Harry Kupfer "leaves no doubt that he is ready to give it to her." His last paragraph, God bless him, is about me:

> The most controversial item in the program book [it was actually an inserted *separatum*] was an article by the American musicologist Richard Taruskin from the end of the 1980s—in response to the apocryphal Shostakovich memoirs brought out by Solomon Volkov—that casts well-founded doubt on the notion that [the opera's] disruptive, seditious content merited the infamous anathema that Stalin pronounced upon it. No matter how far we may wish to follow Taruskin in this ticklish debate, a few traces of ambivalence toward the piece and its titular heroine would have done the performance some good. A new chapter in the opera's reception history was not opened in Munich.[26]

But I'll keep trying. Someday, God willing, directors will listen. If I were rewriting the essay now, I would include some evidence that God has just sent me in the form of Marina Frolova-Walker's study of the deliberations undertaken by juries that awarded the Stalin prizes for music between 1940 and 1956. The documentary publications made possible by the end of the Soviet regime and the opening of the Russian archives (now, alas, in the process of closing once again) have given us some grey, sometimes a lot of grey, with which to revise and lend a bit of credence to the formerly black-and-white portrayals of Soviet life that came to us from both sides during the Cold War. Shostakovich, who in Cold War narratives always appeared passive—as an obedient son of the Communist Party or as a silently suffering and bitter witness, depending on the angle from which he was being described—can now be seen in action, as an honest-to-God agent with honest-to-God agency, in documents relating to his official deeds as a functioning member of Soviet organizations and cultural institutions.

---

26. "Das Programmheft enthielt als streitbarsten Beitrag jenen Artikel des amerikanischen Musikwissenchaftler Richard Taruskin, in dem dieser bereits Ende der 1980er Jahre—ausgehend von den apokryphen, von Solomon Volkow herausgegebenen Schostakowitsch-Memoiren—begründete Zweifel an der regimekritischen Sprengkraft der Oper als Auslöser für Stalins berüchtigten Bannfluch äußerte. Ganz gleich, wie weit man Taruskin in dieser heiklen Debatte folgen mag, ein paar Spuren von Ambivalenz gegenüber dem Stück und seiner Titelheldin hätten dieser Aufführung gut getan. Ein neues Kapitel der Rezeptionsgeschichte ist in München nicht aufgeschlagen worden" (Juan Martin Koch, "Das Herz schlägt im Orchestergraben—Harry Kupfer inszeniert Dmitri Schostakowitschs 'Lady Macbeth von Mzensk' an der Bayerischen Staatsoper," www.nmz.de/online/das-herz-schlaegt-im-orchestergraben-harry-kupfer-inszeniert-dmitri-schostakowitschs-lady-mac).

In a big anthology called *Dmitry Shostakovich in Letters and Documents,* issued in 2001 by the Glinka Museum of Musical Art in Moscow, we finally got to see Shostakovich in action as the First Secretary of the Board of the Union of Composers of the Russian Federation, the post for the sake of which he was pressured into joining the Communist Party in 1960, and the actions we see him perform are those of a canny politician, not a Holy Fool (as Solomon Volkov had explicitly described him). Now Marina Frolova-Walker shows us why we should not have been surprised. On the Stalin Prize jury Shostakovich was outspoken, often to the point of tactlessness, exigent to the point of embarrassing his senior colleagues in pursuit of musical standards—and not only musical ones. Particularly revealing of Shostakovich as a composer of opera, and particularly pertinent to the matters now at hand, are the blunt remarks through which he succeeded in quashing an award to Anatoly Alexandrov (1888–1982), a composer considerably senior to him, for an opera based on the *Bela* chapter from Mikhail Lermontov's novel *A Hero of Our Time.* "For all the excellent musical language, good technique, expressiveness and undoubted talent of the composer," he said (according to a stenographic transcript in the archives),

> the weakest aspect of the opera lies in the lack of any well-defined and expressive characterization. And so Bela sings in more or less the same musical language as Pechorin and the others. I am not insisting on the use of Wagner's leitmotivic principle. There are operas where such leitmotives are lacking, but the characters are still well defined—Carmen and Don José are vivid figures, but here everything is flattened out by the same fine writing of good quality. The main shortcoming here is the lack of definite musical characteristics, and this is exactly what makes an opera, in that high sense of the word which we should demand, a musico-dramatic work.[27]

Reading this, one appreciates anew what it was that made Shostakovich's two operas the great achievements that they were. And such precocious ones: *The Nose* was completed before the composer's twenty-second birthday, *Lady Macbeth* shortly after his twenty-sixth. He obviously had a Mozartian talent for the genre, and that makes it all the more lamentable that his collision with Soviet power made him avoid writing operas ever after. In his critique of Alexandrov's work he showed his grasp of what makes musical drama tick—indeed, what gives it an advantage over spoken drama. A composer controls more than a playwright can control. By determining not just the characters' lines but also the tempo, volume, contour, and register of their delivery, the opera composer in effect combines the jobs of author, actor, and director in fashioning—or, as Shostakovich says, characterizing—a role. And by exercising these multiple functions he controls

---

27. Quoted in Marina Frolova-Walker, *Stalin's Music Prize: Soviet Culture and Politics* (New Haven, CT: Yale University Press, 2016), 119–20.

more than the characters on stage. He also controls the audience's perceptions of the characters and manipulates their reactions to them. That ability to manipulate the audience's response is the source of the composer's power—and a source of music's danger. It is not confined to opera.

IV

Believing along with Susan McClary that it is an important aspect of teaching music within a humanistic curriculum to raise ethical as well as aesthetic issues, and to raise them with respect to the art we value the most, I too have made a habit of trying to incite within my students collisions between their aesthetic and ethical sensibilities. In the classroom my favorite vehicles have been oratorios by Bach and Handel. To make the lesson the more effective I proceeded in both cases by indirection—you might even say by stealth. And because the *Oxford History of Western Music* was basically an amplification of the lectures I had developed in the course of several decades of teaching music history to music majors, my strategies were embodied in that text as well.[28]

The Bach example, as you might well predict, is the *St. John Passion*, which, following its biblical source, names *die Juden*, "the Jews," as the crowd reprehensibly calling for the death of Christ, rather than *das Volk*, "the people," the way the *St. Matthew Passion* does. I began using it as an instrument for raising ethical issues as a result of an incident that took place early in my teaching career, before I had ever thought to depart from the attitudes that had been instilled in me by my training. My earlier habit had been to present the two Passions side by side, representing the *St. Matthew Passion* by its monumental and essentially pictorial opening chorus (characterizing the whole, through it, as a "contemplative" work) and representing the *St. John* with the tense exchange in recitative and *turba* chorus between Pontius Pilate and the crowd who will not allow him to let Jesus off the hook, characterizing the whole, through it, as a more "dramatic," quasi-operatic work. It was a student, made uncomfortable by the characterization of the crowd as Jews, who queried the appropriateness of using that particular part of the *St. John Passion* as illustration. Another student said, "But the Jews, after all, *were* responsible for the death of Christ." I asked him, in preparation for the discussion that I saw we would have to have, how he knew that. "From Bach," was the answer—and it startled me to hear that: for the first time I had actually seen with my own eyes, so to speak, that a great work of art had done someone harm.

The strategy I adopted in response to that observation, now reflected in the *Oxford History*, is to present the two Passions side by side as before, hoping that no

---

28. R. Taruskin, *Music in the Seventeenth and Eighteenth Centuries*, vol. 2 of *The Oxford History of Western Music* (New York: Oxford University Press, 2005), 313–21 (Handel), 377–81, 389–90 (Bach).

one will notice St. John's Jews, so that later I can come back and confront the class (or reader) with the matter and ask them, given that no reputable historian today blames the Jews for the death of Christ (and even the Catholic Church, though not the Lutherans, got around to absolving them of deicide in 1964), whether it is at all objectionable to perform a text that incorporates a libel that has led to bloody persecutions?

There are many possible answers to that question, and I do not necessarily endorse any of them. It is the question that I consider important. And I insist that the question be properly framed: not whether St. John was right or wrong about the Jews, or whether J. S. Bach was personally anti-Semitic, or whether exposure to the work can affect belief (since I have actual empirical evidence to report that it can and has). The question does not involve Bach and the congregation of religious believers that he served with his art but rather we the people who perform the work today, and particularly those who perform the work under secular auspices before religiously and ethnically mixed audiences. What are their (our) ethical responsibilities? Do we even have ethical responsibilities? If so, to whom? "Bach is long dead," I wrote in the *Oxford History*,

> but the *St. John Passion* lives on. Jews not only hear it nowadays, they often participate in performances of it, and are sometimes shocked to learn what it is that they are singing. [Here I was thinking of the incident that took place at Swarthmore College, which brought Prof. Michael Marissen into the discussion and eventually resulted in the publication of his wonderful book *Lutheranism, Anti-Judaism, and Bach's "St. John Passion."*][29] Are they wrong? Does Bach's music redeem the text? Would it impair Bach's work from the standpoint of its present social use if the text were emended to exclude the blood libel? And if people disagree about the answers to these difficult questions, on what basis can they be adjudicated? It is no part of the purpose of this book to provide the answers to these questions. But it is integral to its purpose to raise them.[30]

Do you agree? Not everyone does. The *Oxford History*'s most distinguished reviewer, Charles Rosen, objected vociferously to my raising them: "Taruskin asks if we have the right to listen to the chorus in Bach's *St. John's Passion* where the Jews demand the death of Jesus: he hastens to say that he is only posing the question, not giving an answer, but some questions are too foolish to be asked."[31]

I agree with Rosen. That question is indeed too foolish to be asked. But as I hope and trust you have noticed, it was not my question. To deflect the question onto the

---

29. Michael Marissen, *Lutheranism, Anti-Judaism, and Bach's "St. John's Passion"* (New York: Oxford University Press, 1998).
30. Taruskin, *Music in the Seventeenth and Eighteenth Centuries*, 389.
31. Charles Rosen, "From the Troubadours to Frank Sinatra," *New York Review of Books*, 9 March 2006, 45.

matter of rights makes things very easy for the deflector by yet again stigmatizing ethical concerns as censorship, which then enabled Rosen to admonish me that "the proposal to censor the art of the past to hide unpleasant aspects of history puts Taruskin with one foot in the camp of those who would ban *Huckleberry Finn* from the shelves of our school libraries." Yet as I hope is evident, I am with both feet in the camp of those who would insist on devoting time in the classroom to examining *Huckleberry Finn* precisely and explicitly in an effort to understand unpleasant aspects of history, so as to strengthen our ability to view the beliefs of our ancestors—and our own beliefs as well—freely and critically. That, after all, is the purpose of education, and of scholarship. But perhaps more debatably, I also contend that our promise not to censor implies a promise to critique. And I have been acting on that contention.

The specific purpose that the passage from the *Oxford History* on the *St. John Passion* sought to address was that of exposing rhetorical strategies, both in the historiography of art and in the works of art that are the subject of historiography. The Handel example on which I have relied to teach this lesson is the narration of the ten plagues in *Israel in Egypt*. It is probably the greatest sustained example of word-painting in the whole literature of music, and of course it's a hoot. Take the locusts (please). They come in, as the Bible says, "on the ground," when the cellos, bull fiddles, and bassoons enter with a running bass line in sixteenth notes to join the violins, who had already been imitating flies in thirty-seconds. Nobody who hears this passage ever receives it with a straight face. Before this the audience had made merry over Handel's imitation of frogs in the first and second violins, who play overlapping leaps—yes, leapfrog. And yet, what Handel is imitating here is no benign menagerie but rather the horrors that God visited on the suffering Egyptians. Handel turns this harrowing biblical episode into one of the funniest twenty minutes in all of dramatic music, and it has long been a classroom favorite.

When I used to play it for my music history students, I stopped to examine Handel's portrayal of the darkness, which relies on chromatic harmony and murky timbres (bassoons doubling violins now instead of the basses), which gives us a chance to explore a more sophisticated—because less direct—sort of mimesis. But then came "He SMOTE all the FIRST-born of EEE-GYPT," and we were all laughing again. Here is where I would wheel around and ask the students, "Hey, what are you laughing at?" And we would all realize that we'd been had, that Handel had manipulated us into withholding empathy from the victims, even the innocent little boys among them. That withholding is an essential part of the biblical account of the Exodus, and the scorn of the biblical Israelites (and their religious descendants in Handel's audience) for the ancient oppressor is what enables the success of Handel's strategy of turning an awful tale into a merry entertainment. I get an extra benefit from the example because it illustrates the alliance, seldom explicitly addressed, between musical word-painting and the mechanisms of humor, and serves as a springboard to discussion of more serious and potent resources of musical representation or expression.

But humor itself is a serious business, and a potent one. Handel's musically engineered opposition of self and other through mockery plays into the ideology of nationalism. A great deal of English national pride (or anybody's) depends on a perception of separateness from other nations, and superiority to them. And of course such chauvinism and self-interest are at considerable variance with the liberal ideas we tend to propagate in institutions of higher learning. When the political message of Handel's oratorio is broached, and juxtaposed with contemporary events unfolding in the Middle East, students are apt to feel embarrassed at the way Handel's music had persuaded them to dissociate their reactions as listeners from their ethical sentiments. That cognitive dissonance makes for a memorably "teachable moment," and what I am particularly intent on teaching by means of this example is the power of music—exactly through its (oft-repudiated) representational aspects—to influence thought and behavior: one of the many dangers of music. As always, moreover, the greater the music, the greater the potential mischief.

V

I think it remarkable that my calling attention to this potentiality has made me to any extent at all a controversial figure on today's musical-intellectual scene. People have been writing about the danger of art since Plato—at least. There is no music history text or anthology of source readings that does not include the passages from *The Republic* on the dangers of music. The ethical thread runs through the whole history of music and philosophy: from St. Augustine and any number of other Church fathers, to Vincenzo Galilei and any number of other Florentine humanists, all the way to Wagner, to Nietzsche, to Tolstoy, and into the twentieth century, when people began to laugh at it.

We've all snickered, I'm sure, at the following story, already old in the time of Boethius, who, writing in the sixth century CE, asked:

> Is there anyone who does not know the tale about the young man from Taormina who, drunk and excited by the sound of the hypophrygian mode, was calmed by Pythagoras, who brought him back to his senses by changing the music to a spondee? Whereas a prostitute had been locked up in the house of a rival, and whereas he, in a frenzy, wanted to burn the place down, Pythagoras, who was watching the night sky as usual, and observing the course of the stars, having realized that excited as he was by the Phrygian mode, he would refuse, despite the many warnings of his friends, to

change his mind, advised that the mode be changed, thus tempering the frenzy in the young man's soul, and restoring him to a peaceful state of mind.[32]

I once heard a wonderful old medievalist musicologist named Luther Dittmer get a very easy laugh by telling a version of this story and adding, "Tunings on request, heh heh heh." From then on I got the same laugh in class many times. But it's a nervous laugh. Even if this version of musical ethos is hyperbolic the way parables are always hyperbolic, we all know that the phenomenon it dramatizes is real enough. Modern psychologists attest to it. "I want to report that the two easiest ways of getting peak experiences (in terms of simple statistics in empirical reports) are through music and through sex," the then president of the American Psychological Association, Abraham Maslow, told an audience gathered at Tanglewood in July of 1967 for a symposium on "Music in American Society," having just defined peak experiences as those essential to "becoming fully human."[33] Post-Freudian psychologists might disagree with the terminology, but not with the judgment.

So it is not that musical ethos has been refuted and we no longer believe in it; rather that it has been exorcised and we no longer assent to it—when we are talking, that is, about classical music. In other musical contexts, including academic ones, discussion of musical ethos is allowed. The translation from Boethius's Latin from which I was just quoting comes from the American edition of a very serious study by Gilbert Rouget, a French ethnomusicologist who this past July, incidentally, celebrated his hundredth birthday.[34] Much of the discussion in it is of music and trance in contemporary Africa. In the study of possession cult music from Benin, then, ethos is tolerated. And another area in which American ethnomusicologists and sociologists enthusiastically study musical ethos is in the context of political and social activism. One of the clippings God sent me as I started work on this talk came by way of the AMS-list, the weblist of the American Musicological Society, which on November 9, 2016, sent around an announcement of a conference at UCLA to take place the next April. The propaedeutic accompanying the call for papers contains this pair of paragraphs:

> On both global and local scales, the current state of affairs is at a moment of great flux and portentous adversity. We face issues of global warming, war, oppression, and social violence. As humanists we investigate notions of power structures and knowledge bases, as well as the cultures that give rise to these systems and the resulting contentions. Musical cultures can react to and engage with these issues—it [sic]

---

32. Boethius, *De Institutione musica*, quoted in Gilbert Rouget, *Music and Trance: A Theory of the Relations between Music and Possession* (Chicago: University of Chicago Press, 1985), 229.
33. Abraham Maslow, "Music Education and Peak Experience," *Music Educators Journal* 54 (1968): 164–65, 169; quoted in John Kapusta, "The Self-Actualization of John Adams," *Journal of the Society for American Music* 12 (2018): 318.
34. He died on 8 November 2017 at the age of 101, eleven months after this lecture was delivered.

can express a voice that is perhaps otherwise unheard or silenced by the rest of society.

As an art tradition that historically foments new collective identities and galvanizes movements, music's fluidity and malleability in the service of activism relays a complex relationship between cultural tradition and cultural change. How does music reflect and respond to evolving political climates? What solidarity arises from the unifying effect of music implemented in action? How can music elicit social and political change? This conference seeks to investigate the intricate and infinite ways in which music, culture, and social movements interact.

Mutatis mutandis, that might have been written by St. Basil of Caesarea, two hundred years before Boethius. His homily on the Psalter, also familiar from any number of classroom anthologies, including the one I put together with Piero Weiss in the 1970s, is precisely about the solidarity that arises from the unifying effect of music implemented in action.[35] It might also have been written by Rouget de Lisle, who composed "La Marseillaise"; or by Pierre Degeyter, who composed the music for "L'Internationale"; or by Horst Wessel, if he was indeed the author of the tune to which his lyrics have been sung since Joseph Goebbels declared the so-called "Horst Wessel-Lied" the official anthem of the Nazi Party; or by Andrey Zhdanov, Stalin's culture czar, whose doctrine of Socialist Realism was heavily (though of course tacitly) indebted to Tolstoy's ideas about artistic ethos, and particularly about the "infectious" power of music.[36] All of them have assumed that music can elicit social and political change, and in the order I have listed them they move closer and closer to what we think of as totalitarian modes of political and social thought. So now we may begin to understand the taboo on the matter of musical ethics in the name of pure aesthetics against which I have been working by calling attention to the dangers of music.

For a pithy endorsement of the taboo I call—predictably—upon Igor Stravinsky, the most usual of all suspects, who made the insulation of art one of his life's missions. We can all probably quote his famous pronouncements along these lines, but here is one you may not have heard. In one of the very last of his so-called conversations with his ghostwriter, Robert Craft, he goes on a counteroffensive against the charge of "aestheticism," which he defines, ad hoc, as "the self-sufficiency, or as it may be, the selfishness, of an artist who refuses to come out and play." He of course rejects the charge, suggesting that it originates in "my lack of sympathy with the use of music as an advertisement for extra-musical causes, even the greatest symphony, as I see it, being able to do very little about Hiroshima."[37]

---

35. Weiss and Taruskin (eds.), *Music in the Western World*, 2nd ed., 21–22.

36. See R. Taruskin, "Current Chronicle: Molchanov's *The Dawns Are Quiet Here*," *Musical Quarterly* 62 (1976): 105–15.

37. Robert Craft, *Bravo Stravinsky* (Cleveland: World Publishing Co., 1967), 112; reprinted with minor changes in Igor Stravinsky, *Themes and Conclusions* (London: Faber & Faber, 1972), 98.

Indeed, the greater the symphony, this seems to imply, the less it can do; for one of the things this statement seeks to accomplish is the differentiation of high-art music from the lower, more ephemeral types that, in the words of the UCLA conference announcement, "reflect and respond to evolving political climates." Love it or hate it—and here Stravinsky willy-nilly agrees with Tolstoy (hence with Zhdanov), not to mention Pierre Bourdieu—high art more readily creates social division than it does social solidarity. Stravinsky's opinion could be interpreted as a justification of moral indifference, the debased precinct to which aesthetic autonomy, too zealously defended, will inexorably descend.[38] Or it might be viewed, in a better light, as a defense against the subversion or distortion of artworks in the interests of propaganda. In that sense, classical music has been, literally, a safe space for artists and their audiences.

Literally, yes; but, I would insist, not actually. It is because I do not believe that the space we have created for art is truly safe, and because I do believe that our repression of ethics from the discourse of classical music has harmed it, that I have become so interested in exposing and accounting for the taboo, and bringing its premises, both witting and unwitting, to light, and ultimately bringing them down. You may be getting ready to tell me, as I have so often been told, that I am beating a dead horse. But I have proof that the horse is still kicking.

God sent me the relevant clipping, as he so often does, on the very day I was drafting this part of my text—on 16 November last, if you want to know the date—when I dropped in at the UC Berkeley music department (which I only do sporadically now that I am an emeritus prof) and I found the latest music textbook catalogue from Oxford University Press, containing a full description of a music appreciation text by R. Larry Todd, advertised as "adoptable" for spring 2017, which is to say that it was not yet published, but imminent. It was billed, of course, as innovative (because all textbooks are billed as innovative), but its actual innovations were in technology, not content. One of its format features was a "Why Listen?" paragraph that came at the beginning of each chapter. Here is the one telling us why we should listen to Romantic music:

> Somewhere in the second half of the eighteenth century, the status of music began to rise among the arts. Until then, music had often been regarded as a diversion because of its association with subjective emotional experiences. But with the transformation brought on by the Romantic movement—including its new interest in subjectivity—music acquired new allure and prestige. By the late nineteenth century, music's position among the arts had changed considerably. The influential English critic Walter

---

38. Cf. R. Taruskin, "Is There a Baby in the Bathwater?" *Archiv für Musikwissenschaft* 63 (2006): 163–185, 309–27; rpt. in Taruskin, *Cursed Questions: On Music and Its Social Practices* (Oakland: University of California Press, 2020), 99–146.

Pater captured music's new importance when he wrote that "all art constantly aspires towards the condition of music."[39]

I am well aware that it is unfair to my old friend Larry to appear to be singling him out when he is only doing what we have all been doing for a very long time. But by quoting him in what was then a forthcoming (that is, a not-yet-but-soon-to-be-published) commercial text, I am able to show, irrefutably, that we are still doing it, disseminating the same old ideas on classical music as a way of selling it to the as yet uninitiated. And what we are doing when we quote dear old Walter Pater is removing music—as an art, or insofar as it is art—from the wider world. The "condition of music" did indeed have to do with "subjective emotional experiences," as Larry Todd writes—but only with emotional experiences engendered by music. It was not a mimetic theory, let alone an ethical theory, that Pater and his progeny promoted, and only in the mildest and most decorous way was it an arousal theory, for it placed the highest aesthetic value on form (and, by extension, technique), thus prefiguring all those approaches to art that I have tried to characterize (and challenge) as embodying what I call the poietic fallacy—for a fallacy it is, and we are still working to instill it.

"While in all other kinds of art it is possible to distinguish the matter from the form, and the understanding can always make this distinction, yet it is the constant effort of art to obliterate it," wrote Pater to explain his famous dictum. As to why I regard it as a fallacy: Pater stipulated "that the mere matter of a poem, for instance, its subject, namely, its given incidents or situation, [or] the mere matter of a picture, the actual circumstances of an event, the actual topography of a landscape, [are] nothing without the form, the spirit, of the handling." So far I agree, as would anyone, I suppose. But then Pater goes on to write that "this form, this mode of handling, should become an end in itself," and further, that "this is what all art constantly strives after, and achieves in different degrees," with music, which has no necessary natural model, out in front, thus providing the other arts with an object for emulation.[40] Ultimately form must banish content from our minds. All that should matter to us in this view is the quality of the maker's input; that is why I call it *poietic*, borrowing the term from Jean Molino's *tripartition sémiotique*, which Jean-Jacques Nattiez popularized in musicology for a while.[41] It is a fallacy insofar as it excludes the matching viewpoint of the apprehender, which Molino called

---

39. R. Larry Todd, *Discovering Music* (New York: Oxford University Press, 2017), 299.
40. Walter Pater, *The Renaissance: Studies in Art and Poetry* (1873; London: Macmillan, 1922), 134–35.
41. See Jean-Jacques Nattiez, *Music as Discourse*, trans. Carolyn Abbate (Princeton: Princeton University Press, 1990), following Jean Molino, "Fait musical et sémiologie de la musique," *Musique en jeu* 17 (1975): 37–62, translated by J. A. Underwood as "Musical Fact and the Semiology of Music," *Music Analysis* 9 (1990): 133–156.

esthesic, covering all the things that Pater stigmatizes with the word "mere": matter, subject, incidents, situation, topography. The danger of music is in the perception, not the making; and to ignore the perceptual aspects (even as one affects to be training listeners, as music appreciation claims) is an act of evasion that lowers rather than raises consciousness, hence lowers defenses.

As Larry Todd's citation of Pater shows, music appreciation received its mandate from the Victorians, with Matthew Arnold at their head. In this country it was the viewpoint promoted by the old guard of newspaper critics about whom Joseph Horowitz writes so longingly, beginning with John Sullivan Dwight and proceeding through Henry Krehbiel, Henry T. Finck, W. J. Henderson, and Olin Downes.[42] These were the critics who posited, a priori, that the effect—hence the purpose (though they would never have used the word)—of art was moral uplift, and the higher the art, the higher it lifted you up. That there could be any moral danger in such an enterprise was unthinkable, not to be suggested.

But that is already a danger, a twofold danger. There is the danger, of course, of moral blindness, so well exemplified by Ned Rorem's perfectly insulated tautology: "Art, insofar as it is art, does not change us."[43] (I just love that clause beginning "insofar"!) Because it extends its purview to morals, Rorem's dictum is even smugger than Schoenberg's famous "If it is art, it is not for all, and if it is for all, it is not art."[44] But the other danger is worse. Teaching people that love of art ennobles them teaches them nothing but self-regard. You are left wondering, with George Steiner, "How to explain those who sing Schubert in the evening and torture in the morning?" "I'm going to the end of my life," he told an interviewer, "haunted more and more by the question 'Why did the humanities not humanize?' I don't have an answer."[45] Did you ever hear anything so sad? But that is because the question was wrong.

VI

Where did it go wrong? I blame Immanuel Kant, way back at the dawn of what we call aesthetics, that change in the status of the arts to which Larry Todd draws renewed attention in his new textbook: Kant, with his insistence on disinterestedness in our evaluation of art, and in the making of it as well, insofar as the artist should demonstrate no purpose beyond the sheer purpose of making—what Kant

---

42. See Joseph Horowitz, *Classical Music in America: A History of Its Rise and Fall* (New York: W. W. Norton, 2005); or Horowitz, *Moral Fire: Musical Portraits from America's Fin-de-Siècle* (Berkeley and Los Angeles: University of California Press, 2012).

43. Ned Rorem, "Letters," *New York Times,* 12 May 1991, Arts & Leisure sec., 6.

44. Arnold Schoenberg, "New Music, Outmoded Music, Style and Idea" (1946), in idem, *Style and Idea* (Berkeley and Los Angeles: University of California Press, 1985), 124.

45. Peter Applebome, "A Humanist and Elitist? Perhaps," *New York Times,* 18 April 1998.

called *Zweckmäßigkeit ohne Zweck,* usually translated as "purposiveness without purpose."[46] You would think that with that criterion in mind, Kant would place music at the top of the artistic heap, like Pater; but no, he placed it at the bottom, because it did not convey propositions. So while music was "the highest among those arts that are valued for their pleasantness," nevertheless, if "we estimate the worth of the beautiful arts by the culture they supply to the mind[,] . . . music will have the lowest place . . . because it merely plays with sensations."[47] Like so many literary persons, Kant thought music just a pretty tinkling, or, to use his own analogy, a sonic perfume, a purely sensuous phenomenon; and the only danger music could pose, accordingly, was the same as the danger posed by scent, that of unwelcome diffusion. "Those who recommend the singing of spiritual songs at family prayers do not consider that they inflict a great hardship upon the public by such noisy . . . devotions, for they force their neighbors either to sing with them or to abandon their meditations."[48]

Let's face it: like another otherwise admirable person, Vladimir Nabokov, Kant was militantly tone deaf.[49] And at least one of his contemporaries knew it, and called him out. This is the clipping from God that, although I am presenting it in conclusion, actually started this whole sermon on its way, when I received from the University of California Press a book for blurbing: Philip V. Bohlman's brilliantly annotated edition of the musical writings of Johann Gottfried Herder. I of course knew Herder as the philosopher whose study of Baltic folksongs had laid the foundation for romantic nationalism. (Indeed, the word *folksong—Volkslied—* was his coinage.) And I knew his theories about music and language. But what Bohlman's edition first brought to my attention was *Kalligone,* one of Herder's latest works, written in 1800, the last year of the eighteenth century, when music was on the brink of its fatal embrace of the "work concept," as Lydia Goehr has made us all aware.[50] Like William F. Buckley but a century and a half ahead of schedule, Herder "st[ood] athwart history, yelling Stop."[51] And while nobody ever gets history

---

46. Immanuel Kant, *Kritik der Urteilskraft* (1795), chap. 23.

47. Kant, *Critique of Judgment,* trans. J. H. Bernard (New York: Hafner Publications), 171.

48. Ibid., 174.

49. For Nabokov, see the interview, conducted by Alvin Toffler, that appeared in *Playboy* (January 1964): "The social or economic structure of the ideal state is of little concern to me. My desires are modest. Portraits of the head of the government should not exceed a postage stamp in size. No torture and no executions. No music, except coming through earphones, or played in theaters" (in Robert Golla, ed., *Conversations with Nabokov* [Jackson: University Press of Mississippi, 2017], 83).

50. See her *Imaginary Museum of Musical Works,* 2nd ed. (New York: Oxford University Press, 2007).

51. From the oft-quoted mission statement in the first issue of the *National Review* (1955), proclaiming that it "stands athwart history, yelling Stop, at a time when no one is inclined to do so, or to have much patience with those who so urge it."

to stop, Herder did write the very retort to Kant that I've always wanted to write myself.

Herder never names Kant, but paraphrases him so closely that we are left in no doubt as to whose recent writings on music he found to be "contrary to all experience." "More pleasure than culture," indeed! "A fine art or an applied art?"—how can you even ask? And how can you prefer the visible (painting) to the audible (music)? That is simply a category error. "Space cannot become time, nor time space. The visual cannot be made audible, nor the audible visual. Precisely because the arts exclude each other in their representation do they achieve their distinctiveness."[52] Here, of course, he's paraphrasing another unnamed but easily recognized predecessor, Gotthold Ephraim Lessing and his *Laokoön, or the Limitations of Poetry* (1766), a book I too have often prescribed to the ailing or perplexed.

Wherein lies the distinctiveness of music for Herder? Lessing did not venture to choose between the arts of time and the arts of space, but for Herder, music ineluctably surpasses the arts of the visible. "It *must* surpass them, just as spirit surpasses the *body*, for music is spirit, related to the power of the innermost strength, that of *movement*." Music derives its power from its invisible movement, through which "it speaks to us, moving us with true impact." And, "we ourselves . . . does anyone know how? . . . sense this impact, without opposition, but with real power." And now a truly remarkable passage, which will remind anyone who knows them of famous discussions of music by Arthur Schopenhauer, Eduard Hanslick, Susanne Langer, Roger Sessions, and several of our own contemporaries:

> Every moment is *temporary* for this art, and so it must be, for it is precisely the ways in which it is *shorter* and *longer, stronger* and *weaker, more* and *less,* that produces its *meaning,* its *impression.* In its *arrival* and *departure,* in its *becoming* and *being,* therein lies the conquering strength of sound and its perception. In the ways this or that tone combines with others, in the ways tones rise and fall, disappear, or raise and renew themselves on the string stretched by harmony toward eternal, insoluble laws, therein lies my soul, my courage, my love and hope. . . . You effervescent spirits of the air, come with gentle tones and flee, move my heart and release me to an eternal longing, through you and to you.[53]

Of course this is yet another metaphor . . . but not "just another" metaphor. This one, despite Herder's disclaimer, really explains something. It is the earliest attempt I know to try actually to account for the effects of music described by Plato in that passage from the *Republic* that always comes first in our books of source readings. I'll quote it from the translation in which most of us first encountered it in our musical education, the one that Oliver Strunk chose to open his classic anthology:

---

52. Johann Gottfried Herder and Philip V. Bohlman, *Song Loves the Masses: Herder on Music and Nationalism* (Oakland: University of California Press, 2017), 257.

53. Ibid.

"Education in music is most sovereign, because more than anything else rhythm and harmony find their way to the inmost soul and take strongest hold upon it, bringing with them and imparting grace, if one is rightly trained, and otherwise the contrary."[54] And Herder's idea resonates equally well with one of the latest such avowals, the one in Roger Sessions's "Questions about Music," the book-form publication of the lectures Sessions gave when he held the Charles Eliot Norton professorship of poetry at Harvard in 1968–69, the very forum from which Stravinsky had issued his *Poetics of Music* some three decades earlier. "What music conveys to us," Sessions said,

> —and let it be emphasized, this is the nature of the medium itself, not the consciously formulated purpose of the composer—is the nature of our existence, as embodied in the *movement* that constitutes our innermost life: those inner gestures that lie behind not only our emotions, but our every impulse and action, which are in turn set in motion by these, and which in turn determine the ultimate character of life itself.[55]

Or with W. H. Auden's version:

> If it be asked what such music is "about," I do not think it too controversial to say that it presents a virtual image of our experience of living as temporal, with its double aspect of recurrence and becoming.[56]

These avowals of the powers of music, as I have already implied, are at the same time warnings of the dangers of music. They suggest the reason why Hanslick, possibly having read it in Herder, had the wit to observe that "the concept of motion has up to now been conspicuously neglected in investigations of the nature and effects of music, [but] it seems to us the most important and fruitful concept."[57] Their relevance even extends beyond music, as Lessing might well have pointed out, into the other temporal art media. Writers of words often speak of the music of poetry and even prose, and when they do, they are probably speaking not only about sound correspondences like rhyme, assonance, or alliteration, but also about something more elemental, that Virginia Woolf, for one, was trying to get at in one of her letters to Vita Sackville-West. "Style," she wrote slyly, "is a very simple matter":

> [I]t is all rhythm. Once you get that, you can't use the wrong words. But on the other hand here I am sitting after half the morning, crammed with ideas, and visions, and so on, and can't dislodge them, for lack of the right rhythm. Now this is very

---

54. Trans. Paul Shorey; in Oliver Strunk, *Source Readings in Music History* (New York: W. W. Norton, 1950), 8.
55. Roger Sessions, *Questions about Music* (New York: W. W. Norton, 1971), 45.
56. W. H. Auden, "Music in Shakespeare: Its Dramatic Use in His Plays," *Encounter* 9, no. 6 (December 1957): 31–44, at 33.
57. Eduard Hanslick, *On the Musically Beautiful,* trans. Geoffrey Payzant (Indianapolis: Hackett, 1986), 11.

profound, what rhythm is, and goes far deeper than words. A sight, an emotion, creates this wave in the mind, long before it makes words to fit it; and in writing (such is my present belief) one has to recapture this, and set this working (which has nothing apparently to do with words) and then, as it breaks and tumbles in the mind, it makes words to fit it.[58]

These waves, breaks, and tumbles are all virtual movements—"inner gestures," as Sessions put it. Ursula Le Guin titled a book of essays *The Wave in the Mind* after this very passage. Asked about it, she glossed Woolf's text in a manner that edges even closer to what Sessions had to say about music. "Beneath memory and experience," she said,

> beneath imagination and invention, beneath words, there are rhythms to which memory and imagination and words all move. The writer's job is to go down deep enough to feel that rhythm, find it, move to it, be moved by it, and let it move memory and imagination to find words.[59]

But if, as Auden says, all the temporal arts model temporality—and at that level of generality it is no more than a tautology—music does so most profoundly and indispensably, because it is always already beneath words. That only magnified its power in the minds of those who understood that power's source, and made them fearful. Hanslick, who ensconced the notion of musical motion at the very center of his philosophy with his famously inscrutable (and untranslatable) slogan that music consists of *tönend bewegte Formen,* devoted the rest of his book to a zealous attempt to contain it, frankly acknowledging the danger. "The other arts persuade," he wrote, "but music invades us."[60] Since Sessions's memorable formulation, there have been very few acknowledgments of that invasive power; and whenever I have raised the matter, as you have seen, someone has tried to bat me down. Let us instead press on with our effort to explain it.

As you have perhaps already noticed thanks to Ursula Le Guin's shrewd appropriation from Virginia Woolf, Herder's motion metaphor, now so familiar, is actually a double metaphor, or maybe a pun, playing on the transitive and intransitive meanings of the verb *to move*. Music moves, and because it moves, it moves us. But as Herder also knew, there is an actual, tangible basis for the metaphor— or rather, the many metaphors—of musical motion in the physics of sound production. Thus the levels of motion in music, actual and virtual, are at least three. Herder asks:

---

58. Virginia Woolf to Vita Sackville-West, 16 March 1926, in *The Letters of Virginia Woolf,* ed. Nigel Nicolson, vol. 3 (Boston: Houghton Mifflin, 1980), 247.
59. Ursula K. Le Guin, "The Question I Get Asked Most Often," in *The Wave in the Mind: Talks and Essays on the Writer, the Reader, and the Imagination* (Boulder, CO: Shambhala, 2004), 281.
60. Hanslick, *On the Musically Beautiful,* 50.

Do not all bodies emit a *sound* when they are struck and made to reproduce themselves elastically? Is there not a medium that takes up this sound, carries it forth, and conveys it to other harmonious bodies? What is sound therefore but the *voice of all agitated bodies, projected out from within?* Declaring, softly or loudly, to other *harmonious* beings their suffering, their resistance, their agitated energies?[61]

So music works through *Bewegung,* which in this context I would like to translate as *activation*. Bodies are activated; their vibration activates the air, which activates our sense organs, which through a mental process involving metaphor activate our emotions and ultimately our behavior. Almost as if speaking across the centuries directly to Lydia Goehr and the writers she has interpreted, and almost as if giving voice to my own critique of the poietic fallacy, Herder wrote that "the product of all transitory arts is *effects,* not works."[62] (It works better in German: "Wirkungen, nicht Werke.") He takes this very far, in a passage that Bohlman omitted from his edition—so far as seemingly to deny that there can be such a thing as musical form.

> With regard to the sensations and even shapes that reach us through hearing, we cannot speak of the fixed outlines and forms presented by the eye, for in fact the ear never configures in a fixed manner. Even if tones could constitute forms or parts of forms, they would all last only briefly; each tone takes its form with it and buries it.[63]

This passage will no doubt warm the heart of Justin London or Jerrold Levinson, a music theorist and a philosopher respectively, who have variously questioned the formalist fetish.[64] I question the fetish too, and no less zealously, but I nevertheless recognize and admit that here Herder went too far in opposing it. Our minds can indeed store a series of impressions and constitute them as a shape in memory, and thereafter as an anticipation; and such abstracted shapes can be generalized and classified; and there is no harm in this as long as we remember that these shapes exist in us—in our imaginations—rather than in the music we hear and interpret.

This is how the metaphor of musical form must have started—and eventually it led to *Formenlehre,* the prescriptive study of musical forms, which has done harm. Again, and as promised, we are dealing with a choice between two viable

---

61. Herder, *Kalligone* (Weimar: Hermann Böhlaus Nachfolger, 1955), 35; quoted in Thomas W. Patteson, "'Wirkungen, nicht Werke': The Musical Aesthetics and Influence of Herder's *Kalligone*" (2008), www.thomaspatteson.com/uploads/7/3/8/8/7388316/wirkungen_nicht_werke.pdf (5).
62. Herder, *Kalligone,* 95; quoted Patteson, 6.
63. Herder, *Kalligone,* 228; quoted Patteson, 11.
64. Jerrold Levinson, *Music in the Moment* (Ithaca, NY: Cornell University Press, 1998); Justin London, review of same, *Journal of the American Musicological Society* 52 (1999): 156–62; also London, "*Fernhören* Is Bunk: Jerrold Levinson's *Music in the Moment,*" colloquium presentation, UC Berkeley, October 1998.

metaphors. But the primary effect of music, I hope we can agree, is more as Herder describes it than as Hanslick did when, actively resisting the *Bewegung* in his own "tönend bewegte Formen," he compared music to an arabesque, which is visible and (as Lessing would insist) static, although it must originate in a curving motion (of pen- or brush-holding hand or arm).

What proves the point about primacy for me is the memory of my first full-bore encounter with the man whose genius for musical invasions gave Hanslick the fright that produced his famously regressive, famously evasive theory: who else but Richard Wagner? It took place in January 1960, when I was fourteen. Friends of my parents, who had a subscription to the Metropolitan Opera, were going to a wedding and had to miss a matinee performance of Wagner's *Tristan und Isolde* starring Birgit Nilsson, whose recent Met debut in the role of Isolde had been front-page news.[65] My parents were going to the same wedding, so the ticket holders' grandson and I got the tickets. I was still young for Wagner at full strength, and sitting through the entire opera—even in a box at the Old Met, lucky me—was an endurance contest. But the final aria—you know, "Isoldens Verklärung," which everybody calls the *Liebestod*—hit me with a force such as I had never experienced when listening to music (and by then I was already an avid and somewhat knowledgeable, or at least opinionated, listener). It stayed with me for days. And it was, I think, precisely because I was not anticipating its effects of motion and assimilating them to notions of musical form, but rather allowed myself to be caught up in their real-time unfolding and shattered upon their agonizingly postponed culmination, that they were so strong.

It was harmonic motion, or progression—a metaphor, yes, but it sure seems real—that invaded me and showed me that such a thing was possible. Harmonic motion is an especially tortuous metaphor, and one highly dependent on acculturation (so it could only affect me as it did because I was by then, as I say, an avid and precociously experienced listener), but it was the very metaphor that Wagner consciously invoked when he wrote of navigating the sea of harmony. (Herder does not explicitly employ it, but adumbrates it remarkably when he speaks of music's "arrival and departure.") I have played Nilsson recordings of the *Liebestod* to my classes from the moment I became a college teacher, precisely to show them what music can do thanks to its motion metaphors, and hoping that it will have an effect on them like the one it had on me when I first heard it. But although I still appreciated its force on these subsequent occasions, and was far more consciously aware of how Wagner was achieving that miraculous *Wirkung,* I never felt it again as strongly as I did that first time, partly because it now was form to me: something

---

65. Howard Taubman, "Birgit Nilsson as Isolde Flashes Like New Star in the Met Heavens," *New York Times,* 19 December 1959, 1; Paul Henry Lang, "The Met Has a New Isolde, and She Is a Real Princess," *New York Herald Tribune,* 19 December 1959, 1.

that existed in memory outside of actual elapsing time, that was now apprehended in anticipation and, willy-nilly, braced for.

So there are two main music metaphors, movement and form or "structure," and they are in contradiction. And if the contradiction is not noticed more often, it is because the metaphors themselves are so familiar as to have become naturalized. We often don't even think of them as metaphors, and this applies most especially to structure, which is often assumed to be an immanent property of music, even by today's professional philosophers. Here, for example, is a paragraph from a recent book called *Music and Aesthetic Reality*, by an especially prolific British writer on aesthetics, Nick Zangwill, who casts himself as a faithful follower of the man he refers to, in all earnestness, as "the great Hanslick." It is the crucial paragraph, in fact, which contains the definition of the book's most important term:

> "Realism" is a word familiar to philosophers, but others may not be familiar with it. By "realism" about musical experience, I mean a view that foregrounds the *aesthetic properties* of music and our experience of these properties: musical experience is an awareness of an array of sounds and of the aesthetic properties that they determine. Our experience is directed onto the sound structure and its aesthetic properties. This is the *content* of musical experience. Anything else, such as other mental states caused by such musical experience, is not part of *the intrinsic nature* of musical experience. They are a distraction from *the music itself*. Our basic or primary musical experience is of the music—of the sounds and their aesthetic properties.[66]

I take it as read (as a British philosopher might say) that there are no premeditated metaphors in this passage. Here we are talking, as realists, about the real thing. And yet, as I hope you noticed, one of our basic metaphors is lurking there withal, seemingly unnoticed by the author—namely "structure," which properly refers to complex entities (that is, wholes consisting of parts that define the whole in their mutual relations). I insist that it can *only* be a metaphor when applied to temporal unfoldings, and the dictionary supports me. My trusty desk dictionary, the 1950 edition of the *American College Dictionary*, which has been on my desk for a very long time, gives these meanings for the word, all of which clearly pertain to space, not time:

1. A mode of building, construction, or organization; arrangement of parts, elements, or constituents.
2. Something built or constructed: a building, bridge, dam, framework, etc.
3. A complex system considered from the point of view of the whole rather than of any single part: *the structure of modern science.*
4. Anything composed of parts arranged together in some way; an organization.
5. *Biol.* mode of organization; construction and arrangement of tissues, parts, or organs.

---

66. Nick Zangwill, *Music and Aesthetic Reality: Formalism and the Limits of Description* (New York: Routledge, 2015), 14 (italics added).

6. *Geol.* a. the attitude of a bed or stratum, or of beds or strata of sedimentary rocks, as indicated by the dip and strike. b. coarser features of rocks as contrasted with their texture.
7. The manner in which atoms in a molecule are joined to each other, especially in organic chemistry where it is represented by a diagram of the molecular arrangement.[67]

That last definition is the crucial one for me, for as anyone knows who has ever looked into a music textbook, whether theory or history or appreciation, the "structure" of a musical composition is almost always represented didactically by abstracted diagrams, i.e., visually, which is to say in a form that substitutes space for time. Lessing would object along with me. And that, I suggest, is how classical music creates its safe space. Looking at the score, or at a diagram that statically represents the harmonic trajectory that (as Scott Burnham says David Lewin used to say) "clobbered" fourteen-year-old me in 1960, and has surely clobbered many of you when you heard it with fresh ears, one can easily say, with little Alice, "Why, you're just a pack of notes." Arnold Whittall, defending the poietic fallacy, came very close to saying just this about a score that packs almost as great a wallop as *Tristan*. Acknowledging the pervasiveness of "discords" (his word) in Stravinsky's *Sacre du printemps*, he wrote that "[i]t may indeed be the case that the 'rules' of the game can only be discovered if the discords are 'translated' into some other medium [he means Allen Forte's pitch-class sets], in which they can be examined without the psychological burden of their true character and quality. For *Le Sacre* remains an explosive work, and analysis may be impossible unless the score is first defused."[68] But that defusing took place long ago, not in the academy but in the concert hall, when the ballet that so many disapproved of owing to its grisly subject matter and the musical style that seemed heartlessly to celebrate an ugly ritual the way Handel celebrated the plagues of Egypt (but without the humor) became a key component of the triumphant emancipatory parable of modernist music history, in the course of which it was divested of its original subject and became for most listeners an orchestral showpiece that produces euphoria, never revulsion.[69]

If we really thought about what the piece—when danced as a ballet rather than pranced through as an orchestral track meet or dissected in the sterile music theory lab—is showing us, and even reveling in, we might well be revolted. Just as we might be revolted if we understood the text of Prokofiev's gorgeous-sounding *Zdravitsa*, a hymn of praise to one of the twentieth century's great butchers, or

---

67. *American College Dictionary*, ed. Clarence L. Barnhart (New York: Random House, 1950), 1200.
68. Arnold Whittall, "Music Analysis as Human Science? *Le Sacre du Printemps* in Theory and Practice," *Music Analysis* 1, no. 1 (March 1982): p. 50.
69. See R. Taruskin, "Resisting the Rite," in *Russian Music at Home and Abroad* (Oakland: University of California Press, 2016), 395–428.

Orff's *Carmina burana,* the original "Springtime for Hitler." I especially loved talking about *Carmina burana* with my undergraduate music history classes at Berkeley, because practically everyone in the class had sung it in high school and just adored it. So I just had to tell them all the reasons why they might hate it instead. But I worked the other side of the street, too. When presenting Milton Babbitt's *Composition for Four Instruments,* which the class reliably hated, I gave them reasons why they might love it instead. The main reason, it turns out, is not unrelated to the reason why everyone loves Isolde's *Liebestod.* When the four titular instruments finally play their complementary trichords (the three-note shapes) from which the row that governs the piece is assembled, simply and in order, at the very end, the sense of arrival is palpable and moving—if one has analyzed the music to the point where one can recognize that a process has reached completion. Even a piece of serial music can have a discoverable and meaningful trajectory, a sense of movement and achievement.

So I hope it is obvious that I am not in any simple ideological way opposed to formal analysis, or any of the other things that musicologists do. I too talk about structure. But I try to keep it, along with everything else, in perspective, which is to say that I try to remember that it is a mental construct. That keeps it real. My position may be reminding you of Carolyn Abbate, in her polemic titled "Music—Drastic or Gnostic?," which could be understood as another plea to study *Wirkung* rather than *Werke.*[70] But I reject with indignation the third sentence of that celebrated piece—"Shouldn't this be what we do . . .?" (meaning, of course, what *you* do)—and all that follows from it; and if it were my article I would have called it "Music—Drastic *and* Gnostic." Both need attention. Down with prescriptions: we can go on studying *Werke* alongside *Wirkung.* Fine with me. The thing is to get rid of taboos, not exchange old ones for new. I don't know whether that will stop our orchestras from becoming charities, but if talk about music engages difficult, dangerous issues like the ones I've sought to raise, it may become more engaging, and perhaps more listeners will be engaged by the talk, and then by the music.

---

70. Carolyn Abbate, "Music—Drastic or Gnostic?" *Critical Inquiry* 30 (2004): 505–36.

Laci része

(Laci's Part)

2

Liszt and Bad Taste

[T]here is a right and a wrong to taste, quite as absolute as the death sentence.
—TERRY EAGLETON, *THE IDEOLOGY OF THE AESTHETIC*[1]

[G]ood taste is the enemy of great art.
—BERNARD ASHMOLE[2]

The only unifying element that [Jacques-Émile] Blanche detected in Picasso's work was "taste, taste, always taste." So long as this implied bad taste, the artist might have agreed, but good taste was abhorrent to him.
—JOHN RICHARDSON[3]

To me, bad taste is what entertainment is all about.
—JOHN WATERS[4]

I. ASPERSIONS

My title may appear provocative, but I doubt whether anyone is likely to disagree, first, that of all the great composers, Liszt is the one most frequently accused of bad taste; and second, that somehow these accusations have never threatened his status among the great. Indeed, as Charles Rosen once suggested, the accusations in some sense and to some degree actually identify Liszt's particular position in the pantheon.

Originally given at the international interdisciplinary conference "Liszt and the Arts," Institute for Musicology of the Hungarian Academy of Sciences, Budapest, 19 November 2011; published in *Studia Musicologica Academiae Scientiarum Hungaricae* 54 (2013): 1–17.

1. Terry Eagleton, *The Ideology of the Aesthetic* (Oxford: Basil Blackwell, 1990), 43.
2. Bernard Ashmole, *The Classical Ideal in Greek Sculpture,* Lectures in Memory of Louise Taft Semple, delivered 19 and 20 February 1963 (Cincinnati: University of Cincinnati, 1964), 44 (statement often misattributed to Picasso).
3. John Richardson, *A Life of Picasso,* vol. 3 (New York: Random House, 1991), 479.
4. John Waters, *Shock Value: A Tasteful Book about Bad Taste* (New York: Thunder's Mouth Press, 2005), 2.

Rosen put it in the form of a trumped-up paradox, saying of Liszt that his "early works are vulgar and great; the late works are admirable and minor."[5] Very cagey, this: Liszt's most-admired works, say the *Faust-Symphonie* or the B-minor Sonata, came in between. Take away the invidious comparison, and take away the sophistry, and Rosen's point still resonates. But take away the vulgarity, and Liszt is no longer Liszt. Reviewing the first volume of Alan Walker's Liszt biography in the *New York Review of Books*, Rosen went even further in his baiting, asserting that "to comprehend Liszt's greatness one needs a suspension of distaste, a momentary renunciation of musical scruples." And then, for good measure: "[O]nly a view of Liszt that places the Second Hungarian Rhapsody in the center of his work will do him justice."[6]

That was not an endorsement of the Rhapsody, which Rosen, along with Hanslick and Bartók, thought "trivial and second-rate."[7] What made the provocation doubly surefire was the racial innuendo that tainted not only Liszt and the Rhapsody, but all who came in contact with them. Did not Pierre Boulez say of Bartók that his "most admired works are often the least good, the ones which come closest to the dubious-taste, Liszt-gypsy tradition"?[8] And does that not go a long way toward accounting for Bartók's overt hostility toward a tradition, that of the so-called *verbunkos*, on which he remained covertly dependent?[9] The taint even tainted the tainter; all of which was simply too much for Alfred Brendel, who, exasperated, took Rosen's bait:

> Though enjoying, once in a while, some of the Hungarian Rhapsodies and operatic paraphrases, I wince at Charles Rosen's assertion[s]. . . . In the matter of taste, no composer could be more vulnerable than Liszt. . . . In contrast to Charles Rosen . . ., I consider it a principal task of the Liszt player to cultivate such scruples [as Rosen bids us renounce], and distil the essence of Liszt's nobility. This obligation is linked to the privilege of choosing from Liszt's enormous output works that offer both originality and finish, generosity and control, dignity and fire.[10]

---

5. Charles Rosen, *The Romantic Generation* (Cambridge, MA: Harvard University Press, 1995), 474.

6. Charles Rosen, "The New Sound of Liszt," *New York Review of Books*, 12 April 1984.

7. Dana Gooley, Review of *Liszt's Transcendental Modernism and the Hungarian Gypsy Tradition*, by Shay Loya, *Journal of the American Musicological Society* 66 (2013): 570, summarizing the opinions of Hanslick, Bartók, and Rosen, not stating his own.

8. Pierre Boulez, "Bartók, Béla" (originally a contribution to *Encyclopédie Fasquelle de la musique* [1958]), rpt. in Boulez, *Stocktakings from an Apprenticeship*, trans. Stephen Walsh (Oxford: Clarendon Press, 1991), 241.

9. See David E. Schneider, *Bartók, Hungary, and the Renewal of Tradition* (Berkeley and Los Angeles: University of California Press, 2006), esp. chaps. 1, 2, and 6; also Schneider, "Peasant Music or Gypsy Music: The Implications of Düvö for Bartók's Polemics," *International Journal of Musicology* 9 (2000): 141–68.

10. Alfred Brendel, "The Noble Liszt," *New York Review of Books*, 20 November 1986; rpt. in Brendel, *Music Sounded Out* (New York: Farrar Straus Giroux, 1990), 158–59.

But although I sympathize with his aversion to Rosen's deliberately annoying formulations, I find Brendel's fastidiousness insufficiently generous toward Liszt and the impulses that his work embodies, which, though not always noble, are undoubtedly great. Rosen came closer than Brendel did to pinpointing the fascination that Liszt exerted over his times, and continues to exert over us. Especially worthy of pursuit is Rosen's most irritating pronouncement of all: "Good taste," he teased, "is a barrier to an understanding and appreciation of the nineteenth century."[11]

If the remark grates, it is because of the aspersion it seems to cast on the century that now looms in retrospect as the greatest century of all for music—or at least as the century in which music was accorded the greatest value. But suppose we read the aspersion the other way—as a critique of good taste? Ever since reading the Rosen-Brendel exchange, a quarter of a century ago, I have had an itch to use Liszt and his reception as a tool to situate good taste (along with greatness) in social and intellectual history, and to fathom the profound ambivalence with which virtuosity has always been regarded.

II. WHAT'S GOOD ABOUT IT?

So let me begin again, with another quotation—something that has been rattling in my head even longer—more than half a century by now, ever since, as an undergraduate, I read Thomas Mann's last novel, *The Confessions of Felix Krull, Confidence Man*. At one point the social-climbing title character receives guidance from a titled nobleman, the Marquis de Venosta, whose world he wants to crash. Among the many insights the Marquis offers him is this:

> You come, as one now sees . . ., of a good family—with us members of the nobility, . . . one simply says "of family"; only the bourgeois can come of a *good* family.[12]

What does this mean? What is the difference between "family" and "good family"? What it seems to come down to is that "family" is an existential category, while "good family" is an aspirational one. The bourgeoisie is the aspiring class. The aristocracy simply *is*. And so it is with "taste" and "good taste." "Taste" is something the elect possess and exercise without calculation or necessary self-awareness. "Good taste" is exhibited rather than exercised: it is something attributed to the maker of deliberate and calculated choices in recognition of their correctness, as a mark of

---

11. Rosen, "New Sound of Liszt."

12. Thomas Mann, *Confessions of Felix Krull, Confidence Man*, trans. Denver Lindley (New York: New American Library of World Literature [Signet Books], 1957), 192. "Sie sind also, wie man nicht erst hier und heute sieht, sondern schon immer sah, aus guter Familie—bei uns Adlingen, verzeigen Sie das harte Wort, sagt man einfach »von Familie«; aus guter Familie kann nur der Bürgerliche sein" (Thomas Mann, *Bekenntnisse des Hochstaplers Felix Krull* [Frankfurt: Fischer Bücherei, 1965], 182).

social approval. "Taste" is a matter of predilection, "good taste" of profession. A display of good taste is a mark of aspiration to social approbation, and the standard to which exhibitors of good taste must aspire is never their own. To show good taste is to seek admission to an elite station which the possessor of "taste" occupies as an entitlement. A show of good taste is thus never a mark of election; rather, it marks one as an outsider wanting in. It implies submission as well as aspiration, hence inhibition. Like Felix Krull (which is not necessarily to mark them as *Hochstapler*), people who display their good taste are trying to crash a social world.

Recall now the famous words that Haydn spoke to Leopold Mozart in February 1785:

> Before God, and as an honest man, I tell you that your son is the greatest composer known to me either in person or by name. He has taste, and, what is more, the most profound knowledge of composition.[13]

Imagine for a moment that Haydn had said to Leopold not that Wolfgang "has taste," but that "he has good taste." The compliment would have crumbled. "Taste" (*Geschmack*), in the sense that Haydn used the word, was an existential category. Either you were of the elect or you weren't; and if you didn't have taste as a birthright you couldn't acquire it, even though you had "the most profound knowledge of composition."

But what did it consist of? In this context, clearly enough, "taste" was an unerring and intuitive insider awareness of what was meet, or fitting. The closest any musician came to enunciating such a definition may have been Mattheson in 1744, at the outset of a chapter, "Vom musikalischen Geschmack," in a book devoted to the aesthetics of opera:

> Taste, figuratively speaking, is the inner awareness, preference, and judgment by which our intellect impinges upon sensory matters. If, as Pliny would have it, the tongue has a mind of its own, so the mind can be said to have its own tongue, with which it tastes and evaluates the objects of its attention.[14]

In that figurative sense, "taste" was comparable to the securely inculcated breeding the Marquis de Venosta had in mind when he distinguished "family" from

---

13. Haydn to Leopold Mozart about Wolfgang, quoted by Leopold in a letter to Nannerl, 16 February 1785; translation from Otto Erich Deutsch, *Mozart: A Documentary Biography* (Stanford, CA: Stanford University Press, 1965), 236. "Ich sage ihnen vor Gott, als ein ehrlicher Mann, ihr Sohn ist der größte Componist, den ich von Person und den Namen nach kenne: er hat Geschmack, und über das die größte Compositionswissenschaft."

14. "Der Geschmack, in verblümter Bedeutung, ist die innerliche Empfindung, Wahl und Beurtheilung, die unser Verstand, in sinnreichen Dingen, von sich spüren läßt. Wenn die Zunge ihren eignen Verstand hat . . . so hat der Verstand auch gewissermaßen seine eigne Zunge, womit er seine Gegenstände kostet und prüfet" (Johann Mattheson, *Die neueste Untersuchung der Singspiele, nebst beygefügter musikalischen Geschmacksprobe* [Hamburg: Christian Herold, 1744], 123).

"good family." Mattheson's ingenious, opportunistic inversion of a dimly remembered Pliny[15] provides a link between the literally gustatory and the derivative or conceptual meanings of the term, while also giving off an echo of its social history; for as soon as the word *taste* was elevated beyond its purely sensory meaning in the seventeenth century, it connoted an attribute of aristocracy. The sociologist Stephen Menell locates that origin at the French court, where members of the old *noblesse d'épée*, threatened by the ever-aspiring, ever-rising bourgeoisie, secured positions at court as "specialists in the art of consumption" (at first of food), developing hierarchies of taste and codes of behavior that stressed the restraint of gluttony and refinement of table manners.[16] Taste had become a metaphor for discrimination. The turn from food to art as the arena for the exercise of taste can be traced first in Italy. Giulio Mancini, the personal physician to Pope Urban VIII and a famous collector of fine painting, equated *gusto* and *giudizio* (taste and judgment) in his *Considerazioni sulla pittura*, an essay published in 1623.[17] Half a century later, the attempt to acquire taste without breeding was satirized for all time in Molière's *Bourgeois gentilhomme* (1670). The butt of the satire could be described, long *avant la lettre*, as "good taste," the quality or attainment to which Monsieur Jourdain aspired. Good taste, in effect, was imitation taste, not the real thing.

The notion of taste as an absolute standard, sanctioned by consensus of the capable ("men of sentiment") and associated in the first instance with one of David Hume's most famous essays, has persisted since the eighteenth century despite the rise of less intransigent definitions.[18] Its staying power is attributable to the conviction, among the politically conservative, that (to quote Wye J. Allanbrook) "the agreement of cultivated people about what is good and beautiful was a force for the political cohesion of the community" and a support, or occasional pinch-hitter, for hereditary aristocracy.[19] As Schiller emphasized in *On the Aesthetic Education of Man* (1794), "No privilege, no autocracy of any kind, is tolerated where taste rules";[20]

---

15. According to Enrico Fubini, Mattheson was faultily recalling a passage from Pliny's *Natural History* (2:174): "Intellectus saporum caeteris in prima lingua, homini et in palate" (Other creatures recognize tastes with the tip of their tongue; man also on his palate). See E. Fubini, ed., *Music and Culture in Eighteenth-Century Europe: A Sourcebook* (Chicago: University of Chicago Press, 1994), 295.

16. Stephen Mennell, "On the Civilizing of Appetite," *Theory, Culture, and Society* 4 (1987): 390; quoted in Jukka Gronow, *The Sociology of Taste* (London and New York: Routledge, 1997), 19.

17. Mancini's arguments are summarized in Andrew Dell'Antonio, *Listening as Spiritual Practice in Early Modern Italy* (Berkeley and Los Angeles: University of California Press, 2011), 50.

18. David Hume, "Of the Standard of Taste" (1757), in idem, *Selected Essays*, ed. Stephen Copley and Andrew Edgar (Oxford: Oxford University Press, 1996), 13–54.

19. Wye J. Allanbrook, *The Secular Commedia: Comic Mimesis in Late Eighteenth-Century Music*, ed. Mary Ann Smart and Richard Taruskin (Berkeley and Los Angeles: University of California Press, 2014), 78.

20. Friedrich Schiller, *On the Aesthetic Education of Man*, ed. Elizabeth M. Wilkinson and L. A. Willoughby (Oxford: Oxford University Press, 1967), 217.

but that is because taste itself offered an alternative standard of excellence, working through positive rather than negative reinforcement (the promise of esteem replacing the threat of coercion) to internalize the pressure. Where its autonomy and universality are believed in, spontaneous fellow-feeling and disinterested fraternity can seem to rule. But such belief, far from spontaneous, must be cultivated, or rather, instilled. A century and more after Schiller, T. S. Eliot echoed his sentiments when he defined "the function of criticism" as "roughly speaking, . . . the elucidation of works of art and the correction of taste."[21] This was the formulation of a man who would shortly declare himself to be "classicist in literature, royalist in politics, and Anglo-Catholic in religion."[22] The word for it, and it has become a fighting word, is elitism.

Where Eliot went, Stravinsky tagged dependably behind. In the *Poétique musicale,* his own pinnacle of intransigence delivered at Harvard a decade later, in 1939–40, Stravinsky devoted the last of his six "leçons" ostensibly to musical performance, but in fact made it clear from the outset that the subject matter of the lecture, which outwardly took the form of a diatribe against virtuosos expressly intended as a correction of taste, was in fact *d'ordre éthique plutôt que d'ordre esthétique*—"of an ethical rather than of an aesthetic order."[23] At the height of his dudgeon, Stravinsky declared: "Whereas all social activities are regulated by rules of etiquette and good breeding, performers are still in most cases entirely unaware of the elementary precepts of musical civility, that is to say of musical good breeding—a matter of common decency that a child may learn."[24] And yet, when invoking the *grand thème de la soumission,* the "great principle of submission" that runs like a thread through all six lessons, Stravinsky contradicts himself, proclaiming instead that "this submission demands a flexibility that itself requires, along with technical mastery, a sense of tradition and, commanding the whole, an aristocratic culture that is not merely a question of acquired learning."[25] There is your existential taste: something that one possesses as a birthright, as an aristocrat possesses (and is possessed by) "family."

---

21. T. S. Eliot, "The Function of Criticism" (1923), in *Selected Prose of T. S. Eliot,* ed. Frank Kermode (New York: Harcourt Brace Jovanovich/Farrar, Straus & Giroux, 1975), 69.

22. T. S. Eliot, *For Lancelot Andrewes: Essays on Style and Order* (London: Faber & Gwyer, 1928), ix.

23. Igor Stravinsky, *Poetics of Music in the Form of Six Lessons,* bilingual ed. (Cambridge, MA: Harvard University Press, 1970), 165.

24. "Alors que toutes les activités sociales sont régies par un code de la bienséance et du savoir-vivre, les exécutants en sont encore, le plus souvent, à ignorer les préceptes élémentaires de la civilité musicale, c'est à dire d'un savoir-vivre musical, puéril et honnête" (ibid., 172–73).

25. "Ce soumission exige une souplesse qui requiert elle-même, avec la maîtrise technique, un sens de la tradition et, brochant sur le tout, une culture aristocratique qui n'est pas entièrement susceptible d'acquisition" (ibid., 169–71).

How far this is, we are apt to think, from our colloquial concept of taste as mere personal preference, the thing that is proverbially beyond dispute. That definition, too, has a long history, going back to the anonymous Latin maxim—*De gustibus non est disputandum*—that everybody knows. That maxim, however, is less ancient than it might appear. It is by no classical author. Its origin, rather, is presumed to be medieval and scholastic by virtue of its concern to distinguish between matters open to reason and persuasion and those which philosophers, or at least scholastics, had better leave alone. As the economists George J. Stigler and Gary S. Becker put it, at the outset of a famous article in which they broke the old taboo and embarked on a path that led, for one of them, to the Nobel Prize:

> The venerable admonition not to quarrel over tastes is commonly interpreted as advice to terminate a dispute when it has been resolved into a difference of tastes, presumably because there is no further room for rational persuasion. Tastes are the unchallengeable axioms of a man's behavior.[26]

Taste as axiomatic (and professed) personal preference seems a bulwark of personal autonomy, a democratic or egalitarian notion. As Liszt himself once said, "[I]t is a matter of taste whether the old or the new is more charming. Taste is quite certainly a personal thing."[27] But consider this story, which will bring us back to music. It comes from a famous pamphlet, *Comparaison de la musique italienne et de la musique française*, issued in 1704 by Jean Laurent Lecerf de la Viéville, Lord of Freneuse, in answer to a like-named pamphlet, *Paralèle des Italiens et des Français*, issued in 1702 by another French aristocrat, Abbé François Raguenet. As Lecerf relates, a courtier fond of the brilliance and grandeur of Italian music brought before King Louis XIV a young violinist who had studied under the finest Italian masters for several years, and bade him play the most dazzling piece he knew. When he was finished, the king sent for one of his own violinists and asked the man for a simple air from *Cadmus et Hermione*, an opera by his own court composer, Jean-Baptiste Lully. The violinist was mediocre, the air was plain, nor was *Cadmus* by any means one of Lully's most impressive works. But when the air was finished, the king turned to the courtier and said, "All I can say, sir, is that that is my taste."[28]

The king did effectively put an end to the argument by invoking his taste, but was that because there can be no disputing tastes or because there can be no

---

26. George J. Stigler and Gary S. Becker, "De Gustibus Non Est Disputandum," *American Economic Review* 62, no. 2 (March 1977): 76–90, at 76.

27. Richard Zimdars, trans. and ed., *The Piano Masterclasses of Franz Liszt, 1884–1886: Diary Notes of August Göllerich* (Bloomington: Indiana University Press, 1996), 71 (Weimar, Saturday 27 June 1885).

28. Jacques Bonnet, *Histoire de la musique*, vol. 3 (Amsterdam, 1725), 322; paraphrased in R. Taruskin, *The Oxford History of Western Music*, vol. 2: *Music in the Seventeenth and Eighteenth Centuries*, rev. ed. (New York: Oxford University Press, 2010), 85.

talking back to a king? Lecerf's argument with Raguenet, who had waxed rapturous about the voices of *castrati*, was really all about authority, not taste. In disputes or assertions regarding tastes, authority has many surrogates. Among professionals, including musical professionals, the chief surrogate is experience. Do you remember this famous footnote from Johann David Heinichen's thoroughbass treatise of 1725?

> If experience is needed in any art or science, it is certainly needed in music. . . . But why must we seek experience? I will give you one little word that encompasses the three basic requirements in music (talent, knowledge, and experience), and its heart and its outer limits as well, and all in four letters: *Goût*. Through application, talent, and experience, a composer needs to acquire above all an exceptional sense of taste in music. The distinguishing feature of a composer with well-developed taste is simply the skill with which he makes music pleasing to and beloved by the general, educated public; in other words, the skills by which he pleases our ear and moves our sensibilities. . . . An exceptional sense of taste is the philosopher's stone and principal musical mystery by means of which the emotions are unlocked and the senses won over.[29]

This is the kind of taste—something acquirable through labor and application (provided one has good instruction), hence available not only to the aristocracy of birth but also to an aristocracy of talent and training—to which Francesco Geminiani referred in the title of *A Treatise of Good Taste in the Art of Musick* (ca. 1749), a title that on the surface might seem to offer a counterexample to the distinction between "taste" and "good taste." In the body of the treatise, however, Geminiani (who had lived in London since 1714 and was writing in idiomatic English) usually inserts the indefinite article before "good taste." Thus, at the beginning of the Preface: "[T]he Envy that generally attends every new Discovery in the Arts and Sciences, ha[s] hitherto deferr'd my publishing these rules of Singing and Playing *in a good Taste*"; and, at the end: "Thus I have collected and explain'd all the Ingredients of *a good Taste*."[30]

That indefinite article does a lot of work: it is incompatible with both of the categories of taste with which we are concerned, whether with "taste" as the superior existential endowment Haydn attributed to Mozart, or with the "good taste" in which Liszt was held by Rosen and Brendel to be deficient. When you put Geminiani's odd usage together with the title of his previous treatise, to which *A Treatise of Good Taste* was a supplement and on which it was dependent—that is, *Rules for Playing in a True Taste on the Violin, German Flute, Violoncello, and Harpsichord*

---

29. Johann David Heinichen, *Der General-Bass in der Composition* (1728), trans. George Buelow, in Buelow, *Thorough-Bass Accompaniment according to Johann David Heinichen* (Berkeley: University of California Press, 1966), 273–74 (translation slightly adjusted after comparison with the original).

30. Francesco Geminiani, *A Treatise of Good Taste in the Art of Musick* (London: [the author], 1749); facsimile reprint, ed. Robert Donington (New York: Da Capo Press, 1969), 1, 4; emphasis added.

(London, ca. 1745)—it is clear that the two expressions "a good taste" and "a true taste" are interchangeable equivalents of "correct (or elegant) style." And indeed, it turns out that the *Treatise on Good Taste* is merely a manual on embellishment, consisting of a table of ornaments followed by models for application, chiefly to familiar Scots airs furnished with a thoroughbass. As Robert Donington comments in his Foreword to the facsimile edition:

> "Good taste" was almost a technical term of the period. It was used not merely for a refined and cultured attitude toward music in general; it was used for a refined and cultured ability to invent more or less improvised ornamentation for melodies often notated in plain outline, but requiring such ornamentation in order to be given a complete performance.[31]

Corroboration of this usage in eighteenth-century English comes from Dr. Burney, who in his musical travelogue of 1771 defined *taste* as "the adding, diminishing, or changing [of] a melody, or passage, with judgement and propriety, and in such a manner as to *improve* it."[32] In short, therefore, and ironically, Geminiani's brand of "good taste," insofar as it implies the addition of impromptu passage work to written compositions, virtually coincides with the "bad taste" of which Liszt and his contemporaries would be accused a century after Geminiani's time, and up to the present day. It did not take long for fashions to start changing. At the very end of his *General History of Music*, in the twelfth chapter of the fourth volume, published in 1789, devoted to the "General State of Music in England at our National Theatres, Public Gardens, and Concerts, during the Present Century," the same Dr. Burney wrote off Geminiani's guides to "a good taste" as having appeared "too soon for the present times. Indeed, a treatise on good taste in dress, during the reign of Queen Elizabeth, would now be as useful to a tailor or milliner, as the rules of taste in Music, forty years ago, to a modern musician."[33]

III. SUBJECT AND OBJECT

Yet insofar as Geminiani offered instruction in correct practice, his good taste did imply submission to a standard, a matter of meeting expectations. The taste or ability about which Heinichen and Geminiani wrote was not the personal preference of any particular performer or composer, nor of the authors themselves, nor even the consciously formulated demand of the "general, educated public." Effort and

---

31. Ibid., v.

32. Charles Burney, *The Present State of Music in France and Italy; or, The Journal of a Tour through Those Countries, Undertaken to Collect Materials for a General History of Music* (London: T. Becket, 1771), vii.

33. Charles Burney, *A General History of Music from the Earliest Ages to the Present Period*, vol. 4 (London: The author, 1789), 642; spelling modernized.

education can give us all equal access to correct style: the taste of one is (or ought to be) the taste of all. It is on the promise to impart that universal taste, which all successful composers must master, that the authority of Heinichen's or Geminiani's manuals depended. It was an authority that, in the guise of classicism, could become authoritarian. Take for example Voltaire's article, s.v. *Goût*, in the seventh volume of Diderot and d'Alembert's *Encyclopédie,* issued in 1757—the same year as Hume's seminal essay, but expressing what seems to be a pre-Humean formulation, in which *l'homme du goût,* "the man of taste" (compare Hume's "men of sentiment" or the Marquis de Venosta's "person of family"), is expressly equated with *le connoisseur,* the one who knows the rules of style as the gourmet knows the rules of the kitchen and dining table. "If the gourmet immediately perceives and recognizes a mixture of two liqueurs, so the man of taste, the connoisseur, will see at a glance any mixture of styles"—and, of course, disapprove.[34] The standard is one of purism, and failure to meet it constitutes *le goût dépravé,* debased taste, otherwise known, more simply, as bad taste. When Voltaire admits the phrase *un bon goût,* it is as the back-formed opposite of *un mauvais goût.* Only the latter can be personal. As an idiosyncrasy it is tantamount to a flaw that one must eliminate so as to restore the universal norm, which is simply *le goût,* sans qualifier. "They say there is no point disputing tastes," Voltaire concedes:

> and this is right enough when it is only a matter of sensory taste, . . . because one cannot correct defective organs. It is different with the arts; as their beauties are real, there is a good taste that discerns them and a bad taste that does not; and the mental defect that gives rise to a wayward taste can often be corrected.[35]

Here Voltaire anticipates Eliot: taste, for him, is no mere matter of fallible individual preference, but one of conformity to an established criterion, hence subject to correction. From there, Voltaire connects "good taste" to the idea of perfected style, or what literary historians would eventually christen "classicism":

> The taste of an entire nation can be corrupted. This misfortune usually comes about after periods of perfection. Artists, for fear of being imitators, seek untraveled paths; they flee the natural beauty that their predecessors had embraced; there is some merit in their efforts; this merit covers their faults; the novelty-besotted public runs after them; it soon loses interest, however, and others appear who make new efforts to please; they flee even further from nature; taste disappears amid a welter of novel-

---

34. ". . . si le gourmet sent & reconnoît promptement le mélange de deux liqueurs, l'homme de goût, le connoisseur, verra d'un coup-d'oeil prompt le mélange de deux styles" (*Encyclopédie* 7:761, online at https://artflsrv03.uchicago.edu/philologic4/encyclopedie0521/navigate/7/2520/?byte=8143729).

35. "On dit qu'il ne faut point disputer des goûts, & on a raison quand il n'est question que du goût sensuel, . . . parce qu'on ne peut corriger un défaut d'organes. Il n'en est pas de même dans les Arts; comme ils ont des beautés réelles, il y a un bon goût qui les discerne, & un mauvais goût qui les ignore; & on corrige souvent le défaut d'esprit qui donne un goût de travers" (*Encyclopédie* 7:761).

ties that quickly give way one to another; the public no longer knows where it is, and it longs in vain for the age of good taste that will never return. It has become a relic that a few sound minds now safeguard far from the crowd.[36]

This wholly aristocratic, existential notion of "good taste," ever resistant to destabilizing innovation, is a decreed taste, sanctioned by tradition. Still a child of the seventeenth century, Voltaire locates its source dogmatically in "nature." D'Alembert, the editor of the *Encyclopédie,* in an appendix to Voltaire's article, somewhat modernizes (that is, relativizes) Voltaire's position by vesting the power of decree in "philosophy," which at least implies human agency:

> [I]n matters of taste, a smattering of philosophy can lead us astray, while philosophy better understood can bring us back. It is an insult to literature and philosophy alike to think that they could harm or exclude one another. Everything that pertains, not only to our way of thinking, but also to our way of feeling, is philosophy's true domain.... How could the true spirit of philosophy be opposed to good taste? On the contrary, it is its strongest support, because this spirit consists in returning everything to its true principles, in recognizing that every art has its own particular nature, each condition of the soul its own character, each thing its own particular tint—in one word, that one should never transgress the limits of a given genre.[37]

These extracts exhaust references to *le bon goût* (rather than the more usual *goût,* unmodified) in the *Encyclopédie.* The addition of the adjective does not change the meaning; "good taste" here does not differ from "taste" *tout simple,* the sense of suitability that Haydn recognized as Mozart's mark of election. And that is because the *philosophes* located the criterion of correct discrimination not in the perceiving subject but in the object perceived, rightly apprehended according to

---

36. "Le goût peut se gâter chez une nation; ce malheur arrive d'ordinaire après les siecles de perfection. Les artistes craignant d'être imitateurs, cherchent des routes écartées; ils s'éloignent de la belle nature que leurs prédécesseurs ont saisie: il y a du mérite dans leurs efforts; ce mérite couvre leurs défauts, le public amoureux des nouveautés, court après eux; il s'en dégoûte bientôt, & il en paroit d'autres qui font de nouveaux efforts pour plaire; ils s'éloignent de la nature encore plus que les premiers: le goût se perd, on est entouré de nouveautés qui sont rapidement effacées les unes par les autres; le public ne sait plus où il en est, & il regrette en vain le siecle du bon goût qui ne peut plus revenir; c'est un dépôt que quelques bons esprits conservent alors loin de la foule" (*Encyclopédie* 7:761).

37. "Ainsi dans les matieres de goût, une demi philosophie nous écarte du vrai, & une philosophie mieux entendue nous y ramene. C'est donc faire une double injure aux Belles-Lettres & à la Philosophie, que de croire qu'elles puissent réciproquement se nuire ou s'exclure. Tout ce qui appartient non-seulement à notre maniere de concevoir, mais encore à notre maniere de sentir, est le vrai domaine de la Philosophie: il seroit aussi déraisonnable de la reléguer dans les cieux & de la restraindre au système du monde, que de vouloir borner la Poésie à ne parler que des dieux & de l'amour. Et comment le veritable esprit philosophique seroit-il oppose au bon goût? il en est au contraire le plus ferme appui, puisque cet esprit consiste à remonter en tout aux vrais principes, à reconnoître que chaque art a sa nature propre, chaque situation de l'ame son caractere, chaque chose son coloris, en un mot à ne point confondre les limites de chaque genre" (*Encyclopédie* 7:769).

"its own particular nature," of which philosophy is the arbiter. To acquire taste, on the encyclopedists' terms, one had to submit to their authority. It became a task for a new cohort of eighteenth-century thinkers to emancipate the notion of taste from that of external authority, while nevertheless remaining faithful to the idea of its universality or its status as what Kant called a *sensus communis*, a "common sense," meaning "a sense shared by all."[38] This required some fancy skating.

IV. CONSENSUS

Kant's solution was to posit that taste was subjective in that it concerned not the properties of objects but the pleasure or displeasure of contemplating subjects.[39] Hence "it is absolutely impossible to give a definite objective principle of taste ... for then the judgement would not be one of taste at all."[40] And yet such reactions were ideally universal because they derived from a faculty possessed by humans, only by humans, and by all humans.[41] Within Kant's careful definitions, all have taste, and all have the same taste. It must, therefore, enjoy "a title to subjective universality," or what we now somewhat less paradoxically call *intersubjectivity*.[42]

Evidence of universality is to be sought in consensus, which must be discernible despite the great variety in subjective preference that strikes the casual observer. For Hume, this made it all the more imperative to seek, or establish, "a Standard of Taste: a rule, by which the various sentiments of men may be reconciled; at least, a decision, afforded, confirming one sentiment, and condemning another."[43] The problem for Enlightened theories of universal taste was that of outliers, people of ostensibly normal endowment who nevertheless diverged from the intersubjective consensus. Is it possible to speak of "wrong" taste, even if, as Kant maintained (and as everyone beginning with Hume seems to agree), "the judgment of taste is ... not a judgment of cognition," and therefore cannot be considered factual?[44] If there

---

38. Immanuel Kant, *Critique of Judgment* (1790), trans. J. H. Bernard (New York: Hafner Press, 1951), 160.

39. Ibid., 37–38.

40. Ibid., 186.

41. Ibid., 44. "Pleasantness concerns irrational animals also, but beauty only concerns men, i.e. animal, but still rational, beings—not merely *quâ* rational (e.g. spirits), but *quâ* animal also—and the good concerns every rational being in general."

42. Ibid., 46.

43. Hume, "Of the Standard of Taste," *Selected Essays*, 136. Hume ingeniously infers the existence of such a standard from the durability of aesthetic judgments when compared with scientific or philosophical theories. Rationally constructed theories are invalidated by their successors, while "just expressions of passion and nature are sure, after a little time, to gain public applause, which they maintain forever.... The abstract philosophy of Cicero has lost its credit: The vehemence of his oratory is still the object of our admiration" (148–49).

44. Kant, *Critique of Judgment*, 37.

can be wrong taste, then there can be bad taste; and if there is bad taste, there can be normative good taste—something that can be aspired to. We are approaching the crux of *our* problem.

The most ingenious attempt to account for wrong taste within a universalist theory of taste is found in the introduction to Edmund Burke's famous *Philosophical Enquiry into the Origin of Our Ideas of the Sublime and Beautiful,* first published in 1757, that same bumper year that saw the publication of both the seventh volume of the *Encyclopédie* and Hume's essay on taste. Having defined taste as "that faculty or those faculties of the mind, which are affected with, or which form a judgment of, the works of imagination and the elegant arts,"[45] Burke invoked John Locke's distinction between wit and judgment.[46] "Mr. Locke," he writes, "very justly and finely observes of wit, that it is chiefly conversant in tracing resemblances: he remarks, at the same time, that the business of judgment is rather in finding differences" (17). As we know from experience, wit is much the more pleasurable function, as the perception of resemblances is a matter of immediate sensibility, whereas the discrimination of differences requires expertise and mental effort. Thus, Burke argues, taste being a judgment, its exercise is more or less correct depending not upon what he calls "a superior principle in men," but rather "upon superior knowledge," in the sense of wide acquaintance (19).

This is the crucial move. Once we postulate that taste is not a *simple* idea but a compound of sensibility and knowledge, it follows that a deficiency of taste can be the result of a deficiency in either category. "From a defect in [sensibility]," Burke writes, "arises a want of taste," which is to say an inability or disinclination to render any judgment at all; whereas "a weakness in [knowledge] constitutes a wrong or a bad [taste]" (23). This passage, coeval with Voltaire's *Encyclopédie* entry but the work of a newer breed of thinker, constitutes, to my knowledge, the earliest recognition that there can be such a thing as bad taste, as distinct from a want of taste. The latter can only be deplored or pitied (e.g. by Voltaire, or by Mann's Marquis de Venosta), whereas one can aspire, with Burke or Eliot, to correct the former.

The consequences of this distinction are far-reaching, and baleful; and Burke, to his credit, did not flinch from them. If "the cause of a wrong taste" is "a defect of judgment," he allowed, then the misevaluation of works of art

> may arise from a natural weakness of understanding, . . . or, which is much more commonly the case, it may arise from . . . ignorance, inattention, prejudice, rashness, levity, obstinacy, in short, all those passions, and all those vices, which pervert the

---

45. Edmund Burke, *On Taste, On the Sublime and Beautiful, Reflections on the French Revolution, etc.,* Harvard Classics, ed. Charles W. Eliot, vol. 24 (New York: P. F. Collier & Son, 1909), 13. Further page references to this edition will be made in the text.

46. The distinction is developed in chapter 11 of Locke's treatise, titled "Of Discerning, and Other Operations of the Mind."

judgment in other matters, prejudice it no less in this its more refined and elegant province. (23–24)

But if "bad or wrong taste" can be taken as a symptom of vice or perversion, the door has been opened wide to abuse. Burke recognizes this in an especially pregnant passage that enlarges upon an earlier point—viz., that discrimination diminishes rather than enhances pleasure because it lessens the number of objects from which we can naively derive satisfaction.

> The judgment is for the greater part employed in throwing stumbling-blocks in the way of the imagination, in dissipating the scenes of its enchantment, and in tying us down to the disagreeable yoke of our reason: for almost the only pleasure that men have in judging better than others, consists in a sort of conscious pride and superiority, which arises from thinking rightly; but then, this is an indirect pleasure, a pleasure which does not immediately result from the object which is under contemplation (24).

V. FEAR OF RIDICULE

What we are witnessing here is the birth, or at least the christening, of aesthetic snobbery, which is always and only social snobbery in disguise. An indirect or even perverse pleasure it may be, but snobbery is a powerful pleasure; and Burke's explanation of snobbery, as the sole compensation we receive for the loss of immediacy and naive pleasure that our critical judgment exacts from us, is the best account I have ever encountered of its value to snobs (a category that at times—let's admit it—tempts us all). It amounts, as well, to an account and critique of aspirational "good taste," which arises alongside and in response to aesthetic snobbery, the most quintessentially bourgeois of all snobberies, and might even be deemed tantamount to it.

It is not taste (*pace* Stravinsky) but "good taste" that conflates aesthetic and moral quality, and sits in judgment over them conjointly. Because it is the bastard child of snobbery, "good taste" requires the ever more exacting exercise of negative judgment. Forgetting, or affecting to reject, the Kantian proviso that taste is a property not of contemplated objects but of contemplating subjects, "good taste" constructs spurious existential categories such as "kitsch," a term that arose in the course of the emergence we are now tracing (and Google can tell you how often it is attached to Liszt).[47] As snobbery's surrogate, aspirational "good taste" easily

---

47. Opinions differ as to the origin of the term, whether from the English *sketch* or from the German *verkitschen*, which means to sell cheap or sell off (although the verb may have been a backformation from the noun). It has been traced to the Munich art market of the 1860s. See Matei Calinescu, *Five Faces of Modernity* (Durham, NC: Duke University Press, 1987), 232–37. An experimental googling (on 10 January 2020) linking Liszt and kitsch yielded 95,400 hits.

turns competitive. Critics who earn followings do so (as Louis Menand smirked of Pauline Kael) because they have recognized, and pander to, "the truth" that "people, at least educated people, like not to like movies, especially movies other people like, even more than they like to like them."[48]

The conjoint promise of safety and self-congratulation gives one an incentive to expand the range of objects one can consign to outer darkness, so as to maximize one's "conscious pride and superiority," to recall Burke's more elegant expression. Hence such impressive works of pseudoscholarship as Gillo Dorfles's extravagant compendium *Il Kitsch: Antologia del cattivo gusto* (published in Milan in 1968; translated into English as *Kitsch: The World of Bad Taste*), which contains, alongside what anyone might expect (Nazi and Soviet poster art, eroticized religious images, the Mona Lisa imprinted on bath towels and eyeglass cases), several items that can only have been calculated to shock the reader by their inclusion, e.g., New York's Cloisters, the museum of medieval art endowed by John D. Rockefeller in 1938. A caption explains, "The structure is entirely modern but incorporates authentic architectural features from the cloisters of medieval monasteries. Authentic objects and works of art are displayed in the halls, which are always full of tourists."[49] We are left in little doubt as to what—or rather, whom—the aspersion is meant to degrade.

The inevitable race to the limit in the fastidious exercise of captious "good taste" was well captured by Joseph Wood Krutch when reviewing a book by an especially exigent arbiter. "Her method is one of the safest," he remarked.

> If you deny permanent significance to every new book or play time will prove you right in much more than nine cases out of ten. If you damn what others praise there is always the possibility that your intelligence and taste are superior. But if you permit yourself to praise something then some other superior person can always take you down by saying "So *that* is the sort of thing you like."[50]

That fear afflicts performers as well as critics. There is a coruscating passage on taste in the treatise *Du chant* (1920) by Reynaldo Hahn, the singer, songwriter, and voice teacher who perhaps better than any other musician—and not only because he was Marcel Proust's lover—embodies the spirit of the *belle époque,* a time synonymous with elegance, as elegance may be thought synonymous with taste. But the writing drips with sarcasm:

> When singing is not directed by the heart (and you know that one cannot lightly command the service of the heart), when singing is not guided by feeling, by

---

48. Louis Menand, "Kael's Attack on Sarris," in *Polemic: Critical or Uncritical,* ed. Jane Gallop (New York: Routledge, 2004), 153–78, at 162–63.
49. Gillo Dorfles, *Kitsch: The World of Bad Taste* (New York: Universe Books, 1969), 24.
50. Joseph Wood Krutch, "The Long Claw of Contempt" (review of *Sights and Spectacles,* by Mary McCarthy), *Saturday Review of Literature,* 26 May 1956, 20.

understanding, by the direct outpourings of the heart, it is taste that assumes control, directing and presiding over everything. Then it must be everywhere at once, acting in a hundred different ways. Think of it! Every detail of the vocal offering must be submitted to the dictates of taste.

Let me be precise. By *taste*, I do not mean that superior and transcendent ability to comprehend what is beautiful which leads to good esthetic judgment. In fact, we cannot ask all singers to be people of superior taste, since such a requirement would reduce still further the very limited number of possible singers. By *taste*, I mean a wide-ranging instinct, a sure and rapid perception of even the smallest matters, a particular sensitivity of the spirit which prompts us to reject spontaneously whatever would appear as a blemish in a given context, would alter or weaken a feeling, distort a meaning, accentuate an error, run counter to the purposes of art.

I repeat: A particular sensitivity of the spirit is necessary in this sort of taste, as well as emotion and a certain fear of ridicule. It is no doubt for this reason that women display a better sense of taste in singing than men.[51]

A certain fear of ridicule. It is obvious that Hahn is speaking not of existential but aspirational taste; taste that hedges against the depredations of snobs, who censor idiosyncrasy along with sincerity and force artists (and especially, in Hahn's bigoted view, those of the weaker sex) to retreat into what Russell Lynes, the social historian of art, in a famous article that proclaimed a new social order based not on "wealth or family" but on "high thinking," derided as the "entirely inoffensive and essentially characterless" precincts of "good taste."[52]

Of course, Lynes was writing in the age of Rosen and Brendel, and describes a late stage in the socio-aesthetic process whose beginnings Edmund Burke had charted long before the stultifying category of "good taste" had gained momentum, although he may be said to have predicted it.

Let us return now to Burke's time to make our formal approach to Liszt. At the end of his discussion of (universal) taste, Burke notes optimistically "that the taste . . . is improved exactly as we improve our judgment, by extending our knowledge, by a steady attention to our object, and by frequent exercise" (25). To boil it down to a formula, he proposes that *taste = judgment = knowledge,* and he who knows most judges best. Appeals to the ignorant, therefore, are subversive of taste, because they thwart the advancement of knowledge. Those who seek, or gain, the applause of the ignorant are threats to the maturation of taste.

The stage has been set for our hero.

---

51. Reynaldo Hahn, *On Singers and Singing: Lectures and an Essay,* trans. Leopold Simoneau (Bromley, Kent: Christopher Helm, 1990), 188.

52. Russel Lynes, "Highbrow, Lowbrow, Middlebrow," *Harper's,* February 1949; rpt. *Wilson Quarterly* 1, no. 1 (Autumn 1976): 146.

VI. VIRTUOSOPHOBIA

But before he enters, there remains one last matter to broach, namely the ambiguous character of virtuosity and the ambivalent attitude toward it in Liszt's day on the part, not of audiences, surely, but of the newly professionalized class of tastemakers—what Liszt, in exasperation, called "the aristocracy of mediocrity."[53] Gillen D'Arcy Wood, a social historian of literature and music and their interrelations under romanticism, identifies this wry phrase with "an increasingly influential middle-class cultural regime that wished to be purified of virtuosic display," an aspiration he calls, straightforwardly enough, *virtuosophobia*.[54] Virtuosophobia is obviously akin to what the literary historian Jonas Barish called "the antitheatrical prejudice," in a book that traced from ancient Greece to the mid-twentieth century the curious inconsistency whereby "most epithets derived from the arts"—words like *poetic* or *epic* or *lyric* or *musical* or *graphic* or *sculptural*—"are laudatory when applied to the other arts, or to life," with the conspicuous exception of terms derived from the theater, like *theatrical* or *operatic* or *melodramatic* or *stagey*, which, by contrast, "tend to be hostile or belittling."[55] One reason for the antitheatrical prejudice is that theatrical acting, being by definition an act of dissembling, transgresses against ideals of sincerity; and virtuosos are often similarly accused, the terrific effect of their performances being unrelated, or not necessarily related, to genuine feeling.

This was an observation constantly made about Liszt during his lifetime, and not always invidiously. His American pupil Amy Fay, who attended his Weimar master classes in 1873, wrote in her memoir, *Music Study in Germany*, that

> [w]hen Liszt plays anything pathetic, it sounds as if he had been through everything, and opens all one's wounds afresh.... [He] knows the influence he has on people, for he always fixes his eyes on some one of us when he plays, and I believe he tries to wring our hearts.... But I doubt if he feels any particular emotion himself when he

---

53. According to the *Musical World* 292 (28 October 1841): 276: "M. Liszt is reported to have said that there was 'an aristocracy of *mediocrity* in England, at the head of which was William Sterndale Bennett'; he might, with a vast deal more of truth, have asserted, that there is an aristocracy of hyperbole and nonsense in Paris, of which himself and his friend, the *philosophic* Chopin, are at the summit" (unsigned review of "Souvenir de Pologne," the seventh set of mazurkas by Chopin, probably by the journal's regular reviewer and later editor, John William Davison).

54. Gillen D'Arcy Wood, *Romanticism and Music Culture in Britain, 1770–1840: Virtue and Virtuosity* (Cambridge: Cambridge University Press, 2010), esp. "Introduction: Virtuosophobia," 1–19; the quoted phrase appears on p. 8. Chapter 6 ("The Byron of the Piano," 180–214) is about Liszt's British tour of 1840–41.

55. Jonas Barish, *The Antitheatrical Prejudice* (Berkeley and Los Angeles: University of California Press, 1981), 1.

is piercing you through with his rendering. He is simply hearing every tone, knowing exactly what effect he wishes to produce and how to do it.⁵⁶

To Liszt's manner, Fay contrasted that of Joseph Joachim (once Liszt's protégé, later his most zealous detractor), who exemplified the submissive and antitheatrical attitude later associated with *Werktreue*. Where the one was "a complete actor who intends to carry away the public," the other was (that is, acted) "totally oblivious of it." Where the one "subdues the people to him by the very way he walks on the stage," the other is "'the quiet gentleman artist' who advances in the most unpretentious way, but as he adjusts his violin he looks his audience over with the calm air of a musical monarch, as much as to say, 'I repose wholly on my art, and I've no need of any "ways or manners."'"⁵⁷

Which of course is also a means of taking possession of one's public. What Fay described were two species of charismatic (that is, histrionic) "ways or manners," as she surely knew. (And Liszt was well aware of the alternative species: describing the charismatic playing of John Field he showed the same subtle irony as Fay describing Joachim: "It would be impossible to imagine a more unabashed indifference to the public.... He enchanted the public without knowing it or wishing it.... His calm was all but sleepy, and could be neither disturbed nor affected by thoughts of the impression his playing made on his hearers [since] art was for him in itself sufficient reward.")⁵⁸ The affectation of quiet absorption was the truly romantic ("disinterested") attitude, as was the antitheatrical prejudice itself and the virtuosophobia that was its musical outlet; for it was romanticism that made a fetish of sincerity. As early as 1855, in a famous letter to Clara Schumann explaining his defection from Liszt's orchestra in Weimar, Joachim broadened the antitheatrical, virtuosophobic rhetoric to encompass Liszt's compositions, focusing on the sacred works as especially flagrant breaches of propriety. By the end of the passage, it is impossible to separate the bad taste of Liszt the composer from that of Liszt the performer as the butt of Joachim's righteous indignation.

> For a long time now I have not seen such bitter deception as in Liszt's compositions; I must admit that the vulgar misuse of sacred forms, that a disgusting *coquetterie*

---

56. Amy Fay, *Music Study in Germany, from the Home Correspondence of Amy Fay* (London: Macmillan, 1886), 207–8; quoted in Karen Leistra-Jones, "Staging Authenticity: Joachim, Brahms, and the Politics of *Werktreue* Performance," *Journal of the American Musicological Society* 66 (2013): 397. Recall the second of Richard Strauss's "Ten Golden Rules for the Album of a Young Conductor": "You should not perspire when conducting. Only the audience should get warm" (Richard Strauss, *Recollections and Reflections*, ed. Willi Schuh, trans. T. J. Lawrence [London: Boosey & Hawkes, 1953], 38).

57. Fay, *Music Study in Germany*, 248–49; quoted in Leistra-Jones, "Staging Authenticity," 397–98.

58. L. Ramann, ed., *Gesammelte Schriften von Franz Liszt*, vol. 4: *Leipzig, 1882*, 265–66; trans. R. Taruskin in Piero Weiss and Richard Taruskin, eds., *Music in the Western World: A History in Documents*, 2nd ed. (Belmont, CA: Thomson/Schirmer, 2008), 312–13.

with the loftiest feelings in the service of effect was never intended—the mood of despair, the emotion of sorrow, with which the truly devout man is raised up to God, Liszt mixes with saccharine sentimentality and the look of a martyr at the conductor's podium, so that one hears the falseness of every note and sees the falseness of every action.[59]

Most explicit of all was Nietzsche. In *Der Fall Wagner* he asked, rhetorically, where Wagner belonged, and his answer went beyond Wagner to indict Wagner's father-in-law as well. Wagner belongs "*not* in the history of music. What does he signify nevertheless in that history? *The emergence of the actor in music*: a capital event that invites thought, perhaps also fear. In a formula: 'Wagner and Liszt.'"[60]

At least Wagner did his acting in the theater. Liszt, who turned instrumental performance into a branch of theater, one can only think worse. Nietzsche's peroration, in three italicized "demands," points the final finger at the musician, not the actor; for music is brought down as the theatrical is elevated. "What are the *three demands* for which my wrath, my concern, my love of art has this time opened my mouth?" thunders Nietzsche. They are these:

> *That the theater should not lord it over the arts.*
> *That the actor should not seduce those who are authentic.*
> *That music should not become an art of lying.*[61]

Nor can virtuosos ever be "disinterested," to invoke Kant's principal aesthetic yardstick. Like other theatrical performers, they are never without a *Zweck*, an ulterior purpose, namely to impress us into thunderous vanity-stroking applause and exorbitant pocket-lining expenditures; and our interest in their overcoming obstacles is a human, rather than an aesthetic, interest—the sort of interest that attends to the performances of athletes and prestidigitators as well as musicians. D'Arcy Wood gave this a social twist when writing of the "antagonism," so evident in Georgian England, and especially when Liszt tried to storm its aesthetic barricades with so much less success than he had enjoyed on the continent, "between literary (and academic) culture and the sociable practices of music, between Romantic, middle-class 'virtues' and aristocratic virtuosity."[62]

We are back again to the Marquis de Venosta, and the distinction between "family" and "good family." The former is an unearned status; the latter, a reputation earned through the exercise of virtue—which demanded vigilance against virtue's false cognate. Though etymologically descended from virtue, virtuosity, in the

---

59. Letter of December 1855; translation from Leistra-Jones, "Staging Authenticity," 414.
60. Friedrich Nietzsche, *The Birth of Tragedy and The Case of Wagner*, trans. Walter Kaufmann (New York: Vintage Books, 1967), 179.
61. Ibid., 180.
62. D'Arcy Wood, *Romanticism and Music Culture in Britain*, 270n90.

middle-class view, was sheer vice, inextricably associated with all the other vices, and that remains our incorrigibly Romantic, middle-class view today. The author of a serious scholarly book on Paganini, published in 2012, wanted to know, for example, whether "the greed, lust, pride, and vainglory that [were] manifested in multiple aspects of the virtuoso's life [can] be viewed any longer as separate from the aesthetic of virtuoso performance."[63]

VII. SWEAT AND GRACE

Hence one of the paradoxes of nineteenth-century musical reception that continues to haunt us in the twenty-first century is the simultaneous denigration of virtuosity and fetishizing of difficulty. To unpack it we might begin by returning to Edmund Burke and his famous treatise. The section on the sublime contains a short paragraph, seemingly an afterthought, on difficulty as a "source of greatness":

> When any work seems to have required immense force and labor to effect it, the idea is grand. Stonehenge, neither for disposition nor ornament, has anything admirable; but those huge rude masses of stone, set on end, and piled each on other, turn the mind on the immense force necessary for such a work. Nay, the rudeness of the work increases this cause of grandeur, as it excludes the idea of art and contrivance; for dexterity produces another sort of effect, which is different enough from this.[64]

Thus, difficulty all too dexterously overcome is not sublime; or rather, the dexterous overcoming of difficulty destroys the sublime effect and vitiates the awe that it inspires. Substitute "virtuosity" for Burke's "dexterity" and the reason will become apparent why the English critics who wrote about Liszt in the 1840s so belittled or even deplored his "transcendent" virtuosity, associating it with triviality rather than with grandeur.[65] The very act of transcendence was virtuosity's transgression—a transgression against the virtue of difficulty.

The works of Beethoven were, in Burke's intended sense, the Stonehenge of music. Even before his sketchbooks exposed "the immense force necessary for such a work" to the inquisitive eye, his labor was a proverbial struggle *per aspera ad astra*. And performing his music was likewise a proverbial struggle it became a sacrilege to appear to transcend. The approved attitude toward Beethoven—the tasteful attitude—was Stravinsky's *grand thème de la soumission*, epitomized in Artur Schnabel's famous remark that "I am attracted only to music which I consider to be better than it can be performed. Therefore I feel (rightly or wrongly)

---

63. Mai [Maiko] Kawabata, *Paganini: The Demonic Virtuoso* (Woodbridge, Suffolk: Boydell Press, 2012), 95.

64. Burke, *A Philosophical Inquiry into the Origin of Our Ideas of the Sublime and Beautiful* (1756), pt. 2/sec. 12 in its entirety, Harvard Classics, vol. 24 (see above n. 45), 68.

65. D'Arcy Wood, *Romanticism and Music Culture in Britain*, 178.

that unless a piece of music presents a problem to me, a never-ending problem, it doesn't interest me too much."[66] (Of course Schnabel's submission was as much a boast as a confession, like his answer to a reporter who asked him how his programs differed from those of other pianists; Schnabel replied, "My programs are also boring after the intermission.")[67] And if Schnabel's piety represents the epitome, way beyond epitome was Sir Colin Davis, who said of Beethoven's *Missa solemnis*, "It's such a great work, it should never be performed."[68]

Beethoven's unique social situation was bound up equally with the new attitude toward works and difficulty—or rather, the new valuation placed on old attitudes toward them—and with his removal from society as a result of deafness. It put Beethoven at the opposite social extreme from the virtuoso, who (like Beethoven himself in the earlier stages of his career) was sociability personified. Beethoven's vaunted difficulty was abetted by his aristocratic patrons, while the virtuoso was seen as playing to the common crowd.[69] The newly reified concept of artwork that Beethoven's talent and fate so abetted is our concept still. It is what made possible the notion of "classical music," which is to say, music conceptualized as a permanent and immutable object, at the same level of reification as the products of other artistic media like painting or sculpture: a concrete entity deserving the designation "work."[70] From something that elapses in time, music was thus reconceptualized as something that exists ontologically in an "imaginary museum," as Lydia Goehr put it in the title of her celebrated book—a kind of notional space.[71]

So let us imagine a reified musical work that way—as an article somehow located in a curated space. The humility so demonstratively voiced by Schnabel or Davis (whether or not we accept it at face value) is located below it. It looks *up*, like anything aspirational. The attitude of the virtuoso—who transcends all difficulties, makes light of them, and makes everything seem easy (as the commonplace accolade would have it)—is located, like anything transcendent, above the work. It looks *down*. And therefore it is an arrogant crossing of an ethical line, a hubristic

---

66. Artur Schnabel, *My Life and Music*, ed. Edward Crankshaw (New York: St. Martin's Press, 1961), 121.

67. Quoted in Gregor Piatigorsky, *Cellist* (Garden City, NY: Doubleday, 1965), 132.

68. Quoted in John Canarina, *The New York Philharmonic: From Bernstein to Maazel* (New York: Amadeus Press, 2010), 294.

69. See Tia DeNora, *Beethoven and the Construction of Genius* (Berkeley and Los Angeles: University of California Press, 1996).

70. For the most elaborate account of this aspect of musical ontology, see Roman Ingarden, *The Work of Music and the Problem of Its Identity* (Berkeley and Los Angeles: University of California Press, 1986).

71. Lydia Goehr, *The Imaginary Museum of Musical Works: An Essay in the Philosophy of Music*, rev. ed. (New York: Oxford University Press, 2007).

affront to aspiration; a fortiori, it is an affront to "good taste."[72] A London critic's review of Liszt's rendition of the Emperor Concerto, which casts him in the role of a bad curator, is a perfect summation of these strictures: "The many liberties he took with the text were evidence of no reverential feeling for the composer. The entire concerto seemed rather a glorification of self, than the heart-feeling of the loving disciple."[73]

And yet—as always—one man's transgression is another's transcendence. There is always a more "spiritual" way of viewing virtuosity, i.e., as a literal triumph over the physical. Heine wrote that where others "shine by the dexterity with which they manipulate the stringed wood, . . . with Liszt one no longer thinks of difficulty overcome—the instrument disappears and the music reveals itself." But then he immediately turns around and contradicts himself in his fascination, all but universally shared by those who experienced Liszt in the flesh, with the pianist's physical presence, obsessing over his way of "brush[ing] his hair back over his brow several times," turning his listeners into viewers, or rather voyeurs, who feel "at once anxious and blessed, but still more anxious."[74] The phobia, repressed, returns.

VIII. PERFORMING PENITENCE

The strongest avowal of virtuosophobia, the censorious distinction between virtuosity and difficulty, comes from Liszt himself, in the second of his so-called Baccalaureate Letters, published in the Parisian *Gazette musicale* on 12 February 1837, with a dedication to George Sand. The relevant passage runs as follows:

> In concert halls as well as in private drawing rooms . . ., I often played works of Beethoven, Weber, and Hummel, and I am ashamed to say that for the sake of winning the applause of a public which was slow in appreciating the sublime and beautiful, I did not scruple to change the pace and the ideas of the compositions; nay, I went so far in my frivolity as to interpolate runs and cadenzas which, to be sure, brought me the applause of the musically uneducated, but led me into paths which I fortunately soon abandoned. I cannot tell you how deeply I regret having thus made con-

---

72. Dana Gooley puts it nicely (and sympathetically) at the very outset of his study *The Virtuoso Liszt*: "Virtuosity is about shifting borders. The musician, the athlete, and the magician are potentially virtuosos as soon as they cross a limit—the limit of what seems possible, or what the spectator can imagine. Once this act of transgression is complete, the border shifts, and the boundaries of the possible are redrawn" (*The Virtuoso Liszt* [Cambridge: Cambridge University Press, 2004], 1).

73. Morris Barnett in the *Morning Post*, 18 August 1845; quoted in Dana Gooley, "The Battle against Instrumental Virtuosity in the Early Nineteenth Century," in *Franz Liszt and His World*, ed. Christopher H. Gibbs and Dana Gooley (Princeton, NJ: Princeton University Press, 2006), 109n51.

74. Heinrich Heine, "Über die französische Bühne, zehnte Brief" (1837), quoted and translated by Lawrence Kramer in *Musical Meaning: Toward a Critical History* (Berkeley and Los Angeles: University of California Press, 2002), 73.

cessions to bad taste, which violated the spirit as well as the letter of the music. Since that time absolute reverence for the masterworks of our great men of genius has completely replaced that craving for originality and personal success which I had in the days too near my childhood.[75]

Thus, with a presumed literary assist from Marie d'Agoult, Liszt accuses himself of *mauvais goût,* a locution that was still a novel one at the time of writing. But as we have already observed in the case of Schnabel, confessions can be a form of boasting, and self-abasement a form of self-promotion. I think it pretty clear that Liszt, at that moment engaged in a very public rivalry with Sigismund Thalberg, was using the rhetoric of penitence and contrition in this way, as part of a campaign to show that he, and not his challengers, had become (to quote a famous passage from a letter he had written several years before) "an artist such as is required today."[76] That is to say, an artist who was abreast of the latest intellectual fashions, who was prepared to use the press to establish good public relations, and who was therefore able to maintain preeminence in the new era of publicity. Unlike his rivals, he was displaying himself as an artist who possessed both taste and "good taste," who cultivated the aspirational posture, who looked up, not down, at "the masterworks of our great men of genius."

There is no reason to doubt the sincerity of Liszt's aspirations. But as Kenneth Hamilton has observed, "numerous reviews of his concert tours of the 1840s indicate that [as of 1837], he cultivated an attitude akin to St. Augustine's famous exhortation, 'Oh Lord, grant me chastity—but not yet!'" He was still ready and able, in the words of Carl Reinecke, to "dazzle the ignorant throng."[77] Nevertheless, the

---

75. Second "Lettre d'un bachelier ès musique à un poète voyageur," as translated by Henry T. Finck in "Was Liszt the Paganini of the Piano?" *Etude,* August 1916; rpt. in Finck, *Musical Progress: A Series of Practical Discussions of Present Day Problems in the Tone World* (Bryn Mawr, PA: Theodore Presser, 1923), 121. The original French: "J'exécutais alors fréquemment soit en public, soit dans les salons (où l'on ne manquait jamais de m'observer que je choisissais bien mal mes morceaux), les oeuvres de Beethoven, Hummel et Weber, et, je l'avoue à ma honte, afin d'arracher les bravos d'un public toujours lent à concevoir les belles choses dans leur auguste simplicité, je ne me faisais nul scrupule d'en altérer le mouvement et les intentions; j'allais même jusqu'à y ajouter insolemment une foule de traits et de points d'orgue, qui, en me valant des applaudissements ignares faillirent m'entraîner dans une fausse voie dont heureusement je sus me dégager bientôt. Vous ne sauriez croire mon ami, combien je déplore ces concessions au mauvais goût, ces violations sacrilèges de l'esprit et de la lettre, car le respect le plus absolu pour les chefs-d'oeuvre des grands maîtres a remplacé chez moi le besoin de nouveauté et de personnalité d'une jeunesse encore voisine de l'enfance."

76. Letter to Pierre Wolff, 2 May 1832, in *Letters of Franz Liszt,* ed. La Mara, trans. Constance Bache (New York: Haskell House, 1968), 8.

77. Kenneth Hamilton, *After the Golden Age: Romantic Pianism and Modern Performance* (Oxford: Oxford University Press, 2008), 235. The phrase quoted from Reinecke comes from Adrian Williams, *Portrait of Liszt: By Himself and His Contemporaries* (Oxford: Clarendon Press, 1990), 145. The review cited in n. 73, showing Liszt up to his old tricks eight years after the Baccalaureate Letters, corroborates the point.

social animus in that charge should caution us against too readily slapping a "populist" label on Liszt. Dana Gooley reminds us that some of Liszt's concert practices suggest the opposite. He imposed higher ticket prices than did any of his contemporaries, which Gooley interprets as an attempt "to siphon out the middle bourgeoisie" and ensure that his recitals remained high-prestige events, not popular entertainments.[78] The Baccalaureate Letters themselves, as we have seen, show him striving to found his reputation on "his nearness to the intellectual and political elites of Paris," the "cultural trendsetters."[79]

One of the most revealing portraits of Liszt the composer-performer in all the glorious inconsistency of his behavior, accurately reflecting the ambivalences of mores in transition, is the recollection of Vladimir Vasilievich Stasov, first published in 1889, of the great pianist's St. Petersburg debut forty-seven years earlier, in 1842:

> Everything about this concert was unusual. First of all, Liszt appeared alone on the stage throughout the entire concert: there were no other performers—no orchestra, singers or any other instrumental soloists whatsoever. This was something unheard of, utterly novel, even somewhat brazen. What conceit! What vanity! As if to say, "all you need is me. Listen only to me—you don't need anyone else." Then, this idea of having a small stage erected in the very centre of the hall like an islet in the middle of an ocean, a throne high above the heads of the crowd, from which to pour forth his mighty torrents of sound. And then, what music he chose for his programmes: not just piano pieces, his own, his true métier—no, this could not satisfy his boundless conceit—he had to be both an orchestra and human voices. He took Beethoven's "Adelaïde," Schubert's songs—and dared to replace male and female voices, to play them on the piano alone! He took large orchestral works, overtures, symphonies—and played them too, all alone, in place of a whole orchestra, without any assistance, without the sound of a single violin, French horn, kettledrum! And in such an immense hall! What a strange fellow![80]

In a somewhat earlier memoir, "The Imperial School of Jurisprudence Some Forty Years Ago," Stasov recalled that, after the first item on the program, the *William Tell* Overture, Liszt "moved swiftly to a second piano facing in the opposite direction. Throughout the concert he used these pianos alternately for each piece, facing first one, then the other half of the hall."[81] Stasov was seated near Glinka, and overheard his conversation before the concert. When one noble lady,

---

78. Gooley, *The Virtuoso Liszt*, 69.
79. Ibid., 76.
80. Vladimir V. Stasov, *Selected Essays on Music*, trans. Florence Jonas (New York: Frederick A. Praeger, 1968), 120.
81. Ibid., 121.

Mme Palibina, asked Glinka whether he had already heard Liszt, Glinka replied that he had heard him the previous evening, at an aristocratic salon.

"Well, then, what did you think of him?" inquired Glinka's importunate friend. To my astonishment and indignation, Glinka replied, without the slightest hesitation, that sometimes Liszt played magnificently, like no one else in the world, but other times intolerably, in a highly affected manner, dragging tempi and adding to the works of others, even to those of Chopin, Beethoven, Weber, and Bach, a lot of embellishments of his own that were often tasteless, worthless, and meaningless. I was absolutely scandalized! What! How dare some "mediocre" Russian musician, who had not yet done anything in particular himself [N.B. By that time, Glinka had written both his operas], talk like this about Liszt, the great genius over whom all Europe had gone mad! I was incensed. It seemed that Mme Palibina did not fully share Glinka's opinion either, for she remarked, laughingly, "Allons donc, allons donc, tout cela ce n'est que rivalité de métier!" Glinka chuckled and, shrugging his shoulders, replied, "Perhaps so."[82]

So if Liszt knew enough to pay tribute, or at least lip service, to the new Romantic ideals, his public acclaim and his consummate, irrepressible virtuosity continued to threaten them. Even after his *true* capitulation to good taste, when he withdrew from the concert stage to devote himself to what was considered at the time a particularly high-minded species of modern composition, he was regarded as threatening by musicians with a different notion of high-mindedness. Liszt came to symbolize the danger of the mass audience and those who catered to it—a danger that his composing may have posed even more drastically, in the eyes of some, than his piano playing.

In the later nineteenth century the chief threat to musical idealists was no longer exercised by virtuosos but by composers who subordinated musical values to mixed media: opera composers, to be sure, who as always commanded the largest and least discriminating audiences, but also—and worse—those who tried to turn their instrumental music into wordless operas, as Liszt did in his symphonic poems and programmatic symphonies. Whether embodied in the corruption of texts or in the corruption of media, the corruption that the fastidious really feared was the corruption of taste and mores, which looked to guardians of good taste like corruption of the flesh. In the early correspondence of Brahms and Joseph Joachim, the adjective *Lisztisch* was already a code word. In one letter, Joachim writes to Brahms of a certain passage that Brahms had written: "Es bleibt mir häßlich—ja verzeih's—sogar Lisztisch!" ("I think it's awful, even—forgive me—Lisztish!").[83] Or consider Brahms, in 1869, writing to Clara Schumann:

---

82. Ibid., translation slightly adjusted.

83. Letter of 19 April 1856, in *Johannes Brahms im Briefwechsel mit Joseph Joachim*, vol. 1 (1908; Whitefish, MT: Kessinger Publishing, 2010), 126. My thanks to Styra Avins and Robert W. Eschbach for the reference.

Yesterday Otten [G. D. Otten, conductor of the Hamburg Philharmonic] was the first to introduce works by Liszt into a decent concert: "Loreley," a song, and "Leonore" by Bürger, with melodramatic accompaniment. I was perfectly furious. I expect that he will bring out yet another symphonic poem before the winter is over. The disease spreads more and more and in any event extends the ass's ears of the public and young composers alike."[84]

This diagnosis of social pathology (or what a later anti-Lisztian crusader would call *"Regression des Hörens"*)[85] became quite explicit among the Brahmins, among whom Theodor Billroth, the famous surgeon, was the exemplary figure. Writing to the composer after a performance of Brahms's First Symphony, Billroth gave voice to a new aristocracy of *Bildung*, of education, taste, and culture—or was it just Liszt's old aristocracy of mediocrity?

> I wished I could hear it all by myself, in the dark, and began to understand [the Bavarian] King Ludwig's private concerts. All the silly, everyday people who surround you in the concert hall and of whom in the best case maybe fifty have enough intellect and artistic feeling to grasp the essence of such a work at the first hearing—not to speak of understanding; all that upsets me in advance.[86]

Billroth stands in a resistant line that gathered strength as it moved into the twentieth century: the modernist line that helped create the storied Great Divide between art and mass culture.[87] It passes through Schoenberg—for whom "if it is art, it is not for all, and if it is for all, it is not art"[88]—on its way to the likes of Adorno, Dwight Macdonald, and others who insisted that art identify itself in the twentieth century by creating elite occasions, which is to say occasions for exclusion. Liszt, with his generous, inclusive impulse, created many problems for that project.

As the line of social resistance passed through the twentieth century it got ever shriller, culminating in the pronouncements we have sampled by Rosen and Brendel, allies in snobbery despite their feigned disagreement over Liszt. Charles Rosen has never claimed to be a historian (as anyone knows who has read the

---

84. Quoted in Michael Musgrave, *A Brahms Reader* (New Haven, CT: Yale University Press, 2000), 95.

85. See Theodor Wiesengrund Adorno, "Über den Fetisch-charakter in der Musik und die Regression des Hörens," *Zeitschrift für Sozialforschung* 7 (1938) and widely reprinted; available in English as "On the Fetish-Character in Music and the Regression of Listening," in Adorno, *The Culture Industry: Selected Essays on Mass Culture*, ed. J. M. Bernstein, trans. Anson Rabinbach, Wes Blomster, Thomas Levin, Gordon Finlayson, Nicholas Walker, and Peter Dews (London and New York: Routledge Classics, 2001), 29–60.

86. Billroth to Brahms, 10 December 1876, in *Johannes Brahms and Theodor Billroth: Letters from a Musical Friendship*, trans. Hans Barkan (Norman: University of Oklahoma Press, 1957), 41.

87. Cf. Andreas Huyssen, *After the Great Divide: Modernism, Mass Culture, Postmodernism* (Bloomington: Indiana University Press, 1987).

88. Arnold Schoenberg, "New Music, Outmoded Music, Style and Idea" (1946), in idem, *Style and Idea*, ed. Leonard Stein (Berkeley and Los Angeles: University of California Press, 1985), 124.

introduction to *The Classical Style*), but it takes a singular disregard of history to assert, as he has done, that "'good taste' is a barrier to an understanding and appreciation of the nineteenth century," when in fact good taste was the invention of the nineteenth century. It was the invention of nineteenth-century bourgeois who aspired to the condition of royalty—Billroths who wanted to be Ludwigs; surgeons who wanted to be kings.

IX. CELLOING UP

In its present state of devolution, the line of good taste has descended to the likes of Jack Sullivan, whose Wikipedia entry identifies him as "an American literary scholar, professor, essayist, author, editor, musicologist, concert annotator, and short story writer,"[89] and who was quoted in the *New York Times*, the very day I was drafting the paragraph you are now reading, as complaining in the Carnegie Hall program book about the standard performing version of Chaikovsky's *Variations on a Rococo Theme* for cello and orchestra, as revised after its 1877 premiere by the original performer and dedicatee, Wilhelm Fitzenhagen, at the composer's request. Under the impression that the original version was to be performed by Yo-Yo Ma, with Valeriy Gergiyev and the Mariyinsky Orchestra, and paraphrasing a letter to Chaikovsky from his publisher, Sullivan grumbled that Fitzenhagen had taken Chaikovsky's "cannily constructed Neo-Classical piece and 'celloed it up' for his own grandstanding purposes."[90] Thrice-familiar strictures, these; as is the tone of social derision that the phrase "celloed up" (compare "gussied up" or "lawyered up") is calculated to convey.

In fact, like every self-respecting virtuoso, Yo-Yo Ma had played the Fitzenhagen version, which includes all the passages (like the famous octaves at the end) that have made the Variations a concert perennial instead of the rarity it remained during Chaikovsky's lifetime. "Well, who better than Mr. Ma to play something celloed up," wrote the sharp reviewer for the *Times* (James Oestreich, the paper's music editor), exposing the obtuseness of the class warriors with a well-aimed shaft of contrarian bad taste.[91] As I chuckled, I thought of Charles Baudelaire and

---

89. See http://en.wikipedia.org/wiki/Jack_Sullivan_(literary_scholar).

90. For those who may be wondering, the Russian for "to cello up" is обвиолончелить (*obviolonchelit'*); see Pyotr Ivanovich Jurgenson to Chaikovsky, 3 February 1878: "Противный Фитценхаген! Он непременно желает свою виолончельную пьесу переделать, обвиолончелить и говорит, что ты ему дал полную мочь. Господи! Чайковский revu et corrigé par Fitzengagen!!" (That awful Fitzenhagen! He is set on revising his cello piece, wants to cello it up and says that you gave him free rein. Lordy! Chaikovsky revu et corrigé par Fitzenhagen!!) (P. I. Chaikovsky, *Perepiska s P. I. Yurgensonom*, vol. 1 [Moscow-Leningrad: Muzgiz, 1938], 178).

91. James Oestreich, "Carnegie Echoes of 1891: With Tchaikovsky? Sure," *New York Times*, 7 October 2011.

his immortal sally, "Ce qu'il y a d'enivrant dans le mauvais goût, c'est le plaisir aristocratique de déplaire" (The heady thing about bad taste is the aristocratic pleasure of giving offense).[92] And I recalled the bravura defiance of William Gass, novelist and critic and curmudgeon supreme, in his immortal essay "What Freedom of Expression Means, Especially in Times Like These":

> It is a tough life, living free, but it is a life that lets life be. It is choice and the cost of choosing: to live where I am able, to dress as I please, to pick my spouse and collect my own companions, to take pride and pleasure in my opinions and pursuits, to wear my rue with a difference, *to enjoy my own bad taste* and the smoke of my cooking fires, to tell you where to go while inspecting the ticket you have, in turn, sent me.[93]

What makes this story and its attendant ruminations more than a digression is the letter in which Fitzenhagen reported to Chaikovsky about his first performance, in Wiesbaden in 1879, of the celloed-up version. "I produced a furore," he assured the composer. "I was recalled three times." And then he describes the reaction of one particular member of the audience: "Liszt said to me: 'You carried me away! You played splendidly.' And regarding your piece he observed: 'Now there, at last, is real music!'"[94] Mark that it was the sixty-eight-year-old Liszt who was encouraging Fitzenhagen to cello up, thirty years after his retirement from the concert stage and almost forty years since the baccalaureate letter in which he recanted "runs and cadenzas which [bring] the applause of the musically uneducated, but violated the spirit as well as the letter of the music." Now, at peace, the venerable abbé was declaring his solidarity with the applauders.

In closing, a few words about the Second Hungarian Rhapsody. Yes, of course it is a central work for Liszt; without it, he would not be what he is in our imaginations. But what do those who object to it find objectionable? Why does Brendel exclude it from the category of "works that offer both originality and finish, generosity and control, dignity and fire"? When I hear it well played, I am amazed at the originality with which Liszt imitated the cimbalom, I marvel at the beautifully realized (and "finished") form and pacing of the piece, and cannot see where it is deficient either in control or in dignity. The derision with which it is treated, even by those (like Brendel) who have put in the time and effort to master it, seems a particularly crisp instance of the antitheatrical prejudice as applied to a composition that has become the test par excellence of a pianist's ability to enact the role of virtuoso, an enactment that achieves its zenith with those special performers, like Rachmaninoff or Horowitz or Marc-André Hamelin, who can top the piece off

---

92. Charles Baudelaire, *Fusées* (1867), no. 18.

93. In William Gass, *Life Sentences: Literary Judgments and Accounts* (New York: Alfred A. Knopf, 2012), 33–34 (italics mine).

94. Quoted in David Brown, *Tchaikovsky: The Crisis Years 1874–1878* (New York: W. W. Norton, 1983), 121.

with their own nonchalant cadenzas, the nonchalance signifying the truly *Lisztisch* transgressive transcendence that drives aspirational musicians mad.

And there is more: like a gas (and of course it *is* a gas), the Second Hungarian Rhapsody has escaped its container and leeched out into the popular culture—which is only meet, after all, since that is where its inspiration had come from (and *that*, of course, is what objectors object to). Many other works by nineteenth-century masters had a similar source in restaurant and recruitment music; one need only think of all those Brahms finales—to concertos for piano, for violin, and for cello plus violin, or to his piano quartets. Like Liszt's Rhapsody, they adapted the sounds of environmental music to the special precinct of the concert hall. But unlike Liszt's Rhapsody, they were never reabsorbed into the environment. Liszt's Rhapsody inhabits animated cartoons: Mickey Mouse, Bugs Bunny, and Tom and Jerry have all played it, not to mention (arranged by King Ross) a whole animal orchestra, courtesy of Max Fleischer.[95] It was heard, and *used*, in dance halls; it was in the repertoire of every swing band. It even haunts sports arenas: I am informed by Wikipedia that the St. Louis Cardinals' organist Ernie Hays played Hungarian Rhapsody No. 2 to signal that pitcher Al Hrabosky (nicknamed "The Mad Hungarian") was warming up before appearing as a relief pitcher in the 1970s.[96] It is everywhere. There is even an LP recording of the Rhapsody by a Communist-era Hungarian fakelore ensemble, purporting to return it to an "authentic" environment from which it had never come.[97]

Is this something to condemn, something to resist? Or is this interpenetration of the artistic and the vulgar worlds an ineluctable mark, perhaps the defining mark, of Liszt's greatness? To attempt, like Brendel, to purge Liszt of these impolite associations is indeed to misunderstand his place in our world; but Rosen, too, beholds the vulgar Liszt with distaste. Far better, in the words of Ken Hamilton, is to "embrace our own inner Second Hungarian Rhapsody."[98] We've all got one, and Liszt knew it. To accept his invitation to flout snobbish "good taste" might help us reassert, or recover, taste—which is to say, Mozart's taste as defined by Haydn: namely, a reliable sense of what is fitting, and when.

---

95. See www.youtube.com/watch?v=o5zdHAspBAQ (Mickey Mouse, 1929); www.youtube.com/watch?v=WqGEeymMzQM (Bugs Bunny, 1946); www.youtube.com/watch?v=uKZgio6fVsk (Tom and Jerry, 1947); www.youtube.com/watch?v=UJREpduhgHI ("A Car-Tune Portrait," 1937).

96. http://en.wikipedia.org/wiki/Hungarian_Rhapsody_No._2.

97. *Gypsy and Folk Music of Hungary*, Orchestra and Chorus of the Hungarian State Folk Ensemble, dir. Imre Csenki, cond. Lajos Boross (Angel 65029; recorded on tour in Paris in 1955).

98. Kenneth Hamilton, "Still Wondering If Liszt Was Any Good," *New York Times*, 23 October 2011, Arts and Leisure sec., 20–21.

3

Goldmark's Queen

On Signifiers

I. TEETH

It is an old, old story. I first came across it as an adolescent, browsing in a joke book where it was told about Aimee Semple McPherson, an evangelist who preached to the homeless on the streets of California cities a hundred years ago.[1] But, I have found, it is a lot older than that. The earliest version I know of, now that I have asked Google, was published in 1885, when our protagonist, Karl Goldmark, might have heard it (but probably did not):

> A Presbyterian minister, admonishing freethinking Dr. Russell, the late editor of *The Scotsman*, warned him to flee from the wrath to come, from the place where there is wailing and gnashing of teeth, and paint the joys of heaven, where ransomed sinners chant a new song unto the lamb. "But what will they do with me?" queried Dr. Russell, "who have neither a voice to sing with, nor teeth to gnash?" "Doctor, doctor," answered the minister solemnly, "the teeth will be provided."[2]

Teeth will be provided. The lack of gnashing equipment will not deter us. It can be made to order, and if needed, will be. Can you see why thoughts of Goldmark

---

Keynote address, delivered under the title "Teeth Will Be Provided: On Signifiers" at the international conference "Exoticism, Orientalism, and National Identity in Musical Theatre," Institute for Musicology of the Hungarian Academy of Sciences, Budapest, 11 December 2015; published under the original title in *Studia Musicologica Academiae Scientiarum Hungaricae* 57 (2016): 263–94.

1. Bennett Cerf, *Laughing Stock: Over Six-Hundred Jokes and Anecdotes of Uncertain Vintage* (New York: Grosset & Dunlap, 1945), 231.

2. "Anecdotes," *Our Corner*, vol. 5, ed. Annie Besant (London: Freethought Publishing Co., 1885), 120.

should have led to thoughts of this silly joke? Here's another joke, for a hint. It is a scene from a movie called *A Thousand Clowns*, which I first saw maybe fifty years ago. Never mind what the movie is about. The part I am recalling here can stand alone. It shows a pair of characters entertaining a third by doing impressions of Thomas Jefferson and Alexander Hamilton. When the third character protests that one cannot do impressions of people whose voices no living person remembers, they tell him, "Ha! You missed the funny part."

Again one is undeterred by what ought to be a crippling lack. And so it is with artistic representations, particularly representations of the exotic. Representing the exotic often means representing something we know nothing about. The overcoming of this handicap was Goldmark's particular specialty, his main claim to fame, and he knew it. He actually boasted about it in his memoirs, looking back upon his first and most successful opera, *Die Königin von Saba*, which is set in what we now call the Near or Middle East. "To the musically educated European," he wrote,

> oriental music as a whole sounds alike, a matter of well-known differences in scales and characteristic turns of phrase in the minor. It was clear to me, though, that the musical style adapted to picture the grove of the Indian penitents in the *Sakuntala* [Overture, op. 13, of 1865, the work that made his reputation and established his credentials as an exoticist] could not be used to portray King Solomon's magnificent court; that the music appropriate for either of these scenes would not be appropriate to represent the Arabian Queen of Sheba, or for [her Moorish slave] Astaroth's love call. And still all had to have an oriental character, only each one must be different from the others.[3]

Goldmark here distinguishes four "oriental" idioms: Indian, Israelite, Arabian, and Moorish, of which the last three were to be employed, and needed to be differentiated, in his opera. But that was not all. "There was another very special difficulty," he wrote (and it was one that other composers had faced before him):

---

3. Karl Goldmark, *Notes from the Life of a Viennese Composer*, trans. Alice Goldmark Brandeis (New York: Albert and Charles Boni, 1927), 210; translation adjusted by comparison with the original German, *Erinnerungen aus meinem Leben* (Vienna: Rikola, 1922), 115–16:

> Für den musikalisch gebildeten Europäer besteht die orientalische Musik ohne Unterschied einheitlich und in den bekannten Skalendifferenzen und Moll-Melismen. Mir wurde es jedoch klar, daß der Stil des indischen Büßerhaines in der *Sakuntala* nicht der des prachtliebenden Hofes König Salomons und dieser nicht der der arabischen Königin von Saba und der Lockruf der Astarot sein könne. Und doch sollen alle orientalisches, das heißt verschieden orientalisches Gepräge haben.
>
> Dazu gesellte sich noch eine ganz besondere Schwierigkeit: daß die auch orientalisch gefärbten Tempelgesänge für den europäisch gebildeten Hörer weihevollen, religiösen Eindruck machen sollten, ohne den protestantischen Choral oder katholische Marienlieder hiezu benützen zu können. Ich war nie im Orient, aber die Intuition half mir auch darüber hinweg.

"I wanted the temple hymns with their oriental coloring nevertheless to express a sense of consecration and religious feeling to people familiar only with European music. The problem was to accomplish this without making use of the Protestant chorale or any of the Catholic hymns to the Virgin."

So now we have four contending orientalist idioms in the opera: Moorish, Arabian, and two varieties of Hebrew—one for the court and another for the temple. And then the boast: "I had never been in the Orient," Goldmark informs us, "but intuition helped me even over this lack."

What, though, would it have availed the composer to have visited the Orient? And was it intuition that provided him, so to speak, with teeth?

Die Königin von Saba is most accurately described as an opera with a biblical—that is to say, an ancient-world—setting. The sounds of that world, oriental or occidental, are no longer available for mimicry. Thus, to imitate the music of the ancient Hebrews or Moors is exactly like imitating the speech of Alexander Hamilton or Thomas Jefferson. Authenticity, if that means resemblance to an actual original, is not even an option—nor would it even be desirable, if no one would recognize it. It cannot reasonably be sought. All one can strive for is verisimilitude—not truth, but (to borrow a word from the American fake-news comedian Stephen Colbert) "truthiness." Colbert coined that word to mock the deceptions practiced by American politicians, who tell voters what they believe the voters want to believe, and which will therefore have in the voters' ears a ring of truth even if, as is usually the case, the ring is false. To be satisfied with, or persuaded by, the ring is to confuse truthiness with truth, verisimilitude with authenticity. And we all do it all the time. What sort of ring of truth did Goldmark seek? Where did he seek it? And what do his solutions to these self-imposed problems tell us about his and his audience's cultural assumptions—or ours, come to that? These are the questions I mean to pursue.

Operas or oratorios with an ancient-world setting were common a century or two before Goldmark's time. *Opera seria* usually dramatized subjects from ancient Greek, Roman, or Egyptian history when it was not drawing on ancient myths, and oratorios were almost always dramatizations of stories from the Bible or the Apocrypha. Stylistic verisimilitude of the kind that Goldmark set it as his task to achieve was of no concern to the composers of the seventeenth or eighteenth centuries. The famous Entry of the Queen of Sheba from Handel's oratorio *Solomon* does not sound Arabian in the least, and no one would have wished it to. That was not where Handel's audience expected verisimilitude or where Handel would have thought to provide it. The verisimilitude that was sought in such works was verisimilitude in the portrayal of feeling, which was assumed to be a timeless constant.

The assumption that feelings were universal remained of course in effect in nineteenth-century opera, so that a composer like Goldmark had to strive for fidelity to two standards of truthiness at once, and therefore had to apply what is sometimes called double-coding. Marks of local color, when applied to characters, became marks of ethnicity, which then inflected a traditional repertoire of affective portraiture. Difference thus inflected sameness in a calculus infinitely more supple and shaded than Goldmark's fourfold enumeration implied. His solutions came not from intuition, as I hardly need convince anyone reading this, but from well-honed technique. Observing his mind at work on this problem has certainly enhanced my appreciation of his stature as a musician, which raises another interesting question about him: Why has his music disappeared from the concert and operatic repertories, outside of ceremonial revivals like the one that provided the pretext for this paper?

II. KNOW-HOW

When I was starting life as a concertgoer, radio listener, and record collector, there were at least two Goldmark items that were firmly in current repertory even in America: the Rustic Wedding Symphony and the Violin Concerto. No longer. Goldmark is now a rarity in live performance where I come from. During the first two decades of its existence, however, *Die Königin von Saba* was not only enthusiastically received, but also widely assumed to be a classic in the making, an opera whose popularity would never wane. In 1897, twenty-two years after its Vienna premiere, the opera reached its hundredth performance both in Vienna and in Budapest. By the end of the nineteenth century, three years later, it had been performed on the main German-language stages (Hamburg, Prague, Berlin), as well as in Turin, St. Petersburg, Rotterdam, New York, Madrid, Boston, Warsaw, Riga, Zürich, Antwerp, Buenos Aires, Amsterdam, and Zagreb, in that order. It is listed and described (along with Goldmark's *Merlin*) in the handbook *The Standard Operas* (Chicago, 1899), on which I have long relied for evidence of what deserved to be called "standard" at that time.[4] But between 1900 and 1940, Alfred Loewenberg's *Annals of Opera,* the source of most of the foregoing factoids, records only five productions to compare with the eighteen stagings, on three continents and in only half the time, that I have just enumerated.[5]

When the ten-year-old opera first reached the New World, at the Metropolitan Opera in New York on 2 December 1885, it was greeted with a shower of superlatives from two very distinguished critics. Henry Krehbiel, the music editor of the *New York Herald,* put it in the most majestic, or at least best-rewarded, possible

---

4. George P. Upton, *The Standard Operas: Their Plots, Their Music, and Their Composers* (Chicago, A. C. McClurg & Co., 1899), 117–20. In the preface to his discussion of the opera, the author says of Goldmark: "Four of his compositions during the past fifteen years, the 'Sakuntala' overture, the operas *The Queen of Sheba* and *Merlin,* and 'Die ländliche Hochzeit' (The Country Wedding) symphony[,] have made a permanent reputation for him" (116).

5. Alfred Loewenberg, *Annals of Opera 1597–1940* (Totowa, NJ: Rowman & Littlefield, 1978), 1045–46.

company, writing that "in *The Queen of Sheba* are combined more of the elements which go to make up a successful opera than in any new work that has been seen since Verdi enriched the stage with *Aida,* unless it be *Carmen,* which, for many reasons, must be given a unique position among latter-day creations."[6] Even allowing for the possibly barbed use of the word *successful,* and even if Krehbiel may have been selecting only analogously orientalizing operas for comparison, it is obvious that he foresaw for Goldmark's opera a future comparable to those of Verdi's and Bizet's. The next season, when *Die Königin von Saba* was chosen for the opening night gala at the Met, Krehbiel's rival W. J. Henderson of the *New York Times* wrote that it was certain to be "the artistic and social event of the Winter."

> Since the Metropolitan was opened to the public [three years earlier, in 1883], no audience of like brilliancy has been gathered within its limits. And since opera was first given in the United States, no representation more commendable in point of symmetry and none that could be at all compared with yesterday's in respect of the perfection of the orchestra performance and the completeness and splendor of the *mise en scène* has ever been beheld in the New World. It is simple justice to place these facts on record at the outset of a reference to last night's rendering of *The Queen of Sheba,* for the magnificence of the entertainment and the quality and numbers of the assemblage that witnessed it were the only themes that can be dwelt upon without repeating much that has been already written in this place concerning Goldmark's masterpiece and its chief interpreters in this city.[7]

And yet, less than twenty years later, the opera had been nearly forgotten. Revived in 1905 for the first time since 1890, it moved the anonymous *New York Times* reviewer to ruminate on its disappointing fate. "*The Queen of Sheba,*" he allowed,

> is still a living item in the repertories of the greater German opera houses. But in New York the fifteen years that have gone by since it was produced here have seen some marked changes in the kind of taste that Goldmark's opera appeals to. Its music now makes less of an appeal to ears that have become more attuned to the sources whence Goldmark derived much of his inspiration, and perhaps in certain ways more exacting. And while splendor of theatrical effect will always make its way, and always has, there is such a thing as piling Pelion upon Ossa and wearying by the very superfluity of gorgeousness.[8]

---

6. http://archives.metoperafamily.org/archives/scripts/cgiip.exe/WService=BibSpeed/fullcit.w?xCID=4300.

7. http://archives.metoperafamily.org/archives/scripts/cgiip.exe/WService=BibSpeed/fullcit.w?xCID=5250.

8. "*The Queen of Sheba* at the Metropolitan," *New York Times,* 23 November 1905, 9, www.nytimes.com/1905/11/23/archives/the-queen-of-sheba-at-the-metropolitan-goldmarks-oriental-opera.html.

That last idiom, no longer current, means heaping one mountain atop another—too much of a good thing, or else the compounding of difficulties. Even in the midst of his rapturous review of the Met premiere, Henry Krehbiel had given an inkling of what there may have been too much of, and it is the very thing that interests us. "Herr Goldmark's music is highly spiced," he wrote. "He is plainly an eclectic, whose first aim was to give the drama an investiture which should be in keeping with its character, externally and internally." That much might have been said of *Aida* or *Carmen*, thus by extension of Verdi or Bizet. But then Krehbiel added, "[M]any other composers before him have made use of Oriental cadences and rhythms, but to none have they seemed to come so like native language as to Goldmark." What was said ostensibly in praise in 1885 nevertheless broached a big intractable issue, to which David Brodbeck has devoted a recent book, and which not even the composer's friends (e.g., Brahms) could keep entirely at bay: the charge of being *fremdartig*, the German equivalent of what we now mean when we capitalize the word *Other*.[9]

The charge of eclecticism—the chameleon assumption of many styles rather than the assiduous cultivation of a unique and instantly recognizable personal voice—was one of the charges Wagner leveled at Jews in his notorious tract of 1850, which he had finally owned to having written in 1869, six years before *Die Königin von Saba* had its premiere. Mimicry, even if done with verve and virtuosity, and even if done so persuasively as to create the aura of authenticity, nevertheless transgresses against another sense, perhaps the most exigent one, of the word *authenticity*. For eclecticism impedes the impression of individual vision, also known as integrity, which was more and more insisted upon as romanticism moved into its late, late phase known as modernism. Yet that transgressive eclecticism was precisely the virtue that Goldmark so assertively claimed for himself in the boastful passage from his memoirs about the oriental idiom—or idioms—he contrived for his opera. He did not use the tainted word; he would no doubt have preferred to speak of versatility rather than eclecticism. But versatility is also an antonym of integrity, hence of personal authenticity, the overriding sentiment of self. To value versatility over originality transgressed against what was becoming, with a powerful push from Wagner, a sine qua non.

Meanwhile, Wagner was one of the elements that Goldmark's versatility sought to encompass, although the Wagnerian influence shows up less in the music of his opera than in the dramatic action, the plot being one of the teeth the authors of *Die Königin von Saba* had to provide. The opera's story does not come from the Bible, where the Queen of Sheba (*malkat Sh'ba*) makes only the briefest of appearances,

---

9. See David Brodbeck, *Defining Deutschtum: Political Ideology, German Identity, and Music-Critical Discourse in Liberal Vienna* (New York: Oxford University Press, 2014), to which there will be many references to come.

as recounted twice, in almost identical words, in the tenth chapter of First Book of Kings and ninth chapter of the Second Book of Chronicles. Here is the account from Chronicles in the King James version, slightly abridged:

> [1] And when the queen of Sheba heard of the fame of Solomon, she came to prove Solomon with hard questions at Jerusalem, with a very great company, and camels that bare spices, and gold in abundance, and precious stones: and when she was come to Solomon, she communed with him of all that was in her heart.
>
> [2] And Solomon told her all her questions: and there was nothing hid from Solomon which he told her not.
>
> [3] And when the queen of Sheba had seen the wisdom of Solomon, and the house that he had built,
>
> [4] And the meat of his table, and the sitting of his servants, and the attendance of his ministers, and their apparel; his cupbearers also, and their apparel; and his ascent by which he went up into the house of the Lord; there was no more spirit in her.
>
> [5] And she said to the king, It was a true report which I heard in mine own land of thine acts, and of thy wisdom:
>
> [6] Howbeit I believed not their words, until I came, and mine eyes had seen it: and, behold, the one half of the greatness of thy wisdom was not told me: for thou exceedest the fame that I heard.
>
> [7] Happy are thy men, and happy are these thy servants, which stand continually before thee, and hear thy wisdom. . . .
>
> [9] And she gave the king an hundred and twenty talents of gold, and of spices great abundance, and precious stones: neither was there any such spice as the queen of Sheba gave king Solomon. . . .
>
> [12] And king Solomon gave to the queen of Sheba all her desire, whatsoever she asked, beside that which she had brought unto the king. So she turned, and went away to her own land, she and her servants.

Not much of a story here, which if historical is probably just a reference to a trade mission. The Queen is characterized as rich, not beautiful. I have pruned away some of the great show of opulence that surrounds her in the biblical account, but enough remains to suggest what attracted the attention of so many artists and musicians to the Queen's visit. (One of the attractions for musicians was a verse about harps and psalteries that King Solomon had made from the wood of the algum trees the Queen had given him in tribute.)[10] But there is plenty of room for the imagination, especially when the Bible tells us that "neither was there any such spice as the queen of Sheba gave king Solomon; and king Solomon gave to the queen of Sheba all her desire." It was a snap to associate the Queen of Sheba with the Bride in the Song of Songs, hence with the line best known in St. Jerome's Latin translation, "Nigra sum sed Formosa" ("I am black but comely" according to King

---

10. I Kings 10:12.

James).[11] Building on this, the national saga of Ethiopia, *Kebra Nagast* (thought to date from the fourteenth century), traces the country's ruling dynasty to Menelik ("Son of the wise man" in Amharic), the love-child of Solomon and Sheba.

Handel's Solomon, British to the bone, takes no manly interest in the Queen of Sheba; he is wrapped up in uxorious bliss with his own wife (the Pharaoh's daughter), and in the oratorio's third act, Sheba's, the librettist is too busy "exalt[ing] reason, wisdom, wealth, and cultural ostentation" to spare a thought for sex.[12] But by Goldmark's time, a "Queen of the South," especially one whose South is located in the East, had to be an embodiment of allure. In his memoir Goldmark attributes his first thought of the opera to a chance remark made by the stage manager of the Vienna Court Opera about a fifteen-year-old pupil of Goldmark's who had just made her debut (presumably in the chorus): "Look at that girl! That face! The very image of the Queen of Sheba!"[13] Goldmark immediately sketched a scenario, he tells us, "which contained, in outline, practically all that is now included in the opera."[14] It is, inevitably, a love triangle, in which the Queen performs the role foreordained by romantic orientalist convention as well as ironclad operatic precedent. Here is Brodbeck's efficient summary of the action:

> The story is set into motion when the queen—depicted as an exotic femme fatale—seduces the courtier Assad, who has been sent by Solomon to meet her in the desert and escort her into Jerusalem. The queen privately reveals her attraction to the young man, but in public she denies even knowing him. Driven to frenzy, Assad abandons his betrothed, Sulamith, daughter of the High Priest, at their wedding in the Temple and publicly declares the queen his goddess. At first condemned to death for his blasphemy, Assad is eventually banished instead to the wilderness to work out his salvation by defeating the powers of evil. There, in the end, he rejects the vile queen's entreaties and dies in the faithful Sulamith's arms during a ferocious desert storm.[15]

Unlike her close contemporaries Carmen and Delilah, who were already femmes fatales in their literary sources, the Queen of Sheba had to be transformed into one. Knowledgeable observers had no trouble deducing the path she had traveled to get where Goldmark needed her to be. Krehbiel, for one, assured his readers that *Die Königin von Saba* "is not a biblical opera even in the sense that Mehul's *Joseph* or Rubinstein's *Maccabees* and *Sulamith* are biblical.... The local color of the opera has been borrowed from the old story," he went on, but "the

---

11. Song of Solomon 1:5.
12. Percy M. Young, *Handel* (London: Dent, 1947), quoted in Paul Henry Lang, *George Frideric Handel* (New York: W. W. Norton, 1966), 465.
13. Goldmark, *Notes*, 205. "Das Mädl! Das Gesicht! Die reine Königin von Saba!" (Goldmark, *Erinnerungen aus meinem Leben* [Vienna: Rikola, 1922], 114).
14. Goldmark, *Notes*, 206.
15. Brodbeck, *Defining Deutschtum*, 84.

dramatic motive comes plainly from Wagner's *Tannhäuser,* as will be evident on a moment's reflection."[16]

Thus alerted, we can easily map Goldmark's characters onto Wagner's: Tannhäuser = Assad; Sulamith = Elisabeth; Saba = Venus. Krehbiel tries to extend the triangle into a quadrilateral by paralleling Solomon with Wagner's Wolfram, but Henderson, the reviewer for the rival paper, seems closer to the mark when he observes that "Solomon performs the baritonal functions of a King of Brabant," thus adding *Lohengrin* to the Wagnerian mix. And we can add *Tristan und Isolde* as well, for there is an obvious recollection in the second act of Brangäne's *Tagelied,* when the Watchman of the Temple calls out, at the climax of the love scene between the illicit paramours, "Der Tag ersteht! Söhne Israels zum Morgengebet!"—whereupon we realize that Assad, like Tristan, was the King's emissary to escort a royal visitor from abroad with whom there springs up, as between Tristan and Isolde, a mutual, fatally destructive passion; and to complete the parallel, Assad dies at the end of the opera, like Tristan, as a castaway in the wilderness, and in the arms of his beloved (though not the beloved with whom he sang his second-act duet).

Just as its plot had been concocted from the shards of remembered predecessors, so were the signifiers that defined the opera's various oriental strains. All were taken off the rack. They were products neither of intuition, as Goldmark claimed, nor of his own ineluctable *Fremdartigkeit,* as hostile critics alleged. Rather, they were the fruit of professional know-how, in which Goldmark took an eminently justifiable pride. Brodbeck pinpoints the distinction with precision, recommending that we conceive of *Die Königin von Saba* "not as a Jewish national opera or even a 'Jewish-Oriental' one, but as an out-and-out Orientalist opera." The only part of that definition that I would wish to modify is the squeamish "out-and-out." To call Goldmark an orientalist in this connection need not imply that he wickedly approved of the imperialist exploitation of the backward peoples of the East (although like any affluent European, he can all too easily be shown to have benefited from it). The point relevant to this discussion is that, as he persistently maintained in rebuttal to those who sought to "other" him, he identified with European, and more particularly German, culture, and saw his work as belonging "in its entire structure to German art, ... just as the composer, living among Germans (in Vienna) since his childhood, owes his entire artistic *Bildung* to German art—Beethoven and Bach were his teachers. The 'Fremde' in the work is nothing other than the strong representation of a musical characteristic that is appropriate to the subject matter."[17]

It is that "representation," consisting of Goldmark's orientalist signifiers, to which we are now ready to turn.

---

16. http://archives.metoperafamily.org/archives/scripts/cgiip.exe/WService=BibSpeed/fullcit.w?xCID=4300.

17. Goldmark, "Gedanken über Form und Stil (eine Abwehr)" [Thoughts on Form and Style: A Defense], *Neue Freie Presse,* 4 June 1911; quoted in Brodbeck, *Defining Deutschtum,* 306.

III. PRECEDENTS

There are a great many of them, and if they do not sort quite as neatly as Goldmark implied into four discrete boxes, they are nevertheless quite effectively selected for the purposes they were called upon to serve. In no case had Goldmark been their designer, but he chose them wisely and adapted them inventively.

The most proximate precedent, as Brodbeck has recognized, was set by Anton Rubinstein, who by 1875 had composed two of his so-called biblical operas, as well as the earlier, more generically orientalist *Feramors,* based, like an opera Félicien David was composing at the same time, on Thomas Moore's oriental romance *Lalla Rookh.* (David's opera beat Rubinstein's to the stage by a year, which is why David's is named after Moore's title character, while Rubinstein had to content himself with the name of her lover.) These operas, plus David's prototypical "symphonic ode" *Le Désert* (1844), established the orientalist vocabulary on which Goldmark drew. We know he knew them all, not only because musicians of the late nineteenth century can be presumed to have known them, particularly in the German-speaking countries where Rubinstein's operas were major repertory pieces, but also because Goldmark actually reviewed David's compositions for a Vienna newspaper during an early stint as a paid music journalist,[18] and because he and Rubinstein, to whom he devoted an entire short chapter in his memoirs, were on intimate terms as early as 1860.[19] They even shared a librettist, the Viennese Jewish poet Salomon Hermann Mosenthal, who at the time of his collaboration with Goldmark on *Die Königin von Saba* was fresh from work on *Die Maccabäer,* Rubinstein's most successful opera.

In *Die Maccabäer,* and in the earlier *Der Thurm zu Babel* (first performed in 1870), Rubinstein faced the problem Goldmark described in his memoirs, namely that of differentiating among diverse oriental strains and, in particular, differentiating the Israelites' religious music, which Europeans regarded as an early layer of their own religious and musical tradition, from truly *fremdartig* orientalist styles without making the Israelites sound Christian. It was a problem faced previously by the Russian composer Alexander Serov, whose first opera, *Judith,* performed the same year as Rubinstein's *Feramors* (1863), pitted Israelites against Assyrians. Serov had reserved all the oriental markers for the Assyrians, leaving the Israelite music unmarked, so that it fell into what in his memoirs Goldmark had called the trap of reminding listeners "of the Protestant chorale or . . . Catholic hymns to the Virgin."

It was not a matter of actually imitating the music of the Protestant or Catholic liturgies, only of permitting the Israelites to use the default style of contemporary European music, which in Serov's case (as in Rubinstein's or Goldmark's) was a rather old-fashioned German style, vintage 1840 or so, redolent of Mendelssohn

---

18. Brodbeck, *Defining Deutschtum,* 72.
19. Goldmark, *Notes,* 123–28.

EXAMPLE 3.1. Rubinstein, *Tower of Babel* (New York: G. Schirmer, 1883), "Chorus of the Sons of Shem."

and Schumann. The omission of signifiers was itself a signifier; and that is why it is perhaps better in this context to speak not of signification but rather, using the vocabulary of linguists, of marking. Serov had left the Israelite music unmarked, which, given the expectations of his audience, amounted to marking it Christian. That is why Serov's Assyrian music was much preferred, by audiences and reviewers, to his Israelite idiom. Rubinstein learned from Serov's negative example to differentiate orientalist markers and distribute them among the various groups he needed to characterize.

Especially instructive as an example was *Der Thurm zu Babel* (The Tower of Babel), an opera that, as its plot actually dictated, was all about the differentiation of idioms. At its center are three monumental choruses to mark off from one another the descendants of Noah's three sons, Sem (Shem), Ham, and Japhet, as they are rent asunder into three nations with mutually unintelligible tongues. The children of Sem—that is, the "Semites"—are given the most obvious and predictable orientalist marker, the augmented second (Ex. 3.1). They sing in unison, as do the sons of Ham, whose melody in C-sharp minor, devoid of leading tones, has Phrygian cadences instead, accompanied throughout by a pedal of drone fifths, giving way toward the end to a snaking chromatic bass (Ex. 3.2). The Japhetic

EXAMPLE 3.2. Rubinstein, *Tower of Babel,* "Chorus of the Sons of Ham."

chorus, meanwhile, invokes a *locus classicus,* the "Turkish Dance" from the fourth act of Glinka's *Ruslan and Lyudmila* (compare Ex. 3.3a and Ex. 3.3b).

One can find many similar devices in *Die Königin von Saba,* similarly differentiated and distributed, and critics noticed and reported them at the time of its first performances just as we are doing now. Their interpretation, however, followed a curious trajectory. There were always those who attributed the markers—as we now do (or should)—to what Brodbeck calls "an exoticist strategic choice on the composer's part."[20] But there were always those who, in Goldmark's own words, tended insultingly to attribute his orientalisms not to his *Stück* but to his *Gemüt,* or as his translator put it, "they were attacking my temperament rather than my composition,"[21] aiming their remarks not *ad rem* but *ad hominem.* The same critic, in fact, could at various times argue either way.

Hanslick was one. In 1884 he shrewdly observed that "to the modern composer, the ethnographically sharp differences among Indian [exemplified by Meyerbeer's *L'Africaine* or Delibes's *Lakmé* in addition to Goldmark's *Sakuntala*], Persian

20. Brodbeck, *Defining Deutschtum,* 75.
21. Goldmark, *Notes,* 175.

EXAMPLE 3.3A. Rubinstein, *Tower of Babel*, "Chorus of the Sons of Japhet."

EXAMPLE 3.3B. Glinka, *Ruslan and Lyudmila*, Act IV, Turkish Dance.

[exemplified by *Feramors* or *Lalla Rookh*], Egyptian [*Aida*], Hebraic [*Die Königin* or *Die Maccabäer*] must in any case nearly dissolve into a general idea: oriental music"[22]—by which he meant not that they were all the same, or interchangeable, but that their representation and differentiation were imaginary and arbitrary, so that, as Brodbeck puts it, the markers "relate much more closely to one another than they do to any particular ethnic musical practice."[23] And yet the same Hanslick, writing two years later, backslid into an appalling essentialism. Reviewing the latest Goldmark opera, *Merlin,* he remarked with approval that it was free of the "Jewish-Oriental melodies, whose sickly moaning spoiled for us the undeniable beauties" of *Die Königin von Saba,* and then added:

> The subject matter [of *Die Königin*] certainly justified the Jewish local color in the music, but did not make it any more pleasing. Will *Die Königin von Saba,* precisely because of this striking national character, be judged more original, more "Goldmarkian" than *Merlin*? That may be the case and would not exactly be unfounded. The Oriental, with its passion and colorful display, but also with its unrest, intensity, and exalted solemnity, does not lie merely within the subject matter of *Die Königin von Saba,* but within our composer himself, who grew up under a doubly Oriental influence, the Jewish and the Hungarian.[24]

Take that, residents of Budapest! Goldmark's very ability to produce *Merlin* after writing *Die Königin* should have been enough to refute these silly surmises, had they been actual surmises. Rather than surmises, though, they seem to have been defensive strategies, attributable to the same squeamishness in a German-speaking Jewish immigrant from the outlying provinces to Vienna—Hanslick's identity as well as Goldmark's—that affected the composer's treatment of his orientalist markers, albeit in a manner exactly opposite to what Hanslick was proposing.[25]

I turn with relief from Hanslick's obtuse ruminations to the most intelligent contemporary take on operatic orientalism, that of the Russian critic with German and French names, German (Hermann) Avgustovich Larosh (Laroche), who, reviewing Rubinstein's *Der Thurm zu Babel,* asked rhetorically, "In what does Alexander Serov's masterly characterization of the extinct Assyrians in his opera *Judith* consist, or Anton Rubinstein's of the ancient Semites in his 'sacred opera' *The Tower of Babel?*" and answered, "Obviously, in one thing only: the composers have successfully reproduced *our* subjective idea of the Assyrians and the Semites."[26]

---

22. Eduard Hanslick, "Hofoperntheater," *Neue Freie Presse,* 7 October 1884; quoted in Brodbeck, *Defining Deutschtum,* 215.

23. Brodbeck, *Defining Deutschtum,* 306.

24. Hanslick, "Merlin," *Neue Freie Presse,* 21 November 1886; quoted in Brodbeck, *Defining Deutschtum,* 216.

25. On Hanslick's ethnic and national background, see David Brodbeck, "Hanslick's Smetana and Hanslick's Prague," *Journal of the Royal Musical Association* 134 (2009): 1–36.

26. German Avgustovich Larosh (Hermann Laroche), "'Der Thurm zu Babel' Rubinshteyna," in Larosh, *Muzïkal'no-kriticheskiye stat'i* (St. Petersburg: Bessel, 1894), 117.

This gets everything right. Skirting the poietic fallacy, it places the emphasis not on the composer's input, but on the audience's takeaway, or rather the composer's strategic calculation (as Brodbeck would say) of the audience's likely perception, which enabled the critic to see that teeth were being provided, and that Alexander Hamilton and Thomas Jefferson were being successfully, that is, "truthily," impersonated.

IV. CRAFTY MARKING

So let us take a closer look at that impersonation, or that novel deployment of stereotypes, to put it in terms of an apparent oxymoron that I will try eventually to redeem. Goldmark's treatment of his orientalist markers was subtler and cannier than those thus far surveyed, and—it follows—more interesting and rewarding for study. This applies especially to the most hackneyed signifier of them all. Of course I mean the augmented second.

Augmented seconds are remarkably scarce in *Die Königin von Saba* compared with Rubinstein's operas, or with the exactly contemporaneous *Samson et Dalila* by Saint-Saëns. Everybody remembers the famous Bacchanale from Saint-Saëns's opera (Ex. 3.4). *Die Königin von Saba* has one too. It is the culmination of the ballet at the beginning of Act III, which takes place not among Saint-Saëns's Philistines but at King Solomon's court. As orgies go, Goldmark's Bacchanale is pretty restrained, the way his orientalisms always tend to sound, compared with their French or Russian counterparts (Ex. 3.5).

Partly, as David Brodbeck would (I suspect) agree, it was a matter of *Deutschtum oblige*. Among the ways German art flaunted its sense of superiority was in its civilized, decorous deportment, with which Goldmark, who with determination had weeded his German of all traces of his native Yiddish, strongly identified. It was thus another symptom of the qualms Goldmark must surely have felt on account of his *Judentum*. We have already encountered Henry Krehbiel's assumption that Goldmark was speaking his "native language" in *Die Königin*, and we have seen Hanslick, another assimilated and precariously successful Austrian Jew, react with squeamishness specifically (and solely) to the opera's Jewish palette—a squeamishness, I think it is safe to assume, that was not unrelated to the composer's.

The essentializing process can just as easily work in the other direction. Saint-Saëns was often suspected of being Jewish. During the Dreyfus years the rumor went around that his actual surname was Kohn or Kahn (that is, that he was a member of the big banking family of that name), and the Nazis banned his music.[27]

---

27. Michael Kater, *The Twisted Muse: Musicians and Their Music in the Third Reich* (New York: Oxford University Press, 1997), 85. On Saint-Saëns's genealogy, in express refutation of his rumored Jewishness, see J.-G. Prod'homme, "Camille Saint-Saëns (Oct. 9, 1835–Dec. 16, 1921)," *Musical Quarterly* 8 (1922): 469–86, at 470.

EXAMPLE 3.4. Saint-Saëns, *Samson et Dalila*, Act III, Bacchanale, middle section.

As usual, whatever the Nazis banned, Jewish chauvinists would claim on the same evidence—evidence furnished, in the case of Saint-Saëns, by nothing more than the augmented seconds in *Samson et Dalila*. Here is Gdal Saleski, a Ukrainian-born cellist and amateur writer on music, whose well-known biographical dictionary *Famous Musicians of Jewish Origin* (first published in 1927 as *Famous Musicians of a Wandering Race*) had this to say about Saint-Saëns, who

> embodies one of the many aspects of the French temperament—that in which the mind and intelligence supplant sentiment and emotion, as in the case of a Voltaire, of a Rameau,—that is, of course, as long as Saint-Saëns remained the patriotic Frenchman, a patriot who could attack Wagner for no better reason than that he was a German. But as soon as he dug down to the roots of his own being and for once forgot that he was above all a Frenchman, he succeeded in composing his one immortal work, written on a biblical theme, in which he freely employed the Hebrew scale. In his "Samson et Dalila," not only one of the master's best operas (perhaps the very best), but one of the finest dramatic works produced by any French composer during the last fifty years, Saint-Saëns compelled the admiration of musicians as well as of the general public, possibly for the reason that when he wrote it he did not attempt to please either, but was content to follow ancestral inspiration without *arrière pensées* [*sic*] of any sort.[28]

---

28. Gdal Saleski, *Famous Musicians of Jewish Origin* (New York: Bloch, 1949), 127.

EXAMPLE 3.5. Goldmark, *Königin von Saba* (Bremen: Schweers & Haake, [1881]), Act III, Bacchanale.

And here is Saleski on Goldmark: despite "the influence of Wagner's theories," he wrote, Goldmark "nevertheless shows much originality and individuality. He . . . was much attracted by biblical material, and he brought to it all the passion of his Viennese temperament and all his love for the history of the Jewish nation."[29]

Show me your blood, and I will show you the kind of music you will write; show me your music, and I will show you what kind of blood you have. And if the music and the blood do not match up, your legitimacy is suspect. Obviously Goldmark wanted no part of that—so no augmented seconds in *his* Bacchanale. Not that the music lacks for markers. It abounds in chromatic scales, including a descending one in the bass as in Rubinstein's Hamitic chorus. It has syncopated rhythms galore. It has ostinatos aplenty. But (trust me) there is no "Hebrew scale." Owing to their scarcity, then, Goldmark's augmented seconds are especially telling when they do occur.

And what do his telling seconds tell us? One of their rare appearances occurs near the end of the triumphal march that heralds the title character's entry in Act I. Like its counterpart in *Aida*, Goldmark's march has various contrasting strains that succeed one another as various groups of marchers pass in review. First to appear are soldiers, presumably Solomon's (Ex. 3.6a), followed by women and maidens, accompanied by Solomon's female slaves, strewing roses (Ex. 3.6b). Things get a bit wilder when the Queen's retinue makes its entrance. (They are from Arabia, after all, which makes them *fremdartig*.) First to appear are her male slaves, both white and black, bearing vessels filled with gold dust, pearls, jewels, and spices—and here we may notice drone fifths, again like Rubinstein's in the Hamitic chorus from *Der Thurm zu Babel* (Ex. 3.6c).

And now, as Sigmund Freud would say, we get to where the body's buried, when the female slaves appear, both black and white, and with them augmented seconds galore. After a brief reprise of the music associated with the male slaves, the Queen makes her climactic appearance, borne aloft on a palanquin or covered litter, accompanied by her main personal slave Astaroth, who is designated "eine Mohrin" in the cast of characters (Ex. 6d). *Nota bene:* augmented seconds, thus far held in reserve, make their showy appearance precisely upon the arrival of dark skin and female gender.

This association will hold through the opera, including its most spectacular orientalizing moment. But before getting to that, one slight apparent exception must be acknowledged, namely the first theme in the Prelude to Act I. A couple of solemn introductory phrases apart, these are the very first sounds the audience hears (Ex. 3.7a). Our marker-seeking ears prick up at the augmented second, of course; but as heard in Example 3.7a the interval is as yet a floating signifier, unattached to a referent and therefore not yet, strictly speaking, a signifier at all, except insofar as it identifies the whole opera as "oriental"—something the title has

29. Ibid., 69.

EXAMPLE 3.6A. Goldmark, *Königin von Saba*, Act I, Einzugsmarsch, "Soldaten ziehen auf."

EXAMPLE 3.6B. Goldmark, *Königin von Saba*, Einzugsmarsch, "Aus den Seitenhallen ziehen Frauen u. Jungfrauen, von Sclavinnen begleitet."

EXAMPLE 3.6C. Goldmark, *Königin von Saba*, Einzugsmarsch, "Sclaven und Sclavinnen, Weisse und Mohren."

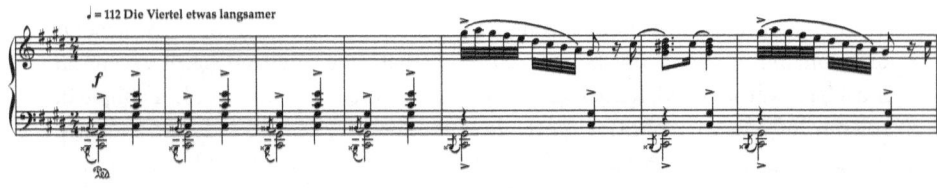

EXAMPLE 3.6D. Goldmark, *Königin von Saba*, Einzugsmarsch, "Weisse und schwarze Sclavinnen."

already done. Not until the beginning of the fifth scene in Act II, the aborted wedding of Assad and Sulamith, does the theme in Example 3.7a become a leitmotif by dint of recurrence, and we learn its meaning. It turns out to be the melody to which the priests sing the beginning of the liturgy: "Danket dem Herrn, denn er ist freundlich! Ewig währt seine Güte!" (Ex. 3.7b).

Here the augmented second (as well as a diminished fourth) is being associated with the Israelites: with "us," you might say, if we are speaking biblically, not "them." Is it then just an all-purpose orientalizing marker, functioning at its most utilitarian to conjure up a generalized "harem" style?[30] Perhaps not. If on first hearing we cannot even be sure that it ought to count as a marker, it is not only because it has yet to be associated with words or image, but also because the augmented second

---

30. For the term "harem style," see R. Taruskin, "*Yevreyi* and *Zhidy*: A Memoir, a Survey, and a Plea," in idem, *On Russian Music* (Berkeley and Los Angeles: University of California Press, 2009), 190–201, at 197.

EXAMPLE 3.7A. Goldmark, *Königin von Saba*, Prelude, mm. 17–20.

EXAMPLE 3.7B. Goldmark, *Königin von Saba*, Act II, "Chor des Volkes."

in Example 3.7b assumes the mildest, most slightly marked form it can take in normal harmonic usage. It is the one that occurs between the sixth and seventh degrees of the harmonic minor scale, which Aryan boys and girls practice on the piano every day. Its use in the Temple scene does make it a marker, but only to the nominal extent Goldmark allowed when writing that he "wanted the temple hymns . . . to express a sense of consecration and religious feeling . . . without making use of the Protestant chorale or any of the Catholic hymns to the Virgin." Thus the Hebrews get the weakest and blandest of oriental tints. Their marking is minimal.

The augmented seconds associated with the Moorish slaves in the Queen's retinue were, by contrast, of a kind that could never occur in normal or unmarked nineteenth-century European harmony. They occur between the third and fourth degrees, as in what was usually called the Gypsy scale or (more euphemistically) the Hungarian minor. That made them *fremdartig*, literally outlandish, and they come clustered with what at least one critic, Richard Specht, called the *Goldmark-triole*, "Goldmark triplets," which, according to Specht, marked Goldmark's *alttestamentarisches, trunkenes Gepräge*, his "Old-Testament, drunken character," even though the device actually went back to *Sakuntala*, the overture inspired by Kalidasa's Sanskrit drama.[31]

More outlandish yet is the so-called *Lockruf*, the weird melody the handmaiden Astaroth sings in the second act as a prelude to the love scene. This is a truly bizarre moment. Astaroth has warned the Queen that Assad is lurking in the vicinity. The Queen gives her an order: "Tiefe Stille rings umher—niemand sieht uns—lock ihn her!" (Deep silence all around—no one sees us—lure him hither!). Whereupon Astaroth sings an incantation, brilliantly recorded in 1925 by Selma Kurz (1874–1933), the reigning coloratura soprano of the Vienna Opera since Mahler's day. Richard Strauss, who wrote the role of Zerbinetta in the revised *Ariadne auf Naxos* for Kurz, surely remembered it when composing *Salome*. (You can hear Kurz's rendition, unbelievable trill and all, at www.youtube.com/watch?v=wcpdM_N1HxQ.) The text is by Mosenthal:

Wie im Schilfe lockt der Reiher,	As reeds attract herons,
Wie der Tauber girrt im Moos,	As doves coo in the moss,
Durch der Nacht verschwieg'nen Schleier	Through the night's concealing veil
Lock ich ihn in deinen Schoss.	I lure him to thy lap.

These verses are all about *locken* (luring), so calling the piece a *Lockruf* makes perfect sense. In the Goldmark literature, such as it is in English, the word is usually translated as "siren song," but the more usual, zoological meaning of the term is "mating call," including the kind that hunters simulate with a specially designed instrument—*Lockmittel* or *Lockpfeife*—to lure their quarry. That is just what the Queen of Sheba is doing here, with Astaroth as her instrument. What Astaroth is singing, then, amounts to a sort of duck call (or, if you remember what Assad means in Arabic, a lion call), and sure enough, in wanders the lion, ensnared, singing the most famous item in the whole opera. We will get to that in a moment, but first let us take a close look at the *Lockruf* melody (Ex. 3.8).

This tune cannot be referred to any single scale. It is a sort of composing-out of the Salome-like progression at the beginning of its orchestral introduction, in which a G-minor scale alternates with a scale that incorporates the diminished-seventh chord containing G. Its modality is thus unstable, but its heavy infusion of weird intervals—the augmented seconds paling next to the cadential tritones—leaves no doubt as to its status. As an orientalist marker it belongs to a very particular class: the kind I have written about at length when describing the erotic

---

31. Richard Specht, "Karl Goldmark, zu seinem hundertsten Geburtstag," *Pester Lloyd* (1930), www.pesterlloyd.net/html/1930spechtgoldmark100.html.

EXAMPLE 3.8. Goldmark, *Königin von Saba,* Act II, Astaroth's "Lockruf."

EXAMPLE 3.9. Goldmark, *Königin von Saba,* Act II, Anathema Scene ("Posaunen auf dem Theater hinter der Scene").

orientalism of Russian operas such as *Ruslan and Lyudmila* or *Prince Igor*—or Rubinstein's *Demon,* to pick an opera that Goldmark is very likely to have known number by number.[32] This last parallel is a reminder of how decisively our reading of any signifier depends on context. Specifically, it reminds us that signifiers generally come in clusters. Thus the cluster tritone-plus-soprano-voice means "come hither"; but a tritone blared out by a team of trombones in unison under a dissonant suspension in the same opera signifies "Anathema" (Ex. 3.9).

Though seldom given as much notice as pitch and rhythm, we are thus reminded, tone color and dynamics play an equally critical role in marking and signification—and this applies as much to voices as it does to instruments. The most famous item in *Die Königin von Saba,* the exhibit we have been postponing, furnishes vivid proof. Recall first that one of the signal points to emerge from an examination of the orientalist markers found in Russian operas was that the orientalizing tropes favored by Glinka, Borodin, and Rubinstein—tropes I have associated with the Russian word *nega,* meaning the sweet lassitude of consummated love—had the effect of emascu-

---

32. See R. Taruskin, "'Entoiling the Falconet': Russian Musical Orientalism in Context," in idem, *Defining Russia Musically: Historical and Hermeneutical Essays* (Princeton, NJ: Princeton University Press, 1997), 152–85.

EXAMPLE 3.10. Goldmark, *Konigin von Saba*, Act II, "Magische Töne," end.

lating the men thus lured.[33] This certainly applies to the number that the *Lockruf* calls forth from Assad in *Die Königin von Saba*—a romance called "Magische Töne," which was recorded time and again by all of the world's most famous tenors when the opera was a repertory item, from Leo Slezak, who was particularly famous in the role of Assad, to Enrico Caruso. Among the treasures now miraculously accessible on YouTube is a recording made in 1903, early enough for Goldmark to have heard it, by the Hungarian tenor Dezső (Desider) Arányi (1868–1923), which exquisitely realizes the demands of the number's ending, ascending as it does into falsetto territory that was increasingly foreign to the technique of twentieth-century *tenori robusti* like Caruso, as Goldmark acknowledged with an *ossia*. If at all possible, one should compare Example 3.10 with www.youtube.com/watch?v=cXshaykDq8o. That eunuch sound, an echo of the old *musico* or alto *travesti*, was an especially potent orientalist marker. Assad at this moment is closely akin to Glinka's Ratmir in *Ruslan and Lyudmila,* a part cast for a contralto in trousers.

Various characteristic instrumental timbres were equally evocative of the East, and Goldmark predictably gives the cor anglais plenty of work to do, especially in Act IV, when the Queen is making her final desperate appeal to Assad. Any biblical opera will have a lot of harp as well, both in the pit and probably on stage; and here,

33. Ibid.

too, Goldmark does his bit. But almost as commonplace was the use of "Turkish" percussion, an old Vienna specialty going back to the eighteenth century. It, too, is often to be found on stage as well as in the pit, and its moment comes in *Die Königin von Saba* when Sulamith's maiden friends, forming themselves into a backup chorus, accompany her confident paean to her betrothed in the first act ("Der Freund ist dein").

The stage directions call for them to play harps, tambourines, and triangles. The harp parts are played in the pit and mimed on stage, but the tambourines and triangles are actually meant to be played by choristers, and their parts are printed, most unusually, in the vocal score (Ex. 3.11). You can hear them clearly even in old recordings of the number, such as the one featuring Mária Németh, another Vienna coloratura star, accessible at www.youtube.com/watch?v=wLPI6xhXoM8. Although there have been fairly recent complete recordings of *Die Königin von Saba*, and though the performances they preserve are creditable enough, century-old recordings of favorite selections remain indispensable for the simple reason that one hundred years ago the world's best singers were singing Goldmark, which they no longer do, and their habits of voice production reinforce the semiotic point of the present discussion in ways that more recent singing might actually impede.

Sulamith's roulades in this her signature number could be likened to arabesques; but without the rest of the signifying cluster, which is to say the accompanying percussion, there would be no reason to think her characterization orientalist. The tonality is straightforward F major, alternating in the middle section with the flat mediant (A♭), a voluptuous effect that Viennese audiences had been enjoying since the time of Schubert. It is the unusual 6/4 rhythm, with its long-held syncopations, that seems most clearly calculated to convey the specifically oriental, luxuriant, languid quality associated in Russian operas with *nega*. The number is reprised at the very end of the opera to accompany Assad's death in Sulamith's arms. The presence of the backup chorus in the wilderness is an improbability that Goldmark was evidently willing to risk for the sake of the poignant musical reminiscence; but the accompanying percussion instruments, along with the harps, are assigned this time not to the terrestrial maidens but to cherubs, who miraculously appear, fully equipped, in the clouds.

V. ANGLE OF SURVEILLANCE

The two characters least marked with orientalizing tropes in *Die Königin von Saba* are King Solomon, whose role appears to have been modeled on that of Sarastro in *Die Zauberflöte*, and, perhaps surprisingly, the title character. Solomon is orientalized, if at all, merely by virtue of a harp-heavy accompaniment when he is being particularly wise (as for example at the end of Act III, when he commutes Assad's death sentence). As for the Arabian Queen, consider the beginning of the second

EXAMPLE 3.11. Goldmark, *Königin von Saba*, Act I, "Der Freund ist dein."

act, the act that exhibits the opera's most blatant orientalisms, including the *Lockruf*. It opens with a long solo *scena*, an internal monologue in which the Queen reveals that, although she had refused to acknowledge Assad in the preceding act, thus precipitating the tragic action, she nonetheless fully reciprocates his passion.

Her music is full of signifiers, but none is in any way *fremdartig*. Rather, they betoken agitated emotion, the primordial operatic stock-in-trade which assumes all human nature to be one. Alone and unobserved, the Queen is stripped bare and exposes her soul, which, being human, exemplifies not any particular subgroup to which she happens to belong (women, queens, Arabs), but only her—which is to say all of us. To be unobserved, in other words, is to be unmarked. A character alone onstage is in no need of differentiation from others, and is consequently to be portrayed as simply—that is, universally—human. Feelings expressed by a soliloquizing soloist belong to everyone. To display them is to stress commonality with the observer beyond the fourth wall, unportrayed but tacitly acknowledged.

Corroborating examples come readily to mind. The second act of Borodin's *Prince Igor* is a riot of oriental color from start to finish, except for the central moment: Igor's soliloquy in which, alone on stage, he sings of his longing for freedom, a moment devoid not only of oriental coloration (which we would not expect of him in any case) but of Russian coloration as well (which we might indeed have expected were we operatic novices). By contrast, the strophic song sung in the first act by Igor's brother-in-law, Prince Galitzky, being what film scholars call a diegetic number (or, to use Carolyn Abbate's language, a "phenomenal" song), performed as such in the presence of others, is for both of these reasons marked "Russian" by the use of stereotypical folkloric turns of phrase (specifically the cadential progression 5–4–1). Another example, perhaps the best known of all: when in the presence of Don José, Carmen expresses herself in habaneras and seguidillas, but when alone onstage (turning cards, for instance), she simply sounds like Bizet the way the Queen of Sheba alone on stage simply sounds like Goldmark.

There is a theoretical side to this, usually tacit, but evidently well enough known to composers of nineteenth-century operas, whether nationalist or exoticist (two sides, after all, of a single coin). The most explicit enunciation I know comes from César Cui's review of Rimsky-Korsakov's first opera, *Pskovityanka* (The Maid of Pskov, 1873). Rimsky had set a love duet for the title character and her star-crossed lover to the tune of a Russian folk song he had found in a published anthology. That, announced Cui (both a paid reviewer and the composer's elder brother kuchkist), was a tyro's mistake:

> One can give a folk song to a chorus representing the folk; one can give it also to individuals who are singing a song; but individual feelings cannot be poured forth in the sounds of a folk song. Here Olga and Tucha are speaking of their own love, of their own feelings; in such a spot the sounds of a folk song are altogether out of place on their lips.[34]

The rule Cui here invokes applied to other-making markers and self-asserting ones alike. Goldmark never stated it as a rule, the way Cui did; but he surely followed it in practice—and in a particularly subtle, self-aware fashion that bespeaks

---

34. *Sanktpeterburgskiye vedomosti*, 9 January 1873; rpt. in César Antonovich Cui, *Izbrannïye stat'i* (Leningrad: Muzgiz, 1952), 220.

high consciousness of the rule. His Queen when unobserved is unmarked; but as soon as she *is* observed, she immediately sprouts exoticist markers. Consider the narrative in which Assad describes to King Solomon his first encounter with the Queen, unclothed and therefore unidentified, but full of sexual allure. After the verses that were often recorded by Leo Slezak and others—evoking the cedars of Lebanon, the plashing of a silvery brook, and so forth—comes the fatally seductive vision.

Goldmark's musical marker of sexual allure had occurred first in the Prelude (Ex. 3.12). My Stravinsky-educated ears certainly pricked up when I heard this sudden excursion into Wagner by way of Liszt. It carried me back to my early investigations, three decades ago and more, into the sources of Stravinsky's harmonic practices. Goldmark's chromatic sequence goes through two progressions encompassing three out of the four members of a circle of minor thirds, and the bass, which links the roots of the chords in the progression with passing tones, performs a complete octatonic scale, to give it a name Goldmark could never have used since it was not coined until 1963.[35] But that tone-semitone scale, when juxtaposed with diatonic harmony, had been a marker of apartness (supernatural, exotic, sublime) since the late 1840s, when Liszt (having observed it in Schubert) made it one of the main constituents of his first symphonic poem, the so-called *Mountain* Symphony, and a whole school of Russian composers, having educed it from Liszt, made it their symbol par excellence of the uncanny.[36]

Goldmark's usage is not systematized the Russian way, and he never takes the circle of thirds through a full fourfold sequence to completion, which suggests that he did not have an a priori conception of his bass line as a particular scale or mode. On its many further appearances in the opera, which consistently identify it with the passionately erotic, illicit liaison between the Queen and Assad, the motif goes through only two sequential progressions. But its preliminary appearance in the Prelude, in a fuller form, makes it instantly recognizable as a leitmotif as it gains context and thus specificity of reference. In its further appearances, including Assad's confessional narrative, it is often placed in conjunction with *Goldmarktriole* and augmented seconds, producing a signifying cluster that associates the Queen (when observed) both with sex and with the inscrutable East. Its appearance in Assad's narrative is heralded, in fact, by a fleeting preliminary reference to the music that will accompany the black slave girls when they appear, in the opera's next scene, as part of the Queen's retinue (Ex. 3.13).

---

35. By Arthur Berger in "Problems of Pitch Organization in Stravinsky," *Perspectives of New Music* 2, no. 1 (1963): 11–42.

36. For the history, see Richard Taruskin, "Chernomor to Kashchei: Harmonic Sorcery; or, Stravinsky's 'Angle,'" *Journal of the American Musicological Society* 38 (1985): 72–142.

EXAMPLE 3.12. Goldmark, *Königin von Saba*, Prelude, mm. 24–35.

This is an especially canny deployment. When delivering his narrative to Solomon, Assad does not yet know that he has seen the Queen of Sheba. All he knows is that he has seen a sexy alien body. And so at this point the augmented seconds signify exactly what they will signify during the Queen's procession in the next scene. But once he has witnessed the Queen's official entrance and—to his horror—recognized hers as the sexy body he had previously encountered, she takes on another identity, and with it, another set of signifiers. Similarly, the proto-octatonic motif that signifies the mutual passion kindled in Assad and the Queen haunts each of them when thinking of the other: it signifies them in each other's eyes as sexually objectified rather than sentient subjects.

Of course, I am using language that would never have occurred to Goldmark. But regardless of the language used to describe them, the composer is making remarkably fine discriminations and distinctions through the use of typical orientalist markers. He differentiates his characters by gender, race, and social class (again using our language for categories to which he might have given other names), and also according to the angle of surveillance—that is, whether a charac-

EXAMPLE 3.13. Goldmark, *Königin von Saba,* Act I, Assad's Narrative.

ter is being observed only by the audience or by other characters with their own points of view. Goldmark's markers convey a wealth of meaning above and beyond the rough breakdown into four categories (Israelite at court and at worship, Arabian, and Moorish) to which he proudly but inadequately called attention in his memoirs. We have seen them all in action and interaction in the characterization of the Queen, of Astaroth, of Assad, of Sulamith, and of King Solomon, as well as in the chorus and the corps de ballet, variously costumed.

But we have seen much more than that. In redeeming his boast, Goldmark showed himself to be the consummate eclectic: a master of a thousand styles, which he could deploy in myriad combinations according to a consummately expert and rationalized technique. In saying this—and obviously I am saying it in admiration—I am well aware that I am describing Goldmark exactly the way Wagner described Jewish musicians so as to denigrate and discredit them. To which Wagner would say: What would you expect from a Jewish musicologist? To which I say: Goldmark's superbly rationalized modus operandi is the modus operandi of all skillful composers, certainly not excluding Wagner, whose mature musical technique—or musical style, which in his case amounted to almost the same thing—was perhaps the most thoroughly willed and rationally contrived in the whole history of European music.

It is only Wagner's incredible success as a propagandist, repackaging and reenergizing a lot of romantic claptrap that still holds too many of us in thrall, that keeps us now from seeing Wagner the way Wagner saw Mendelssohn and Meyerbeer. Karl Goldmark can help us over that obstacle.

4

Why You Cannot Leave Bartók Out

The invitation to address this conference as its keynote speaker was surely among the most gratifying I have ever received. The implied compliment, since—as I probably shouldn't remind you—I am not a card-carrying Bartókian, was seductive. The opportunity to be the guest of those to whom I had long ago played happy host at Berkeley—László Somfai, our distinguished Bloch lecturer of 1989, and Tibor Tallián, who gave us a memorable departmental colloquium talk a few years later—was another irresistible blandishment. And finally, at least one-third of you whom I am now addressing are old friends and acquaintances, not to mention beloved *Doktorkinder;* another third are familiar names to which I am delighted to be able to put faces; and the remaining third a group of likely future friends. So of course I succumbed to temptation and accepted the invitation.

Which left me with a problem—namely, what to say about Bartók to a roomful of people who know more about him than I do. It was a question to which I had no ready answer when I accepted the invitation a year or so ago, but as time went on it began to nag, and made me worry. When the organizers began to press me for a title and an abstract, my worry mounted toward panic. I ransacked my mind for clues as to what I might offer a roomful of Bartókians on their home turf to justify their (that is, your) flattering faith in me. Apologies on behalf of Stravinsky, perhaps? I don't think Igor Fyodorovich would exactly welcome me as a spokesman.

Keynote address at the international conference "Bartók and His Orbit," Institute for Musicology of the Hungarian Academy of Sciences, Budapest, 22 March 2006; published in *Studia Musicologica Academiae Scientiarum Hungaricae* 47 (2006): 265–78.

Greetings from the wider world of musicology, then? Nobody elected me ambassador. Should I aspire to the usual role of the keynote speaker and set an agenda? That would hardly be in character; as my friends and enemies know, my preferred mission in life is not to set agendas but rather to upset them. The longer I thought about it, the harder it became to decide what to do.

And then I received a gift from God. The editors of the journal *Nineteenth-Century Music* invited me to review two big books: *The Cambridge History of Nineteenth-Century Music*, which had come out in 2001, and its companion, *The Cambridge History of Twentieth-Century Music*, which followed in 2004.[1] Like most historical surveys nowadays, these were collaborative volumes, incorporating between them the work of thirty-five scholars from a variety of German- and English-speaking countries. To my amazement and consternation, I discovered that Bartók had been pretty much left out of the twentieth-century volume. This is the kind of thing that can happen when different authors are working independently, and that is why there are editors. But in this case the editor, Nicholas Cook, made a point, in his introduction, of not intervening on Bartók's behalf. "It is hard to know," he wrote, whether the lacuna "is to be seen as an accidental shortcoming that the editors should have remedied, or as symptomatic of a revaluation of twentieth-century classicism that makes Bartók's particular synthesis appear less important than it once did. Time will tell; pending that, our authors' priorities stand."[2]

But the authors had implied no such "priorities." I'm sure they all assumed that *somebody* was covering Bartók—and so, obviously, had Cook himself, or else why make a point of mentioning it in the introduction? In my review, I made an example of his laxness and his failure to do his job properly. But I held back from pressing any further claims on Bartók's behalf, for two reasons. First, as anyone who reads the book (or, to save time, reads my review) will discover, there were plenty of sins of commission to complain about without fussing over omissions. And second, reviews that complain about omissions—and in particular, about the omission of particular persons—usually miss the point. At least I have to think so, since my own recent history of music[3] has suffered so much abuse from Sibelius fans, and Busoni fans, and Elgar fans, and Holst fans, and Vaughan Williams fans (as you see, I'm especially popular in Britain), and Pierre de la Rue fans, and even Florian Gassmann fans—and no, I didn't make that last one up.

What makes the omission of Bartók a more serious offense? If I think it is—and yes, I certainly do—I'll need better reasons than simply my own opinion, however

---

1. My review appeared under the title "Speed Bumps," *Nineteenth-Century Music* 29, no. 2 (2005–6): 185–207.

2. Nicolas Cook, "Introduction," *The Cambridge History of Twentieth-Century Music* (henceforth *CH20*) (Cambridge: Cambridge University Press, 2004), 4.

3. R. Taruskin, *The Oxford History of Western Music* (New York: Oxford University Press, 2005).

widely it may be shared, that he was a better, or at least a more significant, composer than Holst or Gassmann. To argue for any particular figure simply on the basis of your own admiration for him is to fall prey to what I like to call the "poietic fallacy," the assumption (to put it crudely) that history is really collective biography, or (to put it just a bit more urbanely) that creative individuals are the only significant agents in the history of the arts.[4]

I certainly do not believe that to be the case; in fact, since finishing *The Oxford History of Western Music* I seem to have been doing little else but combating the poietic fallacy on many fronts, both offensive and defensive. So if I am to offer an effective critique of Nicholas Cook's decision to allow the inadvertent omission of Bartók from *The Cambridge History of Twentieth-Century Music* to stand, I shall have to do it on other than poietic terms. That is what I now propose to do. And in the course of doing it, I will be offering apologies on behalf of Stravinsky after all, and I will even, perhaps, be advancing—or at least I may lay myself open to accusations of advancing—an agenda.

. . .

It is not as though the name Bartók never appears in *The Cambridge History of Twentieth-Century Music* (any more than the name Sibelius never appears in *The Oxford History of Western Music*). There are eighteen index entries for Bartók. Anyone tracking them down will find Bartók's name in various lists: of composers who explored "the dialectical and reciprocal connections between high-art traditions and popular and folk music";[5] or of composers who "loosened the restrictive bonds of tonality";[6] or of composers "whose music was not consistently associated with specific compositional approaches";[7] or of composers published by Universal Edition;[8] or of composers who "introduced eighteenth-century principles into their works in an innovative way";[9] or of composers who wrote *Weltanschauungsmusik*;[10] or of composers whose music Pierre Boulez did not

---

4. See R. Taruskin, "The Poietic Fallacy," *Musical Times* 145 (Spring 2004): 7–34; rpt. in Taruskin, *The Danger of Music and Other Anti-Utopian Essays* (Berkeley and Los Angeles: University of California Press, 2008), 301–29.

5. Leon Botstein, "Music of a Century: Museum Culture and the Politics of Subsidy," *CH20*, 47.

6. Christopher Butler, "Innovation and the Avant-garde, 1900–20," *CH20*, 75. Another example of Butler's wizened neo-Hegelian rhetoric (73n10): "Bartók's work is an excellent example of the balance between the imperatives of progress, and of assimilation of the new to the traditional."

7. Joseph Auner, "Proclaiming the Mainstream: Schoenberg, Berg, and Webern," *CH20*, 224.

8. Stephen Banfield, "Music, Text, and Stage: Bourgeois Tonality to the Second World War," *CH20*, 115.

9. The unexplained oxymoron is Hermann Danuser's: "Rewriting the Past: Classicisms of the Inter-War Period," *CH20*, 279.

10. Michael Walter, "Music of Seriousness and Commitment: The 1930s and Beyond," *CH20*, 301.

mind conducting;[11] or (yes! still!) of composers "influenced by twelve-tone thinking but retaining tonal features."[12] One will find acknowledgment that Bartók's concertos have joined the standard repertoire for piano and violin; that his string quartets "move beyond those of his predecessors";[13] that his style resonates faintly in film music, that he used "superimposed modal systems";[14] and that he had "an interest in symmetrical forms."[15]

Although I did not use it that way in my review, this little survey of Bartók references certainly exposes—in its contradictions, its hazy formulations, its tendentious errors, and its superannuated rhetoric—the incoherence of the conventional narrative of the history of twentieth-century music that we have been putting up with for so long. Indeed, the insistence that the proliferation of specialized knowledge has made multiple authorship mandatory (asserted by the editors of both Cambridge volumes) insures that incoherence shall remain inviolate, following the hallowed example of the blind men and the elephant. But beyond matters of professional deformation, the list of scattered references to Bartók certainly confirms my diagnosis of the poietic fallacy. Except for the references to Universal Edition and to Pierre Boulez's conducting, from which one can deduce the bare fact that Bartók's music *was* mediated after all by publishers and performers, he is viewed as entirely alone, sitting within the four walls of his workroom, producing scores. One would not learn from *The Cambridge History of Twentieth-Century Music* that Bartók was a performer himself, let alone a great one; one would not learn that he was an admired teacher (though not of composition) who wrote a wealth of pedagogical piano music; one would not learn that he emigrated from Europe to America, or why.

Above all, one would not learn that, shortly after his death, his music was the site of one of the great cruxes, indeed one of the great pitched battles, in the reception history of twentieth-century music. In my view, these matters are far more important than Bartók's use of superimposed modal systems, whatever those might be, or the fact that his string quartets moved beyond those of his predecessors, wherever that may have led them. These more important matters, involving the social mediation and reception of music, and the buffeting the arts and their practitioners have suffered in the turbulent political environment of the twentieth century, are what make Bartók indispensable to the historiography of twentieth-century music.

---

11. Arnold Whittall, "Individualism and Accessibility: The Moderate Mainstream, 1945–75," *CH20*, 366.
12. Ibid., 378.
13. Butler, "Innovation and the Avant-garde," 83.
14. Alastair Williams, "Ageing of the New: The Museum of Musical Modernism," *CH20*, 515.
15. Peter Elsdon with Björn Heile, "Personalia," *CH20*, 618.

But even in a historiography confined to the poietic, Bartók is indispensable, and his absence crippling. Composers' styles and methods will always be an important part of the story, and it should not be supposed that in calling for a broadened musicological perspective I mean to slight or eliminate the poietic from the account. I emphatically reject what I call "the great Either/Or," the insistence (maintained most influentially by Carl Dahlhaus) that one must choose between narrating "the *history* of art" and narrating "the history of *art*."[16] Great artifacts and their makers will always fascinate us. For some of us they will always remain at the center of the story, and there is no reason why they should not do so. All I would insist upon is that they be properly contextualized and explained, and that is why we need the broader purview. I do not want to substitute one partial view for another. I want the whole story. (And that is how you end up writing six-volume histories.)

A proper poietic account of Bartók would emphasize his fascination with symmetries of all kinds—not just formal, but also (and especially) harmonic. The description of that side of his craft was pioneered by George Perle, and magnificently developed by his pupil Elliott Antokoletz.[17] And it is altogether missing from *The Cambridge History of Twentieth-Century Music*, which with preposterous crudity recognizes only two twentieth-century styles, "tonal" and "atonal" (becoming "serial"). There is no discussion of interval cycles, none of octatonic or hexatonic collections, no mention of transpositional or inversional invariance, nor of "modes of limited transposition," let alone matrices of crisscrossing chromatic scales that maintain between them a constant intervallic sum, such as one finds in the work of Bartók and Berg, Strauss and Stravinsky, Debussy and Messiaen. Anyone who has studied such harmonic phenomena and the techniques to which they have given rise knows that they can be most economically and comprehensively demonstrated in the work of Bartók.

That Bartók is unrepresented in the *Cambridge History* is thus a symptom of a greater misrepresentation, and one hallowed by tradition, namely the inveterate, residual Germanocentrism that continues to inform unreflective music historiography. Harmonic symmetry is a strain that, while traceable to Schubert, received its strongest impetus from Liszt and went from Liszt into Bartók, and (via Rimsky-Korsakov) into Ravel and Stravinsky.[18] Eliminate that strain and you are left with

---

16. See Carl Dahlhaus, *Foundations of Music History*, trans. J. B. Robinson (Cambridge: Cambridge University Press, 1982), chap. 2: "The Significance of Art: Historical or Aesthetic?"

17. George Perle, "The String Quartets of Béla Bartók," in *A Musical Offering: Essays in Honor of Martin Bernstein*, ed. Edward H. Clinkscale and Claire Brook (New York: Pendragon Press, 1977), 193–210; Elliott Antokoletz, *The Music of Béla Bartók: A Study of Tonality and Progression in Twentieth-Century Music* (Berkeley and Los Angeles: University of California Press, 1984).

18. See R. Taruskin, "Chernomor to Kashchei: Harmonic Sorcery; or, Stravinsky's 'Angle,'" *Journal of the American Musicological Society* 38 (1985): 72–142.

the Germanic straight-and-narrow, to which Strauss and Berg can now be assimilated without acknowledging their non-Teutonic inheritances. Germanocentrism is so thoroughly ingrained in Anglophone musicology that it has become transparent. The best way of bringing it to light is to study Bartók's work as assiduously as Schoenberg's. But before a bias can be countered, it must be acknowledged. So right there, still within the confines of the poietic, we already have a compelling reason why one cannot leave Bartók out: he is the prime antidote to the Germanocentric infection.

Now, the main symptom of the disorder, as with all ethnocentrisms, is the confusion of the particular with the universal. Germanocentrists never think that they are Germanocentric; hence no one is knowingly or overtly Germanocentric, at least since 1945. The telltale mark of Germanocentrists is that they think of themselves as universalists, in contrast to particularists of various kinds. This is something that observers of American politics will recognize. The rich white men who wield political power in America are always warning against the "special interests," by which they mean the interests of anyone who is not rich, white, or male. The equivalent in music is the notion that there is a classical "mainstream," outside of which we are dealing with regionalisms or folk traditions, representing a less fully developed humanity. "Once," Leoš Janáček recalled, "an educated German said to me: 'What, you grow out of folk song? That is a sign of a lack of culture!' . . . I turned away and let the German be."[19] Or to recall what is surely your favorite Stravinsky quote, his silly condescension toward Bartók: "I never could share his lifelong gusto for his native folklore. This devotion was certainly real and touching, but I couldn't help regretting it in the great musician."[20]

Poor Bartók. Such a remark came with particularly bad grace from Stravinsky, whose Germanocentrism, however belated, was certainly real and touching, but whose tendency to dissemble was regrettable. He had his reasons, of course, and we will come back to them soon enough. But for a third Germanocentric voice, and probably the least self-aware, I give you Robert P. Morgan, and his textbook *Twentieth-Century Music*. He seems at first blush to do all right by Bartók, with a seven-page discussion that goes beyond the composer's debt to folklore. Morgan acknowledges his inheritance from Liszt and his brush with "atonality." But when, a few pages later, Morgan found himself dismissing Janáček in two pages, he justified it with the remark that "it was Bartók who came to be viewed as the dominant compositional voice of Eastern Europe."[21] That remark is classic, not just for its chilling recollection of the *numerus clausus*, but also for the way it evokes another

---

19. Mirka Zemanová, ed., *Janáček's Uncollected Essays on Music* (London: Marion Boyars, 1989), 61.
20. Igor Stravinsky and Robert Craft, *Conversations with Igor Stravinsky* (Garden City, NY: Doubleday, 1959), 82.
21. Robert P. Morgan, *Twentieth-Century Music* (New York: W. W. Norton, 1991), 119.

endearing foible of American politics, known as "tokenism." Having included one East European—or one female, or one gay, or one Black—composer, one is then justified in ignoring the rest. (Stravinsky perpetrated a classic of tokenism when he admitted, to an early biographer, using one folk song in *Le Sacre du printemps* so as to discourage hunting for others.)[22] If these are the terms that gained Bartók admission to Morgan's survey, he might just as well have been excluded.

But let us return to Stravinsky. He and Bartók ought by rights to have become a historiographical pair, a cliché like Bach & Handel, Mozart & Haydn, Debussy & Ravel. Bartók certainly thought so, at least at first. Stravinsky was always his prime exhibit of a composer who had successfully renovated his style on the basis of folklore; and Bartók was so sure of Stravinsky as a kindred spirit that he actually saw as a proposition in need of proof not that Stravinsky quoted folk songs (the proposition for which I had, many years later, to mount such an elaborate proof),[23] but rather that Stravinsky occasionally used themes of his own invention.[24] Stravinsky's extraordinary knack, in his prewar ballets for Diaghilev, and especially in his wartime compositions like *Pribaoutki* or *Svadebka* (*Les Noces*), for blending folklore and modernism gave Bartók enormous encouragement. And beyond themes, it was precisely the most novel aspects of Stravinsky's music, its form and rhythm, that were most heavily indebted to folklore. "Even the origin of the rough-grained, brittle and jerky musical structure backed by ostinatos," Bartók marveled in his Harvard University lecture of 1943, "so different from any structural proceeding of the past, may be sought in the short-breathed Russian peasant motives."[25]

Stravinsky fairly screamed denial until the day he died, but of course Bartók was correct. With the help of an enormous publicity machine, Stravinsky managed to dissociate himself from the early neonationalism that allied him with Bartók, and set himself up, however improbably, as an arbiter of musical universalism in his Parisian and Californian years. Bartók and Stravinsky no longer look like a "natural" pair, and it may be worth noting that the program of this conference contains papers on Bartók and Sibelius, Bartók and Enesco, Bartók and Ravel, Bartók and Schoenberg, and Bartók and Boulez, but no paper on Bartók and Stravinsky (except for this unannounced one).

Needless to say, no music history text would ever exclude Stravinsky, and the *Cambridge History* accords him his usual place as the antipode to Schoenberg, with three sustained discussions corresponding to his Beethovenish trio of

22. See André Schaeffner, *Strawinsky* (Paris: Editions Rieder, 1931), 43n1; also "Table des planches," pl. 21 (217).
23. R. Taruskin, "Russian Folk Melodies in *The Rite of Spring*," *Journal of the American Musicological Society* 33 (1980): 501–43.
24. Béla Bartók, "The Influence of Peasant Music on Modern Music" (1931), in *Béla Bartók Essays*, ed. Benjamin Suchoff (New York: St. Martin's Press, 1976), 343.
25. Ibid.

periods, and a total of seventy index entries, almost four times the number for Bartók. Is that a just dispensation? All of us gathered in this room will surely agree that it is not; but I think those outside should also agree. I think it fair to say, and as a card-carrying Stravinskian I feel not only entitled but bound to say it, that Stravinsky has been as much overrated in conventional music historiography as Bartók was ever underrated. How Stravinsky managed his amazing feat of dissociation and self-reinvention is a subject for another day (and I've told that story before).[26] Here I'd like to consider why he did so.

Stravinsky's vociferous rejection of folklore as a legitimate source for professional music went back to his years as a "white émigré" in Paris. It is sometimes maintained by historians that Stravinsky was not really a "white émigré" on the order of, say, Rachmaninoff, because his expatriation took place before the Russian Revolution. But it was only after 1917 that it became clear to Stravinsky that his expatriation might be permanent, and by 1920, with the final Bolshevik victories over the Whites in the postrevolutionary civil war, Stravinsky allowed himself to be transformed from a gentry liberal who greeted the tsar's abdication with joy,[27] into a passionate enemy of the Bolsheviks, the usurpers who had expropriated his family's property and impoverished him. The change coincided with his move from neutral Switzerland to France, where he divided his time for a while between Paris and Biarritz in the Pyrenees, the main redoubt of the uprooted Russian nobility. In 1940, lecturing in French (also at Harvard University, three years ahead of Bartók), the Parisian Stravinsky went out of his way to deride the "dancing collective farm" and the "symphony of Socialism."[28] These were the musical emblems, popularized by Shostakovich, of the Red Russia that Stravinsky abhorred, where an art "national in form and Socialist in content" (in Stalin's own words) was official, enforceable cultural policy.[29]

By the time Stravinsky dictated to Robert Craft his odious remarks about Bartók he had been living in America for twenty years. By 1959, a dozen years into the Cold War, Stravinsky was following the herd and trying to establish credentials

---

26. R. Taruskin, *Stravinsky and the Russian Traditions* (Berkeley and Los Angeles: University of California Press, 1996).

27. "Toutes nos pensées avec toi dans ces inoubliables jours de bonhuer [sic] que traverse notre chere [sic] Russie liberée [sic]": Telegram from Stravinsky to his mother, Anna Kirillovna Stravinskaya, from Morges, Switzerland, 24 May 1917; in L. S. Dyachkova, ed., *I. F. Stravinskiy: Stat'i i materialï* (Moscow: Sovetskiy kompozitor, 1973), 489.

28. For the most recent edition of his Harvard lectures of 1939–40, see Igor Stravinsky, *Poétique musicale: Sous forme de six leçons*, ed. Myriam Soumagnac (Paris: Flammarion, 2012). The comments on Soviet music are found in the fifth "lesson" ("Les avatars de la musique russe"). For an interpretation of them in the light of Stravinsky's cultural allegiances, see R. Taruskin, "Stravinsky's *Poetics* and Russian Music," in *Russian Music at Home and Abroad* (Oakland: University of California Press, 2016), 421–78.

29. On the Stalinist slogan, see Taruskin, "The Ghetto and the Imperium," in *Russian Music at Home and Abroad*, 233–303, esp. 261–65.

as a twelve-tone composer. That meant seeking the "universal" (and politically safe) truth of numbers to validate his art, rather than the particular (and politically risky) reality of nation. Indeed, a Russian living in the United States in the 1950s might have had especially strong reasons to repudiate his national heritage, in addition to the reasons Stravinsky had while living in Paris in the 1920s. Alongside the aesthetic anxieties that propelled him toward the twelve-tone technique (anxieties that have been touchingly described since Stravinsky's death by Robert Craft, who helped nurse him through them),[30] there must have been some political anxieties as well.

Here the contrast between Stravinsky and Bartók is especially telling. It can be dramatically encapsulated by recalling their differing responses to the Nazi *Entartete Musik* exhibition in 1938. Stravinsky protested that he had been included, Bartók that he had been excluded.[31] That, to me, was Bartók's finest hour, followed two years later by a tragic sequel, his emigration to America—an emigration that was not undertaken (as Stravinsky's was) for the sake of convenience and as a result of a lucky break (the invitation from Harvard), but a most inexpedient one that was undertaken out of principle, and led to privation. Of all twentieth-century musicians, Bartók is the one who in his sacrifice most awe-inspiringly exemplifies for me uncompromising devotion to an exacting humanitarian code.

Is it a coincidence that 1938 also marks a turning point in Bartók's creative biography, discernable in, or even symbolized by, the stylistic gap between the Sonata for Two Pianos and Percussion of 1937, the last work of Bartók's that could fairly be described as esoteric or avant-garde, and the *Contrasts* for violin, clarinet, and piano, composed the next year, in which he reconnected with the kind of popular "verbunkos" Hungarianism he had formerly rejected? That turn in Bartók's style might be compared with the one in Prokofieff's a couple of years earlier, coinciding with his return to Soviet Russia. Again, what is often written off as opportunistic or coerced in the case of the Russian composer appears to be the result of a voluntary commitment on the part of the Hungarian. It brought him no glory in the short run. On the contrary, it has made Bartók a problem for historians wedded to neo-Hegelian deterministic paradigms. For a time it brought about a decline in Bartók's reputation.

And here again the Bartók/Stravinsky dialectic is instructive. In the 1920s, Stravinsky's aggressive early neoclassic idiom knocked Bartók off his feet, and provided the stimulus for his most concentrated modernist phase. David Schneider

---

30. Robert Craft, *Stravinsky: Chronicle of a Friendship, 1948–71*, revised and expanded Ed. (Nashville: Vanderbilt University Press, 1994), 72–73.

31. See Stravinsky, *Selected Correspondence*, vol. 3, ed. Robert Craft (New York: Knopf, 1985), 265 (letter to Willy Strecker of B. Schotts Söhne, 27 May 1938); Béla Bartók, *Letters*, ed. János Demény (New York: St. Martin's Press, 1971), 274 (letter to Hans Priegnitz, 12 January 1939).

has shown how direct an impact Stravinsky's Concerto for Piano and Winds—not only the score, but also Stravinsky's performance of it as pianist in Budapest in 1926—had on Bartók, who was in the audience, and who found Stravinsky's postwar work at once repellent and irresistible. The tension this contradictory reaction created in him was one of the most powerful stimulants he ever received. It roused him from a three-year creative block and led him to his maturest phase. A letter from Ditta Pásztory-Bartók to the composer's mother, quoted by Schneider, gave vivid expression to that ambivalence: "We very, very much enjoyed the evening," she wrote. "Truly one gets caught up in this miraculously beautiful-sounding machine music, music of pulsating rhythm." But it was a music in which "there is absolutely no room for feelings, in which you can find no part that causes tears to come to your eyes." In short, she wrote, "it is not my homeland."[32]

Bartók saw it as his task to reconcile that dynamic pulsation, in which he sensed the lingering reverberation of Stravinsky's earlier neonationalist manner, with a sense of homeland that would restore the missing feelings and tears. His First Piano Concerto, the most direct emulation the pianist-composer Bartók could offer the pianist-composer Stravinsky, was the outcome. The love-hate relationship with Stravinsky is manifest at all levels of the concerto's form and substance, from reflexive near-quotations on the surface to profound transformations in which Stravinsky's monumental, wholly abstract rhythmic gearshifts are made over into what László Somfai calls "Hungarian culmination points": sudden heavy infusions of national style at an abruptly broadened tempo.[33]

Bartók immediately followed up on the First Piano Concerto with his Third and Fourth Quartets, the works that are commonly regarded as his modernist extreme. Here again the Stravinskian pulsation is combined with national style, only now the national style is rendered more abstract by means of the most intensely concentrated preoccupation—elucidated for us all by Elliott Antokoletz[34]—with symmetrical pitch structures that bear a distinct and very traceable relationship to the harmonic idiom of Stravinsky's neoprimitivist music, but distilled and systematized beyond anything Stravinsky ever attempted. That is true emulation: the effort not merely to duplicate, but to surpass.

Far less often noted is the convergence between Bartók's populist swerve, culminating in the Concerto for Orchestra, and the somewhat later but overlapping one that Stravinsky undertook in America during the war years. Here the emblem-

---

32. Quoted in David E. Schneider, "Bartók and Stravinsky: Respect, Competition, Influence, and the Hungarian Reaction to Modernism in the 1920s," in *Bartók and His World*, ed. Peter Laki (Princeton, NJ: Princeton University Press, 1995), 184.

33. See L. Somfai, "A Characteristic Culmination Point in Bartók's Instrumental Forms," in *Conference in Commemoration of Béla Bartók: Budapest 1971* (Budapest: Editio Musica, 1972), 53–64.

34. See E. Antokoletz, "Principles of Pitch Organization in Bartók's Fourth String Quartet," *In Theory Only* 3, no. 6 (September 1977): 3–22; also Antokoletz, *The Music of Béla Bartók* (see n. 17 above), passim.

atic Stravinsky scores would be the Symphony in Three Movements and some lesser-known pieces like the *Scherzo à la russe* and the Sonata for Two Pianos. The war years brought to Stravinsky the same new urgency of communication and the same sense of social solidarity that had already seemed to mitigate Bartók's commitment to stylistic novelty. Stravinsky even, and very unexpectedly, recovered a sense of Russian patriotism in wartime Hollywood. The Scherzo and the Sonata quote Russian folk songs (the Sonata quite secretly: nobody knew or suspected until Lawrence Morton spilled the beans at a Stravinsky centennial conference in 1982),[35] and the scoring of the Symphony in Three Movements pays covert homage to Glinka. Its first movement features a piano obbligato. In the second, a solo harp holds forth. In the third, the two solo instruments play in tandem, producing a silvery tinkle in which any Russian opera lover will recognize the evocation of the bard's *gusli* (the Russian folk psaltery) in the Prologue to Glinka's *Ruslan and Lyudmila*, that great national epic of heroic deeds.

Stravinsky, as we know, lapsed quickly back into modernist respectability and social indifference after the war, whereas Bartók had no postwar period. It is enticing if fruitless to speculate on what sort of music Bartók might have written had he lived as long as Stravinsky (which would have given him until 1970), or what his personal reaction to the early Cold War might have been. Though he had lived for five months under Communism in 1919, he never had to contend with the doctrine of Socialist Realism. But his music did. His legacy suffered terribly during the early Cold War years.

As the wartime alliance devolved into schism and confrontation, Bartók's music, which drew its authenticity in his own eyes from its dialectic of folklore and modernism, was ruthlessly partitioned, like Europe itself, into Eastern and Western zones. Within the Soviet bloc, which included his homeland beginning in 1949, the works in which folklore was perceived to predominate were touted most undialectically, as Danielle Fosler-Lussier has documented in depressing detail, by the culture politicians as obligatory models, and the rest was anathematized or, in some cases, actually banned.[36] The Western European avant-garde, meanwhile, made virtual fetishes out of the Third and Fourth Quartets, which they insisted on misreading as proto-serial, and accused the composer of the Concerto for Orchestra, to recall René Leibowitz's chilling article, published by Jean-Paul Sartre in 1947, of "compromise."[37] That may well rank as the greatest critical injustice ever visited

---

35. See L. Morton, "Stravinsky at Home," in *Confronting Stravinsky: Man, Musician, and Modernist*, ed. Jann Pasler (Berkeley and Los Angeles: University of California Press, 1986), 335–36.

36. See D. Fosler-Lussier, *Music Divided: Bartók's Legacy in Cold War Culture* (Berkeley and Los Angeles: University of California Press, 2007).

37. R. Leibowitz, "Béla Bartók, ou la possibilité de compromis dans la musique contemporaine," *Les Temps modernes* 3, no. 25 (October 1947): 706–34; on Bartók as proto-serialist, see Milton Babbitt, "The String Quartets of Bartók," *Musical Quarterly* 35 (1949): 377–85.

upon a great artist, when we recall the "uncompromising devotion to an exacting humanitarian code," as I put it a moment ago, to which Bartók had sacrificed his personal comfort, fortune, and prestige.

In the 1950s, in the aftermath of his first visit to Europe since before the war, Stravinsky suffered a Schoenberg crisis as profound and transforming as Bartók's Stravinsky crisis had been in the 1920s. Few, though, would claim today, except in pockets of unregenerate Cold War opinion like the music departments of some American and British universities, that Stravinsky weathered his Schoenberg crisis as successfully as Bartók had weathered his Stravinsky crisis, or that his capitulation to historical determinism was less damaging a "compromise" than Bartók's reconciliation with the public had been. By now it is obvious that there was envy, as well as repressed contrition, in the meanspirited barbs Stravinsky hurled not only at Bartók but at practically everyone in the late memoirs he dictated to Robert Craft.

Bartók ended his career in a state of neglect and seeming weakness. In the slow movement of the Third Piano Concerto, written literally on his deathbed, he wistfully paraphrased Beethoven's *Heiliger Dankgesang*, the "Solemn Song of Thanksgiving" from the A-minor String Quartet, op. 132, which celebrated a recovery from illness that Bartók knew he would not duplicate. The injustice of his historical position relative to Stravinsky's persists in the academic literature, as we have seen in the case of the *Cambridge History of Twentieth-Century Music*, but I believe that as the Cold War recedes into history, Bartók's standing in historiography will eventually come into better alignment with his place of honor in the performing repertoire.

Ultimately, to leave Bartók out of the historical narrative means leaving out practically the only redeeming exception to the dismal saga of modernist responses to barbarism. Is the unredeemed version really the story we prefer? Will we try to maintain, even at this late date, the pretense of aesthetic autonomy as enunciated by Schopenhauer a century and a half ago, that "alongside world history there goes, guiltless and not stained with blood, the history of philosophy, science, and the arts"?[38] The history of Bartók's reception refutes that deceitful pose. Having studied it, no one could possibly believe that modern music evolved in lofty or innocent detachment from modern politics.

Historians of the arts who persist in maintaining the old pretense should not wonder that the social or public value of high art has in our lifetimes and within our memories so steeply declined. The figure of Bartók offers a rebuke—and following rebuke, a possible redemption—to the sad history whereby over the course

---

38. Arthur Schopenhauer, *Parerga und Paralipomena* (1851), transcribed here from the vocal score of Hans Pfitzner's *Palestrina* (Berlin: Fürstner, 1916), where it served as epigraph.

of the twentieth century the autonomy of art has degenerated into irrelevance, and the disinterestedness of artists has degenerated into moral indifference. That rebuke, and the redemption that Bartók's example can offer, are something I, for one, am unwilling to leave out.

POSTSCRIPT, 2020

I never expected this innocuous, even unctuous piece to suffer blowback, but there have been two strongly worded retorts to it that raise issues worthy of further discussion. The first came from a distinguished Finnish scholar, Ilkka Oramo, professor of musicology at the Sibelius Academy in Helsinki, who had attended the conference where I delivered it, and asked at the time, despite what I had said, why I had given such short shrift to Sibelius in *The Oxford History of Western Music*. I realized then that my comments on my own omissions could look flippant in the light of my serious points on behalf of Bartók, and while I pointed out again that Sibelius was not literally absent from the *Oxford History*, I knew that such a wan assurance would not placate my interlocutor. His dissatisfaction, and that of the many others who twitted me on behalf of Elgar and Vaughan Williams, did finally cause me to reconsider my choices. These composers, undeniably, were not just favorite sons (although, obviously, they were that, too). They were significant figures, all of them, whose impact on the course of events deserved report; and the disappointment of the many readers from whom I heard, who reasonably expected them to figure in the story, was quite fair. Having decided that they needed to be included, I had to decide what their roles would be—that is, what issues their presence might help illuminate.

My opportunity came in 2008, when Oxford decided it was time for the paperback reissue and asked me for addenda and corrigenda, the proviso being that changes must not affect the existing pagination. This left me with a loophole that would allow me to add a whole section to the book if I did so at the end of a volume, where the pagination would be new. Luckily enough, the third volume (on the nineteenth century) had ended with a chapter called "The Symphony Goes (Inter)national," which tracked the spread of the symphony (newly revived at the hands of Brahms) as well as other late-nineteenth-century orchestral genres, from Germany to Austria (with examples from Bruckner), Bohemia (examples from Dvořák), America (MacDowell, Beach), France (Franck, Saint-Saëns), and Russia (Borodin, Chaikovsky). I extended the chapter with sections on Great Britain (Elgar, Vaughan Williams) and Scandinavia (Grieg, Sibelius). The fact that including Vaughan Williams and Sibelius took the narrative, in seeming anachronism, up to the middle of the twentieth century was actually a plus, I thought. As I put it in the preface to the revised text:

Added partly to rectify the sparse coverage or omission (acknowledged in the preface to the first edition) of several well-known composers, and to provide an appropriate context for them, this new section continues the international survey of late nineteenth-century symphonic music into Britain and Scandinavia and also brings to a close the history of national symphonic "schools." For this reason, it spills over into the twentieth century, at times very far indeed. That spillover is a deliberate reminder that the history of art music in Europe and America, like the history of any cultural phenomenon of comparable scope, is not a single story, but rather a congeries of many narratives, and that there is no one time line along which all may be simultaneously recounted or observed. The histories of various genres and localities are often asynchronous, and the continuation of [the last] chapter past the arbitrary cutoff marked by the turn of century provides a good opportunity to demonstrate and underscore the point.[39]

The decision may not have been quite as deliberate as I claimed, since it was in response to a constraint imposed by the publisher, but I thought it proper and potentially advantageous, and was glad to have made it. There was a move afoot at the time to claim some of these composers (honorifically, I thought, and speciously) as "modernists."[40] Challenging that viewpoint would begin to give my treatment a point of view, which is to say, a *raison d'être* within my narrative. Other issues the newly added authors and works gave me a chance to raise included the reputation of Britain as "the land without music," and the reasons for that; the role of musical centers (in this case, Germany) in legitimizing "peripheral" figures and repertoires; the necessity or desirability of folklore as a resource for a national school of art music; the turning of artists into national heroes or monuments in emergent centers of cultural productivity (indeed, I called the whole newly added section "National Monuments"); and the role of new media in creating and maintaining reputations (previewing a theme that would dominate the fourth and fifth volumes of the *Oxford History*).

Foregrounding these issues, which entailed mediation and ideology, rubbed against the grain of the discourses that had motivated the repeated calls to rectify perceived exclusions of worthy personalities. I did not justify the new inclusions

---

39. R. Taruskin, *Music in the Nineteenth Century*, vol. 3 of *The Oxford History of Western Music*, paperback ed. (New York: Oxford University Press, 2010), xxi–xxii.

40. This propensity is sometimes called modernist "expansionism," after Douglas Mao and Rebecca Walkowitz; see their article "The New Modernist Studies," *PMLA* 123 (2008): 737–48, at 737; cited in Christopher Chowrimootoo, "'Britten Minor': Constructing the Modernist Canon," *Twentieth-Century Music* 13 (2016): 261–90, at 262–63. Among musicologists, the most insistent such writer is J. P. E. Harper-Scott, with two books of this kind: *Edward Elgar, Modernist* (Cambridge: Cambridge University Press, 2009) and *The Quilting Points of Musical Modernism: Revolution, Reaction, and William Walton* (Cambridge: Cambridge University Press, 2012), the latter containing a very heated response to the *Oxford History*. Chowrimootoo also cites as "expansionist" the work of James Hepokoski on Sibelius and Daniel Grimley on Nielsen.

on the basis of their artistic merits any more than I had justified my previous choices on that basis, nor did I argue (or admit) that geographical balance or ethnic inclusivity were in themselves valid criteria for selection. It was because I saw other good reasons for including Elgar and Sibelius (the two most bitterly resented former exclusions) that I went ahead and complied with demands for rectification, always conscious that my reasons might not quite tally with the views of the complainants. Indeed, I took a little perverse pleasure in the thought that they would more likely approve of what I did than of what I said.

So it did not surprise me to find Dr. Oramo renewing his complaint in 2010, a year after my revised text was published, in a paper he read (in English) at the Fifth International Jean Sibelius Conference, held at the University of Oxford in September of that year, with a title, "Why You Cannot Leave Sibelius Out," that parodies (or, as he says, appropriates) my own title, my original keynote address having in the meantime been published in Hungary.[41]

He makes a vigorous case, and with some of it I am in perfect agreement. He ingeniously turns around a point I once made about Schoenberg—that his music "has been influential and controversial out of all proportion to the frequency with which it has ever been performed or otherwise disseminated"—by noting that "exactly the opposite is true of the music of Sibelius," whose music is very widely played but relatively little discussed, and that "this is perhaps the most compelling reason not to leave him out."[42]

By the time Dr. Oramo wrote this, I had already come round, as I have just testified. But thereafter our views diverged. Unacquainted both with the earlier hardcover version of the *Oxford History* and (evidently) with the preface to the revised third volume, where I took note of the restitution and explained its placement, Dr. Oramo felt justified in complaining that in putting Sibelius there I had "push[ed him] back to the nineteenth century," and surmised that in so doing I was following the example of "Carl Dahlhaus's discussion of Sibelius in *Nineteenth-Century Music*."[43] Clearly, I was not giving Sibelius the company Dr. Oramo felt he deserved.

---

41. Dr. Oramo's text has been published only in Finnish translation: Ilkka Oramo, "Miksi Sibeliusta ei voida jättää ulkopuolelle," in *Säteitä 2010*, Sävellyksen ja musiikinteorian osaston vuosikirja 2 (Helsinki: Sibelius-Akatemia, 2010), 7–18; cf. R. Taruskin, "Why You Cannot Leave Bartók Out," *Studia Musicologica Academiae Scientiarum Hungaricae* 47 (2006): 265–78.

42. I. Oramo, "Why You Cannot Leave Sibelius Out" (typescript, kindly provided by the author), 9; p. 18 in the published Finnish text. The quoted phrase is from Taruskin, "The Poietic Fallacy" (see n. 4 above), 7. Further quotations from Dr. Oramo's unpublished typescript will be made without specific citation.

43. That is, the translation, by J. Bradford Robinson, of *Die Musik des 19. Jahrhunderts*, Dahlhaus's volume in the multivolume *Neues Handbuch der Musikwissenschaft* (Laaber bei Regensburg: Laaber-Verlag, 1980); see Carl Dahlhaus, *Nineteenth-Century Music* (Berkeley and Los Angeles: University of California Press, 1989).

In the new section of the *Oxford History* the chief comparison had been with Mahler, and the immediate neighbors were other Scandinavians: Grieg, Harald Saeverud, Carl Nielsen, Allan Pettersson, and Vagn Holmboe. In the fourth volume, *Music in the Early Twentieth Century*, the most sustained discussion of Sibelius portrayed him as a model for younger composers, chiefly British (Walton) and American (Harris), in the 1930s, the decade in which Sibelius's international reputation reached its apex—ironically, just at the time when his productive career was stymied by a creative block he never overcame. (In the fifth volume, *Music in the Late Twentieth Century*, Sibelius was mentioned in a similar connection, this time as an unexpected influence on Sir Peter Maxwell Davies, whose turn away from the avant-garde to a neoromantic orientation was symptomatic of the tendency that used to be called postmodernist.)

These discussions, it seemed to me, were not only accurate in their assessment of Sibelius's reception, but actually, if incidentally, quite flattering to Sibelius, even if I made sure to take note of celebrated dissenters like the inveterately francophiliac Virgil Thomson, who on first exposure to the Finnish composer's music in 1940 (after "twenty years' residence on the European continent," which had "largely spared me Sibelius") found it "vulgar, self-indulgent, and provincial beyond all description."[44] My own summary—and please note that it was an assessment of reception and reputation (a falsifiable fact) rather than an assessment of what I personally take to be the composer's assets and liabilities—ran as follows:

> His ten symphonic poems, composed between 1892 (*En Saga*) and 1926 (*Tapiola*), and, even more decisively, his seven symphonies, composed between 1899 and 1924, gained him widespread recognition at home, in the rest of Scandinavia, and in the English-speaking countries (though significantly less so in Germany and hardly at all in the Romance-speaking world) as the greatest symphonist after Brahms. His reputation has endured vicissitudes and challenges (especially since the 1960s, when Gustav Mahler began to emerge as a repertory composer), and Sibelius has never been without detractors, but the long controversy is in itself testimony to Sibelius's potency.[45]

I went on to observe that "there was hardly a composer of symphonies at this time [the 'interwar' period], especially in Britain and America, who was not profoundly—and often openly, even reverently—beholden to his example."[46] That would seem to accord Sibelius a high enough status to satisfy a modernist assessor, who (as I would enumerate them) judges according to three criteria: innovation, influence, and "difficulty" or "complexity." At least according to the second yardstick, Sibelius made out very well indeed. But Dr. Oramo held out for all three:

---

44. In the endlessly anthologized first review he submitted as the chief music critic for the *New York Herald Tribune*, 11 October 1940.
45. Taruskin, *Music in the Nineteenth Century*, 821.
46. Ibid., 823.

What Taruskin doesn't say, and perhaps doesn't know, is that Sibelius's music has become increasingly influential on contemporary music, especially in the 1980s and 1990s. This is one reason why you cannot leave Sibelius out. And if Taruskin had studied Sibelius's music and the recent literature on it with only half of the intensity with which he has studied Bartók's, he would have noticed that there is no shortage of technical innovation in Sibelius, either. Influence, technical innovation, structure, and craft all belong to the realm of "poietics." When it comes to "the social mediation and reception of music, and the buffeting the arts and their practitioners have suffered in the turbulent political environment of the twentieth century," Sibelius is not a less interesting case in point than Schoenberg and Bartók. Taruskin seems to be aware of that, but he doesn't elaborate on it.

In stylistic idiosyncrasy Sibelius was never lacking, and that is what made him, as no one disputes, a frequent object of emulation. That he is to be regarded for this reason as a technical innovator on a par with Bartók seems a dubious contention. The measure of technical innovation has properly to do precisely with technique, not style, and is best gauged, in terms of modernist historiography, by the extent to which a composer's technique has been abstracted and explicated by music historians and theorists; and here Bartók has been second only to Schoenberg among twentieth-century composers. As I have frequently contended, this criterion is patently, and often preposterously, overvalued in the conventional narrative of twentieth-century music, so I would not myself choose to apply it in assessing the relative stature of creative artists. But it is still widely accepted and employed as a standard, and its assertion identifies the assessor as a modernist: thus I would therefore identify Dr. Oramo, all the more so in view of his dissatisfaction with my acknowledgment of Sibelius's powerful impact on the Walton/Harris generation. In preference to them, he calls attention (citing a survey by Julian Anderson) to Sibelius's resurgent influence on what was, at the time of his writing, contemporary music, attesting to Sibelius's continued historical importance.

In addition to Maxwell Davies, whom I did mention, Anderson calls fitting attention to Sibelius's impact on American minimalists, French spectralists, and a wide variety of other figures, up to and including Morton Feldman.[47] Anderson brings the point home by asserting Sibelius's "bold and experimental attitude towards time, timbre, musical texture and form which transcends the late Romanticism of his origins and places him amongst the most innovative composers of the early twentieth century."[48] Predictably, his Exhibit A is Sibelius's rather trivial, though indubitably experimental, Prelude to *The Tempest* (1925), a sustained study

---

47. Julian Anderson, "Sibelius and Contemporary Music," in *The Cambridge Companion to Sibelius*, ed. Daniel M. Grimley (Cambridge: Cambridge University Press, 2004), 196–216, at 215.

48. Ibid., 197.

in onomatopoeia employing ceaselessly rising and falling whole-tone scales (hardly a novelty in the century's third decade).

Placing such a weight of critical emphasis on so slight a composition is the mark, I'd say, of a tendentious argument, though it is one I am fully prepared to forgive in view of the critical injustices Sibelius has suffered, particularly from the musicians of the "zero hour" avant-garde and their spokesmen, René Leibowitz and Theodor W. Adorno.[49] But it is high time, I'd say, once and for all to let go of the modernist insistence on measuring the stature of composers by investing with spurious aesthetic value the aesthetically neutral criteria that constitute the poietic fallacy. And perhaps, now that practically all the composers of whom Julian Anderson wrote are dead along with Sibelius, we can afford to dispense with the modernist snobbery reflected in Dr. Oramo's concern that Sibelius's debtors constitute a newer and more respectable cohort than the dated ones with which I credited him.

Yet even here I am sympathetic, as would any student of Russian music be who has had to deal with snobbery of another sort, that of "center" toward "periphery." Here Dr. Oramo and I are in the same boat, wincing jointly at condescending pronouncements like this one of Schoenberg's:

> Peace after the First World War granted political independence to nations which culturally were far from ready for it. Nevertheless even small nations of six to ten million people expected to be regarded as cultural units, nations whose national characteristics expressed themselves in many ways: in their applied arts, weaving, ceramics, painting, singing and playing and, finally, even composing music.[50]

Don't you love that "even"? I think I may wince even more sorely than Dr. Oramo at such affronts, because Russia, the country I "represent" in and through my work, is a country of 200 million people, not six or ten, and one that historically had been not only independent but an imperial power in its own right (just ask the composer of *Finlandia*)—and still it gets no respect from the invincibly smug Germanocentric quarter.

---

49. E.g., R. Leibowitz, *Sibelius, le plus mauvais compositeur du monde* (Liège: Éditions Dynamo, 1955); T. W. Adorno, "Glosse über Sibelius," in idem, *Impromptus* (Frankfurt am Main: Suhrkamp, 1968), 88–92 (originally a review of Bengt de Torne, *Sibelius: A Close-Up* [London: Faber & Faber, 1937], *Zeitschrift für Sozialforschung* 7 [1938]: 460–63). Adorno's peroration: "Wenn Sibelius gut ist, dann sind die Maßstäbe der musikalischen Qualität als des Beziehungsreichtums, der Artikulation, der Einheit in der Mannigfaltigkeit, der Vielfalt im Einen hinfällig, die von Bach bis Schönberg perennieren" [If Sibelius is good, then the criteria of musical quality that have endured from Bach to Schönberg—a wealth of relations, articulation, unity in diversity, diversity in unity—are done in once and for all] (trans. Susan H. Gillespie in Daniel M. Grimley, ed., *Jean Sibelius and His World* [Princeton, NJ: Princeton University Press, 2011], 335).

50. Schoenberg, "Folkloristic Symphonies" (1947), in idem, *Style and Idea*, ed. Leonard Stein (Berkeley and Los Angeles: University of California Press, 1975), 161; quoted by Ilkka Oramo in "Why You Cannot Leave Sibelius Out."

But Dr. Oramo's relationship to Finnish music is after all quite different from mine to Russian. For him it is Self; for me (despite what many have presumed on the basis of my name) it is Other.[51] And that removes a pitfall from my path. I am not tempted by my roots into advocacy or the lowering of my critical guard. For Sibelius's countrymen, this temptation is difficult to evade, precisely because it is difficult to acknowledge. We are all trained to honor the ideal of objectivity; and yet, as I put it in the *Oxford History*, ever since Grieg was awarded "a life annuity to guarantee his freedom to compose and thus enhance his nation's musical standing, . . . he has been as crucial to his country's musical self-esteem as Elgar once was for the English."[52] As I learned more recently, in a testy exchange with the English composer Hugh Wood, Elgar is as touchy a subject as he ever was.[53] There is a touch of that touchiness in the complaints I have always received at my coverage of British music, and I have received similar complaints on behalf of the Dutch, the Irish, and the Greeks.[54] All agree, moreover, that I vastly overrate and overrepresent American music in my last volume and attribute my indulgence to personal chauvinism rather than to America's actual emergence as a musical leader since the Second World War.

I realize, of course, that I cannot counter the latter allegation by direct denial, only indirectly, by way of a persuasive argument over the course of the entire lengthy book. But neither I nor any American, I should say, would accord any American classical musician the status that most Finnish musicians, along with most of their countrymen, have accorded Sibelius by virtue of a longstanding tradition, which Dr. Oramo willingly invoked when asked—not by an opponent in debate but by a friendly interviewer—to account for the enviably high level of musical education in Finland, lately reflected in the spectacularly disproportionate prominence of Finnish composers, instrumentalists, and especially conductors on the international musical scene of the early twenty-first century.

> The secret behind the music-love of Finnish people is very simple: Sibelius. Because Sibelius was not only a composer; he was also a national hero, because of certain

---

51. On my status as "other" to Russia and its music, see the Introduction, "Taking It Personally," to R. Taruskin, *On Russian Music* (Berkeley and Los Angeles: University of California Press, 2008), 1–25; and chap. 16 ("*Yevreyi* and *Zhidy*: A Memoir, a Survey, and a Plea"), 190–201.

52. Taruskin, *Music in the Nineteenth Century*, 821.

53. Hugh Wood, "Serenade in B," *Times Literary Supplement*, 21 March 2008, and letters to the editor in the issues of 4 April, 18 April, and 25 April.

54. Karl Kügle, "Past Perfect: Richard Taruskin and Music Historiography in the Early Twenty-First Century," *Tijdschrift van de Koninklijke Vereniging voor Nederlandse Muziekgeschiedenis* 58 (2008): 69–85; Harry White, "The Rules of Engagement: Richard Taruskin and the History of Western Music," *Journal of the Society for Musicology in Ireland* 2 (2007): 21–49. Especially aggrieved are the complaints of Michalis Andronikou and Friedemann Sallis in "Centring the Periphery: Local Identity in the Music of Theodore Antoniou and Other Twentieth-Century Greek Composers," *Intersections* 33 (2012): 11–34.

historical circumstances. And that is why the Finnish people have a respect for classical music, even people who don't themselves play or sing or otherwise are interested in classical music. They respect it. And then I would say that in the 1960s there were some enthusiastic and idealistic people who started to imagine a network of music schools in Finland.[55]

As I say, enviable. And that is obviously a part of the Sibelius narrative that a historian must record, as I did in the new material I added to the *Oxford History* for the paperback reprint, where I noted that since 8 December 1935 (his seventieth) Sibelius's birthday has been for Finns a national holiday. My somewhat ironical remarks in closing about national herohood, partially expressed through a quotation from Aaron Copland ("It takes a long time for a small country to get over a great man," etc.), were certainly not intended to belittle Sibelius's stature among composers, nor minimize the beneficent effect that, as Dr. Oramo pointed out, Sibelius worship has had on the musical life of his country.[56] I do envy what is enviable, as I did many years before when, as an American exchange student in Moscow in 1971, I saw at first hand the mutually sustaining relationship between the Russian concertgoing public and Dmitry Shostakovich.[57] What is not so enviable is the effect hero worship often has on critical thinking, about Shostakovich as well as Sibelius.[58] While I wish that American classical music were given more attention and respect, still more that there were a network of publicly supported music schools in my country that bore comparison to what the Finnish government has fostered, I am glad that there is no musical figure in America who has become quite as much of a sacred cow as Sibelius has long been in Finland. Indeed, whenever I have seen signs of bovine adulation in my own music world, I have, as Schoenberg used to say, sharpened my pen.[59]

So, without opposing or challenging Dr. Oramo's exhortations in favor of greater space for Sibelius, I think my treatment of him in the revised *Oxford*

---

55. Interview with Robert Aubry Davis of WETA (Washington, DC) at the Finnish embassy, posted 21 February 2013: www.youtube.com/watch?v=YdoInfiP_O4&t=443s.

56. Taruskin, *Music in the Nineteenth Century*, 824.

57. Recounted in R. Taruskin, "Double Trouble," *New Republic*, 23 December 2001, 26–34; rpt. under the title "When Serious Music Mattered" in Malcolm Brown, ed., *A Shostakovich Casebook* (Bloomington: Indiana University Press, 2005), 360–84, and in Taruskin, *On Russian Music*, 299–321.

58. See R. Taruskin, "Casting a Great Composer as a Fictional Hero," *New York Times*, 3 March 2000; rpt. in Taruskin, *On Russian Music*, 322–28.

59. Cf. Arnold Schoenberg to Hans Keller (who needed no encouragement), 10 January 1951; in Hans Keller, "Unpublished Schoenberg Letters," *Music Survey* 4 (1952): 465 (also facsimile facing p. 456). Cf. R. Taruskin, "Afterword: Nicht blutbefleckt?" *Journal of Musicology* 26 (2009): 274–84; rpt. with a postscript in idem, *Cursed Questions: On Music and Its Social Practices* (Oakland: University of California Press, 2020), 208–25 (with regard to uncritical adulation of Elliott Carter).

History adequate to my purposes, and respectfully resist calls to expand it further. It is another story when Dr. Oramo seeks to strengthen his case with altogether gratuitous disparagement of Bartók. That is something to be deplored. Referring to what I called "Bartók's finest hour," and specifically to the letter in which the composer twitted an official of the German radio for planning a broadcast of his "degenerate" First Piano Concerto, Dr. Oramo declines to acknowledge it as a protest, calling attention instead to another letter in which Bartók denies having "made, or sent, any statement to German authorities."[60] Bartók's resistance to the Nazis, he wishes us to believe, was just "a rumor," and not a proper subject for a musicologist to investigate—unless, that is, we are talking about the Sixth Quartet, on which Bartók happened to be working when he received news of the Molotov-Ribbentrop Pact and decided at that moment to jettison an already-drafted fast finale and let the opening lament pervade all four movements. Otherwise, Dr. Oramo insists, bringing up what I called Bartók's "uncompromising devotion to an exacting humanitarian code" was "utterly inappropriate" because it is "irrelevant... to the history of music."

I am mystified at the narrowmindedness of this point of view and shudder at the prospect of interpreting it. Had I provoked it by noting that Sibelius was "touted by the Nazis during World War II as a result of his country's alliance with Germany (motivated by a well-grounded fear of Soviet Russia, which had waged a war of aggression against Finland from 1939 to 1940)," and that for this reason he had fallen "into a trough of disdain for a couple of decades, written off as a reactionary during a time of avant-garde ascendency, and only regained full respectability in the 1970s"?[61] Was Dr. Oramo trying to suppress an implicit moral contrast with Bartók? In that case the effort was misguided, because I did not blame Sibelius for the Nazi touting or the German alliance, nor did I level moral censure at him of any kind. Dr. Oramo's tit-for-tat was in vain: there was no "tat."

. . .

But he is not the only debunker now seeking to deprive Bartók of his nimbus. A really lamentable foray has appeared in the *International Review of the Aesthetics and Sociology of Music,* a journal published in Zagreb as an organ of the Croatian Musicological Society, under the title "The Bartók Myth: Fascism, Modernism, and Resistance in Italian Musical Culture." Its author, Nicolò Palazzetti, is an Italian scholar affiliated with the École des hautes études en sciences sociales in Paris. Like Dr. Oramo, Sgr. Palazzetti disparages my "campaign" on behalf of Bartók because it is concerned not with "musical beauty" but rather, and irrelevantly, with "moral

---

60. Bartók, *Letters,* ed. Demény, 266 (letter no. 208, to the editor of *Az est,* Budapest).
61. Taruskin, *Music in the Nineteenth Century,* 823.

beauty."[62] To him, "Why You Cannot Leave Bartók Out" is merely the latest in "a long series of passionate and sometimes bombastic paeans dedicated to the good moral standing of Bartók, his political engagement, exemplary anti-fascism, acute sense of freedom, and heroic resistance" (292). He compares my treatment of Bartók with portrayals of the composer on educational television, in novels, and in comic books. These, he implies, are the venues to which ethical discussion of art ought to be confined—all of which would seem to make Sgr. Palazzetti's contribution to the debate the latest example of what (in a passage that he singles out for derision) I called "the sad history whereby over the course of the twentieth century the autonomy of art has degenerated into irrelevance, and the disinterestedness of artists has degenerated into moral indifference."

According to Sgr. Palazzetti, "Bartók's status as an anti-fascist hero and beacon of freedom" has become "a potent and spellbinding myth of our age," and, as such, "certainly beneficial for the universal canonisation of the composer in post-war Western democracies." Calling it a myth already implies that "it does not stand up to detailed historical scrutiny," which the author now proposes to supply (290). Both he and Dr. Oramo lean heavily on the verdict of Malcolm Gillies, a prominent Bartók scholar, who characterized Bartók's political views and moral stance as perhaps deliberately ambiguous. "Bartók was certainly no Nazi," Dr. Gillies generously allows, just as Sgr. Palazzetti, with equal magnanimity, assures us that he is "far from suggesting that Bartók was actively pro-fascist or that his basic humanism was deficient" (296). Nevertheless, Dr. Gillies continues,

> he was equally not the stalwart figure of resistance beloved of the biographies. Until 1937 he sought performing engagements in Nazi Germany, and even after the outbreak of the Second World War he undertook a concert tour of fascist Italy. On the other hand, he had spoken up for Toscanini when he was attacked by the Italian fascists in 1931, and called for "the protection of the integrity and autonomy of the arts." As a League of Nations committee member he espoused from the early 1930s a "brotherhood of man" philosophy, which reflected his pluralist attitude to compositional sources as well. To see him as an anti-Nazi crusader forced to carry the flicker-

---

62. Nicolò Palazzetti, "The Bartók Myth: Fascism, Modernism, and Resistance in Italian Musical Culture," *International Review of the Aesthetics and Sociology of Music* 47 (2016): 289–314, at 289–90; further page references to this article will be made in the main text. In a book chapter partially derived from the same article, Sgr. Palazzetti goes even further, asserting that "with few exceptions, the widespread agreement on the artistic value of Bartók's oeuvre seemed to be a mere consequence of the shared consensus on his moral value" ("Bartók against the Nazis," in *The Routledge Handbook to Music under German Occupation, 1938–1945*, ed. David Fanning and Erik Levi [London and New York: Routledge, 2020], 489–51, at 490). Most recently Sgr. Palazzetti has published a book based on the dissertation from which the original article was excerpted, *Béla Bartók in Italy: The Politics of Myth-Making* (Woodbridge, Suffolk: Boydell Press, 2021), in which the argument is better contextualized and somewhat moderated.

ing beacon of Hungarian humanity to the New World is, however, fanciful and overlooks the more prosaic and self-interested reasons for his departure.[63]

Does this characterization actually refute the one I presented in my essay or does it merely furnish a distraction? Neither my assessment of Bartók's attitudes and utterances, nor that of any other responsible scholar, casts him as an anti-Nazi crusader. All who have actually looked at his behavior recognize that it was always governed by the composer's inveterate reserve. To remind us, as Sgr. Palazzetti does (citing David E. Schneider), that Bartók's explicit anti-Nazi (and anti-Communist, and anti-revanchist) sentiments were expressed in letters—that is, "documents [that] were private, written to confidantes"—is another distraction.[64] The issue is not one that can be decided by quotation.

One can endlessly cherry-pick words. On the plus side of the ledger there is, in addition to what has already been mentioned, the "Declaration of Writers, Artists, and Scientists Addressed to Members of Parliament Protesting against the Racial Discrimination Law," published in the *Pesti napló* (Pest Diary) in the issue of 5 May 1938, over Bartók's signature along with those of Zoltán Kodály and the folklorist Béla Vikár;[65] and there is his entry in a friend's guest book: "three timely wishes in May 1938: to become free of the Germans' influence on philosophy, economics and culture."[66] On the negative side there is the residual language of racial essentialism that can now appear to mar some of Bartók's scholarly work,[67] not to mention the kind of casually anti-Semitic comments one can find in almost anyone's private correspondence in early twentieth-century Europe.[68] Nevertheless, when Bartók

---

63. Malcolm Gillies, "Bartók in America," in *The Cambridge Companion to Bartók*, ed. Amanda Bayley (Cambridge: Cambridge University Press, 2001), 190–201, at 193; this paragraph is quoted in part by Palazzetti ("Bartók Myth," 295), and in somewhat smaller part by Oramo as well.

64. David E. Schneider, "A Context for Béla Bartók on the Eve of World War II: The Violin Concerto (1938)," *repercussions* 5 (1996): 21–68, at 22; quoted in Palazzetti, "Bartók Myth," 295.

65. For some reason, Sgr. Palazzetti considers it "important to remember that on the same day as Bartók's declaration in *Pesti napló* his *Bluebeard's Castle* was given in Florence" ("Bartók Myth," 300n21).

66. The "Declaration" is shown in facsimile in Ferenc Bónis, *Béla Bartók: His Life in Pictures and Documents* (Budapest: Corvina Kiadó, 1981), 234; also in the more recent, expanded edition: F. Bonis, *Béla Bartók: Pictures of a Life* (Budapest: Balassi, 2016), 410. The peroration: "Let every contemporary think over the responsibility he will have to bear if, in spite of the protest of conscience, a law is enacted here, of which, in time to come, every Hungarian will have to think with shame!" The guest-book entry on "three timely wishes" is shown in *Béla Bartók: His Life in Pictures* at p. 270 and in *Pictures of a Life* at p. 412 (the recipient is Ákos Weress).

67. Most notoriously, the phrase *Csak tiszta forrásból!*, which can be translated in various ways: "Use only pure sources," "Draw only on clean springs," or some other variant. For a thorough consideration, see Klára Móricz, "'From Pure Sources Only': Bartók and the Modernist Quest for Purity," *International Journal of Musicology* 9 (2000): 243–266.

68. And here the most notorious item is his youthful letter to a childhood friend, Irmy Jurkovics (sent from Paris, 15 August 1905), when he was just discovering Hungarian peasant music: "A real

wrote from his American exile an article explicitly titled "Racial Purity in Music," it was with the express purpose of discrediting its value. Immediately recognized as effective antifascist propaganda, it was widely reprinted at the time.[69]

But never mind. We don't need Bartók's words, because we have his deeds. It is they that do him indelible honor, and do indeed set him apart from a majority of his contemporaries. Rather than a crusade, they amounted to a sacrifice of a kind, and on a scale, that should by rights silence the carelessly captious commentaries that have lately surfaced. Unlike Schoenberg or Hindemith, Bartók did not go into exile because he had to. He did not have to fear for his own safety or that of his spouse (although those who have sought to discount his deeds have occasionally spread the rumor that his second wife, Ditta Pásztory-Bartók, was of Jewish ancestry). And unlike Stravinsky, who was fortuitously located in America (lecturing at Harvard) when the war broke out in Europe, and who decided (as then seemed reasonable) to sit out the hostilities on neutral ground that would allow him peace and quiet, Bartók did not leave Europe as a result of a cost-benefit analysis that promised advantages. Without necessity, he suffered privation. He went willingly and knowingly from a position of preeminence to one of obscurity and material want. One can endlessly debate his words, and through them his private thoughts; but his deeds constitute a fact to which neither Dr. Oramo nor Sgr. Palazzetti has offered any rebuttal. One can concede to them all the verbal ambiguities and still condemn the easy way we who live in comfort and security weigh casual words against deeds of sacrifice.

It was the *Anschluss* whereby, in April 1938, Austria became a province of Nazi Germany that decided Bartók on his course of action. "The danger is imminent," he wrote to a friend, "that Hungary will surrender to this regime of thieves and murderers, . . . and how I can then go on living in such a country or—which means the same thing—working, I simply cannot conceive." If that happened, he continued, "I would feel it my duty to emigrate while it is still possible."[70] The death of his

---

Hungarian music can originate only if there is a real *Hungarian* gentry. This is why the Budapest public is so absolutely hopeless. The place has attracted a haphazardly heterogeneous, rootless group of Germans and Jews; they make up the majority of Budapest's population. It's a waste of time trying to educate them in a national spirit. Much better to educate the (Hungarian) provinces" (Bartók, *Letters*, ed. Demény, 50).

69. The peroration: "It is obvious that if there remains any hope for the survival of folk music in the near or distant future (a rather doubtful outcome, considering the rapid intrusion of higher civilization into the more remote parts of the world), an artificial erection of Chinese walls to separate peoples from each other bodes no good for its development. A complete separation from foreign influences means stagnation: well assimilated foreign impulses offer possibilities of enrichment" (Béla Bartók, "Race Purity in Music," *Modern Music* 29 [1942]: 153–55, at 155; rpt. in *Tempo*, no. 8 [September 1944]: 2–3; *Horizon*, December 1944, 403–6; and *Béla Bartók Essays*, ed. Benjamin Suchoff [London: Faber & Faber, 1976], 29–32).

70. Letter of 13 April 1938 to Annie Müller-Widmann, in Bartók, *Letters*, ed. Demény, 267 (translation slightly amended for the sake of idiomatic style); this is also the letter in which Bartók referred scathingly to the "questionnaire about grandfathers, etc." that he (and Kodály) had refused to submit to Universal Edition, their publisher in Vienna, in accordance with new Nazi regulations.

mother late the next year, after the war had begun, severed his last unbreakable bond with his homeland and made it possible for him to leave with a clear conscience. He did not do it heroically, but with silent and cautious resolve, and those who knew him kept it as an open secret.

The most pertinent document testifying to that resolve is a letter, well known in the Hungarian literature but first made available for foreign inspection (in facsimile and German translation) in 2002, in which Bartók confided to Sándor Veress, a fellow composer (who would follow Bartók into emigration—in his case to Switzerland—after the war) that he was wrestling with the question "whether one ought to emigrate (if it is possible)," and that it was for him a question not of advantage but of morality:

> There are various positions one might take. You could argue that anyone who stays here who might have left is thereby showing acquiescence with all that is happening. Nor could one deny it, for that would bring disaster. So remaining here is altogether senseless. Or, one could say that whatever muck your wagon lands in, you should stay home and try to help in any way you can. The question is merely whether there is any hope that things might improve in the foreseeable future. Hindemith has been waiting for this in Germany for five years, but it seems his fortitude is exhausted.
>
> As for me—and this is just my private attitude—I am hopeless. There are some things I still need to do here (for a year at least) because I need access to museum holdings. Nor do I see another country to which it would be worth emigrating if I want to accomplish anything.
>
> So right now I am completely at a loss, although my gut feeling is that anyone who can should leave. But I don't want to influence others in that direction. In February or March of next year I am going to the United States for five or six weeks. So I'll have a look around unless something comes up and makes the whole trip impossible.[71]

Bartók had his American look-around not in February–March but in April–May 1940. What mainly reassured him about prospects in America was learning quite by accident, after a lecture at Harvard, about the Milman Parry collection of untranscribed recorded folk songs collected in Yugoslavia, which suggested the promise of a suitable research project. (A pair of Hungarian-born music professors then at Columbia University, Paul Henry Lang and George Herzog, eventually arranged a sinecure for Bartók at their institution, where he worked on discs that were sent to him from Harvard, where Parry had deposited them.)[72] A month after

---

71. Bartók to Veress, 3 June 1939: Andreas Traub, "Bartóks Gedanken zur Emigration: Ein verschollen geglaubter Brief von Béla Bartók an Sándor Veress," *Dissonanz*, no. 74 (2 April 2002): 26 (facsimile), 27 (translation); my translation is from Traub's German. It was first published in the Hungarian edition of Bartók's letters: *Bartók Béla levelei*, ed. János Demény (Budapest: Zeneműkiadó, 1976), 626; my thanks to Klára Móricz for the reference.

72. On this episode see Tibor Tallián, *Béla Bartók: The Man and His Work* (Budapest: Corvina, 1981), 215.

returning to Budapest, he gave an interview to the weekly magazine *Film, színház, irodalom* (Film, Theater, Literature), in which he reported his plan, "together with my wife, [to] make a second tour . . . for a longer period."[73]

This became the official story, reported in other interviews and news stories at the time. But those who knew him knew that this second concert tour would be more than that. As László Vikárius, the director of the *Bartók Archívum* in Budapest, explains, Bartók

> took with him his complete Romanian, Slovak, Arabic and Turkish [folk song] collections, after he had already had most of his compositional manuscripts sent to America; and when he gave what is always mentioned here as his "farewell concert" at the Music Academy [8 October 1940], nobody had any doubts as to what his alleged "concert tour" meant. His decision was regretted but still considered an act of protest.[74]

Bartók was not altogether without professional prospects at the time of his emigration. He had just signed a contract with Boosey & Hawkes, which had issued *Mikrokosmos* and which was then on the way to its present status as the preeminent publisher of contemporary "serious music." He had several new works in his portfolio: the Sixth Quartet, the Sonata for Two Pianos and Percussion, the Divertimento for string orchestra, and *Contrasts* for violin, clarinet, and piano. But his European reputation as a piano virtuoso did not guarantee sufficient engagements in America, and he fell into greater obscurity than he had anticipated. Neither, needless to say, did he expect so soon to fall ill with an incurable disease. His sacrifices proved to be far greater than he had bargained for.

Still, I find it baffling that a principled act of sacrifice should be devalued because it was not done ostentatiously, with a cathartic flourish, and because it was compounded by bad luck. Malcolm Gillies notwithstanding, acting with moral rectitude and at a high personal cost is to my mind virtually the definition of "stalwart" behavior. Next to this existential act of renunciation, it seems petty to go on quibbling over the nature of Bartók's objections to the performance of his music in Germany or Italy. (Halsey Stevens, and, following him, many others, have seen them as moral; Gillies, and, following him, Palazzetti, see them as venal; still others, including Vikárius, have suggested that Bartók used venal arguments to cloak political ones.)[75] And the suggestion that Bartók has been chosen quite arbitrarily or even deviously (over, say, Stravinsky or Hindemith) as a mythical postwar hero

---

73. Reference courtesy László Vikárius, private email communication, 21 April 2017.
74. Private email communication, 7 April 2017.
75. See Halsey Stevens, *The Life and Music of Béla Bartók*, ed. Malcolm Gillies (Oxford: Oxford University Press, 1993), 81–82; Palazzetti, "Bartók Myth," 294; Vikárius, email cited above.

by nervous Italian and German modernists (who might have chosen Schoenberg) is an odious echo of old calumnies.[76]

In fairness, however, I should give proper mention to one of Sgr. Palazzetti's chief points, which seems to me both ingenious and plausible. He adduces the striking fact that Bartók's music (even *The Miraculous Mandarin!*) continued to be widely performed in Mussolini's Italy long after it had disappeared from Hitler's stages and concert halls, even after the outbreak of the war, but refrains from attributing its popularity there to Bartók himself or his political attitudes. Rather, he writes, retaining Bartók in repertoire was partly a continuation of cultural and political ties between Hungary and Italy that predated the rise of Hitler and, for a time, impeded the Führer's expansionist policies; and partly it was the prospect, well supported by documentation, that "for part of the fascist cultural establishment and Italian intelligentsia, especially towards the end of Mussolini's regime, performing Bartók was a way to resist Nazi political domination" (298–99 et seq.). This status is easily melded with Bartók's postwar reputation as a resister, and, read back on the wartime performances, enabled those who played or listened to Bartók during the war to cast themselves in flattering retrospect as fellow resisters.

If that is what Sgr. Palazzetti means when he refers to "the Bartók myth," I can agree and even applaud. That is correct usage: a myth is not—or at least not necessarily—a falsehood, but rather an uncritically accepted explanatory hypothesis cast in the form of a narrative—in this case a narrative of reception, a myth not about Bartók but about us. To expose the myth is to answer the question, "Why did Bartók become such a powerful symbol of the Italian resistance movement?" (293). And that is a question very much worth asking and answering. So why in that case raise doubts about Bartók's character? Why the effort to ferret out and underscore, or (as it seems to me) merely posit, the "self-interested reasons" that lurked behind the difficult decision to leave his homeland, where he enjoyed an exalted reputation and where he was in no way threatened?

I cannot presume to answer that question, but it does remind me of my own reaction to a book that was once widely read and cited in the English-speaking countries: *Béla Bartók's Last Years: The Naked Face of Genius* by Agatha Fassett, which was published in the United States with the subtitle and modified title reversed: *The Naked Face of Genius: Béla Bartók's American Years*.[77] The author, née Agatha Illés, was a Hungarian émigré pianist, the wife of a prominent American recording engineer and a close friend of Ditta Pásztory-Bartók, the composer's second wife, who had accompanied her husband into exile. Fassett's portrayal of

---

76. See Palazzetti, "Bartók Myth," 296; cf. Leibowitz, "Béla Bartók ou la possibilité de compromis dans la musique contemporaine" (see n. 37).

77. Agatha Fassett, *Béla Bartók's Last Years: The Naked Face of Genius/The Naked Face of Genius: Béla Bartók's American Years* (London: Victor Gollancz/Boston: Houghton Mifflin, 1958).

the expatriated Bartók is frankly and almost literally hagiographic, and like most saints, Fassett's Bartók was an uningratiating personality: exacting, censorious, "uncompromising" in all things great and petty, socially abrupt to the point of rudeness, humorless to the point of priggishness, and just short of abusive toward his wife. Quite unexpectedly and disconcertingly, I liked him less and less as I read, even as my sympathy for his plight was increasingly engaged as he suffered neglect, then privation, finally fatal illness. By the end of the book compassion and vindictiveness were at war within me.

I would have been very grateful for some excuse to find a bit of self-interest in Bartók's insufferably righteous posture. It looks as though I may not have been the only one. It was for me a fleeting feeling, easily cured by renewed exposure to the music, which made me forget my resentment at the composer's moral rigidity and rejoice again in the gift he made us with his art.

Ultimately, of course, it is the art that makes us care about the man who made it—or, as T. S. Eliot would have it, it is always and only the produce of "the mind which creates" that arouses interest in "the man who suffers." For Eliot that interest was never truly justified. He insisted that if the art is good it will suffice, and the man will cease to matter.[78] It is a proposition easier to assent to than to live up to, as many found when, for one conspicuous instance, Eliot's friend Ezra Pound was honored for his poetry after his postwar political disgrace.[79] Since then, as Morris Dickstein has written, Eliot's prescription has "seem[ed] remarkably quaint," and cannot be invoked in the real world without an appearance of evasion.[80] What seems evasive in the case of Pound seems merely gratuitous in the case of Bartók, who had nothing to hide. But in neither case should either man or work be left out.

---

78. "The more perfect the artist, the more completely separate in him will be the man who suffers and the mind which creates; the more perfectly will the mind digest and transmute the passions which are its material" (T. S. Eliot, "Tradition and the Individual Talent" [1919], in idem, *Selected Essays* [London: Faber & Faber 1972], 18).

79. For an account of that uproar, see Robert A. Corrigan, "Ezra Pound and the Bollingen Prize Controversy," *Midcontinent American Studies Journal* 8, no. 2 (Fall 1967): 43–57.

80. Morris Dickstein, *A Mirror in the Roadway: Literature in the Real World* (Princeton, NJ: Princeton University Press, 2005), 184.

5

Liszt's Problems, Bartók's Problems, My Problems

Let me offer apologies at the outset for what must seem the glaring bathos of my title, with its catastrophic descent from Liszt's concerns, through Bartók's, all the way down to mine, about which I hardly expect you to care. And yet the problems about which I have been thinking for many years are not just mine. They are problems that all of us who have devoted our lives to the study of art and culture must face, as I hope you will agree. They are perhaps worth thinking about at least for the length of a lecture.

The progression that I have taken as my frame, from the great Hungarian musicians of the past to me—or us—in the present, was prompted by my efforts to solve another problem: the problem of how to respond appropriately to the great honor done me by the Hungarian Academy of Sciences, which elected me a corresponding member in 2015. The honor entailed an obligation to give an inaugural lecture, which I delivered on 11 December 2017, and from which this essay is adapted. Casting about for the right theme and the right tone, I of course recalled that Bartók and Kodály had been members of the Academy. (Indeed, Kodály was once its president.) I knew the often-reproduced photographs that show Bartók, on 3 February 1936, reading his inaugural lecture in the very room where I would read mine almost eighty-two years later (Fig. 5.1). The room, I found to my amazement and delight, had not changed a bit in the meantime. The same pictures on the wall, the same busts in their sconces; the only alteration was the rotation of the furnishings by ninety degrees, so that I was facing what in the picture is the wall to Bartók's right.

Inaugural lecture, Hungarian Academy of Sciences, Budapest, 11 December 2017; published in *Studia Musicologica Academiae Scientiarum Hungaricae* 58 (2017): 301–19.

FIGURE 5.1. Bartók's inaugural lecture, 3 February 1936.

I of course looked up Bartók's lecture, which (fortunately for me) had been published in an English translation, as a possible guide to what might be an appropriate tone and scope. In the end it gave me much more than that. Bartók took the fiftieth anniversary of Liszt's death in 1936 as an occasion for reflecting on Liszt's significance. His title, "Liszt Problems," prompted mine. Rather than conventional encomia, Bartók offered critical reflections, some of which so resonated with my own preoccupations as to become my own questions, although my answers, as you will see, differ from his. My title, too, differs slightly but significantly. Bartók was not investigating Liszt's problems, but rather "Liszt problems," meaning his problems with Liszt or (more strongly) problems that Liszt created not only for Bartók but for all the Hungarian composers of Bartók's generation.

The biggest, to judge by the amount of space he devoted to it, was the obstacle Liszt had unwittingly placed in the path of modern Hungarian music by mistaking the music of the Romani musicians who performed in urban venues such as restaurants for the authentic folk music of Hungary. As a result, even as he acknowledged and took pride in Liszt's achievements as the genius who had put Hungary on the musical map of Europe, Bartók found it necessary to reject the specifically national side of Liszt's output. Bartók hastened to assure the Academy that Liszt's

Hungarian Rhapsodies were "perfect creations of their own kind." Indeed, he said, "the material that Liszt uses in them could not be treated with greater artistry and beauty." The problem was "that the material itself is not always of value," and as a result, "the general importance of the works is slight and their popularity great."[1]

You have noticed, of course, the use of the conjunction "and" where Bartók might have said "but" or "though." Their popularity with the nonprofessional audience is thus cast as a concomitant of the Hungarian Rhapsodies' slight importance. They are popular, Bartók implies, *because* they are of slight importance. Thus he points to an aesthetic contradiction that had grown since the nineteenth century, when it was first identified by the early Romantics, into a huge dilemma for mid-twentieth-century modernists (or, as I like to call them, after Leonard B. Meyer, my favorite music theorist, the "late, late Romantics").[2] That dilemma, the contradiction Bartók purported to identify between aesthetic value and popularity, and which he saw as a problem for Liszt (but which I see more as a problem for Bartók), gave me the idea of counterposing Liszt's problems with Bartók's problems on the way to my own. A related problem, one that Bartók, together with Kodály, had been wrestling with for thirty years, ever since they issued their first collection of Hungarian peasant songs, was the contradiction between what was truly national in Hungarian music and what was popular.[3]

The ultimate Liszt problem for Bartók was whether, in light of the spuriousness of the national element in Liszt's music (not to mention the fact that Liszt's mother tongue was German, his preferred language French, and that, having left Hungary as a child, he did not return until his musical personality was fully formed), one could nevertheless claim Liszt as a Hungarian musician rather than "a homeless cosmopolitan." For Bartók, the answer was a resounding yes, for Liszt's "art is the antithesis of the excessive density and laboriousness so characteristic of the works of the outstanding German composers of the nineteenth century; it is rather the clarity and transparence of French music that manifests itself in every measure of Liszt's works" (509), together with the pervasive "imprint of the bel canto style of the Italians," which is "plainly to be seen in every work" (502). In sum, therefore, when it comes to characterizing "the style of Liszt's works[, o]ne can say anything of it rather than that it is German." For Bartók, in 1936, as horror of the Germans was mounting toward the point that would eventually cause him to leave Hungary, un-Germanness sufficed to make a great Hungarian out of Liszt.

---

1. B. Bartók, "Liszt Problems," in *Béla Bartók Essays*, ed. Benjamin Suchoff (New York: St. Martin's Press, 1976), 504; further page references to this source will be made in the main text.

2. Cf. Leonard B. Meyer, "A Pride of Prejudices; or, Delight in Diversity," *Music Theory Spectrum* 13 (1991): 241–251, at 241.

3. See *The Selected Writings of Zoltán Kodály*, ed. Ferenc Bonis, trans. Lili Halapy and Fred Macnicol (London: Boosey & Hawkes, 1974), 10.

Bartók's remarks on the Hungarian Rhapsodies leapt out at me and provided the spark that kindled my lecture because I had already taken their equivocal status as the starting point for a talk I had given at a Liszt bicentennial conference at the musicological institute in Buda in 2011, half a dozen years before, titled "Liszt and Bad Taste."[4] Although the title suggested a critique of Liszt, the paper was actually a critique of the other term, bad taste, and its implications, chiefly as regards the relationship between artist and audience. The problem of the audience and its bad taste led Bartók to what in 1936 he characterized as the "distressing conclusion that music-lovers and average musicians . . . liked and accepted, almost exclusively, only [Liszt's] comparatively insignificant and outwardly brilliant works, completely rejecting the most valuable ones which pointed so amazingly ahead of their time." And this in turn became a problem of strategy: how to get listeners to get over their preference for the works "that merely tickle the ears" and begin to prefer "the more interesting but less flashy ones" (501).

In sum, Bartók's solution to the Lisztian dilemma—the dilemma of an indispensable but potentially harmful presence—was to dichotomize Liszt's output, split it into two parts: one to promote, the other as far as possible to suppress. Liszt made this project difficult, owing to what Bartók called the many "concessions he makes to the public, even in his finest works" (504). In part this was attributable to his career as a virtuoso, "fascinated" along with "so many of his contemporaries . . . by frills and decorations, show and glittering ornamentations, [rather] than by perfectly plain, objective [elsewhere in the lecture he calls it 'classical'] simplicity" (506–7). Twentieth-century listeners, Bartók urges, ought to surmount the taste of their "grandfathers" and ignore what is "extravagant, over-loaded and rhapsodic" in Liszt (507). "[T]he essence of [his] works" was to be found not there, but rather in the "new ideas, to which Liszt was the first to give expression, and in [his] prophetic boldnesses"—first and foremost in the "solution of formal problems," such as "the first perfect realization of cyclic sonata form" in the First Piano Concerto (503).

. . .

These were not new arguments in 1936. Connoisseurs of nineteenth-century musical thought will recognize in Bartók's proposals a revival of the campaign mounted on Liszt's behalf by Franz Brendel, the editor of the *Neue Zeitschrift für Musik*, in the writings with which he proclaimed the advent of the *Neudeutsche Schule*, the "New German School," with Liszt as its *spiritus rector*. Beginning with Liszt, and only with Liszt, Brendel asserted, "content creates its own form" in instrumental

---

4. Reprinted as chapter 2 in the present collection. It was published twice in Hungary: in the original English in *Studia Musicologica* 54 (2013): 1–17; and in Hungarian translation (by Balázs Mikusi) as "Liszt és a rossz ízlés," *Magyar zene* 50 (2012): 419–43.

music as it had been doing in opera thanks to Wagner.[5] A little earlier, writing in the same journal, Liszt himself had proposed free forms based on literary plots as one of the "steps forward which the art [of music] has still to take" toward "the poetic solution of instrumental music."[6] How ironic to find Bartók reviving these "New German" claims in the same lecture in which he held Liszt up as the antidote to everything in music that was German.

But that is not the only anomaly. Consider the incongruity between the criteria of value that Bartók applies to the two sides of Liszt's creative output. The characteristics that account for Liszt's appeal to audiences—ear-tickling brilliance, glittering ornamentations, and the like—are matters of immediate sensuous apprehension. That makes them, in the literal and etymological sense of the word, aesthetic characteristics. They are valued (or not) on account of the direct impression they make upon the listener's perceptions (that is to say, in Greek, on account of their *aisthesis,* whence "aesthetics" courtesy of Alexander Baumgarten's treatise of 1735, in which both the word and the philosophical category were coined). The characteristics Bartók asserts on behalf of Liszt's better music—that it was ahead of its time, that it was prophetically bold, that it solved longstanding formal problems—these are not aesthetic traits at all, but rather historical facts and comparative assessments. And so is the point, to which Bartók gives special emphasis, that "Liszt's works had a more fertilizing influence on the following generations than" those of any other composer (even Wagner), and that he "touched upon so many new possibilities in his works ... that he provided an incomparably greater stimulus than" anyone else (505). These traits and virtues are intelligible only with reference to an historical narrative, and they only appear valuable (or not) with respect to a particular theory of history.

That theory, of course, is the neo-Hegelian historicism first applied to the history of music by the same Franz Brendel. It strongly valorized technical innovation and widespread influence on the work of contemporaries and especially on posterity. Both of these are certainly legitimate indicators of historical importance. But to tout them as marks of creative greatness, and high aesthetic value as well, requires the assumption of what I have sometimes called the poietic fallacy: that is, a view that takes only the maker's input (*poiesis* in Greek), not the apprehender's takeaway (*esthesis*), into account in making judgments of value.[7] It is a fallacy because it confuses aesthetic and historical issues, but it has been the dominant historiographical

---

5. Franz Brendel, "Die Aesthetik der Tonkunst," *Neue Zeitschrift für Musik* 46 (1857): 186.

6. Franz Liszt, "Berlioz and his 'Harold' Symphony," *Neue Zeitschrift für Musik* 43 (1855), in Oliver Strunk, ed., *Source Readings in Music History* (New York: W. W. Norton, 1950), 859, 863.

7. See R. Taruskin, "The Poietic Fallacy," *Musical Times* 145 (Spring 2004): 7–34; rpt. in Taruskin, *The Danger of Music and Other Anti-Utopian Essays* (Berkeley and Los Angeles: University of California Press, 2008), 301–29.

standpoint since the late nineteenth century, and in all likelihood Bartók never considered alternatives to it.

Bartók's account of Liszt illustrates the poietic fallacy most clearly when he singles out, for their newness and significance, "the bold harmonic turns, the innumerable modulatory digressions, such as, for instance, the juxtaposition, without any transition at all, of the two keys most distant from each other" (503). This is another passage that leapt out at me as I read, because "the two most distant keys" are those at maximum distance (six degrees of separation) on the circle of fifths, their tonics differing by the interval of the tritone; and Bartók probably knew better than anyone else that this was the harmonic relation on which Stravinsky had staked his chief claim to originality, with *Petrushka*, his second ballet, in 1911. I thought it had been my achievement, in an article I published in 1985, to demonstrate Stravinsky's indebtedness to Liszt;[8] but here was Bartók in 1936, almost half a century earlier, already showing his awareness of it, though without naming names.

This harmonic effect—in early analyses of *Petrushka* called "bitonality"—was famous in Stravinsky for its expressive use. It furnishes the accompaniment to the title character's expressions of rage in the ballet's second tableau. Bartók, however, describes it not in terms of its effect, but only as a technique, adding that to elucidate it and the "many other points" that would serve to valorize the essence of Liszt's music in the eyes of those who have "never see[n] the substance, only the exterior ... would require the use of too many technical terms" (501, 503). The substance, he implies, is only accessible to the informed perception of trained musicians—indeed, only accessible to the perception of what neo-Hegelians would call progressive musicians. (And if we still use that adjective, *progressive,* to describe music, we are still neo-Hegelians.)

But is this not a pessimistic view, and one, moreover, that perhaps unawares undermines the ostensible thrust of Bartók's lecture? How can one make a bid for public recognition of the true, substantial Liszt behind the flashy, ear-tickling exterior, if the substance is irremediably arcane to the uninitiated? If the Lisztian essence was to be sought only in advanced technical innovations, it should be little cause for wonder if, as Bartók admits, despite some progress in popularizing Liszt's more significant work, "we are still not where we could and should be[, a]nd the question keeps coming up—why are the favourite works still mainly the least important ones, ... and why do people still shrink from the more interesting but less flashy ones?" (501). Let this be the first hint—speaking from the vantage point of the early twenty-first century, when popular appreciation of classical music has not only stopped making progress but has actually regressed to a fringe status that

---

8. See R. Taruskin, "Chernomor to Kashchei: Harmonic Sorcery; or, Stravinsky's 'Angle,'" *Journal of the American Musicological Society* 38 (1985): 72–142.

Bartók could never have imagined in 1936—of the problems to which my title alludes at its end.

The final paragraph of Bartók's inaugural lecture suddenly departs from the measured, scholarly tone befitting an academic address and becomes a harangue. After clinching the case for Liszt's acceptance as a true Hungarian and a great one, Bartók turns around and adds a big bewildering "but":

> But—there are important and publicly respected gentlemen in our musical life who are stubbornly opposed to everything new that has happened in Hungarian music since Liszt; who prevent, as far as they can, the following of Liszt's traditions; who, whether as composers or as writers, spend their whole lives crying down Liszt's artistic principles; who, in spite of all this, pharisaically call themselves supporters of Liszt, and pay homage to the memory of an artist whose whole life and work was in absolute opposition to their own. It is these who have the least right to take Liszt's name in vain, to claim him as a Hungarian and to boast of him as a compatriot. (510)

I knew this paragraph before I knew the rest. Pretty much every Anglophone writer on Bartók cites and paraphrases it. It is quoted in full in the recent Bartók biography by David Cooper, who comments that in lashing out this way at his more conservative compatriots Bartók was "implicitly plac[ing] himself as an heir of Liszt's legacy."[9] David Schneider, in his dissertation, of which I was the proud supervisor, and then in his book *Bartók, Hungary, and the Renewal of Tradition*, went further. In his view, Bartók was "using Liszt as his surrogate" to "lodge a thinly veiled complaint at his exclusion from Hungarian concert life."[10] Lynn Hooker agrees and goes further yet. She sees the lecture as a counterpart to Bartók's refusal, the year before, of an award from the Kisfaludy Society for his early Orchestral Suite no. 1 (1905), a work that no longer represented what he saw as his true, as-yet-unrecognized achievement.[11] The resentment that Bartók was feeling at that neglect, she suggests, was what motivated the strategy of "selective embrace of Liszt."[12] "Maintaining this strict separation," she writes, "between the 'bad' Liszt and the 'good' Liszt—or, to be fairer to Bartók, between Liszt as audience-indulging virtuoso with dubious taste in source material, and Liszt as visionary and important modernist precedent—allowed Bartók to imply that his own work represented the fulfillment of Liszt's incomplete promise, a promise that Liszt could not carry out due to the limitations of his time."[13]

---

9. David Cooper, *Béla Bartók* (New Haven, CT: Yale University Press, 2015), 276.

10. David E. Schneider, *Bartók, Hungary, and the Renewal of Tradition* (Berkeley and Los Angeles: University of California Press, 2006), 228.

11. Lynn M. Hooker, *Redefining Hungarian Music from Liszt to Bartók* (New York: Oxford University Press, 2013), 252n15.

12. Ibid., 255.

13. Ibid., 254.

. . .

But, of course, Bartók's strategy implied the possibility of a similarly strict separation with regard to his own works; and thus he left a time bomb ticking at the end of his inaugural lecture. If it served to promote his more recent, more radical, and (therefore) more important work in preference to an "ear-tickling" piece like the First Suite, the opportunistic division could be seen as benign. But such things are rarely benign, and no composer's work was ever more cruelly parsed into its "good" and "bad" components than we now know Bartók's to have been, at a time he never foresaw, after his heartbreakingly premature death in exile, when the defeat of the fascist occupier of Hungary, for which Bartók yearned, was succeeded by a Soviet occupation he did not live to witness.

This hostile division is the subject of a book by another one of my *Doktorkinder*, Danielle Fosler-Lussier. Her title, *Music Divided: Bartók's Legacy in Cold War Culture*, already identifies it as a double parsing—doubly opportunistic, doubly cruel. The division itself was not dissimilar to the one that Bartók imposed on Liszt: the popular folkloric pieces on the one hand, and the advanced, modernistic ones on the other. The double, or complementary parsing was the result of the ideological polarization that took hold of the Euro-American world as postwar shaded into Cold War, and erstwhile allies became enemies.

The two sides of the Cold War divided Bartók just the way they divided Berlin, into eastern and western zones. In the Soviet bloc, where Hungary had landed in 1949, Hungary's greatest composer was lumped with Schoenberg and Stravinsky as one who, in the words of *Sovetskaya muzïka*, the organ of the Union of Soviet Composers, "paid tribute to the glamorous excesses of modernism, creating a series of works that are remote from and alien to the people."[14] Hungarian musicians faced a problem similar to the one Bartók had faced in his evaluation of Liszt: the problem of remaining faithful to a precious emblem of Hungarian achievement in music (as well as a symbol of pertinacious resistance to fascism) and at the same time remaining faithful to an ideology that called his musical commitments into question; or, as Fosler-Lussier puts it, of "simultaneously reclaiming Bartók as a great national composer and denouncing his music as decadent."[15]

The rhetorical solution to this problem can be best observed in a pair of articles by Ferenc Szabo, at the time of writing the head of composition at the Liszt Academy and among composers perhaps "the most active in bringing the ideals of Soviet music to bear in Hungary," in the opinion of one who was in a position to know, namely József Revai, like Szabo a so-called Muscovite, a repatriated com-

---

14. Editorial introduction to Ferenc Szabo, "V zashchitu Bartoka," *Sovetskaya muzïka*, no. 11 (November 1950): 93.

15. Danielle Fosler-Lussier, *Music Divided: Bartók's Legacy in Cold War Culture* (Berkeley and Los Angeles: University of California Press, 2007), 65.

munist who had sought refuge from Hungarian fascism in the Soviet Union, and who served as minister of culture under Mátyás Rákosi.[16] Szabo's articles were commissioned as answers to Western criticism of the musical policies of the new Hungary. The second of them, titled, simply, "Bartók Béla," was published in the magazine *Szovjet kultúra* in September 1950, and reprinted two months later in a Russian version in *Sovetskaya muzïka*, titled "In Defense of Bartók," where I encountered it, and from which I will quote.

This piece was cast as a specific denial of what was in fact an entirely correct report, broadcast by the Voice of America in August 1950, informing listeners that several works of Bartók, including *The Miraculous Mandarin,* the first two piano concertos, the violin sonatas, the third, fourth, and fifth quartets, and several piano works and songs, had been banned from public performance and broadcast, "since the bourgeois influence can be felt most strongly in them."[17] The impassioned conclusion of Szabo's denial recalls Bartók's impassioned defense of the "true" Liszt. "Having embarked on the path of Socialist Realism," Szabo wrote,

> we are striving to reflect in music the building of a new life, the building of socialism.... Enormous tasks confront us, upon us lies the responsibility of marking out the paths along which our art will develop. We will not deviate from this direction, for we are deeply convinced that, following this path, we will preserve the best progressive tendencies in Bartók and thus assure the growth and development of Hungarian music.... Our task today is to restore to his music the social significance of which fascist barbarity and decadent bourgeois art had robbed him.... Therefore we must cleanse the healthy folk roots that remain in Bartók's musical legacy of all alien influences and all that at the present moment can no longer express the spirit of our epoch.
>
> In Hungary we are most apt to play those of his compositions in which the fundamentals of folk music most clearly and decisively show through, together with the principal classical traditions of the past and the aspiration toward realism. We do not maintain, nor do we have the slightest grounds for maintaining Bartók's pessimism, understandable from the human standpoint but altogether unacceptable to us who firmly believe in the triumph of progress and in the further development of human culture.
>
> Bartók did not know this faith. But all the same he is ours, for he is with us and only with us. Bartók is ours. He belongs inseparably to the party of peace. He cannot have anything in common with the igniters of a new war, the dollar imperialists.
>
> We Hungarian musicians demand an end to the heinous comedy the heirs of Goebbels in America and England are perpetrating around the name of Bartók. Keep your dirty hands off our Bartók![18]

---

16. Ibid., 134, paraphrasing a statement by József Revai.
17. Letter from György Pollner of the Agitation and Propaganda Division to Jenő Szell, 9 August 1950; quoted in Fosler-Lussier, *Music Divided,* 54.
18. Szabo, "V zashchitu Bartoka," 95. The final sentence had not appeared in the Hungarian original.

I hope you will forgive me for quoting at such length from such a text, which amounts exactly to a rationalization of the policy whose existence it denies. The comedy to which Szabo refers at the end was the Cold War counterdivision of Bartók in the West, which formed a precise inversion of the one practiced in the East, so that the two Bartóks thus promoted fit one another like two pieces in a jigsaw puzzle. Anyone who studied music in American or western European institutions of higher learning half a century ago, as I did, will know that the list of works that could not be performed in Hungary was precisely the list of works studied and analyzed to death *chez nous,* which earned Bartók his place in the twentieth-century international modernist canon alongside Stravinsky and the Viennese atonalists despite his indulgence in folklore, which Schoenbergians explicitly despised and which Stravinsky nervously (and hypocritically) disavowed. "I never could share his lifelong gusto for his native folklore," Stravinsky said of Bartók in his first book of "conversations" with Robert Craft in 1959.[19] This was as transparent and preposterous a lie as any of Szabo's, but it enabled Stravinsky to condescend to Bartók at a time when such condescension was chic.

The quartets, first performed as a cycle in New York over two concerts in February and March 1949 by the Juilliard String Quartet, were the works that made Bartók respectable in the Cold War academy.[20] Milton Babbitt, the leading American twelve-tone composer of those days, who had written his first "total serial" work, *Three Compositions for Piano,* in 1947, reviewed the quartets in the *Musical Quarterly,* then the premier American musicological journal, and pronounced Bartók's music "completely of its time," because it "achieves a contemporaneity far transcending mere considerations of style or idiom." In this it "reveals a thorough awareness of the crucial problems confronting contemporary musical composition, and attempts to achieve a total and personally unique solution of these problems."[21] Coming from Babbitt, this had to imply a comparison with twelve-tone or serial technique, which composers of the postwar avant-garde regarded as the single viable method for future composition. Babbitt located Bartók's affinity for serial composition in "the identification of linear and vertical statements" in the "developmental nature of the motival structure."[22]

What this means is that any sequence of tones presented successively, as a melody, can also be presented simultaneously, as a chord. What Babbitt had recognized was an "emancipation of dissonance" comparable to Schoenberg's. He acknowledged that "serialization in Bartók is but one of many integrative methods in the

---

19. Igor Stravinsky and Robert Craft, *Conversations with Igor Stravinsky* (Garden City, NY: Doubleday, 1959), 82.

20. Quartets 2, 3, and 5 were in the first concert, on 28 February, and the second, on 28 March, contained 1, 4, and 6.

21. Milton Babbitt, "The String Quartets of Bartók," *Musical Quarterly* 35 (1949): 377.

22. Ibid., 382.

small, and its specific character is determined by the context in which it occurs," adding that "never does it create the context."[23] So Bartók cannot be classified with the serialists, although Babbitt does admit him, against Bartók's own claims, to the company of atonalists insofar as he showed himself "aware of the hazards inherent in the use of a language overladen with connotations" arising from "generalized functional tonal relationships, existing prior to a specific composition."[24] And for this reason Babbitt went out of his way to characterize Bartók's music as "nonprovincial," implying a refusal to acknowledge the national character that allowed musicians on the other side of the Iron Curtain to admit and even promote a portion of Bartók's output.[25]

Yet even on the western side, the national coloration was for most listeners the salient feature. Olin Downes, the *New York Times*'s chief critic, who was hearing the quartets (as performed by the Juilliard Quartet) for the first time, confessed that they were "too unfamiliar ... for the writer to have much perspective or even any very settled ideas about any of them," save that "they 'sound' marvelously, and show incorrigibly original and racial[!] approaches to quartet problems."[26] But you will find no mention in Babbitt's analysis of anything racial, whether Bulgarian rhythms or *parlando-rubato*, or even "Bartók pizzicati." Of the eleven musical examples in Babbitt's essay, ten are drawn from the Fourth Quartet, the one that most convincingly illustrates the verticalization of linear statements, and the remaining example comes from the Fifth Quartet, another item in the Communist regime's *index librorum prohibitorum*.

The nadir of Cold War iniquity toward Bartók and his legacy hooks up in a painfully ironic way with Bartók's academic inaugural lecture of 1936. It is now widely accepted among scholars and commentators on Bartók's career that the period during which he gave that lecture was the high point of tension between him and the Hungarian musical public, which motivated his exaggerated partition of Liszt's legacy. Also widely observed, and variously explained, is the notable relaxation of that tension in the final decade of Bartók's career, which coincided paradoxically with his despairing removal from Hungary and his unhappy exile in America. The last of Bartók's "difficult" works, and the latest one to be listed on the index of prohibited compositions, was the Sonata for Two Pianos and Percussion, composed in 1937, one year after the inaugural lecture. Beginning with *Contrasts* in 1938, Bartók started softening his style and readmitting to it some of the more popular Hungarian idioms, such as *verbunkos*, which he had formerly excluded on

23. Ibid., 382–83.
24. Ibid., 377.
25. Ibid.
26. Olin Downes, "Juilliard Quartet in 3 Bartók Works," *New York Times*, 29 March 1949, 23. See also Downes, "Juilliard Quartet in Music of Bartók," *New York Times*, 1 March 1949, 30.

account of what he thought their dubious legitimacy as resources for modern Hungarian music. As a result, the works he wrote during the last six years of his life—the Second Violin Concerto, the Divertimento, the Sixth Quartet, the Third Piano Concerto, and above all the Concerto for Orchestra—are the ones that have won him his place in the enduring concert repertoire and made him a twentieth-century classic. These were also the works of which it could be said that he made the most successful synthesis between the two sides of his creative output that were being cast after the war as irreconcilably opposed.

That synthesis was of course regarded in the Western academy as backsliding from the fully contemporary into the "racial." Concluding his essay on the quartets, Babbitt expressed this concern as tactfully as he could. "Perhaps more problematical than any aspect of Bartók's music itself," he wrote, "is the future of the attitude it embodies." Babbitt wonders whether Bartók's solution to the problem of what he calls "generalized functionality" can be sustained, or extended by others. "There is some evidence in Bartók's own work that such an exhaustion may have taken place," he wrote, for "the sixth quartet is in many respects a retreat from the position of the fourth and the fifth."[27] And that judgment was corroborated by that of the cultural politicians in Hungary, where Bartók had become in effect the composer of two quartets, the First and the Sixth.

But by the time Babbitt voiced his gentlemanly and musicianly reservations, Bartók had been viciously attacked for his apparent relapse on crypto-political grounds in that infamous article by René Leibowitz, which appeared in Jean-Paul Sartre's journal *Les temps modernes*.[28] Leibowitz was astute enough to notice the synthesis I have described as successful; but for him it was an unacceptable and politically suspect regression from the position of "engagement" that he believed a serious composer was obliged to embody in the postfascist world. So he gave it another, less becoming name: not synthesis but *compromis*. Compromise. Just about the worst thing you could say of a person in the aftermath of the Second World War, and he said it in the journal where it would be widely discussed far beyond the professional world of music, translated into many languages, and widely accepted to the detriment of Bartók's reputation—but also furiously resisted. The first of Ferenc Szabo's manifestos, "Bartók nem alkuszik" (Bartók does not compromise), was an agonized direct reply to Leibowitz, even if Szabo was mainly concerned to defend the composer's personal political integrity rather than vindicate the music.[29]

. . .

27. Babbitt, "String Quartets of Bartók," 385.
28. René Leibowitz, "Béla Bartók, ou la possibilité de compromis dans la musique contemporaine," *Les temps modernes* 3, no. 25 (October 1947): 705–34.
29. See Fosler-Lussier, *Music Divided*, 178n60.

LISZT'S, BARTÓK'S, MY PROBLEMS 137

The real compromise was Szabo's. Danielle Fosler-Lussier, who has investigated his archive, notes that in private or unpublished official documents Szabo testified to his discomfort with the role he was obliged to play in public. Fosler-Lussier quotes the minutes of a meeting of the Communist Action Committee of the Hungarian Musicians' Association in November 1950, just when Szabo's equivocal defenses of Bartók were appearing in the Hungarian and Soviet press. "My own heart draws me strongly toward Bartók," he told his comrades. "I have drawn so much from him. I, who directly occupy myself with musical education, see that we must be very careful in the Bartók question."[30]

When I read this, I thought of a tiny article that appeared in the *New York Times* on Tuesday, 29 March 1949, two days after the Cultural and Scientific Congress for World Peace had concluded its business at New York's Waldorf-Astoria Hotel. That is the famous convocation to which Dmitry Shostakovich was sent as a delegate, and where he read a speech (or rather, sat silent while a translation of a speech was read in his name) that stridently accused the United States of imperialism and warmongering, and denounced the leading modernist composers of the day, and Stravinsky in particular, for their "moral barrenness" and "nihilism."[31] Two days later, the little *Times* article appeared. It was headed "Bartók's Modern Music Soothes Shostakovich," and it read, in toto, as follows:

> After the hurly-burly of the last few days, Dmitri Shostakovich took refugee [sic] at a concert in Times Hall last night. The music consisted of the three string quartets by the late Béla Bartók, and the modern music apparently took precedence over all other engagements and invitations for the Russian composer.
>
> He and a friend sat unobtrusively in the balcony throughout the performance, listening intently. When the music was over, they went backstage to congratulate the performers, members of the Juilliard String Quartet, and then slipped quietly out into the night.[32]

It was probably an ignorant editor who put the word *the* before "three string quartets by the late Béla Bartók" in the reporter's copy. If, as I suspect, the reporter was the same Olin Downes whose review (already quoted) appeared elsewhere in the same issue of the *Times*, he knew perfectly well that the three quartets performed were the First, the Fourth, and the Sixth. There is a report of Shostakovich's participation in the hurly-burly of the Waldorf Conference in *Sovetskaya muzïka*, signed by the composer. That is no guarantee that he wrote it, but still, the article may record some first-hand impressions. Two paragraphs pertain to the concert at which the *Times* reporter spotted Shostakovich in the balcony. (Milton Babbitt, as we know, was also there.)

---

30. Ibid., 178n59.
31. Laurel Fay, *Shostakovich: A Life* (New York: Oxford University Press, 2000), 173.
32. "Bartók's Modern Music Soothes Shostakovich," *New York Times*, 29 March 1949, 3.

> On the evening of 28 March [1949] we dropped in on a very good concert by the Juilliard String Quartet at Times Hall. This quartet, consisting of young musicians, has only existed for the past three years. They devoted both of their concerts to the quartets of Béla Bartók, who died in New York in 1945, as I was told, literally of malnutrition, in a state of dire need.
>
> On this evening they performed the First (1907), the Fourth (1928) and the Sixth (1939) quartets of Béla Bartók. I did not like the Fourth Quartet but very much liked the Sixth. This is an outstanding work by a first-class master. The young quartet played it superbly, and the evening left me feeling very pleased.[33]

As I say, it is impossible to know just what to attribute to Shostakovich in this report. That the author takes the trouble to compare the Fourth Quartet invidiously with the Sixth accords with official Soviet policy, and by so neatly complementing the precisely opposing judgment of Milton Babbitt, crisply illustrates the Cold War dichotomization that played such havoc with the reception of Bartók's music on both sides of the curtain. To my ear, however, the bare fact of Shostakovich's presence at the concert speaks louder than the judgment he submitted for public consumption in the USSR, assuming it was he who submitted it.

Musicians seek out music for their own reasons. In the official speech read at the conference on his behalf, Shostakovich roundly denounced Stravinsky in exactly the terms dictated by the official line. And yet, in his "Travel Notes," we read this:

> I wanted to obtain some records of Stravinsky's music. In not a single record shop on Broadway did the salespeople know the name of this composer; they asked me to look it up in the catalogue. But jazz they knew thoroughly, in every detail, down to the most intimate details of the personal lives of jazz composers and performers.[34]

Whoever wrote up this anecdote for publication evidently intended it as an indictment of American culture, along lines long familiar from Theodor W. Adorno and his many epigones. But what leaps out at me is the fact that Shostakovich, who had just delivered a ringing denunciation of Stravinsky, went out immediately afterwards to rustle up whatever Stravinsky records he could find. His composer's ear hungered for the very sounds he had just condemned—and perhaps even sincerely condemned—for political reasons, or reasons of state. Ferenc Szabo, whose ear and heart were drawn to Bartók even as he participated—again, I can easily believe, out of a sincere ethical commitment—in the suppression of a significant portion of his work, would have sympathized with Shostakovich's ambivalence. I, too, sympathize. I have expressed my own disapproval of performers and audiences who now listen with enthusiasm to works such as Prokofieff's *Zdravitsa*, his

---

33. D. Shostakovich, "Putevïye zametki" [Travel notes], *Sovetskaya muzïka*, no. 5 (1949): 21.
34. Ibid.

cantata in praise of Stalin, because they think it is beautiful. I, too, think it is beautiful—and worth listening to, but not in blissful oblivion. While, unlike Szabo, I deplore censorship, I also deplore the unthinking elevation of aesthetics over ethics, and to that extent perhaps I am like Szabo. We are all, in varying degrees and varying connections, ambivalent.

. . .

So I am wrestling with the same problems as Bartók when it came to Liszt, or Szabo when it came to Bartók, or Shostakovich (or perhaps pseudo-Shostakovich) when it came to Stravinsky—about whom, having spent so many years in close scholarly communion with him, I entertain especially ambivalent feelings. Bartók's problems were especially acute, and especially illustrative of the ambivalence that must attend these questions. The operation he performed on Liszt, for what seemed to him very pressing and necessary reasons, gravely injured him when he posthumously became, so to speak, the operand rather than the operator. Those who operated on him had equally pressing agendas. Thus I broach the last, and shortest, part of this talk, which, as promised in my title, will be about my problems.

My problem is not with agendas as such. I am critical of them all, Bartók's, Szabo's, Babbitt's, Leibowitz's, Adorno's, Shostakovich's, and my own. But I acknowledge their necessity. We all have them, insofar as we have objectives; for an agenda is, quite simply, a list of "things to do." We all believe—do we not?—that there is more to art than the pleasure that it gives, as we, to whom art gives so intense a pleasure that we have devoted our lives to it, have the greatest right—and the greatest obligation—to acknowledge. We all believe that art also plays a social role, that it can do good, or harm, and our view of its social role is not necessarily correlated with our immediate sensory, or visceral, or cognitive response to it.

There has always been a strong tradition in Hungary for such recognition, even on the part of musicians thought of as modernists. Certainly it was true of Bartók, and perhaps even truer of Kodály. Although Bartók figures in this essay as an upholder of the poietic fallacy, that was only one facet of his complex and ambivalent outlook. In my *Oxford History of Western Music* I dealt with Bartók and Kodály, along with Janáček and a few others, in a chapter to which I gave the title "Social Validation," and I took note of the fact that both Bartók and Kodály, in strong contrast to Schoenberg, Stravinsky, and other modernist icons, were vitally concerned with pedagogy (that is, the education of children), the strongest possible testimony to a social conscience in a composer.

Or do we still believe in the social role, and the consequent value, of art—that is, of so-called high art? I am no longer so sure, and that is my chief problem. I can broach it best with a true, and very prosaic story. I have often joked that I know that there is a God in heaven because whenever I am thinking hard about something, especially when I am drafting a text for publication or public delivery, God has a way of sending me clippings. Things happen or come to me out of the blue that help me formulate my thoughts. Sometimes they take strange forms indeed. What I am about to tell you happened to me on the morning of Wednesday, 29 November 2017, while this text was in progress, when I paid a routine visit to the urologist, something I do once or twice a year like many men of a certain age. The fact that a urologist's office is a veritable old men's club is something I normally take for granted and don't pay much attention to; but this time I happened to leave the office with two other men, one of whom remarked to the other that when he goes to the urologist he realizes how old he is. To which the other replied, "If I want to feel somewhat young I have to go to the symphony."

I think you know what he meant. He did not mean that at the symphony he would hobnob exhilaratingly with youth. He meant that at the symphony he would be among people even older than he is. Classical music is losing its audience. The audience is literally dying off. After a century or so of heavy promotion both by governments (in one part of the world) and by commercial interests (in another), it is reverting to its aristocratic niche, which means to a narrowly hedonistic assessment of its value to a very small coterie. The sense of urgency that led to polemics about its social value—Bartók's about Liszt's, Leibowitz's about Bartók's, mine about both of them—is vanishing from our daily discourse.

I am not proclaiming the end of the world when I say this. I don't even deplore the changes to which I am bearing witness, because to do so would be fruitless as well as egotistical. After the experience of barbarism in precisely those countries of Europe that boasted the longest and most distinguished high-art traditions, it is no longer possible to pretend that high art is high for reasons having to do with superior moral or ethical quality. What is, or was, high about high art, as any historian will agree, was its social status, the very thing it has been losing since the middle of the twentieth century.

To account for the loss in full, even were we to confine the question to the world of music, would require an as-yet-unwritten book, and it is a book I am actually thinking I might attempt—not for the purpose of assigning blame: the endless contributing factors, economic, social, cultural, political, demographic, include factors of which I actually feel one must approve, such as the greater seriousness with which my country, for one, now takes the rarely-lived-up-to egalitarian principles on which it was founded. While I do not think the trend is reversible, and do not see it only in terms of loss, I nevertheless have a strong wish—the wish of my academic profession, after all—to understand it. And so I look to the past history of the art, including the history of discourse about the art (the part to which people like me have contributed), for clues about its trajectory, up to the recent past and extending to the future.

Here is where Liszt's problems and Bartók's problems have light to shed on my problems. The tendency, or the attempt, to protect high art by removing it from the concerns of the real world—something that first occurred to artists and philosophers exactly when artists were abandoned by their patrons at the beginning of the period we now call Romantic—was all too successful. It found expression in Kant's notion (asserted in the *Critique of Judgment*) of disinterestedness as an aesthetic sine qua non (indeed, as the very definition of the aesthetic), and in Schopenhauer's classic assertion, in his *Parerga und paralipomena,* of the principle of aesthetic autonomy, which I have quoted more times than I can count because of the damage I think it has done, and so I'll quote it once more: "This intellectual life floats ethereally, like a fragrant cloud rising from fermentation, above the reality of the worldly activities which make up the lives of the peoples, governed by the will; alongside world history there goes, guiltless and unstained by blood, the history of philosophy, science, and the arts."

What Schopenhauer wrote was not true when he wrote it; it had never been true; nor is it true today. But artists (and, as we see, philosophers) needed to believe it in order to carry on after their social abandonment. It laid the intellectual foundation for an unprecedented flowering of the arts, and music especially, in the nineteenth century, but it reached a corrupted and deleterious epitome in the twentieth. It produced what I have already named as the poietic fallacy, the insistence that the maker's technical achievements create the value of the art work, and that the public should be taught to value art the same way professionals judge it. That was the principle that determined Bartók's splitting of Liszt into the bad—the works that appealed to the philistine public—and the good, the ones that influenced the work of later composers like himself. Later, Bartók's own works were split between those that were promoted by political powers who wanted to take control of cultural production and those that were held up as a bulwark by supporters of Schopenhauer's principle of aesthetic autonomy in its debased culminating phase.

It was a contest of mendacity. The politicians pretended to speak for the public. (Soviet newspapers even used to print phony letters from fictitious collective farmers judging the symphonies of Prokofieff or Myaskovsky from the point of view of "the people.")[35] The protectors saw in audience appeal a fatal compromise with totalitarian power. Is it any wonder that over the course of the twentieth century aesthetic autonomy should have shaded into irrelevance and disinterestedness should have shaded into moral indifference?

We in the twenty-first century are paying the price. High art no longer matters the way it did, and perhaps it no longer deserves to matter that much. My effort to

---

35. For a chance example in English, see Alexei A. Ikonnikov, *Myaskowsky: His Life and Work* (New York: Philosophical Library, 1946), 60, quoting what purports to be the enthusiastic reaction of "a peasant" to a broadcast of Myaskovsky's Symphony no. 18 in C Major (1937), his most obedient concession to the templates of Socialist Realism. (The quotation is reproduced in full in this book's chapter 18.)

understand what brought us to this pass, and it has not made me popular in my field, has stemmed from a sense of responsibility that I could not shake—that is, the consciousness that my own profession, that of critics, scholars, and commentators, has contributed, through commission and through omission, not crucially, perhaps, but nevertheless significantly, to the irreversible decline. It leaves me, in my belated, ineffectual way, feeling lonely the way Bartók was feeling when he addressed the Academy of Sciences in 1936. That feeling of sorrowful solidarity has motivated this offering, along with the hope that twenty-first-century musicians may continue to act in the spirit of Bartók's "compromise."

6

Kodály's Pitiful Lament—and Mine

I. GIFTS FROM GOD

Allow me to begin the way the classically educated Kodály so often did, with a phrase of Latin. I come as an *amicus curiae*, a "friend of the court"—that is, an outsider to the case at hand who has agreed to offer testimony and opinion that may prove useful. Anything a foreign visitor has to say at a conference devoted to placing "a national master in an international context" will count as relevant by default, I guess. That (I guess again) must be why I have been invited to visit once more with my Hungarian colleagues and friends, an invitation that I never refuse. But again I face the task I faced the first time I got up to speak in this room, the task of finding something to tell a distinguished audience about a subject that it knows far better than I. The first time it was Bartók; this time it is the man who is, for those who know them only superficially, forever the second in a pair of names like Haydn-and-Mozart or Debussy-and-Ravel. I think I am past that stage by now. I have gotten close enough to Bartók and Kodály to see the contrasts as well as the affinities. But still, what can I tell you about Kodály Zoltán that you do not already know?

As some may remember, my quandary the last time was solved by what I called a gift from God. I unexpectedly received a book for review that had unaccountably neglected Bartók, and explaining and rectifying the slight gave me an opportunity to tell you what Bartók meant to me.[1] Well, I am happy to say that I have received

---

Keynote address, international conference "A National Master in an International Context: Musicological Conference on the Fiftieth Anniversary of Zoltán Kodály's Death," Institute for Musicology of the Hungarian Academy of Sciences, Budapest, 8 December 2017.

1. See "Why You Cannot Leave Bartók Out," chapter 4 in this collection.

another gift from God, an infinitely better one. Between my agreeing to attend this conference and my doing so I have become, for the first time, a grandfather. And believe it or not, my son and daughter-in-law have actually named their little boy Theodore, which, as you may recall, is Greek for—(wait for it)—"a gift from God"! It's the sort of thing that can turn a blasé secularist into a believer.

So how does this latest gift from God help me find my words about Kodály? You know better than I: no musician of comparable stature has ever been more meaningfully and productively involved with children than he. Not that Kodály's activities as an educator of children have been my point of access to him. Like most adult musicians I know him for his adult music, and in the first place for the pieces that everyone knows. I learned the *Háry János* Suite from a record I was given as an adolescent. It was on the other side of—you will surely guess it—*Lieutenant Kijé*, with whom Háry János is as fatally paired as Kodály is with Bartók. But—and I tell you this with hand on heart—although I played it second, the *Háry János* side of the record was the one I kept coming back to. I couldn't get enough of that hilarious Napoleon movement, especially the saxophone solo. And when, years later, I bought a vocal score of the opera (in Moscow, of all places, during my student year there) and saw what the defeated Napoleon sings while that saxophone is playing, I had all my Russian friends singing *Ó, te vén sülülülülülülülü* along with me, and we all thought Kodály the oddest composer ever. But not only that: I studied cello up until my college years, and for me as for any cello student, "the Kodály" (that is, his Sonata for Solo Cello, op. 8) was exactly what Mount Everest was to a mountain climber. (I never set foot on either.)

I also took piano lessons until the age of fourteen, and had the sort of teacher, then somewhat rare in America, who assigned *Mikrokosmos* (I was up to book 4 by the time I quit), so I knew something about Bartók's special interest in musical pediatrics, so to speak, and its relationship to his interest in folklore. I encountered that side of Kodály when I was sixteen and played the cello for a year in New York's All-City High School Orchestra, which gave an annual concert in Carnegie Hall together with the All-City High School Chorus, which that year sang a group of very catchy little numbers by Kodály. So that was another reason to pair the two, even without knowing their biographies and their close personal and collaborative relationship, which lasted more than thirty years. Another thing I did not know when I encountered Bartók and Kodály as writers of music for children was how rare that activity had become among major composers of the twentieth century, let alone that it was regarded by so many as somehow incompatible with major status, or—to use a word I learned later—somehow "compromising."

It was when I embarked on advanced or preprofessional studies in music that I learned about that pitfall—or rather, it was then that I learned that it was regarded as a pitfall. It was in college, when I began studying composition seriously, and especially in graduate school, when I added serious training in musicology to my curriculum, that I was exposed to the doctrine that serious artists had to be "disinterested," and that their work, if it was to be accepted as serious, had to be free of any taint of the utilitarian. The doctrine was especially strong during the period of my education, because that was exactly the time when the Cold War was at its height, and thoughts about art were as politically polarized as thoughts about every other social or cultural issue. Old romantic principles of aesthetic autonomy were conflated, particularly in America, with laissez-faire economics and libertarian politics and, in the Europe of Adorno and Leibowitz, with critical resistance. Administrative involvement with art was suspect as the gateway to totalitarian intrusion, and audiences were the enemy of creative freedom.

You didn't have to write expressly utilitarian music to be tainted with this stigma. I don't have to remind you of Bartók's dual deprecation. Renée Leibowitz did not even have to cite his pediatric output in order to convict him of compromise from the "Western Marxist" perspective. His Concerto for Orchestra, cheered by American audiences, already sufficed to turn him into a sort of Chaikovsky—not even "a better sort of Chaikovsky," as Schoenberg liked to pretend he wanted to be.[2] I am thinking now of a roundtable discussion called "Čajkovskij, musicien type du XIXe siècle?" which appeared in 1970 in *Acta Musicologica,* the organ of the International Musicological Society. Because it appealed to paying audiences, that is, to consumers, Roger Wangermée, the Belgian sociologist of music, dismissed Chaikovsky's music as *la musique de consommation,* as distinguished from *musique de création.* That was his definition of kitsch.[3] Now Bartók—or at least a good half of Bartók (though not *the* good half)—could be assimilated to that category. And if Bartók, who wrote some music that was sufficiently formalist to be banned in the Soviet bloc, could nevertheless be guilty of kitsch, what then of Kodály, who did not write any bannable music?

II. TEETER-TOTTERS

One of the bannables-in-chief can speak to that point. When I gave my old keynote on Bartók I contrasted his attitudes with those of Stravinsky, who very consciously promoted himself as the musical spokesman for modernism at its most intransigent, beginning with that emblematic pronouncement from his ghostwritten autobiography that has become so famous that many of us here, I'm sure, could join me in a chorus as I remind you that "music is, by its very nature, essentially powerless

---

2. Letter to Hans Rosbaud, 12 May 1947; quoted in Sabine Feisst, *Schoenberg's New World: The American Years* (New York: Oxford University Press, 2011), 139.

3. Georg Knepler et al., "Čajkovskij, musicien type du XIXe siècle?" *Acta Musicologica* 43 (1970): 205–235, at 230.

to *express* anything at all."[4] Three decades later Stravinsky was still at it, in a ghost-written program note to his orchestral *Variations*, which ends with a preemptive insult to his audience, still addicted to "the pabulum of our . . . regular concert life": "And there," Stravinsky taunts, "lies the difficulty, mine with you no less than yours with me."[5] That tactical warning—that I did not write it for you; you may not like it and I don't expect you to; in fact I hope you won't—was commonplace in Cold War America. That eleventh-hour modernist strain, the ultimate, ostentatiously flaunted extremity of asocial individualism, prompted Leonard Meyer, the best academic diagnostician of contemporary aesthetics, to call it "the late, late Romantic ideology of our time."[6] Never let it be said that Stravinsky, the man who gave loudest voice to such bluster, was antiromantic.

But as we all know, bravado is the mask worn by insecurity; and the aging Stravinsky, anxiously adopting the serial method when he discovered that young composers had stopped taking him seriously, also let slip his insecurity by going far out of his way, in those late books of "conversations" and in countless interviews, to attack the many musicians whom he had come to regard as threatening. The Hungarian cohort always drew him out. In 1959, he condescended to Bartók in his first "conversation" book.[7] Six years later, he exploded in fury at Kodály ("a sort of Hungarian composer"), whom he caught on television in conversation with Pablo Casals: "And what were the two racy octogenarians talking about?" asked the Russian octogenarian. "Why, they are talking about the trouble with me, which is that I must always be doing the latest thing—*they* say, who have been doing exactly the same old thing for the last hundred and eighty years."[8] Tit for tat, I suppose, but what Stravinsky's kicking down showed most clearly, I think, was that Kodály's remarks had managed to injure Stravinsky's strangely fragile pride.

I say "kicking down," because in the twilight of their lives, Stravinsky's fame so obviously surpassed Kodály's in the West; and Stravinsky's reputation in America, where everyone had forgotten his old flirtations with Mussolini and Hitler, was unsullied by the "totalitarian" associations Kodály could not evade. Kodály, for his part, was a venerated figure at home, but an equivocal one abroad; and even at home he was no longer thought to be a representative composer. Anna Dalos, today's foremost Kodály scholar, in a book I was delighted to edit for publication

---

4. Igor Stravinsky, *An Autobiography* (New York: Simon & Schuster, 1936), 83.
5. Igor Stravinsky and Robert Craft, *Themes and Episodes* (New York: Alfred A. Knopf, 1966), 61.
6. Leonard B. Meyer, "A Pride of Prejudices; or, Delight in Diversity," *Music Theory Spectrum* 13 (1991): 241–51, at 241.
7. "I never could share his lifelong gusto for his native folklore. This devotion was certainly real and touching, but I couldn't help regretting it in the great musician" (Igor Stravinsky and Robert Craft, *Conversations with Igor Stravinsky* [Garden City, NY: Doubleday, 1959], 82).
8. Stravinsky and Craft, *Themes and Episodes*, 102 (originally published as "An Interview with Igor Stravinsky," *New York Review of Books*, 3 June 1965).

in my series "California Studies in Twentieth-Century Music," observed with tender regret that "Kodály had certainly—as his contemporaries believed—outlived his creative career when he died in Budapest on March 6, 1967."[9] The latest of his works in international repertory, the Concerto for Orchestra, dated from 1940. (The Symphony of 1961 was a palpably retrospective composition—in C major, as if to prove a point Schoenberg loved making to his students at the University of California[10]—and received few performances.) He was now firmly identified with what I am calling pediatric activity, which in the world of the 1960s sooner allied him with Kabalevsky than with Bartók. (Kodály and Kabalevsky were, respectively, the second and third honorary presidents of the UNESCO-sponsored International Society for Music Education.) It could even seem that Kodály had sacrificed his composing career to his social and educational commitments, and this by his own admission. In the foreword he was asked to contribute to (and thus authorize) Percy Young's biography, published when he was eighty-two, Kodály wrote:

> I was fifteen, when a German booklet strayed into my hands; author and title are both forgotten, but the idea is still living in me. It depicts the career of an average German composer who, having reached the three-fold figure of Beethoven's opus-numbers, had to realise that he worked in vain; he should rather have used his time to do some work useful to his fellow-citizens. "Less music!—there is too much useless music written."
>
> Since then I always pondered, when some musical idea occurred to me: is it worth while to be written down? This is why I published so few works.[11]

All of which had significantly lessened his prestige, even as Bartók's had soared in the West. But even so, he was under Stravinsky's skin. I think that was because Stravinsky lived the second half of his life in the shadow of the first half, when his new works were eagerly awaited and greeted with public acclaim. The academic prestige he was still able to garner in his late American years, though bolstered by a huge publicity machine and a full schedule of guest-conducting the *Firebird* Suite, did not offer him adequate compensation for the loss of his former audience; and if that were true of Stravinsky, for whom was it not true in late twentieth-century America?

I saw a relationship of another sort between composer and audience when I attended Dmitry Shostakovich's last major premiere, that of his last symphony, the Fifteenth, at the Great Hall of the Moscow Conservatory on 8 January 1972, during my year in Moscow as an exchange student. I have written more than once about

---

9. Anna Dalos, *Zoltán Kodály's World of Music* (Oakland: University of California Press, 2020), 15.

10. "He is fond of telling them that there is still much good music to be written in C major" (Roger Sessions, "Schoenberg in the United States," *Tempo* 9 [December 1944]; in Walter Frisch, ed., *Schoenberg and His World* [Princeton, NJ: Princeton University Press, 1999], 335).

11. "Foreword: A Letter to the Author from Zoltán Kodály," in Percy M. Young, *Zoltán Kodály: A Hungarian Musician* (London: Ernest Benn, 1964), vii.

my amazement at the outpouring of affection that greeted the composer's appearance at the end of the performance, despite the fact that practically no one I asked had really liked the symphony. Shostakovich was not only lionized but loved in a way that no composer of concert music was loved in America; and the kind of music Shostakovich wrote meant more to his audience than such music meant to audiences in my part of the world. In the Soviet Union high art seemed to function as a medium of social solidarity, and composers seemed to receive (and to crave) a sort of social validation that they actively forswore and disdained at home, as we have seen Stravinsky do with such bitter gusto.

The question that of course occurred to me, as an American sojourning in the Soviet bloc during the Cold War, was whether that kind of solidarity was compatible with the creative freedom that I had been taught to value. Could composers enjoy a mutually sustaining relationship with an audience at times and in places where it was not mandated or coerced? Were freedom and social relevance necessarily on a teeter-totter, so that when one went up the other had to go down?

Where I came from, the answer to that question was unequivocally and explicitly yes, as witness a comment by Paul Griffiths, then writing for the *New York Times*, about another symphony by Shostakovich: the Fifth, which began life as a bid for rehabilitation after his opera *The Lady Macbeth of the Mtsensk District* had been savagely attacked in *Pravda*, the official organ of the Soviet Communist Party, and then peremptorily banned, not to be heard again for a quarter of a century. Not only did the Fifth Symphony succeed in its original exculpatory purpose: it had remained, of all Shostakovich's symphonies, with the possible or occasional exception of the Seventh, the most famous and admired one. To all appearances, then, it had transcended the strictures that had called it forth. It had, in Paul Griffiths's words, "entered th[e] high repertory of the great."

For Griffiths—perhaps best known as an enthusiastic spokesman for Elliott Carter, then the American composer with the highest academic and critical prestige—that achievement was something to deplore. His essay appeared just after the leading American orchestras had announced their 2002–3 seasons, and he noted that four of them were programming the Shostakovich Fifth. "One is tempted," he wrote, "to congratulate the Chicago Symphony, which is not only declining to play Shostakovich's Symphony No. 5 in 2002–3 but also going the entire season without performing a note by this composer. The Cleveland Orchestra, alas, merits no such praise." He recognized that Shostakovich's symphony was an important and serious work, especially in view of its history. "It addresses," as he put it, "questions that remain vital and challenging: questions concerning the limits on artistic freedom that might be imposed by a tradition, a public or a government."[12] That reduction of

---

12. Paul Griffiths, "Play That Old Piece If You Must, but Not for Old Time's Sake," *New York Times*, 2 June 2002.

all social function to oppressive social pressure, and the equation of all such pressures irrespective of their source, was a direct echo of Carter, who was often to be heard railing at what he called "the tyranny of the audience."[13] Because of its popularity, Shostakovich's Fifth was for Griffiths an embodiment of that tyranny, whatever its significance may once have been, or what it had since become.

III. WITHOUT BENEFIT OF ZHDANOV

The relationship between social commitment or solidarity, on the one hand, and tyranny on the other was always blurry when speaking of Soviet society, where they coexisted and interacted. So the question has continued to nag at me: was there ever a time and a place when the kind of social cohesion between artist and public that I observed in the Soviet Union existed without any taint of coercion? By the time I wrote *The Oxford History of Western Music*, which I finished drafting almost exactly thirty years after coming home from Russia, I thought I knew the answer, and that is why I gave the chapter in which I discussed the music of Bartók and Kodály (as well as Janáček) the title "Social Validation." Using a vocabulary I had developed earlier in the book, in which the term *maximalism* denoted the employment of radical stylistic means toward accepted or traditional aesthetic ends, I wrote that Bartók was

> as committed a modernist and a maximalist as any . . ., but he felt a need unfelt by the others to justify his stylistic predilections to his social conscience. Grounding in folklore provided a social validation for his art, just as it did for German artists a hundred years before, who remade their art in the spirit of Herder's romanticism. Bartók and the rather less maximalistically inclined Kodály were the only European modernists who remained faithful to this strain of romanticism at a time when it was the complementary strain—the egoistical strain that justified its ways solely on grounds of fidelity to one's own unique subjective self—that captured the imagination of the Germans.[14]

This paragraph is rather blunt and categorical, and I devoted a lot of subsequent words to qualifying its points in various ways; but that Hungarian attitudes did differ from those of other nations, especially those of the German atonalists, could be substantiated from the pens of the composers. I found a particularly quotable passage in Bartók's essay "The Folk Songs of Hungary," which he had written in English for publication in New York. After showing how carefully he and Kodály educed their modernist style from the particularities of Hungarian peasant music, Bartók allowed that "many other (foreign) composers, who do not lean upon folk

---

13. See David Schiff, *The Music of Elliott Carter* (New York: Eulenburg Books, 1983), 114.
14. R. Taruskin, *Oxford History of Western Music*, vol. 4: *Music in the Early Twentieth Century* (New York: Oxford University Press, 2010), 179.

music, have met with similar results at about the same time—only in an intuitive or speculative way, which, evidently, is a procedure equally justifiable." The word *evidently* carries an ironic charge, and Bartók immediately made a claim for the superiority of the Hungarian way: "The difference is that we created through Nature."[15] If you will allow me to modify the Herderian romanticism of this formulation, and if you agree with me that folk music is a social rather than purely natural phenomenon, then the natural basis Bartók is claiming for his art is in fact a social basis—precisely the sort of social basis that Schoenberg or Stravinsky would (and did) reject.

This essay of Bartók's dates from 1928, long before Hungarian composers had to contend with Marxist or Soviet Communist orthodoxies (apart from the five turbulent months of the Hungarian Soviet Republic in 1919). So it would appear to supply the positive answer I had hoped to find to my question about social solidarity without benefit of coercion. By the time of Bartók's death, his stature as an international modern master, and Kodály's nearly equivalent stature, plus Kodály's many years' activity doing what Bartók refused to do—that is, training a school of younger composers who continued the project of synthesizing peasant folklore with advanced academic techniques of composition—gave assurance that when Kodály would have to contend with a Communist regime that Bartók did not live to see, their demonstrated social commitment would ensure that Hungary's musical ways would find favor and not have to suffer totalitarian interference.

As the adviser to Danielle Fosler-Lussier's Berkeley dissertation that was eventually published as *Music Divided*, identified by its subtitle as a study of "Bartók's Legacy in Cold War Culture," I was particularly interested, and particularly moved, by those parts of her book that described the Hungarian response to the so-called *Zhdanovshchina*, the postwar reassertion of Party controls on Soviet art and culture, which culminated in 1948 in the Central Committee's "Resolution on Music." Although it would be another year before one-party Communist rule would be imposed on Hungary, Hungarian musicians saw the *Zhdanovshchina* as writing on the wall, but were hopeful that, as long as Hungarian music remained faithful to the legacy of Bartók and Kodály, "it would not run afoul of Communist principles."[16] Committed Communists like Andras Mihály even hoped that the Soviets would recognize that "the vanguard of socialist music would arise not in the Soviet Union but in Hungary."[17]

Fosler-Lussier recorded Kodály's own fairly sanguine private response to the *Zhdanovshchina*, unpublished until 1989. It accords with this mood of guarded

---

15. *Béla Bartók Essays*, ed. Benjamin Suchoff (New York: St. Martin's Press, 1976), 338.
16. Danielle Fosler-Lussier, *Music Divided: Bartók's Legacy in Cold War Culture* (Berkeley and Los Angeles: University of California Press, 2007), 6.
17. Ibid., 7.

optimism. "Zhdanov's warnings are nothing new to us," he wrote, noting that Hungarians had been voicing similar ideas for thirty years. "I do not mean that we are ahead of them. It is complicated: in some things we are ahead of them, in others they are ahead of us. . . . In any case there are many common problems, and we can learn a lot from each other."[18]

He had, of course, underestimated the complexity of the situation, and overestimated the willingness of the Soviets to learn from those whose territories their armies were now occupying. The main error, as I now see it from my outsider's perspective, was to assume that the longstanding Hungarian commitment to what the Russians called *narodnost'* (very roughly, populism) would be sufficient to fulfill the demands of socialist realism. But no, the Russians insisted on *partiynost'* (submission to party leadership) and *ideynost'* (ideological correctness) as well, which set an inscrutable bar of loyalty to the fluctuating Party line which no one could ever predict or fully measure up to. Nevertheless, Kodály's seniority (he was, after all, approaching seventy at the time of the Communist coup), his world fame, and his sincerely held *narodnïye* principles would assure him a freedom of maneuver that exceeded that of most musicians in the Soviet bloc, and also meant that his work, as well as his person, would be actively promoted by the regime. His universally admired pedagogical methods, to pick the most salient example, were at last officially adopted by the Hungarian government in 1950, at the height of the Rákosi terror. I am not drawing a connection between these things; rather I cite the coincidence as evidence of the complexity to which Kodály referred, which should dissuade us from a one-sided analysis of conditions that—like all conditions at all times—both constrain and enable the historical agents in whom we are interested.

So I will focus on Kodály's *narodnost'*, as it strikes one observer, very much from the outside, basing my observations on the one fairly extensive source that is accessible to me, *The Selected Writings of Zoltán Kodály*, a set of English translations (published by Boosey & Hawkes in 1974) extracted from *Visszatekintés*, the two-volume retrospective collection edited by Ferenc Bónis a decade earlier. A few passages from that book, mainly concerned with music education, attracted my new-grandfatherly attention and prompted me to respond with a gloss. But to set up these glosses, I must first go rather far afield.

IV. ACCEPTING A GIFT

In 1977, a new production of Verdi's *Il Trovatore* was mounted at the Teatro Comunale in Florence, using a new critical edition of the text prepared by the American Verdi scholar David Lawton. In keeping with what he saw as the spirit of the occasion, the conductor, Riccardo Muti, who was then beginning to make a name for

---

18. Quoted (and translated) in Fosler-Lussier, *Music Divided*, 97.

himself as the enforcer of "a rigorous approach to the scores that overshadows even that of the legendary Toscanini" (in the enthusiastic words of Philip Gossett, another rigorous enforcer),[19] forbade the tenor who was singing Manrico to interpolate the traditional and expected high *Do di petto* (high C "in chest") at the end of "Di quella pira," the cabaletta with which the third act reaches its literally blazing culmination. Needless to say, the omission produced a scandal, and the performance has gone down in history as *Il Trovatore senza quel Do* (*Il Trovatore* without that C). Professor Gossett reported it in magazine articles, in a talk to the American Musicological Society (AMS), and finally in his book *Divas and Scholars* of 2006. Each time, he fervently supported Muti's fidelity to the text and did everything he could to discredit the performance tradition on which the audience had been counting. The crowning blow was a quotation from an unidentified Italian critic who called the high C "a gift that the people had given to Verdi."[20] Confident that all would find the idea ridiculous, Professor Gossett gave his rendition of the scandal in *Divas and Scholars* the subheading "Riccardo Muti and the People's Gift to Verdi."

I was in the audience for his AMS talk and I can testify that the quoted remark elicited a big derisive laugh from the assembled musicologists (while I, cringing, wished at that moment that I was something other than a colleague of theirs). I was not cringing on behalf of the high C, about which I cared far less than the *loggionisti* in Florence. I was cringing at yet another snobbish display of contempt for audiences, and beyond that at the implied, typically modernist defense against the social mediation of art, and above all at Professor Gossett's evident (or, as I suspected, feigned) incomprehension of what the Florence audience thought to be at stake. "Why does anyone care so much?" he affected to wonder. "Does it make such a difference if the tenor ascends to that note rather than remaining on the *g*, as in the printed text?" Could an opera scholar really be so clueless?

Kodály understood the difference. He never to my knowledge commented on *Il Trovatore,* but in a lecture he read in 1951 at the Institute of Popular Education, published in translation under the somewhat ambiguous title "Ancient Traditions—Today's Musical Life," he dealt head-on with the issue of social mediation and its role in musical culture. I cannot say how representative this lecture is among Kodály's writings. It is, for one thing, the only text in the translated collection to make conspicuous and approving references to Stalin, something no doubt mandated by its date. For another, to me more attractive, thing, it is the lecture in which Kodály interacts most dynamically with his audience, evidently made up of music teachers. There is a lengthy transcribed question-and-answer session at the end, and

---

19. Philip Gossett, *Divas and Scholars: Performing Italian Opera* (Chicago: University of Chicago Press, 2006), 123.

20. Quoted ibid., 127.

EXAMPLE 6.1. Kalman Simonffy, "Arpád apánk," first stanza.

during the lecture Kodály and his audience join in the singing of several folk songs, beginning with "Peacock," the one every Kodály lover knows because of the big set of orchestral variations on it that Kodály had published in 1939.

Another of these community songs was "Arpád apánk" (Our Father Arpad), a patriotic song that is now all over YouTube, as I have found. Kodály pointed out that it is not actually a folk song but a composed *magyar nóta*, or "art song," by one Kálmán Simonffy (1831–88). I had never heard that name, but even I could have guessed that the song was composed in the nineteenth century by virtue of its opening phrase, which arpeggiates a major triad, and its span of a major hexachord above the tonic note (Ex. 6.1). These are not the features to which Kodály called attention, though. He focused on "the question of tonality":

> There are never any modulations in folksongs. They remain in the same key from beginning to end. But there may be some in composed songs here and there. This can also be a criterion. You certainly know Simonffy's song . . . (*They sing it*). I do not know whom I shall surprise by declaring that this was never written like this by Simonffy. It has become simplified to its present form through being used, being sung by the people, because the original had some little modulation. The second line of the original is different; it has a digression brought about by a rather complicated harmonic process. (*He whistles the original version with the modulation.*)[21]

With some effort I located a version of "Arpád apánk" online that seems to be the original composed song with what Kodály was calling the modulation: not really that complicated a process, just an excursion for the second stanza (or refrain) into the relative minor.[22] Kodály observes:

> In this form the people felt the song too complex and did not use it, so that the simpler variant has completely ousted the original, which can be found only in old editions, in libraries.
> If one likes to potter around with old songs one can discover with amazement that the printed form is sometimes quite different from what one knows, or [from] the version that has become well known later on. Why does this happen? Chiefly,

---

21. *The Selected Writings of Zoltán Kodály* (London: Boosey & Hawkes, 1974), 169.
22. www.youtube.com/watch?v=vE1ornbaYJs (main tune at 0:50, relative minor strain at 1:32).

because these authors were not trained musicians but fumbling dilettanti, who hit upon a good melody and then rounded it off as well as they were able to. But they did not always succeed in giving their tunes a final and unchangeable form[,] and when the songs came to be sung by the people they became changed quite freely. Indeed some authors—even Simonffy himself, for example—sometimes adopted the variant created by the people in singing the tune, and had it printed in later editions.[23]

As Kodály portrayed him, then, Simonffy was happy to accept "a gift from the people." Simonffy, admittedly, was no Verdi, nor was Verdi a fumbling dilettante. I don't know with whom Kodály would have sided that stormy evening in Florence. But I do have some possibly relevant information—or, perhaps I should say, a relevant anecdote that may count as information—about Verdi's attitude. In recounting the story of "Muti and the People's Gift," Professor Gossett made sure to quote "Rossini's famous words to [Enrico] Tamberlick [famous for interpolating a high C-sharp into the role of Arnold in *Guillaume Tell*, bidding him] leave his high C-[sharp] on the hat rack, to be picked up on his way out of the theater."[24] But for the same money, so to speak, he might have quoted from Julian Budden's three-volume study of Verdi's operas, which contains a competing anecdote, related by a famous Manrico, Giovanni Martinelli, in which the same Tamberlick approaches Verdi to ask permission to interpolate the high C into "Di quella pira," having, as he told the composer, "already experimented with it in various provincial theatres where ... it was in great demand with the public. 'Far be it from me,' Verdi had answered, 'to deny the public what it wants. Put in the high C if you like provided it is a good one.'" "From then on," Budden adds, "good or bad, it has come to stay."[25]

The "more complaisant" Verdi of this story (as Budden calls him) agrees with the Kodály of the 1951 lecture that receivers collaborate with producers in the introduction and maintenance of musical traditions, which are not static but evolving. Unlike the Verdi of the story, who regards the process with some irony, Kodály appears to regard the participation of receivers as a necessary validator of the authenticity of musical artifacts. That is the position that my chapter in the *Oxford History* explored: in common with Bartók and Janáček, his companions in that chapter, but also with Vaughan Williams, Grieg, and many nineteenth-century Russians, Kodály asserted explicitly what his music usually implied even without the verbal assist—to wit, that professionally composed music, if it is to last, comes out of (and must come out of) the same ecosystem (to use a word he would not have employed) or stylistic pool (to use a term he would surely have endorsed) as the local folk music. In this way, the professional and the lay musician or listener

---

23. *Selected Writings of Zoltán Kodály*, 169–70.

24. Gossett, *Divas and Scholars*, 127, citing Giuseppe Radiciotti, *Anecdoti rossiniani autentici* (Rome, 1929).

25. Julian Budden, *The Operas of Verdi*, vol. 2 (New York: Oxford University Press, 1979), 98–99.

are united within the tradition, and the music has a chance of surviving. The composers I have just named all come, of course, from areas that the early historians of European art music would have called "peripheral." Composers in the so-called mainstream (that is, from France, Italy, or Germany) did not usually make such assertions, but peripheral composers had no hesitation in applying their view to the products of the mainstream as well.

V. REFUSING ANOTHER

Statements of this kind are so abundant in Kodály's writings that one can open the translated book almost at random to find one. Many of them make what most linguists would probably regard as hyperbolic, untenable claims about language acquisition, especially when Kodály is broaching the matter of musical education. One particularly strong specimen comes from a lecture entitled "Music in the Kindergarten," which Kodály delivered on 3 December 1940, about two months after a despairing Bartók had left Hungary for what would turn out to be for good. That fact may have colored the mood of the piece, which Kodály recalled in 1957 as his "pitiful lament."[26] It amounted to a much more detailed resumption of the complaint embodied in the preface Kodály had written to his and Bartók's original anthology of peasant songs, issued thirty-four years earlier, in 1906. There, he had written that "the overwhelming majority of Hungarians are not yet Hungarian enough, no longer naïve enough and not yet cultured enough to take these songs to their hearts."[27] Here is how he elaborated the point in 1940, with the aid of many musical examples. It is certainly the most narrowly, indeed xenophobically nationalistic passage I have encountered in Kodály's writings:

> Folk traditions, first of all with their singing games and children's songs, are the best foundations for subconscious national features. There are among them some that we share with other peoples of Europe, but there are also differences. We can see the difference if we see on spring days in public parks how a foreign-born governess hammers into Hungarian children's heads the subconscious elements of her own language and music. Such children will have changed souls and will be unable all through their lives to speak and feel Hungarian. When they have grown up and are appointed, thanks to their family, to some leading position, they will not understand either the language or the soul of Hungarians. There is nobody to enlighten such parents as to what they are doing to their children: they are excluding them from the national community. The basic layer of the soul cannot be made from two different substances. A person can have only one mother tongue—musically, too. Anyone who has been brought up on two will never know either. Anyone who has learned a

26. *Selected Writings of Zoltán Kodály,* 149.
27. Ibid., 10.

foreign language at an age under ten will only mix up the different structures of the two languages, their different ways of shaping images. Everybody may have experienced that languages learned under ten will melt like the first snow; they will later have to be started anew; only the wounds inflicted on the Hungarian language will remain in their place. There are innumerable examples of people who started learning foreign languages at the age of ten or over and learned several of them better than those with whom the legacy of the foreign governess was nothing but inexterminable, faulty usages. And today this madness is no longer restricted to wealthy classes; in the foreign-language nursery schools which are springing up like mushrooms it has become available for people with modest incomes as well.[28]

This pungent little screed may have been overheated by the looming threat, in 1940, of a German aggression that went far beyond the musical (the threat that had driven Bartók away from home, to Kodály's agonized regret). Nevertheless, it contains the nucleus of the Kodály method for musical instruction. What was the foreign element that foreign (i.e., German) governesses hammered into children's heads to change their souls? Semitones, of course. Kodály's insistence on the priority of the pentatonic over the diatonic was his theoretical bedrock. In one of his earliest essays, first published in 1917, Kodály called the pentatonic scale "the basis of the music of so many ancient peoples, perhaps even of all peoples." Thus, although his immediate purpose in that essay had been to prove that pentatonicism "is alive and flourishing here, too," that is, in Hungary (and consequently, that the pentatonic peasant music of the countryside was the true and authentic Hungarian music because of its presumable antiquity), the claim he was making on behalf of pentatonicism was a universalist, and therefore exportable, claim.[29] This assertion of precedence was the crucial factor in the spread of what its American adepts customarily call the "Could-die" method far beyond the borders of Hungary. In one American video demonstration, the claim is made outright that the minor third, the larger of the two intervals in the European pentatonic scale, and one said to be endemic to children's chants the world over, is "the first interval people naturally sing."[30]

That, of course, is a conceptual claim rather than an empirical one, and eternally contestable. It is based on the assumption (to recall the old biologists' bromide) that "ontogeny recapitulates phylogeny," so that the musical development of an individual today recapitulates the historical musical development of the species *Homo sapiens*. Kodály asserted it explicitly: "In the same way as the child's development repeats in brief the evolution of mankind," he wrote, "his forms of music represent a history of music; indeed they afford a glimpse into the prehistoric

---

28. Ibid., 131.
29. Kodály, "The Pentatonic Scale in Hungarian Folk Music," in *Selected Writings*, 11–23, at 11.
30. www.youtube.com/watch?v=qcirSqVwHLo&t (see esp. 1:43).

period of music. From the reiteration of the smallest motif, comprising but a couple of notes, we can observe all grades of musical development up to the average stage of the European folksong: the sentence of eight bars."[31]

This assertion comes from the preface to the first volume of the *Corpus Musicae Popularis Hungaricae*, containing children's games, which came out in 1951, the year after Kodály's methods had been institutionalized in Hungary. It can never be confirmed (or rather, more realistically, can never be disproven). It will always remain a hypothesis rather than an observed fact, but it is no mere fallacy. It gains plausibility in the light of that "smallest motif's" prevalence in the volume's many examples, and it was on these examples that Kodály's method so famously built. We do not have to call the minor third natural in order to recognize it as culturally prevalent and therefore familiar; and I take it to be the Kodály method's main advantage that it is grounded in what may be taken (if anything may be so taken) as the universal listening experience of its potential clientele. The advantage is not only to the method's pedagogical efficacy, but also to its claim of social benefit—that is, its claim that music unites people in both actual and figurative harmony.

That claim must surely have made the method attractive to the government that officially implemented it in 1950, always on the lookout for means of social regulation; but the claim can be authorized in other ways as well. When Kodály asked, in 1929, "Is there anything more demonstrative of social solidarity than a choir?" he was not merely speaking on behalf of current or local political authority. His words echoed an ancient theme, famously sounded by St. Basil of Caesarea in the fourth century CE, in a homily about "The Value of Psalms": "Psalmody," wrote the founder of Christian monasticism, "bringing about choral singing, a bond, as it were, toward unity, and joining people into a harmonious union of one choir, produces also the greatest of blessings, love."[32] Kodály never, to my knowledge, quoted these words of St. Basil, but I was much intrigued to find a lengthy quote from the sermons of St. John Chrysostom, an only slightly less ancient church father, in the preface to the third volume of the *Corpus Musicae Popularis Hungaricae*, containing wedding songs, which came out in 1955. That preface also contains the famous exhortation, found in many postclassical authors (Kodály attributing it to Pope [or Saint] Sylvester I), *Aurum in stercore quaerere* ("to seek gold in excrement"), by which Kodály sought to justify "ma[king] available for research" songs with the kind of obscene texts that St. John Chrysostom had deplored.[33] As a specialist in Russian and Soviet music I am of course used to reading political tea leaves, and I cannot help wondering whether these patristic allusions, found in the first volume

---

31. Kodály, "Children's Games," in *Selected Writings*, 40–54, at 46.
32. St. Basil, *Exegetic Homilies*, trans. S. Agnes Clare Way, The Fathers of the Church 46 (Washington, DC: Catholic University of America Press, 1963), 153.
33. *Selected Writings of Zoltán Kodály*, 60–61.

of the *Corpus Musicae Popularis Hungaricae* to appear after the death of Stalin, constitute oblique testimony to the post-Stalinist thaw, and may thus be plausibly read the way such things are often read by people like me, as a signal to readers.

VI. COMMUNITIES

Be all that as it may, Kodály's communitarianism—epitomized, admittedly, during the Stalinist period when he wrote about "the bounden duty of the talented to cultivate their talent to the highest degree, [so as] to be of as much use as possible to their fellow men; for every person's worth is measured by how much he can help his fellow men and serve his country," and when he wrote that "real art is one of the most powerful forces in the rise of mankind and he who renders it accessible to as many people as possible is a benefactor of humanity"[34]—need not be read exclusively in the light of socialist realist teachings. Nor, obviously, is it necessarily read that way, given the enduring worldwide reach of Kodály's pedagogy. So we do not have to interpret in a political context—or at least, in *that* political context—the difference between Kodály's aims and methods and those, say, of Paul Hindemith, set forth in his *Elementary Training for Musicians* (1946), a book from which I myself was instructed when no longer a child.

It makes an interesting comparison, because Hindemith, too, uses anhemitonic melodies—that is, melodies without semitones—to introduce intervals and inculcate sight-singing skills. The reason why I have to resort to this relatively arcane term, *anhemitonic,* is because Hindemith, though he gets to it eventually, steers clear of the pentatonic scale at the outset, precisely (as I see it) for the same reason that Kodály, although he eventually gets to the diatonic scale, accorded such priority to the pentatonic and invested so much in it ideologically (Fig. 6.1).

The four notes introduced in Hindemith's first sight-singing exercise can be identified either as a segment of the diatonic major or natural minor scales (*fa* up to *ti* or *la* up to *re*, respectively) or as a segment of the whole-tone scale. Either way, the segment bears no relationship to folk music, or to children's games, or to any existing repertory save the artificial or, if you prefer, utopian repertory of modern art music. That is the repertory for which the user of Hindemith's book is being trained, and the objective, clearly, is to free the user from predilections born of habit or prior listening experience. Hindemith, in other words, wishes to protect his pupil from the very thing that Kodály's method seeks to instill, harness, and make conscious. By Kodály's standards, then, Hindemith's method is not communitarian, except insofar as it helps form a small, exclusive, and proudly professionalized community of musical specialists; and by Hindemith's standards Kodály's method is not emancipatory in that it fosters conformity with existing repertories

---

34. Ibid., 199.

FIGURE 6.1. Hindemith, *Elementary Training for Musicians* (London: Schott, 1946), 14.

that despite their ordinariness are deemed socially salubrious. In this contrasting pedagogical reliance on competing anhemitonies we see *in nuce* all the big music-aesthetical and music-political debates of the twentieth century.

These debates are inevitably overdrawn in retrospect. We easily forget that Hindemith, in the early 1930s, was known as a communitarian, with a special interest in pedagogy—as his kiddie cantatas advertised (*Wir bauen eine Stadt* in 1930, *Plöner Musiktag* in 1932) and as the Turkish government eagerly recognized in 1934. It was probably his brush with the Nazis that cured him of his civic urges, or at least curbed his civic activity. Living under communism had no such effect on Kodály, even though his continued civic commitments exacted a heavy toll in energy, and eventually in prestige. But how shall we regard these differences in prospect, now that we have lived, as Hindemith and Kodály did not, into the twenty-first century? Both Kodály's authority and Hindemith's are now much diminished, both in their homelands and abroad. The degree to which music education is part of the public school curriculum has suffered a catastrophic decline in my country. I suspect that in other lands, too, there has been decline, albeit (I would certainly hope) less precipitous. The communitarian spirit may not be as strong among Hungarian musicians as it once was, if I may judge by a recent publication, a book of interviews conducted by Bálint András Varga, the Hungarian new-music promoter, called *The Courage of Composers and the Tyranny of Taste*.[35] As the title already suggests, it revives the aggressive individualism of the mid-twentieth-century avant-garde, musicians who willingly sacrificed the building of audiences for the sake of maintaining the pace of stylistic and technical progress as they conceived it. Few would now respond to Kodály's famous warning to his "young colleagues, the composers of symphonies," in a postscript to his "pitiful

---

35. Bálint András Varga, *The Courage of Composers and the Tyranny of Taste* (Rochester, NY: University of Rochester Press, 2017).

lament," exhorting them to "drop in sometimes at the kindergarten, too[, for i]t is there that it is decided whether there will be anybody to understand their works in twenty years' time."[36] The composers Mr. Varga has chosen to interview have given up that hope, and flaunt the fact that they have done so.

And I do not insist that they are wrong. The loss of an audience for contemporary classical or concert music is the result of many economic, cultural, and (especially) demographic factors, and probably owes little enough to the attitudes or decisions of creative individuals. Among these fateful factors, ironically enough, was the very literacy whose spread Kodály strove so hard to foster, which made possible the dispersion of musical style into byways where aural cognition could not follow it. Many have found intolerable this claim of mine, that literacy bears a meed of responsibility for the loss of a musical public; but it is merely a restatement of Plato's millennia-old contention that literacy would disrupt the propagation of true knowledge and culture in the population by destroying memory.[37] Rather than allow it to deflect the present discussion away from Kodály, I would refer doubters to the final chapters of my *Oxford History*. But whether or not one accepts any particular account of it, it would take a heap of denial to contradict the reality of the massive waning of classical music's cultural relevance.

It was already well underway during Kodály's lifetime, despite all his efforts, as he well knew. In 1966, the last full year of his life, Kodály made his last visit to America, during which he gave a televised interview in English at the University of California, Santa Barbara. His interlocutor, Ernő Daniél (1918–77), a Hungarian-born pianist who served as the conductor of the University Orchestra, lobbed him a softball, as we say in America, asking him to comment on a pious quotation from "the Scotchman Fletcher," as Daniél put it (that is, Andrew Fletcher, the early eighteenth-century Scottish patriot), who is reputed to have said, "Let me make the songs of a nation, and I care not who makes its laws." Kodály did not let this idealistic comment pass without reservation. Here is what he said:

> No adult men are able to understand music if they did not learn it in childhood. Therefore [it] is a big difficulty all over the world now to find listeners for music. Many [sic] music is produced, and also good music, but no listeners, too few listeners,

---

36. *Selected Writings of Zoltán Kodály*, 151.

37. *Phaedrus*, 275a–b: "If men learn this, it will implant forgetfulness in their souls; they will cease to exercise memory because they rely on that which is written, calling things to remembrance no longer from within themselves, but by means of external marks. What you have discovered is a recipe not for memory, but for reminder. And it is no true wisdom that you offer your disciples, but only its semblance, for by telling them of many things without teaching them you will make them seem to know much, while for the most part they know nothing, and as men filled, not with wisdom, but with the conceit of wisdom, they will be a burden to their fellows" (*Plato's Phaedrus*, trans. Reginald Hackforth [Cambridge: Cambridge University Press, 1952], 157).

not enough listeners. Just now the listener must be educated—and where? Only in the general schools.[38]

That is what Kodály said after a long lifetime of striving to produce a musically literate and appreciative citizenry at home. He said it smiling, but it was another pitiful lament, and it accords with misgivings he had expressed from the very moment his methods were adopted in the Hungarian schools. In an address he delivered as president of the Bartók Memorial Committee in September 1956, only weeks before the Hungarian polity and its cultural institutions suffered major disruption, he warned that "serious music is threatened by danger," going on to explain that "[i]ts significance is diminishing throughout the world because it is not keeping up with the spread of general education."[39] How much truer is that today! I am sure that you will not disagree when I tell you that there is no classical musician alive today who enjoys the esteem that Kodály enjoyed at the time he issued his warnings and complaints; or that Shostakovich enjoyed in Soviet Russia when I saw him take his bows after the premiere of his last symphony; or that Toscanini (or, after him, Leonard Bernstein) enjoyed in the United States when I was growing up.

Even then classical music was a minority taste, and its promotion in the name of moral or spiritual uplift did not produce social solidarity; in fact it produced the very opposite in the form of a populist backlash. I think everyone sees that now. What Kodály, adopting the German expression, called "serious music" has given up its place—irrevocably, in my opinion—at the center even of the academic curriculum, its last stronghold. It has reverted to its aristocratic niche after a century of optimistic mass promotion on the part of governments in some parts of the world, and commercial interests in other parts. I do not think one could find a musician today who truly believes that classical music is as socially important as Kodály believed it was, let alone Andrew Fletcher—or, for that matter, Andrey Zhdanov. I do not exclude myself from this generalization, nor am I excluding you, my audience. We might wish it otherwise, but the wish will not make it so.

Does that mean that Kodály lived his life in vain? To say that it does would be to say that we have done so too. I am not ever going to say *that*. But the effort to maintain the ascendancy of classical music in the era of mass media and mass politics too obviously contradicted the egalitarian premises on which my country, for one, was founded, and in which I too believe, for me to mourn the loss of its artificially sustained status. Ultimately I have to side with Tolstoy (and with Bourdieu) and recognize that elite art is socially divisive and has never fostered the kind of solidarity that other aspects of expressive culture, including orally

---

38. www.youtube.com/watch?v=NbDvjqzb924, 26:15–26:51.
39. *Selected Writings of Zoltán Kodály*, 112.

transmitted music, have nurtured. I will never give up my devotion to it, but I will not endorse its claim of universal social significance, nor will I deny that there are more important things than what may have mattered most to Kodály, or matter most to me. What has always made Kodály an attractive figure to me is the hunch that, at bottom, he agreed.

Милина часть

(Mila's Part)

7

Russian Responses to Bach

I

In a long lifetime of colloquiums, conferences, and meetings, only once have I ever felt an impulse to walk out on a musicological lecture, and that was at a conference called "Creative Responses to Bach from Mozart to Hindemith." It was the ninth biennial meeting of the American Bach Society, and it took place on my campus, the University of California at Berkeley, in April 1996. Despite its name, the American Bach Society was not an insularly American organization. The roster of speakers at that symposium included British and German scholars, and one of the German guests, Ludwig Finscher, was given the honor of delivering the keynote address, titled "Bach's Posthumous Role in Music History."

The moment of disgust that almost sent me from the room came when, after discussing the impact of Bach's music on Mozart, Haydn, Beethoven, Mendelssohn, Schumann, Wagner, Reger, Busoni (pronounced Bu-ZAWWW-ni, *molto alla tedesca*), Schoenberg, Berg, and Webern, Professor Finscher, moving on to his summation, said, "Now that we have talked about everybody . . ." Hot-head that I then was, I felt a flush. "No, dear professor," my mind shouted, "you have not talked about everybody." A lot of my writing has been expressly aimed at countering the tendency toward German universalism in our discipline, and my strong reaction to Prof. Finscher's talk that day, two decades ago and more, was one of the nudges

---

Keynote address, conference "Back to—and Forward from—J. S. Bach," University of Massachusetts, Amherst, 18 April 2015.

I received toward those efforts, which have won me a reputation (among German universalists at any rate) for xenophobia.[1]

But when I looked for the offending phrase in the published version of the talk, I did not find it.[2] In what I assume was its place, I found something a little milder: "Taking everything together," which does not imply as strongly that the discussion had included everything relevant, only that the summation would pertain to the whole of what had gone before it.[3] Had I only imagined that Prof. Finscher's purview had been so narrow? Indeed not: there was a sentence in the printed version that I had not remembered from the oral delivery, which even more explicitly restricted the scope of the musicologically relevant: "[T]he theoretical and ideological discourse on Bach was dominated by Northern and Middle German authors," the text as published reads, and "the composers' reactions [to Bach] in the nineteenth century constitute a German chapter of compositional history to such a degree that we can leave out French, Italian, English, Russian, and other reactions (and not only because our time is short)."[4]

It is probably a mark of how our field has changed in the past two decades that many listeners would now find such a remark deplorable, whereas no one seemed to react to it in 1996—not even I, if Prof. Finscher actually read aloud then what was printed later. It was not a remarkable thing to say then, nor of course did Prof. Finscher, a man of impeccable manners, mean to offend. But I do wish to wield my privilege as today's keynoter to insist on its incorrectness. Even within the nineteenth century, the ideological and compositional response to Bach was international—*significantly* international—and that was precisely what made it "universal."

Many there are who could set the record straight about prominent nineteenth-century French responses to Bach. There was Franck, who saw himself and was seen by his contemporaries as being, despite his Catholicism, the direct continuer of the Bach organ tradition. There was Saint-Saëns, a major Bach transcriber in many media, whose Second Piano Concerto, according to a famous witticism, "begins with Bach and ends with Offenbach."[5] There was d'Indy, a major dissemi-

---

1. Ian Pace and J. P. E. Harper-Scott are among those who have most forcefully diagnosed it, so perhaps it is something British Germanophiles are best equipped to spot. See J. P. E. Harper-Scott, *The Quilting Points of Musical Modernism: Revolution, Reaction, and William Walton* (Cambridge: Cambridge University Press, 2012), chap. 1, an extended exposé of my xenophobic-capitalist ideology. The analogous rants of Pace and Franklin Cox can be found at http://ianpace.wordpress.com/2012/11/28/a-comprehensive-and-brilliant-critique-of-taruskins-oxford-history-of-western-music.

2. Ludwig Finscher, "Bach's Posthumous Role in Music History," in *Bach Perspectives*, vol. 3, ed. Michael Marissen (Lincoln: University of Nebraska Press, 1998), 1–21.

3. Ibid., 20.

4. Ibid., 9.

5. Zygmunt Stojowski, quoted by his pupil Oscar Levant in *A Smattering of Ignorance* (New York: Doubleday, Doran, 1940), 267.

nator of Bach in pedagogy. And a bit further back there was Berlioz (who said, "Il n'y a pas d'autre Dieu que Bach, et Mendelssohn est son prophète"), not to mention Reicha and Cherubini, the formulators of the French conservatory curriculum—equivocally French, perhaps, by virtue of their foreign birth, but certainly not German, and thoroughgoing Bachians.

But (surprise, surprise) I want to bring the news from Russia. I do so not as a spokesman or vindicator of Russia's cultural importance. I am an even more equivocal representative of Russia than Reicha was of France (just ask my Yiddish-speaking grandparents); and in any case, it is not Russia's distinctiveness as a Bach site that I want to emphasize, but more nearly the opposite. The Russian response to Bach covered the full Finscherian spectrum from "theoretical and ideological discourse" to practical composition, and one can gain an inkling of its full range by focusing discussion on two nineteenth-century Russian Bachians: one who lived early in the century and one who lived late; one who was an aristocratic dilettante and one who was a consummate professional; one for whom Bach was a cultural symbol rather than a source of musical technique, and one for whom Bach was the supreme source of musical technique.

In each of these pairs, the second term—the late nineteenth-century figure, the professional musician, the practicing composer—refers to Sergey Ivanovich Taneyev, who lived from 1856 to 1915, and who I expect is familiar to today's musicians and music scholars at least as a name. But before getting to Taneyev I want to tell you about the other figure—the early nineteenth-century aristocratic dilettante for whom Bach was a potent cultural symbol; and his is a name that I would not expect musicians outside of Russia to recognize: Prince Vladimir Fyodorovich Odoyevsky (whose surname is almost always mispronounced Odoyévsky rather than Odóyevsky by the few in the West who know it, because, I guess, it looks as if it rhymed with Dostoyevsky). He was a prince not because he was heir to any throne but because his hereditary title, *knyaz'*, was the equivalent of the German *Fürst,* and that was high aristocracy indeed. Odoyevsky's family claimed direct descent from Ryurik, the quasi-legendary Viking founder of the first Russian ruling house, the one that culminated in Ivan the Terrible.

At that rank one was not supposed to engage in any profession, or sign one's work if one deigned to publish it, but Odoyevsky, who was born in 1803 and lived until 1869, was an ambitious polymath of Goethean omnivorousness, a scholar and littérateur with a strong interest in everything from natural science to music. He published a great deal of historical research and criticism, including some famous and influential essays on old Russian sacred chant (or *peniye*) and on Glinka's operas. Odoyevsky was best known, however, for his short fiction, and is often called the Russian Hoffmann. His best-known work, a collection of fantasy tales called *Russkiye nochi* (Russian Nights, 1844), was modeled on E. T. A. Hoffmann's *Die Serapionsbrüder,* a Decameron-like series of stories traded by a group of symposiasts. The parallels with Hoffmann go further. Not only did both Odoyevsky and Hoffmann write novellas and criticism; they both also dabbled (Hoffmann the more ambitiously) in musical composition.

Like Hoffmann, Odoyevsky was an exemplary exponent of romanticism in its first idealistic flush. In his music criticism he crusaded tirelessly against the vogue for Italian opera (which meant he had to turn a studied blind eye—or deaf ear—on much of Glinka's work so that he could praise it). To Odoyevsky, Italian music meant *chuvstvennost'*, which is Russian for *Sinnlichkeit*, which is German for *sensuality*. It was half of the cliché binary of German romantic thought, which Odoyevsky lifted right out of Hoffmann's *Serapionsbrüder*, the other half being *Geist*, or (for Odoyevsky) *dukh*, or (for us) *spirit* or *spirituality*. Not unlike his older German contemporaries, Odoyevsky cast contemporary art and its politics as a perpetual war between spirituality and sensuality. It led him into many prejudiced judgments, like the following, from the notes he appended near the end of his life to a projected reissue of *Russian Nights* that was never published. It concerns a work about which he was at best ambivalent: "To the number of proofs of Wagner's greatness, I add the failure of his *Tannhäuser* in Paris, where Meyerbeer's *Ploërmel* and even the so-called operas by Verdi which occupy the same place in music that Chinese works, done in silk and tinsel, occupy in painting, now flourish."[6]

Actually, Odoyevsky preferred the overture to *Tannhäuser* to the rest of the opera.[7] And this was characteristic of him, because he was among the first musical connoisseurs, perhaps the first in Russia, to participate in that great Romantic transvaluation of values that placed instrumental music, for the first time, higher than vocal. And here is where Bach came in for Odoyevsky. For him, Bach represented all that was highest, purest, and most rarefied in art—spirituality without taint of the sensual, which means without taint of the human voice. Obviously, Odoyevsky's Bach was not our Bach, nor even Mendelssohn's Bach (for there was more than one way of romantically receiving Bach). Nor was Odoyevsky's Bach the Bach that became known to the recipients of the Bach-Gesellschaft edition, which began coming out just when an aristocratic intellectual like Odoyevsky might have been expected to sign up for it. The list of subscribers to the first volume of the edition—the ones, that is, whose advance support had enabled its publication—included two Russians, both St. Petersburgers rather than Muscovites like Odoyevsky. One was listed as "Count Wielhorski," which makes his identification tricky, because (as readers of Berlioz's memoirs may recall) there were two Counts Wiel-

---

6. V. F. Odoyevsky, "Notes to *Russian Nights*," in idem, *Russian Nights*, trans. Olga Olienikov and Ralph E. Matlaw (New York: E. P. Dutton, 1965), 27. Meyerbeer's opéra comique *Le Pardon de Ploërmel* (1859) is more often performed under the name *Dinorah*.

7. V. F. Odoyevsky, "Pervïy kontsert Vagnera" (1863), in idem, *Muzïkal'no-literaturnoye naslediye*, ed. G. Bernandt (Moscow: Muzgiz, 1956), 258.

horski (or, in Russian, Viyel'gorsky), Mikhaíl and Matvey, among the aristocratic patrons who oversaw the concert life of the Russian capital. The other Russian subscriber was listed as "Herr Stassow"—not Vladimir Vasil'yevich Stasov, the one we now remember as a prolific arts publicist and egger-on of Russian musical nationalism, but his brother Dmitry (1828–1918), a prominent jurist, who was also a major musical patron. So Odoyevsky did not receive the early publications of cantatas that might have altered his conception of Bach's significance, as they did for so many.

But to judge by Odoyevsky's most sustained literary engagement with Bach (written before the Bach-Gesellschaft edition began to appear), it was probably just as well. *Russian Nights* contains two musical tales. One, composed in 1830, is called "The Last Quartet of Beethoven" and purports to depict the last tortured moments of its imagined subject's life. He is first shown sitting incognito at a rehearsal of the titular quartet, at which the musicians are shown struggling with the unintelligible, to them incoherent, seemingly debased stream of "incomprehensible dissonances, . . . leaps and trills impossible on any instrument, . . . vain attempts to create effects that do not exist in music."[8] Later, at home, he laments in his last moments the futility of contending with the unbridgeable chasm between spirit and flesh:

> The thoughts of a proud creative spirit are humiliated and imprisoned, the lofty effort of the earthly creator, challenging the force of nature, becomes the work of human hands! And people! They come, they listen—as if they were judges, as if you had been creating for them! What do they care that a thought which has assumed an image understandable to them is only a link in the infinite chain of thoughts and sufferings, that the moment when the artist descends to the level of man is only a fragment of the long and painful life of immeasurable feeling; that each of his expressions, each line was born out of the bitter tears of a Seraph who is imprisoned in human flesh and who would give half of his life for a moment of the fresh air of inspiration?[9]

Applied to Beethoven, this portrayal of the tragic isolation of genius is familiar enough—recognizably "Hoffmannesque," in fact. And sure enough, "The Last Quartet of Beethoven" is the one story in *Russian Nights* that actually bears an epigraph from *Die Serapionsbrüder*. But if Odoyevsky's Beethoven fable is exactly what one might have expected from the Russian Hoffmann, the other musical tale is even more Hoffmannesque, but in a more original, somewhat unexpected way.

II

It is called "Sebastian Bach"; it was composed five years later, in 1835; and its title character is another lonely genius, for which reason it is far more at variance with the

---

8. Odoyevsky, *Russian Nights*, 123.
9. Ibid., 128.

facts of its subject's earthly existence than the Beethoven tale. Indeed, the only things Odoyevsky's Bach had in common with the historical J. S. Bach were his name, his profession, and the towns in which the events of his imagined life were situated.[10]

Odoyevsky's Beethoven is the familiar artist of romanticism, choleric and tormented. His Bach, by contrast, might seem a cold fish—but in this he embodies an even higher romanticism. In the words of his fictitious mentor, the Lüneburg organ builder Johann Albrecht, music's domain is

> the highest state of man's soul, which he does not share with nature, which eludes the sculptor's chisel, remains unrevealed by the passionate lines of the poet. This is the state when the soul, proud of its victory over nature, in the full blaze of its glory, grows humble before the Almighty and, suffering bitterly, yearns to prostrate itself at His throne and, like a stranger amid the luxurious delights of a foreign land, sighs for his fatherland. People called the feeling that springs from this lofty state of the soul *the ineffable* [*nevïrazimïm*]. The only language of this feeling is *music*.[11]

Not a thing of nature, then, or even of human nature, music is "a higher organization of the materials nature provides."[12] And the medium through which music can express this higher organization must be suitably artificial rather than natural. Odoyevsky contrives the main event in his fictitious life of Bach as attestation to this aestheticist dogma.

Like so many storied apprentices, Odoyevsky's Sebastian Bach marries his master's daughter. Sure enough, her name is Magdalena (*Magdalina* in Russian orthography). But unlike the historical (Anna) Magdalena Bach (née Wülken), Magdalena Albrecht had an Italian mother. Italian blood thus ran in her veins, and, being Italian, she naturally loved to sing. And Bach, loving her, loved to sing with her. When they resolve to marry and seek Albrecht's blessing, he greets the news with an admonition:

> "I've anticipated this for a long time," he said. "Evidently it is God's will," he added with a sigh. "God bless you, my children; art has united you, and may it be a strong bond for your entire life. Only, don't get attached too much to singing, Sebastian; you sing too often with Magdalena: the voice abounds in human passions; imperceptibly, in the moments of purest inspiration, sounds of another, impure world break into it; the human voice still carries the imprint of the first sinful wail!"[13]

There is an uncanny reverberation here from one of our most ancient musical texts, the ninth-century *Scholia enchiriadis,* when, in answer to the question, How

---

10. The paper-thin factual basis of Odoyevsky's Bach portrait seems to derive more or less exclusively from Carl Philipp Emanuel Bach's obituary of his father, perhaps as mediated by Forkel's 1802 biography.
11. Odoyevsky, *Russian Nights*, 176. Translation of last sentence somewhat adapted to reflect the word order of the original.
12. Ralph Matlaw, "Introduction," in Odoyevsky, *Russian Nights*, 18.
13. Odoyevsky, *Russian Nights*, 179.

is Arithmetic necessary knowledge for a musician, the anonymous author says: "Notes pass away quickly; numbers, however, though stained by the corporeal touch of pitches and motions, remain."[14] This was the Neoplatonic ideal that romanticism revived, in its radical dichotomy of *Geist* and *Sinnlichkeit*, or (to speak Odoyevsky's language) *dukh* and *chuvstvennost'*. Magdalena Bach's Italian blood, and her consequent predisposition toward sensuality, lead to the crisis that provides Odoyevsky's tale with its climax.

A fictitious Venetian musician named Francesco, who announces himself as "the pupil of the famous [fictitious] Abbott Oliva, the follower of the glorious [historical] Cesti," comes north "to pay his respects to the famous Bach," little suspecting what havoc his visit would wreak. "At that time," Odoyevsky informs the reader,

> a new era was beginning in Italian music, the latest development of which we see in Rossini and his followers. Carissimi, Cesti, Cavalli wanted to discard the somewhat antiquated forms of their predecessors' music, and set the voice free. But the followers of these talented men went still further: singing became furious shouting, some passages were now adorned, not for the sake of music itself, but to give the singer a chance to display his voice; invention diminished, and playful roulades and trills replaced well-developed, full harmonies.[15]

Francesco sings for Sebastian and Magdalena a few arias ("this word was being then introduced," Odoyevsky explains) by his teacher, and then "a few popular canzonettas [little ditties], adapted to the new taste."[16] After he has left, Sebastian

> saw Magdalena rush to the clavichord and try to repeat the melodies, the phrases she could still remember. At first Sebastian thought that she was making fun of the Venetian, and he was about to burst out laughing. But he was astonished when Magdalena covered her face with her hands and cried: "That's real music, Sebastian! Real music! Only now do I understand music! How often I tried to recall, as if in a dream, the melodies my mother used to sing to me, rocking me in her arms, but they had vanished from my memory. In vain did I try to find them in your music, in all the music I heard every day! I felt that it lacked something, but I couldn't explain to myself what it was. It was a dream the details of which were forgotten and which had left in me only sweet memories. Only now do I realize what your music lacked; now I remember the songs of my mother. . . . Oh, Sebastian!" she cried out, and, with an unwonted gesture, threw herself into his arms, "throw all your fugues, all your canons into the fire! Write Italian canzonettas; for my sake, write them!"[17]

---

14. Trans. Lawrence Rosenwald, in Piero Weiss and Richard Taruskin, eds., *Music in the Western World: A History in Documents*, 2nd ed. (Belmont, CA: Thomson/Schirmer, 2008), 34.
15. Odoyevsky, *Russian Nights*, 183–84.
16. Odoyevsky, *Muzïkal'no-literaturnoye naslediye*, 431.
17. Odoyevsky, *Russian Nights*, 184–85.

EXAMPLE 7.1. "A famous theme that was later used by Hummel" (From Odoyevsky, *Russian Nights*, p. 187).

This naturalist or sensualist manifesto might as well have been signed Jean-Jacques Rousseau; and in this domestic *querelle des bouffons* we have a case, as they say, of discriminating romanticisms.[18] Odoyevsky stands ready to assist:

> Italian blood, in the course of forty years—forty years!—suppressed by education, way of life, habit, suddenly was awakened by its native sounds; a new, unsuspected world opened before Magdalena. Southern passions, which had long been confined in her soul, now broke loose with all the ardor of fiery youth. To their agony was added the agony experienced by a woman who has understood love only during the decline of her beauty.[19]

Bach tries to humor his wife to the best of his ability. Recalling what Odoyevsky identifies as "a famous theme that was later used by Hummel," he tries to write her a canzonetta (Ex. 7.1).[20]

No sooner had Sebastian invented the theme, Odoyevsky "reports," than his old habits took over: "He noticed how easily it could be developed into a fugue. Indeed, there was a C-sharp major fugue missing in his *Wohltemperirte Clavier* which he was composing at the time; he put six [*recte*: seven] sharps after the clef—and the Italian canzonetta became a fugue to be played for practice."[21]

Magdalena gradually gets back to a semblance of normal, but "in her heart there remained only bitterness, [which] dimmed the glow of her cheeks, penetrated her breast, furrowed her face, and wasted her away."[22] The tale ends with her burial. Such was the price of artistic and spiritual purity.

With its animadversions against things Italian, Odoyevsky's tale is an early example of the Teutonic chauvinism in universalist guise to which I have long objected, albeit not unmixed with a dollop of Russian aristocratic patriotism when

---

18. Cf. Arthur O. Lovejoy, "On the Discrimination of Romanticisms," *Proceedings of the Modern Language Association* 39 (1924): 229–53.

19. Odoyevsky, *Russian Nights*, 185.

20. Hummel's appropriation (if that is what it is—the resemblance is tenuous) is found in his Nocturne in F major, op. 99, for piano four-hands (ca. 1824), which is actually a set of variations (www.youtube.com/watch?v=zgMRmvYVhfI at 3:00). Possibly prompted by Odoyevsky, Glinka orchestrated Hummel's Nocturne in 1854, and gave it a new title, "V pamyat' druzhbï" (Souvenir of Friendship) (www.youtube.com/watch?v=A_WHNb1weeU at 3:18).

21. Odoyevsky, *Russian Nights*, 187.

22. Ibid., 188.

the author goes out of his way to speculate—on the basis of the birthplace of the quasi-legendary founder of the Bach dynasty, the cittern-playing, sixteenth-century Veit (or Focht) Bach, who hailed from what is now Bratislava in Slovakia—that the Bachs "belonged to the Slavs, like Haydn and Pleyel."[23] The same bias motivated Odoyevsky's scholarly efforts to transcribe the neumes of Russian chant and revive the ancient liturgical melodies in contemporary practice—efforts motivated more by a patriotic than by an antiquarian impulse. And it was Odoyevsky who wrote, in the most penetrating review to greet Glinka's first opera, *A Life for the Tsar*, on its 1836 premiere, that its historical significance and its claim to be, in Gogol's words, "a wonderful beginning," was the success with which "Russian melody," formerly confined to comic operas about merry peasants, "is elevated [in it] to a tragic style," endowing its peasant protagonist with the attributes of true nobility.[24]

Elevation was what Odoyevsky always sought in art: *das Erhabene, le sublime*, or (in Odoyevsky's tongue) *vozvïshennost'*, as when he says of Bach that he "became the church organ raised to the level of man" (... *sdelalsya tserkovnïm organom, vozvedennïm na stepen' cheloveka*).[25] But musical pursuits elevate man as well, and he becomes

> oblivious to the storms of his earthly wanderings. In [music], as at the peak of the Alps, there radiates a cloudless sun of harmony. Only the inexplicit, boundless sounds embrace the infinite soul of man; only they can unite the elements of joy and sorrow, sundered by the fall of man; only they can rejuvenate the heart and transport us into the innocent first cradle of the first innocent man.[26]

Yet because Bach, practically alone among earthly musicians, ascended to this realm of immaculate bliss, "we," that is Odoyevsky's contemporaries (and, a fortiori, his progeny), have lost touch with him, living as we do in an age "when music has ceased to be a prayer, when it has become an expression of restless passion, a toy for diversion, a lure for vainglory." To "us"

> Bach's music seems cold and lifeless. We do not understand it, as we fail to understand the impassivity of martyrs burned at the stake by pagans. We look for something comprehensible, something that approximates our indolence, our comforts in life. We are afraid of profound feeling, as we are of profound thought. We are afraid to plunge into our innermost souls lest we reveal our own ugliness. Death has chained all the impulses of our heart—we are afraid of life! We are afraid of things for which there are no words; and what *can* you express in words?[27]

---

23. Ibid., 158.
24. "Pis'mo k lyubitelyu muzïki ob opere g. Glinki: Zhizn' za Tsarya," in Odoyevsky, *Muzïkal'no-literaturnoye naslediye*, 119. Gogol's comment, from "Peterburgskiye zapiski" (1936), may be found in *Sochineniya i pis'ma N. V. Gogolya*, ed. V. V. Kallash (St. Petersburg: Prosveshcheniye, 1896), 7:340.
25. Odoyevsky, *Russian Nights*, 181; Odoyevsky, *Muzïkal'no-literaturnoye naslediye*, 428.
26. Odoyevsky, *Russian Nights*, 176.
27. Ibid., 181–82.

EXAMPLE 7.2. "Known to all is the Bach fugue on the following motif" (Odoyevsky's note).

One does not usually look to Russia for romanticism, where it was a short-lived and fragile bloom, but Odoyevsky, its outstanding Russian exponent, easily out-Hoffmanned Hoffmann in "Sebastian Bach," a story that deserves a place alongside Hoffmann's own essay "Beethovens Instrumentalmusik" in the annals of musical idealism. The strain of purist thought that begins here eventually became the high modernism of the twentieth century. The composers of the so-called Second Viennese School took inspiration, exactly as Odoyevsky did, from Bach's most exquisite and rarefied creations: *Das musikalisches Opfer, Die Kunst der Fuge,* and the organ fugues. Their Bach was his Bach.

Schoenberg's interest in Bach centered on the organ works, of which he made three orchestral arrangements: two of these orchestrations were of chorale preludes and the remaining one, scored for a colossal orchestra, was of the St. Anne Prelude and Fugue in E-flat Major (BWV 552) from the third book of the *Clavierübung.* Odoyevsky, for his part, had singled out Bach's organ fugues (with their thematically related preludes) as the epitome of Bach's "religious inspiration" transmuted into ineffability.[28] Webern arranged the six-part ricercare from the *Musical Offering,* the masterpiece that, for Odoyevsky, had shown the power of musical revelation to outshine the splendor of worldly treasures and inspire awe even in the King of Prussia.[29] Schoenberg and Webern had each appropriated the B-A-C-H cipher from *The Art of Fugue* (Schoenberg in his Variations for Orchestra, op. 31, and Webern in the tone row governing his String Quartet, op. 28). Odoyevsky, fascinated with it as an emblem of the all-pervasiveness of Bach's devotion to his art, printed the cipher as the other musical illustration in his tale (Ex. 7.2).

The utopian, romantic Bach of Odoyevsky's imagination survived robustly into the twentieth century, and if we are more conscious of "Back to Bach" as the rallying cry of an anti-Romantic backlash,[30] we have underestimated the range of Bach's historical resonance and the artful variousness with which his influence was absorbed.

28. Ibid., 182.
29. Ibid., 180.
30. See my "Back to Whom? Neoclassicism as Ideology," *Nineteenth-Century Music* 16 (1993): 286–302; rpt. in Taruskin, *The Danger of Music and Other Anti-Utopian Essays* (Berkeley and Los Angeles: University of California Press, 2008), 382–405.

III

To move on from Odoyevsky to Sergey Taneyev, from the gifted, leisured dilettante to the consummate bustling professional, is already to encapsulate the evolution of Russian music and musical life on the European model in the nineteenth century. Bach furnishes as good a prism as any through which to view that progression.

A musician like Taneyev could not have existed in Odoyevsky's Russia. The first Russian conservatory opened its doors in 1862, in St. Petersburg, the imperial capital. (Anton Rubinstein was its director, Chaikovsky a member of its first graduating class.) Taneyev was then five years old and living in Vladimir, an old cathedral town about 200 kilometers from Moscow. By the time he was a prodigy of nine, and living in Moscow, there was a conservatory there, too. Taneyev was enrolled in *its* first entering class, and Chaikovsky was one of his teachers. He graduated ten years later with the institution's first gold medal. He spent the next three years as a touring piano virtuoso, but when Chaikovsky resigned his teaching post in 1878, Taneyev replaced him as an instructor of harmony, and stayed at the conservatory until 1905, eventually as professor of composition and briefly, in the late 1880s, as its director. Among his pupils were the three great pianist-composers of late nineteenth-century Russia: Rachmaninoff, Scriabin, and Medtner.

Bach's music was a staple of conservatory instruction in Moscow, as it was everywhere; but not until Taneyev did a Russian composer regard Bach as more than a theory assignment, a benchmark of technical mastery, or a model of *stile antico*. Chaikovsky, after whom the Moscow Conservatory is now named, went through a rigorous mill of counterpoint study and seemed to gesture toward Bach in at least one of his mature compositions: the first Suite for Orchestra, op. 43, composed in 1878, which begins with a prelude (or Introduzione) and fugue, in a recognizably Bachian "pathetic" style—recognizable, that is, by virtue of its high level of chromaticism, full of diminished fifths and sevenths, putting a listener in mind of Bach's Chromatic Fantasy or the B-minor Fugue from Book I of the *Well-Tempered Clavier* (Ex. 7.3). The real model here, however, as Chaikovsky confided to his patron Mme von Meck, was not Bach directly, but rather the now forgotten Franz Lachner (1803–90), a specialist in orchestral suites, who included fugal movements or some other sort of neo-Baroque stylization in most of them.[31]

Rimsky-Korsakov, the most academically inclined member of the Mighty Kuchka—not a graduate of the St. Petersburg Conservatory (now named for him) but long a professor there—learned his Bachian lessons well, indeed better than most conservatory pupils, because he was an assiduous autodidact; but like most professionals of his generation, he did not attach a great deal of importance to

---

31. See Chaikovsky's letter to von Meck of 25 August 1878, in P. I. Chaikovsky, *Perepiska s N. F. fon-Mekk*, vol. 1 (Moscow and Leningrad: Academia, 1934), 421.

EXAMPLE 7.3. Chaikovsky, Suite no. 1, opening bassoon solo.

EXAMPLE 7.4. Rimsky-Korsakov, Fugue on B-A-C-H, op. 10, no. 6.

what Bach had taught him. He was content to flaunt Bach in fairly trivial *tours de force* like the little fugue in Example 7.4, from a set of six pieces on B-A-C-H (op. 10) through which he joined (but not really) the distinguished company that included Beethoven, Schumann, Liszt, and Reger, and would eventually encompass Schoenberg and Webern.

This little fugue was the last in the set, preceded by a waltz, an intermezzo, a scherzo, a nocturne, and a prelude to herald the fugue. At once cleverer and even more trivial is another B-A-C-H trifle by Rimsky-Korsakov, from the set of so-called *Paraphrases on an Unchanging Theme* for piano duet (that theme being *Tati-Tati*, the Russian version of *Chopsticks*), in which Rimsky-Korsakov was joined by a cohort of old colleagues and young pupils (Ex. 7.5).

EXAMPLE 7.5. Rimsky-Korsakov, Fughetta (*Paraphrases*).

These little jokes are not the work of a Bach lover. Rimsky made no bones about that, writing in his diary, after attending a performance of the *St. John Passion* at St. Petersburg's Lutheran church: "Beautiful music, but it is music of an altogether different age and to sit through an entire oratorio at the present time is impossible. I am convinced that not only I, but everyone is bored, and if they say they enjoyed it then they're just lying through their teeth."[32]

Thus Rimsky-Korsakov on the likes of Odoyevsky and Taneyev. But even the professed Bach lovers of Rimsky's generation had limits. Vladimir Vasil'yevich

---

32. Mark Yankovsky et al., eds., *Rimskiy-Korsakov: Issledovaniya, materialï, pis'ma* (Moscow: Muzgiz, 1954), 2:16–17.

Stasov, the librarian and arts journalist, so loudly swore by old Sebastian that his friends called him "Bach"—so one finds him referred to in letters by Musorgsky and Rimsky-Korsakov. But as Rimsky-Korsakov himself reported in his memoirs, Stasov only liked the expositions in Bach's fugues, and would complain, when the voices began to weave freely, that "Bach is beginning to grind flour."[33] Like the pronouncement attributed to Debussy, that the development section in symphonic movements was the place where one could go out for a cigarette, Stasov's upholds spontaneous invention over skilled routine, the stance usually cited, in France and Russia alike, as the mark of a "realist" tendency.[34]

But in the same volume of memoirs, Rimsky-Korsakov eventually reconsiders a bit. Recalling the disparaging consensus among the Mighty Kuchka that J. S. Bach was "petrified, yes, even a mere musico-mathematical, feelingless, and deadly nature, composing like a very machine,"[35] he puts it down to immaturity, their failure to realize that "counterpoint had been the poetic language of that composer of genius; that is, it was just as ill-judged to reproach him with his use of counterpoint as to upbraid a poet for using verse and rhyme . . . instead of employing free and easy prose."[36] That reassessment only took Rimsky-Korsakov as far as tolerance. Devotion and sincere emulation had to await Taneyev's generation; but if their fervent dedication passed Rimsky-Korsakov's threshold of comprehension, it was nevertheless a result of a process to which Rimsky-Korsakov had made a fundamental contribution.

IV

That process was academicization, to give it an ugly but precise name. Bach entered the full creative consciousness of practical Russian musicians, including the ones who practiced the art of composition, by way of conservatory curricula. Curricula at both Russian conservatories included courses in music history and aesthetics, and plenty of "theory." The earliest teachers of these subjects were figures the maverick composers of the period loved to hate, and historians of Russian music have often followed suit, marking them out as objects of derision. But we (we academics, that is) needn't join in the mockery of our own kind, especially when their labors bore such magnificent fruit as Taneyev and his works.

33. Rimsky-Korsakov, *My Musical Life*, trans. Judah A. Joffe (London: Eulenburg Books, 1974), 152.
34. See Taruskin, *The Oxford History of Western Music* (New York: Oxford University Press, 2005), 3:22. The Debussy remark has long been engrained in concertgoer lore; written sources I have been able to locate only testify to that status. Charles Rosen, for one, quotes it repeatedly; see, e.g., *Critical Entertainments* (Cambridge, MA: Harvard University Press, 2000), 117; and *The Joy of Playing, the Joy of Thinking* (with Catherine Temerson) (Cambridge, MA: Harvard University Press, 2020), 58.
35. Rimsky-Korsakov, *My Musical Life*, 20.
36. Ibid., 151.

The first such Russian music theorist, and probably the first pedagogue to offer public instruction in harmony and counterpoint in the Russian language, was Nikolai Zaremba (1821–79), who had studied in Berlin with Adolf Bernhard Marx, and who was mercilessly lampooned by Musorgsky—who, obviously, hadn't studied with him—in his song *Rayok* (The Peepshow). When Zaremba ascended into administration, as we now like to say, to become the conservatory's second director (after Rubinstein, the founder), the job of theory instructor went to Hermann Laroche (or German Avgustovich Larosh, 1845–1904), a member of the conservatory's first graduating class and a bigger name in history than Zaremba thanks to his work, later repeatedly anthologized, as a newspaper music critic. He was a close friend of his classmate Chaikovsky, and the Mighty Kuchka's most notorious *bête noire*.

Of course, Zaremba and Laroche amply reciprocated the animosity they inspired in the autodidact composers of the Kuchka generation. It only strengthened their conviction that the only way for Russia to catch up as a music-producing nation would be to recapitulate the phylogeny of European music with a very rigorous, historically oriented program of theory instruction based on counterpoint, starting with Palestrina and even earlier polyphonic masters, and proceeding through Bach. In addition to *Gradus ad Parnassum*, the eighteenth-century classic counterpoint text by Johann Joseph Fux, which he translated into Russian, Laroche used Carl Proske's then-new multivolume anthology *Musica Divina*, a foundational publication of the Cecilian movement. When Laroche transferred from the St. Petersburg Conservatory to the one in Moscow, Taneyev became his pupil in this course.

As we all know, and as those of us who have taught music history at conservatories know all too well, most conservatory students regard these courses as a waste. I have no illusions that things were different at the Moscow Conservatory in the 1870s. But Sergey Taneyev was that one student in ten thousand who catch fire from that study; and it is probably fair to say that he profited more from it than any other conservatory pupil in history. He founded his composing technique on the principles he learned in music history class, God bless him. But what makes him appear to me all the more extraordinary is that this unrivaled assimilation of old contrapuntal practices and devices did not infuse Taneyev's music with antiquarian mannerisms. Like Bruckner before him, he adopted Bachian procedures without adopting a Bachian style. His music is stylistically of its time, and in this way he does seem fairly to merit the sobriquet that he has long been saddled with in superficial historical accounts: the Russian Brahms. Usually it is the fact that Taneyev, very atypically for a Russian composer, wrote a great deal of chamber music that is cited as a reason for calling him that. Nor will it come as a surprise, especially to those who have read their Harold Bloom, to learn that Taneyev detested the soubriquet and (although he had made his debut as a pianist in

Brahms's D-minor Concerto) never lost an opportunity to make his distaste for Brahms manifest.

Nevertheless, the textural and motivic richness his music achieved thanks to his contrapuntal predilections is indeed something that he shared with Brahms, and with Max Reger among his younger contemporaries. But his being Russian and therefore an outsider to the insularly German reception of Bach is what spared him (I would say) the heaviness and the at times risible overloading that many have deplored in Reger.[37] By wearing an equal erudition far more lightly, Taneyev deserves to be described the way Rimsky-Korsakov described Bach himself, as one for whom "counterpoint [was] the poetic language."

Taneyev also surmounted the dichotomies of German music, including the one that affected Bach reception in the nineteenth century, in a way that his being Russian may have actually facilitated. There is no German composer of the nineteenth century (that is, after Beethoven) who made equally prominent and lasting contributions to both the symphonic and operatic repertoires. Outside of Germany there was Saint-Saëns, there was Dvořák, and there was Chaikovsky. And there was Taneyev, whose music has never been canonical or even repertorial outside of Russia, but who has at least one symphony (the fourth, in C minor) and one opera (his only one, *Oresteia* after Aeschylus) firmly ensconced in the Russian repertory.

What this has to do with Bach is that, as Walter Frisch pointed out at the 1996 Bach conference at Berkeley, there was a dual Bach reception in Germany. "One stream," Frisch said, "is dominated by the image of Bach as absolute musician[, k]nown mainly for and through his keyboard works." This was the Bach of Tieck, Wackenroder, Hoffmann (and, as we've seen, Odoyevsky). Frisch quoted Dahlhaus in somewhat dogmatic support: "The 'true" Bach of the nineteenth century ... was the instrumental composer: a 'composer's composer' whose works were held up as paradigms of absolute music."[38] The other stream flowed, a bit later, from Mendelssohn's performance of the *St. Matthew Passion,* and emphasized Bach's role as a church musician, which meant acknowledging the affective and pathetic content of his music, and its morally edifying properties. Frisch's point in raising this issue was to emphasize Brahms's participation in both streams of Bach reception, beginning "in the early 1850s as a composer of 'absolute' or abstract keyboard works[; t]hen, beginning in the later 1850s, he turned his attention to vocal works that, while not liturgical, are clearly imbued with Protestant religious spirit." In this

---

37. For a sensitive treatment of that aspect of Reger's music (and one that also takes note of Harold Bloom's interpretation of creative reception), see Walter Frisch, "Bach, Brahms, and the Emergence of Musical Modernism," in Marissen (ed.), *Bach Perspectives* 3:109–31, esp. 121–27.

38. Ibid., 110; the quotation from Dahlhaus is from "Zur Entstehung der romantischen Bach-Deutung," in idem, *Klassische und romantische Musikästhetik* (Laaber: Laaber-Verlag, 1988).

way, Frisch concluded, "in an instance of ontogeny recapitulating phylogeny, Brahms's early career reflects the nineteenth-century evolution of Bach reception."[39]

Taneyev, whom I have already characterized as an unusually versatile composer despite the relative slenderness of his published output, and who of course came to maturity a couple of decades later than Brahms, did not so much reflect Brahms's evolution as synthesize its components from the beginning. His career was short. The earliest work he let out (as opus 1) was composed in 1884, when he was in his late twenties, and his last completed work, opus 36, was composed over the period 1913–15, and was finished only weeks before Taneyev attended the funeral of the even shorter-lived Scriabin, where he caught a cold that turned into pneumonia and led finally to the heart seizure that ended his life at the age of fifty-eight: an active career lasting barely thirty years from start to finish.

Both Taneyev's opus 1 and his opus 36, his alpha and omega, are concerted choral works on religious themes. The first, *Ioann Damaskin* (John of Damascus), named after the eighth-century Greek church father and homilist known in Slavonic by the epithet Zlatoust ("Golden-mouthed"), is a cantata on funeral verses extracted from a longer poem of the same name by Alexey Konstantinovich Tolstoy, a cousin of the famous novelist. Taneyev was an intimate friend of Lev Tolstoy and his household (indeed, rumors swirled about him and Sophia Andreyevna, the novelist's wife). The cantata is dedicated to the memory of Nikolai Rubinstein, whom Taneyev succeeded as the director of the Moscow Conservatory. Although he had been composing prolifically from an early age, this cantata was the apprehensively self-critical Taneyev's public debut as a composer.

His swan song was in many ways its twin. Entitled *Po prochtenii psalma* (Upon the Reading of the Psalm), it is another multimovement setting of a Christian homiletic text by a nineteenth-century Russian poet, in this case Alexey Stepanovich Khomyakov (1804–50), best known as a religious philosopher. The main difference between these two large choral works is not one of style but of scale. The later one is vast: more than twice as long as its not-insubstantial predecessor, scored for a double mixed choir and very large orchestra, and consisting of an almost unrelieved series of elaborate choral *tours de force*. It was commissioned by Serge Koussevitzky for his then fledgling publishing company, but because Taneyev died so soon after the very successful premiere, the piece had not yet been published when the revolution disrupted the Russian culture industry; and when things settled down, the atmosphere had turned toxic for religious publications in Russia. Taneyev's final masterpiece languished unissued in full score until 1960.

The opening and closing choruses in *Ioann Damaskin* encompass between them the full range of Taneyev's Bachian technique and style. The finale, which evokes the raising of the dead, is a skillful, very energetic, but ultimately orthodox

39. Frisch, "Bach, Brahms, and the Emergence of Musical Modernism," 111.

EXAMPLE 7.6. Taneyev, *Ioann Damaskin*, final chorus, voice parts only. Original text: *V tot den', kogda truba vostrubit mira prestavlenye primi usopshego raba v tvoi nebesnïye selenya.* Translation: On the day when the trumpet shall trumpet the end of the world, admit Thy departed servant to Thy heavenly dwelling.

EXAMPLE 7.6. (continued)

school fugue that ends, impressively, with augmentations and strettos (Ex. 7.6, orchestral doubling omitted).

More characteristic of Taneyev, as he later developed, is the first chorus, which (after a hymnlike orchestral introduction based on a traditional Orthodox funeral chant) describes the groping of a lost soul toward the right path. This chorus, too, uses fugal technique; but as Rimsky-Korsakov would say, it uses the technique less formally, more poetically. The exposition has an independent orchestral accompaniment, and the subject is a melody quite typical of the Russian music of Taneyev's time and place (that is, the Moscow of the so-called Silver Age), reminiscent, I think you will agree, of Rachmaninoff (one of Taneyev's pupils)—but for those in the know (and there were not many in Russia at the time), there is hidden within it an allusion to the *St. Matthew Passion* (Ex. 7.7).

I noticed the reference to the *Matthew Passion* (mm. 5–6 plus pickup) from the first time I listened to the piece, but could not quite pinpoint the spot. It tantalized

EXAMPLE 7.7. Taneyev, *Ioann Damaskin*, opening chorus (*Idu v nevedomïy mne put'*/I travel an unknown road).

me for years until I finally consulted Michael Marissen, the most erudite Bachian I know, who easily identified it as the second phrase (" . . . wenn deine Jünger töricht streiten") from the accompanied recitative "Du lieber Heiland du" preceding "Büss und Reu," the first aria in the work (Ex. 7.8). Despite that homage, Taneyev's chorus could no more be described as partaking of a *stile antico* than could Beethoven's Sonata no. 3 for Piano and Cello, op. 69, which alludes just as unmistakably to the aria "Es ist vollbracht" from the other Bach Passion, the *St. John*.[40]

Before proceeding to the instrumental side of the Bachian dialectic, we might have a look at Taneyev's favorite Bach fugue. How do I know it was his favorite? He never actually called it that, any more than he (or Beethoven) cited his sources for

---

40. For fascinating details, see Christopher Reynolds, *Motives for Allusion: Context and Content in Nineteenth-Century Music* (Cambridge, MA: Harvard University Press, 2003), 1–2, 147–61.

EXAMPLE 7.8. Bach, St. Matthew Passion, no. 5 (accompanied recitative, "Du lieber Heiland, du").

Bachian allusions, but in preparation for writing this essay I put myself through the ordeal of tracing every reference to Bach in the three-volume edition of Taneyev's diaries, which he kept from 1894 to 1909. [41] They are truly private diaries and do not, for the most part, make for exciting reading. As a record of daily activities they are as repetitive as the diaries of any academic might be (any one of ours, for example). Thankfully there is an index in the edition, by the outstanding Soviet musicologist Lyudmila Zinov'yevna Korabel'nikova, so I did not have to skim the three volumes page by page; but since Bach was daily bread for Taneyev, there were a couple of hundred references to run down. In the end it was a rewarding pursuit, because a certain fugue emerged as the one Taneyev returned to most frequently in teaching, in private conversation, and for his own contemplation at the keyboard, and by a very considerable margin. I doubt whether anyone would guess that it was the one in A minor (no. 20) from the first book of the *Well-Tempered Clavier*.

The A minor is not one of the most often played, and certainly not one of the most often praised, among Bach's compositions, but it is one of his most elaborate fugues. Indeed, it is show-offy almost to the point of self-satire. Not only am I tempted to hazard the assertion, unsupported by an actual check (and therefore unhazarded), that there are more *stretti* in it than in any other fugue from the

---

41. S. I. Taneyev, *Dnevniki*, ed. L. Korabel'nikova, 3 vols. (Moscow: Muzïka, 1981–85).

so-called *48*, but it also sports the gaudiest inversion to which Bach ever subjected a subject. When its dramatic downward leap of a diminished seventh is answered by its ascending counterpart (a major seventh), I cannot think we are not meant at least inwardly to laugh. And yet, withal, the fugue produces intense exhilaration in me, as it demonstrably did in Sviatoslav Richter, whose euphoric recording is available on YouTube, and as I vividly imagine it doing to Taneyev, whose manically virtuosic Prelude and Fugue for Piano in G-sharp Minor, op. 29 (1910), seems to vie with it in athletic jubilation, and as (I am confident) it will elicit in any reader who is moved to go online and hear Richter play it, emitting the kind of sounds Taneyev must also have produced when playing the fugue. As an added bonus, one of the YouTube postings provides a color-coded analysis to make sure we don't miss any of the jokes.[42]

Old Stasov was right: this fugue grinds enough flour to feed the multitude, and Taneyev must have pounded away at it as exuberantly as Richter. Surely Taneyev was drawn to technical *tours de force*, both Bach's and his own, not only for the chance to display his mastery, but because of the elation such displays can engender. Memoirs of Taneyev always emphasize his lusty sense of humor (something at which his glum-faced photographs never hint, and which he shared with that other notorious sourpuss Rachmaninoff), and his unpublished works, often described in the literature on him, include many funny items comparable to Rossini's *Péchés de vieillesse,* such as the one (which I am determined to see one day) that treats themes from Chaikovsky's ballets the way Taneyev treated his own themes in his famous sketchbooks: combining them in myriad contrapuntal montages by applying the principles he codified in his celebrated textbook *Podvizhnoy kontrapunkt strogogo pis'ma* (Invertible Counterpoint in the Strict Style).[43] Taneyev was one of those blessed souls for whom John Cage spoke when he told an interviewer that his work was also his entertainment.

For a glimpse of Taneyev at his most flamboyantly contrapuntal and most entertaining, consider two excerpts from the last movement of his String Quintet in G Major (with two cellos), op. 14, composed (simultaneously with another quintet, in C major, with two violas) in 1900–1901.[44] This finale is a huge set of variations on an innocent little theme with a decidedly folkish flavor, such as one might stereotypically expect a Russian composer to employ (Ex. 7.9a). What one would not expect to issue from such a theme (or such a composer) as the final variation would be a triple fugue, with all three subjects based on motives extracted from the folkish theme (Ex. 7.9b). The very excessiveness of the idea is its own excuse, if not its reward.

---

42. www.youtube.com/watch?v=Qj4lPhfG98o&index=18&list=PL9152C783D22D5468 at 0:54.
43. S. I. Taneyev, *Podvizhnoy kontrapunkt strogogo pis'ma* (Leipzig: Belaïeff, 1909).
44. It can be found on YouTube, for example here: www.youtube.com/watch?v=8mkE4IqVyeg.

EXAMPLE 7.9A. Taneyev, String Quintet in G, op. 14, no. 1, IV, Tema.

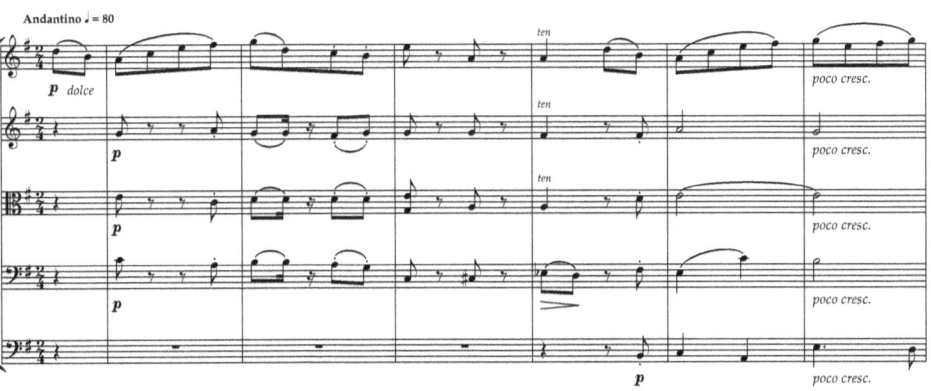

But that is not the only surprise. There is a spot in the ninth and final variation—or, rather, interrupting it—that made me gasp the first time I listened to the piece many years ago: a mysterious passage of *tremolandi* that barges into the fugue right before the inevitable montage of all three subjects, and which turns out to be a quotation from Rimsky-Korsakov's "symphonic picture" *Sadko* (1867). It is a famous theme, which Rimsky reused almost thirty years later when writing an opera on the same subject, the legend of the seafaring merchant of Novgorod whose ship sinks to the bottom of the ocean, where he meets and marries the daughter of the Sea King (Ex. 7.10a). The theme is generally taken to be an illustration of Sadko's underwater plunge, and it has a unique historical significance—one to which, as it happens, I am particularly attuned—since it was the first occurrence in

EXAMPLE 7.9B. Variation 9, Fuga a tre soggetti (beginning of exposition).

Rimsky's music (by his explicit avowal in a letter to Balakirev) of the scale of alternating tones and semitones that he had educed from the work of Liszt, and that we now call octatonic (Ex. 7.10b).[45] Like the allusion to Bach's Passion recitative in *Ioann Damaskin*, it is certainly an homage (corroborated in the quintet's dedication to Rimsky-Korsakov and an actual footnote acknowledging the quotation) and a sort of pun on the intervallic structure of the first fugue subject, which is built on an embellished diminished-seventh chord (one possible way of construing an octatonic scale). The quotation was evidently prompted by a trip Taneyev took to St. Petersburg in January 1901, where he attended a rehearsal of Rimsky's opera at the Mariyinsky Theater.[46]

I would hope it evident that Taneyev deserves release from the Russian ghetto and recognition alongside Busoni and Reger as one of Bach's main late nineteenth-century votaries. But neither should he be classified on that account as an eccentric Russian "non-nationalist," as is so often done, because that only confines and belittles him in another, even more invidious way.[47] As we have seen, his work freely crossed the borders we have erected since. Nor did his Bachian "universalist" affinities prevent his being as committed a Russian patriot as Odoyevsky, with whom he shared a strong attachment to the Orthodox Church.

One of the most intriguing entries in Taneyev's diary (16 March 1895) reports a dispute that arose in conversation with the visiting French conductor Édouard Juda Colonne (1838–1910), for whom Taneyev and Rachmaninoff had just played, on two pianos, Chaikovsky's B-minor Symphony (the *Pathétique*) and his posthumous, as yet unpublished, Third Piano Concerto. Colonne objected to the coda of the concerto's first movement as being out of character with the rest. Taneyev wrote:

> I told him that this was a theme in the style of a Russian song. He said that one shouldn't put folk songs into one's works; that in countries with a rich folk music (Spain, Hungary) professional music is in a bad way; that folk music interferes with musical progress. I said that it is not that folk music interferes with professional music, but on the contrary, that the latter interferes with folk music, that the relationship between them is similar to the relationship between a vernacular and a literary

---

45. For the letter, see Sergey Mikhailovich Lyapunov, "Perepiska M. A. Balakireva i N. A. Rimskogo-Korsakova (1862–1898)," *Muzïkal'nïy sovremennik* 7 (March 1916): 92. For the coining of the term *octatonic*, see Arthur Berger, "Problems of Pitch Organization in Stravinsky," *Perspectives of New Music* 2 (1963): 11–42.

46. Lyudmila Korabel'nikova, *Tvorchestvo S. I. Taneyeva* (Moscow: Muzïka, 1986), 155.

47. For elaboration of this point see R. Taruskin, "Non-Nationalists and Other Nationalists," *Nineteenth-Century Music* 35 (2010–11): 132–143; rpt. in Taruskin, *Russian Music at Home and Abroad* (Oakland: University of California Press, 2016), 33–51—an essay that originated as a talk given at a conference at the University of Leeds, called "Non-Nationalist Russian Opera," that was organized around a performance of Taneyev's *Oresteia*.

EXAMPLE 7.10A. Taneyev, String Quintet in G, op. 14, no. 1, IV: Quotation from *Sadko* at [117].

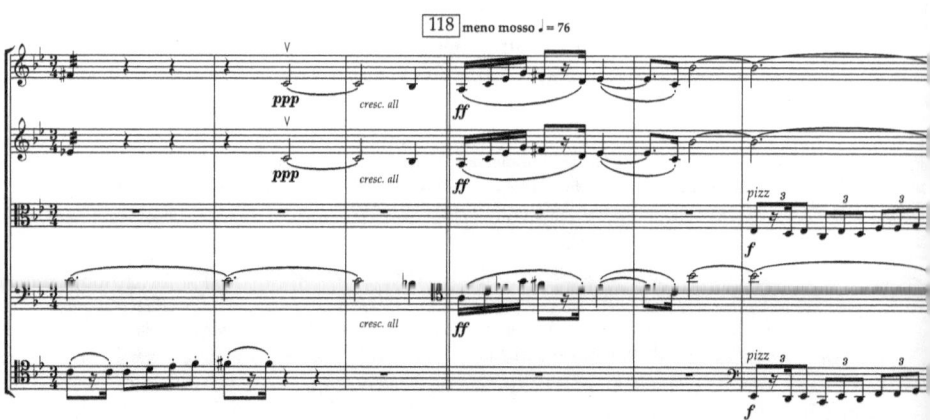

EXAMPLE 7.10B. Rimsky-Korsakov, *Sadko* (1867) (Violin I).

language, that in the middle ages France and Germany were rich in folk songs and these songs helped form the musical language of the contrapuntalist composers. He said that we don't find folk songs in Bach, Mozart, Haydn, [or] Beethoven. I said that Bach wrote many chorales whose themes were mainly folk songs, [and] that since our [Russian] music is young, our composers should work a lot with Russian themes, so as to develop an original style. He said that Russian composers have used enough folk songs in their compositions and that now they can create an international music. He told me how Lalo took the melodies in one of Grieg's works for folk [melodies] and used them in his *Rapsodie norvégienne*. In fact, the tunes were Grieg's own. When Grieg came to Paris and heard the rhapsody he was offended. When they met, Lalo went to one side, Grieg to the other.[48]

Taneyev's side in this argument is not the side a "non-nationalist" would take. It shows that the issue under dispute, so dear to the hearts of us historians, was not really an issue for Russian composers, only for us (or for visiting Frenchmen). Taneyev wrote many contrapuntal exercises, and even real fugues, on themes from folk songs, and as we have heard, his music is full of Russian resonances along with Bachian ones.

But why should that surprise us? Bach was indeed the universal composer, and what could be better proof?

---

48. Taneyev, *Dnevniki*, 1:77. Lalo's *Rapsodie norvégienne* can be found, like everything else, on YouTube, for example here: www.youtube.com/watch?v=2VCTNR3kI6M.

8

So Much More Than a Composer

Der Erneuerer des einfachen Dramas, der Entdecker der Stellung der Künste in der wahren menschlichen Gesellschaft, der dichtende Erklärer vergangener Lebensbetrachtungen, der Philosoph, der Historiker, der Ästhetiker und Kritiker Wagner, der Meister der Sprache, der Mytholog und Mythopoet, . . .

The reviver of pure drama, the discoverer of the place of art in true human society, the poetic exponent of bygone views of life, Wagner the philosopher, the historian, the aesthete and the critic, the master of language, the student and creator of myths, . . .

—NIETZSCHE, RICHARD WAGNER IN BAYREUTH, CHAP. 3

I

Is Wagner reception even a subject for musicologists? From Nietzsche's description, one would never know he was a composer. Literary scholars and social historians have always been in the forefront of Wagner reception studies. Most previous research on Wagner's reception on Slavic soil has been the work of literary historians, and Rosamund Bartlett's *Wagner and Russia* appears in a series called "Cambridge Studies in Russian Literature."[1] The book to which this essay originally served as foreword, *Wagner in Russia, Poland, and the Czech Lands: Musical, Literary and Cultural Perspectives,* was unusual in its distribution, with half the contents devoted to musical matters—that is, reception of Wagner by composers. But, very much as usual, the musical contents of the volume were the coolest and the literary-philosophical the most heated. What might that tell us about Wagner? about music? about literature or philosophy?

First published as foreword to Stephen Muir and Anastasia Belina-Johnson, eds., *Wagner in Russia, Poland, and the Czech Lands: Musical, Literary, and Cultural Perspectives* (Aldershot: Ashgate, 2013), xv–xxxii.

1. Rosamund Bartlett, *Wagner and Russia* (Cambridge: Cambridge University Press, 1995).

With few exceptions, composers were not Wagner's most faithful adepts. Even the best-disposed felt the need to resist. Think of poor Debussy, trying—and failing—to expunge "the ghost of old Klingsor" from *Pelléas*.[2] Think of Schoenberg, often placed by music historians (and not without reason) among the adepts, and his famous essay "Brahms the Progressive," which could just as well have been titled "Wagner the Reactionary."[3] But we are all like that. There is a Wagner hater inside of every Wagner lover. Think of Stravinsky, Wagner's Antichrist (as he loved to say), railing relentlessly against Wagner and "le fameux *Gesammt Kunstwerk*" in his *Poétique musicale*. He got his start, and was profoundly shaped, within an organization, Diaghilev's, wholly devoted to "the idea of the Gesamtkunstwerk, ... for which our circle was ready to give its soul."[4] Wagner, as his many Jewish fans will readily attest, is someone toward whom it is impossible not to be ambivalent.

Russians tried especially hard to overcome their ambivalence and reject Wagner outright after an initial fascination—and not just the musicians among them. There was no greater despiser of Wagner in all the world than Lev Tolstoy, whose late animosity was at least the equal of Nietzsche's early adoration and whose aesthetic treatise *What Is Art?* (1897) contains Wagner mockery much wickeder than Anna Russell's,[5] because it is motivated by real hatred. For Nietzsche and Tolstoy alike, Wagner represented the most powerful challenge to submissive, pacific Christianity, toward which the one was as implacably hostile as the other was devoted. But there was certainly no shortage of purely musical antagonism toward Wagner in Russia.

His concerts, during his single tour of St. Petersburg and Moscow in 1863, were mobbed, successful, and for Wagner very pleasurable as well as lucrative. It was a case of mutual exoticism. "Here I am in Asia, my child, actually in Asia!" Wagner wrote back from Moscow to a woman with whom he was then flirting. "The Kremlin is a convoluted mass of the most amazing buildings, straight out of the Arabian Nights: from the top you can look down on a town of 400,000 inhabitants with

---

2. Letter to Ernest Chausson, 2 October 1893, in Claude Debussy, *Lettres 1884–1918*, ed. F. Lesure (Paris, 1980), 55; for an interpretation, see Carolyn Abbate, "*Tristan* in the Composition of *Pelléas*," *Nineteenth-Century Music* 5 (1981–82): 117–40, still the best study of "anxiety of influence" in music.

3. It can be found in *Style and Idea: Selected Writings of Arnold Schoenberg*, ed. Leonard Stein, trans. Leo Black (London: Faber & Faber, 1975), 398–441.

4. Robert Craft, "My Life with Stravinsky," *New York Review of Books*, 10 June 1982, 6 (for "Wagner's Antichrist"); Igor Stravinsky, *Poetics of Music in the Form of Six Lessons*, bilingual ed. (Cambridge, MA: Harvard University Press, 1970), 76 (for "le fameux *Gesammt Kunstwerk*"); Alexandre Benois, *Reminiscences of the Russian Ballet*, trans. Mary Britnieva (London: Putnam, 1941), 370–71.

5. See, e.g., "The Ring of the Nibelungs (an Analysis)," on *The Anna Russell Album?* (CBS Masterworks, MG 31199, 1972); first released on *Anna Russell Sings! Again?* (Columbia Masterworks ML 4733, 1953); also at www.youtube.com/watch?v=CM33rgC2Fek.

800 churches, many of which have up to 5 towers: everything is very colorful, bright, golden, domed—strange & wonderful."[6]

To the Russians it was Wagner who was strange and wonderful. His programs included excerpts from operas (*Die Walküre, Siegfried, Tristan und Isolde, Die Meistersinger*) that were as yet unperformed in their entirety or still in progress. His second Russian concert, in St. Petersburg on 10 March 1863, was the first occasion at which Wagner presented the *Tristan* prelude joined to the Act III *Isoldens Verklärung* minus Isolde, to form the "Prelude+Liebestod." Alexander Serov, soon to make his debut as a composer with the opera *Judith*, but as yet known mainly as an eccentric St. Petersburg critic and often written off as Wagner's lackey, took heart: "The very novelty of Wagner's music, its unusual and unprecedented, unimaginable boldness in orchestration ... carried the entire audience away to the most extreme limits of ardent appreciation," he wrote.[7] Moscow's most sophisticated musician, actually more of a littérateur, was Prince Vladimir Fyodorovich Odoyevsky, known as "the Russian Hoffmann" for his fantastic stories, but (again like the actual E. T. A. Hoffmann) also a dilettante composer and music scholar. He saw in Wagner's enthusiastic reception the dawn of a new era: "Is there a hope," he wrote, "that instead of Verdi's strings of polkas we will now be able to listen to real operas by such people as Gluck, Mozart, Méhul, Weber, Beethoven and Wagner?"[8]

Not quite yet. Most of the published or otherwise recorded comments from listeners in 1863 attested merely to the satisfaction of their curiosity. Now we know what he's like, most reviewers agreed, and he's too German, or too theoretical, or too utopian for us.[9] Wagner had little chance of influencing the course of Russian composing at the time. It was the precise moment when Russian music was going through the process of academicizing. The best established Russian composer, and the country's principal musical academic, Anton Rubinstein, had long since declared himself opposed to the "New German School," and he educated his pupils, who then included the twenty-two-year-old Chaikovsky, to share his view, or at least compose as if they did. (Unlike Rimsky-Korsakov or Taneyev, Chaikovsky never came round to Wagner. After witnessing the first Bayreuth *Ring* in 1876, he complained: "Before, music strove to delight people—now they are tormented and

---

6. To Mathilde Maier, 21/22 March 1863, in *Selected Letters of Richard Wagner*, trans. and ed. Stewart Spence and Barry Millington (New York: W. W. Norton, 1988), 555–56.

7. Alexander Nikolayevich Serov, "Rikhard Vagner i yego kontsertï v Peterburge," *Yakor'* 2 (1863): 34; quoted in Bartlett, *Wagner and Russia*, 32.

8. Vladimir Fyodorovich Odoyevsky, "Pervïy kontsert Vagnera v Moskve," *Nashe vremya* 57 (1863): 225; quoted in Bartlett, *Wagner and Russia*, 33.

9. See comments by Feofil Matveyevich Tolstoy (Rostislav), Nikolai Alexandrovich Mel'gunov, and others collected by Bartlett in *Wagner and Russia*, 29–33.

exhausted.")[10] The incipient Balakirev circle (then calling itself the "New Russian School" but soon to be christened the Mighty Kuchka) was jealous of their national independence and their direct line from Glinka, and saw Wagner, not unreasonably, as a colonizer. They clung to Berlioz and Liszt, non-Germans who could be upheld against the Teutonic invaders who staffed Rubinstein's orchestra and his conservatory.

Serov was the one committed Wagnerian among Russian musicians, but that was seen by his colleagues as a quirk. His determined maverick stance and his abrasive personality sooner alienated others from his enthusiasms than won them over. When he pushed the score of *Tannhäuser* on Alexander Dargomïzhsky, then known as the composer of *Rusalka,* who was Wagner's exact contemporary and, like Serov, a maverick who proclaimed his idealistic devotion to dramatic truth, he was, to his great surprise, rebuffed. In Wagner's "unnatural vocal melodies," Dargomïzhsky wrote him, "and his overspiced though at times very amusing harmonizations, something tortured lurks: *will und kann nicht*. Truth is truth, all right, but taste as well is needed."[11] Perhaps the best summary of the attitude most Russian musicians adopted toward Wagner was Rachmaninoff's, gloomily following the score while Taneyev was playing through *Tristan* to his pupils: "1,500 pages to go."[12]

Social realities being what they were in Russia, most of the musicians Wagner actually met in 1863 were the titled dilettantes whom Rubinstein was then challenging for the leadership of Russian musical life: Prince Odoyevsky, Count Matvey Wielhorsky, Baron Boris Vietinghoff-Scheel, General Alexei Fyodorovich Lvov. He met them at soirées and tea parties, some arranged by the Grand Duchess Elena Pavlovna (or Hélène, as Wagner called her in his memoirs), the German-born aunt of Emperor Alexander II and Russia's reigning music patron.[13] And here we meet a theme that faithfully dogs the literature of Wagner reception. At the Grand Duchess's salon, which was attended as well by the Grand Duchess Maria Nikolayevna, the daughter of Alexander's predecessor Nicholas I, Wagner was asked to read the "poems" of his as yet unproduced operas, *Die Meistersinger* and the *Ring*.[14] Despite

---

10. Letter to his brother Modest from Vienna, 8 (20) August 1876; quoted in Alexander Poznansky, *Tchaikovsky: The Quest for the Inner Man* (New York: Schirmer Books, 1991), 181.

11. Letter written in the summer of 1856, in *A. S. Dargomïzhsky (1813–1869): Avtobiografiya—pis'ma—vospominaniya sovremennikov,* ed. Nikolai Findeyzen (Peterburg: Gosudarstvennoye izdatel'stvo, 1921), 43.

12. "Остается еще 1500 страниц" (Leonid Sabaneyev, *Vospominaniya o Skryabine* [Moscow: Klassika—XXI, 2000], 16).

13. Richard Wagner, *My Life* (New York: Dodd, Mead, 1927), 856.

14. Ibid., 856–59. In one of his letters from Russia to Mathilde Maier, Wagner testifies to additional social realities: he writes that the Grand Duchess's request to hear him read *Die Meistersinger* embarrassed him "since I had intentionally not brought a copy of it with me, in order not to be held up at the border," whereupon the Grand Duchess immediately ordered one from Berlin by telegraph (letter of 10 March 1863 from St. Petersburg, in *Selected Letters of Richard Wagner,* 552).

Wagner's reputation today as the great synthesizer of artistic media, he appeared in Russia in a dual guise: as conductor of chiefly orchestral concerts at which his music was displayed, and quite separately as a dramatic poet.

II

This was not the paradox it may today appear: first, because the Wagnerian synthesis, now irrevocably linked with the term *Gesamtkunstwerk,* had by 1863 yet to appear in its strongest form (the pre-1849 *Lohengrin* being as of then the latest Wagner opera to have been produced on stage). But second (and more importantly), because the term, as we use it today, was a product of Wagner's posthumous reception. Its meaning in common parlance no longer accords with Wagner's. Wagner coined it in *Die Kunst und die Revolution* (1849) and, both there and in *Das Kunstwerk der Zukunft* (also 1849), always spelled it *Gesammtkunstwerk* (cf. Stravinsky above). It referred in Wagner's own writings not to what we would now call a mixed-media performance but rather to an artwork that had been created as a collective enterprise—most specifically (in the originating phrase), *das große griechische Gesammtkunstwerk,* the collectively created ritual drama of the ancient Greeks, which performed the community-uniting function he wished his own works to achieve.[15]

The conservative Russians who wrote about him in 1863 appear to have understood the term correctly. For Nikolai Melgunov, the *Gesammtkunstwerk* amounted to "aesthetic communism"—something from which nothing individual could arise.[16] Nietzsche understood it this way too, as did Ignacy Matuszewski, Poland's foremost literary critic, and the many other Wagner-worshiping Polish Nietzscheans for whom the composer of *The Ring of the Nibelung* was "a demiurge who gathers all scattered elements around one centre of gravity."[17] Matuszewski's locution hints as well at the other meaning of *gesamt,* the one that Wagner associated not with the *Gesammtkunstwerk* but with what he called "universal" or "all-embracing" art (*allgemeinsame Kunst*), into which Beethoven had wrested music "from out her own peculiar element" by introducing sung words into his media-mixing Choral Symphony.[18] That, rather than Wagner's music as such, was the ideal to which the

---

15. Wagner, *Gesammelte Schriften und Dichtungen*, vol. 3 (Leipzig: C. F. W. Siegel's Musikalienhandlung, 1907), 29.

16. Quoted in Bartlett, *Wagner and Russia*, 33.

17. Ignacy Matuszewski, *Slowacki i nowa sztuka (modernizm)* (1904), ed. Samuel Sandler (Warsaw, 1965), 205; quoted in Radosław Okulicz-Kozaryn, "'Where the King Spirit becomes manifest': Stanisław Wyspiański in Search of the Polish Bayreuth," in Muir and Belina-Johnson (eds.), *Wagner in Russia, Poland, and the Czech Lands*, 137–58, at 146.

18. "Die letzte *Symphonie* Beethovens ist die Erlösung der Musik aus ihrem eigensten Elemente heraus zur allgemeinsamen Kunst" (*Das Kunstwerk der Zukunft*, in R. Wagner, *Sämtliche Schriften und Dichtungen*, Volks-Ausgabe, 6th ed. [Leipzig: Breitkopf & Härtel, n.d.], 3:96; translated phrase above from *Richard Wagner's Prose Works*, trans. William Ashton Ellis [London: Kegan Paul, Trench, Trübner, 1892], 1:126).

late nineteenth-century Wagnerians so ardently responded with grandiose syntheses of their own, in which music was generally far from the most potent or even conspicuous element.

Wagner most nearly approached—or, more precisely, adumbrated—what eventually became the primary meaning of the famous shibboleth in a passage from *Das Kunstwerk der Zukunft* where he describes the *große Gesammtkunstwerk*—not the ancient Greek version this time but its long-gestating successor—as a work that "must gather up each branch [or *genre*] of art and use it as a means, and in some sense to undo it for the common aim of *all*."[19] For Wagner this was merely a default aspect of the communally created *Gesammtkunstwerk*, which, as a collective and collaborative drama, necessarily combined and subsumed the contributions of its various collaborators and their respective media. This aspect of his theory resonated with the aesthetic idealism of earlier German romantics, who radically dissociated the poetic idea from its material realization or embodiment. "The aesthetics of one art is that of the others too," wrote Schumann in the persona of Florestan; "only the materials differ."[20]

In this soft version of the synthetic theory, Schumann sought justification for his own practice of "translating" novels by Jean Paul or E. T. A. Hoffmann into instrumental music. But the tradition on which Schumann relied included statements much closer to Wagner's eventual ideal of all-embracing synergistic union. Schelling's *Philosophie der Kunst* (1803–4) contains an endless sentence that (both in substance and in style) might well have been signed Wagner. It presages not only the link between the two meanings of *gesamt*, but also the strictures that Wagner would register against the contemporary opera in *Oper und Drama* (1851), his main theoretical work. "Let me just note," Schelling wrote ten years before Wagner was born,

> that the most perfect combination of all the arts, the union of poetry and music through song, of poetry and painting through dance, and they in turn synthesized, provides the most composite theatrical phenomenon such as the ancient drama was, of which there remains for us only a caricature, the opera, which in a higher and

---

19. *Richard Wagner's Prose Works*, 1:88. The whole passage in the original German: "Das große Gesamtkunstwerk, das alle Gattungen der Kunst zu umfassen hat, um jede einzelne dieser Gattungen als Mittel gewissermaßen zu verbrauchen, zu vernichten zu Gunsten der Erreichung des Gesamtzwecks aller, nämlich der unbedingten, unmittelbaren Darstellung der vollendeten menschlichen Natur— dieses große Gesamtkunstwerk erkennt er [d.h. unser Geist] nicht als die willkürliche mögliche That des Einzelnen, sondern als das nothwendig denkbare gemeinsame Werk der Menschen der Zukunft" (Wagner, *Sämtliche Schriften und Dichtungen*, 3:74).

20. Robert Schumann, *Gesammelte Schriften über Musik und Musiker* (Leipzig, 1854), 1:43; trans. Piero Weiss in P. Weiss and R. Taruskin, eds., *Music in the Western World: A History in Documents*, 2nd ed. (Belmont, CA: Thomson/Schirmer, 2008), 306.

nobler style, as regards poetry and the other competing arts, would be most likely to lead us back to the performance of the old drama with music and song.²¹

So that is Wagner pre-Wagner. The *fin-de-siècle* post-Wagner Wagner of the Wagnerians arose out of determined steps to expand the *Gesamtkunstwerk* beyond the point to which Wagner took it. They began almost immediately after the Master's death, as Adolphe Appia reports in his *Die Musik und die Inscenierung*, written (in French, as *La Musique et la mise en scène*) in 1892–97 and first published, in German, in 1899. Appia's innovations in stage direction and design were inspired, he tells us, by his exasperation at the "outmoded" sets, costumes, and stagings that prevented Wagner's operas from achieving their potential in Bayreuth. Wagner, he wrote, "considered the conventional forms of staging satisfactory—in need of reform in practice only, not in principle." Unaccountably, for Appia, "his sense of visual form was not appreciably developed beyond this convention," and therefore Appia did not hesitate to call Wagner's visual sense "a defect which explains why he failed to recognize the limitations of the decorative methods of our stage."²² He traced his attempts to improve upon the *Gesamtkunstwerk* to the bleak disappointment he experienced when, in the first production of *Parsifal* (1882), the forest half-light in the first-act "Verwandlung" was dispelled only to reveal a conventional "pasteboard temple" that destroyed for him the otherwise perfect chronotope (as Bakhtin would later call it) of epic antiquity—a mythic "time-location" that created the impression of another world, or a world beyond, both temporally and geographically closed off from ordinary contemporaneity.²³

In seeking a remedy for this deficiency and from the intrusion of mundane realism to which it gave rise, Appia sought in effect to help the Master scale a crucial wall: the one that Lessing had propounded in *Laocoön* between the time arts

---

21. Friedrich Wilhelm Joseph von Schelling, *The Philosophy of Art*, ed. and trans. Douglas W. Stott (Minneapolis: University of Minnesota Press, 1989), 280. The original German: "Ich bemerke nur noch, dass die vollkommenste Zusammensetzung aller Künste, die Vereinigung von Poesie und Musik durch Gesang, von Poesie und Malerei durch Tanz, selbst wieder synthetisiert die komponierteste Theatererscheinung ist, dergleichen das Drama des Altertums war, wovon uns nur eine Karikatur, die Oper, geblieben ist, die in höherem und edlerem Stil von Seiten der Poesie sowohl als der übrigen konkurrierenden Künste uns am ehesten zur Aufführung des alten mit Musik und Gesang verbundenen Dramas zurückführen könnte" (Schelling, *Philosophie der Kunst* [Darmstadt: Wissenschaftliche Buchgesellschaft, 1976], 380).

22. Adolphe Appia, *Music and the Art of the Theatre*, trans. Barnard Hewitt, ed. Robert W. Corrigan and Mary Douglas Dirks (Coral Gables, FL: University of Miami Press, 1962), 114.

23. The whole chronotope idea might be said to have arisen out of Gurnemanz's famously cryptic words to Parsifal in this scene—"Here time becomes space" (*Zum Raum wird hier die Zeit*). For Bakhtin's influential appropriation of the term (from Einstein's theory of relativity, he said), see his 1937 treatise "Forms of Time and of the Chronotope in the Novel" (Формы времени и хронотопа в романе), in *The Dialogic Imagination: Four Essays by M. M. Bakhtin*, ed. and trans. Caryl Emerson and Michael Holquist (Austin: University of Texas Press, 1981), 84–258.

(poetry, drama, music) and space arts (painting, sculpture, architecture). Through ever-fluctuant lighting Appia sought a dialectical synthesis whereby the visual elements could become as dynamic as the aural ones, and thus fulfill Wagner's vision of a union that effectively undid the differences between the media: light musicalized along with poetry, thus to perfect the synaesthetic correspondences that allied the Wagnerian synthesis with the eventual aims of symbolism. Once again the early German romantics were there first. In *Kreisleriana* (1814), E. T. A. Hoffmann had his title character, the Kapellmeister Kreisler, confide:

> Not so much in dreams as in the state of delirium that comes before sleep, especially when I've heard a lot of music, I discover a concord of colors, sounds and scents. It seems as if all had been produced in the same mysterious way by a beam of light and then were made to merge into a wonderful concert.—The scent of dark red carnations acts with strange magical force upon me; involuntarily I sink into a dreamy state and then hear from afar, swelling and again dying away, the deep tones of the basset horn.[24]

Some three decades later, Charles Baudelaire, the first symbolist and the first literary Wagnermaniac, recalled this passage (from memory, putting the oboe in place of the arcane basset horn) in his review of the 1846 salon, as "expressing perfectly my idea" of "a complete scale of colors and feelings,"[25] the idea to which he would give classic, movement-inspiring expression a decade later still in his sonnet "Correspondences" from the *Fleurs du mal*. By 1860, having heard Wagner conduct a concert in Paris (very similar to the ones he would present in Russia three years later; it included one of the earliest performances of the *Tristan* prelude), Baudelaire made Wagner the protagonist of his theories of synaesthesia and the rapture thus induced. He wrote Wagner a letter in which he compared the music he heard (as if

---

24. E. T. A. Hoffmann, *Sämtliche Werke*, vol. 1: *Fantasiestücke in Callots Manier* (Munich and Leipzig: Georg Müller, 1908), 66: "Nicht sowohl im Traume als im Zustande des Delirierens, der dem Einschlafen vorhergeht, vorzüglich wenn ich viel Musik gehört habe, finde ich eine Übereinkunft der Farben, Töne und Düfte. Es kömmt mir vor, als wenn alle auf die gleiche geheimnisvolle Weise durch den Lichtstrahl erzeugt würden und dann sich zu einem wundervollen Konzerte vereinigen müßten.—Der Duft der dunkelroten Nelken wirkt mit sonderbarer magischer Gewalt auf mich; unwillkürlich versinke ich in einen träumerischen Zustand und höre dann wie aus weiter Ferne die anschwellenden und wieder verfließenden tiefen Töne des Bassetthorns."

25. Charles Baudelaire, *Salon de 1846*, ed. David Kelly (Oxford: Clarendon Press, 1975), 93: "J'ignore si quelque analogiste a établi solidement une gamme complète des couleurs et des sentiments, mais je me rappelle un passage d'Hoffmann qui exprime parfaitement mon idée, et qui plaira à tous ceux qui aiment sincèrement la nature : 'Ce n'est pas seulement en rêve, et dans le léger délire qui précède le sommeil, c'est encore éveillé, lorsque j'entends de la musique, que je trouve une analogie et une réunion intime entre les couleurs, les sons et les parfums. Il me semble que toutes ces choses ont été engendrées par un même rayon de lumière, et qu'elles doivent se réunir dans un merveilleux concert. L'odeur des soucis bruns et rouges produit surtout un effet magique sur ma personne. Elle me fait tomber dans une profonde rêverie, et j'entends alors comme dans le lointain les sons graves et profonds du hautbois.'"

reversing "Kreisler's" testimony of sound evoked by color) to "a vast expanse of dark red,... passing through all the transitions of red and pink to the incandescent glow of a furnace," its climax in white expressing "the supreme utterance of a soul at its highest paroxysm." When, referring to a composition (probably the prelude to the first act of *Lohengrin*) that "depicted a religious ecstasy," he confided that "these profound harmonies seemed to me like those stimulants that quicken the pulse of the imagination." By thus adding the effects of liquor and narcotics to the Wagnerian *gesamt*, Baudelaire completed the association of religiose spirituality and sensuality that went by the name of decadence.[26]

III

The Wagner conjured by Baudelaire and the later symbolists, by Nietzsche, and by Appia was the *Mytholog und Mythopoet*, the Wagner of the dandies and decadents as well as the mystics and dreamers of world transformation, the Wagner of the *Revue wagnérienne*, the *Bayreuther Blätter*, and *The Meister*, the presiding spirit of the Russian Silver Age, who inspired the writers—Vyacheslav Ivanov, Dmitry Merezhkovsky, Emiliy Medtner, Andrey Belïy, Valeriy Bryusov, Alexander Blok— to whom Bartlett, Bernice Glatzer Rosenthal, Aleksey Fyodorovich Losev, and the many other literary historians who have written about the eastern Wagnerians have devoted most of their space.[27] This was the Wagner whose cultural significance can seem so oddly unrelated to his having been a composer rather than (or in addition to), as Nietzsche enthused, a "reviver of pure drama, discoverer of the place of art in true human society, poetic exponent of bygone views of life, philosopher, historian, aesthete and critic, master of language," etc. etc. And yet he could have been none of these other things without having been the composer he was, and the littérateurs who cast themselves as his adepts had no chance of emulating his achievements.

---

26. Julien Tiersot, *Lettres françaises de Richard Wagner* (Paris: Editions Bernard Grasset, 1935), 198: "L'un des morceaux les plus étranges et qui m'ont apporté une sensation musicale nouvelle est celui qui est destiné à peindre une extase religieuse.... Généralement ces profondes harmonies me paraissaient ressembler à ces excitants qui accélèrent le pouls de l'imagination.... [J]e suppose devant mes yeux une vaste étendue d'un rouge sombre. Si ce rouge représente la passion, je le vois arriver graduellement, par toutes les transitions de rouge et de rose, à l'incandescence de la fournaise. Il semblerait difficile, impossible même d'arriver à quelque chose de plus ardent; et cependant une dernière fusée vient tracer un sillon plus blanc sur le blanc qui lui sert de fond. Ce sera, si vous voulez, le cri suprême de l'âme montée à son paroxysme."

27. See Bernice Glatzer Rosenthal, "Wagner and Wagnerian Ideas in Russia," in *Wagnerism in European Culture and Politics*, ed. David C. Large and William Weber (Ithaca, NY: Cornell University Press, 1984), 198–245; A. F. Losev, "Istoricheskiy smïsl ėsteticheskogo mirovozzreniya Rikharda Vagnera," in *Rikhard Vagner: Izbrannïye rabotï* (Moscow: Iskusstvo, 1978), 7–48.

I say this not out of any commitment to the Schopenhauerian dogma that so inspired Wagner, according to which music "gives the innermost kernel preceding all forms, or the heart of things," or that it is "by no means like the other arts, namely a copy of Ideas, but a *copy of the will itself.*"[28] With these formulations Schopenhauer sought to explain why it was that "the effect of music is so much more powerful and penetrating than is that of the other arts";[29] but I think it is possible to show why Wagner's music in particular should have made so strong an impression on literary, philosophical, and religious thinkers, precisely to the point where they were no longer conscious that it was music, as the crucially active ingredient in the *Gesamtkunstwerk,* that was creating the effects that so stimulated their imaginations.

These are the very techniques or procedures that are usually adduced as typically Wagnerian by those who have analyzed Wagner's style: the freedom of modulation afforded by the open and endlessly fluctuating "sea of harmony,"[30] with its frequent false sightings of keys and powerful deceptive cadences; and the building up of a musical "past" out of leitmotivs over the whole course of an opera, or even a tetralogy of operas. In neither case was Wagner the inventor of the technique now irrevocably associated with his name, but in both cases he pushed it to a point where difference in degree amounted to a difference in kind. The harmonic technique, which produced what we might call the *Tristan* effect after its most spectacular deployment, is the one that so plays upon the competent listener's expectation of resolution as actually to evoke rather than merely represent desire, the most fundamental of emotions. That sort of manipulation would seem to be what gave Baudelaire the impression (after hearing that very early performance of the *Tristan* prelude) that, as he put it to Wagner in his letter of 17 May 1860, "one feels immediately carried away and dominated" when listening, even of being "penetrated and invaded—a really sensual delight that resembles that of rising in the air or tossing upon the sea."[31] It is what Hanslick, no fan of Wagner, must also have had in mind

---

28. Arthur Schopenhauer, *The World as Will and Representation,* trans. E. F. J. Payne (New York: Dover, 1966), 1:257, 263.

29. Ibid., 1:257.

30. Richard Wagner, *Das Kunstwerk der Zukunft* (Leipzig: Otto Wigand, 1850), 70–71: "Sind Rhythmus und Melodie die Ufer, an denen die Tonkunst die beiden Continente der ihr unverwandte Künste erfaßte und befruchtend berührt, so ist der Ton selbst ihr flüssiges unreinegses Element, die unermeßliche Ausdehnung dieser Flüssigkeit aber das Meer der Harmonie" (If melody and rhythm are the shores through which the art of Tone lays fruitful hands upon twain continents of art, allied to her of yore: so is Sound itself her fluent native element, and its immeasurable expanse of waters make out the sea of Harmony; in *Richard Wagner's Prose Works,* 1:112).

31. Tiersot, *Lettres françaises de Richard Wagner,* 198: "On se sent tout de suite enlevé et subjugué.... Autre chose encore: j'ai éprouvé souvent un sentiment d'une nature assez bizarre, c'est l'orgueil et la jouissance de comprendre, de me sentir pénétrer, envahir, volupté vraiment sensuelle et qui ressemble à celle de monter dans l'air ou de rouler sur la mer."

when he wrote, in combined wonder and fear, that "the other arts persuade, but music invades us."[32]

The gradual saturation of textures by leitmotivs is quintessentially the *Ring* effect, for there it builds over the whole four-opera span until, in *Götterdämmerung*, and especially by the third act, the texture comes to consist of practically nothing except montages of musical memories in which hardly a note is unfraught. Carolyn Abbate has conjectured that it was precisely the equipping of his music with such a store of memory—a "past in music"—that enabled Wagner to feel he had disposed of the problem of excessive narration that had motivated the sprouting of the first three operas in his tetralogy out of the fourth, even though "the narratives, despite Wagner's glee over their elimination, were kept."[33] Being built out of the same web of leitmotivs as the portrayed action, they reinforced the impression of a closed, unique musical time-space in which action and narrative unfolded together in a single mythopoesis. Only the pervasive ambient music—something only a composer can deploy—can give rise to such a closing-off of the chronotope, the aspect that, according to Bakhtin, is peculiar to epic or myth in that it is noncontinuous with present time and space, an "absolute past" sealed off but imaginatively habitable.[34]

In conjunction these two aspects of Wagner's musical technique—both of them aimed at what Wagner called the *Gefühlsverstehen* or nonrational "feelings' understanding"—exerted an irresistible power of suggestion, beginning with Nietzsche's association, in *Der Fall Wagner* (1888), of Wagner's music with hypnosis, a linkage that has become commonplace.[35] That extraordinary combination or conjunction of musical extremes was what produced the grandiose raptures and ecstasies and hysterias that listeners have likened to narcotic or religious experiences, making Wagner so much more than a composer for them that they were able to forget that he was one. But only a composer could have been so much more than a composer. Only a composer (among artists, anyway) could become a "Threat to the Cosmic Order," to cite the delightful title of a book, edited by two medical doctors, that catalogues all the reasons why Wagner has struck so many (again beginning with Nietzsche in *Der Fall*, albeit foreshadowed at a less fevered pitch by Hanslick) as a

---

32. Eduard Hanslick, *On the Musically Beautiful: A Contribution towards the Revision of the Aesthetics of Music*, trans. Geoffrey Payzant (Indianapolis: Hackett, 1986), 50.

33. Carolyn Abbate, *Unsung Voices: Opera and Musical Narrative in the Nineteenth Century* (Princeton, NJ: Princeton University Press, 1991), 161.

34. See Gary Saul Morson and Caryl Emerson, *Mikhail Bakhtin: Creation of a Prosaics* (Stanford, CA: Stanford University Press, 1990), 419–23.

35. Friedrich Nietzsche, *The Birth of Tragedy* and *The Case of Wagner*, trans. Walter Kaufmann (New York: Vintage Books, 1967), 166; also for a general discussion, see James Kennaway, "Musical Hypnosis: Sound and Selfhood from Mesmerism to Brainwashing," *Social History of Medicine* 24 (2011), available at http://shm.oxfordjournals.org/content/early/2011/10/05/shm.hkr143.full.

clear and present threat—to morals, to health, indeed to civilization—precisely the way that Elvis Presley and other charismatic popular musicians were feared in the twentieth century, and for the same reason: they could entrance crowds and create impulsive communities and thus threaten social stability.[36]

IV

And maybe here we have the beginnings of a reason for the enormous gulf between the Master's ecstatic literary-philosophical reception and his cooler, chary, often skeptical composerly reception. Composers contemplating Wagner contemplated a style; writers contemplated an effect for which they could not name the cause, which made the effect uncanny. The composers looked to Wagner for means; the writers and philosophers for ends. Wagner confronted his literary disciples with grandiose unattainable ambitions; he offered musicians implementable procedures which they could take or leave. Seeing in Wagner only a stylistic resource did not necessarily put the lid on enthusiasm. Was there ever a more perfect Wagnerite than Anton Bruckner, in his peculiar way? Yet Bruckner was so uninterested in any aspect of Wagner's dramas save the music they were drenched in, and so oblivious to it all, that he is plausibly reported to have asked, after the first Bayreuth *Walküre*, "Why did they burn Brünnhilde?"[37] As Hans-Hubert Schönzeler observed, no one who could ask a question like that "can ever be termed a 'Wagnerian' in the true sense of the word,"[38] meaning, of course, the sense in which Baudelaire, the young Nietzsche, or the Russian mystic symbolists were Wagnerians.

Compared with such "true" Wagnerians, then, most post-Wagnerian musicians were, perhaps oxymoronically, content to be what Adorno might have called "gemäßigte Wagnerianer"—modest, moderate, limited Wagnerians. They had, after all, more to lose. It was they, not the writers or philosophers, whose individuality was threatened by Wagner's powerful influence. Where the writers happily emulated Wagnerian grandeur, the musicians feared epigonism.

To imitate or duplicate Wagner's style was a technical question, and for a dyed-in-the-wool rationalist like Taneyev or Rimsky-Korsakov, a problem to solve. In

---

36. Peter Ostwald and Leonard S. Zegans, eds., *The Threat to the Cosmic Oder: Psychological, Social, and Health Implications of Richard Wagner's Ring of the Nibelung*, Mental Health Library Series 4 (Madison, CT: International Universities Press, 1997). Most germane to this discussion is chapter 10, "Sickness or Redemption? Wagnerism and the Consequences" by Thomas S. Grey (143–60).

37. This story seems to have originated, or at least seen print for the first time, in Robert Haas, *Anton Bruckner* (Potsdam, Ger.: Athenaion, 1934), 23: "Bei einer Walküreaufführung überraschte [Bruckner] mit der Frage: 'Warum wird Brünhilde verbrannt?'" See Miguel Javier Ramirez, "Analytic Approaches to the Music of Anton Bruckner: Chromatic Third-Relations in Selected Late Compositions" (PhD diss., University of Chicago, 2009), 71.

38. Hans-Hubert Schönzeler, *Bruckner* (New York: Grossman, 1978), 46.

their operatic works, even the ones based on myths, these composers were interested in techniques of conventional representation rather than mythopoesis. Taneyev's modest leitmotiv technique in his *Oresteia* amounts to not much more than the pre-Wagnerian technique of reminiscence. Rimsky-Korsakov's "Wagnerism" amounted to even less, confined as it usually was to orchestral imagery: forest murmurs, magic fire, snowstorms, and aerial rides. There is no opera by Rimsky-Korsakov that adopts what could be described as Wagnerian formal principles—or nonprinciples, Wagner being the epitome of the "New German" principle that content creates its own form. Rimsky insisted to the end with schoolmasterly pertinacity (as he put it explicitly in his "Notes on production and performance" to *The Legend of the Invisible City of Kitezh*, often cited as his most Wagnerian opera, even as the "Russian *Parsifal*") that "[a]s in previous publications of his operatic works, the author insists again on this occasion that such works are, according to his conviction, above all to be regarded as *musical works*," by which he meant works in traditional musical forms, to be performed with traditional vocal production (i.e., no shouting or gasping or grunting).[39] No *Gesam(m)tkunstwerk* for him.[40]

In particular, Rimsky mocked the very aspects of Wagner on which "Wagnerians" placed the highest premium. He dismissed the supersaturated web of leitmotivs with obtuse, even philistine literalism: "If character A, finding himself in a certain mood, were to speak with character B about character C, and if in the accompanying music we hear the contrapuntally interwoven motives A, B, and C, perhaps with the addition of a fourth denoting their mood, can one then clearly distinguish such a situation from the reverse: i.e., where C speaks to A about B, or B and C discuss A?"[41] As for the ceaseless modulatory undertow of Wagner's "sea of harmony," the ex-naval cadet Rimsky-Korsakov unaccountably thought not of a sea but rather of a building that consisted "entirely of a staircase leading from the entrance to the exit."[42]

The cases of Dvořák and Janáček are not dissimilar. Both Czech composers experimented with Wagnerian style, but neither was ever wed to it. Dvořák, especially, was a proud eclectic—possibly the most versatile of all nineteenth-century composers. What other composer contributed major works to so many genres—opera, symphony *and* symphonic poem, chamber music, oratorio, even piano music (not a major genre with him, perhaps, but it did include the ubiquitous

---

39. N. Rimsky-Korsakov, *Skazaniye o nevidimom grade Kitezhe i deve Fevronii* (Leipzig: M. P. Belaïeff, 1906), 3.

40. See his essay "Vagner: Sovokupnoye proizvedeniye dvukh iskusstv, ili muzïkal'naya drama" [Wagner: The Joint Work of Two Arts, or Music Drama], *Polnoye sobraniye sochineniy: Literaturnïye proizvedeniya i perepiska*, vol. 2 (Moscow: Muzgiz, 1963), 47–60.

41. Ibid., 52.

42. Ibid., 57.

Humoresque).⁴³ The stylistic patrimony Dvořák commanded was as diverse as his generic output: a chronological list of his models would begin with Bach and Handel and end with Wagner and Brahms, with Mozart, Schubert, Mendelssohn, and Schumann in between. That extraordinary variegation, which somehow did not efface Dvořák's individuality, seems remarkably modern, as does Rimsky-Korsakov's rationalism.

Just as plausibly, though, these traits could be designated "classical." Either way, they offer a challenge to Carl Dahlhaus's famous contention that late nineteenth-century music was romantic in an unromantic age.⁴⁴ If the relatively long-lived and late-blooming Wagner set the standard of romanticism with his profound connections to the ur-Romantic aesthetic of Schelling and Hoffmann, then he was an undeniably great yet perhaps unrepresentative figure among the musicians who knew the work of his maturity. (And the enthusiastic neo-Wagnerians in the literary world would constitute a counterexample to Dahlhaus's contention from the opposite side; they are evidence that the age, Darwin and Comte notwithstanding, was perhaps not so utterly antiromantic after all.) The rationalism of Rimsky-Korsakov and the eclecticism of Dvořák are easily correlated with the "positivist zeitgeist" from which, Dahlhaus claims, music was "alienated."⁴⁵

The obvious exception among Russian composers was Scriabin, who practically alone among his contemporaries saw himself without any doubt or conflict in a direct line from Wagner, the only other musician besides himself whom he regarded as a genius.⁴⁶ Indeed, he was the one musician anywhere who wholeheartedly accepted the challenge of emulating all of Wagner, means and ends alike, casting himself in the world-transforming Orphic image that all his composing contemporaries rejected, determined as he was, in the words of Bernice Glatzer Rosenthal, "to out-Wagner Wagner."⁴⁷ It is obvious to any knowledgeable listener that the end of the *Poème de l'extase* is an attempt to surpass the cataclysmic end of *Tristan und Isolde* in specific technical terms: damming up the energy of an excruciatingly prolonged dominant pedal until it is finally discharged in a single

---

43. The sole possible rival would seem to be Saint-Saëns (and perhaps Chaikovsky, minus oratorio).

44. See his essay "'Neo-romanticism,'" in Carl Dahlhaus, *Between Romanticism and Modernism: Four Studies in the Music of the Later Nineteenth Century*, trans. Mary Whittall (Berkeley and Los Angeles: University of California Press, 1980), 1–18. The essential claim is that "after the middle of the century music, in which something of romanticism lived on, was the odd art out in a cultural climate that was predominantly anti-romantic" (7–8). The problem with the claim would appear to be that, as often with Dahlhaus, Wagner was the implicit—or even explicit—synecdoche for "music."

45. Ibid., 8.

46. Sabaneyev, *Vospominaniya o Skryabine* (Moscow: Muzïkal'nïy sektor Gos. izd-va, 1925), 103; quoted in Bartlett, *Wagner and Russia*, 114.

47. Rosenthal, "Wagner and Wagnerian Ideas in Russia," 221.

shattering cadence to the tonic. A listener both knowledgeable and sympathetic might even call the attempt successful. The *Mysterium* was just as obviously an attempt—unsuccessful in that it remained unfinished (and perhaps unfinishable)—to surpass the Wagner of *Götterdämmerung* as eschatological mythopoet.[48] For these reasons, in a move adumbrating Dahlhaus, Scriabin's brother-in-(common)-law Boris Schloezer characterized Scriabin as the one romantic composer of his generation among classicists.[49]

V

With scads of chamber music and nine nonchoral symphonies to his credit, and with his unwillingness to forgo a show-stopping "Song to the Moon" even in his most seemingly Wagnerian (because mythological) opera, Dvořák would seem an archetypal classicist or pattern-designer next to Wagner, let alone Scriabin. And yet the line could be blurry between pattern-designer and tone-poet (to reappropriate the Beethovenian *mot juste* that Wagner had earlier appropriated). Consider the *New World* Symphony, probably Dvořák's best-known composition after *Humoresque*. It is usually classified as a not-quite-programmatic "motto" symphony, because like Chaikovsky's Fourth and Fifth, or Franck's Symphony in D Minor, it recycles themes from movement to movement. But no other "cyclic" symphony (and here we could instance many others in the wake of Franck's, by such pupils of his as Chausson, D'Indy, or Ropartz) ever recycled so many themes, or montaged them so thoroughly into contrapuntal webs. By the end of the finale, we are confronted by the same situation as at the end of *Götterdämmerung*: the symphony's themes—all of them!—have become leitmotivs; everything is reminiscence, everything is fraught, and the symphony, endowed with a "past in music," has taken up residence in the epic chronotope. Little wonder, then, if, as many are now convinced, the *New World* is the residue of an opera or oratorio (or at least a melodrama) after *The Song of Hiawatha*, Longfellow's attempt to write an American epic to give the United States a national myth like the *Kalevala*, on which the poem, with its heavy trochaic tread, was so transparently modeled.[50]

It was an obviously Wagnerian, because "mythopoetic," task, and Dvořák attempted a truly Wagnerian solution to it, one that went beyond the general,

---

48. See Simon Morrison, "Skryabin and the Impossible," *Journal of the American Musicological Society* 51 (1998): 283–330.

49. See *Scriabin: Artist and Mystic*, trans. Nicolas Slonimsky (Berkeley and Los Angeles: University of California Press, 1987). For Schloezer, "classical" was equivalent to decorative; cf. G. B. Shaw's distinction, in his discussion of Wagnerism in *The Sanity of Art* (New York: Boni & Liveright, 1918), 30–43, between "pattern-designing" and dramatic music.

50. See the four chapters in part 2 ("Dvořák and Hiawatha") of Michael Beckerman, *New Worlds of Dvořák: Searching in America for the Composer's Inner Life* (New York: W. W. Norton, 2003), 23–75.

somewhat vague stylistic influence one notes in many of Dvořák's works, into a consciously chosen Wagnerian *procedure*—chosen to suit the nature of the task. And the effect is Wagnerian too: not merely in the sense that, by the end of the finale, "character A, finding himself in a certain mood, speaks with character B about character C," but because the music has joined the *Ring* in tenseless mythological time. How suggestive to learn that during his time in New York Dvořák met regularly with Anton Seidl, the Wagner intimate who eventually conducted the *New World* Symphony's premiere with the New York Philharmonic, and that they "discussed avidly Wagner's music and working methods."[51] The results of these discussions have mainly been cited in connection with Dvořák's revisions to his grand opera *Dimitrij*; but why not the *New World*? If his secretary Kovařík reported that "during his exchanges with Seidl Dvořák *was insistent* that *Tannhäuser* was the greatest of Wagner's operas," that would imply that Seidl was arguing another position.[52] The *New World* might be evidence that Seidl eventually won Dvořák over to the *Ring*.

But if so, it was not without reservations. Like Brahms in his First Symphony, Dvořák supplied an instrumental counterpart to a work that had flaunted "the redemption of Music from out her own peculiar element." Friedrich Chrysander, Brahms's musicologist friend, recognized Brahms's intention: far from the "weak and impotent imitation" the Wagnerians were calling it, Brahms had created, Chrysander wrote, "a counterpart to the last sections of the Ninth Symphony that achieve the same effect in nature and intensity without calling on the assistance of song."[53] One would not claim for the *New World* Symphony quite the same effect as *Götterdämmerung* in conception or intensity. Dvořák fastidiously held back from Wagner's "progressive" tonality—that is, the unpredictable tonal navigations on the sea of harmony that did not circle back to port but ever sought new shores— and in that sense, compared with Wagner, Dvořák did indeed remain a "classicist." But the use of an advanced or even extreme music-dramatic technique in an instrumental composition could seem, no less pointedly than Brahms's example, an affirmation of the continuing relevance of "absolute music" after its demise had been so confidently proclaimed by the New Germans and their followers. The fact that the symphony's music probably originated in a programmatic context does not contradict the point. The point is actually strengthened by the knowledge that a program had been entertained and then dispensed with. For "absolute music" was never looked upon by its adepts as meaningless. It was, rather, ineffable. It said

---

51. Jan Smaczny, "'The Great Little Man': Dvořák and Wagner," chap. 5 in Muir and Belina-Johnson (eds.), *Wagner in Russia, Poland, and the Czech Lands*, 93–117, at 112.

52. Ibid., my italics.

53. Friedrich Chrysander, performance review, *Allgemeine musikalische Zeitung* 13 (1878): col. 94; quoted in David Brodbeck, *Brahms: Symphony No. 1* (Cambridge: Cambridge University Press, 1997), 86.

something words could not say—something, indeed, beyond the power of words to convey, and something that the presence of words in conjunction with music prevents music from saying.

Nietzsche acknowledged the necessity of music to the epic or mythic chronotope, although he obviously could not have used that word for it. In *Richard Wagner in Bayreuth,* his most eulogistic Wagner essay and the source of the epigraph that stands above this chapter, Nietzsche allowed that if

> the heroes and gods of mythical dramas, as understood by Wagner, were to express themselves plainly in words, there would be a danger (inasmuch as the language of words might tend to awaken the theoretical side in us) of our finding ourselves transported from the world of myth to the world of ideas, and the result would be not only that we should fail to understand with greater ease, but that we should probably not understand at all.[54]

From this standpoint, Dvořák's translation of his Hiawatha epic into the form of a wordless symphony might seem a radical act of liberation rather than a retreat. And at a certain point in his Wagnerian trajectory, Nietzsche might even have agreed. In *The Birth of Tragedy* he addressed a question to "genuine musicians"— that is, to "those who, immediately related to music have in it, as it were, their motherly womb and are related to things almost exclusively through unconscious musical relations"—whether they can imagine "a human being who would be able to perceive the third act of *Tristan and Isolde,* without any aid of word and image, purely as a tremendous symphonic movement, without expiring in a spasmodic unharnessing of all the wings of the soul?"[55]

Without the rational, "theoretical" (yes, Apollonian) restraining force of words, Nietzsche implies, Wagner's Dionysiac art might prove lethal. Scriabin certainly agreed, and hoped, in his *Mysterium,* to put Nietzsche's notion to the ultimate test. Mahler, too, nurtured hopes that people might "do away with themselves" on hearing his symphonies.[56] Franck gave backhanded, jocular credence to Nietzsche's conceit when he pasted a skull-and-crossbones "poison" label on his *Tristan* score.[57] Dvořák, a man who related to music as his motherly womb if anyone did, might also have been a believer—enough so, at any rate, to restrain himself from going the whole Wagnerian hog harmonically even as he adopted a more thoroughgoing Wagnerian technique in his final symphony than any other symphonist ever dared.

---

54. Friedrich Nietzsche, *The Untimely Meditations* (*Thoughts Out of Season,* Parts I and II), trans. Anthony M. Ludovici and Adrian Collins (Lawrence, KS: Digireads.com, 2010), 82.

55. Nietzsche, *The Birth of Tragedy* and *The Case of Wagner,* 126–27.

56. Bruno Walter, *Gustav Mahler,* trans. James Galston (New York: Greystone Press, 1941), 59.

57. James R. Briscoe, "Debussy, Franck, and the 'Idea of Sacrifice,'" *Revue belge de musicologie/Belgisch tijdschrift voor muziekwetenschap* 45 (1991): 37 (special issue, "César Franck et son temps").

VI

To a certain extent, this little essay, like most forewords, has been an attempt to find a standpoint or context that would lend coherence to a fortuitous assemblage of independently conceived essays—essays that in the present instance do not really isolate any peculiarly Eastern European Wagnerian discourse. Only, perhaps, when Aleksey Losev is shown blasting Adorno's anti-Wagnerian qualms as "petty bourgeois" and casting Wagner's anti-Semitism as "love of one's own" rather than hatred of the other (within an overall discourse that is, somewhat astoundingly, said to be "anti-nationalist and anti-racist") do I feel a distinctly Eastern European breeze wafting air from a planet that one recalls with little nostalgia.[58] Otherwise, the Eastern Europe presented herein is partial and perhaps unrepresentative, consisting of three nations selected as if at random, with each constituent represented, moreover, by an assortment of strange musical bedfellows.

This is true even of the pair of Czech chapters, devoted respectively to a Bohemian and a Moravian. Janáček, the Moravian, identified strongly as a Slav with other Slavs, especially Russians, and the Wagnerian flirtation his chapter traces was a youthful fling that left few traces on the mature musical dramatist. By contrast, Dvořák, the Bohemian, although he was on cordial if sporadic terms with Chaikovsky and praised *Eugene Onegin* very warmly,[59] could appear so thoroughly Viennese and Brahmsian in orientation as to lead to ugly politically motivated denunciations in the decade following his death—especially from a self-proclaimed "progressive" camp whose rudest spokesman, Zdeněk Nejedlý (later notorious as the culture czar in the early years of Communist rule), did not hesitate to make crudely invidious comparisons with Mendelssohn ostensibly on the basis of eclecticism, but *au fond* nationalistic in a manner redolent of the very worst in Wagner.[60]

That worst is among the reasons why the ambivalence toward Wagner that so pervasively suffuses the Wagner literature continues unabated to this day—to the point where, asked to furnish a foreword to a new edition of Adorno's *In Search of Wagner*, Slavoj Žižek thought it suitable to title his contribution "Why Is Wagner

---

58. Vladimir Marchenkov, "Prophecy of a Revolution: Aleksey Losev on Wagner's Aesthetic Outlook," chap. 4 in Muir and Belina-Johnson (eds.), *Wagner in Russia, Poland, and the Czech Lands*, 71–91, at 88.

59. See his letter to Chaikovsky of 2/14 January 1889, and Chaikovsky's answer of 18/30 January, the former in Nikolai Alexeyevich Alexeyev, ed., *Chaikovskiy i zarubezhnïye muzïkantï: Izbrannïye pis'ma inostrannïkh korrespondentov* (Leningrad: Muzïka, 1970), 219; the latter in P. I. Chaikovsky, *Polnoye sobraniye sochineniy: Literaturnïye proizvedeniya i perepiska*, vol. 15a (Moscow: Muzïka, 1976), 32.

60. See Marta Ottlová, "The 'Dvořák Battles' in Bohemia: Czech Criticism of Antonín Dvořák, 1911–15," in *Rethinking Dvořák: Views from Five Countries*, ed. David Beveridge (Oxford: Clarendon Press, 1996), 125–33.

Worth Saving?"⁶¹ I have always assumed, when it came to writing about Wagner, that it is precisely our agreement that he is, in spite of everything, worth saving that motivates our continuing efforts to understand him in as many contexts as possible. But I have also assumed that every study of Wagner is at least implicitly a study in the ambivalence that has furnished me with my principal theme. As long as that ambivalence remains salient, Wagner scholarship in the twenty-first century has all the *raison d'être* it needs.

---

61. Slavoj Žižek, "Foreword: Why Is Wagner Worth Saving?" in Theodor Adorno, *In Search of Wagner*, trans. Rodney Livingstone (London: Verso, 2005), viii–xxvii.

9

Rimsky-Korsakov Catches Up

I

The easiest way to start an argument among Russians or those who study them is to espouse a position—any position at all—on the relationship between Russia and "the West," however defined. That is the mother of all "cursed questions," as the Russians call them, the questions that can never be answered, and that never go away.[1] It became an acute question for music when the organization of Russian musical life became an issue of social and political concern: first when Tsar Nikolai I was persuaded to endow an international (which meant an Italian) opera theater in his capital in 1843, and later, during the reign of his brother and successor, Alexander II, when Anton Grigoryevich Rubinstein persuaded the Tsar's German-born aunt, *Velikaya knyaginya* (or Grand Duchess) Elena Pavlovna, born Princess Charlotte of Württemberg, to sponsor, in 1859, a permanent German orchestra in the capital, to be known as the orchestra of the Russian Musical Society, and, three

---

Keynote address, international conference "Year by Year: Rimsky-Korsakov—175," St. Petersburg, 21 March 2019; published, as "Римский-Корсаков догоняет," trans. Vladimir Khavrov, in *God za godom. Rimskiy-Korsakov—175. Materialï mezhdunarodnoy nauchnoy konferentsii 18–21 Marta 2019 g.*, ed. Lidiya Olegovna Ader (St. Petersburg: Sankt-Peterburgskoye gosudarstvennoye byudzhetnoye uchrezhdeniye kulturï/Sankt-Peterburgskiy gosudarstvenniy muzey teatral'nogo i muzïkal'nogo iskusstva, 2019), 3–21.

    1. The term "cursed questions" (проклятые вопросы) entered the Russian sphere by way of Heine's poem *Zum Lazarus*, as translated by Mikhaíl Larionovich Mikhailov; for a whole book of them, see R. Taruskin, *Cursed Questions: On Music and Its Social Practices* (Oakland: University of California Press, 2020). The term is introduced and explained on pp. 1–2.

years later, a conservatory to staff it, with an imported German faculty that would educate a class of Russian musicians in the traditions of advanced instrumental music, which Rubinstein explicitly identified as "a *German* art."[2]

This is a story that deserves to be told by all historians of Russia, not just music historians, because it is the crispest possible illustration of the difference—a really crucial difference, the importance of which is reflected in newspapers all over today's world—between patriotism and nationalism.

The institution of the St. Petersburg Italian Opera and the St. Petersburg Conservatory were patriotic acts, as understood within the context of Russian aristocratic or dynastic politics. The primary benefit of the Italian opera, in the eyes of its sponsors, was the enhancement of their country's prestige among the powerful states of Europe. That was an eminently patriotic aspiration, but its establishment created nearly insuperable obstacles to the development of an indigenous Russian operatic repertory. That made it an antinationalistic act, at least in the eyes of indigenous Russian musical nationalists, who had a completely different set of values and aspirations, and a different idea of nationhood, ethnic rather than political. They felt as much affronted by the imposition of the conservatory, from which they felt excluded, as they did by the opera, which many of them could not afford to attend. The whole history of Russian music as an institution can (and, I believe, should) be narrated as the history of the often clashing claims of nationalism and patriotism and their always provisional negotiation.

One particularly piquant moment in that history took place in the summer of 1871, when the twenty-seven-year old naval officer Nikolai Andreyevich Rimsky-Korsakov, on the strength of his early musical compositions, one of which, the symphonic picture *Sadko,* had been successfully performed at a concert by the German-staffed Russian Musical Society, was invited to join the faculty of the conservatory as a professor of practical composition and instrumentation, and also to conduct the school orchestra. As everyone knows who has read the *Chronicle of My Musical Life* (*Letopis' moyey muzïkal'noy zhizni*), his uncommonly frank and unsparing autobiography, Rimsky-Korsakov had never studied the subjects he was now hired to teach. It was a mark of his outstanding talent that *Sadko* had impressed the professionals, and in particular Mikhail Pavlovich Azanchevsky, who had just replaced the founder, Rubinstein, as director of the Conservatory, and who now welcomed Rimsky-Korsakov to its staff.

Balakirev and Stasov, Rimsky's mentors in the little band of brothers now known as the Mighty Kuchka, assured him that his success in passing himself off as a trained composer was proof that training was unnecessary. As Rimsky looked back on the moment thirty years later, Balakirev had cynically fostered what in retrospect Rimsky called his "delusions" of competence. As the only member of the

---

2. Rubinstein, *Muzïka i yeyo predstaviteli* (Moscow: P. Jurgenson, 1891), 40; italics original.

Kuchka who did have some professional standing, Balakirev was "the only one to realize how unprepared" the new professor really was; but he saw a chance "to get one of his own men into the hostile Conservatory," that is, to place a nationalist spy among the patriots.[3]

After finishing *Pskovityanka,* his first opera, and accepting the post, Rimsky-Korsakov woke up to the reality of his situation. His sense of shame produced a creative block, and a resolve to catch up. In what is probably the most famous sentence from Rimsky's *Chronicle,* he wrote that "having been undeservedly accepted at the Conservatory as a professor, I soon became one of its best and possibly its very best *pupil!*"[4]

But just what, exactly, did he learn? The short answer couldn't be simpler: He learned what he needed to learn in order to write the rest of his music. But if we want a more exact or detailed answer, and one that might shed some light on the relations of Russia and "the West," what will be our evidence?

II

The most frequently cited testimonial to Rimsky-Korsakov's self-administered crash course in conservatory lore is his correspondence with Chaikovsky, the first fully professional, conservatory-trained composer in the history of Russian music, who became Rimsky's informal mentor for a while. In the summer of 1875, Rimsky-Korsakov sent Chaikovsky for inspection a sheaf of ten fugues he had composed, out of a total summer harvest, he said, of sixty-one in which he had tried to apply every device of traditional counterpoint. Having received them, Chaikovsky responded to Rimsky that "I simply bow down in reverence before your noble artistic modesty and astounding strength of character."[5] In one of his most celebrated letters to his patron, Mme von Meck, written a couple of years later, Chaikovsky was a little more skeptical, Rimsky's about-face having struck him as too radical to be altogether genuine. Having by this time heard a couple of Rimsky-Korsakov's actual compositions—his String Quartet in F Major, op. 12, eventually published by Jurgenson in 1878, and his Symphony in C Major, unpublished until 1888 as op. 32—Chaikovsky wrote that he was "[e]vidently ... going through a crisis right now, and how it will end will be difficult to predict. Either he will come out of it a great master, or he will get completely bogged down in contrapuntal tricks."[6]

---

3. Rimsky-Korsakov, *My Musical Life,* trans. Judah A. Joffe (London: Eulenburg Books, 1974), 116.
4. Ibid., 118–19.
5. Chaikovsky to Rimsky-Korsakov, 10 September 1875, in P.I. Chaikovsky, *Polnoye sobraniye sochineniy: Literaturnïye proizvedeniya i perepiska,* 17 vols. (Moscow: Muzgiz, 1940–81), 5:412.
6. Chaikovsky to von Meck, from San Remo, 24 December 1977/5 January 1878, in Chaikovsky, *Polnoye sobraniye sochineniy,* 6:367.

Recalling the quartet in his *Chronicle,* even Rimsky admitted getting bogged down in contrapuntal tricks. The work's most salient feature is abuse of fugato in all four movements, stemming, Rimsky confessed, from his overly zealous application to Cherubini's *Cours de contrepoint et de fugue* (1841) and Johann Gottfried Heinrich Bellermann's *Der Contrapunct oder Anleitung zur Stimmführung in der musikalischen Composition* (Counterpoint; or, Instructions for Voice Leading in Musical Composition, 1862), to give it its full title. These were the textbooks then in use in the conservatories of Paris and Berlin. He had composed the quartet, Rimsky wrote to Chaikovsky, as a break from working in the strict (or "Palestrina") style, but he carried the strict style over into the quartet to the point where, to quote the *Chronicle,* "it got boring."[7] Still, the old professor who wrote the *Chronicle* did point with pride to one of the contrapuntal tricks in the finale, where the young professor had succeeded in recombining the two themes that had formerly served as subjects in a double fugue, to form a double canon in the stretto (Ex. 9.1).

That was the stuff the young Rimsky-Korsakov understandably wanted to strut, but for me there is something more interesting to be found in his quartet, something that broaches the true subject of this paper. Consider the opening theme in the first movement. From the point of view of contrapuntal tricks it is a little laughable, so blatantly does it advertise that it, and the movement, will be all about inversions (Ex. 9.2). And yet its contrapuntal banality seems curiously related to the one aspect of the movement that is altogether unconventional and intriguing. The second theme, which in an F major sonata movement one would expect to be in C major, is cast instead, or at least begins, in D-flat major, approached through what we would now call a modal mixture (Ex. 9.3).

One could argue that the local tonic here is that of the second phrase, in A-flat, in which case the D-flat was a subdominant on the way to it. One could even argue that the tonic here is that of the third phrase, in E-flat, which continues a reversed circle of fifths through one more progression. That, of course, would please those who want their Russian music always to be plagal. But we can let that point remain moot, since eventually the key of C major is reached for the closing theme, so that the apparent vagary into flatted territory could be described—and justified, if need be—as part of the transition.

Even so, that transition contains a theme with a full cadence in a most unconventional key, whether we call it the flat submediant (D-flat), the flat mediant (A-flat), or the unclassifiably "modal" flat seventh (E-flat) with respect to the tonic F. The mixture that prepares it, F minor for F major, can be described as a tonic mixture in terms of the opening theme, or as a subdominant mixture in terms of the eventual closing theme. Which of these Rimsky had in mind will, I think, eventually become evident.

7. Rimsky-Korsakov, *My Musical Life,* 150 ("wearisome" in Joffe's translation).

EXAMPLE 9.1. Rimsky-Korsakov, String Quartet in F Major, op. 12, IV, mm. 235–245.

But if that were all there was to this tonal vagary, I would not have stopped to take note of it. What is finally of compelling interest is its counterpart in the recapitulation (Ex. 9.4). Here the opposite or reciprocal modal mixture is introduced: D major for D minor, a submediant mixture placing the second theme a half-step higher than in the exposition, so that the second phrase is in A major cadencing on E, rather than A-flat cadencing on E-flat, as presented the first time around. I can't help regarding the D-flat major of the exposition and the A major of the recapitulation as a reciprocal pair, symmetrically surrounding the tonic F with chromaticized mediants.

EXAMPLE 9.2. Rimsky-Korsakov, String Quartet in F Major, op. 12, I, mm. 1–12.

EXAMPLE 9.3. Rimsky-Korsakov, String Quartet in F Major, op. 12, I, mm. 63–79.

EXAMPLE 9.4. Rimsky-Korsakov, String Quartet in F Major, op. 12, I, mm. 213–229.

III

Why do I see it this way? Because I know Rimsky's later music, as do you. And you probably know as well as I do where Rimsky himself located the source of these harmonic relationships. Before naming names, though, I want to consider a similar passage from the Symphony in C Major, the other piece on which Chaikovsky based his assessment of Rimsky-Korsakov's work as sent to Mme von Meck in 1877.

Chaikovsky knew it in the long-unpublished version of 1873. Rimsky began composing it in 1872, immediately after finishing *Pskovityanka* and after his very stressful first year as a conservatory professor, as part of his heroic effort to catch up with his colleagues (and—all the more humiliating for him at first, as he tells us in the *Chronicle*—with his early pupils). The symphony was, in its way, Rimsky's *diplomnaya rabota* or graduation piece, his demonstration of competence within his newly professional environment; and like many such works it is, like the string quartet but even more so, a very labored affair. By the time it was issued by M. P. Belaïeff, Leipzig, as Symphony no. 3, op. 32 (1888), Rimsky-Korsakov had subjected it to the sort of ruthless revision he eventually lavished on all his early compositions (sometimes more than once), as well as on many works by his friends Musorgsky, Dargomïzhsky, and Borodin, for which he has not always been thanked by posterity.

The 1873 version of the symphony was not published until 1959, in the complete academic edition of Rimsky-Korsakov's works. In the *Chronicle*, Rimsky treated it harshly. "Work . . . was slow . . . and beset with difficulties; I strove to crowd in as much counterpoint as possible; but being unskilled in it and hard put to combine the themes and motives, I drained my immediate flow of imagination considerably."[8] The texture abounds in strettos, augmentations, and overwrought contrapuntal montages, as well as a stilted return in the finale to the first movement's opening theme (and other themes from previous movements as well)—practically all of which were mercifully pruned out of the eventually published revision.

Needless to say, the other kuchkists hated the piece. As Rimsky put it in the *Chronicle* with his inimitable dry wit, "The symphony pleased my musical friends extremely moderately."[9] Their mole in the conservatory, it turned out, was not infusing that German institution with Russian nationalism. Just the opposite: their junior member was, under its institutional influence, becoming a German. You probably remember what Borodin, who actually liked it better than the others, said about it—that the composer "appeared to him as a professor who had put on his spectacles and composed *Eine grosse Symphonie in C-dur*, as befitted his rank."[10]

As a parenthesis, or another counterpoint by inversion, I cannot refrain from adding that in his public voice, as critic for the *Sankt-Peterburgskiye vedomosti*, the many-faced and volatile César Cui, who had one week earlier published his notoriously mixed review of Musorgsky's *Boris Godunov*, praised Professor Rimsky-Korsakov's Third Symphony to the skies, and in great detail, when it was performed under the composer's direction—his conducting debut—at a concert to benefit victims of a famine in the Samara *guberniya* on 18 February (2 March) 1874: "A capital work, the best of all Korsakov's symphonic works, it is the fruit of mature thought, happy inspiration, strong talent united with solid and profound technical knowledge—everything, in short, that a work of art should be."[11] Chaikovsky also reviewed the symphony, which happened to be performed (in Moscow in December 1874 under Nikolai Rubinstein's direction) during the short period when Chaikovsky was a paid reviewer for the newspaper *Russkiye vedomosti*. He was less kind than Cui but not unfair, and certainly more truthful, remarking that the dominant impression was that of "preponderance of technique over the quality of ideas,

---

8. Ibid., 133–34.
9. "Симфония понравилась моим музыкальным друзьям весьма умеренно" (Rimsky-Korsakov, *Polnoye sobraniye sochineniy*, 1:83).
10. Rimsky-Korsakov, *My Musical Life*, 141 (" . . . в ней я представляюсь ему профессором, надевшим очки и сочинившим подобающую сему званию Eine grosse Symphonie in C" [Rimsky-Korsakov, *Polnoye sobraniye sochineniy*, 1:83]).
11. César Cui, *Izbrannïye stat'i* (Leningrad: Muzgiz, 1952), 244.

a lack of inspiration and impulse in exchange for proficiency and a great variety of elegant details, to the point of excess." Anticipating his letter to von Meck, Chaikovsky wrote that "Mr. Rimsky-Korsakov is apparently undergoing a transition; he is trying to find a footing, vacillating between the inclination for novelty that has been noticeable in him from the beginning and a furtive attraction to archaic, Old Testament musical forms. He is an unsophisticated conservative at heart, carried away for a while into the arena of free-thinkers but now beating a timid retreat."[12]

That hit home, evidently, because it was after this review had appeared that Rimsky began sending Chaikovsky his work for inspection, relying on the reviewer's prediction, eerily reminiscent of Schumann's salute to the young Brahms, that if Rimsky finds his terra firma, "from him will emerge the great symphonist of our day, one who will sooner ally himself with classicism, toward which his musical nature gravitates, rather than the disheveled romantic school of Berlioz and Liszt."[13]

Yet neither Cui nor Chaikovsky, nor any other commentator of whom I am aware, called attention to the tonal plan of the symphony's first movement, or the unclassical, indeed disheveled moment that corresponds to the modulation we have already examined in the string quartet. Once again the second theme is pitched not at the dominant but at a chromaticized mediant with respect to the tonic. On reaching G, the expected goal, Rimsky tightens the meter from a triple to a duple measure and continues the chromatic motion, carried now by an extracted thematic motive, upward in the bass until it zeroes in, unexpectedly, on the dominant of E-flat: once again a flat mediant with respect to the tonic, but a flat submediant with respect to the dominant key for which it is serving as substitute (Ex. 9.5).

Both Cui and Chaikovsky singled out this chromatic sequential passage for its piquant originality, but neither of them took note of its destination. Were there precedents for it? I can think, offhand, of only one previous piece in sonata form that has a first theme in C major and a second theme in E-flat major, and that is the great string quintet, D. 956, by Franz Schubert, the composer whose name I deliberately withheld a moment ago. It was first published posthumously in 1853 and was still fairly little known in the 1870s. I therefore abstain from naming it as Rimsky's precedent, although Rimsky did comment, decades later, while his wife and his pupil Igor Stravinsky were playing Schubert's "Great" C-Major Symphony four-hands at his parlor piano, that "Schubert was the first composer in whom one can meet such bold and unexpected modulations."[14]

Any reader who knows the Schubert quintet is surely objecting by now that the key of E-flat is only seemingly the tonality of its famously lyrical second theme,

---

12. P. I. Chaikovsky, *Muzïkal'no-kriticheskiye stat'i* (Leningrad: Muzïka, 1986), 198.
13. Ibid., 198–99.
14. Vasiliy Vasiliyevich Yastrebtsev, *Nikolai Andreyevich Rimskiy-Korsakov: Vospominaniya, 1886–1908*, ed. A. V. Ossovsky, vol. 2 (Leningrad: Gos. muzïkal'noye izd-vo, 1960), 374 (25 January 1906).

EXAMPLE 9.5. Symphony in C Major (1873), I, mm. 73–103 in keyboard reduction.

played as a duet by the two cellos (Ex. 9.6). It is preceded by the conventional dominant key of G, achieved by a strongly articulated (though plagal) cadence, and then, while one of the cellos holds the G, the other slips down by chromatic degrees to E-flat, leaving no doubt that the strange key is to be heard as the flat submediant of the dominant rather than the flat mediant of the tonic. And as anyone who knows the tune will recall, its best moment is the transfiguring slip back into G at the end.

So Schubert's theme is no real precedent for Rimsky's. It is not "really" in E-flat, only feints toward it (albeit spectacularly), whereas Rimsky's theme really is in the submediant key, until the written-out repeat of the exposition, in which the second theme comes where the textbook says it belongs, in G (which may have prompted Chaikovsky's cruel remark about Rimsky's "timid retreat").

But for us this only prompts the question, Why did he make the unconventional modulation in the first place in a composition wherein, as Chaikovsky correctly observed, he was making every effort to conform to classical models, a composition that I have been characterizing as a sort of *diplomnaya rabota*, the last place you'd look for audacity or surprise. Was it just a relapse into the world of *Antar*,

EXAMPLE 9.6. Schubert, Quintet in C, D. 956 (1828), I, mm. 53–80 in keyboard reduction.

Rimsky's programmatic Second Symphony? Was the movement by thirds just a habit acquired during a youth misspent in the company of Balakirev and the vicarious company of Liszt? That may have been the origin of Rimsky's lifelong love affair with mediant relationships, but by the time he was composing the Third Symphony, one has to suspect he had found ways of rationalizing them. By then, I think we have to suppose, he needed to be able to justify his practice by means of a theory. Where would he have found that theoretical justification?

IV

If you take its whole creative history into account, the Third Symphony occupies a doubly significant place in Rimsky's creative biography, especially in relation to his academic work. He began writing it as the summation of a year's cramming—intense, relentless application to the rulebooks. Which books? Which rules? Those remain our questions. Switch now to the other end of the symphony's creative history. Rimsky began thinking about rewriting it, he tells us in the *Chronicle*, in the summer of 1885—which is to say, right after he wrote the first version of his own harmony textbook, *Prakticheskiy uchebnik garmonii* (Practical Manual of Harmony), which he undertook when he inherited the harmony class at the Imperial Chapel Choir School (*Pridvornaya kapèlla*) and in which, he tells us, he set out "a wholly new system as regards pedagogic methods and sequence of exposition."[15] This first edition of the textbook was issued in lithographic form and distributed only to the pupils in the class.

Rimsky did most of the work on revising the symphony during the academic year 1885–86, exactly while he was revising the textbook for publication as a printed book for adoption at the conservatory. The book was issued in 1886 by the St. Petersburg music publisher A. Büttner, whose firm had previously published a number of Rimsky's romances and minor piano pieces. The revised symphony was first performed in October of the same year, at a Belyayev-sponsored Russian Symphony Concert. So the revised symphony was a sort of twin of the revised textbook. Was there a family resemblance?

On the face of it, this might seem to be an unpromising question, because Rimsky's textbook is a very terse introduction to its subject, which sought to give novices a maximum of elementary instruction in the fewest possible words. As Rimsky wrote to his Moscow friend Semyon Kruglikov about the original lithographed edition, "You won't find any philosophizing or words of wisdom or any 'whys and wherefores'—its epigraph might be: 'Do as I command thee, and it will be good.'"[16] But in the lithographed edition, there is a peculiarity that has attracted the attention of theorists, one that Rimsky himself mentioned in his usual tight-lipped way in the *Chronicle* after announcing his "wholly new system" of instruction. "Four scales were taken as the basis of harmony," he wrote, "the natural major and minor and the harmonic major and minor."[17]

Now, unless you have studied from the Rimsky-Korsakov textbook at the St. Petersburg or Leningrad Conservatory, you will likely never have heard of the harmonic major. It turns out to be a parallel major to the harmonic minor, with a major third instead of a minor one, but with the same augmented second between the sixth and seventh degrees. In other words, where the harmonic minor is a natural minor with a raised seventh degree, the harmonic major is the ordinary major with a lowered sixth. When, to test the obscurity of the scale, I've asked friends and colleagues in America about the harmonic major, the usual response has been "What's

---

15. Rimsky-Korsakov, *My Musical Life*, 271–72.
16. Letter of 17 October 1884, in Rimsky-Korsakov, *Polnoye sobraniye sochineniy*, 8a:138.
17. Rimsky-Korsakov, *Polnoye sobraniye sochineniy*, 1:155.

EXAMPLE 9.7. Rimsky-Korsakov, *Polnoye sobraniye sochineniy: Literaturnïye proizvedeniya i perepiska*, 4:246 (the four scales).

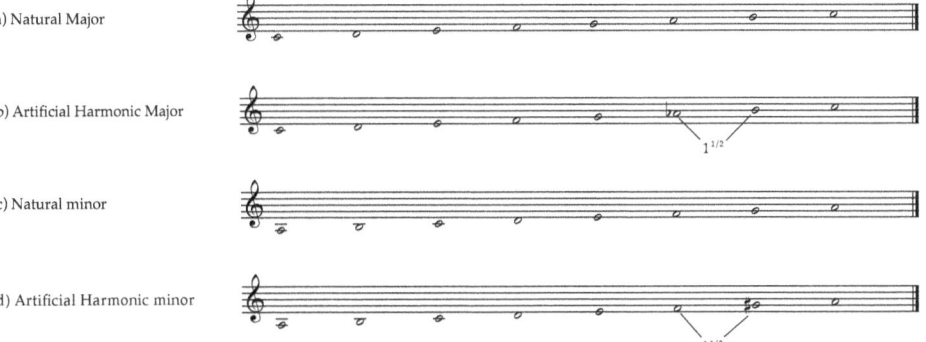

that?" And when I have explained what it is, the usual response was, "Who needs it?" The rest of this paper will be an attempt to answer that question.

In keeping with his resolve to offer no explanations, just dogmatic prescriptions, Rimsky simply listed the four scales in the printed, 1886 edition of the harmony textbook, all pitched on C under the rubric "natural and artificial scales" (*natural'nïye i iskusstvennïye ladï*) (Ex. 9.7), without any further justification.

In the initial, lithographed edition of 1885, however, he interrupted the section headed "Preliminary Notions about Triads" (*Predvaritel'nïye ponyatiya o trezvuchiyakh*) with an elaborate, rather tortuously written, and seemingly inappropriate rationalization of the third item in the list, under the subheading "The Minor Subdominant Triad in the Major Mode" (*Minornoye subdominantovoye trezvuchiye v mazhornom lade*). This unadvertised bunch of "whys and wherefores" is worth quoting in full:

> If we turn our attention to the relationship of the triads on the V and I degrees of the minor mode, in which the major V is a fourth below the minor I:
>
>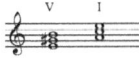
>
> we will come to the conclusion that we do not encounter a similar relationship between the triads of the major mode; meanwhile this progression, completely natural to the ear [i.e., from a major triad up a fourth to a minor one], would be very

desirable to apply to the major mode as well. Indeed, if in order to form the harmonic minor scale we resort to the alteration of the natural minor scale by means of an accidental that raises its seventh degree, then it appears possible to resort to the same artificial alteration of the major scale. If we introduce an accidental in the major scale that lowers its sixth degree, we will get the following artificial variety of the major scale, called the harmonic major as opposed to the natural:

The primary triads constructed on its degrees will be the following:

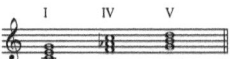

Thus, by introducing the aforementioned accidental in the major scale we obtain the relationship we are seeking between the I and IV triads, the same as between the V and I in the harmonic minor:

If we write out the artificial major scale in ascending order and the harmonic minor in descending:

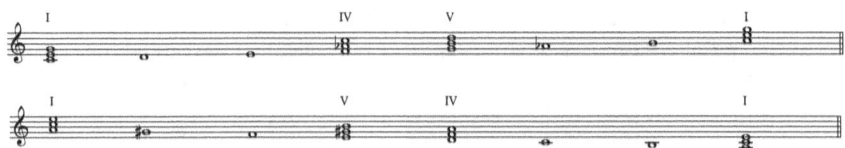

we will see that our alteration of the sixth degree in the major is perfectly analogous to the generally accepted alteration of the seventh degree in the minor: to wit, if the third of the dominant triad in the minor is raised by an accidental, then the third of the subdominant in the major is lowered.

On account of the obvious euphony of such an alteration of the subdominant in the major, throughout this manual we will consider two forms of the subdominant in the major: the major form (natural) and the minor (artificial); thus, the primary triads of the major or harmonic major mode will be the following:

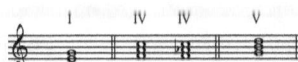

And the primary triads of the minor remain these:

The artificial lowering of the VI degree will alter many other chords in the major, as we shall see.[18]

At least one prominent Russian music theorist of the Soviet period, Yuriy Nikolayevich Tyulin (1893–1978), touted the harmonic major, together with its altered harmonies, as Rimsky's innovation.[19] But it was not; and it is likely that Rimsky-Korsakov not only knew that, but also knew where the harmonic major did come from. Right before announcing his "wholly new method" of teaching harmony, Rimsky acknowledged in the *Chronicle* that he had adapted the methods of two local predecessors in the field of music pedagogy:

> Upon the ancient Hunke's leaving the Chapel [*Pridvornaya kapèlla*],[20] I took over his harmony class, and became extremely interested in teaching this subject. The system of Chaikovsky, to whose textbook I had previously confined myself when giving private lessons, did not satisfy me. Constantly discussing the matter with Anatoly [Lyadov], I became acquainted with his system and techniques of instruction and resolved to write a harmony textbook using a wholly new system in terms of teaching methods and the sequence of topics. In essence, Lyadov's system grew out of the system of his Professor, Yu[liy Ivanovich] Iogansen, and mine grew out of Lyadov's.[21]

Then comes the description of the four scales and all the rest, strongly implying that they were in fact the ideas that had come to Rimsky-Korsakov by way of Lyadov and Iogansen and the pedagogical tradition they represented. The 1886 printed edition of the textbook carries another oblique acknowledgment of this debt:

> Although I am convinced that my textbook abounds in multiple shortcomings, still and all I am inclined to think that I have succeeded in setting out the methods for harmonizing melodies and for modulating, and have done so fully enough and also gradually, proceeding from the simplest means to the more complex, for which I am

---

18. Ibid., 4:9–10
19. Yury Tyulin, "Ob istoricheskom znachenii uchebnika garmonii N. A. Rimskogo-Korsakova," in *N. A. Rimskiy-Korsakov i muzïkal'noye obrazovaniye: Stat'i i materialï*, ed. S. L. Ginzburg (Leningrad: Muzgiz, 1959), 81–93, at 92–93. To be exact, it was the inclusion of the minor subdominant (inherent in the harmonic major) as a closely related key that Tyulin mistakenly credited to Rimsky-Korsakov as an original contribution. See Larisa P. Jackson, *Rimsky-Korsakov's Harmonic Theory: "Practical Manual of Harmony," Its Sources, History, and Traditions* (Denton, TX: University of North Texas Press, forthcoming 2022), typescript p. 137.
20. That is, Osip Karlovich Hunke (Gunke in Russian, 1802–83), a Bohemian immigrant who joined the faculty at the *Pridvornaya kapèlla* after serving as organist and violinist in the Imperial Theaters orchestra. Hunke gave private lessons as well to a number of Russian composers, including Alexander Serov.
21. Rimsky-Korsakov, *Polnoye sobraniye sochineniy*, 1:155.

FIGURE 9.1. Yuliy Ivanovich Iogansen (Julius Ernst Christian Johannsen, 1826–1904).

indebted to the friendly collaboration of Anatoly Konstantinovich Lyadov, to whom I gratefully dedicate this work.[22]

But since Lyadov had been the pupil of Iogansen, who is also mentioned in the *Chronicle* in connection with the harmony text, interest settles on this usually neglected figure.

Yuliy Ivanovich Iogansen (Fig. 9.1) taught at the Conservatory from 1866, when he was brought in by Anton Rubinstein, the founder, until his retirement in 1898. For the last seven years of his thirty-two-year tenure he served as director of the Conservatory. So he was one of Rubinstein's "Germans," and that accounts, I guess, for his being ignored by historians of Russian music. Actually, though, he was not quite a German: he was born Julius Ernst Christian Johannsen in Copenhagen in 1826, and had his preliminary training in the city of his birth. Starting in 1845, however, he spent three years at the Leipzig Conservatory, which definitely made him a German by training. He studied composition with Mendelssohn and Gade (his countryman), piano with Moscheles, counterpoint with Ernst Friedrich

---

22. Ibid., 4:237.

FIGURE 9.2. Moritz Hauptmann (1792–1868).

Richter, and harmony with Moritz Hauptmann, the most eminent German theorist of the mid-nineteenth century (Fig. 9.2), who was also Bach's successor as cantor of the Thomaskirche. Azanchevsky, the man who hired Rimsky-Korsakov to the Conservatory faculty, was also a Hauptmann pupil in Leipzig, some seventeen years later than Iogansen. Thus, it seems probable that the Hauptmann tradition informed theory instruction at the St. Petersburg Conservatory, and that Rimsky's acknowledgment of his debt to Lyadov and Iogansen was indirect testimony to that fact. Indeed, the parts of Rimsky's harmony textbook that have been quoted so far as most distinctive are also the best evidence for Hauptmann's presence behind the scenes; for, it transpires, it was Hauptmann who had introduced the harmonic major into nineteenth-century music theory, albeit under the name *Molldurtonart* (minor/major key).

V

The connection between Hauptmann and Rimsky-Korsakov has not gone altogether unnoticed in the existing literature. Most extensive is the account given by Larisa Petrushkevich Jackson in her Columbia University dissertation, "Modulation and Tonal Space in the 'Practical Manual of Harmony': Rimsky-Korsakov's Harmonic Theory and Its Historical Antecedents" (1996), to which I am indebted for the idea that sparked this paper. More recently Matthew Riley included Rimsky-Korsakov in the Hauptmann lineage, and adopted Rimsky's nomenclature in preference to Hauptmann's.[23]

Rimsky's way of presenting and accounting for the mode thus variously named differed greatly from Hauptmann's, as anyone who knows the both of them would only expect. Hauptmann was surely the most esoterically philosophical and idealistic of German music theorists—which, of course, is saying a great deal. He gave the components of the fundamental major triad names reminiscent of the Hegelian triad: the root is *Einheit*, "unity," the fifth *Entzweiung*, "duality" or "split," and the mediating third between them *Verbindung*, "union" or "connection." (Compare that with thesis-antithesis-synthesis, or compare *Einheit* vs. *Verbindung* with *Sein* vs. *Werden*, "being" vs. "becoming.") The minor triad is conceptualized not as the inversion of the major, nor as its complement, but as its dialectical negation.

From all such philosophical explanations and analogies, Rimsky-Korsakov stood, as we know, at the opposite extreme. His justification of the harmonic major is naively empirical: we need it, he says, for the sake of the pleasing chord progressions it supports. Matthew Riley's article, essentially a census of minor subdominants in major keys, follows suit.

In Hauptmann's heavily philosophical discussion there was infinitely more at stake than sensuous enjoyment. He justifies the necessity of his "minor/major key" in terms of positive and negative forces and the need to balance them. Never equating modes or keys with scales, he defines them in terms of functions, representing them graphically as a tonic triad flanked on the left by the subdominant, its fifth coinciding with the tonic root, and by the dominant on the right, its root coinciding with the tonic fifth. A collection of notes that the keyboard lays out in a

---

23. Matthew Riley, "The 'Harmonic Major' Mode in Nineteenth-Century Theory and Practice," *Music Analysis* 23 (2004): 1–26, at 6 (including a musical example from Rimsky-Korsakov's textbook).

scale is thus conceptualized, alternatively, as the sum of the three primary triads with the tonic represented, quite literally, as the balancing point in the center.

Within this system, the minor/major key functions as a mitigation of the minor's negative vector, thus:

> In the minor ... the negative element, the negation of the positive, or major, triad, which is assumed first, is determined to be the principal thing, the middle or tonic. But we may also conceive the notion of the key-system, so that it shall contain the negation, the minor triad, as essential determination, yet not give it prominence as principal element, i.e. not place it in the middle of the system. Then the positive, or major, triad represents the middle, and its negation, the minor triad, occupies the place of subdominant chord [to the left of the tonic as represented graphically]. For the dominant chord there results, by continuing the positive series, evidently a major triad [to the right].[24]

We do get a whiff of Rimsky's purely aesthetic justification when Hauptmann writes that "although it is unusual for the minor-major key to be formally made the basis of a piece of music, yet it does occur, oftener in the sentimental style of modern music than in the older." Moreover, he adds, "Wherever the diminished chord of the Seventh is resolved into the major triad as tonic, there this key is present; in fact it is then contained in its whole compass in the notes of the two chords."[25] (He means that the constituent notes of a major triad plus the diminished seventh chord constructed on its leading tone may be represented graphically as a harmonic major scale.) And, as if reciprocally, we get a whiff of Hauptmann's philosophizing in Rimsky's account, when he casts the relationship between the harmonic major and the ordinary harmonic minor as a sort of complementation: major V to tonic in the minor mirroring minor iv to tonic in the major.

By the time Hauptmann wrote his last treatise, *Die Natur der Harmonik und der Metrik: Zur Theorie der Musik* (1853), he had arrived at a globally symmetrical model of musical structure—something that, his English translator suggests, had only lately been conceivable with the assistance of idealistic philosophy:

> The system of music is wonderfully symmetrical. Yet its development has never been ruled by considerations of outward symmetry, but only by the feeling or intuition of what is right in music. Sound having been made the vehicle of expressing ideas, [however,] a symmetrical construction has resulted: symmetry has unconsciously been attained.[26]

In this final treatise of Hauptmann's, the exchange of chord quality and function had become for him as well as for Rimsky the conceptual basis of the minor/major

---

24. Moritz Hauptmann, *The Nature of Harmony and Metre*, trans. W. E. Heathcote (London: Swan Sonnenschein, 1888), 21.
25. Ibid., 22.
26. William Edward Heathcote, Introductory essay in Hauptmann, *The Nature of Harmony and Metre*, xxxi.

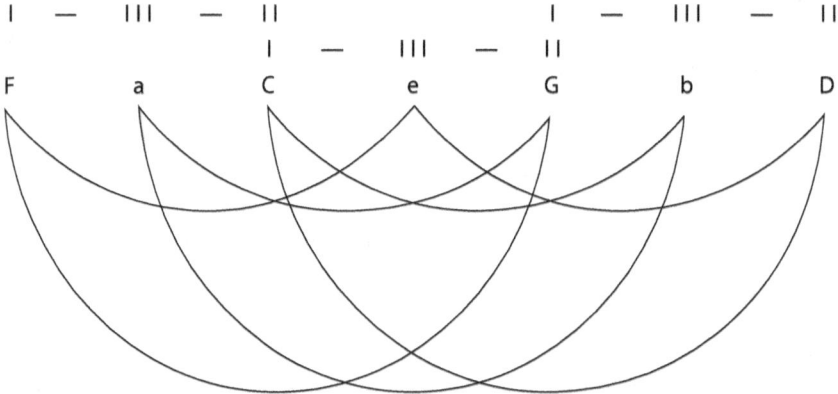

FIGURE 9.3. Hauptmann's diagram of the key of C major.

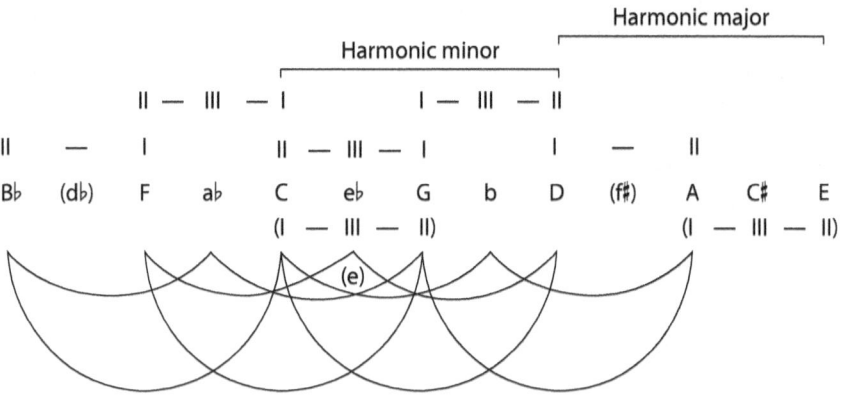

FIGURE 9.4. Hauptmann's diagram of the *Molldurtonart* (adapted).

key, and Hauptmann's *Molldurtonart* was now fully comparable in usage and effect to Rimsky's harmonic major.

Hauptmann's *The Nature of Harmony and Meter* may be the only treatise on harmony that contains not a single example in musical notation, only note names arranged in diagrams. Figure 9.3 shows Hauptmann's representation of the major mode centered on C, while Figure 9.4 is adapted from his composite diagram of the natural minor on C, side by side with his signature *Molldurtonart* extended so as to encompass the harmonic minor and harmonic major centered on G—all represented as triads linked by common tones.

Hauptmann's emphasis on such links has given rise to a branch of theory that has recently received a powerful new impetus in Anglo-American scholarship under the name "neo-Riemannian," so called because it builds on further developments of Hauptmannian symmetry in the work of Hugo Riemann. What has intrigued neo-Riemannian analysts like David Lewin and Richard Cohn in these relationships of reciprocity and complementation is the possibility of tracing harmonic linkages that bypass the circle of fifths, the way actual late nineteenth-century harmony was apt to do. It has furnished a means of connecting post-Wagnerian harmonic practice with various post-tonal idioms in the twentieth century. Adopting a term that was coined by the mathematician Leonhard Euler in a treatise he published in 1739 during his stay in St. Petersburg (so it was in a way already part of the history of music in Russia),[27] these theorists call the graphic representation of such a tonal complex a *Tonnetz* or tonal network (Fig. 9.5), mapping what is now conceptualized as musical space.

Hauptmann's representation of a key through linkages by common tones was already an incipient *Tonnetz*. In his representation the dominant is derived from the tonic by means of ascending replication from the fifth of the major triad, and the subdominant is derived by means of descending (hence inverted) replication from the root. Major and minor are generated by a similar process of complementation by inversion, so that they function as a sort of yin and yang.

By this token, the *Molldurtonart* (or Rimsky's harmonic major), as well as its counterpart the *Durmolltonart* (our familiar harmonic minor), more fully represent that dualistic complementation than the natural major or minor, because the mirror relationship of the complementary dominant and subdominant functions is at the same time a mirror complementation of intervallic content of the triads. The minor subdominant in major, like the major dominant in minor, mirrors its counterpart in a double sense, both as to function and as to intervallic content (hence sonority), thus providing a theoretical basis for what Rimsky rather loosely called the "perfectly analogous" relationship between the lowered sixth degree in the harmonic major and the raised seventh in the harmonic minor.

Hauptmann and (I am guessing) Iogansen showed this by means of a more rigorous analogy. If the minor subdominant descends from the tonic root, then the parallel minor can be derived by strict intervallic inversion from the fifth of the major triad (Ex. 9.8a), just as the whole natural minor scale can be derived by strict intervallic inversion from the fifth degree of the major scale at the fifth (Ex. 9.8b), and the harmonic major can be similarly derived from the fifth degree of the harmonic minor (Ex. 9.8c).

---

27. *Tentamen novae theoriae musicae ex certissismis harmoniae principiis dilucide expositae* [An exposition of a new theory of music derived from basic harmonic principles] (St. Petersburg: Academy, 1739).

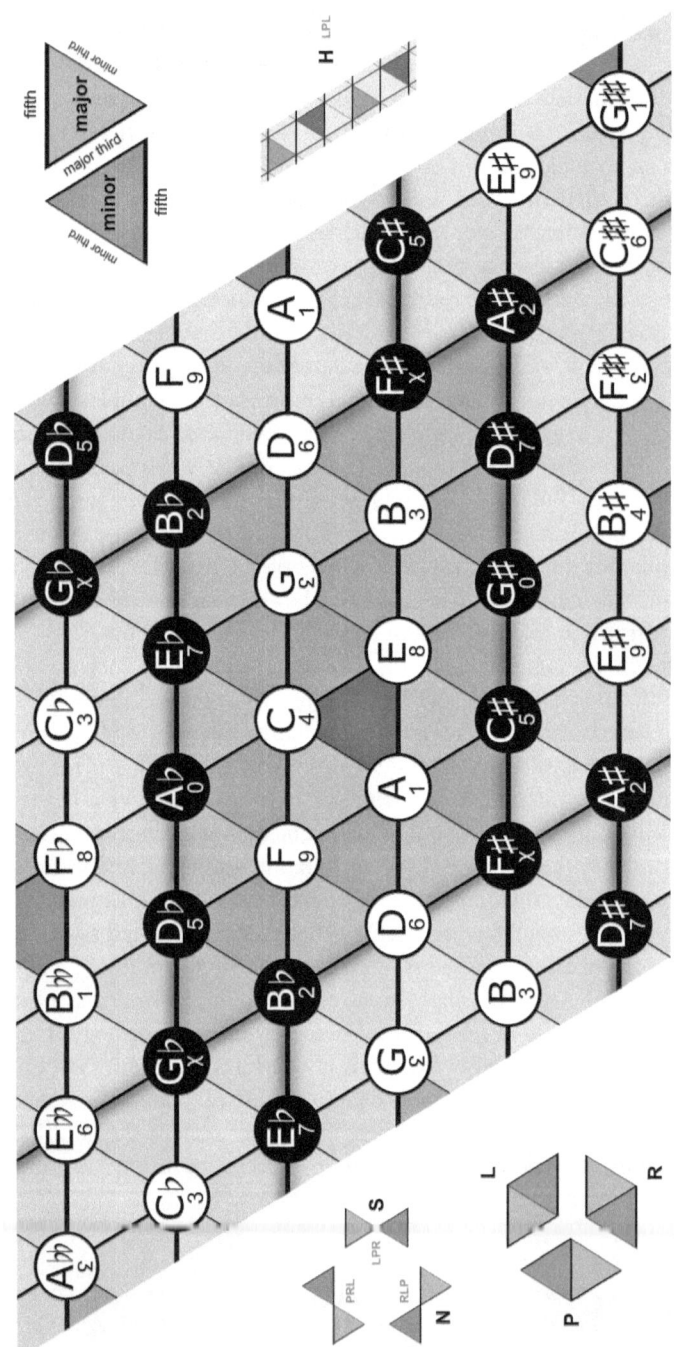

FIGURE 9.5. The neo-Riemannian *Tonnetz*.

EXAMPLE 9.8A–C. Hauptmannian derivations by inversion of parallel minor, harmonic minor, and harmonic major.

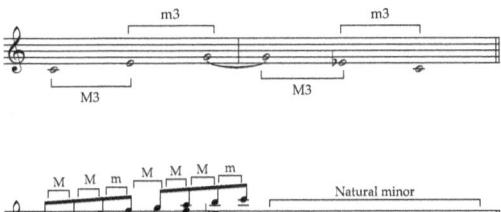

I will venture the further guess that Iogansen's pupil Lyadov showed all this, or a good bit of it, to Rimsky-Korsakov, and that the practical-minded Rimsky Korsakov then took from it only what he needed to justify the harmonic devices that gratified his ear, and that he wanted his pupils to use. For a practicing composer-pedagogue, he evidently reasoned, that was justification aplenty.

Chaikovsky certainly agreed, if anything even more emphatically. The tiny modicum of justification Rimsky-Korsakov did include in the early version of his harmony textbook was already too much for him. In the margins of the copy Rimsky sent him for comment, Chaikovsky pounced on the long digression quoted above on behalf of the minor subdominant. "Всей этой галиматьи не понимаю!" he scribbled in the margin; or as Larisa Jackson translates it, "I don't understand this whole load of rubbish." What made it rubbish was the confusion of practical advice with abstract theorizing. "How can you talk at all about the euphoniousness of a progression when we don't know anything yet?" Chaikovsky wanted to know. More generally, he argued—rightly, I think—that euphony is not a proper criterion for evaluating theoretical precepts: "One can derive all kinds of things from this kind of reasoning, since 'apparently pleasing sonority' means nothing."[28] So it may actually have been Chaikovsky who got Rimsky-Korsakov to take that disruptive digression out of his treatise in time for its publication as a printed book.

28. Chaikovsky, *Polnoye sobraniye sochineniy*, 3a:230.

VI

Without it, how much of Hauptmann actually remains in Rimsky's textbook?

I am far from suggesting that Rimsky-Korsakov took anything directly from Hauptmann, let alone that he had actually read Hauptmann's unreadable book. Hauptmann himself realized that his theoretical work was of little use to practical musicians. He sent a copy of *The Nature of Harmony and Meter* to his friend Louis Spohr with a note: "I am venturing to send you a book on the Theory of Music, hoping that you will be so kind as to accept it, and let it take its place on your bookshelves. I shall not expect you to read it. It is by nature abstract, and, happily for the world, your business is with the concrete."[29] Even Larisa Jackson, whose dissertation first uncovered the relationship between Hauptmann's theory and Rimsky's textbook some two decades ago, and first mapped its probable route to him through Iogansen and Lyadov, cautioned that the minor subdominant can be found in Rimsky-Korsakov's works long before his conservatory years, and that this "greatly reduces the possibility of an outside theoretical influence on a mature composer."[30] But Jackson's work nevertheless convinces me that there was such an influence, although it is not to be sought in the use of a particular scale or chord.

As one fairly recently educated in the American academy, Larisa Jackson is well aware of *Tonnetz* theory. Accordingly, she made a special point of mapping musical space as conceived or configured by a large sampling of nineteenth-century theorists, both German and Russian, as deduced from their discussions of modulation and their various definitions of the relative closeness or distance of key relations (this being another area where Hauptmann's predilection for symmetry and reciprocity shows up). In this survey Hauptmann's map of tonal space is the most symmetrically disposed such conception of all, save one. And, as I probably do not even have to say aloud at this point, that one exceptional mapping is Rimsky-Korsakov's. Only Hauptmann's and Rimsky's maps, as abstracted and rendered by Jackson, show paths through cycles of thirds like the diagonals in Figure 9.5 above.

I readily concede that we already knew about Rimsky's extreme, longstanding penchant toward symmetrically disposed harmonies and tonal trajectories without benefit of Jackson; indeed, my work has provided a lot of the evidence for that. So Jackson's own caveat might seem to apply here, too: Rimsky hardly needed Hauptmann to show him the way to what for him was already home. But the works of Rimsky-Korsakov that go furthest in the direction of systematically symmetrical disposition all date from after the appearance of his harmony textbook, which culminates in a bunch of exercises in what the author called "false progressions along the circle of major and minor thirds," which is to say, along the diagonals in

---

29. Letter of 3 March 1853, in *The Letters of a Leipzig Cantor*, ed. Alfred Schöne and Ferdinand Hiller, trans. A. D. Coleridge, vol. 2 (New York: Vienna House, 1972), 211.

30. Jackson, *Rimsky-Korsakov's Harmonic Theory*, typescript p. 157.

Figure 9.5. These progressions also show up clearly in Hauptmann's symmetrically disposed tonal space, as Lyadov surely knew from his harmony lessons with Iogansen. By showing models that connect the roots along those diagonals with passing tones in descending basses, Rimsky-Korsakov teaches the readers of his textbook to construct hexatonic scales (including, but not limited to, the whole-tone variety) and octatonic ones as well—thus reinventing the wheels that Schubert had constructed in 1828, his last earthly year, in the Sanctus of his Mass in E-flat (whole-tone) and the finale of the G-major Quartet (octatonic).[31]

It was the operas of Rimsky-Korsakov, beginning with *Mlada*, that furnished me with most of the examples in "Chernomor to Kashchei," the article I published at the outset of my investigations into Igor Stravinsky's early style and his Russian heritage.[32] *Mlada*, composed in 1889–90, was the first opera Rimsky wrote after completing the harmony textbook. *Sadko*, from 1895, was the first to show a really systematic or cyclic approach to third-related harmonies, now liberated from the descending bass progressions, yet still linked as if in a *Tonnetz*. But the earliest composition in which I have identified harmonic mirror writing of this kind is none other than the Third Symphony, in the revised version composed alongside the textbook and first performed in the year the textbook was published. The mirroring device shows up most dramatically at the spot corresponding to the one already displayed as Example 9.5, from the earlier version of the symphony: the transition to, and placement of, the tonality of the second theme in the first movement.

As seen in Example 9.5, that earlier version pitched the second theme in the key of E-flat major, construable either as the flat mediant of the tonic or as the flat submediant of the dominant (and if the latter, then pitched precisely on the altered degree of the harmonic major scale). Example 9.9 shows the analogous spot in the revised version, beginning with the transition from the tonic. This time the second theme is cast in E major rather than E-flat: the diatonic mediant key rather than its flatted variant; and this time the dominant is altogether preempted. The exposition actually ends in E major, the mediant key. So one might say that, reversing the conventional wisdom about Rimsky-Korsakov, the revised version is actually a bit more adventurous than the initial one.

But now let us repeat the experiment we performed on Rimsky's F-major String Quartet and compare the analogous spot in the recapitulation. We didn't do this when sampling the earlier version of the symphony because in that version the first movement had no conventional recapitulation, only a montage of fugati, augmentations and diminutions in the tonic key. The revised version sports a full

---

31. For the relevant passages in Schubert, see R. Taruskin, *The Oxford History of Western Music*, vol. 3: *Music in the Nineteenth Century* (New York: Oxford University Press, 2009), 103–7.

32. Taruskin, "Chernomor to Kashchei: Harmonic Sorcery; or, Stravinsky's 'Angle,'" *Journal of the American Musicological Society* 38 (1985): 72–142.

EXAMPLE 9.9. Rimsky-Korsakov, Symphony no. 3 (revised version, 1886), I, 99–151 in keyboard reduction.

formal recapitulation, and in my teaching days, before playing it for my classes, I loved to ask them to guess in what key the second theme would be recapitulated. Only now and then would some bright and imaginative student who had caught on to the mature Rimsky's habits of thought guess right. But after hearing all about Hauptmann and *Tonnetze,* I am guessing that the answer will now be easy enough for the reader to predict (Ex. 9.10).

The key of A-flat makes perfect Riemannian/Hauptmannian sense. It's right along the *Tonnetz* diagonal, the recapitulation mirroring mediant with submedi-

EXAMPLE 9.10. Rimsky-Korsakov, Symphony no. 3 (revised version, 1886), I, mm. 470–523 in keyboard reduction.

ant, a major third up mirrored by a major third down. These symmetrical measurements have been made in a conceptual space that has quite superseded the old major mode, an alternative space that theories like Hauptmann's were the first to explore systematically.

Once again I hasten to assure my readers that I do not imagine Rimsky-Korsakov taking this or any idea straight from Hauptmann, to whom he may never have given a moment's thought. It was, rather, the experience of writing the textbook on the model provided by Lyadov, with significant prior input from the Leipzig-trained Iogansen, that seems to have prompted the very orderly, quasi-didactic layout of symmetrical conceptual space one finds beginning in the revised C-major Symphony, thence in the later operas as well.

Evidence of this orderliness is especially abundant in the revised symphony's finale. The earlier version had been full of rotations along circles of major and minor thirds such as had already abounded in *Antar*. It was a technique the young, pre-Conservatory Rimsky-Korsakov had educed (as he actually reported in the *Chronicle* and in contemporary letters) from Liszt's symphonic poems, beginning with *Ce qu'on entend sur la montagne*, the so-called *Mountain* Symphony. In the revised finale, the third relations remain, but they have been systematized in a manner that actually helps clarify the movement's form, as detailed in Examples 9.11a–e:

- The second theme in the exposition, in A minor, surrounds the tonic (C major) with its ordinary diatonic mediant and submediant, ending, like the first movement's exposition, in E (minor this time; Ex. 9.11a).
- The tonic is regained at the end of the development section through a rotation around the circle of major thirds (E–A♭–C) equivalent to the diagonal vector in the *Tonnetz* (Ex. 9.11b).
- In the recapitulation the diatonic mediant is replaced by E-flat, so as to surround the tonic C with its upper and lower minor thirds, equivalent to the opposite diagonal vector in the *Tonnetz* (and note the preparation: a pristine use of the harmonic major scale of C; Ex. 9.11c).
- At the second theme in the recapitulation, the diatonic mediant (E) is reinstated and applied as a dominant to the diatonic submediant (A) to prepare a properly cadential ending to the symphony (Ex. 9.11d).
- Finally, the coda makes a couple of playful feints toward both mediants (that is, both altered and diatonic) in advance of the actual cadential reapproach to the tonic, which begins, significantly enough, by way of Rimsky's pet, the minor subdominant or F minor (Ex. 9.11e), so that the harmonic minor (V–i in A minor) is immediately juxtaposed with the harmonic major (iv–I in C major), as if expressly to bring to life that notorious digression at the beginning of the harmony textbook which asserts their analogical relationship.

Rimsky surely meant his listeners to notice his bass-line's genuflection toward the coda of the *Ruslan and Lyudmila* overture in the coda of his own finale (Ex. 9.12a). But unlike the Chernomor scale in *Ruslan* (Ex. 9.12b), Rimsky's was not a simple whole-tone bass connecting the roots in a cycle of major thirds; it was a Hauptmannian (which is probably to say, as far as Rimsky-Korsakov was concerned, a Iogansennian) alternation of major and minor thirds like the ones in the diagrams displayed in Figures 9.4 and 9.5: C (I)–A–F–D–B♭–G (V).

EXAMPLE 9.11A. Rimsky-Korsakov, Symphony no. 3 (revised version, 1886), IV, mm. 70–85 in keyboard reduction.

EXAMPLE 9.11B. Rimsky-Korsakov, Symphony no. 3 (revised version, 1886), IV, mm. 122–141 in keyboard reduction.

EXAMPLE 9.11C. Rimsky-Korsakov, Symphony no. 3 (revised version, 1886), IV, mm. 152–161, 170–186 in keyboard reduction.

EXAMPLE 9.11D. Rimsky-Korsakov, Symphony no. 3 (revised version, 1886), IV, mm. 187–198 in keyboard reduction.

EXAMPLE 9.11E. Rimsky-Korsakov, Symphony no. 3 (revised version, 1886), IV, mm. 246–258 in keyboard reduction.

EXAMPLE 9.12A. Rimsky-Korsakov, Symphony no. 3 in C Major, op. 32, IV, mm. 272–277 (Animato).

EXAMPLE 9.12B. Glinka, Overture to *Ruslan and Lyudmila*, Coda (transposed from D major to C major to facilitate comparison).

VII

The Third Symphony thus provides some of the earliest indications of that Rimskian paradox, whereby the composer's procedures became more orderly even as his thinking became bolder. Setting the symphony in the context of the composer's herculean self-education suggests that some old-fashioned German schooling may have played a part, more specific and explicit than usually acknowledged, in that curious process whereby the composer's imagination was at once tamed and liberated. It did not in any way Germanize the sound or style of his music. Rimsky loaded the Third Symphony chock-full of melodic and harmonic turns that, by the time he wrote it, had been strongly marked (in the first instance by Balakirev) as stylistically Russian. Alongside the obvious reference to *Ruslan*, there are abundant, perhaps involuntary resonances with earlier compositions by Rimsky himself, most noticeably *Snegurochka*. So any linkage between Rimsky's practice and Hauptmann's teaching, with Iogansen, Azanchevsky, and Lyadov standing as intermediaries, is strictly biographical and technical rather than style-critical.

Still, I have to wonder how welcome this news will be in St. Petersburg. The first time I spoke about Rimsky-Korsakov in his own city, I described the resistance I encountered when pointing out Stravinsky's debt to his teacher.[33] That resistance came from my colleagues back home, who thought it compromised Stravinsky's cosmopolitan (read: modernist) credentials. In St. Petersburg the news was more than welcome, so I have continued to be a frequent (and grateful) guest. This time, in a paper whose title inverts that of its predecessor, I hazard a suggestion that Russian-educated scholars, even Larisa Jackson, whose research first uncovered Rimsky's possible debt to Hauptmann, have striven to minimize—out of a comparable or reciprocal aversion (or so it strikes me) lest it compromise Rimsky's national credentials in the eyes of his compatriots.

Do we have here, in this ironic symmetry of squeamish repudiation, a trace of the old iron curtain—or the even older Chinese wall—that once excluded Russian music from the legitimate domain of musicology in the West, and that still persists—anachronistically, I'd say—in the institutional structure of Russian musicology, which (to me, inexplicably) retains the old parallel tracks pitting faculties concerned with Russian music (*russkaya muzïka*) against those devoted to (I hate to say it) *zarubezhnaya muzïka*, "foreign music," an ineluctably invidious term? It

---

33. R. Taruskin, "Catching up with Rimsky-Korsakov," keynote address delivered at conference "N. A. Rimsky-Korsakov and His Heritage in Historical Perspective," St. Petersburg, 20 March 2010; published under its original title in *Music Theory Spectrum* 33, no. 2 (2011): 169–85, 229 (rpt. in R. Taruskin, *Russian Music at Home and Abroad* [Oakland: University of California Press, 2016], 78–119); and trans. Olga Panteleeva as "Dogonyaya Rimskogo-Korsakova" in *N.A. Rimskiy-Korsakov i yego naslediye v istoricheskoy perspektive, materialï mezhdunarodnoy muzïkovedcheskoy konferentsii 19–22 Marta 2010*, ed. Lidiya Olegovna Ader (St. Petersburg: Dom-muzey N. A. Rimskogo-Korsakova, 2010), 287–306.

creates obstacles to perceiving anything as complex as the history of Russian music—or any music, really, that has a history—in its full spectrum of eclecticism, heterogeneity, hybridity, miscegenation, call it what you will.

But ought not hybridity or eclecticism be by now the default assumption? When Stravinsky, in his *Sonate* for piano of 1924—one of his exemplary neoclassical, demonstratively cosmopolitan compositions—casts the three movements in a circle of major thirds (first movement in C, second in A-flat, third in E), or when in his *Concerto per due pianoforti soli* of 1935, an even more militant manifesto on behalf of "pure music," he casts the *quattro variazioni* and concluding *fuga* in the finale in a circle of minor thirds (G, C-sharp, B-flat, E), ending in the Concerto's opening tonality, we can say (as I said in 1985) that he is following Rimsky as Rimsky had followed Liszt.[34] Alternatively, we can point in the light of the present discussion to the two diagonal tracks on the *Tonnetz*, and speak of Stravinsky's indirect reception, through Rimsky, of the German tradition that Rimsky had received through Lyadov and Iogansen from Hauptmann, and Hauptmann from Euler (who, completing the circle, was writing in Russia). Neither explanation can be proven false; nor is either of them exhaustively true. Either way, the *russkaya* and the *zarubezhnaya* are hopelessly intermixed, never to be fully parsed or disentangled.

And thus one circles back to this paper's point of entry: the endless debates about Russia vs. its big other to the west. Let's end these debates. Rimsky-Korsakov's career can show us the way; more precisely, it is the afterlife of his work, which we are gathered here to celebrate, that can show us. He has long been a musician of world stature—taking "world" now to mean that part of the globe where the classical music of nineteenth- and early twentieth-century Europe is performed, a territory that now takes in far more than Europe. The whole world of nineteenth-century European music shaped his work and equipped it to travel. To paraphrase the words of Arnold Schoenberg, who probably enjoyed Rimsky-Korsakov's music about as well as Rimsky-Korsakov, had he lived to hear it, would have enjoyed Schoenberg's, but nevertheless pertinently, Rimsky's music, "being based on tradition," was "destined to become tradition"—everywhere.[35]

---

34. Taruskin, "Chernomor to Kashchei," 141.

35. Cf. Schoenberg: "Ich maße mir das Verdienst an, eine wahrhaft neue Musik geschrieben zu haben, welche, wie sie auf der Tradition beruht, zur Tradition zu werden bestimmt ist" (Arnold Schönberg, *Stil und Gedanke: Aufsätze zur Musik, Gesammelte Schriften*, vol. 1, ed. Ivan Vojtech [Frankfurt am Main: S. Fischer Verlag, 1976], 254).

10

Prokofieff's Problems—and Ours

[Tallis's O nata lux de lumine] shows as clearly as [Palestrina's] Missa Papae Marcelli that coercion can be met with creative imaginativeness, and that artists can find opportunity in constraint.[1]

Last sentences are often worst sentences. Having so often reached for them and been mortified by finding them quoted, I apologize for what I am about to do—namely mortify Stanley Dale Krebs, the author of a very perceptive chapter on Prokofieff in a pioneering book that ought not be forgotten, by quoting its conclusion. It will help crystallize the problems that I have taken as my theme. "Although his position on the concert stage is emphatically assured," Krebs wrote,

> Prokofieff left little to excite today's aspirant composer. No crueler thing could be said, for this was the point of much of his life's struggle: a success that transcends the concert hall or opera theatre. For many reasons, both political and personal, it was denied. He would have been the Musorgsky of his century: he was its Borodin—no small accomplishment.[2]

So many of the prejudices that hampered the thinking of those who wrote about music in the mid-twentieth century are reflected in this summation. There is, of course, the modernist—or as Leonard Meyer brilliantly put it, the "late, late Romantic"—prejudice that looks for something that transcends the approval of audiences.[3] Krebs actually began the chapter by observing that "[o]f all music

---

Keynote address, international symposium "Prokofiev and the Russian Tradition, "Louisiana State University, 25 February 2016; abridged in Rita McAllister and Christina Guillaumier, eds., *Rethinking Prokofiev* (New York: Oxford University Press, 2020), 449–72.

1. R. Taruskin, *The Oxford History of Western Music*, vol. 1: *From the Earliest Notations to the Sixteenth Century*, rev. ed. (Oxford: Oxford University Press, 2009), 674.

2. Stanley Dale Krebs, *Soviet Composers and the Development of Soviet Music* (New York: W. W. Norton, 1970), 164.

3. Leonard B. Meyer, "A Pride of Prejudices; or, Delight in Diversity," *Music Theory Spectrum* 13 (1991): 241.

written since 1900, Prokofieff's is the most played today throughout the world."[4] That's not enough? No, of course not: the true measure of artistic significance in the late-late-Romantic view is influence on "aspirant composers." But here again Prokofieff seems to have done better than Krebs wants to admit. Soviet music in his day was to a very large extent the work of Prokofieff epigones. And if their imitations were not successful, it was only because Prokofieff was inimitable. That, too, is something rare and wonderful—yet Krebs seems to deny it.

But the worst sentence, as promised, is the last, because it shows how difficult it was (and is) to compare Russian composers with any but other Russian composers—that is, how hard it is to imagine them other than within the ghetto to which Russian composers have always been confined. (The Russians helped build the ghetto, to be sure, but that does not make their confinement any fairer.) By saying Prokofieff wished to be a Musorgsky but ended up a Borodin, Krebs seems to have wanted to say that he aimed for greatness but had to settle for popularity, as if the one precluded the other. That only compounded nationalist prejudice with modernist prejudice. So let me propose what I think is the proper comparison, and in so doing attempt to surmount both prejudices at once. Prokofieff, I would contend, was neither the twentieth-century Musorgsky nor the twentieth-century Borodin. Prokofieff was the twentieth-century Mozart.

Surprised? I knew you'd be, but the claim, I think, is not only defensible but illuminating. Was there, to begin with, any other twentieth-century composer who can be compared with Mozart as a creative prodigy? We've probably seen the picture of nine-year-old Seryozha seated at his *pianino* with the score of *Velikan*, his twelve-page opera in three acts, open on the music rack. Like Mozart, and unlike most prodigies, Prokofieff developed from a wunderkind into a prodigiously fertile and inventive adult composer, who has attracted the adjective *Mozartian* not just from me. (I'm thinking of Simon Morrison's description of the "Mozartian clip" at which Prokofieff was turning out masterpieces in his first happy days of Soviet residence.)[5] Mozart began writing works that could only have been his around the age of nineteen, with his set of violin concertos, five of them, between K. 207 and K. 219, composed in 1775. Prokofieff became truly Prokofieff around the same age.

There is a recording I have treasured since my early teens, sent to me by my Moscow uncle as a gift. It was a then new Melodiya LP that featured Sviatoslav Richter playing two First Concertos back to back, Rachmaninoff's and Prokofieff's. (You may know this record from its various reissues—some licensed, some pirated—on American and Western European labels.) Both concertos were

---

4. Krebs, *Soviet Composers*, 138.
5. Simon Morrison, *The People's Artist: Prokofiev's Soviet Years* (New York: Oxford University Press, 2009), 46.

EXAMPLE 10.1. Prokofieff, Piano Concerto no. 1, beginning of the solo part.

written by teenagers. Rachmaninoff began his when he was only seventeen (although the version that was published and recorded was heavily revised when he was in his forties). Prokofieff wrote his at nineteen and first performed it at twenty. Two years later he rode the piece to victory in competition for the St. Petersburg Conservatory's Anton Rubinstein Prize, despite the opposition of Glazunov, the conservatory's rector.

Glazunov's opposition is an indication of the difference between Rachmaninoff's student concerto and Prokofieff's. Listening to Rachmaninoff's, you know exactly on whom he was modeling his early style: behind him lurks Chaikovsky, and behind Chaikovsky lurks Schumann. Chaikovsky recognized the compliment Rachmaninoff was paying him, and returned it, recommending that the young genius be awarded a grade of ten on a scale of one to five. Chaikovsky said it about the opera *Aleko*, Rachmaninoff's graduation piece from the Moscow Conservatory, but it is easy to imagine him saying it of this concerto as well. Its first theme is something Chaikovsky would have been glad to have written. The vertiginous first theme from Prokofieff's concerto is not so obviously ingratiating, but has been for me an invincible earworm ever since I first heard it at thirteen (Ex. 10.1). Who knows where it came from?

I'll gladly entertain suggestions from those who think they know, but I think we can all agree that it did not come from Chaikovsky, nor from Rachmaninoff, nor from Glazunov, nor Balakirev, nor any of the usual suspects as of 1911, when it was written. Interestingly enough, Prokofieff does not seem to be interested in the most "advanced" models then available for aspirant composers, either. Most unusually for his age group, he was never much of a Scriabinian. His concerto already sounds to me like something only he could have written, but it was also fairly conventional, not radical, in style; that earworm of a first theme turns out, on inspection, to be just an embellished arpeggio. And in this, too, Prokofieff resembles Mozart— "radical, conventional Mozart" in Charles Rosen's wonderful formulation.[6]

---

6. In the title to a bicentennial essay in the *New York Review of Books*, 19 December 1991.

More than any other twentieth-century composer's music, but yet again like Mozart's, Prokofieff's conforms to the three axioms by which John Keats defined great poetry:

> First, I think Poetry should surprise by a fine excess and not by singularity; It should strike the Reader as a wording of his own highest thoughts, and appear almost a Remembrance. Second, its touches of Beauty should never be half way, thereby making the reader breathless instead of content. The rise, the progress, the setting of Imagery should like the Sun come natural to him, shine over him and set soberly, although in magnificence, leaving him in the Luxury of twilight. But it is easier to think what Poetry should be than to write it, and this leads me on to another axiom. That if Poetry comes not as naturally as the Leaves to a tree it had better not come at all.[7]

In exemplifying these precepts, Prokofieff wrote with well-nigh unbelievable fecundity and facility throughout his career. Come what may, the music continued. The best evidence of his powers of sheer grind-it-out productivity comes at the other end of his career, in the list of what he managed to produce during his tortured last half-decade, when he was a physically and morally broken man, supervised by doctors who forcibly curtailed his working schedule, and depressed beyond anything I can imagine by the political pressure to which he was being subjected, which prevented the dissemination of his work and pauperized him in consequence; by perfidious colleagues whose envy had turned in those dark days into schadenfreude; and possibly most of all by the consciousness that his career miscalculations had wrecked the lives of his wife and sons. And still he managed to complete one opera and start another, and to compose a four-act ballet (not to mention two suites, a fantasy, and a rhapsody derived from it), a symphony, a symphony-concerto, a large "festive poem" for orchestra, a huge oratorio, a smaller cantata for children's voices, a cello sonata, several revisions of earlier works, including one of the Fifth Piano Sonata that was so extensive as to require a new opus number, and a marching song for chorus. And on top of all that Prokofieff still left, as Bartók put it when his own premature death was approaching, "with a full trunk."[8] Besides the opera I've already mentioned, Prokofieff had six works in progress at the time of his death. What happy and healthy composer ever did better?

There were composers who could grind it out at an even more astounding rate than Prokofieff, even in the twentieth century when high outputs were suspect. Here Milhaud was the champion, I suppose. One of my pupils at Berkeley once

---

7. John Keats to John Taylor, 27 February 1818, in *Selected Letters of John Keats: Based on the Texts of Hyder Edward Rollins*, rev. ed., ed. Grant F. Scott (Cambridge, MA: Harvard University Press, 2002), 96–97.

8. Marilyn Berkery, "Hungary at Last to Welcome Home Bartok's Remains," *Los Angeles Times*, 20 June 1988 (quoting Peter Bartók).

referred in a paper to Milhaud's "wartime output for the viola," and I had to marvel. Milhaud was surely the only composer who ever lived of whom it was meaningful to speak of a wartime output for the viola. He ended his career in 1973 with a lifetime total of 443 opuses as against Prokofieff's 138 (if you include the unfinished and projected works). Of course, Milhaud had twenty more creative years than Prokofieff had; at age sixty-one, the age at which Prokofieff died, Milhaud had logged a mere 333. But neither Milhaud nor Hovhaness, nor any other composer who outstripped Prokofieff in sheer Stakhanovite yield, saw as high a proportion of his output join the standard or canonical repertory in every genre. Not a single symphony or opera by Milhaud is part of that standard rep, while at least two of Prokofieff's seven symphonies and two of his eight operas (including the massive and insanely expensive *War and Peace*) are now canonical. Even among the works of Prokofieff's agonized last five years, the two works for cello—the sonata and the symphony-concerto—are firmly ensconced in the core repertory for that instrument, thanks partly to Rostropovich, who inspired and promoted them.

Beyond sheer quantity, one can only marvel at Prokofieff's versatility. He made a lasting contribution to all the main genres of his day, both vocal and instrumental, and here once again he was alone with Mozart. That permanent legacy, moreover, includes works written up to and including the 1950s, by which time the classical repertory had ossified and, for all practical purposes, closed. Prokofieff was the last—that is, the youngest—composer to make a permanent and many-sided contribution to the repertory of classical music as the general public defines it. No one younger than he, whether Shostakovich or Poulenc or Britten or Copland, matched its extent or its variety. Which is only to restate what Stanley Krebs asserted at the beginning of the chapter that ended with such a harsh verdict, albeit rendered more in sorrow than in pique.

So if you agree with me, after this lengthy attempt at a proof, that Mozart and Prokofieff were comparable figures (and I haven't even broached the clincher, their dual capacities as performer-composers), and if you agree that they deserve to be regarded and perhaps even ranked similarly, then you might find yourself wondering, as I have often wondered, why the thought is so surprising. You might also agree with me that Prokofieff is more likely to be ranked alongside Chaikovsky, Dvořák, or Saint-Saëns than alongside Mozart, who is normally accorded a much higher echelon. Mozart is a mantelpiece bust, Prokofieff is not.[9] So answering the question means interrogating not the ranks but the ranking, the criteria according to which echelons are defined.

To make a long story very short, Mozart was the very last composer to flourish before the qualities that Stanley Krebs saw fit to dichotomize in evaluating Prokofieff had been put asunder by Romanticism. Mozart's time did not dichotomize

---

9. See Michael Beckerman, "A Tradition, from Boom to Bust," *New York Times*, 19 December 1993.

artistic greatness and popularity. (That dichotomizing began with Beethoven, and that's the long story.) So Mozart does not suffer denigration on account of his popularity, or his performing virtuosity, the way all subsequent composers did who, like Chaikovsky, Dvořák, Saint-Saëns (not to mention Liszt, the paradigmatic virtuoso), enjoyed, as did Prokofieff, an easy relationship with a broad public.

Finally, both Mozart and Prokofieff suffered notorious vicissitudes in their careers. Their life stories are compelling narratives, often romanticized, mythologized, fictionalized—but also profitably mined for historical insight, especially for insight into the sociology of the musical profession. Both stories are often viewed as sad or calamitous. They are stories of maladaptation, and even more specifically, of thwarted quests. In both cases, what was sought but not found was the perfect patron. Yet where Mozart's unhappy ending is regarded as merely unlucky, Prokofieff's life story is often regarded—and, I believe, justly—as tragic, delivering a full dose of pity and terror.

Its exemplary quality has long reminded me of Wagner as viewed by Thomas Mann in his immortal memorial essay "Leiden und Größe Richard Wagners" (Sufferings and Greatness of Richard Wagner),[10] which he delivered in 1933 on the fiftieth anniversary of Wagner's death, and which became the proximate cause of Mann's exile from his homeland. "Suffering and great as that nineteenth century whose complete expression he is, the mental image of Richard Wagner stands before my eyes," Mann's oration begins. "Scored through and through with all his century's unmistakable traits, surcharged with all its driving forces, so I see his image." Prokofieff, in his different sort of suffering and different sort of greatness, was just as complete an expression of the twentieth century, with its displacements, its pressures, its din, its cruelties. And in that parallel also lay the difference from Wagner, after all an even unlikelier bedfellow for Prokofieff than Mozart. Mann went on to speak of "the century during most of which [Wagner] lived his restless, harassed, tormented, possessed, miscomprehended life, and in which, in a blaze of glory, he died."[11] Prokofieff's life was also restless, harassed, tormented, possessed, and miscomprehended, but it did not end in a blaze of glory, for it was misguided as well. The twentieth century defeated Prokofieff, and the rest of this essay will dwell on that defeat, and on what we might learn from it.

ENDGAME

Prokofieff is one composer—perhaps *the* one composer—whose career, even if Wilhelm von Lenz had never written a word about Beethoven, would have three

---

10. In *Essays by Thomas Mann*, trans. H. T. Lowe-Porter (New York: Vintage Books, 1957), 197–254.
11. Ibid., 197.

periods.¹² Born and educated in Tsarist Russia, he joined the huge postrevolutionary brain drain and spent the middle of his career in America and Western Europe, before returning home to Soviet Russia, an entirely different country from the one he had left. These changes inevitably, and profoundly, marked his life and work. Prokofieff's vicissitudes epitomize the turbulent history of the twentieth century. Three key moments in his life can illustrate its dramatic trajectory.

I've already sketched the first, Prokofieff's winning the Rubinstein Prize with his precocious concerto. It shows not only the dazzling magnitude of his talent, but also his uncanny ability to present himself as an *enfant terrible* and still win the prize, to make a show of breaking the rules and still get an A. There was an implied contradiction in that. You could describe it benignly and indulgently, the way Harlow Robinson did in his Prokofieff biography, where he quite perceptively described his man as a "teacher's pet,"¹³ or you could do it with hostility, using the terms Stravinsky summoned in describing a man he hated: Maximilian Steinberg, his own teacher's pet. Steinberg, he told Robert Craft one day, was "one of these ephemeral, prize-winning, front-page types, in whose eyes conceit for ever burns, like an electric light in daytime."¹⁴ That was Prokofieff, too, except that he was not ephemeral. He knew what he had to do to keep the approval coming on which he was fatally dependent—or, he thought he knew.

Let us move now directly to the endgame, to what has always seemed to me the worst moment in Prokofieff's life. It took place in a hotel room in Leningrad, on 3 December 1948. Prokofieff was in town for the *pokaz*, the trial performance of his opera *The Story of a Real Man* (*Povest' o nastoyashchem cheloveke*), op. 117. This was the opera through which Prokofieff sought expressly to regain favor after the Zhdanovshchina, the public denunciation of the leading composers of the Soviet Union for "formalism," on the way to the "Resolution on Music of the Central Committee of the Communist Party of the Soviet Union (Bolshevik)," promulgated in February 1948. In a letter to the Central Committee "greeting" the Resolution, Prokofieff described the opera in some detail to show his willingness to reform. "I am highly gratified," he wrote,

> that the Resolution has pointed out the desirability of polyphony, particularly in choral and ensemble singing. This is indeed an interesting task for a composer, promising a great pleasure to the listener. In my new opera on a contemporary Soviet sub-

---

12. Cf. Wilhelm von Lenz, *Beethoven et ses trois styles* (St. Petersburg: Bernard, 1852), which decreed the tripartite division of every subsequent composer's life and works.

13. Harlow Robinson, *Sergei Prokofiev: A Biography* (New York: Viking, 1987), 72: "Despite his superficial rebelliousness, Prokofiev had something of the 'teacher's pet' in his personality and had always wanted to please the authority figures in his life."

14. Igor Stravinsky and Robert Craft, *Expositions and Developments* (Berkeley and Los Angeles: University of California Press, 1962), 45.

ject, *The Story of a Real Man* by [Boris] Polevoy, I intend to introduce trios, duets, and contrapuntally developed choruses, for which I will make use of some interesting northern Russian folk songs. Lucid melody, and as far as possible, a simple harmonic language, are elements which I intend to use in my opera. In conclusion, I should like to express my gratitude to our Party for the precise directives of the Resolution, which will help me in my search of a musical language accessible and natural to our people, worthy of our people and of our great country.[15]

Anyone who knows Prokofieff's previous operas will know how drastically he now proposed to alter his procedures and simplify his style, and to what an extent this notoriously and justifiably proud man had been forced to eat crow. But if he really thought that the Resolution had furnished him with firm directives, and that by following them he would be assured of meeting the Central Committee's requirements and producing an acceptable Socialist Realist opera, he was deluded. Soviet directives, such as those in the Resolution on Music, were not made to be followed. Worded loosely and vaguely, they admitted great latitude in interpretation. Because of this, no one could ever be assured of meeting any requirements. As Jiří Smrž put it in his study of Soviet musical policy, that vagueness permitted the Party and its agents to redefine goals *ad libitum,* so that "Soviet composers could be found perennially lacking in accomplishment, and Soviet critics perennially lacking vigilance."[16]

And so it was with Prokofieff. The scene in the opera that shows most clearly how Prokofieff interpreted the directives he thought he was being given is the one depicting the dramatic turning point. The titular hero, Alexey Meresyev (altered for some reason from Maresyev, the actual surname of the "real man" as given in the novella), is a fighter pilot in the Great Patriotic War, who was shot down and injured so that his legs have had to be amputated, but who with miraculous, superhuman determination overcomes his handicap and manages to return to active duty with the help of a double prosthesis. In the early scenes he is shown despondent; but then he is brought round by an old commissar he meets in the hospital, who inspires him by reminding him that he is, after all, a *sovetskiy chelovek,* a Soviet man.

The scene is played against the opera's main leitmotif, which is derived from one of Prokofieff's mass songs of the 1940s, *Pesnya o rodine* (Song of the Fatherland), although Prokofieff's letter to the Central Committee seemed to imply that its source was one of those northern Russian folk songs on which he promised in the letter to draw. It is first heard as a motto at the very outset of the opera, sung to metaphorical words about the growth of a hardy oak tree—words that the melody

---

15. Trans. Nicolas Slonimsky in idem, *Music since 1900,* 4th ed. (New York: Charles Scribner's Sons, 1971), 1374.

16. Jiří Smrž, *Symphonic Stalinism: Claiming Russian Musical Classics for the New Soviet Listener, 1932–53* (Berlin: LIT Verlag, 2011), 21.

will thereafter repeatedly recall. In the scene with the commissar, the melody is carried by the orchestra while the characters sing in naturalistic recitative, the way Prokofieff had preferred in his earlier operas. Only when the commissar sings "A ved', tï zhe sovetskiy chelovek!" (But look, you are a Soviet man!) does his part coincide with the concurrent leitmotif, as if to attach his words to a higher reality than naturalistic methods can portray: nothing less, one imagines, than "the truthful, historically concrete representation of reality in its revolutionary development," to quote the original formulation of the Socialist Realist method from the founding statutes of the Union of Soviet Writers, as promulgated in 1932.[17] Each time the commissar repeats the phrase in answer to Meresyev's various objections, he jacks it up a half-step. After he is wheeled offstage, Meresyev jacks it up two more half-steps and is left a changed man.

One could expound at length on all the ways this scene successfully, and in a musically satisfying way, embodies the goals of Socialist Realist art, particularly as regards the depiction of the individual agent in relation to the community that forms him. One could speak of *stanovleniye lichnosti*, the formation of a personality in harmony with its epoch, the way the Red Count, Alexey Tolstoy, interpreted the *dramaturgiya* of Shostakovich's Fifth Symphony, the work that won for Shostakovich after his 1936 disgrace the sort of rehabilitation that Prokofieff was now seeking to achieve with *The Story of a Real Man*.[18]

One could, that is, if one wished. Or, one could say this:

> Have we managed to liquidate from our creative work the formalist tendency that had reigned in Soviet music before the Resolution of the Central Committee? Have we managed, by giving active support to realistic work, to help it improve its standing and assume the reigning position in our musical art?
>
> To this question one must answer that the overwhelming majority of composers have sincerely and energetically embarked on the realist path. However, formalist tendencies continue to show themselves in the work of certain composers, who have not managed as yet to draw the correct conclusions from the Resolution of the Central Committee of our Party.
>
> The clearest evidence of this is the new opera by Sergei Prokofieff, *The Story of a Real Man*, in which the music is formalist to an extreme and blatantly contradicts the procedures of Boris Polevoy's novella. It is not surprising that the trial concert performance at the Kirov Theater in Leningrad was met with indignation on the part of those who saw it. The appearance of this opera shows that for Prokofieff the fashion-

---

17. Quoted from Andrey Alexandrovich Zhdanov, "Soviet Literature—The Richest in Ideas, the Most Advanced Literature," speech delivered at the first plenary meeting of the Union of Soviet Composers, August 1934, in M. Gorky, K. Radek, N. Bukharin, A. Zhdanov et al., *Soviet Writers' Congress 1934* (London: Lawrence & Wishart, 1977), 15–26, at 22.

18. Aleksey Konstantinovich Tolstoy, "Pyataya simfoniya Shostakovicha," *Izvestiya*, 28 December 1937.

ing of individual slick effects and the contrivance of naturalistic details are more important than the creation by musical means of a true image of a heroic Soviet man and his determination, his powerful, life-affirming will. And this observation points to the unwholesomeness of Prokofieff's musical thinking, as seen primarily in his aversion to melody, the predominance of a dry recitative that is capable only of expressing the most graphic and external aspects of the text, never the characters' inner world. If Prokofieff believed more in the power of the collective, did not cut himself off all this time from his own professional organization, if he had not so resolutely rejected all talk of a preliminary showing at the Composers' Union, if he had not held his finished opera back from public opinion before its concert showing, it is possible, and very likely, that the timely critical interventions of his comrades might have made him aware of the depravity of his chosen path, might have caused him to reconsider the views he nurtured in isolation, and might have enabled him to achieve success in the creation of a new opera on such a significant and sensitive theme.

We hope that this experience, which has led to such sad consequences, will serve as a lesson to Prokofieff and to certain other composers, who as yet have not had the fortitude to overcome their habitual individualism.[19]

That is the final verdict on *The Story of a Real Man,* delivered by Tikhon Nikolayevich Khrennikov in his second official report as the head of the Union of Soviet Composers and read at a meeting at the end of 1948, when memories of the fiasco in Leningrad were fresh. It was published in *Sovetskaya muzïka* in January 1949 under the title "The Work of Composers and Musicologists since the Resolution of the Central Committee of the Communist Party on the Opera *The Great Friendship.*" It offers a rationalization of the opera's failure; but that is all it is—a rationalization. There is nothing Prokofieff could have done—and as we have seen, he did a great deal—to avert this harsh negative judgment, altogether arbitrary and preconceived, which was mandated by the political moment—the *kon"yunktura,* as the Russians would say—and reinforced, as Khrennikov makes all too clear, by jealousy, and by the personal animus that years of haughty Prokofieff behavior had elicited.

Stanley Dale Krebs, whose primary informant was Yury Shaporin, a composer of Prokofieff's generation, described his behavior toward colleagues, as witnessed at the Composers' Union retreat at Ivanovo. "Curt and unapproachable, . . . he ridiculed others, snubbed Shostakovich, teased Kabalevsky, and would not acknowledge the likes of Khrennikov and Belyi. Indeed, he tolerated only his two old companions, Gliere and Miaskovsky."[20] Now he was being paid back.

That is what dawned on him at last that evening of 3 December, when Mira Mendelson, his second (common-law) wife, came back from the discussion

---

19. Tikhon Nikolayevich Khrennikov, "Tvorchestvo kompozitorov i muzïkovedov posle Postanovleniya TsK VKP(b) ob opere 'Velikaya druzhba,'" *Sovetskaya muzïka,* no. 1 (1949): 24–25.
20. Krebs, *Soviet Composers and the Development of Soviet Music,* 161n.

following the ill-fated *pokaz* with the awful news that the opera had been not only rejected but bitterly denounced. Simon Morrison has summarized her unpublished memoir of the occasion in *The People's Artist*, where we may read the pronouncements that were heaped on the opera by all who were present—except the popular songwriter Vasiliy Solovyov-Sedoy, who was not yet world-famous for writing "Moscow Nights," and who was, in defending Prokofieff, probably counting on his relative insignificance to protect him.

The bigger fish, if I may mix metaphors, all fell in line. The pianist Pavel Serebryakov, who was at the time the rector of the Leningrad Conservatory, derided the opera as "a parody" that lacked "both Russianness and feeling." Leonid Entelis, a composer of agitprop songs who was perhaps better known as a critic for the Leningrad press, found that the opera expressed "neither truth nor heroism"; he then had a little field day of schadenfreude, gloating: "Prokofieff is finished. Prokofieff is no more." That base calumniator Marian Koval', a Party enforcer who had (on account of *Yemel'yan Pugachov*, an oratorio of 1939 that became an opera of 1942 and won the USSR State Prize in 1943) a reputation as the exemplary exponent of Socialist Realism in music to protect, and who had over the course of the previous year piled on Shostakovich a three-part exposé in *Sovetskaya muzïka* titled "Dmitry Shostakovich's Creative Path" (*Tvorcheskiy put' D. Shostakovicha*), on account of which he had been made the journal's editor, delivered himself of such a baroque fulmination that I asked Simon Morrison to let me see the full Russian text, and he kindly obliged. Here is what Mira Mendelson reported:

> M. Koval said that "The Story [of a Real Man]" was misplaced self-confidence and conceit embodied in sound. In the orchestra he noted the complete disintegration of sonority, tricks, the breakdown of mastery; the vocal writing couldn't stand comparison with what second-rate or even third-rate composers write; dramaturgically it is a hopeless mess, music that follows the novel page by page; this opera is a document of the composer's unwillingness to reform.[21]

It got even worse. Prokofieff learned that Boris Khaikin, who had conducted the run-through at the Kirov, and whom the composer had thought a loyal friend, had actually intrigued against the opera in the run-up to the occasion, writing behind Prokofieff's back to the Committee on Arts Affairs to warn them of the likely out-

---

21. "М. Коваль сказал, что 'Повесть'—это 'самоуверенность, зазнайство, воплощенное в звук.' В оркестре он отметил разложение звучности, фокусы, падение мастерства; вокальная фактура не выдерживает сравнения с тем, как пишут не только второстепенные, но и третьестепенные композиторы; драматургически это беспомощное произведение; музыка, написанная на страницы романа; опера эта—документ нежелания композитора перестроиться" (Mira Mendel'son-Prokof'yeva, "Vospominaniya o Sergeye Prokof'yeve. Fragment: 1946–1950 godï," RGALI f. 1929, op. 3, yed. khr. 375, l. 160 [pp. 112–13], kindly supplied by Simon Morrison; citations in the preceding paragraph are from Morrison, *The People's Artist*, 329–30).

come. Khaikin's perfidy was the product of fear—a fear that everyone connected with the project was feeling. Nor was it unfounded. In Khrennikov's follow-up report on the way things were going since the Resolution, the lashing out against Prokofieff gave way to this chilling paragraph:

> To this I feel it is necessary to add the following: even now there remain in our midst people who not only have not taken part along with the rest of us in the fight against formalist composing, but constantly demonstrate their devotion to their former formalist idols. These people constitute a numerically small contingent, perhaps, but nevertheless an environment that favors the conservation of formalist thinking in certain composers and impedes their ideological and creative reform. To this contingent, without doubt, belong the conductor Khaikin, who has played a truly disastrous role in the whole history of Prokofieff's new opera, and the conductor Mravinsky, who behaved in such a defiant and tactless manner on the stage after his performance in Leningrad of Shostakovich's Fifth Symphony.[22]

Caught between a rock and a hard place, Khaikin had evidently panicked. Prokofieff, deeply wounded, never forgave him. Mendelson's description of the night of 3 December ends this way:

> He wandered around the room and several times he said: "I don't get it." He took what happened like a man, only several times he said: "I just don't get it."[23]

That scene of Prokofieff walking around and muttering at the futility of all his efforts has haunted me for years. That is the image of suffering that has always put me in mind of Mann's essay on Wagner when I think of Prokofieff. But actually, it seems, he did get it; or rather, that night he finally got it. He understood his vulnerability, his helplessness, and his friendlessness. That is why I think of that day, 3 December 1948, as Prokofieff's nadir. And, as we know, he would never manage to climb out of that hole.

PINNACLE

But let us now rise from the nadir to the zenith, as depicted in a little-noticed memoir by Alice Berezowsky, the wife of the minor Russian émigré composer Nicolai Tikhonovich Berezowsky (1900–1953), who was better known during his lifetime as a violinist with the New York Philharmonic and the Coolidge Quartet. Simon Morrison has referred to this memoir, in his book *Lina and Serge,* as "charming," and it is

---

22. Khrennikov, "Tvorchestvo kompozitorov i muzïkovedov," 25. The reference to Mravinsky's defiant behavior pertains to his holding up the score of Shostakovich's symphony during the ovation that followed the performance as an act of solidarity with the beleaguered composer.

23. "Он ходил по комнате и несколько раз сказал: 'Ничего не понимаю.' Он принял происшедшее мужественно, только несколько раз сказал: 'Ничего не понимаю.'"

indeed gracefully written, by a witty and cultivated southern belle whose marriage to an impecunious Russian refugee was a tragedy for her parents.[24] It is at times very funny, which makes the prospect of quoting from it at length irresistible—and forgivable, I hope, in view of its rarity (the book from which it comes, called *Duet with Nicky,* having been published in 1943 and never reprinted). To me it seems not so much charming as terrifying, and that is why I began with the endgame or nadir, to give us the context within which we can receive this account of the apex with a suitable dose of irony. It is the most revealing glimpse I know of the émigré Prokofieff outside of Prokofieff's own diaries, and in some ways more revealing than his or anyone's own account could possibly be. Like the memoir in Nicolas Nabokov's *Old Friends and New Music,* it illustrates something of the dynamic of his marriage with Lina Ivanovna, his first wife, and like the memoir in Vernon Duke's *Passport to Paris,* it shows Prokofieff poised on the cusp of repatriation (Duke's right before, Berezowsky's right after), so that it provides insight into what remains, even after all the light that Simon has shed on it, the biggest enigma in our composer's biography.[25]

It begins on the morning of 6 January 1937. The Berezowskys had just received an invitation from Serge Koussevitzky, who was giving some concerts in New York with the Boston Symphony Orchestra, to lunch with the Prokofieffs, who were also in town on a concert tour. "I was almost as pleased as Nicky at the prospect of meeting the Prokofieffs," Alice wrote,

> and equally pleased at the thought of being able to observe at close range two such distinguished citizens of Soviet Russia. I was curious about their looks, their behavior and their point of view in matters artistic, economic and social.
>
> I put on my most chic hat and my best dress and jewelry to go to the luncheon. I always dressed up to go to the Koussevitzkys, for Natalia Constantinovna [that is, Mrs. Koussevitzky, née Ushkova, the tea heiress who had bankrolled her husband's career] paid a great deal of attention to fashion, dressed beautifully, and was very observant of what others wore.
>
> "How do I look?" I asked Nicky when it was almost time to leave.
>
> "Ally dear, must you wear that hat?" he said. "It's much too chic for lunch with Soviet composer. In Russia everything is simple. You be simple."
>
> Reluctantly I went to change my hat.
>
> "Is this better?" I asked.
>
> "Yes, but why you have to wear such a dressy dress? Haven't you something not so conspicuous?"

---

24. Simon Morrison, *Lina and Serge* (New York: Houghton Mifflin Harcourt, 2013), 183.

25. Nicolas Nabokov, *Old Friends and New Music* (Boston: Little, Brown, 1951), chap. 8 (pp. 141–83), "Srg Srgvtch Prkfv"; Vernon Duke, *Passport to Paris* (Boston: Little, Brown, 1955), passim, esp. 199, 367. The Prokofieff diaries have been published, trans. Antony Phillips, in three volumes: Sergey Prokofiev, *Diaries,* vol. 1: *Prodigious Youth: 1907–1914;* vol. 2: *Behind the Mask: 1915–1922;* vol. 3: *Prodigal Son: 1924–33* (Ithaca, NY: Cornell University Press, 2006–13).

Once again I went to my room, pulled an everyday dress from its hanger and put it on.

"That's better," he said. "If you take off your jewelry you'll be all right."

I took off the jewelry, picked up a coat and some furs and went to join him.

"Now you look all right, but you better leave your furs home, they're too pretentious," he advised. After a moment's reflection he added, "Be still better if you take off your lipstick."

I wiped off the lipstick, dropped the furs on a chair and rang for the elevator. We went to the Koussevitzky's suite and found that the Prokofieffs were not yet there. Natalia Constantinovna kissed us, then looked at me and said, "Don't you feel well today, Alice?" When I replied that I felt fine, she said nothing further but kept looking at me as though I were someone else. A room clerk announced that the Prokofieffs were on their way up. Koussevitzky's valet went to open the door and Natalia Constantinovna and Sergei Alexandrovich stood expectantly in the vestibule. In a moment or two, the Koussevitzkys and the Prokofieffs, embracing and kissing each other warmly, came into the salon.[26]

Of course you know what's coming:

Madame Prokofieff, to my astonishment, was an extremely pretty, petite brunette with a perfect figure. She had on a wine-colored suit with a sable collar, wore a sable toque on her fashionably upswept dark curls and carried an enormous sable muff. Her furs were superb Russian sables so fine in quality that tiny silver hairs glistened among the thick dark brown ones. Clipped on her toque and her collar were two large gold discs studded with huge emeralds and rubies. The stones were not "reconstructed" or "simulated"; they were rare jewels that shone with oriental fire and brilliance. She wore the sheerest possible stockings on her good-looking legs, and wine colored antelope pumps on her small delicate feet.

"Well, Alice, aren't you going to say how do you do?" dryly asked Natalia Constantinovna.

Luncheon was served in the salon. Since the three musicians wanted to talk music to their hearts' content without feminine interruption, they sat at one end of the table and Madame Koussevitzky, Madame Prokofieff and I sat at the other. While the two ladies exchanged amenities I stared at Prokofieff. Try as I might, I could see nothing unusual about him. He was tall and bald-headed and looked exactly like a well-to-do American business man. His suit was a conservative English tweed; his tie a small patterned foulard, and his unremarkable pleasant face was clean shaved.

Alice began directing her attention to the husbands' conversation:

Koussevitzky inquired about Prokofieff's sons and said he had heard that the composer had recently written a work for children. Prokofieff then spoke of the splendid government-sponsored children's concerts held in Moscow and said that he had

---

26. Alice Berezowsky, *Duet with Nicky* (Philadelphia: J. B. Lippincott, 1943), 208–14, at 208–9; all quotations from Berezowsky's memoir are from this passage in the book.

written a work called "Peter and the Wolf" for them which had been given a successful première by the Moscow Philharmonic. Koussevitzky expressed keen interest in seeing the score and the composer promised to have it sent to him and to give him the rights to the first American performance.

On this occasion Prokofieff would have called the piece "Kak pion'yer Petya poymal volka" (How Pioneer Pete Caught the Wolf). And while it was not surprising that the Prokofieffs were traveling abroad without their children, who had to go to school, we know that whole Soviet families were never allowed to go abroad together. After Prokofieff's next tour, a long one, from late in 1937 to April 1938, he was classified *nevïyezdnoy*, ineligible for an exit visa. After 1938 he never saw the West again. But at lunch that day in the Savoy-Plaza Hotel, thoughts of the children led in a different direction. As Alice Berezowsky recalled,

> The subject . . . afforded me the best possible opening for a friendly conversation with Madame Prokofieff, so I turned and asked her to tell me about her boys.
> "You can't imagine how I miss them," said Lina Ivanovna. "It seems so long since I've seen them. Even when I'm at home I rarely see enough of them as they both go away to school."
> "Oh, please, tell me about their schooling," I asked. "I'm so interested in hearing about Soviet education."
> "Well, I can't tell you very much," she answered. "You see, our boys go to private English school in Russia. By the way," she said, turning to Natalia Constantinovna, "it's just as well they've been away from home, we've been having such servant troubles. You can't imagine how difficult it is to get a good cook at home. All the good ones are pre-revolution and the prices they ask . . . terrific! We had a good one, but there was the constant problem of getting her to and from church in a car. Sergei is always so busy he needs his Rolls, and somehow I always seem to have something I must do just when others need mine. I don't know why, but there's always so much for women to do . . . going to meetings and dinners and teas and shopping for clothes."
> "That's a stunning suit you're wearing," said Natalia Constantinovna.
> "Thank you. I rather like it," said Lina Ivanovna. "I bought the material in Paris but had the suit made at home. I have such a good dressmaker in Moscow and besides, no one understands and handles furs so well as a Russian furrier."

So this is why resentful colleagues used to call the repatriated Prokofieff "that *frantsuz*" (that Frenchman), and why later he was deserted in his hour of need. He and Lina were indeed keeping up a Parisian lifestyle during their early Soviet years. Servants, chauffeurs, furriers, milliners, cooks. That English school, though, would close the next year, as xenophobic panic seized the USSR in the grip of the purge. Just how oblivious the Prokofieffs were of what was going on around them came out in the next turn the luncheon conversation took that January day in New York.

Natalia Constantinovna and Lina Ivanovna carried on a long conversation about furs, clothes and the servant problem. Finally Natalia Constantinovna changed the subject and hesitantly inquired for some old friends of hers.

"You know, it's too bad but I think he must have been a little indiscreet. I heard they were both in Siberia," said Lina Ivanovna, exactly in the tone I might have used had I said that a dear friend had suffered a slight illness and was sent by his physician to Palm Beach to recuperate.

But it didn't fully register on Alice Berezowsky, either. It couldn't. The extent of the Stalinist repressions, then just getting under way, is still debated. And for the moment, Alice Berezowsky was dazzled:

> After lunch we sat gossiping about friends in Paris and New York and then the men joined us and took part in our superficial talk. The Koussevitzkys invited all of us to their box at Carnegie Hall for the Boston Symphony concert on the following evening and we said goodbye.
>
> I spent two hours dressing for the concert. When I was ready to go I pounced on Nicky before he had a chance to open his mouth.
>
> "Don't you dare say one word!" I said. "Simple Russians . . . my eye!"
>
> No matter how she was dressed, every woman who went to a box in Carnegie Hall that night might as well have worn sackcloth or calico. When Madame Prokofieff took her seat in the Koussevitzkys' box, everyone within lorgnette range gazed at her. As she let a magnificent sable cape slip from her shoulders, she revealed her exquisitely cut, shimmering lamé evening dress. In her hair, around her neck and on her arms and fingers she wore a set of enormous antique topazes. The stones were mounted in massive ultra-modern gold settings that she told me had been designed by a jeweler in Paris. Unaware of the attention she was attracting, Lina Ivanovna sat through the evening listening to the music, laughing and chatting between numbers, and looking like a queen.

Here's a parenthesis. I've told the story before of how I unexpectedly met Lina Ivanovna Prokofieva in Moscow in the winter of 1972.[27] Afterward I asked about her when visiting the *podpol'nïy* (underground) composer Nikolai Karetnikov, who shocked me by telling me about Lina Ivanovna's incarceration in 1948, something that was not yet generally known about, at least in the West. One detail that really impressed me in Kolya Karetnikov's telling was that Lina Ivanovna had told him that one of the things that sustained her during her eight years in the gulag was memories of the wonderful musical performances she had heard in the course of her life with Prokofieff. In the light of Mrs. Berezowsky's memoir, one can see that there was more to those memories than the music.

---

27. R. Taruskin, "Two Serendipities," *Journal of Musicology* 33 (2016): 401–31; rpt. in Taruskin, *Russian Music at Home and Abroad* (Oakland: University of California Press, 2016), 303–31.

After her sparkling night out with Lina and Serge, Mrs. Berezowsky reports a conversation with her husband that, all unwittingly, shows us exactly why the Soviets were so avid to lure Prokofieff back home:

> "Nicky," I said, on the way home in a taxi after [the] concert, "I owe you an apology. I never really believed you when you said that in Russia artists are a privileged class and that the Soviet Government gives them the best of everything. Seeing Lina Ivanovna convinces me. If that's the Russian system, I'm all for it!"

As long as Prokofieff was free to travel abroad—and, at first, even to continue publishing his music with Koussevitzky's émigré firm *Rossiyskoye muzïkal'noye izdatel'stvo*, better known as the *Russischer Musikverlag* or *Éditions russes de musique*—keeping him happy was a propaganda bonanza. And it seems quite obvious that Lina and Serge knew this—that is, knew that they were a pair of walking showcases for the regime, and that their cooperation in the propaganda game would keep the perquisites coming. When Prokofieff continued his concert tour, Lina Ivanovna stayed behind in New York and regularly visited with the Berezowskys. "We became good friends," Alice reports:

> When she felt more at ease with us, Lina Ivanovna often talked about her life in Russia. She explained that although both she and her husband had spent many years on the European continent and knew the United States well, they greatly preferred life in Soviet Russia. Time and time again she repeated her conviction that nowhere else in the world could creative artists enjoy such fine working conditions, dignified position and freedom from financial worries as they do in Russia. She spoke of the many gifted young composers there, of their harmonious relationship to each other and earnest desire to glorify their native land by their works. I asked her if the government forced her husband to write propaganda music. Her expression showed that she considered my question puerile.
>
> "Anyone who knows Sergei Sergeievitch knows that he would never permit anything or anyone to prejudice his work. He can work only when he's happy, and he's completely happy in Russia, in *Soviet* Russia." [...]
>
> "Tell me, Lina Ivanovna," I said, "what kind of life do you lead at home? You're so pretty and so typically *mondaine*, don't you miss dressing up and leading a social life when you're in Russia?"
>
> "But I don't dress any differently in Russia. What makes you think I do? I dress the same, I act the same, I talk the same and I lead the life I want to lead."
>
> "But I thought all Russians had to dress . . . "
>
> "Look here," she interrupted, "I know what you think. All I can say is that you're wrong. My husband and I fulfill our duty to the community in which we live, and we don't exploit those around us. Artists have an obligation to the world as well as to themselves. As long as we try to do our duty, I assure you that the Soviet Government doesn't concern itself with our private lives. As to the clothes question," and she smiled at me indulgently, "Russians are among the most artistic people in the world. They fully enjoy every form of the applied arts. We Russians have set out to perform

gigantic tasks. When we've accomplished them we'll devote our increased leisure to the beautification of our homes, ourselves and everything around us." Turning to Nicky she said, "As a native Russian, Nicolai Tikhonovitch, you'll agree with me, I'm sure, that art is as necessary to the people of Russia as bread. All the major arts flourish there now. All the minor arts will flourish there in the future!"

This might as well have been a TASS communiqué. Which is not to say that Lina Ivanovna was insincere. At this point the Prokofieffs and the Soviet regime no doubt viewed their relations, from both perspectives, in terms of mutual obligations and mutual benefits. The ingenuousness of that view, so obvious to us now, and reinforced (as Simon Morrison informs us) by Christian Science and its resolute inattention to the phenomenal world, only shows how thoroughly the benefit of hindsight can be a detriment to compassion.[28] (It can be hard to sympathize with those who seem blithely intent upon their own destruction.) But a passage I skipped in the part I just quoted really tests the limits of one's empathy, because it shows more than an inability to predict what was still an unpredictable future. It also shows blindness to portents that were completely *nalitso*, as the Russians say—there for all to see—and also an absence of empathy on the part of the speaker that was perhaps attributable at this point more to the power of denial than to heartlessness.

Here is what I skipped. When Mrs. Prokofieff asserted that her husband was completely happy in Russia, Mrs. Berezowsky brought up a then much discussed apparent counterexample:

> "Well, perhaps [you are so contented] because your husband is so great," I said. "Look what the government has done to Shostakovich. No one seems to know what's become of him. Some papers say he's in disgrace, others say he's been liquidated."
>
> "But the government hasn't done anything to Shostakovich," she said. "We saw him just before we left home. He's working hard, living quietly with his family and getting along fine. Just because he wrote a work which didn't meet with success doesn't mean that he's in disgrace. Shostakovich experienced something which happens to every composer, no matter how talented he is . . . a failure. But no one punished him for it, nor is it true that he's in disgrace. Naturally, when a creative artist experiences a rebuff he suffers, and he'd rather suffer in private than in public. But a really gifted artist always enjoys a rebound after a defeat. You'll see, Shostakovich will write new works and have greater success than ever before."

And so he did, actually—when he began "doing his duty." But the setback Shostakovich suffered in 1936 was not just the sort of failure that every composer endures, nor was the pair of articles in *Pravda* denouncing him merely a pair of bad reviews. Unsigned, they came not from any individual critic expressing his

---

28. Morrison, *The People's Artist*, 4, 330–31, and passim.

own taste but from *sovetskaya vlast'* itself, the impersonal source of absolute political power, and unlike a negative review, these articles harbored a mortal threat—or have you forgotten the passage where it says that Shostakovich was "trifling with difficult matters," and that "it might end very badly"?[29] Once again Lina Ivanovna was speaking in the voice of official Soviet propaganda. I won't presume to attempt an assessment as to whether she and her husband were put up to it as part of their bargain (as part, she might have said, of their duty) or whether she had donned her own set of rose-tinted spectacles.

BOMBASTIC OPTIMISM

We know that Sergei Sergeyevich's powers of denial were capable of even greater feats than this. He was able to read propitious portents when Vsevolod Meyerhold was arrested and unpersoned while *Semyon Kotko,* Prokofieff's first Soviet opera, on which they were collaborating, was in production, and yet the production was not canceled, merely handed over to another director, Serafima Birman. It took a very long time indeed for Prokofieff to give up the conceit that in coming home to Soviet Russia after making his spurs abroad, he had found his Esterházys. "Here's how I feel about it," he told Vernon Duke:

> I care nothing for politics—I'm a composer first and last. Any government that lets me write my music in peace, publishes everything I compose before the ink is dry, and performs every note that comes from my pen is all right with me. In Europe we all have to fish for performances, cajole conductors and theater directors; in Russia they come to me—I can hardly keep up with the demand. What's more, I have a comfortable flat in Moscow, a delightful *datcha* in the country and a brand-new car. My boys go to a fine English school in Moscow. It's true, Lina Ivanovna whimpers now and then—but you know her. Being a composer's wife isn't easy.[30]

This was about a year before the meeting with the Berezowskys, and Simon Morrison has pointed out that Prokofieff did not yet have the car or the dacha when he bragged about them to Vernon Duke.[31] Simon attributed the inaccuracy to Duke's faulty memory or his wish to embroider on an amusing anecdote, but it seems to me at least as likely that it was Prokofieff who was doing the exaggerating. Duke describes him during his penultimate visit to America as "radiating . . . a kind of bombastic optimism." (How's that for a definition of Socialist Realism, by the

---

29. "Это игра в заумные вещи, которая может кончиться очень плохо" ("Sumbur vmesto muzïki," *Pravda,* 28 January 1936, 6). The author, we now know, was David Zaslavsky (1880–1965), a *Pravda* staff writer.
30. Duke, *Passport to Paris,* 344–45.
31. Morrison, *The People's Artist,* 53, 419n86.

way?) It made Duke skeptical—and with good reason, I should say.[32] Recall that famous maxim of Reinhold Niebuhr's: "Frantic orthodoxy is never rooted in faith but in doubt; it is when we are unsure that we are doubly sure."[33] Prokofieff gave many signs of that unsureness, along with that double sureness, in the reports that filled his letters to Duke after he had gone home. In September 1936, to pick one example, he boasted that

> the four-act ballet which I just finished composing and am now orchestrating [*Romeo and Juliet*] will be staged at both the Bolshoy Theatre and the Marinsky. . . . I'm spending the summer in Bolshoy Theatre's estate near Serpukhov [about 60 miles south of Moscow]. . . . I have a separate minuscule house with a Bluthner piano, and a terrace opening on the river Oka, with all the peace I need for productive work. . . . I spend *eight* hours a day scoring. I also wrote the Second Violin Concerto, two symphonic suites, two piano cycles and an album of children's pieces.

And then he added this:

> I am flattered that you find certain works of mine "timeless." It's possible that therein lies the reason why men who are *too much of our time* often fail to understand my language.[34]

Duke interpreted "the phrase about men 'who are too much of our time'" as "the first indication of an already-existing, ideological friction between the composer and the Soviet musical authorities."[35] That may be putting it rather too bluntly, or wishfully, or (at least) with benefit of hindsight. But we know that the Bolshoy and the Mariyinsky did not stage *Romeo and Juliet* in a timely fashion, and that the actual, belated, premiere did not even take place in the Soviet Union but in Brno, in what was then "bourgeois" Czechoslovakia, in 1938. I should think that bureaucratic delays and interference (even with the orchestration) troubled Prokofieff much more than he could allow himself to let on. Surely he saw shades of *The Fiery Angel*—the fiasco from which he was reeling at the time he was negotiating his return to Soviet Russia. It was the worst kind of fiasco—not a bad reception, but a failure to get the piece even produced. (Prokofieff never got to see this opera, which he never stopped regarding as his masterpiece.) Such obstacles were exactly what his move back to Soviet Russia was supposed to eliminate from his path. And here they were again.

A year later, Prokofieff sent Duke another *otchot*—an accounting of his accomplishments. "Everything is going well," he exulted:

---

32. Duke, *Passport to Paris*, 343.
33. Reinhold Niebuhr, *An Interpretation of Christian Ethics* (New York: Harper, 1935), 14.
34. Duke, *Passport to Paris*, 313–14.
35. Ibid., 314.

I just completed the sketches for a Cantata, commemorating the 20th anniversary of U.S.S.R.—a huge machine for orchestra, two choirs, military band, a percussion "choir" and an orchestra of *garmoshkis* [slang for accordions]. When I think of the number of notes that I'll have to put on paper to orchestrate all this, I become seized with terror! The first "Romeo and Juliet" suite is being engraved. The car has arrived and, with a good chauffeur, it makes life much easier.[36]

But that Cantata, over which Prokofieff was laboring so, suffered exactly the same fate as *The Fiery Angel*—never performed during his lifetime. And whereas the difficulties that thwarted *The Fiery Angel* were of the kind Prokofieff had described to Duke when complaining of having to "fish for performances, cajole conductors and theater directors"—i.e., the difficulties that made relocation to Soviet Russia an attractive proposition—the impediments to performing the Cantata came from the same source as the *Pravda* attacks on Shostakovich, and could not be appealed. It was the beginning of the long process of humiliation that culminated on the awful night of 3 December 1948.

Over the year that followed this second letter, the English school the Prokofieff boys were attending was closed down for political reasons and, as we know, their parents were stripped of their travel privileges. Whereas up to now the children had been hostages, at this point the whole family became in effect prisoners of the Soviet state. Prokofieff was now living the life described by Andrey Sinyavsky, writing as Abram Tertz, in *The Trial Begins*. A young man under arrest—his name, chillingly enough, is Seryozha—is asked by his interrogator to give the names of the foreign agents with whom he has been consorting:

"What kind of idiotic joke is that?" Seryozha paled. "Please remember, I have not so far been condemned. I am only on trial."

The Interrogator looked amused and drew the curtain back. The daylight was so clean and so transparent that you felt like taking a deep breath of it.

"Come here. D'you hear me? It's you I'm talking to."

"Now he's going to strike me," thought Seryozha, his face stiffening.

"Look through the window."

Seryozha saw the square which he had often crossed in the old days, tiny people diving through the entrance to the subway, others travelling in toy cars and trolley-buses, all free to go where they pleased. Snow, real snow, was coming down on them out of the sky.

"That's where they are, the people who are on trial. See how many of them?"

The Interrogator pointed at the crowds milling below. Then he stroked Seryozha's shorn head and explained gently:

"You're different now, my boy. You're not on trial, you're condemned."[37]

36. Ibid., 348.
37. Abram Tertz, *The Trial Begins and On Socialist Realism,* trans. Max Hayward (New York: Vintage Books, 1965), 104.

For writing what I have just quoted, as you no doubt remember, Sinyavsky was sent to prison. That fate never befell Prokofieff; unlike the fictional Seryozha, he remained on trial until the end. But Lina got the full package, and for precisely the offense for which Sinyavsky's Seryozha was condemned—consorting with foreign agents, which in Lina's case was the result of her desperate wish to get out of the country. And that is another turn of events, the effect of which on Prokofieff's morale I cannot begin to fathom. To the weight of frustration was now added an incalculable weight of guilt. The older son, Svyatoslav, gave a laconic interview many years later about this catastrophe and its effect on all concerned, and in its studied matter-of-factness it makes a searing effect for the same reason that Alice Berezowsky's light-hearted memoir is so agonizing to read.[38] Or maybe, in a sense, it is the opposite reason: Alice Berezowsky's memoir of Prokofieff at the zenith is made poignant by our knowledge of his nadir; Svyatoslav Prokofiev's account of the nadir is made unbearable by our knowledge of the zenith.

RUIN

And that is why *catastrophe* is the only possible word to describe Prokofieff's Soviet experience. It means a downward turn, a fall, and it is the word used to describe the fate of a tragic hero. Did ever a creative artist fall further than Prokofieff? It was indeed a classically tragic fall, as Aristotle himself described it in the thirteenth chapter of his *Poetics*, where we find the definition of tragedy that everyone has been quoting now for at least 2,400 years—namely, a drama that produces, or induces, catharsis by arousing pity and terror: *pity*, because the misfortune portrayed is unmerited, and *terror* because the suffering protagonist is a man like ourselves, but preferably greater than we—not in moral character but in prosperity and renown.[39]

But while unmerited, the fall is not without cause. Aristotle called it ἁμαρτία (*amartía*), the inner quality that prompts within the protagonist the impulse to commit the actions that drive the plot toward its dénouement and make it inevitable, and which is usually translated by the familiar phrase "tragic flaw."

In modern Greek (following the use of a related word, ἁμαρτάνω [*amartáno*], in the New Testament), the word means "sin." For this reason, Aristotle's concept of *amartía* or tragic flaw is often equated with vice or wickedness. In Prokofieff's case it is all too easy to ascribe his decision to return to Soviet Russia to moral blindness

---

38. Svyatoslav Sergeyevich Prokof'yev, "O moikh roditelyakh: Beseda sïna kompozitora s Nataliyey Savkinoy," in *Sergey Prokof'yev 1891–1991: Dnevnik, pis'ma, besedï, vospominaniya*, ed. M. E. Tarakanov (Moscow: Sovetskiy kompozitor, 1991), 212–32.

39. For the source of this and all other citations or paraphrases from Aristotle, see *The Poetics of Aristotle*, ed. with critical notes and a translation by S. H. Butcher (London: Macmillan, 1895), 40–45.

born of arrogance or cynicism, or careerism, or self-centered conceit breeding self-delusion. But that is not what Aristotle meant by a tragic flaw, if that is how we want to keep translating the word *amartía*. In fact Aristotle warns against such an interpretation of a tragic action, because, he says, the portrayal of a downfall brought about by vice or moral depravity "would, doubtless, satisfy the moral sense, but it would inspire neither pity nor fear." It would not be edifying, merely repulsive. Because I have been accused of sitting in heartless judgment over Prokofieff in some of my earlier writings, I want to assert as explicitly as I know how that I do not think Prokofieff suffered the fate that he deserved. No one deserved, or could possibly deserve, such a fate. To regard the choices and behavior that brought it about as villainous would amount to no more than schadenfreude.

Rather, let us stick with Aristotle, who insisted that in order to resemble "us," the tragic protagonist must not be located morally at either extreme. He should be "a man who is not eminently good and just"—in other words, not Job, to pick an example Aristotle would not have known, but who does exemplify the case of one whose sufferings produce pity but no fear; nor should the tragic hero's suffering be brought about, as we have already learned, "by vice or depravity." Rather, they are the result of *amartía*, which, if it does not entail vice or depravity, must entail something else.

Modern Aristotelians interpret the word not according to its Christian usage, but according to its Greek etymology. Both *amartía* and *amartáno* derive, it is thought, from μέρος (*meros*), meaning part, portion, or share, whence one's lot or one's due, plus the negative particle "ἀ" (as in "atonal"). So *amartáno* means missing out on one's deserts or not receiving one's due, and *amartía*, rather than a moral quality, is an act—the act or choice that prevents one from achieving what one deserves, but instead brings about the very opposite. Unable to choose between them, Samuel Henry Butcher rendered the word, in his widely used translation of the *Poetics* (I'm still using the copy I bought as a college freshman), as "error or frailty" that leads to a wrong turn, or a missing of the mark—a blunder. And, interestingly enough, that is also the etymological meaning of חטא (*khayt*, rhyming with "hate"), the Hebrew word for what is atoned for on Yom Kippur, and which, again, is usually translated as "sin." It, too, means a wrong turn.

That fits our story. By the end of his life, Prokofieff surely regarded the decision to return to Russia as his greatest blunder. It was, in the most literal sense of the word, a wrong turn. And his arrogance, cynicism, etc., are surely more charitably viewed as weakness rather than vice. The main criterion of genuine tragedy is surely met: namely, that through *amartía*, the tragic hero visits his own fate upon himself. That is what makes his life story, like those of the heroes Aristotle names—Oedipus, Orestes, and all the rest—so edifying, arresting, pitiable, and terrifying.

Is there another story like it in the annals of music and musicians? And could it have taken place in any other century than the twentieth? Thomas Mann would not have had to invent his protagonist if he had based *Doktor Faustus* on Prokofieff rather than a mythologized Schoenberg. In Prokofieff, twentieth-century music has a real-life Faust, replete with devil's bargain and damnation. That is further testimony to Prokofieff's unique and in its way unmatched position among twentieth-century composers, as I proposed at the outset.

But wait. Do you accept the proposition that the drama of Prokofieff's life, being an authentic Aristotelian tragedy, transcends moral concerns? I certainly don't. There are many moral implications that complicate the story far beyond the rather simplistic tale I've been telling of wrong turns and bad consequences. I have been telling the story as if it concerned only Prokofieff, his family, and their problems, as my title has it. But there is far more to it. There is his music, for the sake of which he sacrificed his and his family's well-being. And because there is his music, there is also us. We are in the picture too, as beneficiaries of Prokofieff's *amartía*. Our relationship to his music is fraught willy-nilly with moral implications, and these are our problems, not his.

HIS MISERY, OUR BONANZA

Raising such issues never makes one popular. Thomas Mann found that out with his Wagner tribute. It was written in all innocence to mark an anniversary, the semicentennial of the composer's death. But by 10 February 1933, three days before the actual anniversary date, when Mann delivered an abridgment of it at the University of Munich, a phalanx of Wagner's self-designated heirs had (eleven days earlier) assumed political power in Germany. On 16 April 1933 a group of musical luminaries headed by Hans Knappertsbusch, Generalmusikdirektor of the Bavarian State Opera, and including Hans Pfitzner and Richard Strauss, issued a public protest at Mann's "lukewarm and patronising praise" of Wagner, which so flouted Hans Sachs's injunction to *Ehrt eure deutschen Meister* ("Honor your German masters").[40] Mann's Wagner tribute also led to his expulsion from the Munich Rotary Club on 3 April 1933, which led in turn to Mann's decision not to come home from a little tour in the course of which he repeated his Wagner lecture in Amsterdam (on 13 February), Brussels, and Paris.[41] He ended up, as you may recall,

---

40. "Protest der Richard-Wagner-Stadt-München," *Münchener Neueste Nachrichten*, 16 April 1933, as quoted in Michael Tanner, "Richard Wagner at 200/In Defence of Wagner," *The Spectator*, 13 April 2013. The original can be found in Klaus Bäumler, "Thomas Mann und der 'Protest der Richard-Wagner-Stadt München' (1933)," in *München und der Nationalsozialismus: Menschen. Orte. Strukturen*, ed. Stefanie Hajak and Jürgen Zarusky (Berlin: Metropol, 2008), 273–302, at 289–91.

41. See Hansjörg Franzius, "Rotary in Deutschland vor dem 2. Weltkrieg. Teil II," 2014, https://memorial-rotary.de/dokumente/28; idem, "Diskussion um Thomas Mann," *Rotary Magazin*, no. 7 (2008): 6, https://memorial-rotary.de/dokumente/345; and René Nehring, "A Difficult Way Back: The Rotary Club and the German Jews," *Jewish Voice from Germany*, 3 January 2012, http://jewish-voice-from-germany.de/cms/a-difficult-way-back.

in Pacific Palisades, California. In the words of Michael Tanner, "The Sufferings and Greatness of Richard Wagner" "earned him 12 years of exile."[42]

My writings on Prokofieff have earned me no such prize. I do not compare myself with Thomas Mann, nor my occasional pieces on our composer with his great essay—and I certainly do not compare my opponents in debate with Nazis. But I do feel a certain sense of kinship when I read Mann's take on Wagner, for he and I do share one particular tenet that I have held to in the face of opposition, namely the conviction that we honor our great artists best not with shallow festivity but with renewed serious, which of course means critical, engagement.

My reputation as a hater began quite like Mann's, with an anniversary piece, this one in the *New York Times* on Sergei Sergeyevich's centennial in 1991 (appearing two days in advance of the actual centennial date).[43] It elicited enough vehement ripostes to fill the *Times*'s Arts and Leisure letters column a few weeks later. One of my enraged correspondents was actually Harlow Robinson, whose deft *aperçu* it was that Prokofieff's wrong turn was related to the "teacher's pet" mentality that rendered him fatally dependent on external approval; and it was in a review of Harlow Robinson's Prokofieff biography in the *New Republic* that I first broached what still seems to me the central paradox—or at least the central moral irony—of Prokofieff's tragic career.[44]

To reopen it, let's go back to *How Pioneer Pete Caught the Wolf*. Even Russian-language work-lists now give the title of that piece in depoliticized form, as *Petya i Volk (simfonicheskaya skazka)* (Peter and the Wolf: A Symphonic Tale), for that is the title that has taken it around the world and made Prokofieff a household name. How many twentieth-century classical composers have ever become household names? One, I think, and he's the one. And I can prove it.

In March 1953 I was in the third grade. On the fifth day of that month Iosif Stalin died. It was not even eight years since the end of the war in which the United States of America and the Union of Soviet Socialist Republics were allies, and the newly installed president of the United States, Dwight David Eisenhower, who had commanded the Allied forces in Western Europe and who had stood as Stalin's guest atop the Lenin Mausoleum on Red Square for Victory Day in 1945, ordered the flags on U.S. government buildings to fly at half-mast. That included my school, and our teacher, Miss O'Hara, told us about the custom, which we had not seen enacted before, of flying flags that way in memoriam, and told us that it was happening because Stalin had died.

---

42. Tanner, "Richard Wagner at 200."
43. "Prokofiev, Hail . . . and Farewell?" *New York Times*, 21 April 1991, Arts & Leisure sec.
44. R. Taruskin, "Sergei and the Bear," review of *Sergei Prokofiev: A Biography*, by Harlow Robinson, *New Republic* 196, no. 14 (6 April 1987): 33–37.

Along with the new president, a new Congress was seated at the beginning of 1953, a Republican Congress that had the Cold War, not the World War, on its mind. Republican politicians raised a hue and cry about honoring Stalin with official memorials, and so, the next day, Miss O'Hara told us, "Children, remember the flag yesterday? Well, it was not flying at half-mast because of Stalin, but because of Prokofieff—you know, the composer of *Peter and the Wolf.*" And we did know, all of us. We had probably all heard it performed live, since parents in those days took their kids to concerts. And even more probably, we all had recordings of it.

The first recording ever was made by the Boston Symphony Orchestra under Serge Koussevitzky, whose expression of interest in it over lunch with the Prokofieffs was overheard by Alice Berezowsky in 1937. Koussy was good as his word. I learned the piece from what was probably the second recording with orchestra (there having been a recording with piano in between). This one was by Leopold Stokowski conducting a youth orchestra called the All-American Symphony, with Basil Rathbone, the famous Sherlock Holmes from the movies, doing the reciting. It was a set of four 78-RPM shellac discs made in 1941, before I was born, and my older brother had learned the piece from this recording and could sing all the tunes, my mother boasted, when he was three years old. We could easily believe that Prokofieff merited a flag at half-mast.

Miss O'Hara's explanation differed from the official one. According to the *New York Times* of 7 March 1953, the flag atop New York's City Hall had been flown at half-mast, it was announced, not in honor of Stalin but in honor of Cornelius A. Hall, the retired borough president of Richmond, better known as Staten Island, who brought to three the number of luminaries who died on that same Thursday, 5 March 1953. (Here is the end of the *Times*'s report: "What with the confusion caused by the coincidental deaths of Mr. Stalin and Mr. Hall, scores of calls were received at City Hall and Police Headquarters from persons who considered President Eisenhower's formal expression of regret adequate for the occasion of Mr. Stalin's passing. The operators explained about Mr. Hall. The callers, they reported, were 'awfully sorry'—about Mr. Hall.")[45]

But back to Pioneer Pete. Even though the piece had been heavily popularized in America (and, of course, elsewhere), would Prokofieff have written it—*could* he have written it—were it not for his Soviet commitments? How many twentieth-century composers of the first rank wrote major works for the entertainment or instruction of children? Besides Prokofieff I can think only of Bartók, whose children's music was pedagogical (for kids learning piano or violin). Prokofieff wrote an album of learners' pieces, as did many others (even Stravinsky!), but these were not major works. There were famous composers who wrote learners' pieces in quantity, like Kabalevsky, but who would place him in the first rank? (Certainly not

---

45. "Half-Staff Flags Here Stir Confusion," *New York Times,* 7 March 1953.

Prokofieff.) Writing socially useful music was not first-rank behavior in the twentieth century in countries that honored creative freedom, according to the Cold War cliché (or that honored aesthetically autonomous music, according to an older cliché).

But it's only lately that Prokofieff has been uncontroversially admitted to the first rank—or has he been? The first time I ever read a paper at a meeting of the American Musicological Society it was at a session organized by Malcolm H. Brown in 1978 to commemorate yet another anniversary, the twenty-fifth from the day of Prokofieff's—not to mention Cornelius A. Hall's—death. (Besides Malcolm and me, the participants were Miloš Velimirović and Boris Schwarz, with William A. Austin as respondent—to me all greatly beloved and regretted.) Much was made of the fact that it was the first session honoring a Russian composer at the AMS, but the sparse attendance eloquently gauged its importance to the members of that body. Since then, of course, the range of subject matter considered *kosher für Musikwissenschaft* has expanded exponentially; but like equal pay for women, equal respect for repertory composers (as opposed to canonical composers) commands universal professed assent, even if it is by no means universally practiced.[46]

Prokofieff remains a repertory composer—and that's okay, because as I have already contended, his greatest distinction is the unequaled contribution he has made to the performing repertory in all genres. But he would not have achieved that unequaled status were it not for his return to Soviet Russia, with all its unhappy consequences. When you tabulate the works that have given him his unshakable place in repertory, you find that most of them date from the Soviet period, and of the rest, most come from the period before his emigration. From the émigré years, when Prokofieff was competing with Stravinsky for canonical status, only two repertory items date: *The Love for Three Oranges* and the Third Piano Concerto. From the Soviet period the list is very long, beginning with the Suite from *Lieutenant Kijé* (his first Soviet commission, composed in Russia albeit before his permanent relocation there), and including *War and Peace, Romeo and Juliet, Cinderella, Alexander Nevsky, Peter and the Wolf,* the Fifth Symphony, the Symphony-Concerto, the Seventh Piano Sonata, the Second Violin Sonata (originally for flute), the Cello Sonata—and I've only named titles that I felt sure would not be challenged. I could have extended the list by another half-dozen items without feeling that I was padding it.

Exactly when the émigré period ended and the Soviet period began is a matter of some contention. But if we allow that the span 1933–36 was one of overlap and include it in both periods, Prokofieff had eighteen émigré years and twenty Soviet ones—roughly equal. But what a difference in the ratio of hits and misses. The

---

46. Well, not quite universal: see Karol Berger, "The Ends of Music History, or: The Old Masters in the Supermarket of Cultures," *The Journal of Musicology*, 31 (2014): 186–198.

return to Soviet Russia was for Prokofieff a personal tragedy, but for his music it was a salvation. He spoke of material advantages and of relief from the pressure of scrounging after performances and the necessity of performing to earn a living. But the greatest benefit the move to Soviet Russia conferred on Prokofieff, it seems to me, was relief from the pressure of competing with Stravinsky in chic innovation.

That pressure had led him into a cul-de-sac, as he came to realize when (as he confessed to Myaskovsky) he found his own drastically overloaded Second Symphony unappealing when he heard it performed by Koussevitzky.[47] Soviet Russia wanted the music he was singularly equipped to write. Going back home after achieving an eminence that he thought would protect him from the troubles others faced seemed to solve all his problems. He must have thought he'd lucked out handsomely. He may also have thought he'd been very shrewd.

But no, it was *we*, not he, who lucked out. He and his family got personal misery, and we got a musical bonanza. Better not think of the costs when enjoying it. Thinking about human cost is always a problem for art lovers, however we may react to the thought. Dismissing the problem leads to moral indifference, but confronting the problem can lead to moral snobbery. Shall we deprive our kids of *Peter and Wolf* because Lina Prokofieff paid for it in the gulag? Put *Mansfield Park* on the index of forbidden books because Jane Austen sweetened her tea with sugar harvested by enslaved persons?[48] That sort of thing can give more appropriate reflections a bad name.

ABSTRACT MUSICAL WORTH AND ITS DISCONTENTS

In the case of Prokofieff, such appropriate reflections surround the works Lina rationalized, in conversation with Alice Berezowsky, as "doing our duty"—the many occasional pieces Prokofieff supplied to glorify the Soviet state and the person of its leader. There are more of these in his catalogue than there are in those of Shostakovich or Myaskovsky, the Soviet composers with whom he was usually compared in his day. They include that huge "machine," as he put it in his letter to Vernon Duke, commemorating the twentieth anniversary of the Bolshevik coup, or what the Soviets called the October Revolution. There is also a less often cited cantata for the thirtieth anniversary of the same event, called *Rassvetai, moguchiy krai* (Flourish, Mighty Land), a vocal-orchestral cycle, *Pesni nashikh dney* (Songs of Our Time), and the oratorio *Na strazhe mira* (Guarding the Peace), with its lullaby about the godly protector in the Kremlin; and, of course, there is *Zdravitsa*,

---

47. Letter of 18 June 1927, in *Selected Letters of Sergei Prokofiev*, ed. and trans. Harlow Robinson (Boston: Northeastern University Press, 1998), 268.

48. Cf. Edward W. Said, *Culture and Imperialism* (New York: Alfred A. Knopf, 1993), 80–97 ("Jane Austen and Empire").

the toast to Stalin on his sixtieth birthday, for which a weird vogue has arisen since the Soviet collapse.

Despite what one is often told, these pieces are just as beautiful as the ones in the other list. Just listen sometime to the section of the twentieth-anniversary machine that sets the famous line from Marx's rather unpromising *Theses on Feuerbach* (you know, "Philosophers describe the world but we need to change it"). It is one of the great gorgeous moments in twentieth-century music. *Zdravitsa* has the same soaring lyricism at its outset and again at its peroration; so it is not hard to understand those who want to silence objections to its performance by citing its "abstract musical worth."[49] Far be it from me to deny its musical quality, the way I do dismiss attempts to read secret anti-Soviet messages into Prokofieff's work. Those messages may be chimerical, but the musical quality is simply undeniable.

The claim of closet dissidence, everyone seems to agree by now, is a desperate, wishful claim, and one hears it only rarely as justification for performance. But the claim of musical value, while irrefutable, is no more effective an argument, because it merely reasserts the problem from the other side; for were it not for Prokofieff's peerless musical gifts, and the extraordinary quality of the music he could not help creating, there would be no problem for us. The Stalinist odes and paeans by Prokofieff's legions of contemporaries, the ones who, as he wrote to Vernon Duke, "*sont des zéro-virgule-zéro,*" are, as we say, "not a problem."[50] Prokofieff's music is our problem precisely because it is so good—and it is a problem we minimize at our peril.

To decree that the objectionable text vitiates the merits of the music will not solve the problem; the mere desirability of a claim does not render it truthful. The contrary notion, that the musical beauty of *Zdravitsa* redeems it, is even less effective, for it rivals in its strange amalgam of naïveté and cynicism the naïve and cynical calculation that motivated Prokofieff's catastrophic decision to return to his Stalinized homeland. It, too, is an *amartía,* a tragic blunder, and the debased status of classical music as we enter the twenty-first century is its consequence. Our problem has broadened to become music's problem.

Of course, I am assuming that you agree with me that the texts of Prokofieff's tribute or "duty" pieces are objectionable. Not everyone does. Objections like mine are often written off as anachronistic or even nostalgic—atavistic remnants of cold-warfare that the world has left behind. And the question of where to draw the line that marks the onset of objectionability is always contentious, always negotiable. Honorable disagreement is to be expected.

---

49. John Rockwell, in the program book for the 1996 Lincoln Center Festival; see R. Taruskin, *On Russian Music* (Berkeley and Los Angeles: University of California Press, 2009), 279.

50. Duke, *Passport to Paris,* 314. "0,0" parodies the way prices are written in French: no francs and no centimes.

In my journalistic writing I have actually courted such disagreement as a way of encouraging engagement with our Prokofieff problems rather than their avoidance, deliberately drawing the circle of objectionability as wide as possible, so that it would encompass some of Prokofieff's more popular works, including the wonderful scores he wrote for Eisenstein's films. Not that I have dissembled: the nausea I experienced, two weeks after the Berlin wall was breached, when Kurt Masur conducted a rousing performance of the *Alexander Nevsky* cantata in San Francisco, was real and palpable.[51] By now I can respond again to the rousing, triumphal qualities of this work that I had always loved without qualms. Is my regained equanimity evidence of moral inconstancy, or evidence that the music is after all inoffensive? I think not. We never experience anything except in a context, and as contexts change so does experience. I'll never understand why Kurt Masur, fresh from his leadership of the Leipzig resistance, did not change a program that had become inopportune, unless it was to avoid any appearance, however specious, of censorship. But the confusion of discretion with suppression is a vice—my idea of an atavistic remnant of cold-warfare.

Or take *Ivan Groznïy* (Ivan the Terrible), the other Prokofieff-Eisenstein collaboration, which, like the *Alexander Nevsky* score, is now often performed in concert as variously arranged by Levon Atovmyan, Abram Stasevich, and others. Here censorship is an even more intractable, paradoxical issue because the suppressed second part of the trilogy, which shows the *oprichniki* (Ivan's NKVD, you might say, as more than hinted in the film) swearing allegiance to their leader, promising "На Руси государю как пёс служить" (to serve Russia's ruler like a dog), is the more objectionable one, so that objections to its content are in tension with discomfort at its suppression.

That chorus of *oprichniki* made it into the cantata, and when a performance of Stasevich's *Ivan Groznïy* cantata was scheduled amidst lots of hoopla in New York in 1995, I seized the chance to turn it into what we like to call a teachable moment. I stated the case against performing the piece, and for once (of exactly twice in my career as a writer for the *New York Times*) I also succeeded in writing the headline that the editors agreed to run above it: "Great Artists Serving Stalin Like a Dog."[52] When reprinting the piece fifteen years later, I was able to report on, and answer, the angry mail it elicited. I did not report, however, on what seemed at the time a more ephemeral response (because it took place on the air), but one that is especially pertinent to the issues now under scrutiny.

It came from the organizers of a symposium on *Ivan Groznïy*, to whom I had issued a mock challenge in the *Times* to defend the piece against my specific

---

51. Taruskin, "Prokofieff's Return," in *On Russian Music*, 233–45, at 233–37.

52. *New York Times*, 28 May 1995, Arts & Leisure sec.; rpt. with an update in Taruskin, *On Russian Music*, 270–76.

strictures. National Public Radio invited them to answer me (and me to give a sur-rebuttal, but I declined). It was broadcast, if I am not mistaken, during the *Morning Edition* program. (A colleague, who was up early that day and listening, called me and told me to tune in, pronto, so I heard most of it.) I was rather sorry that NPR had bothered the organizers, because one of them thus put on the spot was Oleg Prokofiev, the composer's younger son, whom I had no wish to confront or embarrass.

What makes his statement on the air so pertinent today is the way it nearly paraphrased his father's rationalization of his return (or his mother's assurances to Alice Berezowsky about "doing our duty"). There was nothing objectionable, he said, in pieces like *Ivan Groznïy* or *Zdravitsa*, because they only did what any number of works by Lully or Haydn did, namely pay tribute to those who paid the piper (in Lully's case a king, in Haydn's a count). If we listen to Lully or Haydn without protest or discomfort, and of course we do, then it is unfairly inconsistent to object when Prokofieff's tributes to his patron are performed. Harlow Robinson, the other organizer, with whom I have been fated repeatedly to clash, put it more strongly a couple of years later, in the introduction to a book of Prokofieff letters. "To condemn the hopelessly apolitical Prokofiev as a scheming apologist for Stalinism is no less absurd than describing Mozart as a cynical lackey of the Hapsburg emperors."[53]

There is a lot here to dispute, and to correct. Mozart never had a chance to be the emperor's lackey. No one ever accused Prokofieff of scheming, just of building a career, the way any artist has to do. His own political beliefs have never even entered into this discussion, nor should they. They are irrelevant to our problem, which involves not Prokofieff's relationship to his patrons but, rather, ours. How many of us know anything about Nikolaus Esterházy except that he was Haydn's employer and played the baryton? A good egg, we're apt to think, viewing him entirely from the perspective of the composer, with whom we have unconsciously (or even consciously) identified ourselves. Most of us probably know a bit more about Louis XIV, and so we do not see him wholly as Lully did. We may even disapprove of him in one way or another, as the personification of royal absolutism, or the divine right of kings, or for revoking the Edict of Nantes, or for having (as he is said to have confessed on his deathbed) "undertaken war too lightly and . . . sustained it for vanity."[54]

But still, he is no Stalin, and I use the present tense advisedly, since the relevant standard is that of the present, not the past. The difference is not magnitude of iniquity. Time eventually makes a difference in kind. Unless we are historians, we don't know the Protestants who faced persecution under Louis XIV or the con-

---

53. Robinson (ed.), *Selected Letters of Sergei Prokofiev*, xiv.

54. *Journal du Marquis de Dangeaux*, quoted in John Hajdu Heyer, *The Lure and Legacy of Music at Versailles: Louis XIV and the Aix School* (Cambridge: Cambridge University Press, 2014), 219.

scripts who died for the sake of his vanity, any more than we know the serfs who perished so that Peter the Great's metropolitan monument to himself could be built. Stalin's victims, or rather those who mourn them, are still among us. They include relatives of mine. It is in part for their sake that I object to hearing Stalin praised from the stage of Carnegie Hall, and in particular to seeing comfortable and oblivious people cheering at the end of a panegyric to Stalin because Prokofieff has given it such a nice package.

I don't condemn Prokofieff for doing what he could to better his lot and that of his family, and I am especially inclined to forgive him his *amartía* in view of its untoward results, and the pity and terror to which they give rise. I agree that opposing the performance of *Zdravitsa* is in one sense an injustice to Prokofieff, who was not responsible for Stalin's crimes, and who lavished his talent and his hard work on the score. But those who protest that avoiding it subjects Prokofieff to a second martyrdom are, I think, misguided. Since 5 March 1953 there is nothing we can do to harm the composer, or earn his gratitude. The debate, if we wish to go on debating, is not about Prokofieff. It's about us. Our problem.

And it is for us to solve it—or rather, to keep solving it, for our solutions can only be provisional, pending changing times and changing needs. Prokofieff won't help us, as Thomas Mann knew very well. "It is idle," he wrote at the beginning of the long closing paragraph to his Wagner essay,

> to conjure great men out of eternity into our now and here—to the end of asking them their views upon questions that were put differently in their day and thus are foreign to their spirit. How would Richard Wagner [or, I'll add, Serge Prokofieff] stand toward our problems, our needs and the tasks before us? That "would" has a hollow sound, the position is unthinkable. Views are of secondary importance, even in their own present.[55]

Yes, views are secondary. What counts are deeds, which have consequences. Prokofieff's deeds—his *amartía*—have had consequences not only for him, but for us as well, and that is why his story is so endlessly fascinating and compelling as we come to grips, we twenty-first-century historians and listeners, with the twentieth century, its displacements, its coercions, its mass politics from which no one could escape, its suffering, and, withal, its greatness.

---

55. *Essays by Thomas Mann*, 253–54.

11

Коле посвящается (for Kolya)

I have not formally studied the late-Soviet nonconformist music scene, but I lived in proximity to it for a year, just when it was at a high point of—what to call it?—conspicuous inactivity. You couldn't hear the work of Denisov or Schnittke in concert halls in 1971 or 1972, but in the Moscow Conservatory dorm, where I lived for nine months over those years, you heard them constantly discussed in reverent whispers, along with the even more shadowy Philipp Gershkovich, an actual Webern pupil then living, improbably enough, in darkest Moscow, about whom I heard plenty from Dima Smirnov, now long a resident of the United Kingdom where his composing career has flourished, who then lived on my floor and often dropped in to my room.[1] Russian students use the familiar second person when talking among themselves, and once that form of address is established it is set for life. So when twenty years later, in 1991, Dima and I met again at a conference on late Soviet music in Columbus, Ohio, when the Soviet Union was about to dissolve and travel restrictions had been much relaxed, the many Soviet participants were astounded to hear Dima call to me, "*Privet Richard, kak tï pozhivayesh'?*" (Hi Rich-

---

Keynote address, international conference "Found in Time," University of Chicago, 5 October 2017; published, as "Коле Посвящается," trans. Anton Svynarenko, in Julia Vaingurt and William Nickell, eds., *Nestandart: Zabïtïye èksperimentï v sovetskoy kul'ture, 1934–1964 godï* (Moscow: Nauchnoye Literaturnoye Obozreniye, 2020).

1. And now there is a book about him, by the same Dima: Dmitri Smirnov, *A Geometer of Sound Crystals: A Book on Philipp Hershkowitz* (Berlin: Ernst Kuhn Verlag, 2003). Rather than emend the text, I will just add here the sad news that Dima died in London on 9 April 2020, an early victim of the Covid-19 pandemic.

ard, how're you doing?)—or something like that. I can serve here not as a scholar but as a sort of informant.

And what I want to inform you about is my brief but intense friendship with a composer who was then even more conspicuously inactive than Denisov, Schnittke, Gubaidulina, or Ustvolskaya. He was literally celebrated for being unknown. You may be familiar with the book, edited by Valeria Tsenova, that was originally published in Moscow in 1994 under the title *Muzïka iz bïvshego SSSR* (Music from the Former USSR) and later published in somewhat awkward English translation as *Underground Music from the Former USSR*. The lurid additional word in the English gives a taste of the old Cold War bromides that I have made a career of trying to surmount. But that word *podpol'naya*, or "underground," was indeed a word that was often applied in those days, with varying degrees of pertinence, to the sort of musician or work that we are met here to discuss. (Nowadays the colloquial Russian for it is *andergraund*, which suffices to tell a long story.) Even within Tsenova's collection, the chapter devoted to the composer I want to talk about today, by Mikhaíl Yevgen'yevich Tarakanov, a very distinguished musicologist of my generation (and the author of the first Soviet book on the music of Alban Berg), singled him out as furthest underground of all.[2]

Tarakanov's chapter was based on an essay of his that had appeared as a lead article in *Sovetskaya muzïka*, the official organ of the Union of Soviet Composers, in 1990—year three of perestroika and the last full year of Soviet power—under the provocative title "Apologıya neprıznaniya," which might be translated as "In Defense of Nonrecognition." That article had begun with a somewhat hackneyed metaphor in which master composers are arranged on what the author called the *obshchestvenno-tvorcheskaya "piramida,"* "the social and artistic pyramid," or what we would call the ladder of success. "Some," he wrote,

> achieve world recognition—their works are heard in prestigious musical venues, and critics hold them up as the leaders of the nation's musical culture; others prosper as functionaries in the system of cultural institutions, among which the Composers' Union is by no means the least. But a third group remains to one side—they are granted at best an honorable mention in whatever few remarks by professional critics might somehow get into print.[3]

But no, he insists: this is not going to be a protest against "the cruel Darwinian law of the struggle for existence" and its misapplication to matters of the spirit. Nor is it going to be a wishful prediction of the "posthumous triumph of those who in life found no place in the sun, but bore the mark of neglect stamped upon them by the verdict of public opinion, which is not subject to appeal." Indeed, he continues,

---

2. Mikhaíl Tarakanov, *Muzïkal'nïy teatr Al'bana Berga* (Moscow: Sovetskiy kompozitor, 1976)
3. Mikhaíl Tarakanov, "Apologiya nepriznaniya," *Sovetskaya muzïka*, 1990, no. 7, 6–13, at 6.

> [f]or me the current boom around certain names that had formerly suffered public ostracism carries a whiff of blatant *spekulyatsiya* [I leave that obvious cognate of "speculation" in Russian—where it can only mean shady commercial dealings—so that it can convey its full dose of negative vibration—RT]. At best it only affirms the eternal verity that there is no prophet in his native land [*sic*], since rehabilitation applies mainly to those creative figures and artistic values that are long since recognized "over there." It might seem that now, in the time of *glasnost'* and the removal of the ruthless controls once exercised by state censorship, the possibility would open up for the free flowering of creative individuality, when the main criterion for recognition would simply be the aesthetic value of the work of art. But no, in our time of still far from perfect creative freedom, the path of an independent artist who wishes not to take any political side, whether nativist or westernizing, has become if anything even more hedged with pitfalls than in those bad old days when the fate of a creative artist was decided by ham-fisted functionaries and incompetent bureaucrats, and the only opposition that could be halfway grudgingly tolerated was aesthetic opposition. Even now a lone artist is an outcast who feels out of his element among confrères who are sharply defined, if one may say so, by their sociopolitical sympathies . . .
>
> I needed this long preamble because in the present article I will be talking about precisely this sort of artist, who for long years was neither the beneficiary of those in a position to smooth his creative path, nor their fierce antagonist who has thus won (and not wrongly!) a secure position in the global musical marketplace. With unerring instinct they have sensed him "not one of their own," by virtue of the consistent nonconformism of his music and at the same time the absence of any urge to keep out in front, hastily grabbing hold of the *dernier cri* in foreign fashion.[4]

At the end of the article, after describing his subject's frustrated career and some of his neglected works, Tarakanov reaches for an even higher rhetorical pitch:

> Still and all, there is something downright inspiring in prolonged non-recognition. For only a master who writes for himself alone is completely free. He does not need to reckon or calculate, as little heeding the tastes of the public—who cares anymore about the people who visit our half-empty theaters and concert halls?—as he does the whims of performers or the clandestine arbiters of fashion. Nobody is going to push him around, and he can polish his masterworks as much as his artistic conscience demands. Finally, he is spared the risk of disappointment, when his works, on seeing the light, are for any number of reasons shattered against the wall of incomprehension. Isn't it better to keep one's creations to oneself, jealously protecting them from the judgment of fools and the laughter of the uncaring mob, never letting them out of one's hands, knowing all too well that they will even so remain unclaimed and

---

4. Ibid., 6–7. Misquotation from the Bible is par for the Soviet course. Tarakanov's "eternal verity" is something Jesus says in all four gospels, e.g. Matthew 13:57 in the King James version: "A prophet is not without honor, save in his own country."

unappreciated? Inasmuch as the new millennium will give rise to new problems and new people to whom much that the twentieth century took seriously will look ridiculous, the creator of an unknown masterpiece needn't envy the cunning nonentity. He knows what his accomplishment is worth. . . .[5]

And so on, in compulsive superfluity. By the time this romantic credo had been adapted for Tsenova's book, the Soviet regime had collapsed, and by the time the English translation was published, under the title "A Drama of Non-recognition," the subject of the piece had died. That only intensified the author's ardor, and emboldened him to make at the outset the direct comparisons that prudence had formerly forbidden. Here, with apologies for the unidiomatic translation that it somehow seems appropriate to retain, is the rewritten first paragraph as translated by Romela Kohanovskaya for publication in 1998, in which its subject was now identified as

> belong[ing] to the ranks of Russian master musicians kept in the background for many years and even decades. The composer seemed to be haunted by persistent neglect in his homeland and the indifference on the part of those in the West who promoted some of his fellow-countrymen. He did not share in the currently successful careers of the recognized leaders of the Soviet avant-garde represented by "the magnificent three": Edison Denisov, Alfred Schnittke and Sophia Gubaidulina. The ominous shadow of non-recognition has been cast upon his name, with his compositions remaining still unclaimed.[6]

This kind of writing makes an equivocal impression; but I thought it worth quoting at some length to establish the fact that we are dealing with someone who exemplified to a superlative, even mythic degree, both in his own time and since, the characteristics that we are here to evaluate, as regards both the creative protagonist and also the environment within which he operated. He was indeed the quintessential, unrivaled outsider among Soviet composers who had major reputations despite the rarity with which their works were allowed exposure to audiences. And if you have been treating all of this preludizing, both mine and Tarakanov's, as a guessing game, as I have been more or less begging you to do, you

---

5. Ibid., 13.
6. Mikhaíl Tarakanov, "A Drama of Non-recognition: A Profile of Nikolai Karetnikov's Life and Work," in *Underground Music from the Former USSR*, ed. Valeria Tsenova (Amsterdam: Harwood Academic Publishers, 1998), 98–109, at 98. The reference to the "magnificent three" alludes to the historic concert of 15 April 1982 in the Great Hall of the Moscow Conservatory, where these three composers were officially canonized in performances by the handpicked orchestra of the USSR Ministry of Culture under Gennady Rozhdestvensky. The program consisted of *Zhivopis'* (*Peinture* or Painting) by Denisov (1970); Gubaidulina's *Offertorium* for violin and orchestra (presented under the neutralized title Concerto), with Oleg Kagan as soloist; and Schnittke's "Gogol Suite," assembled from his incidental music to various productions at the Taganka Theater—all framed by a March that Rozhdestvensky had commissioned from all three in collaboration. The concert was recorded and widely distributed.

may well have guessed by now that the composer I have been so elaborately adumbrating is Nikolai Nikolayevich Karetnikov, who was born in Moscow in 1930 and who alas died there, long before his time, in 1994.

His name is far less obscure now than at the time of his death. A lot of his music, I have learned to my pleasant surprise, can be found on YouTube, in performances by such leading post-Soviet conductors as Valeriy Gergiyev and Alexander Lazarev. Some of it has been recorded for commercial release. There has been a biography in Russian, originally published in 1997 in a press run of only five hundred copies, issued in the small city of Rostov-on-Don, where the author, Alexander Yakovlevich Selitsky, happened to live, but reissued in 2011 in an expanded edition published in Moscow.[7] It is now possible to learn the facts of his life and hear the sound of his music to an extent that was not possible when I knew him; so I do not have to tell you facts that you can easily look up, and I will only talk about such music of his that I had occasion to talk about with him. My subject is my friend Kolya as I knew him in Moscow in 1971 and 1972, which was indeed the period in which this most isolated figure was at his most isolated. In the preface to his second edition, Selitsky writes that

> among composers of the next generation, those born in the fifties, it is widely thought that the persecution suffered by many masters of the Soviet epoch at the hands of the authorities is either a myth or else something the persecuted purposely organized themselves. One contemporary of ours, respected, highly talented, and very successful, has put it about that those devastating articles in the main newspapers were instigated by the friends of Alfred Schnittke so as to fire up interest in him in the West. He goes on to say, "I would recommend that one read carefully the big books on the lives of Schnittke, Denisov, or Karetnikov. If one looks at it objectively, one will have to affirm that all this talk about their problems is just a myth." . . . One reason for reissuing this book is to remind readers that the rudely scathing critiques, the "beating up" on authors, the prohibitions on performances of their music, and on foreign travel so as to prevent their presence at premieres, and much else, was alas no myth.[8]

---

7. A. Y. Selitsky, *Nikolai Karetnikov: Vïbor sud'bï* (Rostov-on-Don: Kompozitor, 1997; 2nd ed., 2011).

8. Ibid., 4–5 (2nd ed.): "Среди композиторов следующего поколения, то есть рожденных в 50-е годы, распространено убеждение, что гонения, которым со стороны властей подвергались многие мастера советской эпохи,—либо миф, либо эти гонения чуть ли не специально организовывались самим и гонимыми. Один из наших современников, уважаемый, высокоталантливый и весьма успешный, огласил версию, согласно которой разгромные статьи в центральных газетах инициировали друзья А. Шнитке с целью подогреть интерес к нему на Западе. Далее он говорит: « . . . Я советую очень внимательно читать толстые книги с жизнеописаниями А. Шнитке, Э. Денисова, Н. Каретникова. Если объективно посмотреть . . . то приходится констатировать, что все разговоры об их проблемах—*просто миф*». . . . И может быть, одна из целей ее переиздания—напомнить, что грубая «разносная» критика, «проработки» авторов, запреты на исполнения музыки, на поездки композиторов за рубеж с целью присутствовать на премьере своих произведений и многое другое—увы, не миф."

We almost did not meet, Kolya and I. I was given his address by an American acquaintance who had preceded me on the Graduate Student/Young Faculty fellowship program of the International Research and Exchanges Board (IREX). I sent Kolya a postcard from the dormitory of the Moscow Conservatory, where I was the only English-speaking resident except for a British ballet student who was studying at the Bolshoi Theater's school, and whose name, as it happened, was also Richard. For about a month I heard nothing from Kolya, then was called to the phone to receive a message. He apologized for the long delay and said he would explain it when I came. Turned out he did call back when he got my card, asked for Richard, and was connected with the ballet school Richard, who went in my place and, as Kolya put it to me when we did meet, "decided to play you" (*reshil sigrat' vas*). He kept up the pretense for a couple of hours, Kolya said, very amused.

Lots of things amused Kolya, and he was very amusing. He did not project an affect of suffering. His manner was cool and ironic, and he loved to talk. He was in fact a terrific raconteur, and his book of memoir vignettes (or novellas, as he called them), *Themes and Variations* (*Temï s variatsiami*)—which was previewed in the famous literary magazine *Yunost'*, went through two Russian editions, and was translated into French and Japanese—is a marvelous, often hilarious, read.[9] (I don't know whether the title was a deliberate parody of the titles of the Stravinsky-Craft books, but that would have been characteristic of him.) His music does often project an anguished mood, however, especially the work of his I know best because he played it for me on the day of our first meeting, and it remains his best-known piece: the Fourth Symphony, composed in 1962–63 but only published in 1982 (in an edition of only two hundred copies), long after he and I had lost touch. (I spotted it in the catalogue of the German music dealer Otto Harrassowitz, then the chief Western European importer of Soviet music publications, and bought it when it appeared.) Kolya sat me down on his sofa, in front of a huge old German tape player (you can see it in Figure 11.1, a picture from *Themes and Variations* taken in the apartment where I met him) and gave me the manuscript score to follow. After we had listened to it he patted my shoulder and said I was the only listener who managed to turn the pages at the right time. I doubt whether that was true (and in fact he had helped me a couple of times with the pages), but I realized I had been tested. Later I read, in *Themes and Variations*, about the time Dmitry Kabalevsky, the book's main villain, failed that test with Kolya's Third Symphony—his first twelve-tone work, and the beginning of his clash with the musical establishment.

So I had not really aced the test, and I'll bet Kabalevsky didn't really flunk completely; but something about me appealed to Kolya and he knew I was a keeper even before testing. I think I know what it was, and it had nothing to do with

---

9. A couple of chapters have been published in English: Nikolai Karetnikov, "Two Novellas," *Tempo*, no. 173 (June 1990): 44–47.

FIGURE 11.1. Kolya Karetnikov in his apartment near Lefortovsky val, Moscow, 1969 (*Temï s variatsiami*, 84–85).

music. I have never seen it referred to in the by now not inconsiderable literature about him, but his second-biggest passion after music was stamp collecting. And those of you who know me, whether personally or by reputation, have probably never guessed that I too am a collector and have been one since the age of six. (The front cover of the first edition of *Themes and Variations,* which I received through Peter Schmelz with an inscription from Olga Karetnikova—Kolya's fourth wife, I believe, but the one who lasted and survived him—shows a couple of foreign stamps mixed in with a mélange of snapshots and manuscripts, but that is the only public allusion to his hobby that I have ever seen.)

I noticed his stamp albums in a bookcase during our first meeting, and he took great pleasure in showing off his gems. He asked me at one point to shut my eyes and then open them. When I did so I saw that he had put a very early (and quite valuable) Japanese stamp on my hand. It was made of rice paper and was so light that I had not felt it. "*Vidite,*" he said; "*eyo netu*" (See? It isn't even there). By the end of the evening he would have said "*Vidish'.*" We went very quickly to *tutoyer* terms, which was not automatic with us the way it was with my friends at the Conservatory dormitory, because we were fifteen years apart in age. We always devoted a part of our meetings to stamps, about which he found me more knowledgeable than any of his other music friends. One time I brought him a gift of stamps from the American embassy—not American stamps but Finnish and Austrian ones, which we exchange students bought at the embassy to put on letters that were traveling out of Russia by diplomatic pouch as far as Helsinki or Vienna. They were of course unused. "*Ooh,*" Kolya said when I produced them, "*chisten'kiye!*" (Minties!) I think he enjoyed getting those stamps even more than he enjoyed getting (again via the embassy) LP records of recent American music, including the very late works of Igor Stravinsky, who was of course an American composer at the time of his death, which had taken place earlier that same year, 1971. "*Akh, starik,*" he said when I produced these; "*nakonets on ponyal*": "Ah, the old man—he finally understood," meaning he finally understood what Kolya also understood, that *seriynaya dodekafoniya*—"serial dodecaphony," which was how Kolya always referred to the twelve-tone technique—was the only viable method for a serious composer in the late twentieth century.

I of course did not agree with him about that. I came from a place where students wrote twelve-tone music under duress, the way Kolya had written his Socialist Realist student works, including an oratorio called *Julius Fučík*, which memorialized not the composer of the immortal "Entry of the Gladiators," who lived from 1872 to 1916 and was known as the Bohemian Sousa, but rather the Czech Communist journalist, who was born in 1903 and was hanged by the Nazis in 1943. It was Kolya's graduation piece, and he graduated in 1953. Note the year. It makes a perfect match with the year of his admission to the Moscow Conservatory, 1948. His years of intensive training coincided exactly with the years of the *Zhdanovshchina*, the most draconian years of Soviet policy in the arts as in everything else. I understood his intransigence on behalf of twelve-tone music the same way I understood my friend at Columbia, who one day in the big room where all of us TAs had our desks, cried out, "I'm from Iowa. Why am I taking my seventh course on hexachordal combinatoriality?"

The classic statement of this kind in America came from Steve Reich, whose name was as unmentionable in American university classrooms in those days as Karetnikov's was in the classrooms of the Moscow Conservatory. Reacting to Pierre Boulez's contention (not so far from things I used to hear Kolya say) that composers who resisted twelve-tone technique were "useless," Reich wrote in 1987 that Stockhausen, Berio, and Boulez

> were portraying in very honest terms what it was like to pick up the pieces after World War II. But for some American in 1948 or 1958 or 1968—in the real context of tailfins, Chuck Berry and millions of burgers sold—to pretend that instead we're really going to have the dark brown Angst of Vienna is a lie, a musical lie.[10]

10. Quoted in Robert Fink, *Repeating Ourselves: American Minimal Music as Cultural Practice* (Berkeley and Los Angeles: University of California Press, 2005), 118.

Kolya's attitude was the inverse of that, and of course I never debated the point with him. I didn't even disagree, given the context in which he and I were speaking. In the Soviet environment where we met, the bombastically optimistic works of Kabalevsky and Khrennikov were the musical lies, and it was easy to see Kolya as speaking truth to power (except that power never heard him speak). With the perspective of years I see a more complex picture, and I will try to sketch it in a bit here. But it is just as appropriate, and perhaps more important right now, to keep things in the original context, where I was privileged to see up close a figure who lived in the shadows, and to transmit as faithfully as I can my eyewitness impressions.

So back to our first encounter, and the Fourth Symphony. The piece was very difficult (to follow with the score, never mind play) and the performance on the tape Kolya shared with me was superb. I asked who was playing, since I was under the impression the work had never been publicly performed. The Leningrad Philharmonic, he replied, under Gennady Rozhdestvensky (1931–2018), at the time of the recording the chief conductor at the Moscow Bolshoi Theater and one of the most adventurous of Soviet musicians. I was surprised. So it was performed in Leningrad? I asked. No, Kolya replied. It was a performance recorded there for broadcast abroad. Why was that? I asked. "To show that we too have ugliness," he replied, chuckling (*chtobï pokazat', chto u nas tozhe yest' gadosti*).[11] He went on to tell me that the work had been given a live performance abroad as well, at the Prague Spring festival in 1967, a year before the Soviet tanks rolled in, but that he was not present at that performance because he was not granted an exit visa. I was indignant to hear that the Soviet arts establishment was happy to exploit for the sake of foreign prestige the work of composers whose careers it thwarted at home, but Kolya told me about it without evident rancor. For him it was business as usual.

A year or so later, after I had returned from my Moscow year, I became even more indignant. There was a magazine in those days called *Krugozor* (Horizon, Outlook, Perspective, Field of Vision, Spectrum, something like that; literally, it's "glance-around"), which featured twelve floppy-plastic seven-inch LP discs interleaved and spiral-bound together with the printed pages. I subscribed to it because one or two of those recordings were usually devoted to classical music, and often contained interesting or unusual items. Like most magazines, my *Krugozor*s tended to pile up and I would occasionally devote an evening to working through them. On one such evening I was going down the stack and I found a recorded souvenir of the Prague Spring. I put it on and, to my amazement, I heard a familiar passage.

---

11. A later recording by a different ensemble but the same conductor from a 7 March 1985 concert in the Large Hall of the Moscow Conservatory, proclaimed as the "first performance in the USSR," was released by Melodiya in 2020 and is available on most streaming platforms. See https://melody.su/catalog/classic/44041/ and https://youtube.com/playlist?list=OLAK5uy_ng-GMluxGA3TF-dpgm4gbfPN-jytfAkJLQ.

The voice-over identified it as the Fourth Symphony by the Soviet composer Nikolai Nikolayevich Karetnikov, and the *naibol'shiy uspekh* at the festival—the biggest hit.¹² That really disgusted me. The piece could not be heard at home, but it was vaunted abroad as a showpiece—not only *naibol'shoye*, but also *pokaznoye*. And although the piece was *pokaznoye*, for show, the composer was *nevïyezdnoy*, not entitled to travel abroad where he could hear the showing off of his own showpiece. And *Krugozor* was brazenly touting it to its subscribers, who also had no access to it beyond the recorded snippet. The plain contempt for all concerned was palpable and breathtaking; and that is why I used to joke during my first year home from the academic exchange that I went to Moscow a bleeding heart and came back to the right of Reagan.

My disgust was instructive, though. It gave me a little taste of Kolya's frustration, but also some insight into what you might call the aristocracy of the excluded—the process whereby the injustices of a system of incentives and penalties designed to elicit compliance and docility (as patronage regimes usually do) could in certain temperaments not only stiffen resistance but actually provide a sort of moral compensation for the indignities one suffered for nonconformity.

Kolya was a very proud nonconformist. His marginality went beyond strict commitment to *seriynaya dodekafoniya*, which he had encountered for the first time in 1957 when he heard a homemade tape recording of Glenn Gould's now legendary performance at the Moscow Conservatory of Anton Webern's Variations for Piano, op. 27.¹³ After showing me the Fourth Symphony, he told me about his opera project (conceived, actually, as an oratorio), which he was then calling the *Misteriya*, but which when completed (sixteen years after our meeting) bore as its full title the name *Misteriya apostola Pavla* (The Mystery of the Apostle Paul). When I learned from this that Kolya's other major commitment was to religious themes, I remember thinking, perhaps infected by then with his ironic disposition, "Wow, what an instinct for success."

Having recently watched a documentary film called *Professiya kompozitor* (My Profession Is Composer), made in 1992 and now (like practically everything else on the face of the earth) available for watching on YouTube,¹⁴ I know something Kolya did not tell me at the time—namely, that he had just then resolved to profess the Orthodox faith actively under the guidance of a spiritual tutor, Archpriest Alexander Men', to whom the *Misteriya* was eventually dedicated.¹⁵ In the film he

12. This recording (and the accompanying article, which does not mention Karetnikov at all) is available at www.krugozor-kolobok.ru; see issue no. 8, 1967, p. 14, track 7.
13. www.youtube.com/watch?v=3tf8bhi1ovQ.
14. www.youtube.com/watch?v=jEAirdEw36g.
15. Alexander Vladimirovich Men' (1935–90) was then just coming into his own as a proselytizer among the disaffected Soviet intelligentsia. His works were widely disseminated in *samizdat*. His assassination on the eve of the Soviet collapse remains an unsolved crime.

refers to himself as a *veruyushchiy chelovek,* a believer—and that, of course, was the ultimate act of bridge-burning with the Soviet establishment. It reminded me, inevitably, of Stravinsky, who began professing Orthodoxy exactly when he began identifying himself with the postrevolutionary "white" emigration.

Neither in Stravinsky's case nor in Kolya's is it my intention, nor have I any right, to assess the sincerity of their religious professions, but in both cases the open religious act, precisely insofar as it was openly professed, had a political dimension—or at the very least, had political repercussions—that inevitably stimulate the imagination. Kolya's profession was clearly the riskier one. It entailed a substantial renunciation, and what he renounced, unambiguously, was any chance for the Soviet success toward which he had at first seemed inexorably headed. He once told me, in his usual supercilious way, that Tikhon Khrennikov, the *khozyayin,* or boss, of Soviet music, handpicked for the position by Stalin himself in 1948, had once pronounced my friend Kolya the "white hope" of Soviet music. He wasn't just boasting; there was an element of confession in it too. Like other white hopes before him, he first attracted attention with pieces he wrote while still a student at the Conservatory. His Fučík cantata may remind you, if you are a reader of *JAMS* (the *Journal of the American Musicological Society*), of Alfred Schnittke's graduation piece, also an oratorio, about which Peter Schmelz wrote a very perceptive article a few years ago. Schnittke's offering, completed in 1958, was called *Nagasaki,* and was a "safe protest" against the threat of renewed American nuclear aggression, despite the presence in it of a cacophonous depiction of an atomic explosion that managed to attract some typical censure for "formalism."[16] Karetnikov's dissertation cantata, completed five years earlier under infinitely more stringent political conditions, contained no such transgression. It proclaimed not only talent but also political reliability and obedience.

Kolya's status as a golden boy was confirmed when, owing at first to a fortunate friendship with Vladimir Vasilyov and Natalia Kasatkina, the husband-and-wife team of Bolshoi Theater choreographers, he received at the age of twenty-nine a commission for a ballet, *Vanina Vanini,* after Stendhal's novel of star-crossed Risorgimento-era love between a Roman princess and a *carbonaro* (another impeccable theme for Soviet consumption), to be performed in the Soviet Union's premier musical theater. At the time of the premiere, in 1961, Kolya was thirty. Thus he came near to paralleling the meteoric rise of Rodion Shchedrin (b. 1932), whose first ballet, *Konyok gorbunok* (The Little Humpbacked Horse) was given at the Bolshoi the year before, when the composer was twenty-eight. Shchedrin, of course, went on to marry Maya Plisetskaya, win Lenin Prizes (and, post-collapse, the Russian Federation State Prize, awarded by Boris Yeltsin), and remains a golden

---

16. See Peter J. Schmelz, "Alfred Schnittke's *Nagasaki:* Soviet Nuclear Culture, Radio Moscow, and the Global Cold War," *Journal of the American Musicological Society* 62 (2009): 413–72.

boy to this day, as he approaches ninety. By contrast, Kolya's conflicts had already begun by the time *Vanina Vanini* was performed; indeed, by the time it was composed he had already received his fatal initiation, via Glenn Gould, into the underworld of *seriynaya dodekafoniya*.

Kolya's ballet has been described (by the composer as well as other writers) as a twelve-tone composition, the first such (and the only one?) ever performed at the Bolshoi. Peter Schmelz has shown this to be an exaggeration.[17] The work, like many Soviet compositions of the 1960s, is better described as *dvenadtsatitonovïy*, or (as Schmelz translates it) "twelve-tonish." It had a chromatic surface, including themes that sounded all the pitch classes in succession in the manner of a tone row, and that were often subjected to the sort of variegated and perambulating scoring techniques one finds in Schoenberg's "expressionist" pieces, described in his *Harmonielehre* as "Klangfarbenmelodie." But it had a more traditional harmonic underpinning and an altogether traditional numbers format. Nevertheless, it was far enough out to elicit a *spornïy*, or controversial, reception—not so much from critics or culture bureaucrats, but from fellow musicians, which Kolya found especially wounding and alienating. He described it to me more than once, and also recounted it in *Themes and Variations*, under the title "Lekarstvo ot tshcheslaviya," or "An Antidote to Vainglory." As recounted there:

> Nervous tension arose at the very first rehearsal. The musicians did not understand or accept the music. They turned their heads in bewilderment every time a phrase was continued by a different instrument from the one that started it. Gradually both they and I became convinced that they would not be able to give it a clean performance. Everyone became defensive, and to forestall any accusation of professional incompetence the orchestra made a decision about which no one bothered to inform me.
>
> When we went from the rehearsal room to the actual theater, the dancers immediately began shouting from the stage that they couldn't hear the music, and I too, sitting in the empty hall, heard right away that the orchestra sounded as though it had been tightly wrapped in cotton wadding. So ... after the rehearsal I took home the orchestral parts and penciled in some doublings. The next day I didn't notice any greater weight to the sound and again took home the parts and entered more doublings. The players, knowing I was taking the parts home, entered into correspondence with me. Mainly they wrote abusive or sarcastic little notes to me, or else pathetic exclamations commiserating about the horrible fate that must await me. In one of the parts someone had even pasted in a page ripped from a calendar with a portrait of Chaikovsky and a quote from him: "Melody is the soul of music." I answered a few messages that appealed to me.
>
> The next morning at rehearsal, I stationed myself at the orchestra pit and watched as the players ran from stand to stand reading my answers; my presence did not

---

17. Peter J. Schmelz, *Such Freedom, If Only Musical: Unofficial Soviet Music during the Thaw* (New York: Oxford University Press, 2009), 132–33.

inhibit them in the least. The orchestra was animated, but when they began to play, there was no difference in the sound they made. I began to despair.... People from the Composers Union began to appear in the hall, mostly what you call "middle managers." They silently took seats here and there around the sides, listened, and left before the rehearsal was over. The players, without hiding it from me, were saying that at the next meeting of the artistic board [*khudsovet*] they would do what they could to get my ballet canceled. Especially ferocious were the first-desk first fiddles—you know, the "aristocrats of the orchestra."...

On the ninth day of rehearsing, during a break, one of the violinists, who had gone to music school with me, finally let me know the reason for the orchestra's lack of sonority: "Our guys were organizing an 'Italian' strike," he said. "We conspired to play everything pianissimo." When Algis Žiūraitis, who was conducting my ballet, resumed the rehearsal, I went up to him from behind, stopped the music, and told him everything. He turned to the orchestra: "If you don't give me a real fortissimo right now, I will go immediately and report you to the theater directorate!" He gave a downbeat and from the pit came a huge crash. I stopped the rehearsal again and, turning to the orchestra, cried out, "Don't play the notes in pencil!" On stage everyone could suddenly hear, and the sound in the hall suited me fine. In three days the dress rehearsal was called.

Now here is where the story really gets interesting:

The day before, I called Shostakovich on the phone. "Dmitry Dmitrievich! Are you free tomorrow morning for two or three hours?" Shostakovich answered that he was free. I explained the situation. "I really need you to come and, if you like the music, defend it!" D. D. answered, "I will certainly, certainly that is, come, and I'll try to do everything, that is everything, that you need me to do!"

To Bolshoi dress rehearsals they used to invite any performers who were not engaged at the moment, as well as students at the ballet school, retired performers, members of the Composers Union, and the press. This time the doors were locked, and there was a crowd milling in confusion at the entrance. In the empty hall a little group of Ministry representatives was sitting, along with members of the artistic board and a few middle managers from the Composers Union. Shostakovich was there. The orchestra played as well as it could. Some messed up the even bars, some the odd, some both, but still and all you could make out what the music was like. Everyone then went to the director's office. When I came in, the first fiddles were already there, arms akimbo. Their faces wore the expression of wolves about to tear a lamb to pieces. Shostakovich was given the privilege of going first. Dmitry Dmitrievich stood up and told a barefaced lie: "I congratulate, that is, with all my heart I congratulate the orchestra of the Bolshoi Theater, who have so brilliantly, brilliantly managed to perform this most difficult, that is most difficult score!" Then he explained to all those present the various properties of my symphonic style. The matter was decided.

The fiddlers let their arms drop to their sides, their faces melted, and no one who followed D. D. dared contradict him. The ballet was passed for performance. When the first performance had ended, from the hall one could hear stormy applause and shouts of "Bravo!" The curtain went up again and again, and I went out to bow. You can easily imagine how I felt in these minutes: I was thirty years old, I had come to the Bolshoi not as anyone's protégé, without a recommendation from the Ministry of Culture, I had endured heavy fighting with the orchestra, and here I was taking my bows in the main theater of the Soviet Union! I had won! The orchestra section, the balconies, the loges, the huge chandelier, the denizens of Parnassus painted on the ceiling, the light projectors, all of this was tumbling down upon me and I was filled to bursting with pride and vainglory. Making my bows I finally glanced down and spied the orchestra .... They were all standing, applauding, some with their palms, others on the backs of their instruments. They had whirled around like a weather vane.

And I understood that my success wasn't worth a damn thing.[18]

This story is meant in its published context as an explanation for the composer's disaffection. But what was it, exactly, that produced disaffection—or, to put it another way, that served as the titular antidote to vainglory? The story seems to be about the orchestra's perfidy, and then its fickleness. That is something that often surprises readers "over here," who imagine that Soviet musicians were united in opposition to the "authorities," and would always be on the side of what in the West would have been classified as "progressive." The story illustrates a more complicated reality, in which even musicians as proficient as those in the Bolshoi Theater orchestra, raised in an educational hothouse that exposed them to intense indoctrination and kept them in creative isolation, could develop provincial attitudes and behave like philistines. But that is the way educational hothouses operate everywhere. You would have found the same narrow horizons and resistance to contemporary music in Juilliard jocks in those days. That was not a peculiarity of the Soviet regime, and it was not the source of Kolya's bitter reflections at the end. That aspect of the narrative was artful indirection.

For the real story, reconsider the vainglorious thoughts Kolya reports having had while bowing: "I was thirty years old, I had come to the Bolshoi not as anyone's protégé, without a recommendation from the Ministry of Culture, I had endured heavy fighting with the orchestra, and here I was taking my bows in the main theater of the Soviet Union! I had won!" But of course, as he has just shown us, these thoughts were utterly fallacious. He had received the commission for the score because of lucky friendships, and he had won against the orchestra's intrigues only because he had had Shostakovich's protection. As much as anyone, he had gotten where he was *po blatu,* as the saying went, "through pull," even though the crucial pull in this case was honorable and came from someone who was acting not in the name of the Party but in the name of human decency. Realizing that was

18. Nikolai Nikolayevich Karetnikov, *Temï s variatsiami* (Moscow: Kinotsentr, 1990), 41–46.

the true antidote to vainglory. If you need to win without pull, the story is saying, you will always lose. Told from the vantage point of the later "underground" Karetnikov, it is a manifesto of the aristocracy of the excluded. His whole career had been dedicated to the renunciation and denunciation of pull, and he had suffered the consequences.

It was a very obdurate sort of elitism. It led Kolya to disown the music he had written before his conversion to *dvenadtsatitonovost'*, or twelve-tonishness—which is to say, all of the music of his that was then in circulation. At the time I knew him, he had seven works in print. Six of them were in small keyboard and vocal genres, including choral arrangements of Russian folk songs. There was, however, one major work among them: *Dramaticheskaya poèma* (Dramatic Poem) for large orchestra, op. 12, adapted in 1960 from music originally composed for a film, *Veter'* (The Wind, 1958). In 1964, it had been choreographed by Kasatkina and Vasilyov for a second Karetnikov ballet at the Bolshoi Theater called *Geologi* (Geologists), and subtitled *Geroicheskaya poèma* (Heroic Poem). The score was published in 1969 in an edition of just 125 copies, and I found one of those copies, minus the front cover, while rummaging one day in the second-hand bins of the little music shop right next to the Conservatory on Herzen Street (now renamed, as in prerevolutionary times, Bol'shaya Nikitskaya). Next time I visited Kolya I showed him what I had bought and asked him to sign it as a souvenir. "*Akh, dorogoy, ne mogu*," he answered: "Sorry, I can't." It was in his older style, he explained, and "*uzhe yeyo ne priznayú*" (I don't acknowledge it anymore). Sure enough, in the worklist in back of Selitsky's biography the piece carries an asterisk, identifying it, according to a legend accompanying the list, as an item that the composer no longer included in his own worklist.

Well, that was OK. I have plenty of signed letters from him. True, they are signed "Kolya," but on the envelopes the handwritten return address says "N. Karetnikov," so I have all the autographs I need. But still, his refusal to sign the score for an admiring friend struck me as a needlessly inflexible gesture. Now I know, from reading Selitsky, as well as an article on *Geologi* by Anna Melovatskaya, a ballet historian, that Karetnikov had intended his Fourth Symphony to be used for that ballet but that, according to Melovatskaya, "the atmosphere in the country was clearly inimical to such 'experiments.' It was obvious that a ballet with such music would not be cleared for production. So it was decided to substitute the *Dramaticheskaya poèma* for the Fourth Symphony."[19]

The piece had become a sore point—too sore, apparently, even to tell me about. The style of the music might also have contributed to Kolya's embarrassment. It is in the heroic vein of movie music the world over, with a main theme, proclaimed by six horns in unison doubled by a tenor trombone for good measure, which

---

19. Anna Melovatskaya, "Balet 'Geologi' v postanovke N. Kasatkina i V. Vasilyova," *Voprosï teatra*, 2012, nos. 3–4, 178–185, at 181.

would not have been out of place in a tone poem by Strauss. Its first four notes happened to coincide with the familiar DSCH Shostakovich monogram, albeit as "SDHC" (E-flat, D, B, C) with both pairs of notes reversed, so I will assume it was a coincidence. By the time it was published it must have looked to Kolya like a misrepresentation and a reminder of his earlier conformism. *Veter'*, the movie for which the music was originally written, might also have been an embarrassment to him by the time I knew him. The earliest work by the eventually famous directorial team of Alexander Alov and Vladimir Naumov (with whom Kolya collaborated five times), it was a smoothly executed but utterly conventional Socialist Realist celebration of revolutionary heroism of a type that in the West, too, would have been relegated to "genre" status. It partook of two related genres, in fact: road movie and buddy movie. The plot concerned a trio of railroad workers in 1918 who decide to trek to Moscow, 1,500 kilometers away, to attend the first Komsomol congress. On the way they pick up a reformed prostitute and, one of the fixtures of that era, a *besprizornik* (homeless child), on a journey that takes them through White territory. Only one of the original three, plus the *besprizornik*, makes it to the congress. The movie ends with the survivor's fiery revolutionary oration to a rapturous Komsomol reception. The opening theme of Kolya's *Dramaticheskaya poèma* is of course the title music (Fig. 11.2),[20] and it returns in many guises to underscore every major dramatic turn. Indeed, pretty much all Kolya had to do to assemble his symphonic score was lay these cues end to end so that they formed a series of variations. The very end of the movie corresponds to the very end of the *Poèma*, except that in the symphonic score the final triumphant sounding of the theme is accompanied by a huge orchestral tutti that (I'll bet) the directors decided to reduce to bare unison brass so as not to compete with the verbal rhetoric.[21]

You may be thinking that you didn't come to a conference on nonconformist Soviet art to hear about the likes of this film or its music—examples, both of them, of the sort of stuff to which our designated heroes were antithetical. But I want to challenge the antithesis somewhat. The high, rhetorical, *bol'shoy sovetskiy stil'* (grand Soviet style) one can hear in his *Dramaticheskaya poèma* survived Kolya's serial conversion. His rhetoric remained what it had been, just as another sort of sublime rhetoric distinguished Galina Ustvolskaya's "nonconformist" music from its counterparts in the "Western" avant-garde. The Soviet avant-garde was indeed the *Soviet* avant-garde, and thus the terms of our propaedeutic—Socialist Realism vs. artistic innovation, bold experiment vs. dominant aesthetic, and so on—should be cast not in terms of static binary oppositions but in terms of dialectics. Although Kolya Karetnikov was well

---

20. The movie is available on YouTube; the title music, corresponding to Ex. 1, can be found here: www.youtube.com/watch?v=sugdNI6u0aw&t=65s (1:05–2:13).

21. Here is the relevant cue: https://www.youtube.com/watch?v=sugdNI6u0aw&t=5460s (1:31:00–1:33:35).

FIGURE 11.2. Karetnikov, *Dramaticheskaya poèma,* first page in facsimile.

and truly alienated from the Soviet musical establishment, we should not make the mistake "Westerners" so often make about Soviet "dissidents." Always remember Solzhenitsyn's scathing 1970 Nobel lecture, which so confounded commentators who assumed that if he was not one of "them," then he was one of "us." It was a great lesson in the vacuity of binaries.[22] I learned a lesson like that from Kolya, too.

We were talking one day about contemporary music as usual, and he was expressing his usual contempt for most of the figures who came up. When I would ask him *"kak ti otnosish'sya,"* which is Russian for "what do you think of" but literally translated would be "how do you relate to" so-and-so, his answer, nine times out of ten, would be *"skverno"* (really really badly). One day I asked him about Boulez, and he surprised me when he said, "You know, if I thought, the way he does, that music is just a play of sounds [*zvukovaya igra*], I could write a symphony every week." And then he added these words, and I've never forgotten how he sounded when he said them: *"No k sozhaleniyu, yest' i dramaturgiya"* (But unfortunately, there is also dramaturgy). And at this I thought, still in Russian, *"Akh, dorogoy, ti vsyo-taki sovetskiy kompozitor"* (Ah, my dear, you're a Soviet composer after all). I didn't say it out loud.

Dramaturgiya was one of the most banal words in the Soviet critical vocabulary. It stood for the assumption that music always had an implied plot or scenario, and that its thematic processes were analogous to the processes of dramatic action, which involved, in the first place, conflict and resolution. Soviet criticism, like a lot of conventional "music appreciation" talk in the West, was devoted to the uncovering and interpretation of such plots and action, often by means of literalistic paraphrase. The authenticity and propriety of the plots (as embodied in "intonations" and "imagery") were as much the concern of critics as the style, sound, or structure of the music—or what a Soviet critic would have called the composer's musical language (*muzikal'niy yazik*). And as you may have noticed, I have been using a vocabulary partly drawn from the theories of Boris Asafyev, whose work was foundational to Soviet criticism because it proposed a practical methodology both for the contrivance and the analysis of music from the standpoint of Socialist Realist aesthetics.

Kolya raised the matter of implicit emplotment in one of the anecdotes in *Temï s variatsiami*, in which Alexander Gauk, a very senior (and, in Kolya's telling, especially stupid) Soviet conductor, to whom Kolya had submitted his Second Symphony, heard the intonations of a funeral march and asked Kolya whom he was burying. I suspect that as a fledgling composer Kolya saw his funeral march primarily in relation to the funeral marches in Mahler's symphonies. As he told Gauk, he was asserting through it what he called (after the title of a then widely discussed

---

22. The text is available online at www.nobelprize.org/nobel_prizes/literature/laureates/1970/solzhenitsyn-lecture.html.

essay on Soviet film) his *pravo na tragediyu,* his "right to [express] tragedy."²³ To Gauk, a funeral march, if it was to be taken seriously as an "intonation," had to refer to a life experience, and he threw Kolya out of the room. Yet at the time I knew him, Kolya was still speaking this language. It should not have surprised me the way it did, perhaps. I had heard the Fourth Symphony, and I had heard how full it was of plot-implying intonations. It was the only twelve-tone instrumental music I had ever heard of which that could be said, except Berg's *Lyric Suite* and Violin Concerto, as well, perhaps, as Schoenberg's *Begleitungsmusik zu einer Lichtspielszene,* op. 34, an accompaniment to an imaginary silent film, which is more a spoof than an embodiment of the idea that music can "tell a story." But Kolya's Fourth Symphony does indeed tell a story, and although I never asked him to paraphrase it, I had no trouble grasping it, and he had no trouble expounding it when asked.

I mentioned Berg and Schoenberg as possible precedents for the sort of twelve-tone music that Kolya was writing, but his actual twelve-tone techniques had more in common with Webern's—which means, of course, that his music did not imitate that of any one of the Viennese trinity, but was an original synthesis of their collective achievement, and one that perhaps only a Soviet composer could have made. The tone row on which the symphony is based, like many of Webern's, is a so-called degenerative row, which can be broken into a lot of fragments of similar shape— "motivic segments," in the jargon of classroom analysis. The one in the Fourth Symphony breaks down into two-note semitone progressions, just like the row in Webern's Piano Variations, to recall the piece that first introduced Kolya to dodecaphony. These semitones (usually expanded, by inversion or by registral shifts, into characteristically Webernian sevenths and ninths) are salient to anyone who knows to look for them, but the rhetoric is worlds away from Webern, at least from Webern's twelve-tone music. The symphony begins with six French horns in unison, bells in the air, just like the old *Dramaticheskaya poèma.* That opening gesture, once reminiscent of Richard Strauss, now proclaims kinship with Webern insofar as Karetnikov and Webern shared a common descent from Mahler (Fig. 11.3).²⁴

The sort of kinship Karetnikov shared with Webern he also shared with Shostakovich, and that is the kinship that is apt to come first to mind now, as it surely did to Shostakovich himself when he so willingly offered Karetnikov protection in the period immediately preceding this symphony, when Karetnikov survived the crucible of *Vanina Vanini* and resolved on the creative path that led him to the straits in which I found him—the straits that actually furnished the Fourth Symphony with the dramatic program that lay behind the vivid gestural surface. As Kolya tells

---

23. See Semyon Izrailevich Freylich, "Pravo na tragediyu," *Iskusstvo kino,* 1957, no. 12. Mainly devoted to Grigoriy Chukhrai's film *The Forty-First,* a controversial love story set during the postrevolutionary civil war, the article was one of the bellwethers of the post-Stalin "thaw."

24. www.youtube.com/watch?v=T-osyopbhxE (through 0:43).

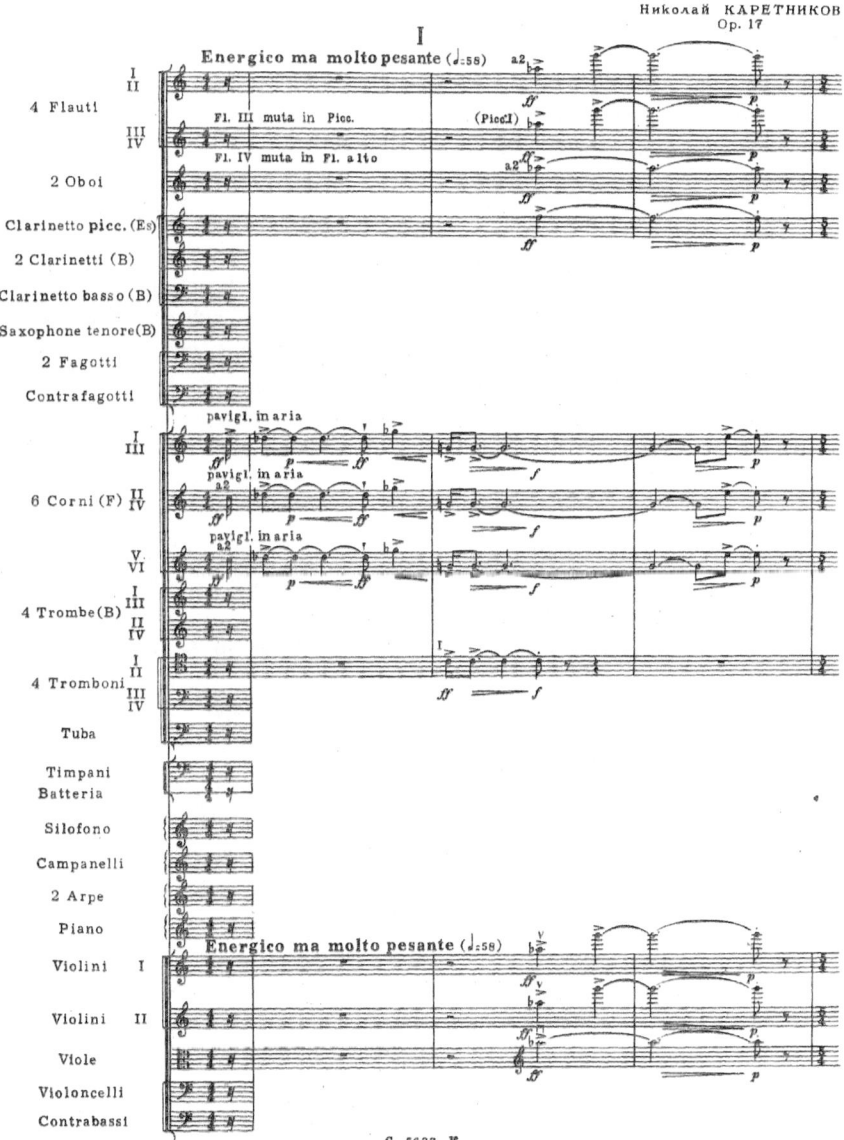

FIGURE 11.3. Karetnikov, Fourth Symphony, first page.

the unseen interlocutor in the *Professiya kompozitor* documentary, the symphony portrays the depths of his isolation and despair. He says in the film that he could not write such a work "now," meaning in 1992, which I take to be an oblique reference to his religious faith. Given its expressive purpose, it is no surprise to learn that the fourth of the Fourth Symphony's five movements reclaims the composer's *pravo na tragediyu*, his "right to tragedy," in the teeth of Gauk's dismissal, by once again resorting to the *topos* (as we would say) or the *intonatsiya* (as Asafyev would say) of the funeral march (Fig. 11.4).[25] Nor will it surprise us that the fifth and last movement is cast as a passacaglia, emphatically asserting kinship with Shostakovich in conclusion (and if the genre itself does not suffice to bring Shostakovich to mind, the use of the piano as a doubling color in the orchestra certainly will).[26]

All three of these excerpts from the Fourth Symphony, moreover, have in common a device (or *priyom*, to adopt the language of Russian formalism) that runs through the whole symphony like the proverbial red thread: pairs of repeated notes that are frequently extended into multiple repetitions, and that in the very middle of the symphony create a climactic impasse that it takes a Mahlerian breakthrough (i.e. *Durchbruch*, as Adorno called the device in his very influential book on Mahler) to surmount, leading directly into the equally Mahlerian funeral march.[27] The vividness of its imagery and the scale of its rhetoric certainly put this symphony in the grand line of traditional Soviet *simfonizm*. The fact that it is composed according to twelve-tone technique no longer seems its most essential or noteworthy characteristic. A phrase I once used to characterize Alfred Schnittke's music seems equally applicable to Kolya's: Socialist Realism minus socialism. What I might say to an audience as sophisticated as my present one is that it is Socialist Realism minus *partiynost'*, or Party-mindedness, but lacking neither *ideynost'* nor *obraznost'*, neither philosophical content nor imagery. It certainly speaks to me in that language, as I believe its composer intended it to do.

But that must be partly because Kolya Karetnikov the man spoke so often to me, and I cannot separate the music, especially the music I once listened to in his presence, from the man who wrote it, and who was briefly but fervidly my friend. When I was starting to write my book on Stravinsky in 1983, I sent chapter outlines to various people with strong Stravinskian credentials to see what they thought. The most helpful, voluble, and encouraging response came from Lawrence Morton, the man who ran the Monday Evening Concerts in Los Angeles, and who knew Stravinsky intimately in the last decades of the composer's life. I'll never forget one thing he said. He told me that I was very lucky I did not know Stravinsky

25. www.youtube.com/watch?v=K_pkp4nOHXw (at 0:25).
26. www.youtube.com/watch?v=64r2pEoDT80 (at 1:27).
27. See T. W. Adorno, *Mahler: Eine musikalische Physiognomik* (Munich: Suhrkamp, 1992); trans. by Edmund Jephcott as *Mahler: A Musical Physiognomy* (Chicago: University of Chicago Press, 1996).

FIGURE 11.4. Karetnikov, Fourth Symphony, beginning of fourth movement.

personally. I remembered then that Morton had once announced that he would write Stravinsky's biography but never did. The burden of his friendship with the composer, or perhaps I should say the burden of loyalty to him, made the task impossible. I don't expect ever to write again about Kolya Karetnikov, and I do not regard what I have told you today as a professional musicological account. To the extent that my words have been trenchant, they have also been at times disloyal, and the consciousness of my potential disloyalty has been very inhibiting, so my words have not been very trenchant. I did not tell you everything I know or much of what I think, nor will I do so. That is not a worthy admission coming from a scholar, but it's the least a friend can do.

12

In from the Cold

Nicolas Nabokov: A Life in Freedom and Music by Vincent Giroud, Oxford University Press, 2015, 562 pp., $39.95

I did not know him personally, but I had a connection to the subject of Vincent Giroud's *Nicolas Nabokov: A Life in Freedom and Music* that I ought perhaps to disclose. I was college friends with his great-nephew Alexander Ledkovsky, a grandson of his sister Sofia Dmitrievna Nabokova (known in the family, and in the book, as Onya). Alex's father Boris was a famous émigré Russian Orthodox kapellmeister, and Alex, who alas died in 2002 long before his time, followed in his footsteps. Owing to my consuming interest in modern Russian music (very much including that of émigré composers like Nabokov), I had, even before meeting Alex, discovered the two works by his Uncle Nicky that had been issued—or that would ever be issued—on LP records, both of them commissioned and recorded by the Louisville Orchestra, a minor organization but one with major foundation support. I was the only person Alex knew outside the family who knew them (or of them), so Uncle Nicky became for us an even more frequent topic of conversation than Uncle Volodya (the author of *Lolita*), and Alex showed me the scores of unrecorded compositions, most with inscriptions to Onya.

One of them was *Vozvrashcheniye Pushkina* (Pushkin's Return), an "Elegie in three movements" for solo voice and orchestra, which (I now learn from Giroud's book) was Uncle Nicky's favorite among his works. Alex and I played and sang it through. The music appealed to me, as did the other pieces I knew (one of them another solo cantata with orchestra called *Symboli chrestiani*, the other an opera

---

Review of *Nicolas Nabokov: A Life in Freedom and Music* by Vincent Giroud, *Times Literary Supplement*, 3 August 2016, 3–5.

about the death of Rasputin). It was attractively reminiscent of Stravinsky, Nabokov's mentor and friend, but more conventionally tuneful. I was struck, though, by the joshing inscription: *Ot tvoyego brata, polukompozitora*, "From your brother the half-composer." It seemed to betoken a sense of himself as *manqué*. I asked Alex about it. "Well, he's more famous for other things," he said.

And so he remains. Giroud's is not the first book about him. In 2002 there appeared a much shorter study, *Music on the Frontline: Nicolas Nabokov's Struggle against Communism and Middlebrow Culture* by Ian Wellens, in which, if the author had not mentioned the fact in passing, you would never have guessed that he was writing about a composer. Although he would be citing Nabokov's writings at length, Wellens announced, he would ignore the music, "simply because there seemed to be nothing of value along that route.... To be sure," he allowed, "it would have been possible to locate a few dusty, neglected scores, but I make no apology for not having done so: I am convinced that what we need to know we can learn from the writings."

That is a sad fate for a composer, and it goes beyond neglect of his music. The struggle against communism and middlebrow culture—a.k.a. the Cultural Cold War—has by now generated a sizable, fast-growing literature, through which Uncle Nicky clanks his way like the ghost of Jacob Marley, weighed down by a ponderous chain he forged in life as a diplomat and politician of the arts. Of his own free will he wore it sixteen years as Secretary-General of the Congress for Cultural Freedom (CCF), known as the "liberal conspiracy" after the title of Peter Coleman's pioneering account of 1989. And historians have labored on it since, to the point where in some tellings, notably Frances Stonor Saunders's ominously titled, widely cited *Who Paid the Piper? The CIA and the Cultural Cold War* of 1999, Nabokov is recklessly caricatured as some kind of reverse-engineered Goldfinger or Dr. No, owing to the connection between the CCF and the Central Intelligence Agency that has become the One Big Thing that hedgehogs know about him.

That vindictiveness raises its own questions. And I do not exaggerate it. Nabokov's work as a composer is mentioned only once in Saunders's book, in the epilogue, where his last major work, the ballet *Don Quixote* (composed for George Balanchine), is brought up just so that the author can quote Andrew Porter's withering review, following which a ludicrous bit of gossip—literally an old wives' tale, about all five of the women Nabokov had married at one time or another showing up to mutual consternation at his funeral—is retailed on the strength of the uncorroborated testimony of an interviewee who wasn't even there. An animus that induces such bad behavior in an ostensibly serious investigator only heightens curiosity about the man who inspired it, and I approached Giroud's biography in keen anticipation. Written with the cooperation of the surviving widow, Dominique Cibiel Nabokov, who supplied many of the documents on which it is based, it aims explicitly to place Nabokov in a better-rounded context than previous authors had been interested in providing, and certainly a more forgiving one.

Yet even Giroud has a problem dealing with the music, simply because it is so inaccessible. Not one work by Nabokov is currently available in a commercial recording (although a couple can be found on YouTube), and, as the book is aimed at a general readership, there are no notated examples. While musically knowledgeable (having published a survey of French opera), the author attempts no detailed stylistic or technical descriptions. Like Saunders, he mainly quotes reviews, albeit more favorable ones (though if you are willing to run down a reference to a book in Polish, you can learn that Witold Gombrowicz called Nabokov's music *straszne gowno*, which Google can translate for you). Critical evaluations are informative only when you know something about the critics (Andrew Porter, heavily biased in favor of tough "progressive" music over Nabokov's comfy *gemässigte Moderne*, being an obvious case in point). So while Giroud takes account of every one of Nabokov's musical works, and though he has diligently compiled a complete and quite informative catalogue of them all in an appendix (the first ever, and at seventy-nine items quite respectable as to bulk), I regret to say that the musical discussions, while occupying a lot of space, make rather a nugatory impression, unsatisfying to those, like me, who know something and wish to know more, probably skipworthy to those who don't.

Nabokov's two most significant works—both ballets, and both predating his career in cultural politics—were recorded on a CD of which eleven used copies are available, as I write, at Amazon.com: *Ode* (1925–28), through which he made a gaudy Paris debut thanks to Serge Diaghilev, and *Union Pacific* (1933–34), his first American work, to a scenario by Archibald MacLeish, which had a successful nationwide tour that seemed to augur a major career. That career somehow never materialized, forcing the composer, temporarily, into academic employment. Like the even more garrulous Ned Rorem, Nabokov was better known during his lifetime for his autobiographical writings than for his music. He published two very lively books of memoirs, which, inevitably, were major sources for Giroud (though the new book is no mere recycling: the author had access to the full typescript texts, including many parts that were never published).

The first memoir, published in 1951, right before his stint with the CCF, was called *Old Friends and New Music;* the second, published in 1975, was called *Bagazh.* The snappy titles now ring with irony. *Bagazh,* French hiding behind transliterated Cyrillic, purported to evoke the busy peripatetic life of "a Russian cosmopolitan," as the subtitle identified the author; but no one who knows the one thing about Nabokov that everybody knows can read it without thinking of the ton of political baggage with which the CIA connection saddled him. And the title of the other book chiefly registers the fact that, before he achieved notoriety as a political operative, the bright, suave, and gregarious Nabokov was chiefly known for knowing people. Its chapters might as well have been titled "Diaghilev and Me," "Prokofieff and Me," "Stravinsky and Me," and so on, up to "Shostakovich and Me," the segue into the operative phase and the later book.

The pictures in Giroud's biography tell a similar story: there is NN with Prokofieff, NN with Milhaud, NN with Stravinsky, with Balanchine, with Virgil Thomson, with Auden, with Stephen Spender, with Rostropovich, with Willy Brandt, Jacques Maritain, Isaiah Berlin, Elliott Carter; and of course with cousin Volodya. And with the whole serial harem of wives. And in every case save that of the wives (and not even invariably in their case, since one of them was Patricia Blake), Nabokov is the lesser-known member of the pair, the one compared with others rather than the one with whom others are compared. His books, like his essays on music, are fairly insubstantial compendia of polished anecdotes and table talk, and though his biographer works hard toward greater gravitas, he can't wholly shake the sense that Nabokov's life amounted to a big bunch of amusing incidents.

Only the CCF years, and those immediately before (when he served as a cultural attaché with the American army of occupation in Germany) and after (when he ran the musical *Festwochen* in West Berlin), lent Nabokov's life a coherent sense of purpose, and his projects genuine historical interest. Unfortunately, Giroud's treatment of this most important phase of Nabokov's career starts off on the wrong foot with a misguided complaint. "It does Nabokov a grave injustice," he writes, "to see him primarily—or only—as a Cold War cultural warrior, which he never really was in any case, being above all passionately hostile to fascism and totalitarianism in all their forms." That is a strange claim to make about the man who came up to New York from Baltimore expressly to give Shostakovich what the latter remembered ever after as "the worst moment of my life," and who had shortly before that signed a manifesto identifying "Stalinism as the main enemy in Europe."

If Nabokov wasn't "really" a cold warrior, then neither were Michael Josselson, Irving Brown, or Melvin Lasky, three knowing CIA operatives or cooperators who worked alongside Nabokov in the CCF. Josselson recruited Nabokov to be their front man; Brown disbursed the CIA's money to the CCF as the ostensible agent of Julius Fleischmann Jr., the yeast king, whose bogus "Farfield Foundation" was the CCF's officially advertised sponsor; and Lasky (an uncanny Lenin lookalike) was the editor of *Der Monat*, a journal of liberal opinion established by the American military government in postwar Germany. *Der Monat* was the model for *Encounter* and all the other magazines published by the CCF to influence European popular opinion. Josselson, Brown, and Lasky had all served with the American forces in Germany before recruitment by the CIA. Their transition from antifascist to anticommunist as wartime shaded into postwar and then into cold war was the normal route by which one became a "cold warrior."

Nabokov met his future handlers while serving as a civilian cultural adviser to the Information Control Division, which handled denazification proceedings. It was his horror at the forced repatriation of displaced persons to the Soviet Union, where he knew harsh fates awaited them, that determined his path into active anti-Soviet work. Although the CCF paid occasional attention to oppression from the right (which is to say Spain), everyone knew who the "totalitarians" were that the organization was set up to counter. Franco, after all, was not bombarding Western Europe with propaganda or organizing peace conferences. So while one can agree that Nabokov has been unfairly treated by anti-anticommunist writers, Giroud's attempt at spurious (and unnecessary) exculpation rings false and undermines credibility.

What turned out to be Nabokov's audition for the CCF was his celebrated confrontation with Shostakovich at the Cultural and Scientific Conference for World Peace at New York's Waldorf-Astoria Hotel in March 1949, which Shostakovich attended as a member of an official Soviet delegation and Nabokov as an infiltrator from a rump faction masterminded by the philosopher Sidney Hook, dubbed Americans for Intellectual Freedom for the occasion. The tale has been endlessly spun in histories, in memoirs both genuine and faked, and in flat-out fiction, their versions competing in boorishness and banality, pitting the cowardly bully Nabokov, the failed composer, in a sort of cage match against the pathetic victim Shostakovich, the great composer of the *Leningrad* Symphony, fresh from humiliation at the hands of Andrey Zhdanov for "formalist" transgressions. Actually, it was a two-minute exchange in which Nabokov asked Shostakovich personally to corroborate the vilifications of Schoenberg, Hindemith, and Stravinsky that had just been read out in his name by a translator from a prepared text, to a standing ovation. Shostakovich did so, to no one's surprise.

Saunders excoriates the bully for "throwing punches at a man whose arms were tied behind his back." Julian Barnes, in his recent novelization of the event in *The Noise of Time*, has his fictional Nabokov acting with theatrical impudence, "looking around the hall as if expecting applause." Giroud points out, correctly, that the target of Nabokov's intervention was not the man but the occasion, and that this was well enough understood by those present that, as reported for example by *Time* magazine, Nabokov's performance was met with "unanimous, ferocious booing." To do what Nabokov did took some courage, actually.

But of course we now regard the protagonists of this exchange through a retrospective scrim, seeing the victim in the calculated Cold War glare of *Testimony*, Solomon Volkov's faked Shostakovich memoirs (both Barnes's source and Saunders's), and Nabokov, in the light of subsequent revelations, as a Washington lackey. Barnes, stepping out of his protected zone as a fictioneer in a very ill-considered "Author's Note," claims in blithe anachronism that "Nicolas Nabokov, [Shostakovich's] tormentor at the New York Peace Congress, was indeed funded by the CIA"— this at a time when the CCF had not yet been envisaged. Saunders, for her part, insinuates that Nabokov was by then an actual agent. This he never became, but neither was Shostakovich a mere victim. Far from defenseless, he had actually leveraged his world fame, in a phone conversation with Stalin (or possibly, it is now thought, with the dictator's right-hand man, Alexander Poskryobyshev), to exchange his attendance at the Waldorf for a lifting of the post-Zhdanov ban on his music and that of his colleagues. It is time to restore some gray to the Cold War black and white, and Giroud, after his initial gaffe, does this with some success.

He is also helpful, though circumspect, when it comes to the big question: *Did he know?* Was Nabokov in on the CIA charade? After reading the book, I think it safe to say he was not. Or, to be maximally careful: He was not told, and knew better than to ask. Despite its catchiness, Peter Coleman's titular phrase was inapt. The CCF was not a liberal conspiracy. It was a co-option of liberals. As Noam Chomsky never tires of pointing out, if you appoint the right people to do your dirty work, you do not have to conspire with them. Saunders, perhaps unwittingly, gave Nabokov a compelling alibi when she cited an official document issued in 1950, the year of the CCF's inception, by the National Security Council's Select Committee to Study Governmental Operations with Respect to Intelligence Activities. The section on psychological warfare allows that "the most effective kind of propaganda" was the kind "where the subject moves in the direction you desire for reasons he believes to be his own"—a perfect definition of co-option. A subjective sense of autonomy is essential to morale and motivation, and Nabokov enjoyed a superlative level of both during his CCF years. Thanks to his auspicious placement and fortunate friendships, he got to play a role that looks (to me, at any rate, so I rather fancy to him as well) like the one Diaghilev had aspired to play, as his country's—you could even say the Free World's—de facto minister of culture.

Needless to say, Nabokov did not accomplish in that role anything like what Diaghilev accomplished. He did not actually commission a single new work of art, let alone a slew of masterpieces, just organized lavish and prestigious festivals of music and the arts in Europe (later in Latin America and Asia as well), along with dozens of exhibits and symposia—ephemeral events but star-studded, splashy, and serving a purpose thought important enough to justify enormous outlays: that of swaying the European intelligentsia away from its flirtation with communism or neutralism toward support for bourgeois democracy, by advertising the fruits of laissez-faire policies and practices in the field of cultural production.

The finest fruit, it was then agreed, was diversity, as showcased both in Nabokov's extravaganzas and in the journals of opinion which were the CCF's most durable legacy (especially *Encounter,* which outlasted the CIA revelations and the CCF itself by more than two decades). One easily forgets now that in the early years of the Cold War the strongest antitotalitarian position was assumed to be liberalism, not conservatism. The idea of an anticommunist left, a casualty of the Vietnam War and the subsequent rise of neoconservatism, seems almost as quaint now as the enlistment of high culture as a weapon of foreign policy. Nabokov's monster spectacles, the month-long Paris orgy *L'Oeuvre du XXème siècle* in 1952 and the 1954 mini-orgy in Rome, *La musica nel XX secolo,* were the greatest, some would say the final, monuments to these values.

They brought many American artists to Europe for the first time, the most expensive being George Balanchine's New York City Ballet, the sensation of 1952. In his proposal, Nabokov assured Irving Brown that showing them off "will help to destroy the pernicious European myth (successfully cultivated by the Stalinists) of American cultural inferiority," and that "it will be a challenge of the culture of the free world to the un-culture of the totalitarian world and a source of courage and *redressement morale*, in particular for the French intellectuals." His *chef d'oeuvre* as a planner was a *Soirée Schoenberg-Stravinsky*, pitting the former's *Erwartung* (which Stravinsky detested) against the latter's *Oedipus Rex* (which Schoenberg detested). It was a program that could not have been presented under the fascists (for whom Schoenberg was anathema) or the Soviets (who anathematized both), or even at avant-garde centers like Darmstadt or Donaueschingen, where the neoclassical Stravinsky was scorned. It was time, this concert said, to put away petty rivalries in the face of a common foe. Nothing could have better touted the "free world" message of ecumenical liberality, or the message that *l'art pour l'art*, when left alone, would be implicitly *engagé*.

Less subtle was the program at which the RIAS Orchestra (or, to give its full name, the *Rundfunk im amerikanischen Sektor Sinfonie-Orchester Berlin* or Radio Orchestra of the American Sector of West Berlin), itself an artifact of the Cold War, performed works by Soviet composers that were banned at home. Nabokov had scoured Western Europe and America for performance materials that would enable a production of Shostakovich's *The Lady Macbeth of the Mtsensk District*, the great *cause célèbre* of Soviet music censorship, but could only come up with a concert suite, which he programmed alongside the neoprimitivist *Scythian Suite*, Prokofieff's answer to his one-time friend and fellow émigré Stravinsky's *Sacre du printemps* (which was prominently featured on another program in a performance by the Boston Symphony Orchestra under *Le Sacre*'s original conductor, Pierre Monteux).

Nabokov's panoramic program essay, his most serious piece of writing, cast the history of music in terms that attributed the modern flowering of the art not to audacious enterprise or benevolent patronage, but to the rise and spread, despite obstacles, of political freedom. The essay was given preliminary publication, ironically enough, in the same (April 1952) issue of *La Revue musicale* that contained Pierre Boulez's celebrated burst of intolerance ("tout musicien qui n'a pas ressenti ... la nécessité du langage dodécaphonique est INUTILE" [any musician who has not felt the necessity of the dodecaphonic language is USELESS])—two contrasting views, the one intransigent, the other demonstratively liberal, both emblematic of the geopolitical moment and its tensions. Nabokov, in his liberality, gladly indulged the intransigent position: Boulez's *Structures Ia*, the very apogee of strictly algorithmic serial composition, was given its first performance (under the neutral title *Musique pour deux pianos*) at *L'Oeuvre du XXème siècle*. The de facto culture minister was having a ball, doing the Lord's work and receiving not only pay but an incalculably higher prestige in the world that mattered to him than he could ever have achieved as a composer. He was the one on whom others now depended, as he had once depended on Diaghilev. It gratified his expansive nature to be making such a big difference in so many careers—those of George Balanchine and Jerome Robbins particularly in 1952, and his old friend Elliott Carter in 1954, when the Parrenin Quartet performed Carter's First String Quartet at *La musica nel XX secolo* and launched the composer's extraordinary run as the preeminent American standard-bearer of elite modernism in music.

If Nabokov did not wonder whether the financial cornucopia he was privileged to administer might have been coming not only from private foundations but from the American taxpayers as well, he would have been the only one who didn't. Indeed, Giroud quotes a passage from one of the unpublished *Bagazh* typescripts that shows Nabokov to have had all the evidence he needed to draw that conclusion in 1961, but chose not to. As long as that dawn lasted, bliss it was to be alive, and ignorance was bliss. But then came the newspaper leaks of 1966 and the unapologetic admissions of 1967, and it all went up in smoke.

The story broke in the *New York Times*, in a series of articles that the government had tried vainly to suppress, devoted to an exposé, in the wake of a congressional investigation, of covert CIA operations, some of which were clearly illegal. The bean-spilling piece, headlined "Electronic Prying Grows," was ostensibly devoted to a mainly admiring description of new technologies and equipment, but halfway through, long past the jump, it turned to "secret warfare" in Guatemala and Nicaragua, and several columns later still it reached operations that "channel research and propaganda money through foundations—legitimate ones or dummy fronts." Foundations supporting academic research, it noted, had "warned that this practice casts suspicion on all traveling scholars," and called for the curtailment of clandestine CIA support. And then the *coup de massue*: "Through similar channels, the C.I.A. has supported groups of exiles from Cuba and refugees from Communism in Europe, and anti-Communist but liberal organizations of intellectuals, such as the Congress for Cultural Freedom and some of their newspapers and magazines."

Frantic letters to the editor of the *Times* followed, from Nabokov (promising his own investigation), from John Kenneth Galbraith, George Kennan, Robert Oppenheimer, and Arthur Schlesinger Jr. (testifying on behalf of Congress to "the independence of its policy, the integrity of its officials [and] the value of its contribution"), and, on behalf of *Encounter*, from Stephen Spender, Melvin Lasky, and Irving Kristol, who attempted outright (mendacious) denial. Their panic was well founded. Of all agencies of the United States government, the CIA was the last with which any respectable or responsible intellectual could afford to be associated. Were it, say, the State Department instead, long openly and legally engaged in cultural diplomacy, there would have been no ruinous stigma. In 1959, for example, the State Department had sent Leonard Bernstein (a fellow-traveling participant, incidentally, in the Waldorf Conference a decade earlier) and the New York Philharmonic on a Soviet tour that included the first Russian performances in decades of *Le Sacre du printemps,* long since under a de facto Soviet ban (as well as performances of Shostakovich's Fifth Symphony, which thrilled the composer, who rushed onstage to embrace the conductor despite the fact that Bernstein had played the ending at twice the indicated speed, thus creating an alternative—and politically divisive—performing tradition for the piece). Bernstein was thus able to confront Soviet arts policy with United States government support without incurring the sort of opprobrium that now descended on Congress and its functionaries, whose protestations were cruelly undercut the next year by an interview with Michael Josselson in *Ramparts* magazine and by the celebrated in-your-facery of Tom Braden, the head of the CIA's covert action arm, who had been responsible for all the secret disbursements.

This was confirmation from the horse's mouth. Under the headline "I'm Glad the CIA is 'Immoral,'" Braden confessed, in the jingoistic *Saturday Evening Post,*

> the enormous joy I got when the Boston Symphony Orchestra won more acclaim for the U.S. in Paris than John Foster Dulles or Dwight D. Eisenhower could have bought with a hundred speeches. And then there was *Encounter,* the magazine published in England and dedicated to the proposition that cultural achievement and political freedom were interdependent. Money for both the orchestra's tour and the magazine's publication came from the CIA, and few outside the CIA knew about it. We had placed one agent in a Europe-based organization of intellectuals called the Congress for Cultural Freedom. Another agent became an editor of *Encounter.*

These agents never having been fingered by name, everyone involved with the CCF was now a suspect. Nabokov wrote in agony to Oppenheimer of the "poetic irony" whereby it might now look "to people outside (and within the Congress community) that 'I' and not 'Others' have been an agent of a certain distinguished Agency." No one, Saunders apart, has ever explicitly accused him of that. But he (and Spender, and Kristol, and many others) had been exposed as "unwitting assets" in the jargon of the CIA, or what Lenin would have called useful idiots. Worse, it made them all look like "dupes," to use the mean epithet that opponents mercilessly applied to the men and women who had cheered Shostakovich and jeered Nabokov at the Waldorf Conference in 1949. Witting or unwitting, they were all effectively discredited, because what the revelations truly revealed, in Saunders's words, was "the sublime paradox" whereby "in order to promote an acceptance of art produced in (and vaunted as the expression of) democracy, the democratic process itself had to be circumvented."

But do we still need to demonize them? Let us recall the famous sentence from John Maynard Keynes's *Tract on Monetary Reform* which reminds us that "in the long run we are all dead." My pet variant, as alumni of my music history seminars will attest, is "in the long run we are all wrong," which applies not only to scholarly hypotheses but also to political attitudes in the light of changing conditions. All sides of the cultural cold war are wrong by now. Their positions have been superseded. The particular totalitarian threat to artists and thinkers against which the CCF did battle has withered away, and rightly, but the individualistic modernism the CCF defended has also lost its sheen. That supersession has its emblem in Giroud's narrative when Nabokov and Shostakovich meet again, in 1967, right after the crisis that finished the CCF—this time at a birthday party for one of Rostropovich's daughters at the cellist's dacha outside Moscow: "nor did Shostakovich appear to bear Nabokov the slightest grudge." If Shostakovich could afford to let him off the hook, so can we.

My musicological colleagues, to begin with, ought to stop equating Nabokov with the CCF and the CCF with the CIA. This fallacy has seriously hampered assessment of Stravinsky's late career, in particular his celebrated "conversion" to the twelve-tone technique pioneered by his old rival Schoenberg, who died the same year Nabokov assumed his duties at the CCF. As one of Stravinsky's closest friends, and surely his best-connected one, Nabokov often acted as Stravinsky's de facto agent, arranging commissions and performances for many of the works Stravinsky wrote in America, beginning with *The Rake's Progress*. Thereafter, he served as facilitator for *Canticum sacrum* (1955), *Movements* for Piano and Orchestra (1958–59), *The Flood* (1962), *Abraham and Isaac* (1962–63), and, perhaps most emblematically, *Threni* (1957–58), Stravinsky's first wholly twelve-tone composition.

These works were variously commissioned: *Canticum sacrum* by the Venice Biennale; *Movements* by a Swiss industrialist on behalf of his pianist wife; *Abraham and Isaac* by the Israeli government; *The Flood* by the Hamburg Staatsoper and CBS Television; *Threni* by the Norddeutscher Rundfunk. Yet because Nabokov was involved in the negotiations, it has been authoritatively asserted, by Anne C. Shreffler of Harvard University, that these commissions were all "initiated and presumably [!] financed by the CCF while appearing to come from a third party." But the CCF never engaged on its own account in clandestine sponsorship. It was the visible arm. Its patronage role was always proudly proclaimed, and to be able to claim proprietary credit for a new Stravinsky composition would have been the very opposite of a dirty secret. Nevertheless, since the *Ramparts* revelations, and particularly since Saunders's defamatory elaborations, anything Uncle Nicky has touched has been prejudicially tainted by his reputation, and that of the organizations he wittingly and unwittingly assisted. If Vincent Giroud's biography succeeds in mitigating that injustice, it will, despite its musical longueurs and its occasional overreaches, have served a worthwhile purpose.

13

Flesh and Blood Juke Box

Moscow Nights: The Van Cliburn Story—How One Man and His Piano Transformed the Cold War by Nigel Cliff, Harper, 2016, 452 pp., $28.99

Obituaries for Van Cliburn, who died at seventy-eight at the end of February 2013, were wistful. He was a man of a moment, a moment long past. Many readers surely reacted to the news the way I just did to Zsa Zsa Gabor's obits (oh, was *she* still alive?). Although Nigel Cliff works hard to ramp up his hero's exploits into something world-historical, his book, too, strikes an elegiac note. It is more about the moment than the man.

In case you blinked: Van Cliburn (born Harvey Lavan Cliburn Jr. in Shreveport, Louisiana, in 1934) was the American pianist who, at the age of twenty-three, won the first International Tchaikovsky Competition in Moscow in 1958, a few months after Sputnik and a few months before the Cuban revolution. Immediately co-opted into the rhetoric and diplomacy of the Cold War, he was fêted like no other classical musician in America, before or since. He shook hands with Nikita Khrushchev one week, with Dwight David Eisenhower the next. He was given a Broadway ticker-tape parade. He had fan clubs (one of them conspicuously defecting to him from Elvis Presley). His recordings of his war horses, the big Tchaikovsky Concerto and the even bigger "Rach 3," were huge sellers, and the Tchaikovsky disk is still the best-selling classical record of all time. It is impossible to think of him in any other context than the one that made him suddenly and sensationally famous. He is sooner seen as the American counterpart to Yuri Gagarin, the first cosmonaut, rather than in relation to other American pianists of his generation, such as John Browning or Byron Janis, or the rather better known pianists of slightly older

Review of *Moscow Nights: The Van Cliburn Story—How One Man and His Piano Transformed the Cold War* by Nigel Cliff, *Times Literary Supplement*, 3 March 2017, 3–5.

vintage such as Gary Graffman or Leon Fleisher—let alone Emil Gilels or Sviatoslav Richter, the celebrity Soviet pianists who, as members of the jury that awarded him his prize, proclaimed him their peer.

Which is a pity and an injustice. Cliburn *was* their peer. He could have been one of the great twentieth-century pianists rather than a fabled flash in the pan. His recordings prove that, as do, even more convincingly, a set of five Video Artists International DVDs, easily available for online purchase, that preserve his Soviet performances in recital and with orchestra over a period of fourteen years. (A few can be found even more easily on YouTube.) Watching as well as hearing him, one immediately sees what his peers and preceptors saw: an absolutely colossal aptitude for piano performance, beginning with ideal pianist hands: huge, like those of Rachmaninoff (he and Cliburn having been of comparable height), but with even longer, slimmer fingers. And how well they were trained, those hands, at first by his mother, his only teacher before he went to Juilliard at the age of seventeen, where he became the star pupil of Rosina Lhévinne, Juilliard's star teacher, who had graduated with a gold medal from the Moscow Conservatory in 1898 (sixty years before Cliburn's triumph in that very building), and who rated him "the most promising student I have had."

Even before the Tchaikovsky he was known among pianists as fortune's child. In 1954, at the age of nineteen, he won the Edgar M. Leventritt Award, a competition, judged by no-nonsense types like George Szell and Rudolf Serkin, to which one was admitted only by invitation or recommendation, and in which there were no runners-up, and often no winner. It paid its laureates in prestige and exposure: Cliburn played a solo recital in Carnegie Hall and the Tchaikovsky Concerto with the New York Philharmonic. Nigel Cliff reports good-but-not-great reviews for these performances, but Cliburn also got to appear on *The Tonight Show,* then in its first year, with Steve Allen, its first host, and made an extraordinary impression, setting the pattern for his whole career. He would always be admired by professionals and loved by audiences, and he would always be a whipping boy for the intellectual lower middle class, that is to say most critics. After his appearance on the air, his first manager was deluged with inquiries about the "guy with the hair we saw on TV" (71).

Did I mention the hair? It added three inches to his height and turned its lanky owner into a cartoon Texan. (Harvey L. Cliburn Sr., a low-level oil executive, had moved the family from Shreveport to Kilgore, Texas, when Junior was five years old.) That look was magic for him, precisely for the way it jarred with the sounds he made: for he was in every way save the accident of birth, long before he ever saw Moscow or even Rosina Lhévinne, a Russian pianist. His mother, née Rildia Bee O'Bryan, though she might have looked the part of an East Texas piano teacher, had been a devoted pupil of Arthur Friedheim, a Russian despite his name, who had been a devoted pupil of Anton Rubinstein in St. Petersburg, and who had moved on from Rubinstein to Liszt himself. As for Lhévinne, she was a prizewinning pupil of Vasiliy Safonoff, who had been a pupil of Theodor Leschetitzky (who had studied with Carl Czerny, who had studied with Beethoven).

Cliburn lived up to his formidable pedigree in a fashion that made him irresistible to the pianists who would judge him in 1958. You can hear what they heard in Cliburn's altogether astonishing rendition of Scriabin's Nocturne for the Left Hand, op. 9, no. 2, preserved from a finals round of the Tchaikovsky Competition itself, and available for audition on YouTube (www.youtube.com/watch?v=Mzs9PBaQAoM, at 27:38). What makes this particular piece a touchstone of Russian style is the way it depends on shades of "color," that is, of touch—tiny, telling gradations of pressure and length of contact with the key that can make the piano such a marvelous elucidator of complex musical textures. Like practically all pieces for the left hand alone, Scriabin's Nocturne seeks to create the illusion of two-handed playing. (There are hardly any pieces for the right hand alone because of the way the weight of human hands is distributed: the thumb—"my tenor thumb," Brahms called it—is at the "top" of the left hand at the keyboard and can easily bring out the tunes.) It may be the most successful of all in this deception—see if your friends can tell when you play them Cliburn's performance that he's using only one hand—but only if the performer can realize its demands: partly a matter of canny pedaling, but, far more important, of being able constantly to change the hand position while insuring that note follows note in each "voice" in the texture with exactly the right weight and articulation in relation to its predecessor and successor, no matter which finger has to play it. It requires a muscular control far rarer than the more easily noticed feats of velocity or digital marksmanship that to nonprofessional audiences define bravura "technique." Pianists known for this ability—Rachmaninoff, Medtner, Horowitz, Moisiewitsch, Sofronitsky, Josef Lhévinne (Rosina's husband), Genrikh Neygauz (aka Heinrich Neuhaus, the teacher of Gilels and Richter)—were Russians to a man.

Cliburn, too, had it to a superlative degree, which means his mother must have worked toward instilling it from the beginning; and you can hear it as well in his two-handed playing. Few pianists were as capable of modulating the tone of the instrument, judging the shape of a phrase and realizing it vividly, than Cliburn in his early days, when the imprint of the Russian style was most marked upon him. (For an exquisite demonstration of two-handed touch control, *watch* Cliburn play the end of Liszt's *Sonetto 123 della Petrarca*—a Sofronitsky specialty—on one of the VAI DVDs, with its dissonant notes struck by the left hand and resolved by the right.) Gilels, Richter, and their seniors on the Moscow jury, like the venerable Alexander Goldenweiser (a friend of Rachmaninoff and Tolstoy), were uniquely attuned to Cliburn's special virtues. Nigel Cliff describes their ecstatic reaction to his playing at the competition, which made the young Cliburn's victory inevitable, as well as richly deserved.

But his playing coarsened with time. You can hear it happening if you compare his many performances of Liszt's famous transcription of Schumann's song "Widmung" (Dedication), op. 25, no. 1. It was his favorite encore, and he recorded it during every phase of his short career. A favorite of many pianists, the piece is often held up by the fastidious as evidence of Liszt's bad taste—so often, indeed, that the authors of the play on which *Song of Love* (1947), the Hollywood Schumann biopic, was based worked in a scene in which Clara Schumann (played in the movie by Katharine Hepburn) dresses Liszt down for turning her husband's loving wedding gift to her into a garish star turn. Modeling his transcription on his own *Liebestraum* (also a transcription of a song, in this case his own), Liszt piled on repetitions, each more ornately festooned with arpeggios than the last, including a gratuitous climactic statement, marked *fortissimo, con somma passione,* that turns intimate confession into some sort of alpine cow call. A curious book by a disciple of the great German music historian Carl Dahlhaus, called *Probleme der musikalischen Wertästhetik im 19. Jahrhundert: Ein Versuch zur schlechten Musik* (Problems in the Aesthetic Evaluation of Music in the Nineteenth Century: An Essay on Bad Music), gives Liszt's "Widmung" a whole chapter.

The author, Eva Eggli, remarks that such a piece can only come off as "artistic" if the virtuoso embellishments are treated as "colors" applied nonchalantly (*quasi improvisando*) rather than "rendered ostentatiously as in an étude." Sound advice, and in his early renditions Cliburn seemed to be heeding it—not surprisingly, since that emphasis on color accords completely with his "Russian" training. A little recital he recorded in Moscow right after winning his gold medal, issued on a ten-inch LP by the Soviet Melodiya label, puts both the piece and the performer in a fresh, appealing light. Even the *somma passione* is kept in perspective—a spontaneous, touching swell of feeling that gushes up and immediately subsides. That brief impulsive outburst (and, much harder to achieve, its subsidence) requires the most exacting and strategic calibration of manual weight—something that only pianists who have been there will fully appreciate.

You may have to take my description of this early Cliburn performance on faith; as a teenager I was lucky enough to get a copy in the mail from doting Russian relatives. The Cliburn "Widmungs" you will find on YouTube are later performances. The version that had the widest circulation comes from an RCA Victor LP called *My Favorite Encores,* issued in 1970. Here, the *somma passione* has morphed into a tsunami, the arpeggios that introduce it have grown oceanic, and subsidence is minimal. It is a Texas-sized performance by someone used to bringing down huge houses. At twenty-three Cliburn had been a precociously refined artist; as he approached forty he had regressed into a conservatory jock, responding and catering to what Eggli calls *bürgerlichen Publikumsgeschmack,* the taste of the bourgeois public. (Schumann, of course, would have spoken of *Philister,* Philistines.)

Do I sound like a snob? I hope not: first, because I have actually listened and compared; but second, because I well remember the snobbish way Cliburn was written off by the prejudiced and the envious in his glory days, and by none more loftily than us junior aesthetes at New York's High School of Music and Art, where I was a sophomore in his time of triumph. *That drawling, lugubrious bohunk from Texas,* we thought. (The phrase is John Updike's, describing Lyndon Johnson, but it can't be bettered.) A churchgoing Baptist, a mama's boy, "a naïve domestic Burgundy without any breeding," as James Thurber might have said—who needed to hear *him*? By October 1960 there was the romantically exotic, and undeniably great, Sviatoslav Richter to gawk at and worship. Formerly kept at home as politically unreliable, Richter was sent on a ten-week American tour as if to show that, Cliburn or no Cliburn, the Soviets had the best pianists as well as the best rockets. We certainly thought so. One of my classmates sent him a poem—"Rikhter—Mad condor / clipped winged / Struggling against the sun / Piano, / player, / and harpy footed stool shall rise," etc.—and had an answer: "It is a tremendous thing to receive such a letter!" Would Cliburn with all his fan clubs elicit or respond to such a poem? Well, then! The very best part of Nigel Cliff's book is the refutation it delivers, half a century on, to puncture our airs. Citing the archived ballots and minutes of the 1958 Tchaikovsky jury, he reveals that it was none other than Richter who, having seen a kindred spirit and proclaimed him a genius, lobbied most intensely for Cliburn, even resorting to chicanery like giving zeros to his rivals (on a scale from 1 to 25) to knock them out of the running.

The story of how Richter's widely shared but politically fraught judgment ultimately prevailed is now one of the legends of twentieth-century music, but it is not very well understood. Cliff is helpful. There was never a doubt in the competition hall who deserved to win. But there were doubts aplenty about the integrity of the contest. Back home, once reports of Cliburn's progress through the rounds began seeping out, the question was not whether the competition would be fixed, but how. Those who thought the whole thing a sham engineered to enhance Soviet claims of cultural superiority assumed that the winner—perhaps all the winners—would have to be chosen from among the Soviet entrants. (This actually came close to happening on the violin side of the contest, with six of eight prizes, including the gold medal, going to the home team.) Those who thought the objective was to impress the world with Soviet magnanimity (as even stronger evidence of confident superiority) assumed that they would award the prize to a foreigner. After Cliburn's victory they thought their surmise vindicated. What Cliff's account reveals is that the judging of the competition was honest, but at all times subjected to political vetting: at first by some of the Soviet jury members, Dmitry Kabalevsky most prominently, who accused the Cliburn supporters of a lack of patriotism; then by Nikolai Mikhailov, the minister of culture, to whom the dispute was referred, but who quailed at the prospect of assuming responsibility for the outcome; and so, third, by Nikita Khrushchev himself, who was shrewd enough to see that awarding the prize to an American would be a propaganda coup—though even he did not foresee how right he would turn out to be.

And this returns us to the matter of Cliburn's sad regression. Cassandra prophecies and cautionary tales greet all sudden and spectacular ascents, and the critics outdid themselves where the rawboned Cliburn was concerned. One was truly prescient: Paul Henry Lang, a musicologist who had been appointed chief critic for the *New York Herald Tribune*. Writing after the Carnegie Hall concert at which Cliburn repeated his winning Moscow combo of Tchaik 1 and Rach 3, Lang warned that he might become "a flesh and blood juke box which at the insertion of the proper coin always plays the same tune" (226).

That is just what happened. His complaisant nature, combined with high-power, high-pressure management, ensured that Cliburn would be—in a sense quite far removed from the Soviet meaning of the title but just as real—a People's Artist, "performing" (as he put it himself) "for all people all over the world; not just musicians, but for everyone," and that his repertoire would become stagnant. His audience expected always to relive his triumphant exploits at his concerts, and so his stagnant repertoire became hackneyed as well. Cliff lists his seventeen concertos at one point, and what a predictable menu they were. If you know anything about the habits of what Rachmaninoff called "elephants" (championship-level performers), you can reel them off. Of Beethoven's five, only the last three made the cut, along with two of Rachmaninoff's four (the middle two, plus the Paganini Rhapsody), only one of Prokofieff's five (the Third), both of Brahms's and both of Liszt's, the Firsts by Chopin and Tchaikovsky, the Grieg and Schumann singletons, and one lonely concerto out of Mozart's twenty-seven—the big C-Major, K. 503, the only blockbuster in the lot. If you've been keeping count, you know that there is one more, and if you are a canny concert manager like Arthur Judson, you know it has to be the MacDowell Second (not the First, which nobody plays), as befits the repertoire of an American cultural ambassador. That was the list, the whole list, and for Cliburn it would be nothing but the list—a life sentence.

The life got sadder as it lengthened, culminating in a colossal burnout in 1978, which ushered in a sixteen-year hiatus, or—the managers' euphemism—"sabbatical," from which Cliburn tried to emerge in 1994. A documentary film made that year to herald the comeback tour, *Van Cliburn: Concert Pianist*, ends on a note of purported triumph, but it depressed me to watch it on YouTube, where you can easily find it. It shows Cliburn at Chicago's Grant Park, playing to an outdoor, nonpaying audience estimated at 350,000, accompanied as in the old days by the Moscow Philharmonic Orchestra, with the American conductor Leonard Slatkin standing in for Cliburn's old Soviet partner Kirill Kondrashin (who had died during the sabbatical), as if to memorialize Cliburn's place as a walking buffer between the superpowers. But Russia was no longer a superpower in 1994, and unlike Vladimir

Horowitz, who in 1965 had returned from twelve years of psychological paralysis a new man with a whole new repertoire (making comparisons inevitable), Cliburn had not grown in retreat. Just as Lang had predicted thirty-six years earlier, the coin dropped and out came the Cliburn theme song, Tchaik 1, which the fifty-nine-year-old pianist had been performing since the age of twelve, now slowed down and bloated up to a lumbering *grandioso,* with every phrase, once the piano got the tune, mauled into an inflated, affected *espressivo.* The tour ended in a fiasco on Cliburn's sixtieth birthday in July when, just before a concert at the Hollywood Bowl, he lost his nerve, canceled Rach 3, and offered instead a bouquet of badly received and mercilessly reviewed "favorite encores" that—inevitably—included "Widmung."

Yet if that late outing with Tchaik 1 was Cliburn's nadir, you can see him at his zenith on one of the VAI DVDs, at a 1962 concert in Moscow, playing the same concerto before an audience that included Khrushchev, Anastas Mikoyan (the great survivor from Stalin's Politburo), Alexey Kosygin (who two years later would supplant Khrushchev as Soviet premier), and (according to Nigel Cliff) an unseen Andrey Gromyko, the Soviet foreign minister. It is a thrilling performance, perhaps the best I have ever seen or heard of that ubiquitous piece. Cliburn plays assertively, indeed commandingly, no longer a talented boy who has been superbly trained by the last living mistress of a great tradition, but as one of its living masters, a great pianist, peaking prematurely at the age of twenty-eight. Afterward, in endearingly broken Russian, he announces an encore, Chopin's F-minor Fantasy, op. 49, "which I want to play for Nikita Sergeyevich Khrushchev." The Soviet premier, we learn from Nigel Cliff, had told Cliburn in 1958 that it was his favorite piece. To hear it, Khrushchev and the other bosses have to be summoned back from the green room, to which, thinking the concert was over, they had repaired to congratulate the pianist. He comes out into his box to laughter and cheers from the audience and bows graciously to Cliburn, clapping the while. While Cliburn plays the Fantasy (which, in Cliff's somewhat improbable version, Khrushchev had cited in 1958 by its opus number), the camera lingers on Nikita Sergeyevich, who is cradling his head with his right hand and dreamily conducting along with his left. The following weekend, he invited Cliburn to a family picnic at his dacha.

This little summit meeting is the one fleeting justification in the book for the author's hyperbolic portrayal of his hero as a Cold War leading man. The early chapters alternate vignettes from the lives of Cliburn and Khrushchev, as if limning parallel ascents. We get perfectly gratuitous, if adroitly narrated, vignettes of Stalin's death, Khrushchev's "secret speech," the Sputnik launch, Khrushchev's "kitchen debate" with Nixon, his visit to the United States, the U-2 debacle, the Berlin Wall, the Cuban missile crisis, and so on, as if Cliburn had something to do with them. Casting the 1958 Tchaikovsky Competition as a Cold War turning point is a footless conceit, even if it lends the book a vivid shape, just as it is a misreading of Cliburn's role in musical and diplomatic affairs to see him as an American cultural ambassador.

If anything, he was a Soviet ambassador. He was never sent to Russia by the American government, the way the State Department sent orchestras and jazz greats. The name Cliburn is not even to be found in the index of Danielle Fosler-Lussier's recent *Music in America's Cold War Diplomacy* (University of California Press, 2015), the most comprehensive account of the subject. But he does figure prominently—and fittingly—in Kiril Tomoff's *Virtuosi Abroad: Soviet Music and Imperial Competition during the Early Cold War, 1945–1958* (Cornell University Press, 2015), whose jacket sports a picture of Cliburn playing Tchaik 1 in the final round of the book's culminating event. He had entered the Tchaikovsky Competition on his own (or rather, Mme Lhévinne's) initiative, with the aid of a Martha Baird Rockefeller Fellowship, a private foundation grant. His victory took the American authorities, and the American musical establishment, equally by surprise. (The Juilliard dean, Mark Schubart, hurried to Moscow to see his winning round only after learning that it was unexpectedly looming.) It was furiously spun by both sides as a propaganda victory, but the Soviets got by far the greater share of cultural capital from it, for it was they, after all, who had recognized "Vanya" Cliburn and effectively created his myth.

Vanya could always be depended on thereafter to speak well of the country and its people, and could do it with impunity even at the tensest moments. On his triumphant return from Moscow in 1958, giving the first of countless interviews to American media, he said of the Soviets, "They are very warm individuals. They love very strongly. And yes, they are very sincere as a people. As a matter of fact, I couldn't refrain from telling them that they are very much like Texans." That was the kind of talk that was fondly supposed to ease tensions between the superpowers, and the older Cliburn, forgotten by everyone but the Soviets, went on being trotted out as an affable relic or *monstre sacré* to soften the Soviets up at difficult moments—right up to the end, when he was summoned out of his sabbatical to a command performance at the Reagan-Gorbachev White House summit in 1987. He played the expected juke box selections, including three items he had recorded on that 10-inch Melodiya disk twenty-nine years earlier ("Widmung" dependably among them), and ended with the Soviet pop chestnut, by Vasiliy Solovyov-Sedoy, whose title Nigel Cliff has appropriated for the title of his book. In 1958 he had charmed his hosts by making it the last encore in his postcontest concert; three decades later, singing along himself, he gets the whole Russian delegation to chime in, amid laughter and applause.

Cliff's reading of its effect is starry-eyed. "The next day," he writes,

> every network will lead with the scene of "Moscow Nights" at the White House, and Van will once again make front page headlines around the world for drawing out the humanity of a Soviet leader. Nancy Reagan will call the performance one of the great-

est moments of her husband's presidency. And Mikhail Gorbachev will be noticeably warmer as [he and the president] begin negotiations on the most ambitious arms control treaty in history. (358)

On the next page, getting reckless, he credits Cliburn with something even more momentous. "As Western values seeped in, with music in the vanguard," he writes, "the Soviet state lost credibility with its own people." And then, this:

> Van Cliburn's secret was that he lovingly played back to Russia the passionate, soul-searching intensity that was its culture's great contribution to the world, while embodying the freedom that most Americans took for granted and the Soviets sorely lacked. It was a devastating combination. (358–59)

But wily George Will (quoted by Cliff, who seems not to notice the divergence of opinion) got it right when, after Cliburn has the room singing, he "leans over to Adm. William Crowe, chairman of the joint Chiefs of Staff, and whispers, 'That song just cost you 200 ships'" (357). Will understood who had softened up whom.

It will never happen again. The strongest reaction I felt while reading this book was a pang of recognition that classical music is no longer seen, even fatuously, as an arena for national policy. It no longer represents nations, only (often rapacious) elites. That, rather than the end of superpower competition, is the big change that Cliburn's decline symbolizes. He was indeed a significant figure, and worthy of a book that says so, but Cliff puts him in the wrong context. He was the protagonist—or perhaps, more accurately, the figurehead—of the moment when classical music enjoyed a pinnacle of popularity and prestige from which it would plummet almost immediately. The sixties were the decade in which, as sociologists have shown and sought to explain, big changes in musical taste and consumption patterns, reflecting changes in demography and social attitudes, caused classical music to return to its tiny social niche after a couple of decades of pumped-up status vouchsafed by the New Deal and the touting of middlebrow culture.

Educated people, who until the 1960s habitually "graduated" from popular music to genres with higher social status—classical, jazz, coffeehouse "folk"—upon entering college, began retaining their popular music allegiances into adulthood, as they still do. Since then, no classical musician who was not already popular in the 1950s (perhaps only Leonard Bernstein besides Cliburn) has figured as a mass cultural or political icon, and such icons as still existed were worshiped nostalgically, by aging fans. The preconcert interviews at Grant Park in 1994, preserved in Cliburn's documentary video, showed this vividly. The huge audience that had assembled to hear his comeback consisted mainly of Medicare recipients, who were still comparing him with Elvis. The Cold War created the specific conditions that brought Cliburn to his unique, never to be equaled, peak, but it also created the trap that caught him and prevented his full maturation as an artist.

Just as Nigel Cliff portrays Cliburn in dual ascent with Khrushchev, they effectively come to a dual end in his book as well. Cliburn's post-Khrushchev years were wan, and Cliff allots less than one-tenth of the book's space to them. Ferdinand and Imelda Marcos of the Philippines became, *faute de mieux,* his patrons; how much further could one get from the Soviet-tinctured idealism Cliburn loved so long to profess? (And how symbolic of the kind of company classical music is now forced to keep.) He was hit with a palimony suit that, although dismissed, outed him against his will as gay. The last two decades, after the aborted comeback tour, merit only eight bleak pages. The piano competition that a consortium of Texas businessmen endowed in his name in 1962 continues to this day as a monument to his career, but neither it nor the Tchaikovsky Competition, which still limps back into quadrennial undeath in Moscow, arouse the kind of notice they once commanded. They have not, and will never, produce another Van Cliburn.

14

Tales of Push and Pull

Classics for the Masses: Shaping Soviet Musical Identity under Lenin and Stalin by Pauline Fairclough, Yale University Press, 2016, 283 pp., $45

Stalin's Music Prize: Soviet Culture and Politics by Marina Frolova-Walker, Yale University Press, 2016, 369 pp., $65

It is an oddity in Arnold Schoenberg's biography that, faced with life under the Nazis, he contemplated removal not to Western Europe and eventually the United States, the path he actually took, but to the Soviet Union—quite the opposite direction in more ways than one. Could that really be true, I always wondered. What could the inventor of twelve-tone music (and a monarchist revanchist besides) have been thinking? Where, other than Germany, the country he was fleeing, would he have been less welcome? Now I learn from *Classics for the Masses*, Pauline Fairclough's scrupulous archival study of the evolving Soviet performing repertory and the policies that conditioned it, that within the Soviet musical community there was a faction, led by Ivan Sollertinsky (the young Shostakovich's bosom friend), who believed that putting Schoenberg in charge of composition at the Moscow Conservatory "would . . . guarantee the Soviet Union's cultural pre-eminence." Following up on Fairclough's references, I further learned that Schoenberg was sounded out by his former pupil Hanns Eisler, an ardent Communist, and that he took the prospect seriously enough to send in a proposal "for the establishment of a musical institute" in the Soviet capital, as he put it in a 1934 letter to Fritz Stiedry, the German conductor then leading the Leningrad Philharmonic Orchestra.

Thirty years later, Stiedry recalled warning Schoenberg off of this "crazy idea," adding that "Russia was under the totally reactionary whip of Stalin," so that "friend Schoenberg would have been the least suitable musician imaginable." So I thought,

Review of *Classics for the Masses: Shaping Soviet Musical Identity under Lenin and Stalin* by Pauline Fairclough and *Stalin's Music Prize: Soviet Culture and Politics* by Marina Frolova-Walker; published as "Play It Again, Stalin," *Times Literary Supplement*, 4 August 2017, 3–5.

too; but after reading Fairclough's book I wonder whether Stiedry's memory had not been colored, as mine obviously was, by subsequent events, beginning in 1936 when the denunciation of Shostakovich's opera *The Lady Macbeth of the Mtsensk District* ushered in the draconian arts policies that became synonymous with Stalinism and with the Soviet regime. In 1935, between the sounding out of Schoenberg and the chewing out of Shostakovich, Stiedry led a performance in Leningrad of Schoenberg's Variations for Orchestra, the first big symphonic work to be written using twelve-tone technique, hence the very emblem of uncompromising modernism in those days. (According to Schoenberg's biographer Hans Heinz Stuckenschmidt, Shostakovich attended every rehearsal.)

As Fairclough shows (and it is one of many nuances she adds to our crude collective memory of Soviet music), there was a window between the Communist Party resolution of 1932 dissolving the "proletarian" associations of writers and musicians opposing modernist trends, and the clampdown of 1936, which coincided with the beginning of the bloody purges now known as the Great Terror. During that time, compositions using advanced academic techniques could be programmed at the discretion of performers. (Besides Schoenberg's Variations, she lists twelve-tone works by Berg and Krenek in the Leningrad repertoire). Still, it was a good thing Schoenberg stayed away. In a couple of years he would have been in even worse trouble than Prokofieff, who had been wooed back to his Sovietized homeland with promises of creative autonomy on which he felt, during the "window," he could rely.

The two books here under review give fuller, finer-grained, and better-shaded accounts of Soviet policy ups and downs and their impact on musicians than any previous study except Kiril Tomoff's pioneering *Creative Union* (2006), a similarly archive-based chronicle of the Union of Soviet Composers. Their purviews differ: Fairclough's is a panorama; *Stalin's Music Prize*, by Marina Frolova-Walker, is a minute close-up on the workings of a prestige machine. But they will, I hope, have similar salutary impacts. Almost to the end of the twentieth century, Russian music studies, and studies of Soviet music in particular, suffered from a dearth of documentation and a plethora of prejudice and hearsay. The field was notoriously prey to fabrications and suppressions, irresponsible assertions and reprehensible invective. With the arrival of these books—Anglophone heirs to a tradition that began in the first post-Soviet decade with spadework by such Russian scholars as Leonid Maksimenkov and Yekaterina Vlasova (who were attracted first, and understandably, to the crisis years 1936 and 1948)—I dare hope that the silly season of Russian musical scholarship is at its long-awaited end.

Fairclough's panorama sheds light on three especially murky areas. One, as noted, is modernism. The relationship between mass politics and modern art has always been tense and unstable. To the extent that it is viewed as hermetic or elitist, modern art will seem just another excrescence of aristocratic privilege. But there has always been a countervailing tendency to see modernized art as an embodiment of a modernized, which is to say progressive, reality. The simple view of modernism's trajectory in Soviet policy was a steady backslide from the second position to the first, from the radical (futurist, constructivist) twenties, epitomized for music by Shostakovich's wild Second Symphony ("To October") and Mosolov's cacophonous *Zavod* (Factory; known in English for some reason as *The Iron Foundry*), to the philistine, bureaucratically hamstrung, and increasingly nationalistic late thirties, so gleefully derided in Stravinsky's *Poetics of Music* ("the dancing kolkhoz," "the symphony of socialism"), the promulgation of Socialist Realism in 1934 serving as watershed. Rather than a linear descent, Fairclough traces a tremulous fever chart, examining deeds and events rather than rhetoric.

The second area of illumination is sacred music, a touchy matter in a country where "religious propaganda" was outlawed. For many years (into the 1970s, as I can attest from experience), Church Slavonic texts were suppressed and Orthodox choral compositions, when performed outside of church, became vocalises. (There were exceptions, though: Fairclough documents a program of Orthodox sacred music the Moscow Patriarchate was allowed to present in the Great Hall of the Moscow Conservatory in 1945, as a reward for the church's wartime loyalty to the regime.) The sacred works of major canonical composers, mainly in Latin or German, presented a more subtle problem, solutions to which amounted to another fever chart that Fairclough traces for the first time in detail. She has a fine eye for the paradoxes and quandaries that arise when artworks with strongly ideological content are justified on purely "aesthetic" grounds. She quotes a proletarianist commentator, writing in 1927, who sees Bach's *St. John Passion* scheduled for performance at the House of Unions, usually a site for workers' concerts, and rubs his eyes in bewilderment: "Then I heard that, though the 'Passion' is spiritual music, at the same time it is interesting in this or in that way. In the end I just couldn't understand why we have to have 'The Passion of Our Lord.' When the Passion ended it was 'And now listen to "Sleeping Beauty."'"

I sympathize with this man whenever I hear Prokofieff's *Zdravitsa*, a paean to Stalin, Lord of another church, performed and cheered by those who think its tunes are pretty. Of course, I'd join the protest if it were ever banned. But as Fairclough shows, Bach was never banned in the USSR. The fact, moreover, that his sacred music could be aesthetically justified there exposes Soviet arts policies, whatever the proletarian rhetoric, as thoroughly bourgeois, very much in keeping with the class background of the cultural policy makers, whatever their political professions.

Bans were rarer in Russia than we might assume. Take Rachmaninoff, a composer often reviled in the Soviet press as a "white émigré," but irreversibly (and increasingly) popular with audiences. The one organized campaign against him came in March 1931, when the Russian Association of Proletarian Musicians (RAPM) called for the removal of his works from the concert repertoire because they are "reactionary, reflecting a decadent mood of the petite bourgeoisie, and . . . particularly harmful in the bitter conditions of class struggle." Fairclough wonders why he of all composers was singled out for "aggressive motions," evidently unaware that two months earlier Rachmaninoff had been among the signers of an incendiary letter to the *New York Times* complaining that Rabindranath Tagore, interviewed after a visit to Russia, had failed to denounce "the horrors perpetrated by the Soviet government and the Ogpu [secret police] in particular." So RAPM was responding to a provocation rather than launching an offensive. But while they succeeded in getting a few performances canceled, there was never a ban on performing Rachmaninoff's concert works, which enjoyed full canonical status—especially during the war, when many émigrés, especially those in Allied countries, were forgiven.

Also forgiven were many great cultural figures of the tsarist past whose class backgrounds and political views had formerly counted against them, as resurgent nationalism supplanted class consciousness. This is the third area Fairclough lights up. Centenaries were always handy opportunities for reassessment. Pushkin's, in 1937, was the most conspicuous. In the 1920s, it had been a special mission of Nadezhda Krupskaya, Lenin's wife, to root "that nobleman" out of Soviet lending libraries to protect young Soviet minds. His rehabilitation dovetailed nicely with Chaikovsky's, whose centennial followed in 1940 (and whose most popular operas—the most popular Russian operas of all—were both based on Pushkin). Chaikovsky's "pessimism" (as at the end of his "Pathetic" Symphony), once considered antirevolutionary, now became the manly requiem of his dying class, available for optimistic reading by successor classes. The only Chaikovsky-related postcentennial ban was on public references to his homosexuality (which contradicted the manly image), formerly a topic of frank discussion. The most radical interpretive revision concerned Musorgsky, whose centennial fell between Pushkin's and Chaikovsky's. Much more of an aristocrat than Chaikovsky, his talent for writing crowd scenes insured that Musorgsky would always be read in Soviet Russia as the musical equivalent of the "populists" (*narodniki*) and nihilists who were his contemporaries, but with whom he had precious little in common.

Fairclough provides a time line on which all aspects of evolving Soviet musical reception—performance, critical assessment, historiography—can be tracked and interrelated against the background of evolving official policy. The two evolutions are portrayed in a dialectical relationship, a constant push-pull that neither conforms to the old "totalitarian" model that, invoked to explain everything, explained nothing, nor ascribes disproportionately autonomous agency to the musicians, as post-Soviet revisionists were doing for a while. Although she does not say so, her descriptions accord with the "affordance" model, widely adopted in the social sciences since it was proposed by ecological psychologists in the 1970s, according to which agents react to, and reciprocally affect, the enabling and constraining properties of their environments.

Stalin's Music Prize turns out to be a case study of precisely this kind, loaded with fascinating tales of push and pull, Frolova-Walker's stated objective being to demythologize and de-exoticize the old riddle-wrapped-in-a-mystery-inside-an-enigma that was Russia under Stalin. The environment Frolova-Walker describes is a sometimes peculiar but recognizably terrestrial milieu inhabited by recognizable human beings, not excluding the one with the power of life and death over the rest, who is portrayed in collaboration with others as the acknowledged first among . . . well, not equals, but agents all the same. The administration of the Stalin Prize, awarded annually in the arts and sciences over a rough decade beginning in 1941, while undeniably unique in some ways owing to that radical lopsidedness of power, was in other ways quite like that of other incentive systems, and therefore not only explicable but revealing—not merely of the capricious personal predilections of a tyrant, but of a set of competing social values.

Caricatural exaggerations of Stalin's role in its administration began at least as early as Nikita Khrushchev's so-called secret speech, "The Cult of the Person and Its Consequences," delivered in February 1956 to the Twentieth Congress of the Soviet Communist Party. The Stalin Prizes were among the megalomaniacal excesses Khrushchev purported to expose. "Comrades!" he urged (as recorded in the official stenographic transcript), "Let us take the matter of the Stalin Prizes. (*Movement in the hall.*) Not even the Tsars created prizes which they named after themselves!" They are now a laughing stock, fatally linked to the scientific frauds they once ratified (like the bogus genetics of Trofim Lysenko, one of the earliest recipients), not to mention the secret awards for nuclear bomb development. Frolova-Walker's book sports as its dust-jacket illustration one of the better-known examples of that laughter: *The Origins* (1983), from the series "Nostalgic Socialist Realism" by the ex-Soviet "post-art" team of Vitaly Komar and Alexander Melamid. The painting shows a monumentalized Stalin, wearing the white generalissimo's uniform he wore when descending from the sky at the end of the film *The Fall of Berlin* (Stalin Prize first class, 1950), sitting at the base of what looks to be a Greek temple, staring off into the future while his profile is being traced by what looks to be a seminude, caressing Minerva (Fig. 14.1). Without actually referring to this picture in her text, Frolova-Walker nevertheless provides it with an apt running commentary, using the history of the Stalin Prize to give—by way of practical examples, the only reliable way—a more coherent definition than any I had previously encountered of just what the unstable compound of heroism and classicism known as Socialist Realism entailed.

She also gives a plausible account of the institution of the prize in 1939, relying on a story told long after the fact, but by someone in a position to know: Alexander Nikolayevich Poskryobyshev, Stalin's closest aide, who as the head of the so-called Special Section of the Central Committee was, in plainer language, the official keeper of secrets. The institution of what amounted to Soviet Nobel Prizes, he said, was a solution to the problem of disposing of large sums earned in foreign royalties

FIGURE 14.1. Vitaly Komar and Alexander Melamid, "Rozhdeniye Sotsrealizma" (1983).

by the writings of Stalin and other high-ranking members of the Party. The project reflected the grandiosity of Stalinist thinking. Its name was not—or not just—a caprice of vanity. As Jeffrey Brooks showed in *Thank You, Comrade Stalin! Soviet Public Culture from Revolution to Cold War* (1999), his study of the Stalinist gift economy, the cult of Stalin's person served an administrative purpose, very successfully reinforcing in the population a sense of dependency on the state and its guiding force, the Party. (Or as Stalin himself is said to have put it to his adopted son: "You're not Stalin and I'm not Stalin. Stalin is Soviet power. Stalin is what he is in the newspapers and the portraits, not you, not even me!")

So although recipients did tend to convey personal thanks to Stalin, he did not pick them. Or rather, he was one of the participants in a multilevel process of selection, which, working from a ton of archived documentation, Frolova-Walker has reconstructed. It began, like virtually all such processes, with a nominating committee of professionals: she calls it the KSP, from the Russian initials for Stalin Prize Committee. The KSP's recommendations were referred for vetting first to the Committee on Artistic Affairs (renamed the Ministry of Culture in 1946) and to Agitprop, the Central Committee's Department of Agitation and Propaganda, thence up the ladder to the Politburo, sometimes aided at this higher stage as well by representatives (usually the general secretaries) of the relevant creative or scientific unions. Here is where Stalin (never chairing the session, of course, or sitting at the head of the table) took part; but as the record makes clear (to that extent confirming assumptions), he had veto power and was thus the final arbiter of the process, though never (well, hardly ever) the initiator.

Stalin wielded his authority in proportion to his level of interest. He was a most active intervener when it came to literature and film, where he considered himself an expert. The lists he was given at those selection meetings are covered with his marginalia (at which we get some fascinating peeks). He also took active, often peremptory part in discussions of paintings and sculpture. Classical music was evidently of little concern to him; his preserved notations relating to music are sparse, and mainly affected awards for folk and popular performers, not the major composers who are likely to command our interest today. But this absence itself is of the greatest interest, for it bears eloquent testimony to matters of recent furious debate.

Solomon Volkov's *Shostakovich and Stalin: The Extraordinary Relationship between the Great Composer and the Brutal Dictator* (2004), a big seller, was his second book about Shostakovich. It was expressly intended to substantiate the first, *Testimony* (1979), a true bestseller, which had been marketed as Shostakovich's dictated memoirs, though that was effectively discredited by its better-informed academic reviewers. The "extraordinary relationship" that Volkov purported to describe was one of intense mutual obsession. His Stalin was modeled on Tsar Nikolai I, who had undertaken to serve as Pushkin's (= Shostakovich's) personal censor.

One of Volkov's chief exhibits in support of his mythology was the first round of Stalin Prizes, in which one of the lavish first-class awards in music went to Shostakovich's Piano Quintet (1940), still commonly rated among his best works. Volkov pointed to the modesty of its genre—chamber music, and with a quiet ending to boot—as evidence that it contradicted the requirements of Socialist Realism for monumentality and optimism, epitomized for all time by one of the other first-class award winners that year, Vera Mukhina's flamboyant sculpture *Rabochiy i kolkhoznitsa* (Worker and Collective Farm Woman), in which the figures held aloft, respectively, the hammer and sickle. It had stood atop the Soviet pavilion at the Paris Exposition of 1937 before becoming the emblem of Mosfilm, which made it familiar to moviegoers the world over as the huge emblem of its mammoth motherland. A mere piano quintet could never be considered alongside it for a major Soviet award, Volkov insisted, without the personal intervention of the dictator, with his singular freedom of transgression.

As perverse corroboration, Volkov adduced a letter to Stalin from a well-known music bureaucrat that called upon the ruler to override the KSP's selection of a composition that exemplified "unhealthy tendencies" and that "lacks any connection with the life of the People." (The letter was published in 1995 in an early post-Soviet roundup of formerly inaccessible government documents, which is how it came to Volkov's attention.) "They tried to talk Stalin out of this decision," Volkov wrote; and since they failed, it can only mean that "Stalin listened to Shostakovich's music and liked it." That is how myths are made. The actual selection documents, by contrast, give no evidence of Stalin's participation, and much evidence of enthusiastic support by those actually charged with the decision. The ultimate resting place for the dissenting letter, Frolova-Walker observes, suggests that it was not forwarded to the dictator, but rather, and typically, "went down the steps of the bureaucratic ladder," ultimately reaching the Committee on Artistic Affairs, the likely end of the road.

Frolova-Walker breezily admits that Volkov's fable makes a better story than hers; but in fact, her version of these events forms part of the best story we have yet been told about music and its vicissitudes under Soviet political pressure. Intervention from on high varies inversely with initiative from below. Stalin's relative apathy toward music serves as a quirky guarantee that music will be the area where the records of the Stalin Prize will give us the least obstructed view of genuine artistic—or more generally, professional—agency, on two levels: that of the creative practitioners, and that of the administrators. In the present case, when the dust had settled, first-class prizes were awarded to Shostakovich for his quintet and to the venerable Nikolai Myaskovsky for his Twenty-First Symphony, still the best known of his twenty-seven, which had been commissioned by the Chicago Symphony Orchestra for its fiftieth anniversary alongside works by Stravinsky (his Symphony in C), Darius Milhaud, Zoltán Kodály, William Walton, and Roy Harris. It, too, was a work of comparatively modest dimensions, and like Shostakovich's quintet, it ended quietly. But it, too, represented Soviet music as world-class art.

Then the administrators started meddling. The remaining first-class award, to Yury Shaporin for his cantata *On the Field of Kulikovo*, commemorating the 1380 victory by Prince Dmitri Donskoy over the Golden Horde, conforms to the stereotype of crypto-nationalistic Socialist Realist art; and the five second-class awards, the product of a lot of ministry-level horse-trading which Frolova-Walker tracks in absorbing detail, ended up as what American politicians call a balanced ticket: one apiece to the five major music-producing non-Russian "nationalities" of the Soviet Union as embodied in the Ukrainian, the Belorussian, and the three Transcaucasian republics. Balloting and haggling thus produced a compromise between aesthetic and sociopolitical criteria; and so, in varying proportions, did all the other Stalin Prize deliberations concerning music—not so different, in fact, from the outcomes of prize competitions everywhere. Frolova-Walker's account is topical rather than chronological, her chapters displaying that bargaining process from many angles of interest to students of Soviet society and culture: Russian vs. "national," "high" genres vs. "low," performance values, the crisis of 1948, and finally the collapse of the whole enterprise following the death of the man in whose name it had been instituted. There are also chapters devoted to the three individuals of greatest interest to biographers: Prokofieff, Myaskovsky, and, of course Shostakovich, who gets two.

The second of these is probably the most surprising and instructive chapter in the book. It concerns Shostakovich as an intermittent member of the KSP beginning in 1947, and it stunningly contradicts the image of the composer as Holy Fool advanced by Volkov and other Shostakovich fabulists. On the KSP Shostakovich was not a holy fool but a holy terror, described by a fellow panelist as the only composer on the committee who actually spoke his mind rather than equivocating (like Myaskovsky and Shaporin) or holding a finger to the wind (like Glière). His interventions were not always constructive. Frolova-Walker found herself taken aback by transcripts of the last meetings of the committee, which showed Shostakovich in vindictive pursuit of Alexander Mosolov, of *Iron Foundry* fame but by then thoroughly tamed, who was being considered for a third-class prize for an innocuous folk-song arrangement. The other members of the committee wanted to recognize his efforts at "self-correction." Not Shostakovich. "I don't believe in his talent," he said, "and his modernist compositions were just as talentless as this."

"To speak dismissively of Mosolov's later work was perhaps unpleasant, but frank," Frolova-Walker allows; but "dismissing his earlier work was another matter, and perhaps [alluding now to the time of his own humiliation] Shostakovich himself had a little of the spirit of January 1948 lurking within him." Summing up, she cites his "strong desire to participate in public life," which

> sometimes allowed him to make a principled stand, or to help out friends, and at other times drew him into shabby compromises, or indeed into joining the Communist Party. [And yet] without that innate need to speak up, to interfere, whether to take a stand or to find official approval, we wouldn't have had either the Seventh or the Thirteenth Symphony, nor, on the other side, *Song of the Forests* or the Twelfth Symphony.

These are the refreshing words of a scholar, not a fabulist. They serve not to pave the way to satisfying redemptive myths, but seek a footing along the tortuous, asymptotic path toward understanding the often awful twentieth century. Pauline Fairclough and Marina Frolova-Walker are doing work it takes a twenty-first-century musicologist to do. I wish them many competitors.

15

Was Shostakovich a Martyr, or Is That Just Fiction?

Novelists have every right to use historical data to lend their works verisimilitude, and they are free to range beyond the facts, wherever their fancy leads them. Historians enjoy no such liberty. They (or, I should say, we) are bound by circumstances, constrained by the record, condemned to whatever partial, obstructed view their sources grant them. Their only recourse is to keep on looking and pray. Meanwhile, novelists soar aloft and gain an untrammeled vista.

But what are they actually seeing? Sometimes they deliberately describe what never was. Counterfactual fiction, like Philip Roth's *The Plot against America*, imagining a Lindbergh presidency and its dire consequences for American Jews, can be fun in a ghastly sort of way, as well as morally instructive. But some novelists aspire to something nearer the opposite of counterfactual. In a draft for *War and Peace*, Tolstoy wrote that he really wanted to tell the history of Russia's Napoleonic war, but that if he attempted the task without fictional admixture, it would "force me to be governed by historical documents rather than the truth."

What is that truth, which goes beyond the documents? Whatever it is, Tolstoy's pursuit of it gave us *War and Peace*. But more recently, it has given us Julian Barnes's novel *The Noise of Time*, which pretends to give us the truth, not just the facts, about Dmitri Shostakovich, the greatest composer the Soviet Union ever produced. And since I think Mr. Barnes's book a beautifully written botch, I have been wondering anew about truth.

Review of *The Noise of Time* by Julian Barnes; published, quite cut to ribbons, in *The New York Times*, 28 August 2016, Arts & Leisure sec., and, in Russian, as "Bïl li Shostakovich muchenikom? Ili éto tol'ko vïmïsel?" trans. Pavel Raigorodsky, *Muzïkal'noye obozreniye*, 2017, no. 11, 10.

I have plenty of company—not in my opinion of Mr. Barnes's book, which has been garnering extravagant praise, but in wondering about truth. People have been doing that for a long time—since Pilate confronted Christ, at least. And the wrangling over what the truth might be about Shostakovich and his experiences under Stalin has been going on, it sometimes seems, almost as long.

Contention—between those who believe that Shostakovich was a blameless martyr, opposed to and victimized by the Soviet regime, and those of us who believe he made pragmatic compromises to survive and prosper—reached such a pitch that if you search for "Shostakovich wars" on Google, it will fetch thousands of hits. Shostakovich warriors, those who have sought to portray him as disaffected and tacitly hostile to the Soviets, distinguish the literal truth of the letters, journals, and memoirs we have from what some have called "the essential truth" that only inspired speculation can reveal.

The fallacy of such thinking is to regard that essential truth as something revealed rather than created. Tolstoy did not make that mistake. He knew that the difference between real and fictional worlds is that a fictional world is wholly known. Nothing could remain hidden from Tolstoy about his imagined Napoleonic Russia and its Natashas, Pierres, and Andreys. But no matter how diligently he or we may burrow in the archives, things will elude us. There will always be more documents somewhere; some may contradict the ones we know, and there is no end to what was never recorded to begin with. The whole documentary truth can never be known. (Which is fine for business, historians will murmur.)

I don't think that Julian Barnes would necessarily disagree. But he has not lived up to his calling as a free ranger. He might have invented his own Shostakovich—and had he done so, he might have done as he did in his marvelous novel *The Porcupine*, which fictionalizes Todor Zhivkov, the fallen Communist ruler of Bulgaria, and lets us hear his inner voice as he faces trial. Like all the main characters in *War and Peace*, the owner of that voice is given a fictional name in the book, which frees the author from the factual record, and frees us from expectations based upon it.

So why, then, is Shostakovich given his own name in *The Noise of Time* (as are all the other characters)? If Mr. Barnes had called his hero, say, Ivan Ivanovich Ivanov, and let the reader divine the resemblance to Shostakovich, I would accept his work without demur. But Mr. Barnes evidently wanted to capitalize on the interest that frenzied debate has drummed up in his subject, and to claim implicitly to have settled the issues that scholars dispute. In a bumptious "Author's Note" appended to the novel, he advertises his fidelity to his sources and his superior insights. He is trying to have it both ways. He wants the novelist's freedom and also the historian's authority. But in trying for both he achieves neither.

Mr. Barnes's view of Shostakovich conforms in every detail to the sentimental Cold War fable of a passive, pathetic yet saintly figure buffeted by an obtuse, implacable force. This stereotype goes beyond Shostakovich and beyond his music, all the way to music itself, imagined as pure and spotless, utterly truthful the way mathematics is truthful, unresistant to martyrdom and co-option yet ultimately triumphant. These are the naïve assumptions of pop Romanticism. Somehow a fine novelist thinks that's good enough for music.

The sources on which Mr. Barnes has most conspicuously and uninventively relied are the two canonical texts of the Shostakovich wars. One is the now-discredited *Testimony,* a bestseller that appeared in 1979, subtitled "The Memoirs of Dmitri Shostakovich as Related to and Edited by Solomon Volkov." The other is the invaluable *Shostakovich: A Life Remembered* (1994; 2nd ed., 2006) by Elizabeth Wilson, a compendium of third-person accounts by people who knew the composer. The one is a proven fake, a mixture of recycled material that Shostakovich had approved for republication and fabrications inserted after his death; the other makes no truth claims about its contents but presents a great gabble of conflicting viewpoints from which we are invited to draw our own conclusions.

Mr. Barnes has purportedly done just that. But the remarkable, disappointing fact is that his fictional Shostakovich is not his own. He has adopted a readymade: the version of Shostakovich peddled by *Testimony,* supplemented by the most famously lurid tales from Ms. Wilson's argosy and a published letter or two. The resulting narrative, a salad of stale anecdotes and romantic clichés, is familiar to anyone who has followed the Shostakovich wars. I call it the Shostakovich Apocrypha.

It consists of three books. The first is The Book of Muddle. It tells of the anonymous *Pravda* editorial of 28 January 1936, "Muddle Instead of Music," which denounced Shostakovich's wildly successful opera *The Lady Macbeth of the Mtsensk District.* It not only led to a ban on the opera, but also put the composer under a cloud of suspicion that brought him within a hair's breadth of being "repressed," as the saying went, in the Stalinist purges of 1936–38.

The second is The Book of Waldorf. It tells of the Cultural and Scientific Conference for World Peace, held at the Waldorf-Astoria Hotel in New York in March 1949, where Shostakovich, fresh from a second denunciation at the hands of Andrey Zhdanov, Stalin's culture czar, was sent against his will as a member of the official Soviet delegation, only to be humiliated again in a confrontation with the composer Nicolas Nabokov, who would later head the Congress for Cultural Freedom, an agency funded by the CIA.

The third is The Book of Victims. It tells of Nikita Khrushchev's successful effort to browbeat Shostakovich into joining the Soviet Communist Party in 1960 so that he could serve as titular head of the Russian Federation's Union of Soviet Composers, after which the composer was so demoralized and filled with shame that he wrote a string quartet about it—his Eighth, often regarded as his masterpiece, in which the themes, all derived from his initials, represent his wounded subject persona, bearing witness to his status (in the words of the quartet's dedication) among the twentieth century's "Victims of War and Fascism." (Here the most relevant document is a letter from Shostakovich to his friend Isaak Glikman, which Mr. Barnes also cites in his Author's Note.)

The three books of the Shostakovich Apocrypha correspond exactly to the three chapters of *The Noise of Time,* and there is nothing in Mr. Barnes's account that cannot be found in the sources he cites. His open fictionalization achieves nothing beyond what previous covert fictionalizations had achieved: Mr. Volkov's, which has been exposed as such; the uncorroborated hazy reminiscences of Shostakovich's friend Veniamin Basner, based on a bibulous long-ago (and long after the fact) conversation as recounted by Elizabeth Wilson; and the connections already drawn by Isaak Glikman between the changes in Shostakovich's life in 1960 and the implied narrative of the Eighth Quartet.

Meanwhile, all three apocryphal books would have been fine fodder for creative novelization, were the novelist truly enterprising and curious about his subject. In the Muddle chapter, Mr. Barnes has his hackneyed Shostakovich musing not only that Stalin had "inspired and approved the *Pravda* editorial" lambasting his opera, but that he had "perhaps even written it himself." Nobody thought that in Russia in 1936 (though Mr. Volkov raised the possibility in *Testimony* to beguile gullible Westerners). Nor did anyone seriously think it the work of any other member of the Soviet leadership. Such jobs were done by professionals, and now we know who it was.

"Muddle Instead of Music" was the work of David Iosifovich Zaslavsky (1880–1965; Fig. 15.1), a literary critic and journalist who in 1934 had been handpicked by Stalin to be a *Pravda* staff editorialist over the objections of many of his future colleagues. From the standpoint of Stalinist orthodoxy, Zaslavsky had a dubious, even a shady, past life as a Menshevik and a high-ranking member of the Jewish Labor Bund. He belonged, in other words, to prerevolutionary factions opposed to Lenin's. His early published work had been in Yiddish. Stalin, nothing if not a shrewd psychologist, knew how to pick his underlings. Some former Mensheviks or Bundists emigrated after the revolution. Others were arrested and condemned. A few, however, joined the ranks of Stalin's trusted henchmen, peerlessly loyal because they were motivated by unassuageable fear.

Andrey Vyshinsky, the prosecutor of the show trials through which Stalin's rivals were eliminated (and later the first Soviet delegate to the United Nations), was one of them. David Zaslavsky was another. Drafts of "Muddle" and diary references to it were found in his archive after his death, along with drafts of equally slanderous and almost equally notorious editorials denouncing Osip Mandelstam and Boris Pasternak.[1] Even the supremely odious "On a Certain Antipatriotic

---

1. See Yevgeniy Yefimov, *Sumbur vokrug "sumbura" i odnogo "malen'kogo zhurnalista"* (Moscow: Flinta, 2006).

FIGURE 15.1. David Zaslavsky, the anonymous author of "Muddle Instead of Music," in his *Pravda* office, ca. 1947.

Group of Theater Critics," one of the publications that unleashed the 1948 anti-Semitic campaign against "rootless cosmopolitans," turned out to be Zaslavsky's work. Imagine what went on in the head of the man who wrote these infamous texts. When I think of the novel Julian Barnes might have written had he taken David Zaslavsky as his subject, rather than recycling the threadbare Shostakovich Apocrypha, his banalities seem all the more deplorable.

The Book of Waldorf also abounds in food for ironic thought. The portrayal of Shostakovich as a passive pawn in Stalin's clutches does scant justice to a man whose collisions with power had educated him in the rules of a complicated game, one he had learned to play with exceeding self-concealing skill. In his one actual person-to-person encounter with Stalin (or possibly, it is now thought, with Alexander Nikolayevich Poskryobyshev, the despot's right-hand man) by phone in March 1949, through which the ruler sought to coerce the composer's attendance in New York, Shostakovich leveraged the world fame that made him indispensable as a showcase exhibit into a rescinding of the broadcast and performance ban on his own and his colleagues' works that followed the "formalist" denunciations at Zhdanov's hands the previous year.

After his return from abroad, Shostakovich composed a pair of tribute works, an oratorio called *Song of the Forests* and the soundtrack score for the film *The*

Fall of Berlin, which won him Stalin Prizes in 1950, with bountiful purses that lifted him out of the financial straits the ban had imposed. These pieces are often dismissed as cheap potboilers by those who know them only by reputation. Yet as the British musicologist Pauline Fairclough has shown in a patient analysis, they do not suffer by comparison with the more respectable works of the period. The Shostakovich of history did not separate his works, as we now tend to do, into those written for "them" and those written for "him." No one writes badly on purpose, especially one who knows his work is unsurpassable.

If Mr. Barnes had explored the ambivalences and inconsistencies that caused an outstanding ex-Soviet musicologist, Margarita Mazo, to stand up at a Boston meeting of the American Musicological Society, where the Apocrypha was being smugly and dogmatically touted, and shut the touters' mouths by saying (and showing) that Shostakovich's "hands were dirty," *The Noise of Time* would have been worthy of *The Porcupine*. No one could make a career as successful as the one Shostakovich made in Soviet Russia while maintaining the kind of moral and aesthetic purity his mythologizers attribute to him. No one makes a successful career anywhere without learning and executing a complicated social dance.

The best evidence of all can be found in the real events that the third book of the Apocrypha, The Book of Victims, distorts. There is no reason to think that Shostakovich sought either the Party membership or the leadership of the Russian Composers Union that were thrust upon him in 1960. Like another perquisite of fame, his 1947 "election" to the Supreme Soviet, the USSR's rubberstamp parliament, they were far more a distraction than an honor. But once in possession of political power, Shostakovich behaved not like a saint but like a politician. Among the documents published since the Soviet collapse is his correspondence as Union secretary. It can make grimly humorous reading when you know its context. Shostakovich was not above settling scores.

In 1948, the worst thing anyone said about him at the hearings that preceded the Central Committee's "Resolution on Music," and the imposition of the ban, came from the foul mouth of Vladimir Zakharov, who as director of the Pyatnitsky Choir, the Soviet Union's leading song-and-dance ensemble (and not at all a bad musician), was the country's number-one fakelorist. "From the point of view of the People," Zakharov taunted, Shostakovich's Eighth Symphony "is not a musical work at all; it is a 'composition' which has nothing whatever to do with the art of music." At the very first Union meeting over which he presided as chair, Shostakovich paid his tormentor back (posthumously) with a scorching attack on the Choir's repertory, which still consisted mainly of Zakharov arrangements; and to one of the ensemble's then active arrangers he wrote that the hapless fellow's setting of one particularly famous song "has nothing in common with the art of music," echoing nearly verbatim Zakharov's old insult, which had been published and widely circulated. Yes, Shostakovich's hands were indeed dirty. Everyone's were.

The author of *The Porcupine* knew that. What lured him into hagiography when Shostakovich became his subject? Were I a novelist I might speculate; but that he has, saddeningly, followed the uncomprehending crowd is a fact.

16

How to Win a Stalin Prize
Shostakovich and His Quintet

I

I'll start with someone from whom it is always a pleasure to quote: Marina Frolova-Walker, a Russian-born professor at the University of Cambridge who is at present the foremost student of Russian and Soviet music in the United Kingdom. On being awarded the Dent Medal, one of the high honors in the world of musicology, she delivered a lecture to the Royal Musical Association that she later revised for publication as an article in the Association's *Journal*. Its title took the form of a question: "An Inclusive History for a Divided World?" Now that the Cold War is over—or (at least) now that we seem to be in a lull between cold wars—it is time, she proposes, to find ways of integrating what used to be the parallel histories of twentieth-century music in the "Soviet bloc" and the "free world" into a single, unified music historiography. As one who has long lamented the ghettoization of Russian music on both sides of the old divide, I of course applaud Prof. Frolova-Walker's proposal, even if I am among those twitted in (I assure you) a friendly way for maintaining the bad old rift. Neither her argument nor her gentle reproof surprised me, because the discussion circled around the figure of Shostakovich, a world-class eminence by anyone's standards, yet one habitually treated in isolation from others of comparable stature—and thus, ineluctably, diminished. "He remains in a historical and musicological ghetto," Prof. Frolova-Walker

---

Originally delivered at the Blavatnik School of Government, University of Oxford, 8 May 2018, as part of the Kyoto Prize at Oxford exercises; published in the *International Review of the Aesthetics and Sociology of Music* 50 (2019): 19–46.

objected, "trapped within narratives of oppression and resistance, collaboration and victimhood."¹

It's been a hard habit to break. Narratives of oppression and resistance have done wonders for Shostakovich's popularity with audiences. Cycles of his fifteen string quartets—very taxing works on players and audiences alike—are (allowing for the relatively tiny and shrinking presence of classical music on today's cultural scene) reliable box-office attractions. The last of these quartets, a series of six Adagios, long, slow, and dismal, would be impossible to sell to audiences if it were signed with a name like Schoenberg or Krenek, but signed Shostakovich it is an allegory of intense human suffering to which audiences respond empathically. So I am not sure that we are ready to dispense with those old narratives just yet. Integration within the modernist narrative alongside Schoenberg and Krenek might bring Shostakovich additional prestige within the professional discourse of musicology, but there would be a price to pay.

The main discussion of Shostakovich in my *Oxford History of Western Music* comes, to Prof. Frolova-Walker's disappointment, in a chapter called "Music and Totalitarian Society." I am the first to agree that that is a one-sided view of Shostakovich. But what I needed as a historian at that point was precisely a discussion of music and totalitarian society, and Shostakovich was by orders of magnitude the most significant figure with which to populate that particular landscape—much more important, I would argue, than Ottorino Respighi or Alfredo Casella, my prime exhibits for fascist Italy, or Carl Orff, my preeminent representative of Nazi Germany (with a bothersome side glance at Webern). Since I do not believe that art historiography should be a collective biography of artists, I was content to live with that seemingly inequitable treatment of Shostakovich. I was more concerned with the changing landscape than with the lives of its individual inhabitants.

There are of course many other ways of viewing Shostakovich, and in other contexts than a general history of music I would be glad to try them out. Can we keep politics out of the picture? Can we look at Shostakovich in relation to his non-Russian, non-Soviet contemporaries? If that is our aim, we would do best to stay with his chamber music rather than his frequently programmatic symphonies or any music that carried a text. Chamber music did not have a long or distinguished history in Russia. What history it had was closely associated with aristocratic patronage. The most famous Russian name that comes to mind when thinking about classical string quartets is that of Count Andrey Kirillovich Razumovsky, the Russian ambassador to the Austrian Empire in Beethoven's day, who commissioned from Beethoven the three quartets, op. 59, that now bear his name in popular parlance. If you have done a bit of reading, you might know that there was another Russian aristocrat, Prince Nikolai Borisovich Golitsyn (or, as Beethoven spelled it,

---

1. Marina Frolova-Walker, "An Inclusive History for a Divided World?" *Journal of the Royal Musical Association* 143 (2018): 1–20, at 1.

Galitzin), who also commissioned three quartets from Beethoven, later ones. In two of the Razumovsky quartets, probably as specified in the commission, Beethoven quoted Russian folk songs from a big anthology that had been published in St. Petersburg in 1790.[2] That made it possible for me, when writing an essay to accompany a double cycle of Beethoven and Shostakovich quartets, to observe that all the Russian folk songs in the cycle will be contributed by Beethoven rather than Shostakovich, so that by one stereotyped standard Beethoven was the more Russian composer of the two.[3] I too like to subvert the old clichés when I can.

If you try to think of Russian composers of string quartets before the twentieth century, you will come up, I think, with no more than four names. If you have a degree in musicology you might know about Alexander Alexandrovich Alyabiev, a somewhat older contemporary of Pushkin and Glinka, who wrote three quartets that you will probably never hear.[4] Otherwise there was Chaikovsky, Russia's first fully professional, conservatory-trained composer, who also wrote three quartets, of which the first is a repertory piece, at least in Russia, and Borodin, who did not go to conservatory but was the very cultured son (illegitimate, but we don't mind) of a Georgian nobleman and amateur cellist (Borodin was also an amateur composer: chemistry was his profession). He wrote two quartets, the second of which is the only Russian quartet from which you can probably whistle a couple of tunes—that is, if you are old enough to have seen the Broadway show *Kismet*: the quartet's two middle movements formed the basis for two of its songs, "Baubles, Bangles and Beads" and "This Is My Beloved." That's three composers so far. Let the fourth remain nameless for now.

Anything aristocratic being suspect in Soviet eyes, especially early and unjaded Soviet eyes, it is not surprising that the younger Shostakovich, whose higher education in music took place in Soviet Russia, showed little interest in chamber music. That registers now as an ironic fact, given Shostakovich's reputation as perhaps the greatest composer of string quartets since Bartók. But Shostakovich did not write his first string quartet until he had already written five symphonies, both of his operas, all three of his ballets, eight incidental scores for plays both old and new, and a full baker's dozen of film scores. The relative frequency of genres in this list is a reliable guide to early Soviet aesthetics. The highest priority was the medium of highest technology and widest dissemination, namely film, followed by theatrical genres and orchestral music that were also capable of reaching large audiences.

---

2. For a superbly annotated facsimile edition, see Nikolai L'vov and Ivan Prach, *A Collection of Russian Folk Songs*, ed. Malcolm Hamrick Brown (Ann Arbor, MI: UMI Research Press, 1987).

3. R. Taruskin, "Hearing Cycles," in *On Russian Music* (Berkeley and Los Angeles: University of California Press, 2008), 340–56; originally published in the Aldeburgh Festival program book, June 2000.

4. Although you can if you wish: the first and third were excellently recorded long ago (1948) by the Beethoven Quartet (most recently reissued in 1999 on a Boheme Music CD). The slow movement of the third, which consists of variations on Alyabiev's famous song "Solovey" (The Nightingale), can be found (like almost everything else that ever was) on YouTube: www.youtube.com/watch?v=eLXEtR5S3_Q.

Two of the symphonies were commemorative works devoted to revolutionary themes: the Second (1927) a celebration of the tenth anniversary of the revolution and the Third (1930) a celebration of May Day, the international labor holiday. What would be the place of chamber music in a revolutionary society that considered itself the most modern place on earth?

So it becomes a pressing question: not only why Shostakovich should eventually have decided to compose a string quartet, but why he did so precisely in 1938. It surely has something to do with the great *perelom* his career suffered in 1936. I'm using a Russian word, *perelom,* to describe it because that word covers a range of meanings that no single English word can match. Literally, a *perelom* is a break or fracture, as of a bone. Figuratively, it means a turning point or critical period, or any sudden, difficult change. And in January 1936, at the age of twenty-nine, Shostakovich suddenly changed from being the coddled darling of Soviet culture, the brash young musical protagonist of a brash young society, into the chastened figure whose Fifth Symphony, premiered the next year, was received as "a Soviet artist's creative reply to just criticism." The catalyst of that change was an unsigned editorial in *Pravda,* the official organ of the Soviet Communist Party, called "Muddle Instead of Music," denouncing his most famous work, an opera that had been played all over the world, as a "left deviation," a term otherwise then reserved, at the outset of the great purges, for Trotskyites, and warning the composer that he was trifling with important matters and that "it could end very badly."[5] He was being put on notice that he would have to change not only his style, but his whole aesthetic outlook. And he did.

That is why it is a fruitless task to speak of Shostakovich's music without taking his political and social environment into account. That environment did not allow itself to be ignored or resisted. It actively intruded on the composer's creative development, and that development cannot be understood solely on its own terms. But neither can anything else be so understood, nor *anyone's* creative development, no matter where or when. Nothing exists solely on its own terms. Change is always overdetermined; it comes about through a dynamic or dialectical interaction between agents and the environments within which they act according to their affordances. Not everyone, however, is forced to undergo a *perelom.*

What adds insult to injury from the perspective of conventional music historiography is that Shostakovich's *perelom* appeared to be a backslide against the narrative of perpetual technical and stylistic innovation that confers prestige on its protagonists. Until 1936 Shostakovich could be ranked among the modernists. Since its first publication in the year 2000, in a book of Shostakovich letters and documents now held by the Glinka Museum of Musical Culture, one of the most widely touted source texts relating to Shostakovich's biography has been a long

---

5. [David Zaslavsky], "Sumbur vmesto muzïki," *Pravda,* 28 January 1936, 4.

questionnaire that the twenty-year-old Shostakovich filled out at the request of a musicologist named Roman Ilyich Gruber in 1927, the first year of his world fame following Bruno Walter's Berlin performance of the First Symphony. One of its most frequently quoted passages is the answer to a question concerning "your attitude toward the education you received." Shostakovich replied in two very long paragraphs, of which this is the first:

> During the time I was going through the course in Theory of Composition at the conservatory, I looked on it as an "unavoidable evil," to which I submitted passively, to some extent. On finishing the course, I felt it impossible to compose freely, spontaneously; I was obliged somehow to "squeeze out" a series of works (in the summer of 1925, a symphony and two movements of a string octet . . .); starting in the fall of 1925 through December 1926, I kept trying to compose, but unsuccessfully (during that early period after finishing the conservatory, I had turned into too narrow a "professional," putting matters of technical fluency above everything else, unwittingly trying to make everything I wrote turn out "correctly" and fluently): my creative consciousness could not escape the bounds inculcated by academic canons. From the fall of 1926, I turned to the study of contemporary Western composers (Schoenberg, Béla Bartók, Hindemith, Krenek), which apparently provided the immediate stimulus for "liberating" my musical faculties: my first compositions from this new period were composed in white heat (from the end of 1926 through 1927): the [first] Piano Sonata, "Aphorisms" for piano, the "Symphonic Poem for the Tenth Anniversary of the October Revolution" [now known as the Second Symphony], and the first act of the opera based on Gogol's story *The Nose* (August 1927).[6]

In the second paragraph, Shostakovich derides his teacher, Maximilian Steinberg (Rimsky-Korsakov's son-in-law), whose advice he boasts of never following; he mocks the teaching of musical form: for example, that "'Sonata form consists of (a) an exposition, (b) a development, and (c) a recapitulation; the exposition consists of (a) a principal theme, (b) a subordinate theme, and (c) a closing theme,' etc. etc."; but meanwhile "not a word was uttered about the expressive character of the musical line, about *statika, dinamika,* and *dialektika.*"[7]

This pushes every modernist button, and in particular abjures anything traditional or insularly Russian. Shostakovich portrays himself here exactly the way Marina Frolova-Walker would like to see him portrayed in the new "inclusive" history she advocates—as a counterpart to Schoenberg, Bartók, Hindemith, and

---

6. "Responses of Shostakovich to a Questionnaire on the Psychology of the Creative Process," trans. Malcolm Hamrick Brown, in *Shostakovich and His World,* ed. Laurel E. Fay (Princeton, NJ: Princeton University Press, 2004), 29–30. First published as "Anketa po psikhologii tvorcheskogo protsessa" in *Dmitriy Shostakovich v pis'makh i dokumentakh,* ed. I. Bobïkina (Moscow: Gosudarstvennïy tsentral'nïy muzey muzïkal'noy kul'turï imeni M. I. Glinki, 2000), 470–81.

7. "Responses of Shostakovich," 30. Brown translates *statika, dinamika i dialektika* as "relaxation, tension and dialectical form."

Krenek, rather than Prokofieff, Myaskovsky, Khachaturyan, or Kabalevsky. She wants to "take the next step by, for example, discussing how *Lady Macbeth* was given wide international exposure, leaving its mark on the development of twentieth-century opera (on Britten, for example)."[8] I would like to see this too, but not at the sacrifice of the other. The ghetto, while grossly exaggerated and at times enforced by historiography, was not created by historiography. It was part of the reality of Russian music both in the nineteenth century and in the twentieth, and it must be reported and assessed. As for the *perelom,* without taking it into account, there is no way of explaining how or why the Piano Quintet—the main subject of this essay, still regarded, alongside Shostakovich's modernist peaks like the Second Symphony and *The Nose,* as among his best and most characteristic works—ever got written. The effect of the *perelom* on his style and outlook must stop looking like a backslide, but rather as the next stage in an evolution in which all of Soviet music took part, one which gave the evolution of Soviet music its particular character and significance within the larger narrative of music in the twentieth century. And in order for it to stop looking like a backslide, it must stop being so portrayed and deplored.

One perfectly accurate way of describing the effect of the *perelom* would be to say that it forced Shostakovich at last to take seriously and attempt sincerely to embody in his work the precepts and methods that were in 1932 first codified and in 1934 first promulgated as a requirement under the rubric Socialist Realism. That Shostakovich's embodiment of Socialist Realist principles was sincere, rather than the cynical sop to authority that it is often portrayed as being, is proved, I believe, by the fact that when in 1961 *Lady Macbeth* was allowed back on stage after a quarter-century ban, it came back in a revised form that Shostakovich described approvingly in a private letter to his close friend Isaak Glikman, which conformed in many ways to the implicit prescription of the famous 1936 denunciation. What is more, Shostakovich took steps to discourage or even prevent stagings of the original version abroad.[9] That is why I would say that citing Socialist Realism is a legitimate key to Shostakovich's *perelom* and (to recall a word we used to import into English) his *perestroika;* and yet, without a basic definition of the operative term the statement is paradoxical and incomprehensible. For Socialist Realism

---

8. Frolova-Walker, "An Inclusive History," 4.

9. Letter of 21 March 1955, in Isaak Davïdovich Glikman, *Pis'ma k drugu: Dmitriy Shostakovich-Isaaku Glikmanu* (Moscow: DSCH; St. Petersburg: Kompozitor, 1993), 109–10; or in *Story of a Friendship: The Letters of Dmitry Shostakovich to Isaak Glikman 1941–1975,* trans. Anthony Phillips (London: Faber & Faber, 2001), 55–57. The production Shostakovich tried to deter with news that an improved version was on the way was mounted in Düsseldorf in 1959–60; it was actually advertised, as a direct result of Shostakovich's attempted interference, as "the last time the work would be shown in its original version" (Laurel Fay, *Shostakovich: A Life* [New York: Oxford University Press, 2000], 237).

seems to make demands with which no string quartet or piano quintet could ever comply.

As originally defined for literature and literary criticism by Andrey Zhdanov, Stalin's culture czar, in 1932, in the statutes of the newly formed Union of Soviet Writers (and later in his keynote address at the Union's first congress), Socialist Realism "demands of the artist the truthful, historically concrete representation of reality in its revolutionary development." Moreover, the definition continues, "the truthfulness and historical concreteness of the artistic representation of reality must be linked with the task of ideological transformation and education of workers in the spirit of socialism."[10] Out of this last proviso a set of guidelines emerged in the form of three desiderata: *partiynost'*, which meant, roughly, "party-mindedness," or conformity to what the Communist Party defined at a given moment as the truth; *ideynost'*, which refers to the demand that art must contribute to the "ideological transformation" of its beholders; and *narodnost'*, which is a very capacious term derived from *narod*, the Russian word that means "people" or "nation." At the most basic level, *narodnost'* means that the art embodying it must have some "connection to the life of the people," to cite a frequent critical cliché, and thus be accessible to nonprofessional audiences. Later, the term took on another connotation, as traditional Russian nationalism began to seep back into Soviet ideology, replacing the Marxist internationalism of the revolutionary period. *Narodnost'* could now be construed as a demand that art conform to established national traditions, whether folkloric or artistic.

One can easily see how a novel may be judged according to these prescriptions, or a play, or an opera like *Lady Macbeth*. Indeed, "Muddle Instead of Music" is one of the primary documents of Socialist Realism in practical criticism and as political intervention. But how does one apply such a standard to nontheatrical instrumental music? Obviously, by modifying it appropriately; and Shostakovich's Fifth Symphony, or rather the critical discourse that grew up around it, showed the way. As applied to musical compositions, Socialist Realism amounted to what I once identified, in an essay specifically about Shostakovich's Fifth Symphony, as "heroic classicism."[11] "Heroic" is a term relating to scale, or to what in Russian is called *bol'shoy stil'*, "big style" or "grand manner." The *bol'shoy sovetskiy stil'* or "Great Soviet style" was a concept originating in architecture and sculpture. The standard example is the unrealized plan of the architect Boris Mikhailovich Iofan for the projected Palace of Soviets, the Moscow house of parliament (the statue at its top

10. Maxim Gorky, Karl Radek, Nikolai Bukharin, Andrey Zhdanov et al., *Soviet Writers' Congress 1934* (London: Lawrence & Wishart, 1977), 15–16.

11. R. Taruskin, "Public Lies and Unspeakable Truth: Interpreting Shostakovich's Fifth Symphony," in *Shostakovich Studies*, ed. David Fanning (Cambridge: Cambridge University Press, 1995), 17–56; rpt. in Taruskin, *Defining Russia Musically* (Princeton, NJ: Princeton University Press, 1997), 511–44, and in Mark Carroll, ed., *Music and Ideology* (London: Routledge, 2017), 263–302.

was reassigned to the Soviet Pavilion at the New York World's Fair of 1939). And in sculpture, the paradigmatic work was one that was indeed realized, and famous: the statue *Worker and Collective Farm Girl* (*Rabochiy i kolkhoznitsa*) by Vera Mukhina that first adorned the Soviet pavilion at the World Exposition in Paris in 1937 and then became the logo for Mosfilm studios.

Shostakovich's symphonies were also examples of *bol'shoy sovetskiy stil'*, especially the Fourth (1936), which languished unperformed until 1961 because it transgressed against the other part of the definition, which required classicism, or conformity with time-honored canons of style, form, and taste. The Fifth Symphony was almost as big as the Fourth, but it was safely classical. This difference can be seen most clearly in their respective first movements. The first movement of the Fourth has a shape that is completely *sui generis*. There is none other quite like it. It can only be described specifically, not generically. The first movement of the Fifth follows exactly the textbook model of sonata form that Shostakovich derided in his answer to Roman Gruber's questionnaire in 1927. That is one obvious reason why Shostakovich was so often accused by Western modernists of backsliding; but I continue to reject that charge on Shostakovich's behalf. Anyone who knows his style and knows the conditions that shaped its evolution could easily tell on first audition that the Fifth is a later work than the Fourth, just as one can tell that Prokofieff's Soviet works are later than those wilder ones written during his emigration.

And there is one other way in which Shostakovich's Fifth Symphony exemplified Socialist Realism whereas the Fourth Symphony had transgressed its canons. The Fourth starts with a bang and ends with a whimper, while the Fifth begins in severity and ends in an affirmation so over the top that it has often been read against the grain as a parody rather than as a sincere effort—as if Shostakovich would have risked that in 1937, the bloodiest year of Soviet political terror. The most tangible aspect of *ideynost'* as applied to music was optimism—or *zhizneutverzhdeniye*, "life affirmation," to cite what is perhaps the most hackneyed word in all of Soviet arts criticism. That, after all, was what "revolutionary development" was all about, in that basic definition of Socialist Realist art as the "truthful, historically concrete representation of reality in its revolutionary development." That Shostakovich explicitly intended his Fifth Symphony as a sort of "correction" of the Fourth was widely assumed on the basis of the article titled "My Creative Response," which appeared over Shostakovich's byline in a Moscow newspaper before the Moscow premiere in 1938, in which the symphony was dubbed "a Soviet artist's creative response to just criticism."[12]

It was in the aftermath of the Fifth Symphony's tumultuous reception and his restoration to the good graces of Soviet authority that Shostakovich wrote his First

---

12. "Деловой творческий ответ советского художника на справедливую критику" (D. Shostakovich, "Moy tvorcheskiy otvet," *Vechernyaya Moskva*, 25 January 1938, 3).

Quartet. It is so far over on the other end of the spectrum from *bol'shoy sovetskiy stil'* that no one could think of it as anything but an implicit commentary on the insignificance of its genre. It's a pretty little culinary confection, as Brecht might have said, a divertimento in four movements that's all over in fifteen minutes. (After fifteen minutes, the first movement of the Fourth Symphony is barely more than half over.) The quartet's first two movements are in a ruminative, pastoral vein; the last two are lively and humorous. The third movement is the standout: a wispy scherzo with a middle section that recalls Chaikovsky's Italianate style. Nothing heroic about it, but it certainly is classical, in a manner that still calls Hindemith to mind—but the Hindemith of the thirties, who had also undergone a stylistic metamorphosis since the wild early twenties and was now writing in a distinctly academic manner as befitted his appointment in 1927 to a chair in composition in Berlin. (Shostakovich had been given a similar appointment in Leningrad in 1937, becoming a professor at the same age as Hindemith before him; stylistic changes are overdetermined everywhere.) There was nothing in this piece to suggest that Shostakovich would become a major composer of string quartets, something no Russian composer had ever been. And to prove it, let me read you a paragraph from the official biography of Shostakovich by David Abramovich Rabinovich that came out in 1959, by which time Shostakovich had written eleven of his fifteen symphonies but only six of his fifteen quartets:

> In the period between the Fifth and Sixth symphonies he wrote his First String Quartet (op. 49, 1938), one of the few compositions that stand alone, by themselves, and far away from the big problems that were disturbing the composer's mind at the time. The Quartet is not in any way connected with Shostakovich's symphonic music of the late thirties, neither in concept nor in the coincidence of musical phrases. Nevertheless the Quartet also reflected the radical change that occurred in Shostakovich's attitude to music and life, and expressed it no less clearly although in a different way. The bright, clear, "spring" music of the piece bore witness to something new that had come to maturity in the composer's heart, something that was the opposite to the procession of images that had been there before.[13]

The ensuing discussion emphasizes lyricism, tranquility, transparency, grace, and (for the first time) "the spirit of classical Russian chamber music." Of the suddenly boisterous final movement, Rabinovich writes that it is "deliberately noisy like a child who has been sitting quietly, listening attentively, let us say, to a tale and has then suddenly jumped up from his place and run away, and is immediately up to his amusing and inoffensive pranks."[14] That is what classical chamber music was to Russians as of 1938: something amusing and inoffensive—in a word, cute.

13. D. A. Rabinovich, *Dmitry Shostakovich: Composer*, trans. George Hanna (Moscow: Foreign Languages Publishing House, 1959), 58.
14. Ibid.

II

Shostakovich's cute little one-off was given its first performance in Leningrad by what was then the leading professional string quartet in Soviet Russia: the Glazunov Quartet, which had been founded in 1919 at the then Petrograd Conservatory and was named after the composer who was then the institution's director (and who was also among the most prolific Russian composers of string quartets, with five completed out of an eventual seven). Their counterpart and rival at the Moscow Conservatory was a very long lived organization called the Beethoven Quartet, which was founded in 1923 by four newly graduated players, two of whom were still playing in the quartet when I heard them during my year as an exchange student at the Moscow Conservatory in 1971–72, half a century later. To get even with the Glazunovs, the Beethovens pestered Shostakovich to write a second quartet and give it to them. But according to a memoir by Isaak Glikman, Shostakovich had a better idea. He'd write a part for himself into the new work. "And you know why?" he asked Glikman.

> "So that I would have to perform it with them and get to travel around with them to various cities and other places. Now the Glazunovs and Beethovens, who go everywhere, will have to take me along! So I will also see the world." We laughed. "Aren't you joking?" I asked. "Not at all," Dmitry Dmitrievich answered. "You are an incurable homebody but me, I am an incurable wanderer!"[15]

And that is how the quartet became the Piano Quintet, op. 57. Memoirs are rarely to be trusted, especially when they are trying to be funny; but our image of Shostakovich has become so solemn and tragic that it is always worth remembering that he was, according to all accounts, an inveterate joker. Dmitry Tsyganov, the leader of the Beethoven Quartet, recalled Shostakovich telling him not only that he was going to write himself into the piece he'd promised them, but also that he'd make sure that his part would be easier than theirs.[16] (That much, as any pianist will agree, is untrue.) All these jokes, moreover, confirm the general rule that the more weighty the work, the more flippant the author's commentary is likely to be.

In fact, the eventual Piano Quintet, when it was first performed on the evening of 23 November 1940, took everyone by surprise. David Rabinovich, from whose official biography I quoted to show how trifling an impression the First Quartet had made, was sitting in the audience at the Quintet's premiere, so that his book at this point becomes an eyewitness report. The premiere took place during a so-called *dekada*, one of the most typical cultural events of the Stalinist years, when

---

15. Glikman, *Pis'ma k drugu*, 21.
16. D. Tsyganov, "Vstrechi s Shostakovichem za dvadtsat' let" (1944), in *Shostakovichu posvyashchayetsya: sbornik statey k 90-letiyu kompozitora*, ed. E. Dolinskaya (Moscow: Kompozitor, 1997), 162; quoted in Fay, *Shostakovich*, 116.

the cultural life of the Soviet Union was being reorganized and centralized. The term *dekada* in Russian does not signify a period of ten years, but rather ten days: it's a rough equivalent of the English "fortnight." In the culture jargon of Stalinist Russia, a *dekada* was a cultural showcase, a series of performances when many new works would be introduced at one fell swoop, or when performing ensembles from the so-called Union Republics, the non-Russian outlying areas of the reconstituted Russian empire, would come to the capital to show their cultural wares. Ultimately, the word *dekada* became synonymous with tedium. And now we are ready for Rabinovich's report:

> One cannot forget the atmosphere that reigned in the Smaller Hall of the Moscow Conservatoire during the *première* of the Quintet. It came at the end of a concert after three new quartets by three leading Soviet composers had been played. The audience was growing tired. But when the Beethoven Quartet, so well known to Moscow music-lovers, appeared on the stage with Shostakovich himself, and when the first strains of the Quintet resounded, all workaday, dearly-beloved and accustomed sensations disappeared without leaving a trace. Obviously something important was happening in the hall, something that was outside the scope of "current" musical events.[17]

One can hear from the very start of the opening piano solo that Shostakovich was writing a piece that would belie the reputation of chamber music in Russia. Nevertheless, there was a Russian model for it, one that every conservatory graduate in Russia certainly would have known, and that precedent, I am quite sure, accounts far more cogently than Shostakovich's funny stories for his choice of string quartet plus piano as his medium and for the way he treated it. Any Russian musician listening to me now knows that I am about to name the composer whose name I made a show of withholding when sketching the early history of the string quartet in Russia: Sergey Ivanovich Taneyev (1856–1915), who completed nine quartets between 1880 and 1905, and left unfinished works in the genre at either end of his career. He may not be among the best-known Russian composers abroad, but Taneyev was (and remains) a revered figure at home, especially at the Moscow Conservatory, where he had been pupil, professor, and director, and where his name, carved larger than all the rest, heads the honor plaque listing all the gold medalists that is still proudly displayed over the main staircase. His best-remembered chamber work—and, many have said, the *chef d'oeuvre* of his career—was the Piano Quintet in G-minor, op. 30, composed in 1911, four years before the composer's death at the age of fifty-nine.

It is the big blockbuster of Russian chamber music, very much in the line of such previous blockbuster quintets as Schumann's in E-flat, Brahms's in F minor,

---

17. Rabinovich, *Dmitry Shostakovich: Composer*, 59.

and César Franck's, also in F minor. These works, and Taneyev's, too, are fashioned on an almost orchestral scale, like piano concertos in miniature, the string writing full of doublings, multiple stops, bariolage, tremolo, anything to make a lot of noise. Shostakovich's writing, as suited the time, was a bit sparer. Nevertheless, by writing a quintet, especially by writing a quintet in the same key as Taneyev's, Shostakovich was obviously invoking it, thus committing himself to the grand style, and to the new demand for heroic classicism, as enunciated by Zhdanov in 1934 and enforced by *Pravda* in 1936.

There is more. Taneyev's Quintet sounds no more Russian than Schumann's, Brahms's, or Franck's. It is resolutely "mainstream," which of course meant, basically, German in style. Anyone who knows Taneyev at all by reputation, knows that he was nicknamed the Russian Brahms.[18] He resisted the epithet, but it was not unfounded. Like Brahms (and like Schumann and Franck, come to that), Taneyev was unusually drawn to the old contrapuntal genres. He was celebrated at the conservatory for his counterpoint classes, for which he wrote a famous textbook;[19] and he was also known for making innumerable contrapuntal sketches for his works, which were distinguished for their dense and intricate, some said overladen, textures. He even wrote compositions in the forms associated with Bach and Handel. He was, for example, the only composer of his generation to write preludes and fugues not for the classroom but actually for publication (except for Glazunov, another "Russian Brahms" and the director of the other conservatory, in St. Petersburg). By emulating Taneyev, the very model of an academic composer, Shostakovich was characterizing himself the same way, which as we know signaled a big change of direction.

What clinches the connection between Shostakovich's Quintet and Taneyev's is the self-conscious reference in both to Baroque genres. In Taneyev's case it was the slow third movement, which is untitled but very obviously a passacaglia, with a ground bass consisting of a stately one-measure descent through an octave, relentlessly reiterated throughout the movement. Shostakovich's answer to that was to

---

18. Nikolai Medtner (Taneyev's pupil), Alexander Glazunov, and Paul Juon were also called Russian Brahmses in their day. As his contemporary Alexander Kastalsky wrote in Taneyev's obituary, "no matter how much the deceased waved it away, they went on sticking the label on him" (как ни отмахивался покойный—прилепили-таки ему ярлык; "Po povodu obnovleniya" [1915], in *Aleksandr Kastal'skiy: Stat'i, materialï, vospominaniya, perepiska*, ed. S. G. Zverev, Russkaya dukhovnaya muzïka v dokumentakh i materialakh, vol. 5 [Moscow: Znak, 2006], 110). Others have begrudged it as well, on behalf of other claimants and other climes: "Taneyev is known as the Russian Brahms, and on Wednesday his String Quintet No. 1 in G showed why, with its chunky counterpoint and vigorous development of motifs. There is, however, more Brahms-like music in the late 19th century—some of Stanford's, for example" (Adrian Jack, "The Stars Come Out for 'The Russian Brahms,'" *The Independent*, 18 January 2002).

19. S. I. Taneyev, *Podvizhnoy kontrapunkt strogogo pis'ma* (Leipzig: M. P. Belaïeff, 1909); trans. G. Ackley Brower as *Convertible Counterpoint in the Strict Style* (Boston: Bruce Humphries, 1962).

cast the first two movements of his Quintet in the form of a prelude and fugue: the "Präludium" starting grandiloquently in the typical Baroque manner (*baroque* at first actually meaning grandiloquent), and the fugue a remarkably sustained construction of 171 measures, satisfying the implied dual requirement that Socialist Realist art achieve heroic scale in addition to classical design.

Thus, insofar as one could manage the feat with only five musicians on the stage, and even though its Baroque grandiloquence adopts stylistic features that had their sources in monarchial pomp and religious ceremony, Shostakovich's Quintet was an exemplary Socialist Realist composition according to the de facto standards by which such things were judged at the time. Despite what some have said about it, and we will get to them, it is a piece that in 1940 could only have been written in the Soviet Union, and having been so recognized, it was rewarded accordingly. That is where my somewhat ironic title comes in, because the Stalin Prizes, the Soviet Nobels, were instituted in 1939 and first awarded in 1941 for achievements in the arts and sciences precisely up to the year 1940, which is to say just in time for Shostakovich's Piano Quintet. It was chosen to receive one of the first batch of first-class awards, right alongside Vera Mukhina's *Worker and Collective Farm Girl*, so we have it on the most reliable authority that this nonprogrammatic and not especially Russian-sounding work was officially accepted as an example of *bol'shoy sovetskiy stil'*, "the grand Soviet manner" at its greatest and grandest and most quintessentially Soviet. The rest of this essay will be an attempt to show how and why it was so regarded.

III

But first, one last funny story.

This essay is based on a talk that I agreed to give as part of the Oxford Kyoto Prize exercises in 2018. Before assenting, I had to overcome considerable reluctance. I don't like lecturing about Shostakovich. Like many of us in the Anglophone world of Russian music studies, I am battle-scarred by the so-called Shostakovich wars that raged in the 1980s and 90s in the wake of several sensationalistic publications, beginning in 1979 with *Testimony*, a bestseller whose lengthy subtitle identified it as "the memoirs of Dmitri Shostakovich as related to and edited by Solomon Volkov."[20] Very opportunely timed to the last phases of the Cold War (the Reagan presidency, the Afghanistan invasion), it portrayed Shostakovich as an embittered dissident. Widely publicized and eagerly believed, it led to a wholesale revision of popular opinion about the composer; but it also led, more troublingly, to a massive reinterpretation of his works as so many messages in a bottle. All of this ideological movement vastly increased public interest in Shostakovich and led

20. Solomon Volkov, *Testimony* (New York: Harper & Row, 1979).

to a huge upswing in performances of his works, which was a fine thing to observe; but it also led to a massive flattening out of interpretation, each and every one of those works being seen as retellings of one encompassing and increasingly tedious tale.

Musicologists felt the brunt of this tedium. Just as when the movie version of Peter Schaffer's Mozart play *Amadeus* was at the height of its popularity one couldn't get through a dinner party without being asked, "Was he really like that hyena?" now one always had to answer the was-he-or-wasn't-he question about Shostakovich. What was a mild annoyance at parties became an exasperating distraction in public symposia and conferences when, no matter what the ostensible topic of one's presentation, one was inevitably waylaid and sidetracked during the Q&A. The Shostakovich stakes were high. Nobody had much invested in Mozart's hyenahood, but to question Shostakovich's dissident credentials led inexorably to bruising political confrontations, especially if one was at pains to explain why scholars were bound to oppose simple black-and-white, yes-or-no frames.

All of this was over and above the more immediate questions as to the authenticity of Volkov's book, and its veracity. And the first difficulty was in getting people to see that these were two separate questions, requiring different strategies of investigation and different criteria for acceptance. I already feel that this talk is in danger of getting bogged down in just the way I spent the whole centennial year 2006 trying to avoid, so I will just skip to the present and say that Volkov's book has by now been well exposed as a mixture of recycled material that Shostakovich approved for republication and fabrications inserted after his death. It is no longer quotable in serious scholarly work. But the seductive stories it contains have continued to circulate, along with the revised opinions that it fostered. The Piano Quintet actually provides a good arena for testing them anew. So that is why I accepted the invitation to launch once more unto the breach.

There is not much in *Testimony* about the Quintet; but Volkov and his supporters have continued to publish books reasserting their allegations, and in one of these Volkov came back to it. The new book's title, *Shostakovich and Stalin: The Extraordinary Relationship between the Great Composer and the Brutal Dictator*, reiterates one of *Testimony*'s chief allegations: that the great one and the brutal one were mutually obsessed. The story of the Quintet and its Stalin Prize seemed grist for that mill, especially if one supposed that Stalin personally selected the winners of the prizes that bore his name.

That seems a natural enough assumption, given our casual notions about "totalitarianism" generally and the ruthlessness with which Stalin was known at times to have wielded his unlimited power. The actual workings of the award, as now very meticulously traced by Marina Frolova-Walker in a fascinating book called *Stalin's Music Prize*, were a far more complicated process than mere dictatorial fiat—as indeed it had to be; for total dictatorial fiat would have implied a practically endless expenditure of dictatorial time in reading nominations and personally judging the merits of candidates not only in the arts but in all of the sciences as well.

At the very least, a dictator needs a little help from his friends; thus bureaucracies are born and, with them, paper trails. The administration of the Stalin Prize left a huge one, and it contained one particular document that gratified Solomon Volkov's prejudices both as to Stalin's personal manipulation of the prizes and as to his fixation on Shostakovich. A letter of denunciation of a fairly commonplace sort, it was addressed to Stalin personally in January 1941 by a disgruntled musical administrator and long-time Party member named Moisei Abramovich Grinberg, who had recently been demoted from a high position overseeing musical organizations, and who therefore needed to curry favor.[21] Invoking the tritest of Socialist Realist slogans, he warned Stalin that Shostakovich's Piano Quintet "lacks any connection with the life of the People."[22] Even to consider awarding such a prize to such a work, rather than to an opera on a heroic historical theme, such as Ivan Dzerzhinsky's *Quiet Flows the Don*, based on Sholokhov's novel of the postrevolutionary civil war, or a work full of vivacious folk-like tunes such as Khachaturyan's already very popular Violin Concerto, which had been given its first performance about two months before Shostakovich's Quintet, showed that "certain unhealthy tendencies are emerging in our music." "The prize awarded in your name," Grinberg told Stalin, must not go to such a "contrived" composition, in which "there are so many abstract formal pursuits and so little genuine beauty or strength." While it "may stand out for its formal perfection, . . . this form is nourished by rationalism and the air of the hothouse, rather than by any living human energy." Just listen to it, Grinberg implored, together with the other, more deserving works he had proposed. "You will see perfectly well for yourself," he assured Stalin, "for you are familiar with works in all the other arts media—literature, painting, architecture and drama."

Volkov drew a strange conclusion from this document: that Stalin listened, as requested, and then decided, with the magisterial arbitrariness that was his alone to exercise, to award the prize to Shostakovich's Quintet anyway. Affirming the logic of Grinberg's position within the doctrinaire Soviet arts establishment, and admiring the slanderer's political adroitness in promoting Dzerzhinsky's opera, which Stalin himself had praised in a press interview just before Shostakovich's *Lady Macbeth of the Mtsensk District* was denounced, Volkov bade his readers

> Imagine the shock for Grinberg and his numerous allies when they opened *Pravda* on 16 March 1941 and saw the list of names and photographs of the laureates.

21. Information on Grinberg from Frolova-Walker, *Stalin's Music Prize* (New Haven, CT: Yale University Press, 2016), 52–53.
22. M. Grinberg, letter to Stalin of 7 January 1941, quoted in Frolova-Walker, *Stalin's Music Prize*, 54. All quotations from the letter are taken from the same book, pp. 53–56.

Shostakovich's Piano Quintet received the First Class prize, and his portrait was placed ahead of the other winners, clearly out of alphabetical order. Dzerzhinsky got nothing.

This decision could only have been made by Stalin.[23]

Defending his take to a skeptical Russian interviewer, Volkov said: "We know from documents that they tried to talk Stalin out of this decision. Why can't we imagine that Stalin listened to Shostakovich's music and liked it?"[24] Marina Frolova-Walker gives two reasons why we can't. First, and as you may have noticed, Grinberg's denunciation already implies that Stalin took less interest in, and interfered less with, the music prizes than those in "the other arts media—literature, painting, architecture and drama." Frolova-Walker has confirmed this inference by examining Stalin's own ballots in the prize adjudications. The ones concerning literature, film, and the visual arts are covered with his marginalia while the music ballots are for the most part pristine. And second, she deduces from its current location in the archive that Grinberg's letter was not handed up the bureaucratic ladder to Stalin but went the other way, to the so-called Committee on Artistic Affairs. (And that, by the way, is how Volkov came to know of it: it was published in an early roundup of documents from formerly closed archives, shortly after the Soviet collapse;[25] Volkov read it in isolation and fell into a common trap for the unwary or the opportunistic.)

IV

But there is a more basic reason to discount Volkov's little fable of Stalin's intervention just to show who's boss. Its very point of departure was fallacious. Whatever our casual assumptions might be, despite Volkov's prejudices and the apparent evidence of Grinberg's letter, there was in fact no obstacle so great that only Stalin could surmount it to the awarding of a Stalin Prize to a sophisticated chamber composition, even one that ends as quietly and nontriumphantly as Shostakovich's Quintet. We have already seen that the Quintet was rapturously received at the 1940 *dekada* that preceded the prize deliberations. The question of its fidelity to the tenets of Socialist Realism was explicitly raised and resolved both in the critical

---

23. Solomon Volkov, *Shostakovich and Stalin: The Extraordinary Relationship between the Great Composer and the Brutal Dictator* (New York: Alfred A. Knopf, 2004), 166.

24. "Мы знаем из документов, что Сталина пытались отговорить от этого решения. Почему мы не можем предположить, что Сталин прослушал музыку Шостаковича и она ему понравилась?" (Irina Chaikovskaya, "Solomon Volkov: 'Umer on velikim sovetskim kompozitorom,' Dmitriy Dmitriyevich Shostakovich—za i protiv: Beseda pisatelya i kul'turologa. Chast' vtoraya. Soprotivleniye muzïkoy," *Chastnïy korrespondent*, 1 October 2011 [available at www.chayka.org/node/4597]; also quoted in Frolova-Walker, *Stalin's Music Prize*, 37).

25. *Istochnik* 5 (1995): 156–58.

press and in a crucial document that has been mostly overlooked in the Shostakovich literature: a report in *Sovetskaya muzïka*, the official organ of the Union of Soviet Composers, of a discussion following the *dekada*, in which prominent composers and musicologists evaluated the event and the works that had been heard there. Shostakovich's Quintet, unsurprisingly, received the lion's share of attention, with detailed reactions by professionals in both categories: first a prominent musicologist and then a celebrity composer.

The musicologist was Daniel Vladimirovich Zhitomirsky, a long-lived Ukrainian-born scholar who was Shostakovich's exact contemporary, and who remained active as a commentator on the composer until his death in 1992, which is to say, past the end of the Soviet regime.[26] He had published one of the many positive reviews of the Quintet right after the premiere, and his contribution to the slightly later published discussion is cast as if it were a direct refutation of Grinberg's letter. "Sometimes," he allowed,

> it is asked whether this lyrical composition is typical of our music, whether it is connected with its basic tasks. Such doubts call forth a protest from me. Could it be that the embodiment of high ethical qualities, the creation of an image of a full-grown human being, with strong, finely honed, noble yet uncomplicated feelings—could it be that all this is not one of the chief tasks of socialist art?[27]

The trouble, Zhitomirsky asserted, was that "a fully realistic, universally human content is expressed in a form that is by no means the usual, simple, plain and easy way. And this has already aroused in certain musicians a spirit of opposition toward Shostakovich." The first mistake such musicians make, according to Zhitomirsky, is to "imagine the establishment of some sort of universal Soviet style or even some sort of universal Soviet artwork—fetchingly 'folksy,' fetchingly 'optimistic,' in which everything is reflected as it should be, without a hitch, without a snag [*net ni suchka, ni zadorinki*]—but also without a trace of life." Turning the tables on Shostakovich's critics (alluding to some prominent reviews that all who heard his remarks would have recognized), Zhitomirsky went on:

> That this mistaken idea exists is proven by certain critical interventions. They even tried to convince Shostakovich that in his Fifth Symphony the relationship between the first three movements and the finale should be different. The composer realized

---

26. His last article, "Shostakovich: ofitsial'nïy i podlinnïy" (Shostakovich: The Official One and the Authentic One), first published in the Latvian journal *Daugava* on the eve of Latvian independence (1990, nos. 3–4, 88–100; no. 4, 97–108), was reprinted, titled, simply, "Shostakovich," in *Muzïkal'naya akademiya* (1993, no. 3, 15–30), the successor journal to *Sovetskaya muzïka*; English translation in Allan B. Ho and Dmitry Feofanov, ed., *Shostakovich Reconsidered* (London: Toccata Press, 1998), 419–71.

27. D. V. Zhitomirsky, "Obsuzhdeniye IV dekadï sovetskoy muzïki: vïstupleniye D. Zhitomirskogo," *Sovetskaya muzïka*, 1941, no. 2, 70–71; all citations from Zhitomirsky's contribution are from these pages. (My thanks to Laurel Fay for supplying a photocopy of the document.)

his very profound and truthful conception—and they try to pin him down to an abstract scheme! Don't we see the same thing in literature, in certain articles devoted to *Quiet Flows the Don,* that pinnacle of Soviet literature? All these are just attempts to make the rich, many-sided human content of Soviet art conform to some pitiful standard.

In the case of Shostakovich's Quintet, the problem was that it expressed "great and authentic feelings," but transmitted them "through a prism of thought." This filtering process produced a sense of "tediousness" (*skuchnovatost'*) in those who sought from art only an immediate rush of raw emotion. Zhitomirsky commends this "tediousness" for the way it shows Shostakovich's Quintet to have been "purified of concrete, empirical images," leaving only "an exalted synthesis of abstract thought." Such a creation, he admits,

> will naturally make the process of apprehension a bit more difficult, relatively speaking. This type of art may of course provide the highest aesthetic enjoyment, albeit not always with blazing immediacy, nor will it be attainable at all levels of musical discernment. This last [point] is very important. Sometimes we tend to equate the idea of what is democratic (or belonging to the people [*narodnoye*]) in art with what is immediately comprehensible. But from that standpoint many of the greatest achievements of human culture will seem undemocratic [*nenarodnïmi*], for far from all of them, even in our country, the most democratic in the world, are truly accessible (in the sense of being capable of complete inner assimilation) by a wide audience.
>
> Do we need this intellectual type of art? Of course we do: it is needed, and deeply to be valued, as a particular artistic genre, alongside other genres, neither replacing them nor contradicting them.

Zhitomirsky even seems to take up the comparison with Khachaturyan's concertos that Grinberg advanced against Shostakovich's Quintet (or rather more likely, it was Grinberg who responded to Zhitomirsky, since Grinberg probably attended the same meeting at the Moscow Composers' House where Zhitomirsky had delivered his remarks, on 7 December 1940, about a month before Grinberg posted his letter to Stalin). "Sometimes," Zhitomirsky said,

> one encounters a failure to understand that works of the intellectually rigorous variety in no way contradict or threaten the existence of vividly sensuous lyricism, as in the Khachaturyan concertos. But actually this variety of genres and styles is one of the most attractive properties of the present moment in the development of Soviet music. One also encounters at times a failure to understand the fundamental aesthetic and ideological value of what is the strongest side of Khachaturyan's talent: his elementally vivid emotionality, his remarkable feeling for folklore, his ability boldly and inventively to make elements of vernacular language his own. And in this misunderstanding I have personally sensed something that comes from an aristocratic aesthetic, from the armchair, shunning "excessively" open and realistic emotionalism in art, along with language that is "excessively" familiar. But what Khachaturyan

wields with such skill is actually one of the most important sources for Soviet musical culture taken as a whole. And many major masters of Soviet music show their greatest deficiency precisely here. I think, for example, that a shortness of lyrical breath, of openness and fullness of feeling constitutes the most vulnerable side of Prokofieff's opera *Semyon Kotko*.

And in gratuitously naming and piling on that unfortunate work whereby Prokofieff had just suffered his first and most public failure as a newly repatriated Soviet composer, Zhitomirsky, having gone pretty far out on a limb on behalf of Shostakovich's Quintet, was obviously covering his left flank. But until that digression into safe territory, you may have been thinking that Zhitomirsky's defense of Shostakovich's intellectually rigorous and exalted synthesis of abstract thought hardly sounded like a Soviet opinion—and yet there it was, in the official organ of the Union of Soviet Composers, selected for publication there as one of two commentaries from a meeting at which many had spoken. And if we find that paradoxical, it shows how one-sided and stereotyped our idea of Soviet opinion remains in the lingering aftermath of the Cold War.

Zhitomirsky's opinion, which as we know represented what had to have been a consensus of opinion, given the Quintet's place within the first harvest of Stalin Prizes, was obviously a pre–Cold War opinion. It could not have been expressed during one of the periods of high ideological pressure that colors our retrospective view of Soviet culture. Right after "Muddle Instead of Music" in 1936, such a defense of Shostakovich would have been impolitic, to say the least, and after the so-called *Zhdanovshchina* of 1946–48, when the big so-called antiformalist campaigns were underway, it would have been unthinkable. But in 1940, and early in 1941, a window had opened for it. It quickly closed tight, and no one is ever thanked for remembering it, but right now we do need to remember it if we are to understand why and how Shostakovich's Quintet took the form it did and merited the shower of praise and recognition that greeted it.

In 1940, World War II was on. But neither of the countries that would eventually be the protagonists of the Cold War was as yet taking part. The United States was hoping to remain neutral, just as it had hoped at first to stay out of the previous Great War, and was resisting Great Britain's urgent pleas for assistance against the Blitz. As for the Soviet Union, it was actually allied at the time with Nazi Germany. The world has done Russia the favor, by and large, of forgetting this little episode, but it had a bearing on Soviet policy, including arts policy. It is a bit jarring to look into the issues of *Sovetskaya muzïka* that came out between the summer of 1939 and the summer of 1941, and find so much news of Soviet-German musical ties and cooperation.

The best-known case is the 1940 production of Wagner's *Die Walküre* at the Moscow Bolshoi Theater to greet Joachim von Ribbentrop, the German foreign minister, who along with Vyacheslav Molotov, his Soviet counterpart, had signed the August 1939 pact between the two "sworn friends" (*zaklyatïye druz'ya*), as the phrase then went. It was staged by Sergei Eisenstein, the great film director, fresh from working with Prokofieff on *Alexander Nevsky*, a film that portrayed the Germans as Russia's evil enemies and was then under a pact-related ban. For me, however, the signal event was Wilhelm Furtwängler's performances of Shostakovich's Fifth Symphony in Berlin.[28] (*Those* are something I wish I could have heard.) So it would seem that Zhitomirsky had read accurately the temper of what the Russians call the *kon"yunktura*, the particular moment in Soviet arts policy when a bit of German idealism was welcome in critical evaluations of music—and perhaps, as we'll see, in its composition, too.

Certainly Zhitomirsky read the moment better than the other featured speaker at the meeting called by the Union of Composers to discuss the recent *dekada* and its presentations. That speaker was Sergei Prokofieff, making his one and only extended comment on Shostakovich. In retrospect, the situation is heavy with ironies. Having closed his Paris apartment only four years earlier, Prokofieff was still enjoying the extraordinary privileges that were promised him as inducements to return. He had made an extensive tour of Western Europe and America in 1938, and was planning another American tour when the war began. He did not know it yet in December 1940, when he made his public comments about the Shostakovich Quintet, but *we* now know that his right to travel abroad had been permanently canceled by the authorities, and he would no longer be the coddled and protected figure he had bargained on remaining.[29] That adds another layer of irony to the patronizing tone he adopted in commenting on this much-touted offering by Shostakovich, toward whom his attitude was—to say the least—complicated.

A vain, competitive, and blissfully self-centered man, Prokofieff actually saw the appearance of the *Pravda* editorial excoriating Shostakovich's *Lady Macbeth* early in 1936 as a good omen for his own preeminence among Soviet composers, and it probably helped nudge him toward the worst decision of his life: to retreat, later that very year, to Soviet Russia from Paris, where Stravinsky was uncontestably dominant.[30] Another little irony: the first Western engagement that Prokofieff had to cancel because of wartime restrictions on travel was a date conducting the New York Philharmonic-Symphony Orchestra in April 1940. As the *New York Times*

---

28. As reported in *Sovetskaya muzïka*: "The great German conductor Wilhelm Furtwängler has included in the program of his concerts the Fifth Symphony of D. Shostakovich" (Крупный германский дирижер Вильгельм Фуртвенглер включил в программу своих концертов 5-ю симфонию Д. Шостаковича). "Muzïkal'naya zhizn' za rubezhom," *Sovetskaya muzïka*, 1940, no. 4, 92. The same page contains a report of a production of Glinka's *Ivan Susanin* (the Soviet redaction of *A Life for the Tsar*) at the Berlin State Opera.

29. Simon Morrison, *The People's Artist: Prokofiev's Soviet Years* (New York: Oxford University Press, 2008), 112–13.

30. Ibid., 41.

announced, "Igor Stravinsky will conduct in his place." (I hope Prokofieff did not actually see that announcement.)[31] Once he came to realize his virtual imprisonment in his new home, Prokofieff must have resented deeply Shostakovich's full pardon after the Fifth Symphony and the younger composer's ever-mounting prestige within the Soviet musical establishment, culminating in 1941 when Prokofieff was passed over for the Stalin Prize, in favor of the very Quintet on which he had commented with a condescension that made an awkward counterpoint to Zhitomirsky's defense of the work.

Although Prokofieff ended his report by calling the Quintet "a remarkable composition," he also complained, in the same final sentence, that it "lacked momentum and climaxes," despite its "unusually clear basic design."[32] Although he carps at length, and clearly meant to put the younger composer in his place, Prokofieff's laser-focused composer's ears led him to make one really discerning and illuminating point about the piece, concerning its treatment of the medium, which (in keeping with the generally thin textures that most composers preferred in what we now call the "interwar" period) was airy and fresh without sacrificing weight. "Listening to the first movement," Prokofieff says,

> you get the really distinct feeling that Shostakovich thought up this piece with exactly this combination of instruments in mind. The fact that he puts the four voices of the string quartet in the middle, and separates the two voices of the piano so that one is above and the other below, produces an impression of a sextet and immediately lends an extraordinary clarity and a completely new character to the sonority.

He is actually talking about the opening section of the Prelude, marked *Lento* (slow), the striking effect of which got everyone, as we know from Rabinovich's report, to sit up and take notice. When the strings enter after a dramatic piano solo modeled on Bach's organ toccata style, they are indeed bunched together in the middle range, and in a very unconventional voicing, with the cello on top, playing

---

31. "Prokofieff Unable to Come to America," *New York Times*, 10 January 1940, 24. The whole tiny article in its entirety:

> Serge Prokofieff, Russian composer, will be unable to come to America this season to fill his engagement as guest conductor of the Philharmonic-Symphony Orchestra, it was announced yesterday. Political conditions have made it impossible for him to obtain the necessary visas.
>
> In his place Igor Stravinsky will conduct the concerts of April 3, 5, 6 and 7. Mr. Stravinsky will direct his own "Sacre du Printemps" on all four programs. On the first two programs he will also lead his Divertimento and "Chant du Rossignol." On the final two programs he will repeat his "Petrushka" and "Firebird" Suites, which he conducted at Carnegie Hall last week.

Stravinsky's Philharmonic performances of *Petrushka* and *Le Sacre du printemps* were recorded by Columbia Records and issued later that year.

32. "Obsuzhdeniye IV dekadï sovetskoy muzïki: vïstupleniye S. Prokof'yeva," *Sovetskaya muzïka*, 1941, no. 2, 71–72; all citations from Prokofieff's contribution are from these pages. (Thanks again to Laurel Fay for the photocopy.)

at the upper extremity of its compass. This really does give the sound an extraordinary intensity; and when the pianist reenters, the right hand is indeed above the strings and the left hand below, just as Prokofieff described. The unusual disposition of instruments continues in the Fugue: the string instruments enter one by one with the subject, each one lower than the last—with the viola, rather than the cello, last and lowest, only to be trumped by the piano playing lower than any of the string instruments can go. Again, the sound is strange and fresh, even if the writing is academically disciplined.

But now the relentless carping begins. "I don't know how Shostakovich goes about composing," Prokofieff said. "Most of us write at the keyboard; but it seems to me that in working on the Quintet, he thought through a lot of it without going to the piano," and as a result all the movements came out too long, producing "a certain feeling of fatigue by the time you get to the fourth and fifth movements." Indeed, Prokofieff all but yawns as he describes the piece.

> It saddens me a little that in the first movement he uses Bachian and even pre-Bachian mannerisms. That's nothing new, and it seems to me that for an opening gesture he should have tried something else. As it is, there is a certain carelessness of approach: "Bach wrote like this, and that's good, so I'll use this figure." It would have been better to do without this and take it as one's goal to write a different figure. Then the first movement would have become much more original in substance.

That is some niggling. The only movement Prokofieff praises without reservation is the Fugue. Despite its Bachian inspiration, he said,

> I regard the fugue as the best and most interesting movement in the Quintet. Why? Because Bach wrote such a variety of fugues and other composers have added to them so much more that lately it has seemed utterly impossible to write a fugue that sounded novel and interesting. While abroad I saw people taking the most desperate measures to write a fugue that would be more or less original in sound. Rarely did anyone succeed; in Hindemith's sonatas you'll find a little something of interest in this direction. One has to hand it to Shostakovich: in his fugue, as far as the general impression it makes, there is an unusual amount that's new. I don't even know whether it's a good fugue from the technical standpoint. But musically it's good.

Prokofieff was quite right to mention Hindemith; we already know that Shostakovich studied and emulated his music. Shostakovich's "Bach" was really Hindemith, as Prokofieff was hinting. When he gets to the Scherzo, against which he can register no complaints, Prokofieff gives it all of one sentence: "Everybody agrees that the Scherzo is a brilliant number." It is the one movement in which the instruments saw away the way they do in Taneyev or Franck, yet even here Shostakovich maintains the texture that so impressed Prokofieff, the piano playing in multiple octaves both above and below the strings. With the fourth movement, a lengthy Intermezzo, Prokofieff is back to displaying his singular lack of tact, both toward Shostakovich and toward his audience:

> [W]ith regard to [this] movement I feel I must register some objection. The Handelian device used here—an elongated, endless melody over a pizzicato bass—was a very good invention in Handel's time. In the postwar period in Paris positively everybody was getting into it—and finally it became a bore. If it makes any impression at all on us now, it's only because we don't know that literature. It seems to me that Shostakovich, with all the colossal inventiveness that manifests itself all through the Quintet, could have avoided this device. And whenever that Handel bass unexpectedly lets up in the fourth movement, immediately good music starts up, because the real Shostakovich starts up instead of the Handel-pastiching Shostakovich. And for a final thought, I am somewhat amazed to find such excessive refinement in a young composer who is now in the full bloom of his creative powers. In this composition there is not a single moment where he really lets fly. If Shostakovich were sixty years old, then for someone wise in years this habit of pondering every note might seem a remarkable virtue. But at present it threatens to become a vice.

Surely Prokofieff intended to sound like a benevolent mentor, but I think you will agree that he sooner comes off as a crank and (as usual) utterly obtuse in reading the moment. The constant reminder that he'd heard it all before in Paris, and that those who found the work impressive were yokels, was typical of him, and explains why his fellow Soviet composers thought him a snob, called him "that Frenchman" behind his back, and did nothing to defend him when, in 1948, it was his turn to be attacked. But how strange that, although Prokofieff said the final movement was one of the tiresome ones, he never describes it. That can only be because it did not fit his characterization of the Quintet as a whole. Its tempo designation, *Allegretto*, already telegraphs a lightening of tone, and it turns out to be an exquisite pastoral. At the end you can almost see frolicsome lambs a-gamboling, something of which the preceding four movements had offered scant premonition. David Rabinovich did it greater justice than Prokofieff by simply reporting its first-night reception and the Quintet's subsequent reputation. After remarking that "encores at . . . a [chamber-music] concert are a great rarity," he noted that insistent between-movements applause mandated the repetition of the Scherzo, and the prolonged applause at the end impelled the performers to repeat the Finale as well. As a result, he wrote, "the wits say that Shostakovich's Quintet is a piece in five movements of which there are seven," because the repetition of the Scherzo and the Finale had become a "tradition."[33]

When I hear the sweet, gentle, cheery Finale in context, I can't help thinking of the Stalinist mantra of the late 1930s, "Жить ста́ло лу́чше, жить ста́ло веселе́е!" (*Zhit' stalo luchshe, zhit' stalo veseleye,* or Life has become better, life has become

---

33. Rabinovich, *Dmitry Shostakovich, Composer,* 59.

merrier!), words uttered by the Gensek (General Secretary, Stalin's official title) himself on 17 November 1935 at a meeting of so-called Stakhanovites or shock workers, zealous laborers who overfulfilled quotas in the five-year plans and ushered in what Stalin proclaimed to be "novuyu, spokoynuyu i sïtnuyu zhizn'," a new, peaceful, plentiful life.[34] Shostakovich was catching the spirit of the times, in more ways than one. Both the implied message of the Quintet and its style were just right for the *kon"yunktura*.

V

The message was in effect the old Beethovenian progression from dark to light—*per aspera ad astra*, "through suffering to the stars," if you prefer Latin; or *Kampf und Sieg*, "struggle and victory," if you prefer German, but modulated in a manner suitable for the age not of heroes but of the *prostoy narod*, the common folk. It is the program of the Fifth Symphony (Beethoven's or Shostakovich's, take your pick), cut down to scale. It begins not in a tortured mood, just a sober one, and ends not in a paroxysm of rejoicing but a sigh of contentment.

As to style—and this is what Prokofieff utterly failed to understand—the touch of Bachian or Handelian "universalism" was just what the moment required in Soviet music. It built a modest bridge to the moderate modernism (what T. W. Adorno was just then disparaging as *die gemäßigte Moderne*)[35] of Hindemith, that longstanding influence on Shostakovich, whose stylistic evolution from brash to decorous paralleled Shostakovich's own (so you see, it was not something confined to the Soviet sphere). Alternatively, it was a bridge to what we now call the *Boulangerie* (literally "the bakery") after Nadia Boulanger, who schooled her pupils (including a lot of Americans) in tame Stravinskian neoclassicism; not that anyone in the Soviet Union would dare to name Stravinsky in the same breath as Shostakovich—nor Hindemith by then, for that matter, for he had fallen out of favor with the Nazis (their sworn friends) and was, like Stravinsky, in America by 1940. (Of this, too, Prokofieff was oblivious, as we have seen.) But their styles defined an international norm to which Soviet music was just then encouraged to conform, as Prokofieff was forced, backhandedly and gauchely, to concede.

The Stalin Prizes were an instrument of such encouragement—not only in the case of the Shostakovich Quintet, but also in that of Nikolai Myaskovsky's one-movement Twenty-First Symphony, originally titled *Simfoniya-fantaziya*, which was one of several works by internationally famous composers that the Chicago

---

34. You can actually see him do it on YouTube: www.youtube.com/watch?v=b9g7RGypnTI.
35. "Falsch klingt die gemäßigte Moderne selber" (T. W. Adorno, "Ad vocem Hindemith. Eine Dokumentation" (1939), in idem, *Gesammelte Schriften* 17, *Musikalische Schriften* 4 (Frankfurt am Main: Suhrkamp, 1982), 232.

Symphony commissioned in honor of its fiftieth anniversary in 1940. (Another was Stravinsky's Symphony in C, the first composition Stravinsky completed in America.)[36] Having an international reputation and an international style was at that particular juncture a plus. A few years later, when World War II and its temporary alliances were over, and postwar was giving way to Cold War, Soviet arts policies would turn xenophobic again and Shostakovich, Myaskovsky, Prokofieff, and even folksy Khachaturyan would be accused of "formalism" and "kowtowing to the West" (*nizkopoklonstvo pered zapadom*).[37] That is the attitude we now tend to remember when we think of Soviet arts policy, but there were many fluctuations. Some musicians were better attuned to the changes than others. Shostakovich was always better attuned than Prokofieff.

Does it sound to you as if I am belittling or demeaning Shostakovich when I say this? Do we prefer seeing him as a victim to seeing him as a prizewinner? As a saint rather than as a success? As someone who took no cognizance of the surrounding world and its *kon"yunktura*s when composing? If so, we are idealizing him, as we are taught by our popular culture to idealize the creators of high art—seeing him, that is to say, not as a human being but as an icon of our own manufacture. In the case of the real human beings that we know, including all the composers we have actually met, or in the case of ourselves, insofar as we can know ourselves, we know that our feelings, moods, ideas, techniques, strategies, and so on are not entirely endogenous. They do not always (or perhaps ever) arise utterly spontaneously from within. They are often (or perhaps always) in some measure a response to stimuli from without. Our actions, which in the aggregate constitute our lives, are dialectically connected with our environments, which furnish our affordances, the conditions that determine our possibilities of action, within which we make our choices. Our choices are better or worse depending both on our inner resources and on the resourcefulness with which we respond to the environment that both enables and constrains us.

Shostakovich was a better chooser than Prokofieff; his life achieved a better synthesis of personal integrity and necessary adaptation. The Quintet is a beautiful example of such adaptation—adaptation to the demands of Socialist Realism, grand style, life-affirmation, and all, and an adaptation to new affordances vouch-

---

36. Grigoriy Shneyerson announced the work in *Sovetskaya muzïka* as "the just-completed symphony (on Biblical themes)," evidently confusing it with the *Symphony of Psalms*, written for the Boston Symphony ten years earlier ("Za rubezhom," *Sovetskaya muzïka*, 1940, no. 6, 91).

37. The dread phrase was adapted from the earliest of the three Resolutions that collectively constituted the Zhdanovshchina: the one on literature (officially, "the Resolution of the Central Committee of the Soviet Communist Party on the magazines *Zvezda* [The Star] and *Leningrad*"), indicting "произведения, культивирующие несвойственный советским людям дух низкопоклонства перед современной буржуазной культурой Запада" (works that cultivate a spirit, uncharacteristic of Soviet people, of kowtowing to the contemporary bourgeois culture of the West).

safed by a particularly "German" moment in Soviet culture. In making this very successful and well-rewarded synthesis, Shostakovich was acting in a manner that can be called self-serving—or could be called that, were "self-serving" not a term so ineluctably tinged, in ordinary English, with cynicism. Success need not be cynical. Shostakovich's success in fashioning his Quintet is evidence that he could find his way to a combination of style and message that satisfied his own creative urges and critical standards while also turning the demands of the *kon"yunktura* to his advantage. It's something we all try to do, Stalin Prize winners and Kyoto Prize winners alike. He did it better than Prokofieff, and better than most of us. The fact that, having weathered so many vicissitudes, he ended up the most officially decorated of all Soviet composers, and at the same time an inspiration to the nascent Soviet counterculture, is evidence that this publicly taciturn man who let people think him a holy fool was in fact the champion player of the only game in town.

Pars Ricardi Primi

(Ricardus Primus's Part)

17

Shooting a White Elephant

Simon P. Keefe, ed., *The Cambridge History of Eighteenth-Century Music*, Cambridge University Press, 2009, xvii + 798 pp.

Reviewer's Note: Although Simon P. Keefe is listed on the title page as editor and signs the Editor's Preface alone, the last paragraph of the preface contains an acknowledgment to David Wyn Jones "for his planning of the volume and his solid advice throughout" (xvii). Since matters of editorial responsibility and performance receive a great deal of emphasis in this review, the ambiguity thus introduced prompts me to refer to the editor(s) throughout as "Editor," rather than naming names.

I

The Editor's Preface begins with a strong claim: "The eighteenth century perhaps boasts a more remarkable coterie of totemic musical figures, and a more engaging combination of genres, styles and aesthetic orientations, than any century before or since" (xv).

Totemic figures for sure. When the publisher asked me which of the six volumes of the original hardcover edition of *The Oxford History of Western Music* I wanted sent to bookstores to tease potential buyers, I unhesitatingly recommended the second, which encompasses the seventeenth and eighteenth centuries, precisely because the composers best known to, and best loved by, the shrinking radio-listening, concert-attending, and CD-buying audience for "classical music" were all denizens of the eighteenth century. Their popularity is not an unmixed compliment. One of the virtues that broadcast music must exhibit is that of not being overly "engaging," to cite the other encomiastic adjective from the preface. But at whatever price, the eighteenth century provides the unshakeable bedrock of our scholarly and performing canons—canons that started forming precisely during

Review of *The Cambridge History of Eighteenth-Century Music*, ed. Simon P. Keefe, *Eighteenth-Century Music* 8 (2011): 117–29.

the eighteenth century and for eighteenth-century reasons, and continue, for better and worse, to sustain our musical occupations and institutions.

That is surely enough to justify a new comprehensive treatment. And yet, as every reader of this journal will be aware, since the late 1960s the status of the eighteenth century as a musical-historical period has been very much in question. These four decades–plus exactly coincide with my own professional activity as a music historian. The question, therefore, has been with me for the duration of my career, and I vividly recall its early formulations.

My earliest encounter with the eighteenth-century problem was private, but authoritative and indelibly impressive. My most eminent professor, Paul Henry Lang, was an eighteenth-century specialist—though that is not something I will assume that every reader will remember, since his name occurs nowhere within the covers of the volume under review, and his most important contribution within his specialty, a weighty biography of Handel (1966), has long been superseded. In addition to editing the *Musical Quarterly* (where he succeeded Carl Engel), serving as chief music critic for the *New York Herald Tribune* (where he succeeded Virgil Thomson), and putting in time as officer in every professional organization (including a term as president of the International Musicological Society [IMS]), this indefatigable man, now best remembered for his first book, *Music in Western Civilization* (1941), was W.W. Norton's acquisitions editor for music from the 1940s to the 1960s, which meant that he was responsible for the legendary series of historical surveys from which early generations of American musicologists learned their basics: Reese for the Middle Ages and Renaissance, Bukofzer for the Baroque, Einstein for the Romantic era, and Adolfo Salazar, a composer by trade and a refugee from the Spanish civil war, wanly bringing up the rear with *Music in Our Time*, a translation of a book first published in Argentina in 1944, on a subject that at the time was not *kosher für Musikwissenschaft*. (Later it was replaced by William Austin's very comprehensive survey.) And looming over all was Lang's own *Universalgeschichte*, from which one omitted to quote, in those days, at one's peril.

You will notice that there was no Norton history of the "classical period." Lang often told us why that lacuna persisted. He had first assigned the volume to Alfred Einstein on the strength of the latter's Mozartean credentials, but Einstein had begged off, for a reason that still resonates: we don't yet know enough, Lang said he said, about the origins of the Haydn-Mozart style to write its history. That is why Einstein ended up writing (not too well) about the nineteenth century instead. Whereupon, with typical self-assurance, Lang decided to take on the job himself, but, as he told us, he shortly came up against an insurmountable barrier: the mountains, as he put it, of southern Italian church music that had never been prospected, and which contained, he was certain, the key to the origins and essence of eighteenth-century classicism.[1] The unwritten book, Lang averred, would remain unwritten for a long time. And it did.

The man who brought the eighteenth-century problem to the attention of the musicological world at large was Daniel Heartz, in an article—published, as it happens, in a Lang retirement festschrift that formed a special section within an early issue of *Current Musicology* (no. 9, 1969), the Columbia graduate student publication that was then edited by Neal Zaslaw, one of Lang's most redoubtable protégés. In terms of impact per unit length, I nominate this four-page, two-thousand-word essay, "Approaching a History of Eighteenth-Century Music," as the most influential article in the history of musicology. (It had been preceded by a somewhat more detailed challenge, "Opera and the Periodization of 18th-Century Music," delivered at the 1967 IMS meeting in Ljubljana but not published until the appearance of that conference's proceedings in 1970.) No musicologist today, certainly no reader of *Eighteenth-Century Music*, can be unaware of its thesis, or unresponsive to it. Heartz argued that all attempts at writing the history of eighteenth-century music up to then had been misguided because all had been looking for ways of connecting the style of Bach and Handel to the style of Haydn and Mozart. The wizened among us will remember all the proposed missing links: the Mannheim school, the Tyrolean school, the Italian keyboard school, *e tutti quanti*. Heartz, New Hampshire Yankee that he was, was playing the part of the Down East farmer who, asked for directions by tourists in an old joke, hems and haws awhile and finally blurts, "Ya cahn't get theah fiom heah." And the missing links were especially otiose, Heartz insisted, because they were all drawn from the realm of instrumental music under the misapprehension (still adamantly maintained by Charles Rosen) that High Classicism was an essentially instrumental style.[2]

There have been three responses to Heartz's gauntlet over the years. One, Rosen's in *The Classical Style* (1971), was simply to dodge the question, writing about

---

1. According to a memoir by Daniel Heartz, supported by relevant quotations from his correspondence with Lang, Lang at this point "quietly palmed off the job on [Friedrich] Blume," who "two years later handed it back to me [that is, Lang]; he got stuck at exactly the same spot—Italian opera in the first half of the century" (Lang to Heartz, 21 September 1968, quoted in Daniel Heartz, "A Pilgrim's Progress Report Concerning 'Music in the Classic Era,'" in *Music, Libraries, and the Academy: Essays in Honor of Lenore Coral*, ed. James P. Cassaro (Middleton, WI: A-R Editions, 2007), 24. Heartz suspects that Manfred Bukofzer was also "in the running" for the classical assignment, since at the time of his death in 1955 he was working on "a substantial revision of his University of California syllabus 'Music in the Classic Period'" ("A Pilgrim's Progress Report," 24–25).

2. In the same long letter to Heartz, Lang recalled mooting the possibility that the genealogy of High Classicism went back to *opera buffa* at the International Musicological Society Congress in Basel as early as 1948, whereupon the veteran Danish scholar Jens Peter Larsen "became quite agitated. 'You are ruining your reputation,' he said, with all the nonsense of 'deriving the symphony from opera'" (Heartz, "A Pilgrim's Progress Report," 24).

Haydn, Mozart, and Beethoven as though their styles had no history at all
except in terms of their mutual relations and a few proximate influences, mainly
C.P.E. Bach. (Rosen's introduction very elaborately disavowed any interest in
music history, which is why it has always amused—or bemused—me to find Rosen
so often listed among the music historians.) Heartz's own response is found in his
Music in European Capitals: The Galant Style, 1720-1780 (2003)—a thousand-page
bodying forth of his four-page blueprint, in which he effectively posits a "short
eighteenth century" to cover what in the gauntlet piece he dubbed the "main evolution" that the century witnessed, namely the one that led to Haydn and Mozart,
with Bach and Handel simply excluded as the end of a previous line of no real
eighteenth-century import. This book, by the way, plus the two almost equally
hefty bricks Heartz published on either side of it,[3] constitutes the missing volume
in the Norton series that Lang so long bemoaned, which the publisher formally
passed on to Heartz in 1971 after Lang had officially given up on the project. I wish
Lang, who died in 1991, had lived to see Heartz's formidable trilogy, if only to hear
the inevitable wisecracks with which he would have greeted it.

Heartz's solution to the eighteenth-century problem is certain to become even
more influential than it already has been. It is trickling down. Just last week I
received a review copy of *The Concise History of Western Music*, fourth edition,
by Barbara Russano Hanning (2010), the latest condensation of the Burkholder/
Palisca/Grout textbook that has over the last half-century established itself as the
most widely used music history text in the history of music. While the latest edition of "Grout" as of this writing (the eighth, published in 2009) continues to
apportion its contents according to calendrical centuries, each divided into several
roughly chronological chapters, the new concise edition divides its matter up into
six parts, of which the third is now called "The Long Seventeenth Century." The last
of that third section's five chapters is titled "Baroque Music in the Early Eighteenth
Century," and is further broken down into "national" sections covering Vivaldi
(Italy), Couperin + Rameau (France), Bach (Germany), and Handel (England).
Part Four, titled "The Eighteenth Century," is in fact Heartz's short eighteenth. It
opens with a chapter called "The Early Classic Period: Opera and Vocal Music,"
which, after a brief introduction, begins, just as Heartz had preached and later
practiced, with *opera buffa* (followed by sections on *opera seria* and "Opera
Reform"). (In response to a query of mine, Peter Burkholder writes that, although
he recognizes the virtues of the approach Heartz has proposed, he does not plan to
adopt it in future "Grouts": "I like my caesurae at 1700 and 1800, instead of the old
divides I learned as an undergrad between 'Baroque' and 'Classical' and between
'Classical' and 'Romantic' . . . because seeing the centuries as units allows me as a

---

3. Daniel Heartz, *Haydn, Mozart, and the Viennese School, 1740-1780* (New York: W.W. Norton, 1995); and idem, *Mozart, Haydn, and Early Beethoven, 1781-1802* (New York: W.W. Norton, 2008).

teacher to emphasize the conflicts and changes of taste. In a sense, it seems better to take an obviously artificial division at a century mark rather than a somewhat constructed one elsewhere.")

The third response was the one this journal had the honor of presenting in what amounted to the keynote address in its maiden issue: James Webster's "The Eighteenth Century as a Music-Historical Period?"—in whose title the question mark did all the work. Webster's solution was the opposite of Heartz's. He accepted Heartz's posited "main evolution" as the central component of a tripartite scheme that encompassed a late-Baroque half-century (1670–1720) leading up to it and an unnamed half-century (1780–1830) that realized its implications, encompassing (to quote from his abstract) "the rise of the 'regulative work-concept' (Goehr) and 'pre-Romanticism' (Dahlhaus) [but why 'pre-'?], and the Europe-wide triumph of 'Viennese modernism,' including the first autonomous instrumental music and a central role in the rise of the modern (post-revolutionary) world symbolized by Haydn's sublime in *The Creation*."

While one can agree with Webster that his "long" eighteenth century "seems more nearly adequate than either baroque/classical or 1700–1800 as a single, undifferentiated period," it strains plausibility to call it, at 160 years' duration, in any sense a century, or even a separable music-historical period—although as I write this I am aware that I have claimed, in the *Oxford History* and in my classroom teaching, that the whole two-hundred-year span 1680–1880 is defensibly a unitary period insofar as those dates circumscribe the time during which musical form was primarily determined by harmonic relations. So let me modify my objection to Webster: I don't see in his "long" century a criterion that lends coherence to the whole. As for Heartz's "short" century, one could complain with equal justice that it leaves out all the best parts. So the problem remains a problem, and *The Cambridge History of Eighteenth-Century Music* (henceforth *CH18*) has a perfect right to attempt a new solution.

The decision to cast all the Cambridge histories by calendrical centuries was clearly made before individual editors were engaged, and so it was presumably not something that Editor was free to negotiate. But the editor of a volume like this one is nonetheless answerable for its overall approach and performance.[4] And Editor *has* shouldered responsibility. As stipulated in the "Editor's preface," his solution shares with the two others (Rosen's arch nonsolution aside) the elimination of the artificial divider at midcentury between Baroque and Classical, while still allowing the calendar to define the span:

---

4. I feel I have to state the obvious here because other Cambridge editors have tried to fob editorial accountability onto the individual chapter authors: see my review of the Cambridge histories of nineteenth- and twentieth-century music, published under the title "Speed Bumps" in *Nineteenth-Century Music* 29 (2005–6): 185–207.

Whatever the merits of an approach determined by a mid-century partition, the sense of musical continuity across the century as a whole is invariably lost as a result, as is the inter-generic and intra-generic ebb and flow of musical development. By rejecting Baroque and Classical periodizations as a means of organizing this volume ... it is hoped that eighteenth-century musical activities will be portrayed as richer, more diverse and more complex than is often the case in single- or multi-authored historical volumes. By eschewing a chronological approach across the volume as a whole, we encourage our reader to think less in terms of overtly teleological developments than of interacting and mutually stimulating musical cultures and practices. (xv–xvi)

II

Editor presents this as a new line of attack: "instead of relying on temporal, periodic and composer-related phenomena, then, we organize our volume by genre." But we've been there and done that. That is how the unlamented *New Oxford History of Music* (*NOHM*) was organized, to virtually everyone's dissatisfaction. That project was conceived in some antediluvian, preheartzian era (actually I know from conversations with Gerald Abraham that it was the late 1940s), although the individual volumes took forever and a day to see the light. Eighteenth-century material was covered (along with earlier and later material) over a span of four volumes (V–VIII) published (not in that order) between 1973 and 1986, and their various chapter breakdowns were almost the same as the ones now served up by *CH18*:

CH18	*NOHM*
1 PRELUDE: The Musical Map of Europe c. 1700 (Stephen Rose)	
PART I: MUSIC FOR THE CHURCH	
2 Catholic Church Music in Italy, and the Spanish and Portuguese Empires (Paul R. Laird)	V:6 Church Music and Oratorio in Italy and Central and Eastern Europe (H. C. Wolff, P. Smith)
	VII:4 Church Music and Oratorio (E. Olleson)
3 Catholic Sacred Music in Austria (Jen-Yen Chen)	(VII:4 cont'd)
4 Catholic Church Music in France (Jean-Paul C. Montagnier)	V:7 Church Music in France (D. Launay, J. R. Anthony)
5 Lutheran Church Music (Stephen Rose)	V:9 German Church Music (P. Steinitz)
	VI:10 Organ Music 1700–1750 (W. Emery)

6 Protestant Church Music in England and America (Charles E. Brewer)

V:8 English Church Music (A. Lewis)

7 INTERLUDE: Listening, Thinking, and Writing (David Schroeder)

PART II: MUSIC FOR THE THEATRE

8 Italian Opera in the Eighteenth Century (Margaret R. Butler)

V:2 Italian Opera 1700–1750 (H. C. Wolff)
VII:1 Opera in Italy and the Holy Roman Empire (A. A. Abert, H. C. Robbins Landon)

9 Opera in Paris from Campra to Rameau (Lois Rosow)

V:4 French Opera from Lully to Rameau (P.-M. Masson)
VII:2 Opera in France (M. Cooper)

10 An Instinct for Parody and a Spirit for Revolution: Parisian Opera, 1752–1800 (Michael Fend)

(VII:2 cont'd)

11 German Opera from Reinhard Keiser to Peter Winter (Claudia Maurer Zenck)

V:5 Opera in England and Germany (J. A. Westrup)
(VII:1 and 2 cont'd)

12 The Lure of Aria, Procession, and Spectacle: Opera in Eighteenth-Century London (Michael Burden)

(V:5 cont'd)

13 Music Theatre in Spain (Rainer Kleinertz)

VII:3 Opera in Other Countries (R. Fiske, G. Seaman, G. Abraham)

14 Opera in Sweden (Gerger Andersson)

(VII:3 cont'd)

15 INTERLUDE: Performance in the Eighteenth Century (John Irving)

PART III: MUSIC FOR THE SALON AND CONCERT ROOM

16 Keyboard Music from Couperin to Early Beethoven (Rohan Stewart-MacDonald)

VI:9 Harpsichord Music, 1700–1750 (P. Radcliffe)
VII:10 Keyboard Music (P. Radcliffe)

17 The Serenata in the Eighteenth Century (Stefanie Tcharos)

18 Private Music in Public Spheres: Chamber Cantata and Song (Berta Joncus)

VI:2 Solo Song and Vocal Duet (H. J. Marx, I. Spink, D. Tunley)
VII:5 Solo Song (R. Hughes)

19 Handel and English Oratorio (Eva Zöllner)

VI:1 Ode and Oratorio in England (R. McGuinness, A. Hicks, G. Abraham)

20 The Overture-Suite, Concerto Grosso, Ripieno Concerto and *Harmoniemusik* in the Eighteenth Century (Steven Zohn)

VI:4 Orchestral Music in the Early Eighteenth Century (W. Kolneder)

21 Concerto of the Individual (Simon McVeigh)

VI:5 The Solo Concerto (W. Kolneder)
VII:7 The Concerto (E. Wellesz and F. Sternfeld)

22 Eighteenth-Century Symphonies: An Unfinished Dialogue (Richard Will)

VII:6 The Early Symphony (E. Wellesz)
VII:11 Instrumental Masterworks and Aspects of Formal Design (F. Sternfeld)

23 The String Quartet (Cliff Eisen)

VII:8 The Divertimento and Cognate Forms (G. Hausswald)
VII:9 The Rise of Chamber Music (K. Geiringer)

24 POSTLUDE: Across the Divide: Currents of Musical Thought in Europe, c. 1790–1810 (Simon P. Keefe)

VIII:1 General Musical Conditions (A. Hyatt King)

I will not undertake any direct comparisons between the coverage in *CH18* and *NOHM*; one may take it for granted that the newer chapters have the benefit of more recent research and exhibit more recent attitudes, at times quite self-consciously and by no means always to the good. (Is there anything more hackneyed by now than scare quotes around the word *great*? Anything staler than the use of *radical* and *radically* as general intensifiers or encomia? Anything more pretentious than the misappropriation of technical terms from other disciplines, like *performative*, which does *not* mean, simply, "pertaining to performance"?) All the same, the organization of the contents by genre was a deplorable decision, because it prevents (or absolves) this purported history of eighteenth-century music from ever engaging with the historiographical problems I have been discussing.

A couple of exceptional chapters aside, the book hardly qualifies as history at all. Instead, it is a repertory survey, a genre that differs from historiography precisely as synchronic differs from diachronic.

There has been a certain vogue within musicology for synchronic studies in recent decades, given a notable stimulus by Gary Tomlinson in his still widely discussed article "The Web of Culture: A Context for Musicology," which argued for the anthropological turn that Tomlinson has been advocating by precept and example for a long time.[5] The model of contextualization Tomlinson promoted there was that of the cultural anthropologist Clifford Geertz, whose name for it— "thick description"—was itself an appropriation from the philosopher Gilbert Ryle and his celebrated parable of blinking boys, which made Tomlinson's "prescription for the modern musicologist," as he was not ashamed to call it, doubly derivative.

My problems with the enterprise are two. The objective of thick description is to explain more or interpret better by broadening the amplitude of the field under observation (often compared with widening the angle of a photographer's lens). The thickest description of an artifact or gesture or any product of culture is a maximally informative description. The way you can distinguish a thick description from a thin one, on Ryle's model, is that it enables one to see and elucidate "what constitutes the difference between externally similar factors" (in Ryle's example, thence Geertz's and finally Tomlinson's, knowing whether an apparent wink is an involuntary twitch or an actual conspiratorial gesture or a parody of the latter or a preparatory exercise to do the last). But—to pose my first problem—how does the objective of thick description, hence of the new culturally anthropological musicology, differ from the *Verstehen* of *Geistesgeschichte* (which is to say, from the model of scholarship that musicologists of my now-senior generation were taught by their Central European émigré teachers—which is to say, the foundational model of the discipline and the most old-fashioned of all humanistic ideals)? And—to adumbrate the second problem—the quote in the sentence before last ("what constitutes the difference" etc.) is not from Geertz or Ryle, let alone Tomlinson, but from the preface to *Music in the Baroque Era* by Manfred Bukofzer (1947), one of those same Central European émigrés, who was as ardently devoted to "internalist" methods as Tomlinson is (or was) to external contextualization, and as insistent that informative comparisons were in essence diachronic (or in Tomlinson's paradoxical vocabulary, "presentist") as Tomlinson is (or was) that comparisons be drawn laterally, so as to reconstruct the "webs of significance he himself has spun," in which "man is an animal suspended" (as Tomlinson quotes Geertz, who was paraphrasing Max Weber). The avowedly antihistorical Rosen apart, for whom history is just a series of begats, no one to my knowledge has ever

---

5. Gary Tomlinson, "The Web of Culture: A Context for Musicology," *Nineteenth-Century Music* 7 (1983–84): 350–62.

actually propounded the sort of narrowly causal historical narrative that Tomlinson condemns as thin description. What is so new about the method?

Nothing is new about it, and as the comparison between *CH18* and *NOHM* has already suggested, the synchronic approach has already been given a fair trial and convicted. Especially in multitopical, multiauthored surveys, the generic approach is untenable, because its underlying assumption—that a multiplicity of synchronic accounts will somehow combine to imply a coherent diachronic narrative—is utopian. Can a multiply authored text ever produce such a narrative? Probably not, unless the editor is prepared to control things to the point where he or she might as well have been the author; and today's editors, like today's conductors, are rarely equipped by temperament or circumstance to be the tyrants they once were. As I will show later with examples, the editing of this volume has been unusually lenient even by current standards, and that has virtually precluded the achievement of a coherent diachronic narrative. But if such a narrative is not the goal, why assemble books like *CH18*?

Well, I *would* say that, wouldn't I? (But can you show me a counterexample?) In the Introduction to the *Oxford History*, now reprinted in each of the volumes of the five-volume paperback edition, I insisted upon the fundamental and invidious distinction I am again developing here, writing (in a passage that elicited a great deal of indignant commentary) that "most books that call themselves histories of Western music, or of any of its traditional 'style periods,' are in fact surveys, which cover—and celebrate—the relevant repertoire, but make little effort truly to explain why and how things happened as they did. This set of books is an attempt at a true history." Much of the annoyance at this passage stemmed from what appeared to be an intolerable hubris: that what I wrote was true (and that what others wrote was, by implication, false). That was not my claim. I claimed only that I tried to explain the whys and hows, and that only books that made that attempt truly deserved to be called histories. Histories track and account for change over time, something Editor quite wrongly equates with "overtly teleological developments," while surveys are content to describe things as they are or were—which is to say, statically (however richly, diversely, or complicatedly).

That the absence in *CH18* of a dynamic historical narrative is not inadvertent but very much the intention is evident from the very outset—with the survey of "the musical map of Europe, c. 1700," with which the volume begins. I welcomed it at first encounter, but that was because I was laboring under what proved to be the false expectation that it would be balanced at the end by a similarly static, synchronic survey of the musical map c. 1800. That would be one way, I thought, of trying to supply a sense of the century's dynamic, albeit one that the reader would have to infer. And why not? Letting the reader do the work might even have been an effective heuristic. But the final chapter, by Simon P. Keefe, is not a counterpart to the first. Instead, it amounts to a somewhat cranky and in any case futile complaint that the canonization of Haydn, Mozart, and Beethoven had already been locked into place by the time Ernst Ludwig Gerber reissued his *Historisch-biographisches Lexicon der Tonkünstler* of 1790–92 (as the *Neues historisch-biographisches Lexicon*) in 1810. It is indeed striking that Gerber's canon of dead white eighteenth-century males—J. S. Bach, C. P. E. Bach, Handel, Gluck, Joseph and Michael Haydn, and Mozart (as Keefe lists them on p. 668)—nearly matches (Michael Haydn apart) not only the academic canon but also the performing repertory of today; but calling it an "ossification" (672), or implying that the exclusion of such formerly popular figures as Pleyel may have been unjust (681–84), is an unhelpful counterfactual exercise, and prissily rebuking Beethoven's cadenza to the first movement of Mozart's D-minor Concerto, K. 466, for its "brazen virtuosity" (immediately upped, four lines further down on p. 676, to "gushing virtuosity") merely reinforces stereotypes of "Classical" effeteness. In *Expositions and Developments* (1962), Stravinsky told Robert Craft that after hearing a run-through of *Pulcinella*, Diaghilev "went about for a long time with a look that suggested The Offended Eighteenth Century." It was a silly look for him, and an even sillier one for a scholar; but it's typical of surveys, which all too often fall into advocacy at the expense of critical understanding (of canonization, for example). Dr. Keefe might have thought them a throwaway, but the last two sentences in *CH18* strike me, unhappily, as an apt summation of the book in their combination of platitudinous salesmanship and complacent non sequitur: "Perhaps many precariously placed musicians at the turn of the century ... longed for a better life in the nineteenth century than the life they had experienced at the very end of the eighteenth, but they could scarcely have yearned for richer or more vibrant musical cultures. The brightest of musical pasts and presents guaranteed the brightest of musical futures."

III

Substantiating a negative claim is always difficult. Only by reading the whole book will readers of this review be able to satisfy themselves that what I say is missing from *The Cambridge History of Eighteenth-Century Music* (namely, history) is truly missing. The best I can do is cite a few places where various chapter authors managed to sneak a reference, implicitly or obliquely, to the dynamic or dialectical processes the book fails to address. (The only chapter that presents a truly historical account at its core rather than in the margins is Richard Will's on the eighteenth-century symphony, which puts production in fruitful dialogue with social reception—the "unfinished dialogue" of his title, which continues to the present—and educes out of the dialectic "between musical sources and the interests, experiences and imaginations of those who encounter them" a narrative of significant change.)

The general failure, I hasten to reiterate, is Editor's, not the authors'. When one is asked to contribute one tile to a mosaic, one bears no responsibility for the whole picture. The only one who could have supplied the dynamic framework is the one in possession of all the tiles. Only that one could have told the others what they needed to add or remove so that gaps and redundancies could be minimized and superfluities mitigated. The chapter authors were justified in assuming that, in the instances I will describe, they were alluding to matters more fully addressed elsewhere in the book. Nor is it their fault that they were asked to produce perhaps the most lifeless and least attractive of all literary genres: the minimally fleshed out list, which mimics narrative but only amasses detail.

And what a careless clutter, those details! Have you always yearned to know the names of the viola players in the Madrid court theater's pit band in 1758? You can look them up on p. 411, along with the bassoonists, the copyist, the keyboard tuner, and the other twenty-three members of the crew. On pp. 408–10 there is a table listing, right out of the author's database, every opera performed in Madrid between 1731 and 1746. While extreme, the chapter on Spanish theater music is not unrepresentative. The chapter on Italian opera, at sixty-nine pages predictably (and rightly) the longest in the book, has a laudable premise: that the proper method for studying the genre is not by composers and not by works but by theaters, for that is the only way in which Italian opera can be fully understood as a social practice. Having stated the premise, however, the author proceeds theater by theater throughout the length and breadth of Europe (or as much of Europe as musicologists acknowledge), detailing the repertory of every last one. Given the way in which famous operas and librettos circulated, you can imagine how much unbearable overlap these many lists incorporate.

Telling details are the gems in any history, but indiscriminately ladled details like these are a morass. And byways can be delightful, but if Sweden was worth a chapter, why then—forgive me—not the Slavic lands? (Gerald Abraham covered them economically and effectively in *NOHM,* so their omission this time seems gratuitously invidious. Are we still smarting over the Battle of Poltava?) From the unexpected chapter on the *serenata* I carried away a useful nugget that I should already have possessed, and for which I am grateful: I learned that the word derives not from *sera* but from *sereno* (Italian for clear sky), referring not to the genre's usual time of day but to its al fresco location. But once the author had made it clear that a *serenata* was defined by its performance location and celebratory purpose rather than by its formal or dramatic content, and that a work called *serenata* could be called lots of other things as well, I had to wonder why it rated a chapter.

Thus the problems that made for the almost uniformly poor reception of the ill-fated *NOHM* continue to bedevil its Cantabrigian successor. They are much more severe this time around because the *NOHM* was generous with musical examples. The authors of its chapters could actually exhibit the artifacts they were describing and classifying, while *CH18* contains a mere ten examples in staff notation totaling twenty-two systems, of which five are found in chapter 5 (how did that one rate?)

and the rest are scattered without apparent rhyme or reason among chapters 16, 17, 18, and 24. Many of the chapters, especially those dealing with lesser-known repertories, were evidently written in the expectation that there would be examples. The lengthy prose descriptions that had to be concocted to take their place are a vain, near-unreadable substitute. Try this one, on a villancico by Antonio Soler:

> The *obertura* is a Vivace and in rounded binary form, followed by a brief, harmonically ambiguous *introducción* in which the voices announce a contest between Fire and Water. The *estribillo*, in a triumphant D major with bows towards F-sharp major and B minor, highlights the contest, with soloists at times urging on Fire while the choir calls for Water's victory. The villancico concludes with a *recitado* and *aria*, the former predictable but with interesting chromaticism. The da capo aria is for solo tenor, usually doubled by the oboe. The tempo is unmarked, but apparently an Andante, with a florid vocal line. There are long melismas and ornaments on appropriate words, and the B section is in the relative minor with vocal trills and semiquavers in the violins to emphasize the word "fire." The polychoral forces join the tenor and orchestra for the repeat of the A section, providing effective punctuation to the elaborate tenor line. (50)

In other words, nothing about the piece is in any way unusual, and the original purpose of illustrating it must have been precisely to show its typicality— something that can be accomplished without a descriptive commentary. Its chapter, like several others, is studded with similar paragraphs, often peppered with complimentary adjectives (*charming, delightful, profoundly beautiful,* and, of course, *forward-looking*) that one is given no chance to corroborate. Again, one commiserates rather than remonstrates with the authors; the publisher made them do it. But one is also aggrieved on their behalf that they got so little help from the astonishingly lax editing. An editor who would print this sentence—

> It is undoubtedly true that the concerto as a genre encouraged both an approachable idiom and direct melodic appeal. (602)

—without, at the very least, lopping off the first five words is no friend of the author, or the reader. Further down on the same page we read, "It is striking that J. C. Bach completely abandoned the strenuous style of his teacher and half-brother ... " A nominal weeding of drone clauses and gratuitous modifiers would have shortened the book, I would guess, by the length of one of its briefer chapters, and removing the pointless descriptive commentaries would have shortened it by another. And who should take the blame for the fact that in one of the chapters in which he appears, Piccinni is shorn of an *n*? (It happens repeatedly, and only in that chapter, so it cannot be a typo.) One has to wonder if anyone actually read the copy before it was handed to the printer. In an age of digital texts and e-mail, not even the printer would have had to read it. I won't say that the chapters I am describing were unreadable, since I did in fact succeed in reading them. But as a reviewer I was constrained by an honor bond, without which I surely would have scamped or skimmed.

But I have been putting off the matters of organization and intellectual substance where I felt, as a reader, the greatest disappointment. As many will have noticed from the listing above, the chapters in *CH18* are ordered according to a time-honored device, the "three styles" (within "two practices")—*ecclesiasticus, cubicularis, theatralis*—proposed by Marco Scacchi in his *Breve discorso sopra la musica moderna* of 1649 (if not earlier) and endlessly parroted thereafter, a list in which the church style was placed first out of mandated decorum. Still, when I saw that the chapters on the *stylus ecclesiasticus* came first I felt a rush of anticipation, recalling Lang's old contention that it was in church music that the secrets of the eighteenth century lay concealed. But the choice turned out to be a miscalculation, since all of the authors agree, having actually surveyed it, that (*pace* Lang) the church music of the eighteenth century was uniformly parasitic on theatrical genres, so that the early chapters constantly foreshadow material that is not fully expounded until the middle of the book; and by the time that essential matter receives its full exposition it abounds in redundancies.

One of these prefigurings epitomizes *CH18*'s most characteristic failing. Discussing the "progressive" Viennese composers (the adjective is Bruce MacIntyre's) whose masses incorporated theatrical forms, Jen-Yen Chen comments that "despite the heated criticism that it sometimes engendered in the late eighteenth century, the assimilation of operatic styles within Viennese sacred music certainly did not begin in this period, as the earlier examination of the work of Fux and Caldara clearly demonstrates" (79). And to this he appends a footnote:

> What was new, though, was the "entry" of comic opera into the church. Cf. Friedrich Nicolai, *Beschreibung einer Reise durch Deutschland und die Schweiz* (Berlin 1784), vol. 4, pp. 544–45: "With respect to composition, Catholic Church music up until several years ago still had much of its own special character. But nowadays operatic music also forces its way into churches everywhere, and, what is worse, [it is] the insipid Italian opera music of the new style. In Vienna, too, I found it all too conspicuous. During many a Credo or Benedictus I knew not whether perhaps I was hearing music from an Italian opera buffa." Cited (in translation) in MacIntyre, *The Viennese Concerted Mass*, p. 54.

This is what in the newsroom they call "burying the lede." The whole "main evolution" toward the Classical or symphonic style—as signaled by Heartz in 1969, and even more emphatically (via an admixture of topical analysis) by the late Wye J. Allanbrook in *The Secular Commedia: Comic Mimesis in Late Eighteenth-Century Music*, left unfinished at her death but published as edited from her notes by Mary Ann Smart and the present writer by the University of California Press in 2014—is presaged within this little footnote. It is not something for which we have only the word of modern scholars and contemporaneous complainers. There is also this pregnant passage from Johann Adam Hiller (1728–1804), who figures very prominently in *CH18* both as a composer and as a reporter or theorist:

> Comic opera is not precisely the best school for singers; but it has become much the best for today's composers. Symphonies, concertos, trios, sonatas—all, nowadays, borrow something of its style, and there would be nothing to object to here, if only the low elements in it and the poor taste could always be avoided with success.[6]

This passage is not quoted in *CH18*, nor, amazing to relate, is the development Hiller describes ever pursued (the result, it seems, of Editor's declared aversion to a "chronological approach" out of a misplaced fear of "overtly teleological developments"). And so throughout the volume we hear about this momentous stylistic transformation only as if inadvertently, as in Dr. Chen's little footnote, or when Margaret R. Butler snatches a moment from her survey of Italian opera centers and theaters to comment, with reference to the comic intermezzo, that "its musical features have been acknowledged as a primary source for the Classical style" (231). An alert editor should have taken this as a hint that something important needed addressing, albeit not under the rubric "Classical" if (as I agree) that is now considered an outmoded signifier. But jettisoning the signified along with the signifier puts one in mind of babies and bathwater.

Another hint, somewhat more oblique, should have come from Claudia Maurer Zenck's chapter, whose title, "German Opera from Reinhard Keiser to Peter Winter," propounds one of those aporias that have so plagued the study of eighteenth-century music. To Zenck's credit, she forthrightly acknowledges that you can't get from Keiser to Winter, that she is telling not one but two quite unrelated stories, and that the second of them, the rise of the singspiel, must remain sketchy owing to the obscurity of its origins. "It has to be remembered," she writes, "that dating depends on the material that survives [in written form] and that the practice of equipping spoken texts with [musical] insertions ... was standard practice both before and after 1752 [the date of the earliest surviving score]" (351). The shape of her chapter replicates in miniature the shape of the century itself when forced into the mold on which Editor insists when he asserts the necessity of preserving a "sense of musical continuity across the century as a whole." Zenck's chapter should have served as a prompt to Editor that his vaunted sense of continuity was imaginary, and that, consequently, there was an elephant in his study.

That elephant virtually trumpets and charges when the author of the chapter on the solo concerto commits a telling gaffe. Writing about the dual impact of

---

6. Johann Adam Hiller in *Wöchentliche Nachrichten und Anmerkungen, die Musik betreffend* 3, no. 8 (22 August 1768): 62; trans. Piero Weiss in *Music in the Western World: A History in Documents*, ed. Piero Weiss and Richard Taruskin, 2nd ed. (Belmont, CA: Thomson-Schirmer, 2008), 239–40.

symphony and sonata on the later eighteenth-century concerto as exemplified by those of J. C. Bach, he observes that the balance between the two parent genres was later upset, "the two sides . . . thrown into still sharper relief by the arrival of the modern symphonic idiom, not to mention the sheer size of the forces involved" (599). Idioms whose development has gone untraced for six hundred pages will inevitably seem suddenly to "arrive" of their own volition. That is probably the most insidious consequence of the misplaced emphasis on genres. When genres take center stage, the stage is effectively depopulated. The result is a history without effective agency—no history at all.

For me the most piquant trace of stories left untold comes at the beginning of the keyboard chapter, one of the most provocative in the book, in one of the infrequent musical examples. Rohan Stewart-MacDonald, the chapter's author, tries extra hard, and quite resourcefully, to construct that unbroken century-spanning continuity that Editor has posited as the book's ideal. One of his keenest points, reminiscent of arguments advanced by Charles Rosen on behalf of Beethoven or Chopin, is that the composers of "serious" keyboard music at the end of the century often went back to J. S. Bach for their inspiration, bringing the century's musical developments full circle. The example (458) juxtaposes the beginning of the sarabande in Bach's second English suite (in A minor) with the beginning of the second movement (*Adagio sostenuto e patetico*) in Clementi's sonata in A minor, op. 50, no. 1. The top voice is identical in the first measure of both pieces, and both pieces proceed by two-measure phrases, so that one is quite willing to accept the author's suggestion that the Clementi was modeled directly on the Bach. "Clementi," he writes, "appears to have borrowed a good deal from the earlier suite movement, including its key, time signature, thematic substance and sarabande style; but he has strenuously reinterpreted the material within the expanded possibilities of a later keyboard idiom, adorning it with chromaticism and intensifying the texture" (457). What he does not report, and does not seem to notice, is that Bach's two phrases are both constructed over the same cadential progression, reiterating an approach to A (bridged the first time by a deceptive cadence). Clementi, meanwhile, separates the two phrases with a beat's caesura and transposes the second so that it cadences not on A but on D. The two phrases are therefore not only complementary and reiterative, but also progressive, in the original meaning (rather than the currently fashionable politicized meaning) of the word. The first phrase is harmonically directed at the second in accordance with the circle of fifths.

Viewed from this angle, the juxtaposition of Bach and Clementi becomes an instantiation of the thesis embodied in Karol Berger's recent monograph, *Bach's Cycle, Mozart's Arrow: An Essay on the Origins of Musical Modernity* (2007). Berger's is perhaps the most radical enunciation of the bifurcated eighteenth century that *CH18* works so hard to elide. I am among those who find Berger's thesis overdrawn, but I find it so mainly with respect to the cycle, not the arrow. The greater discreteness in the phrasing as well as the harmonic trajectory associates Clementi's work as much with the tradition described by Hiller as with those described by Tia DeNora or Anselm Gerhard, the authorities on whom Stewart-MacDonald relies. Unlike Bach, Clementi had comic opera in his heritage; and the author's silence about this aspect of the comparison he has engineered greatly weakens his argument and calls attention once again to the great gaping conceptual hole at the center of *CH18*.

IV

As you see, reading *CH18* left me feeling piqued; and my vexation may seem disproportionate, because I have not yet fully accounted for it. I crossed the threshold from ennui into exasperation when I read the blast of propaganda that lies at the very center of *CH18*, John Irving's "Interlude" on "performance in the eighteenth century." One expects a multiauthored book to be uneven, and one is prepared to forgive the inevitable lapses and contrasts in style, even the longueurs, so long as one is convinced that all concerned have done their best in the face of hindrances. But with Irving's Interlude everything changes, and we hear not the voice of a scholar addressing colleagues but the voice of a Simon Callow or Simon Schama condescending to an NPR or BBC audience of a Sunday morning:

> Take yourself back in time. It is 1700 and you are in the studio of your teacher, Arcangelo Corelli, in Rome. He has just demonstrated to you a passage from his newly published Sonate a Violino e Violone o Cimbalo, and now asks you: "*Non l'intendite parlare?*" "Do you not hear it speak?" In that question, Corelli captures the essentials of musical performance in the eighteenth century. (435)

From what, exactly, is the author quoting here? From the memoirs of the fly on the wall? In a book belonging to a genre in which all citations are presumed to have a source, and the source is to be named, this bit of folklore from Roger North,[7] which was not contemporary with Corelli, and which has become a standby for performance-practice fantasists ever since,[8] is unsourced. From the standpoint of scholarly standards, it is contraband. It then becomes a watchword: "The composer

---

7. Here it is in situ, from *Memoirs of Musick by the Honourable Roger North, Attorney-General to James II*, ed. E. F. Rimbault (London: George Bell, 1846), 128–30: "the works of the great Corelli... became the onely musick relished for a long time.... And no wonder after the Great Master made that instrument speak as it were with humane voice, saying to his scollars—*Non udite lo parlare?* ('Do you not hear it speak?')." North, writing around 1725, is marveling in this passage at the late Corelli's popularity in England, where he never appeared as a player; the Italian phrase, North's invention, refers to the quality of the composition, not the performance.

8. See, for example, Bruce Haynes, *The End of Early Music* (New York: Oxford University Press, 2007), 123.

(who in the eighteenth century was so often also the performer) expected his music to be rendered sensible, expressive, meaningful by *being spoken.*" Thence follows a pretense of corroboration using properly sourced extracts, none of which, however, contains the crucial word, *speak*. The closest the author comes is a bait-and-switch, first equating speech with rhetoric and then quoting the harpsichord treatise by Monsieur de Saint-Lambert, who writes, "Just as a piece of rhetoric [*une pièce d'Éloquence*] is a whole unit which is most often made up of several parts, each of which is composed of sentences, each having a complete meaning, these sentences being composed of phrases, the phrases of words, and the words of letters, so the melody of a piece of music is a whole unit which is always composed of several sections."[9] But this description refers not to the act of speaking but (again) to the structure of the utterance as composed, not performed. Irving's ruling concept, musical speech, is Irving's invention—unless he pinched it from Nikolaus Harnoncourt's *Musik als Klangrede* (1982). He educes from it, as performance-practice scholars were wont to do in the bad old days, a set of prescriptions for the modern performer, couched dogmatically in the language of ethics or morality—*dogmatically* because musical speech is nowhere defined in relation to other possible performance ideals, such as faux-Tartini's *"per ben suonare, bisogna ben cantare"* (to play well you have to sing well), which connotes something rather different about the relationship between violins and voices, and which has a pedigree no worse than faux-Corelli's.[10] Here, in any case, are Irving's exaggerated and overconfident (and impressively arcane) prescriptions:

> The performer (whether or not synonymous with the composer) had a *duty* [italics mine] to make that music speak by reading the signs it contained (whether notated or not) and applying performance conventions to them that differed widely across Europe, and were diversely recorded in vocal and instrumental treatises published throughout the century in many places and in many languages. All such treatises, though, presumed the same thing: that the performer will afford the music a way of being spoken. The instrument or voice was a related tool (combining with the performer's skill) that allowed the music to speak, and to speak appropriately. (435)

A familiar mystique is being constructed, and a footnote appended to the word *appropriately* completes the edifice:

> That is, with a sound that the composer would have conceived. This includes, for example, the sound production of baroque bows on violins with gut strings, perhaps

---

9. *Les Principes de Clavecin* [sic] (1702), trans. and ed. Rebecca Harris-Warwick (Cambridge: Cambridge University Press, 1984), 32; I looked up and supplied the crucial phrase in the original French, which Harris-Warwick included but Irving suppressed.

10. It comes from Pierre Baillot's *Notice sur J.-B. Viotti* (Paris: Hocquet, 1825), an obituary for an eminent "grand pupil" of Tartini, who is said to have heard it from his teacher Pugnani, a representative of the middle generation.

on instruments strung to equal tension, with smaller bridges and with shorter necks set at different angles from violins built later, or else adapted later to suit nineteenth-, twentieth- or twenty-first-century principles and purposes. Or it might include clarinets with only five keys, with wooden mouthpieces and producing a sound whose tuning, colour and intensity varies unequally across the range. Or it might include particular temperaments (by Vallotti, Young, Werckmeister or Kirnberger, say), enhancing the characteristics of tonal inter-relations in a piece, which are rendered uniform—and arguably diminished—in equal temperament. This is not a chapter on organology or a defence of using only original instruments or copies of historical fortepianos, violins, flutes, horns and timpani to perform eighteenth-century music. The music may be (and sometimes is) very well played on modern instruments, of course. But we restrict our opportunities to explore those eighteenth-century sound-worlds and the extent to which they highlight an *unwritten* part of the musical vocabulary of the time by playing the repertory on instruments built for later and different expressive purposes. (435n1)

This is not . . . a defence of using only original instruments. Oh yes it is, but worry not: I am not about to unpack the wonted rhetoric for the millionth time. I don't have to—not only because it has been discredited so many times over by so many writers besides me, including the more responsible performance-practice historians (like José Bowen or Bernard Sherman), but also because Irving's *musealer Klangmaterialismus* (to give it the term Hans Redlich invented for it some seventy-four years ago) is so patently anachronistic with respect to the eighteenth-century performance practices Irving himself describes, which entail the free alteration of the notes and the scoring far beyond any difference the use of "original instruments" could make. Yet even as he reports Geminiani's orchestral arrangements of Corelli's solo sonatas, or Clementi's edition of the same sonatas with supplementary dynamics, or the extent to which Mozart updated Handel at van Swieten's request, or embellished (and expected others to embellish) the solos in his own concertos, or C. P. E. Bach's insistence on spontaneous (or seemingly spontaneous) variation in notes, dynamics, and articulation; and even as he casts fashionable aspersions at "museum-like practices of enshrining and representing the musical canon in concert culture and in intellectual traditions of pedagogy, criticism and scholarship" (445), Irving also insists on the need to "police the style of such embellishments" on behalf of the composer's intentions, and returns obsessively to the matter of original instruments, particularly where his own instrument, the so-called fortepiano, is concerned. He even repeats the canard, which seems to have originated with Malcolm Bilson (not Corelli's contemporary but ours), about the physical impossibility of articulating eighteenth-century music on a modern piano:

> Because of the immediacy of the fortepiano sound, beginning with a pitch, rather than the "thud-then-note" of a modern piano, and also because of the much more

rapid decay of the sound (on a modern piano, the sound "blooms" well after the hammer has struck the massive, high-tension, overwound string, causing it to vibrate, and it then takes some time to die away), the rests Haydn notates so carefully in his score are much more noticeable as silence in distinction to sound. On a fortepiano, then, it becomes possible to "speak" Haydn's music (that is, to interpret it in relation to the sonorous possibilities of an appropriate instrument) as a dialogue between sound and silence, in the course of which music first intrudes into silence's space, then fills it, retreating again at the mid-point before sound once more seems to triumph in the fortissimos, before being cloaked finally in silence. (451)

Reading this, I was carried back to the many splendid demonstrations I've been privileged to witness at which Malcolm Bilson played a phrase from Haydn or Mozart on a fortepiano with all the skill and refinement one expects from him, then donned his boxing gloves and showed that one simply can't get the same exquisite effect from a Steinway. I have always forgiven him his excesses, of course, dear friend that he is, because he is a crusader, not a scholar, and because the cause for which he crusades is so eminently worthy if it wins talented performers to the side of the Classical repertory. I suspect I'd forgive John Irving, too, the moment he sat down to play. Nor can one really fault a hardware salesman for making his pitch. There can be no forgiving Editor, though, for allowing that pitch into such an inappropriate venue. It is one of many ways in which the editing of this volume failed both publisher and readers, and rendered this book a £120/$200 white elephant.

18

Is This a Thing?

The Cambridge History of Music Criticism, ed. Christopher Dingle, Cambridge: Cambridge University Press, 2019, xvi + 826pp.

I

"It would have been easy," writes Christopher Dingle, the editor of *The Cambridge History of Music Criticism* (henceforth *CHMC*), "to start with the rise of the press in northern Europe, broadly coinciding with the Industrial Revolution, and concentrate on the principal centres of Western art music." Instead he has chosen, he says, a path of greater effort and reward, its purview expanded to encompass whatever may be described as "the chronicle and discourse of music," so that it might potentially "cover all music, of all times, all places and all types where there is evidence of discussion and reflection upon it." Conceived in this broader way, he writes, "a history of music criticism itself becomes an alternate history of music, considering those who do the observing, chronicling and critiquing rather than the object of their musings" (3).

I wish he had taken the easy path. Confinement to the area of music reviewing—which (as the editor admits) is what we mean by "music criticism" in usual parlance—would have defined it as an activity with a traceable history, tellable in terms of material and social affordances, institutions, issues, and consequences, and one that will be of special interest and relevance to readers of this journal. Widening the scope to indefinable infinity produces haze and confusion, ensures a largely anecdotal coverage with an unwarranted though irresistible emphasis on individual personalities ("those who do," etc.), and, of course, is doomed to failure, like any

Review of *The Cambridge History of Music Criticism*, ed. Christopher Dingle, *Nineteenth-Century Music Review* 19 (2022): 317–61 (https://doi.org/10.1017/S1479409821000239).

attempt to encompass the unencompassable. So the book must begin with an editorial disclaimer—"All histories are partial. All histories are simplifications" (1)—which rehearses a truism that could have gone without saying, and probably would have but for the editor's evident bad conscience about his governing decision. And it leaves authors as well as readers in a quandary of inclarity as to what to provide or expect. One author, Mark Berry, actually spoofs the situation, beginning his chapter ("The Feuilleton and Beyond: Criticism in the Federal Republic of Germany and Austria after the Second World War") with three pages of Hamletic maundering (what to include? where to begin?) that might not amuse readers as much as it did author and editor (590–92). But it does underscore the volume's most persistent problem: continually deferring an answer to the question, *Is this a thing?*

There are precedents. The large, multiply authored article "Criticism" in the *New Grove 2* has a preamble by Fred Everett Maus that chimes almost faultlessly with the Introduction to *CHMC*:

> Music criticism may be defined broadly or narrowly. Understood narrowly, it is a genre of professional writing, typically created for prompt publication, evaluating aspects of music and musical life. Musical commentary in newspapers and other periodical publications is criticism in this sense. More broadly, it is a kind of thought that can occur in professional critical writing but also appears in many other settings.[1]

And, like Prof. Dingle's Introduction, it goes on to announce that it will travel the broad way "in order to see the continuity among various activities of musical interpretation and evaluation." But that continuity, not observed but merely asserted, is fictitious. It gives rise not to a narrative but to an arbitrary list (or parataxis, if that makes you feel better)—which may do for a dictionary article, but not for a book that calls itself a history, not even if its components are ordered chronologically. Prof. Dingle has marshaled the contents of *CHMC* into six parts, enumerated with Roman numerals, plus a Postlude contemplating the possible future. Part I ("The Early History of Music Criticism") comprises six chapters devoted to periods ostensibly antedating "The Rise of the Press" (Part II), following which the subject actually does effectively narrow down in the main to what we all know as music reviewing. Thus it was for the sake of these earliest chapters, on writings that were never called criticism in their day, that all the disclaimers had to be made and clear definitions sacrificed. (The earliest use of the actual term seems to have been Johann Mattheson's in his journal *Critica musica*, from 1722.) As it turns out, moreover, only two of them—"Speaking of Plainsong in the Middle Ages" by Christopher Page and "Music Criticism in the Late-Medieval and Renaissance Era" by

---

1. Fred Everett Maus, Glenn Stanley, Katharine Ellis, et al., "Criticism," *Grove Music Online*, 2001, https://doi.org/10.1093/gmo/9781561592630.article.40589.

Stefano Mengozzi—really do cover topics that precede the rise of the press. Were they worth their price?

Why plainsong to begin with? Just because it is the traditional starting point for "histories of Western music"? The best the very resourceful author can do to justify the chapter he was assigned is to ferret out words like *dulcedo* (sweetness) and *lascivia* (gratification) in descriptions of liturgical chanting. He works hard to educe from them a dialectical pair, portending an early round in the contest between ethics and aesthetics (but where is St. Augustine?), or perhaps, more improbably, a scuffle, centuries *avant la lettre,* in the name of aesthetic autonomy. Meanwhile, I thought it strange that while mentioning Boethius, who died about two decades before Pope Gregory I was born, as an early model of "musical teaching and codification" (11), Prof. Page neglects to tell his readers what I would have expected to be his chapter's big news, that at the top of the musical food chain—above the *citharode* who plays or sings the song, and above the *poeta* who makes the song, both of whom *a musicae scientiae intellectu seiuncti sunt* ("are shut off from an understanding of musical science")—this late-classical philosopher placed the one *quod judicandi peritiam sumit* ("who can judge from experience"), and who is therefore the true *musicus* (musician). In a word as yet uncoined, he means a critic. Never again would that third one—he's talking, dear reader, about the likes of you and me—be rated so high. But Prof. Page never mentions him or defines his role.

It is Prof. Mengozzi who, almost in spite of himself, manages to broach a workable definition of *CHMC*'s titular subject, by first proposing and then shaking off the notion, popular among composers and theorists, that music criticism is "closely aligned" with their domains—even to the extent that (as Mengozzi paraphrases Maus) "the very act of assembling tones to create a melody implies a conscious act of self-criticism on the part of the musician," since any selection implies rejection (25). But if that is all it is, then music criticism as a separate activity would seem devoid of a *raison d'être* (as theorists and composers might readily agree). Happily, Prof. Mengozzi's very next sentence, while intended as amplification, finally narrows things down usefully: criticism properly so called does not concern the making alone (that being grammar), but is motivated by "the awareness of the affective power of organized sound upon listeners," so that it becomes study of "meticulous quantifications of the structures of musical pitch (scales, intervals, proportions, temperament, etc.) in conjunction with a consideration of the psychological and social effects of those same structures" (25).

Criticism, in short, and in keeping with Molino's once-popular *tripartition sémiologique,* requires, and is defined by, responsiveness to "esthesic" concerns. And, it also follows, though no author says so outright within the covers of *CHMC,* that theory (like censorship) can be a priori, while criticism, whether positive or negative, is necessarily a posteriori. Thus, to pick two evaluative texts that Prof. Mengozzi offers as examples of criticism, Pope John XXII's bull *Docta sanctorum,* warning prescriptively against minims and hockets, does not really qualify according to his criterion, while Tinctoris's *Liber de arte contrapuncti*, with its *obiter dicta* on solecisms in specific compositions by Faugues, Caron, or Busnoys (not to mention its blanket dismissal of any music more than forty years old), can be fairly so called—as can Glareanus's *Dodekachordon*, with its enthusiastic *Wunderkabinett* of a last chapter, *De symphonetarum ingenio* ("On the Skillfulness of Composers").

So much for prehistory. As early as the third chapter, the press starts surreptitiously to rise, and we get the first of several surveys dealing with writings that are (on unspecified terms) dubbed "musical discourse" or "music criticism" in Italy, France, Britain, and the germanophone lands up to the eighteenth century. That division of the material by countries or languages will recur many times; but alongside this potential superfluity there remain shortages to report. The bane of random or haphazard coverage is never dispelled. I was surprised to find that, once the period of actual music reviewing is reached, there is virtually no attempt to cover those other kinds of "chronicle and discourse, . . . discussion and reflection" on which the editor so insists in his introduction, including some very conspicuous types that have actually been called "criticism" since the nineteenth century.

There is, for example, no treatment, nor is cognizance even taken, of what the nineteenth century termed *Stilkritik*, or "style criticism," which came to musicography with the founding documents of *Musikwissenschaft*, and which over the next century and a half produced a huge literature that is still current, if attenuated. Its chief early protagonist, Guido Adler, who introduced it as a curricular subject in 1885, and who fifty years later authored an article on it that was still prescribed to musicology novices when I was one, appears only once in *CHMC*, when Kelly St. Pierre, the author of a chapter on Czech and Slovak music criticism, casually records his appointment to the faculty of the German University in Prague (443).

Nor is there any discussion of a *querelle* through which many of the older readers of this review will have lived, when Joseph Kerman, first in an article called "A Profile for American Musicology" (1965) and then in a book called *Contemplating Music: Challenges to Musicology* (1985), made strenuous efforts to get American musical scholarship to incorporate the type of ahistorical (or transhistorical) evaluative and explicative writing that in literature went, beginning in the 1940s, under the name of New Criticism ("the way of looking at art," in Kerman's definition, "that tries to take into account the meaning [music] conveys, the pleasure it initiates, and the value it assumes, for us today").[2] Kerman is mentioned only twice in *CHMC*, both times in passing, first as a commentator on musical canon-formation ("repertoires are determined by performers, canons by critics," quoted on pp. 232–33) and the other time with a reference to his "influential and controversial" book

---

2. J. Kerman, "A Profile for American Musicology," *Journal of the American Musicological Society* 18 (1965): 61–69, at 63.

of 1985, in what Kerman would surely have regarded as the bizarre context of Soviet critical debates, and without any description of the controversies it inspired at home (581).

I thought for a moment that new-critical modes were being adumbrated as early as *CHMC*'s third chapter, Carrie Churnside's "Musical Discourse in Italy, 1500–1800," when Baldassare Castiglione's *Il cortegiano* (Book of the Courtier, 1528) and Cosimo Bartoli's gloss on Dante (*Ragionamenti accademici sopra alcuni luoghi difficili di Dante*, 1567) are adduced as "discussions that took place between music-loving amateurs" (44) and I recalled R. P. Blackmur, Kerman's secret mentor, whose celebrated, "winsomely snobbish" definition of criticism was "the formal discourse of an amateur."[3] But no, Dr. Churnside makes straight for Luigi Dentice's *Duo dialoghi della musica* (1552) "because," she writes, "it contains an early concert review" (45)—and from then on it is the nascent professional commentariat (alongside the still ill-fitting theorists) that commands her interest, and that of practically all her fellow authors.

Finally, discussion of the vast congeries of viewpoints and methods that travels under the umbrella of Critical Theory, which has informed so much public and academic writing about music in the past half-century, is confined to a single chapter, Mark Berry's on West German and Austrian music criticism in the aftermath of the Second World War, as if that were the extent of its relevance. (T. W. Adorno gets one additional mention, when Raffaele Pozzi, in a chapter on Italy in the twentieth century, credits him with "an important role in the renovation of music criticism in Italy," though without specifying its nature [621].)

II

The editor might have forestalled these complaints had he only announced that *CHMC* would omit coverage of academic criticism. But such an announcement, it seems, would have contradicted too flatly the brave assertions on which the enterprise had been staked; and so unresolved issues bedevil the book's range of topics and their treatment at every turn. In the end, the unannounced and unjustified limitations are dwarfed by much more conspicuous redundancy and supererogation, by-products of what probably seemed a self-evident principle by which to subdivide and organize the contents and commission the chapters.

That principle is nationality. Nations—"national schools"—are the primary categories into which art has been sorted (concert programs constructed, museums hung, anthologies compiled) since the late eighteenth century, when concerts,

---

3. Richard P. Blackmur, "A Critic's Job of Work," in idem, *The Double Agent: Essays in Craft and Elucidation* (New York: Arrow Editions, 1935), 269; the lovely characterization is from James Coakley, review of *The Esthetic of Jean Cocteau* by Lydia Crowson, *Comparative Drama* 15 (1981): 283.

museums, and printed anthologies began proliferating. Ironically enough, its conceptual source is *Stilkritik,* one of the critical practices so conspicuously scamped in *CHMC,* first theorized by Johann Joachim Winckelmann and already taken for granted in the earliest mappings of music history. It would seem only natural, then, that if you are constructing "an alternate history of music," as the editor of *CHMC* has described it, you will proceed analogously. But in a multiply authored book that combines the national principle with a periodized chronology, this turns out to have been a major miscalculation. With one exception, every section of the book is repetitively subdivided into chapters representing nations, among which, as in a United Nations council, there are permanent members and a random assortment of transients. We have already seen that the first section of the book contains chapters on Italy, France, Britain, and Germany. The second ("The Rise of the Press") has chapters on Italy, France, Britain, Germany, and Russia. The fourth ("Entering the Twentieth Century") has chapters on France, Britain, Germany, the United States and Canada, Portugal, Spain, Norway, Hungary, and Czechoslovakia. The fifth ("New Areas") introduces new musical genres as they begin to be written about, but the nationality principle persists, with chapters on the United States, Cuba, and Singapore. The sixth and last ("Developments since the Second World War") reverts to chapters on Italy, France, Britain, Germany/Austria, the USSR, and the United States. The third section ("Critical Influence and Influences") is the exceptional one, organized by issues rather than nations: canon formation (Laura Hamer), recordings (the editor), and women (Hamer again), first as critics and then as objects of critique.

That exceptional section is also, not by accident, exceptionally interesting and rewarding to read. Elsewhere, wheels are constantly reinvented as author after author tells the same stories of burgeoning public spheres, exploding (later receding) print cultures, mushrooming nationalism, political and commercial pressures, factions, aesthetic and stylistic disputes, critical role-playing, gatekeeping, canon constructing, ethical dilemmas, contests over authenticity, and so on, none of them coterminous with national boundaries—*especially* not nationalism. And though invented again and again, none is a complete and viable wheel, for in their confinement to a single bailiwick (and their probable—quite reasonable—assumption that basic matters will have been attended to up front) the various authors give partial and (inevitably) contradictory views, passing along to readers the task of synthesis that a single author would have been obliged to perform, or that a fully functioning editor might have undertaken in his introduction.

Should they choose to accept it, moreover, the readers' mission is far from easy. Synthesis comes slowly, and not without wasted effort. Only in rare cases do authors even explicitly announce their purviews. Not until chapter 33 ("Music Criticism in France since the Second World War" by Christopher Brent Murray), practically at book's end, do we get a really explicit—and oh so welcome—

definition of scope, the author informing us that he will address "writing in the general, non-academic press," embracing, besides reviews, "editorial pieces, reporting on musical life and... interviews," but not "philosophical criticism destined for specialised, intellectual readerships" (648). In other chapters the purview must be laboriously deduced. These difficulties all stem from that original, never-defended decision to order the contents of the book country by country. My guess is that, fitting as well as it did with an anachronistic institutional habit, it promised ease in identifying contributors. But the book might have critiqued the old received idea rather than reflexively endorse it. As it is, I cannot imagine anyone but a reviewer reading straight through, chapter by chapter, a narrative of such unendurable inefficiency. The more I slogged, the more insistently the question nagged, how else might the book have been structured?

One of the "national" chapters unexpectedly suggested an alternative model—but only, in apparent paradox, when the nation was filtered out of it. Paulo Ferreira de Castro's short chapter on Portugal, a country whose inclusion I would not have predicted, and whose critics (and composers) I would be hard-pressed to name, is assigned to the section on the early twentieth century; but it is actually concerned with the whole history of Portuguese music-critical activity from its nineteenth-century beginnings to the present, and is therefore, despite its compactness, one of the few chapters to raise a full range of historical issues. Its author, a Portuguese musicologist trained in Great Britain (and with an interest, as I have reason to know, in Russian music), has sufficient international perspective to see the situation in his small country as typical (or perhaps synecdochical) rather than distinctive. "In Portugal," he writes, "*as elsewhere* the development of music criticism has been closely linked to the flourishing of the periodical press" (318; my italics), and that sense of *pars pro toto* is maintained throughout. Possibly because he recognizes his country (at least since the time of Domenico Scarlatti) as receiving territory, devoid of bulking and distracting personalities, he allows big general themes—"questions of authorship and readership," as he puts it (310)—to emerge the more saliently. As a result, his chapter, which is more likely than most to be overlooked by those who (following the editor's implicit advice) consult this book as an adjunct to the study of their favorite musical repertoires, actually provides a better introduction to the main issues than the editor's Introduction.

The chapter's analysis is especially illuminating because it is deconstructive, in the precise and technical meaning of that grossly overused adjective. "Whatever form it may assume," de Castro writes, "music criticism tends to thrive on the production of differential schemata (beautiful versus ugly, imitation versus imagination, foreign versus national, traditional versus modern, serious versus frivolous, etc." (319). He has a bit of fun adding binaries as he goes along, establishing increasing distance, either by the use of scare quotes ("'artificial' versus 'expressive'") or by actual decoding: "'Italianism' versus 'Germanism' as easily politicized ciphers for 'routine' (conservatism) and 'progress' (evolution, 'the future') respectively"—or, most generally, by casting the role of the critic "either as a reinforcer of prejudice or as a producer of difference," then adding that "the fact that these and other polarities often disguise larger issues of authority and power should come as no surprise" (330).

He thus broaches what I have always regarded as the most important difference among critics, the ancient contest between those who regard themselves as the public's preceptor—or what Simon Frith, the sociologist of popular music, defines two hundred pages later as "critics who see their task as giving shape to a potential taste community" (525n80)—and those who see themselves as the voice or public spokesperson for existing communities, a dichotomy that grew directly out of the old dialogues of ancients and moderns (as reported as early as the third chapter of *CHMC*, e.g. in disputes between Pietro della Valle and Lelio Giudiccioni over the merits of Frescobaldi [49]).

It is, in any case, always a good question to ask of critics, regardless of time or place, whether they come before or after the taste communities for which they purport to speak. Not that they will always answer truthfully or correctly, or even know the answer; and not that one can always tell the difference. But the question is clarifying. Neither position is necessarily to be preferred; either can be abused, and abuse often takes the form of a false flag.

Take, for example, "Muddle Instead of Music" (*Sumbur vmesto muzïki*) on Shostakovich's *The Lady Macbeth of the Mtsensk District*, the unsigned *Pravda* editorial of 28 January 1936, probably the twentieth century's most famous music review, which Peter J. Schmelz analyzes in his chapter, "Music Criticism in the USSR from Asafyev to Cherednichenko." For whom did it speak? *Pravda* was the voice of the Soviet Communist Party, but the Party claimed to speak for the people. Maxim Gorky fastened on precisely this point in a complaint about the article he addressed directly to Stalin, in a letter that became public in 1993, writing that "critics should give a technical assessment of Shostakovich's music," so as to instruct and educate listeners and thus create a proper taste community for Socialist Realist art. Instead, "what the *Pravda* article did was to authorise hundreds of talentless people, hacks of all kinds, to persecute Shostakovich" (quoted on p. 576), and this because it couched its complaint on behalf not of qualified preceptors but—falsely—on behalf of the existing audience (ignoring the fact that the opera had had a wildly successful two-year run by the time of the "review"). "The composer apparently never considered the problem of what the Soviet audience looks for and expects in music," reads the unsigned indictment (now known to have been written by the notorious David Zaslavsky, dubbed "*Pravda*'s journalistic revenge weapon" by *Time* magazine),[4] catering rather to "the effete 'formalists' who had lost all their

---

4. "Russia: Red on White," *Time*, 18 December 1944, http://content.time.com/time/subscriber /article/0,33009,778271,00.html.

wholesome taste, ignoring the demand of Soviet culture that all coarseness and savagery be abolished from every corner of Soviet life."[5] This pretense, writes Prof. Schmelz, initiated and empowered "an attack on the elites in the name of the (anonymous) masses" (577).

The same ploy can of course be used as an incentive as well as a deterrent. The biography of Nikolai Myaskovsky by Alexei Ikonnikov, which has long been available in English, contains an example I have long been dying to quote. It comes, ostensibly, from a peasant (or "collective farmer–pensioner" [*kolkhoznik-invalid*], as he is identified in the original Russian text) named Sergei Ivanovich Korsakov, who, it seems, wrote a letter to the musicologist Arnold Alexandrovich Alshvang, who passed it along to Myaskovsky, who passed it along to Ikonnikov. After listening to a broadcast of Myaskovsky's folksy, bouncy Eighteenth Symphony (in C major, composed in 1937, the most intense year of Stalinist political terror, and dedicated to the twentieth anniversary of the October Revolution), Korsakov wrote: "I simply can't tell you how much I enjoy it. It's so full of vim and gusto, and brimful of good spirits. Especially in the first movement. There's a particularly fine passage there, you know, which is repeated three or four times, and occurs again in the finale. Of course, you can guess which passage I mean.... That particular passage from the first movement is in my ears all the time."[6] In his cover letter to the composer Alshvang wrote that his peasant correspondent "expresses fresher and more profound opinions than many of our would-be pundits."[7] How I would love to see that letter!

This little digression into Soviet territory will, I hope, signal the range of fruitful issues broached *en passant* by Paulo de Castro's unpretentious little chapter on Portugal. Similarly transferable is the chronological trajectory the chapter describes. Of the conditions that summoned the music-critical profession into existence, Prof. de Castro writes that "in the inaugural issue of *O trovador*," the earliest specialist music periodical in Portugal (1855), "the pianist and composer Emilio Lami denounced the lack of musically authoritative voices in the press, calling for a more professional kind of criticism at a time when, as he put it, music

---

5. "Sumbur vmesto muzïki," *Pravda*, 28 January 1936, https://sutalkmusic.files.wordpress.com/2012/11/muddle-instead-of-music.pdf.

6. "За последнее время я по уши влюбился в некоторые новые произведения, и среди них первое место занимает XVIII симфония Мясковского. До чего она мне нравится, и сказать не умею. В ее музыке много жизнерадостности и задорного веселья. Особенно в первой части (там, знаете, есть такой замечательный один пассажик, который повторяется раза 3–4, присутствует он и в финале. Вы, конечно, догадываетесь, о каком пассаже я говорю) ... (А пассаж из первой части так вот около уха и вьется)."

7. "... будучи человеком одаренным, высказывает суждения более свежие и глубокие, чем наша 'присяжная критика'" (Alexei Alexandrovich Ikonnikov, *Khudozhnik nashikh dney N. Ya. Myaskovskiy* [Moscow: Muzgiz, 1940], 240; translated from the Russian as Alexei A. Ikonnikov, *Myaskovsky: His Life and Work* [New York: Philosophical Library, 1946], 59–60).

was increasingly regarded as a social necessity rather than a mere pleasure, thus staking out a new position for the musical specialist in the cultural sphere" (322). Similarly economical is the characterization of Fernando Lopes Graça (1906–94), nominated as the foremost Portuguese critic of the twentieth century, whose writings are said to "touch upon virtually all the major issues of Portuguese musical life," to wit: "the social responsibility of the artist, the conflicting forces of nationalism and cosmopolitanism, the impact of modernism on the European periphery, the political uses of folklore and the vexed question of 'Portugueseness' in music" (328).

These pithy sentences sketch a pair of historical *Zustände,* as the Germans would say, evoking both a situation and its informing conditions, and their juxtaposition gives a sense of the historical movement from the mid-nineteenth century, when the enhanced status of music and of musicians elevated the potential status of a writer on music (who was then positioned to lobby in turn for the musical profession), to the mid-twentieth, when political authority forcibly impinged (*as elsewhere*) on cultural affairs. A wealth of recurrent topics—power, professionalism, social necessity, social responsibility, social status, pleasurableness, contemporaneity, nationality—that will resurface in practically every chapter of the book, are set forth in an unusually dialectical (i.e., mutually implicative) fashion. (And, once again, this applies particularly to nationality, the author taking care to remind us that—as in all "peripheral" lands—"the label 'national' was . . . tantamount to bad publicity for a product of Portuguese art or industry" [325]—until it became the very opposite.) The chapter's conclusion sketches a third *Zustand,* the one that every author must confront whose remit extends into the twenty-first century, with its "crisis of the traditional press and the expansion of so-called social media," as reflected in "the shrinking of space given to music reviews in generalist newspapers, partly replaced since the late 1990s by digital platforms such as the weblog ('blog')—whose ephemerality, incidentally, renders listings instantly obsolete and may prove a huge challenge to documentation and research purposes in the future" (330).

In its tandem of comprehensiveness and concision, Prof. de Castro's chapter provides the best general enunciation to be found within *CHMC* of constant themes (each of them worthy of chapter-length treatment), and is one of the few that convey a dynamic sense both of temporal evolution and of interaction between agents and affordances. I would prescribe it for perusal alongside whichever other ones individual readers may be prompted by their particular interests to consult. Many such chapters are informative and well written and can profitably serve the adjunctive purpose the editor foresees for them as components within "an alternate history of music," but they will do so the more effectively within the framework de Castro's chapter supplies.

III

Those who follow their interests, however, may miss the best fruit on this tree. Shzr Ee Tan's "Cultural Anxieties, Aspirational Cosmopolitanism and Capacity Building: Music Criticism in Singapore," a synchronic essay set in what at the time of its writing was the present, and with an Asian purview to boot, is a chapter that readers of this journal might be especially prone to overlook; but it is perhaps the best granular description I've read of the critic's actual job. Its actual subject is the globalized musical culture toward which many of the later chapters in *CHMC* gesture—and its discontents. That certainly earns it a place of singular pertinence within a historical, chiefly Eurocentric survey. An exercise in retrospective participant-observation by an ethnomusicologist who came to academic work from a journalistic career covering Western classical music for a Singapore newspaper (the *Straits Times*), it focuses on the quotidian push and pull of working life: pressures and resistance, blandishment and risk, pursuit of livelihood and status, with emblematic twenty-first-century precarity looming over all. The opening anecdote recounts the reprisals to which the author was subjected after publishing an insufficiently positive review of a performance by a young violinist with a politically connected mother, and proceeds from there to a general consideration of her job as "a negotiation of subjectivities governed by bigger ecosystems of musical, cultural, socio-economic and political activity" (545).

Having left active employment within these systems and gained some critical distance, she views her former profession in terms of its compromises. Critics, in her telling, are poised between "networks of local listeners" and "global conglomerates of distribution and consumption," communicating with both "via multinational media companies and the Internet" (548). Determined to transcend simple binary "opposition between industry and critic," and relying for her initial formulation on the pioneer cultural ecologist John Holden, she "posits music criticism within 'connections, symbiosis, feedback loops, and flows of people, product, ideas and money'" (545). The story she tells is one of contest among critics for fluctuating privilege and prestige, and of service to competing masters. I can hardly imagine a better short sociological take on music as public activity, or on music critics as mediators, and I write as one whose eye is always out for such things. No reader should miss it.

It is particularly refreshing because it follows another chapter, "Working in the Cool Capitalism Complex: The Role of Critics in the World Music Field" by Timothy D. Taylor, which treats similar content in the loftiest sociologese, the most immediate effect of which is to finesse agency, the very thing Dr. Tan most vividly illuminates. To get the full clarifying effect of her account, even to the extent that I have quoted it thus far, compare Prof. Taylor's topic paragraph:

The rise of world music and its (continuing) genrefication and fieldification was thus the result of a series of processes of the industrialisation and management of the world musics by the international music industry. The rise of specialty labels, specialty magazines and websites, the rise of a system of charts and awards, were all part of this institutionalisation. Criticism had and continues to have an important role to play in all of these processes, as it does with any field of cultural production. (531)

All these -*ation* words, freezing (or friezing) action into abstract nouns! "Rise," whether noun or verb, is a handy lever (along with "emerge" or "emergence") for removing people from the scene (unless one holds with Mitt Romney that corporations, or international music industries, "are people, my friend"); and even "production," which does imply a producer, is identified not with persons but, à la Bourdieu, with a collective "field." It will not be easy to define the role of any actual person within such an impersonal or depopulated world, especially when the word *critic* is applied to the assembler of a passage like this:

> Nowadays the music you play needs to be sophisticated but not obtrusive, easy to take but not at all bland, unfamiliar without being patronizing. World music gives the American listener a sense of freedom from the constraints of standardized Anglo-American pop. . . . World music is both entertaining and different. It takes the listener to a place where the world's various cultures meet happily and in the spirit of festival. It is a force for understanding and goodwill in an increasingly dark world. (Peter Spencer, *World Beat: A Listener's Guide to Contemporary World Music on CD* [2007], quoted on p. 532)

That is advertising copy. And though I put it more bluntly than Prof. Taylor does, my characterization accords with his. He defines the writing of "critics" like Peter Spencer as an "attempt to make a product or a commodity more than just a product or a commodity, but a trusted entity that enjoys complex relationships with consumers, involving memories of past experiences of pleasure, community with others, feelings of satisfaction and self-satisfaction, membership in a special club of consumers, and much more" (538). Such hype, while distinct from what I would call criticism (as a priori is distinct from a posteriori), is certainly not without cultural significance. Prof. Taylor shows it at work, as paratext, in the most interesting part of his chapter, tracing the transformation of the word *authenticity* from a label connoting purity to one connoting hybridity (533–36 passim). What ultimately defines the "critics' role in what one could call the Cool Capitalism Complex," as Prof. Taylor sums it up, is their usefulness in branding,

> since they, and others who discover or create and promote the hip, cool, edgy, trendy, are slowly destabilising cultural hierarchies in the West and, perhaps especially, in the United States, as cultural capital as defined by knowledge of the fine arts declines in importance as a way of displaying and maintaining cultural superiority and dominance. Such knowledge is increasingly replaced by knowledge of the hip and the cool,

a new form of capital measured by one's familiarity with the latest indie rock album or independent film, and even, sometimes, knowledge of an obscure world music artist. And with this knowledge increasingly comes cultural capital in the neoliberal world. (541)

If this transcends the crude "opposition between industry and critic," which Dr. Tan's chapter seeks to complicate, it is only because Prof. Taylor sees no contest at all. Once the dread word *neoliberal* is out, moreover, and the Cool Capitalism Complex duly tainted, it can be explicitly denounced for its complicity in the "promotion of musicians thought to be cool, or potentially cool, and its discarding or ignorance of many other musicians" and morally equated with "the well-known Military Industrial Complex," known for "making far too many people far too much money in the United States and promoting endless war." Really? The one is "no less pernicious" (541) than the other? Such overheated overstatement oversimplifies the problem which both Dr. Tan's and Prof. Taylor's chapters identify, namely co-option.

Most of us can name prominent critics—Michael Steinberg, Nicholas Kenyon, for two—who have gone over to the other side and become salesmen (Steinberg on behalf of the San Francisco Symphony and later the Minnesota Orchestra, Kenyon to run the London Proms, the BBC music division, and currently the Barbican Center);[8] but all critics are under pressure to play ball with the moneyed interests of whose products they are the appointed (or self-appointed) judges, and the moneyed interests don't always wear identifying badges when one encounters them in daily life. In place of Prof. Taylor's static condemnation of a fait accompli, Dr. Tan shows us the process and pressures of co-option at ground level and in real time.

The paper for which she worked, she reports, recognized four "music beats": (1) Anglo-American Pop/Rock, (2) Chinese/Asian Pop (broken down into "Mandopop, Cantopop, K-pop and J-pop"), (3) Classical Music (both Western European and Chinese Conservatory), and (4) Jazz and World Music (one beat, not two), as she lists them. The first and third (not the fourth!) represented "supercultures," and the other two "took place under the collective guise of secondary 'beats,' with genres taxonomised along class-based hierarchies of listenership and ethnic-based categorisations of 'other' musics" (554–55). The relative prestige of critics followed that of their beats. But exceptions followed their own rules, which Dr. Tan diagnoses according to a criterion she dubs "aspirational cosmopolitanism" (547). Thus,

state or classist agenda could trump potential readership: an editor could privilege print space for a national ensemble over a small community group, or tokenistically

---

8. Nick Kenyon's salesmanship is on full display in his *The Life of Music: New Adventures in the Western Classical Tradition* (New Haven, CT: Yale University Press, 2021). Steinberg, a subtler huckster, produced a series of comprehensive "Listener's Guides," all published by Oxford University Press (*The Symphony* in 1998, *The Concerto* in 2000, *Choral Masterworks* in 2008).

highlight projects operating under the nation-building banner of multicultural performance. They could also make space for connoisseur jazz reviews in order to lift the newspaper's cultural "tone." (555)

All of which tended to lure critics into civic boosterism, touting "the international reputation of the city as a focal point for the arts" (552). The pressure was evidently at its greatest in Singapore, a "translocal and international" city-state, as Dr. Tan puts it, with a sovereign foreign policy (548). But critics in the United States are hardly immune to such suasions, and there have been occasional notorious casualties (e.g., Donald Rosenberg of the Cleveland *Plain Dealer,* who was barred in 2008 from reviewing the Cleveland Orchestra and ultimately, in 2013, laid off). Nor is such conflict necessarily between management and labor: it is easily internalized. Dr. Tan quotes a former colleague: "If it's a lousy concert, whether local or foreign, I'd rather not review" (552–53). Have we not all felt this way at times, when asked, say, to review manuscripts for publishers or serve on ad hoc committees?

IV

Another sort of internalized pressure that in music criticism still counts as a dirty secret, though it has had a thorough airing in metacritical writing on the visual arts, is the one Dr. Tan calls "overcomprehension" after the film theorist Robert B. Ray, a form of subtle (or not-so-subtle) intimidation that leads critics "to praise everything, because *anything* could be the next Elvis" (556). Ray traces it back to Théophile Gautier's review of the 1868 Salon, in which an aging aesthete, well used to the comfortable risk-aversion of snobbery (which counsels omnibus dismissal), reacted with nervous banter to the discourse of an avant-garde that held incomprehensibility and concomitant critical rejection to be infallible earnests of aesthetic value:

> Faced with this paradox in painting, one may seem, even without admitting it, to be frightened lest one be taken for a philistine, a bourgeois, a Joseph Proud'homme, a cretin with a fancy for miniatures and copies of paintings on porcelain, or worse still, as an old fogey who finds merit in David's *Rape of the Sabines*. . . . It is probable that the pictures of Courbet, Manet, Monet, and others of their ilk conceal beauties that elude us, with our old romantic manes already shot with silver threads.[9]

---

9. Théophile Gautier, "Salon de 1868," *Moniteur universel,* 11 May 1868, quoted (differently translated) in Robert B. Ray, "Critical Senility vs. Overcomprehension: Rock Criticism and the Lesson of the Avant-Garde," in *Pop Music and the Press,* ed. Steve Jones (Philadelphia: Temple University Press, 2002), 72–78, at 75; original text (cited from Bettina B. Cenerelli, *Dichtung und Kunst: Die "Transposition d'art" bei Théophile Gautier* [Stuttgart: J. B. Metzler, 2000], 254): "En face de ce paradoxe en peinture, il semble qu'on ait peur, si on ne l'admet pas, de passer pour un philistin, un bourgeois, un Joseph Proud'homme, un goîtreux aimant les miniatures et les copies sur porcelaine, ou pis encore, un retardataire trouvant

In classical music one would speak of the next *Eroica* or *Rite of Spring*: just ask Nicolas Slonimsky, whose old favorite, the *Lexicon of Musical Invective* (originally published in 1953 and since reprinted in many editions), is probably the heaviest, most concentrated preemptive guilt-trip ever administered to immunize the new from hostile critique. (It was not without models: Slonimsky himself refers to the *Schimpflexikon* [mock-dictionary], a German genre whose outstanding musical representative was a compilation of anti-Wagnerian abuse assembled by Wilhelm Tappert in 1877, whose interminable title Slominsky took characteristic pleasure in citing: *Ein Wagner-Lexicon, Wörterbuch der Unhöflichkeit enthaltend grobe, höhnende, gehässige und verleumderische Ausdrücke welche gegen den Meister Richard Wagner, seine Werke und seine Anhänger von den Feinden und Spöttern gebraucht worden sind zur Gemütsergötzung in müssigen Stunden gesammelt* [A Wagner lexicon, dictionary of rudeness containing coarse, scornful, hateful, and slanderous expressions which were used against the master Richard Wagner, his works, and his followers by enemies and scoffers, collected in idle hours purely for pleasure].)

Dr. Tan discusses overcomprehension with cool and humorous detachment, the way she discusses everything. Less self-aware contributors to *CHMC* often display its symptoms. They show up right on schedule in the opening chapter of Part IV, "Entering the Twentieth Century," when Mark McKnight, the author of the chapter titled "Music Criticism in the United States and Canada up to the Second World War," starts noting, as a means of separating sheep from goats, how "receptive to modern trends" a critic showed himself to be (313). His main sheep, predictably enough, are Carl Van Vechten and Paul Rosenfeld. The major goat, also predictably, is Olin Downes, whose advocacy of Sibelius is held up, just as in the days of René Leibowitz and T. W. Adorno (not to mention Virgil Thomson), as a black mark against him. But the old modernist judgments (especially that one) have lately been giving off a musty smell.

And they can be hasty. Downes is accused of having "vehemently denounced" Stravinsky alongside the inevitable Schoenberg. But the two cases were not comparable, or even contemporaneous. Downes's review of Schoenberg's Five Pieces for Orchestra, long ensconced in Slonimsky's *Lexicon*, complained of the music's unpleasant depiction of "raw and tortured nerves"—a not-inaccurate report, actually, of the composer's intention and achievement. It dates from 1914, at the very beginning of Downes's career, when he was working at the *Boston Post*. The Stravinsky review was written eleven years later, when the composer was making

---

du mérite à *l'Enlèvement des Sabines* de David.... Il est probable que les tableaux de Courbet, Manet, Monet et tutti quanti renferment des beautés qui nous échappent à nous autres anciennes chevelures romantiques déjà mêlées de fils d'argent." Joseph Proud'homme was the creation of the caricature artist Henry Monnier (1799–1877) to embody the obtuse bourgeoisie—a French counterpart to Papa Biedermeier.

his American debut as a conductor with the New York Philharmonic at Carnegie Hall, and Downes was one year into his tenure at the *New York Times*, where he would serve as chief music critic until his death in 1955. The composition under review was *Pulcinella*, and the charge was backsliding: "[T]here is little question," Downes wrote, "that the bewildering rise of Igor Stravinsky from apparent creative nonentity to the position of composer of the *Sacre du printemps* has been followed by a decline fully as rapid and destructive of the high hopes of those who believed that in him there was a prophet of a new age" (quoted on p. 313). What Dr. McKnight does not report, and may not know, is that Downes had been among the highest hopers the year before, when Pierre Monteux conducted the Boston Symphony Orchestra in the American premiere of *Le Sacre* in the same hall. Downes's rapturous review of that performance puts an altogether different complexion on his aversion to Stravinsky's neoclassicism, which now might seem to anticipate Boulez's by thirty years.[10] To paraphrase Morton Feldman, chortling at Darmstadt in 1984: "The people who you think are sheep might really be goats, and the people who you think are goats might really be sheep."[11]

Consider, in this light, the chapter by Caroline Rae on the music criticism of the Swiss-born Cuban novelist Alejo Carpentier ("Catalysing Latin American Identities: Alejo Carpentier's Music Criticism as a Cuban Case Study"), *CHMC*'s single portrait study. The sudden close-up on this peculiar figure, possibly included for the sake of geographical distribution, gives a precious glimpse of modern-music thinking in the quick, before its ossification into our familiar master narrative. Carpentier (1904–80) had a professional-level training in music theory and composition, worked sporadically as a music journalist both at home and in Paris, and called neoclassicism "the most inexplicable, most sterile, most fruitless movement in the history of music" (quoted on p. 495).[12] An eclectic cosmopolitan—or, conversely, a universal outlander—Carpentier was both at home and abroad wherever he went. "In Cuba," the author writes, "he was considered almost French, but in France he was also a foreigner and an importer of the culturally exotic" (486). His preferences were often for today's cringeworthies, like Poulenc's opus 1, the *Rapso-*

---

10. Olin Downes, "Music: 'Sacre du Printemps' Played," *New York Times*, 1 February 1924; for a commentary, see R. Taruskin, "Resisting *The Rite*," in *Russian Music at Home and Abroad* (Oakland: University of California Press, 2016), 395–427, at 416.

11. Or, to quote him exactly: " . . . many times you're living in a fantasy. For example, you think I'm loose. I might have been stricter than the people you thought were strict. The people who you think are radicals might really be conservatives. The people who you think are conservative might really be radical" (Morton Feldman, "Darmstadt Lecture 1984," transcribed by Ken Muller and Hanfried Blume, www.cnvill.net/mfdarmstadt1984.pdf). And then, as the transcript shows (and as Alex Ross, who has quoted it repeatedly, loves to point out), "he began to hum the Sibelius Fifth" (Ross, *The Rest Is Noise: Listening to the Twentieth Century* [New York: Farrar, Straus & Giroux, 2007], 193).

12. "El movement más inexplicable, más estéril, más inútil, de la historia de la música."

die nègre (text—if you can call it that—by "Makoko Kangourou"). He was a walking embodiment of the paradoxical, long-repressed union of the ultramodern and the neoprimitive.

I received a fine shock of recognition when I learned of Carpentier's strong reaction to Villa-Lobos, to whom he was obviously affine in so many ways. One of the many composers I have taken heat for excluding from the *Oxford History of Western Music* (although like many another *refusé*, a composer whose music I frequently enjoy), Villa-Lobos has—I trust we can all agree—fallen completely out of the academic canon. Like most South Americans, he is thought of as a minor back-to-Bacher, or a minor regionalist, or a minor post-Impressionist—in any case minor, wherever he is slotted. But Villa-Lobos was absolutely huge in Paris in the 1920s, whither he was sent by Arthur Rubinstein (and an assist from the Brazilian government) to knock 'em dead—which he unquestionably did in a series of spectacular premieres, including the *Noneto* with chorus (1924), *Rudepoema* (introduced by Rubinstein in 1927), the ballet *Amazonas* (1929), and especially a series of *Chôros*, nos. 8–14, spaced throughout the decade.[13] Carpentier's view of his fellow New Worlder summed up the general reaction: according to Dr. Rae, the critic "underplayed the French impressionist colourings of Villa-Lobos's early ballets, preferring to emphasise parallels with Varèse and the Russian works of Stravinsky; he reserved praise precisely for those who escaped what he considered the 'dangerous' influence of Debussy" (495).

Carpentier was not the only one to link Villa-Lobos and Varèse. They shared many programs, including the concert on 30 May 1929 at the Salle Gaveau at which the conductor Marius-François Gaillard (1900–1973), both a neoprimitivist composer in his own right and a friend and promoter of Varèse, scored a *succès fou* with his pick-up orchestra in the premieres of Villa-Lobos's *Amazonas* and Varèse's *Amériques*. In that company the Varèse already takes on a different color from the one now assigned to it, or to him. An earlier piece on Carpentier by Dr. Rae fills in many details of Varèse's Parisian interactions with Latin American contemporaries, including Carpentier's countrymen Amadeo Roldán (like Carpentier European-born) and Alejandro García Caturla. "Given that the only work Varèse managed to finish during his Paris years was *Ionisation* for solo percussion (with Cuban instruments)," she writes, "it is interesting to ponder whether, thanks to Carpentier, Varèse also had knowledge of the solo percussion pieces by Roldán [*Ritmicas* V and VI], which pre-date *Ionisation* by two years."[14]

13. Scholarly interest in such works may be reviving: see Chelsea Burns, "'Musique cannibale': The Evolving Sound of Indigeneity in Heitor Villa-Lobos's *Tres poèmas indigenas*," *Music Theory Spectrum* 43 (2021): 91–113, about another conspicuous Parisian triumph, this one assisted by press interviews hyping the composer's made-up adventures among the savages.

14. Caroline Rae, "In Havana and Paris: The Musical Activities of Alejo Carpentier," *Music and Letters* 89 (2008): 373–95, at 391.

FIGURE 18.1. Edgar Varèse (age 45) and Heitor Villa-Lobos (age 42), Paris 1929.

I have indeed pondered that—or rather, I have pondered why we don't ponder it, and now I have the perfect pretext to print one of the many pictures I was forced to omit from the *Oxford History* (Fig. 18.1). It shows our two Vs, looking very much like twins. Their juxtaposition took me by surprise at first encounter, and I have since (as we now say) interrogated my surprise. Nobody puts these two composers in the same box nowadays, although (as the music criticism of the past will prove) they are as "natural" a pair as Debussy/Ravel or Bartók/Kodály. Yet the modernist canon is as unthinkable without Varèse as Villa-Lobos would be unthinkable within it. How they became embedded in separate narratives would be a wonderful topic for investigation. In *The Ox* I made a stab at accounting for Varèse's overcoming of the neoprimitivist taint, partly by dint of his later indelible associations with high technology. Another factor elevating Varèse above Villa-Lobos must have to do with productivity—the latter's, that is (and it is something for which many in the twentieth century—Milhaud, Hindemith, Hovhaness, Persichetti—have paid a price in prestige). A mere dozen pieces by the one (with a legendary dry spell to account for it), versus, according to most sources, "about 2,000 works" (to quote the *Encyclopedia Britannica*) by the other.[15] For the one, composition was abnormally easy; for the other, supremely difficult—and we all know which of the two adjectives is a fetish and which a stigma. Villa-Lobos's catalogue contains, besides the impressive compositions that made his Parisian reputation, a number of popular items (the Aria from *Bachianas Brasileiras* no. 5; the preludes for guitar; *The Little Train of the Caipira* from *Bachianas* no. 2) that have been known to function as ambient music. (Just try to imagine Varèse that way—though it's not impossible if you know his *Dance for Burgess*, which could have furnished theme music for *The Twilight Zone*.) For one of them, and only one, one must summon one's overcomprehension. For the other, snobbery comes unbidden.

V

Overcomprehension dominates with particular clarity a pair of consecutive chapters on postwar Britain and France—the first by the editor, the other by Christopher Brent Murray—in which the primary sheep-and-goats gauge turns out to be what Dr. Murray calls the "perceived divide between composers and the audiences of traditional classical concerts" (649), with critics classified as if according to the old Pete Seeger song, *Which side are you on, boys, which side are you on?* "Perceived" is a trusty amulet for writers who want to impugn without saying so. Others are less inhibited. Once past its opening soliloquy, Mark Berry's chapter on West Germany makes no pretense at what the author must regard as the hypocritical stance of disinterested reportage. It ends with a defense of *Regieoper* by way of a truculent offen-

15. www.britannica.com/biography/Heitor-Villa-Lobos.

sive against its critical opponents. One has to wonder that the editor condoned such a campaign of just-askin' innuendo, in which individual critics are speculatively saddled with the editorial policies of their papers. Of a critic who expresses easily corroborated doubts about the audience appeal of radical, ideologically didactic (and heavily subsidized) restagings of popular operas, Dr. Berry asks, "Might one draw connections with *Die Presse*'s worship of the free market, the 'normal' opera-goer knowing best?" (605). But neoliberalism is only the mildest dart in Dr. Berry's quiver. Suggestions of homophobia are next, together with the imputation that a writer for the *Kronen Zeitung* must therefore be "a supporter of Kurt Waldheim's presidential candidacy" (606). One sees where all this is headed, but the final paragraph breaks through to a level of insinuation I had not seen since the Shostakovich wars. First a decoy disclaimer: "Whilst we should remain on our guard against too-easy identification of reactionary and/or Radical Right aesthetics and politics, there are, then, strong indications that there would be much to learn from further study of such connections" (607–8). And then, of course, a beeline to the too-easy:

> For the moment, . . . we might remind ourselves why conservative aesthetic stances are long likely to prove more problematic in Germany and Austria than in many other countries, and ask where German-language music criticism had most notoriously heard such claims before. One notorious instance would be Goebbels's insistence that performances be described and not discussed, that they be entertainment, not politically explorative. (608)

Would Dr. Tan care to comment? Dr. Berry hounds his quarries even more zealously than Singapore politicians. As an example of lax editing, it makes a teachable moment, albeit at Prof. Dingle's expense; but since Dr. Tan's, the best chapter, is arguably as much the product of editorial leniency as Dr. Berry's, the worst, laxity (or alternatively, accommodation) as such would seem to be as neutral a category as censorship (or discretion)—to be blamed or thanked (or even named) depending on one's evaluation of the outcome.

Dr. Tan confronts the crypto-political with an analytical rather than an accusing eye. Hers is one of the more discerning dismantlings of the status privileges accorded classical music (as a "universal" or "superculture") among the genres. "On the one hand," she writes, such glossing

> operates on the back of an unquestioning stance of its classical reviewers; they are unwilling to confront the postcolonial implications of the genre's widespread entrenchment across the island as shorthand for any kind of formal music education. On the other hand, this seeming historico-cultural amnesia might well be reunderstood as an unashamed declaration of successful Asian postcoloniality in the twenty-first century: why fixate over justifying the presence of any "foreign" musical genre, if listeners and critics on the island were cosmopolitan enough to stake appreciatory claims on it in the name of egalitarianism? (563)

Her discussion adumbrates the reappraisals of white privilege or "white framing" that by now have spread from places like Singapore to countries, like the USA, with longer postcolonial histories, and that have proliferated in the academy. As elsewhere, resistance to the issue in Singapore "reflects a circumvention of any discussion of postcolonial historicity and class (heavily implicated in the political and elite nature of Singapore's classical scene), so that readers can focus on potentially loftier concerns of 'art for art's sake.'" In particular, she observes, classical reviewers are uniquely licensed, as elsewhere, to pitch their "writing to 'insiders' in a style that privileged textual, connoisseurial and genre exclusivity" (563).

Indeed, that connoisseurial, insider pitch was the tone to which reviewers of other genres began to aspire, once the door was opened (in response to new consumption patterns in the 1960s) to "serious" criticism of categories formerly excluded as "commercial." No fewer than four chapters in CHMC (two of them by the editor) cite William Mann's 1963 welcome to the Beatles in the London Times as the defining moment, from which, in the words of Simon Frith, still the most authoritative British scholar of popular music and author of the relevant chapter in CHMC, "a new way of writing about music was established in European and North American journalism" (502). But was it that? Or was it a new application of an old way of writing about music—one that had previously colonized jazz, as early as the 1920s? Laura Hamer had already settled the matter within CHMC in her chapter, "Critiquing the Canon: The Role of Criticism in Canon Formation," hundreds of pages earlier, writing that "canonical values which critics developed to describe works contained within the nineteenth-century Austro-German canon still echo strongly in the criticism of other musical canons (especially rock) to this day" (232). Would Prof. Frith really want to contest that assertion, or seriously deny that classical music has set the terms for canonization no matter what the repertoire or genre?

It is especially evident now, when there is so much political pressure on the traditional canon, that its values are sooner appropriated than contested by those who are exerting the pressure. Prof. Hamer notes the frequency with which honorifics like "classic," "model," or "masterpiece" are applied to pieces in competing genres to elevate them to the high status that critics may think they are challenging (236). She notes Frith's insistence (not in this book but in his seminal *Sound Effects*) on "transgression" as a rock-specific canonical value, along with the "clear genre hierarchy ... between 'authentic' rock music and 'commercialised' pop music" (243). On these criteria, as Prof. Frith notes within CHMC, "rock writers quickly established networks and hierarchies that could be ostentatiously exclusive" (518). But transgression was a modernist (or as Leonard B. Meyer blessedly put it, a "late, late Romantic")[16] value long before it was applied to rock, and the denigration of

---

16. See L. B. Meyer, "A Pride of Prejudices; or, Delight in Diversity," *Music Theory Spectrum* 13 (1991): 241–251, at 241.

commerce, appropriated, in the case of jazz or pop, directly from Adorno's blanket denigration of culture-industrial detritus, was already a snob value in Jane Austen's day. Applied to rock it can look silly, as Prof. Hamer shows when, quoting Stuart Borthwick and Ron Moy's *Popular Music Genres*, she asks "how . . . an act that sells millions of albums [can] be considered 'uncommercial'" (246).

Relying on Carys Wyn Jones, another perceptive piper-upper in the emperor's crowd, Prof. Hamer notes the rise of "auteur" theory in the construction of the rock canon—that is, a "tendency . . . to construct 'canonic' songs and albums as the autonomous product of a single individual, generally the lead singer-songwriter, and to downplay the input of others, including band members, session musicians, sound engineers, agents and producers" (245). (Calling Dr. Becker, Dr. Howard S. Becker!)[17] Prof. Frith quotes from an Edinburgh undergraduate thesis the revelation that "authenticity can be shown to be a subjective label, attributed to artists whom [sic], at that moment, lead the writer to perceive certain qualities pertaining to the means by which the music has been created, produced and consumed" (Frances Boyson, quoted on p. 522). Why yes indeed, that it can. Readers of this journal will take note that nineteenth-century values are alive and well in the twenty-first.

It is the opposite move, down the staircase—like the one canny Philip Ewell has made defending his take on music theory's "white racial frame" ("Beethoven Was an Above-Average Composer: Let's Leave It at That")—that gets cultural work done now.[18] Recognizing these vectors is important, especially if one is interested in contesting "classical" values. After an initial period of high connoisseurship, rock and pop criticism did begin leading the way back from detached elitism to a more engaged mode of address, so that now it is classical reviewing that is pressed to catch up—against strong resistance from fans, I can attest on the basis of my experience in writing for the *New York Times*. (I will never forget what Robert Commanday wrote about *The Death of Klinghoffer* in the *San Francisco Chronicle*: "as the authors' approach to this sensitive subject is classical, no 'sides' are taken." Those scare quotes!)[19]

Once again, it is Shzr Ee Tan, writing from and about semiauthoritarian Singapore, who best describes the attendant issues. "The closely networked nature of the classical music community" works to limit the viability of "alternative discourses," which must "function within the broader conservatism of the scene itself," discouraging overt contextualization. "At most, grumblings are heard about the technicalities of lackluster performances; commentaries rarely critique cultural impe-

---

17. . . . whose *Art Worlds* (Berkeley and Los Angeles: University of California Press, 1982) remains an excellent antidote to auteurism and other romantic maladies.

18. https://musictheoryswhiteracialframe.wordpress.com/2020/04/24/beethoven-was-an-above-average-composer-lets-leave-it-at-that.

19. Robert Commanday, "'Klinghoffer' Soars into S.F.," *San Francisco Chronicle*, 1 November 1992, Datebook sec., 42.

tuses or political implications of creativity." She juxtaposes this perspective with that of "the pop arena," where freer discussion is facilitated by the rise of digital media. "Discussions on these platforms," she writes, "have ranged from the banning of music videos owing to issues of alleged LGBTQ+ agenda, to the promotion of propaganda in national songs, to scandals over the multiple state purchases of Steinway pianos for national music campaigns" (565).

The old way of writing about music is now everywhere in decline, along with its platforms—and along with the music it was designed to advance. The chapters in the last section of *CHMC* contemplate these multiple falls with varying levels of denial. Raffaele Pozzi's, on Italy, ends on a note of "crisis" (628). The next one, the editor's on his home turf, starts right off by seconding the "straightforward and disheartening" picture his predecessor had sketched (629). Sophie Redfern's chapter, "Old Divisions and New Debates: Music Criticism in Post-War America," records the ravages of a zero-sum game "[a]s jazz, pop and rock claimed the mainstream, leaving classical music an increasingly marginalised interest" (671). The editor works hard, both in his British chapter and in the concluding Postlude, to find mitigation—in dumbing down (citing his own glossy forum, *BBC Music Magazine*, as an effort "to attract the new potential audience for classical music revealed by the success of *The Three Tenors*" [633]), in relaxed ethics (promoting and reviewing the same events), and in evidence that classical coverage is not declining any faster than other features in the publications housing it (is that really consoling?)—but the brave face wavers when he concludes, in attempted palliating echo of his gambit, that "[t]he story of British music criticism since the Second World War is neither straightforward nor necessarily disheartening" (647)—the sop vitiated by a too-obvious resort to another amulet-word, *necessarily*. Chapter, and book, end in equivocation.

The mood of the music-reviewing community in the twenty-first century is glum, even among those with the steadiest jobs. Alex Ross, the *New Yorker*'s classical music man, at the very top of his profession, describes himself (in a piece titled "The Fate of the Critic in the Clickbait Age") as participating "in an exceedingly dull, slow version of Agatha Christie's *And Then There Were None*" (quoted on p. 691). Tom Sutcliffe, a veteran reviewer interviewed in a dissertation quoted by Prof. Dingle, shudders that

> editors don't really see any distinction between the different forms of music.... They feel that classical music doesn't have as large an audience, isn't as interesting to their readers, their young readers in particular ... so they feel they are still doing a perfectly good job even though the perception among classical music critics of the Critics' Circle, of which I'm Chairman, is that the situation is a complete disaster. (643)

But readers interested in a serious diagnosis of this situation, or a real analysis of its causes, will have to look elsewhere than in *CHMC*. Rarely have I seen so elaborate a sweeping of urgent matters under the rug as in the Postlude's final paragraph, which chucks historiography once and for all:

> It is tempting to say that whether the arrival of the Internet and subsequent upheavals in the printed press are regarded as disastrous or as creating new opportunities merely reflects whether the observer is a pessimist or optimist, seeing the glass as either half-empty or half-full. However, it is more pertinent to remember that wine was previously drunk out of pewter, clay or leather goblets, cups and tankards. Moreover, as generations of students will testify, if the glass breaks, another receptacle will be found. One lesson of this volume has been that whenever and wherever music is made, in whatever genre, there will be those who wish to discuss, describe and debate it, argue, attack or advocate it, read, reflect and write about it in whatever medium is available. They may or may not be paid or labelled a music critic, they may or may not write or speak eloquently, and they may or may not be perceptive and insightful, but, whether on paper, on the airwaves, on a computer screen or some medium not yet conceived, music criticism will continue. (705–6)

Which only raises, or reraises, the old question: *Is this (still) a thing?*

19

Exoticism and Authenticity

I. TRUTHINESS

I'll begin with a juxtaposition of the sublime and the ridiculous, and you can decide which is which. First, a bit of dialogue from a movie, *The Noose Hangs High*, released in 1948. It was a parody gangster film starring the burlesque team Abbott and Costello, who always found ways of working their old routines into the plot. Many of them took a form I like to think of as post-Socratic dialogues. This one is called "I Bet That You Aren't Here," and in the movie they are playing a pair of furniture movers who are being watched over by a gangster. The whole scene can be accessed on YouTube.[1] Here is an abridgment of the repartee:

Bud Abbott: I'll bet you you're not here! Ten dollars says you're not here!
Gangster: Alright, alright, prove it that I'm not here.
Bud Abbott: You're not in Chicago, are you?
Gangster: Why, certainly not!
Bud Abbott: No . . . you're not in Philadelphia, are you?
Gangster: No!
Bud Abbott: No . . . you're not in Saint Louis, are you?
Gangster: Course not!
Bud Abbott: Well, wait a moment . . . you're not in Chicago, you're not in Philadelphia, and you're not in Saint Louis, you must be someplace else!

Keynote address, international conference "Erik Bergman 100 vuotta/100 år Symposium," Svenska Kulturfonden, Helsinki, 21 November 2011.

1. www.youtube.com/watch?v=2KGk_oooFbY.

Gangster: That's right!

Bud Abbott: Well, if you're someplace else, you can't be here!

Gangster: Hey, that's a good one! I'm gonna play it on my boss! He could use a little humor.

Bud Abbott: Sure, sure!

Gangster: (to Lou) Hey you, get up out of there. Hey! (rouses Lou) Get up, get up!

Lou Costello: What'd you get me up for?

Gangster: I wanna bet you ten dollars that you're not here. Are you ready?

Lou Costello: Yes.

Gangster: Now I'm gonna prove to you that you're not here. Now, you're not in Chicago, are you?

Lou Costello: No sir, but I've got an aunt there . . .

Gangster: No, you're not in Chicago, are you?

Lou Costello: No, sir.

Gangster: And you're not in Saint Louis?

Lou Costello: No, sir.

Gangster: And you're not in Philadelphia?

Lou Costello: No, sir.

Gangster: Now if you're not in Chicago, and you're not in Saint Louis, and you're not in Philadelphia then you must be someplace else!

Lou Costello: That's right.

Gangster: And if you're someplace else, you're not here!

Lou Costello: Yes. (Lou takes the money) That's right.

Gangster: Hey, give me back my money!

Lou Costello: Who took your money? Didn't you say I wasn't in Chicago?

Gangster: That's right.

Lou Costello: And I wasn't in Philadelphia?

Gangster: Yeah, yeah!

Lou Costello: And I wasn't in Saint Louis?

Gangster: That's right!

Lou Costello: Well if I'm not in Chicago, and I'm not in Saint Louis or Philadelphia, I must be someplace else.

Gangster: That's right.

Lou Costello: And if I'm someplace else, I couldn't be here, isn't that right?

Gangster: That's right.

Lou Costello: If I'm not here, how could I take your money?

You really can base a philosophy lesson on an Abbott and Costello sketch. From the difference between the two outcomes in this one, we learn the difference between the conceptual and the empirical. Costello's "If I'm not here, how could I take your money?" is a parody of Samuel Johnson's empirical refutation of Bishop Berkeley's idealism: "[S]triking his foot with mighty force against a large stone, till he rebounded from it," Boswell tells us, Dr. Johnson announced, "'I refute it *thus.*'"[2] But the trick as played the first time gives us an interesting conceptual take on the terms in my title. We learn from it that "someplace else" is not a place—not here, but also not Chicago, not Saint Louis, and not Philadelphia. The list could go on forever. *Someplace else* corresponds to no place at all. It is purely an idea, and so is its Greek equivalent, εξωτικός (*exotikos*), from which we get our word *exotic*. More literally, *exotikos* means "from the [unspecified] outside," hence "strange," as when the same Dr. Johnson, in his *Lives of the Poets,* called opera (which, to an Englishman, was indeed from someplace else) "an exotick and irrational entertainment" ("which," he added, "has been always combated, and always has prevailed").[3]

To Abbott and Costello's I will juxtapose a lesson from Roland Barthes: a short essay he published in 1968, called "L'Effet de réel," or (as translated by Richard Howard) "The Reality Effect."[4] It begins with what Barthes presents as a pair of problematical passages, drawn respectively from the novelist Flaubert and the historian Michelet, in which Barthes identifies a seemingly superfluous detail, so characterized because it does not, in his view, contribute meaningfully to the construction of a scene. "Flaubert, describing the room occupied by Mme Aubain, Félicité's employer [in "Un Coeur simple" from *Trois Contes* (1877)], tells us that 'an old piano supported, under a barometer, a pyramidal heap of boxes and cartons.'" Meanwhile, "Michelet, recounting the death of Charlotte Corday" in his history of the French Revolution (1847–53), reports "that, before the executioner's arrival, she was visited in prison by an artist who painted her portrait," and he "includes the detail that 'after an hour and a half, there was a gentle knock at a little door behind her'" (141).

In Flaubert's description, Barthes observes, "It is just possible to see in the notation of the piano an indication of its owner's bourgeois standing and in that of the cartons a sign of disorder and a kind of lapse in status likely to connote the atmosphere of the Aubain household, [but] no purpose seems to justify reference to the barometer, an object neither incongruous nor significant, and therefore not participating, at first

---

2. James Boswell, *The Life of Samuel Johnson,* ed. Christopher Hibbert (New York: Penguin Classics, 1986), 122.
3. Samuel Johnson, *Prefaces, Biological and Critical, to the Works of the English Poets,* vol. 4 (1781), s.v. "Hughes."
4. Roland Barthes, "The Reality Effect," in *The Rustle of Language,* trans. Richard Howard (Berkeley and Los Angeles: University of California Press, 1989). (Page references to this source will be made in the main text.) The essay has attracted considerable attention from Finnish semioticians: e.g., Sirkka Knuuttila, "*L'effet de réel* Revisited: Barthes and the Affective Image," *Sign Systems Studies* 36, no. 1 (2008): 113–33.

glance, in the order of the notable." And in Michelet's sentence, "[W]e have the same difficulty in accounting structurally for all the details: that the executioner came after the painter is all that is necessary to the account; how long the sitting lasted, the dimension and location of the door are useless" (141–42).

Hence, Barthes concludes, in language surprising in its severity, "such notations are scandalous (from the point of view of structure), or, what is even more disturbing, they seem to correspond to a kind of narrative luxury," which merely "increase[s] the cost of narrative information" (141). Finally, of course, he will identify their rationale—that being the whole point and purpose of the essay, as telegraphed in its title. But W. S. Gilbert, in the libretto to *The Mikado* (1885), had anticipated Barthes by eighty-three years. After Pooh-Bah, Ko-Ko, and Pitti-Sing had concocted a story about an execution to satisfy the bloodthirsty title character, each embroidering it, in accordance with his or her own predilections, in just the manner Barthes calls scandalous and luxurious, they discover that their alleged victim was the emperor's own disguised son; whereupon they start exchanging reproaches. "Well, a nice mess you've got us into, with your nodding head and the deference due to a man of pedigree!" Ko-Ko tells Pooh-Bah, listing the elements corresponding to Flaubert's barometer or Michelet's little door. To which Pooh-Bah retorts that the superfluities were "[m]erely corroborative detail, intended to give artistic verisimilitude to an otherwise bald and unconvincing narrative."[5]

Precisely. *Verisimilitude,* though *veritas* is one of its roots, is not the same as truth. It is not the real that we apprehend as realistic. Barthes insists that there is always something left—the irreducible residue, as he calls it—when the functionally meaningful has been fully accounted for by analysis. These "insignificant gestures, transitory attitudes, insignificant objects, redundant words," he writes, "denote what is ordinarily called 'concrete reality'" (146). And now the explanatory theory: "The pure and simple 'representation' of the 'real,' the naked relation of 'what is' (or has been) thus appears as a resistance to meaning; this resistance confirms the great mythic opposition of the *true-to-life* (the lifelike) and the *intelligible*" (146). So if we want our narrative to be accepted as true (or rather, *vraisemblable*, "verisimilar"), we must take care not to eliminate the unintelligible, the redundant, the insignificant—i.e., the barometers and the little doors. These, Barthes concludes, "say nothing but this: *we are the real;* it is the category of 'the real' (and not its contingent contents) which is then signified" (148).

These "useless" extras, it turns out, have an important use: they provide a bit of seepage from what William James called the "great blooming, buzzing confusion" of unmediated reality, the world as it presents itself to babies, who have not yet

---

5. *The Mikado* (1885), act 2, in *The Complete Plays of Gilbert and Sullivan* (New York: Modern Library, 1936), 227.

formed any notion of categories.⁶ Accomplished liars have always known this; we all know that we must avoid stories that are too neat. Artists, too, know how to avoid the neatness that kills persuasion. Above all, Barthes advises that one must follow the advice of the seventeenth-century philosopher Pierre Nicole, and "not consider things as they are in themselves, nor as they are known to be by one who speaks or writes, but only in relation to what is known of them by those who read or hear" (quoted on p. 147).⁷

Barthes calls this strategy of couching one's discourse according to the presumed expectations of one's readers or hearers the "referential illusion." When I read Nicole's dictum as quoted by Barthes, I immediately thought of some wise words of the nineteenth-century Russian music critic Herman Laroche, which had served me so well, decades ago, when it came to characterizing Russian musical orientalism. "In what," Laroche asked, "does [Alexander] Serov's masterly characterization of the extinct Assyrians [in his opera *Judith* of 1863] consist, or [Anton] Rubinstein's of the ancient Semites [in his "sacred opera" *The Tower of Babel* of 1869]? Obviously, in one thing only: the composers have successfully reproduced *our* subjective idea of the Assyrians and the Semites."⁸

It took more than a century for the thoughts of this perceptive critic to find echo in the discourse of musicology, when Jonathan Bellman, in the introduction to a collection of essays called *The Exotic in Western Music,* wrote that the exotic is defined not by distance but by strangeness. Bellman's next point, that "musical exoticism is not equivalent to ethnomusicological verisimilitude," requires a little tweak if it is truly to reflect Laroche's insight (which I take to have been Bellman's as well). We need to substitute "veracity" for *verisimilitude;* for (as Laroche said and Bellman clearly meant), artistic representations are judged not by their actual truthfulness, which we are in most cases in no position to judge, but by their "truthlikeness" (or, to quote the fake news comedian Stephen Colbert, their "truthiness")⁹—the ring of truth in the ear of the beholder. We judge them, just as Laroche said we do, on the basis of our prejudices, and therefore it is indeed ethnomusicological verisimilitude that we do look for when judging musical exoticism.

Verisimilitude thus implies conformity with preconception and predisposition rather than with empirical observation. Representations are successful to the

---

6. William James, *Principles of Psychology* (1890; New York: Dover Publications, 1950), 462.

7. "Il ne faut regarder les choses comme elles sont en elles-mêmes, ni telles que les sait celui qui parle ou qui écrit, mais par rapport seulement à ce qu'en savent ceux qui lisent ou qui entendent" (Pierre Nicole, Preface, *Recueil de poésies chrétiennes et diverses,* 1671).

8. "'Der Thurm zu Babel' Rubinshteyna" (1870) in German Avgustovich Larosh, *Muzïkal'no-kriticheskiye stat'i* (St. Petersburg: Bessel, 1894), 117.

9. As coined in the maiden episode of *The Colbert Report,* 17 October 2005; it was quickly taken up in the popular press, and the American Dialect Society selected *truthiness* as its 2005 Word of the Year (see www.americandialect.org/Words_of_the_Year_2005.pdf).

extent that they are convincing, and they are convincing to the extent that we are predisposed to believe them. That belief is not to be confused with merely being taken in. We unconsciously collude with the reality effect for the sake of the emotional payoff it makes available. Or even consciously collude. Here is Roger Scruton, a philosopher known for his commitment to traditional rites and values, objecting on that account to the concept of "early music," which for him merely "cocoon[s] the past in a wad of phoney scholarship, . . . elevate[s] musicology over music, and . . . confine[s] Bach and his contemporaries to an acoustic time-warp." Rejecting the whole project of historical performance practice, he maintains that only by making the music sound as acoustically familiar as possible can we repossess the exotic content that the musical sounds convey to ears properly attuned:

> It is precisely because the tradition of Western music still lives that we can gain access, through music of previous generations, to states of mind that we no longer encounter in our daily experience. The unbroken tradition of polyphonic writing enables us to hear, in Victoria's great *Responsories for Tenebrae*, exactly *what it was like* to believe as Victoria believed, seeing the world in terms of the Christian drama. This experience is overwhelming: it redeems for us a moment of past time, which could never be redeemed by factual knowledge. It makes a vanished experience present in our own emotions, and instructs us, through the imagination, in spiritual possibilities that our lives deny.[10]

The nervous italics are original, and betray, I would surmise, the writer's awareness that the overwhelming experience he describes is in fact a willingly enacted charade. Perfectly cognizant of the difference between veracity and verisimilitude (but perhaps hoping that his reader is not), Scruton votes enthusiastically for the latter. We need not vote, but we do need the distinction. Having made the necessary adjustment, we can appreciate Bellman's point as amended—that "musical exoticism is not equivalent to ethnomusicological *veracity*"—as a fundamental truth. Bellman's further point, that "the exotic equation is a balance of familiar and unfamiliar: just enough 'there' to spice the 'here' but remain comprehensible," places the crucial emphasis just where it belongs (and where Barthes had already placed it): not on accuracy but on legibility. "Exoticism," Bellman affirms, "is not about the earnest study of foreign cultures; it is about drama, effect, and evocation."[11]

And it is about something else as well: something that is often valued more highly than drama, effect, or evocation, because it makes an actual, if unsustainable, truth claim. It is about "authenticity," the name we give the reality effect when we encounter it in music. Now, "authenticity" (a word that, as used in this essay, must always be surrounded mentally by scare quotes) is something about which

---

10. Roger Scruton, *The Aesthetics of Music* (Oxford: Clarendon Press, 1997), 448–49.
11. Jonathan Bellman, "Introduction," in *The Exotic in Western Music*, ed. Bellman (Boston: Northeastern University Press, 1998), xii–xiii.

I've had a lot to say. My take on it quite resembles Barthes's, although I had not yet read Barthes's essay when I did most of my writing on the subject. I too have posited a "referential illusion" by which musicians have managed, like Roger Scruton, to claim possession of unpossessable knowledge in support of insupportable claims. The "authenticity effect," as I might now name it, after Barthes, is produced by a comparable set of devices that enable us to imagine seepage from historical or geographical realities to which we have no real access. I don't propose to waste words rehashing old questions, reopening old wounds, or unsettling old scores. But one aspect of the old debates is worth recalling as a springboard to a new discussion, one that will bridge my two preliminary exhibits and launch us into matters broached by my title.

What first put me onto the hunch that, despite its claims of veracity, early-music performance practice was a modernist practice rather than an historical one was a review by Robert Winter of a recording of Beethoven's *Missa solemnis*. Winter complained of a difference in approach between the instrumentalists in that particular recorded performance and the singers. The instrumentalists were well within the style Winter identified as "historical performance" (which was generally defined, in those days, by its difference from so-called "modern"—that is, ordinary, or unmarked—performance practice); and yet, he wrote,

> I would be hard pressed to point up any significant difference between the vocal styles applied here and those in any of a half dozen representative modern recordings. There is something specious about arguing for instrumental authenticity while largely ignoring the vocal domain. It is certainly true that we know less about vocal techniques and performance styles than we do about instrumental performance. But that is no reason to abandon the search.[12]

"Search for what?" I had to wonder when I first read this. Winter did not seem to know. But he did seem to know that familiar vocal techniques and performance styles could not be authentic. Unlike the traditionalist Roger Scruton, who radically distinguished the sound of music from its meaning, and who sought ancient meanings in modern sounds, Winter was committed to the modernist view that the two were coterminous. Therefore an indispensable earnest of authenticity, for him, was sonic strangeness. It was in the sounds themselves that Winter, and other performance-practice modernists, needed to find Samuel Johnson's "exotick." Since formulating it in response to Winter[13] I have been testing this proposition on many

---

12. Robert Winter, "The Emperor's New Clothes: Nineteenth-Century Instruments Revisited," *Nineteenth-Century Music* 7 (1983–84): 255.
13. R. Taruskin, "The Pastness of the Present and the Presence of the Past," in *Authenticity and Early Music: A Symposium*, ed. Nicholas Kenyon (Oxford: Oxford University Press, 1988), 137–210; rpt. in Taruskin, *Text and Act: Essays on Music and Performance* (New York: Oxford University Press, 1995), 90–154.

styles of composition and performance, and I have come to the conclusion that the exotic—the sense of being from "someplace else"—is a fundamental and often indispensable aspect of the reality (or authenticity) effect in music. Authenticity—which, according to the Merriam-Webster online dictionary, means "conforming to an original so as to reproduce essential features" or "made or done the same way as an original,"[14] or according to Dictionary.com, "having the origin supported by unquestionable evidence"[15]—comes in two flavors, since there are two kinds of stipulated origin that interest authenticators: original time and original place. Whether we are talking about temporal or geographical provenience, I believe (and will try to demonstrate) that we are willing, like the listeners about whom Laroche and Bellman have written, to accept exoticism at its face value as evidence that an artifact conforms to an original of which we have (and in many cases, of which we *can* have) no actual knowledge. Thus, I maintain, rather than on the basis of evidence, we still ratify aesthetic objects as authentic on the basis of stereotypes and prejudices. Why else has art forgery always been so profitable? But that is another story.

II. INSPIRED SCREECHING

Let us begin with the matter Robert Winter broached in his *Missa solemnis* review, that of "historical" vocal techniques and performance styles. At the time Winter was writing, high hopes were vested in a singer named Jantina Noorman. She was born in Holland in 1930 and moved to the United States with her family in 1947. She entered the University of Illinois as a music education major, and there she became a charter member of a *collegium musicum* directed by George Hunter (1918–2011), an alumnus of Paul Hindemith's *collegium* at Yale. (They made a well-received recording of music by Guillaume de Machaut in 1955, released the next year on the Westminster label.) At the end of the 1950s, Noorman moved to England and studied voice with Margaret Ritchie, a famous oratorio singer. In 1960, at a summer school that Ritchie was running, Noorman was approached by John Beckett (1927–2007), an Irish harpsichordist and conductor, who together with Michael Morrow (1929–94), an Irish painter and lutenist, was then forming a group called Musica Reservata. They invited her to join. Morrow, she recalled years later,

> discovered my ability to imitate several vocal styles. For his interpretation of "early" music he did not want a "trained" voice, but a voice that sounded like "ordinary" people's voices. He was particularly fascinated by the way people from the Balkans sang. He told me that the voice should sound like the instruments that accompany the

14. www.merriam-webster.com/dictionary/authentic.
15. http://dictionary.reference.com/browse/authentic.

singer. He played the bagpipes himself; so when I sang with him my voice had to be loud. However, when I sang with a crumhorn, for instance, that required a different way of singing. I think you can compare it to pop music, as most pop musicians are not trained musicians as well.[16]

Whether Noorman's style of singing was like Balkan singing or like pop music (or, for that matter, like "'ordinary' people") you can decide for yourself on the basis of a recording of hers that for a while was famous: the estampie "Kalenda maya" by the troubadour Raimbaut de Vaqueras, recorded by Musica Reservata around 1977 and still available on YouTube (where—*sic transit*—it has attracted few hits).[17] I think it is quite obvious that, despite what Noorman told her interviewer, this way of singing was not an imitation of anything. Indeed, she told another singer, Judith Milardo (who then told the same interviewer), that she "created her own 'Reservata Sound' for her performances with the London Musica Reservata, and did not care whether or not her sound fitted in with the vocal conventions of that time." But of course that is not quite right, either. Morrow's objective was precisely a sound that did not fit with the vocal conventions of any time. It was pure canny invention. For a while it was very successful—and, I am tempted to say, influential, although no one, to my knowledge, ever actually ventured to imitate Noorman's singing. It was too distinctive to be imitated; one would end up sounding like a medieval Elvis impersonator. Nevertheless, she told her interviewer, "[m]ost people appreciated our way of interpreting 'early' music."

Where it was particularly influential was among academics. Joseph Kerman, in his very prescriptive musicological manual *Contemplating Music* of 1985, touted it this way:

> Much is speculated about singing without vibrato, or with vibrato of a very different kind than is heard in the modern opera house (or, for that matter, the modern Oxbridge chapel). Such singing can be heard in non-Western musical traditions, but in the performance of Western music only [Michael] Morrow's lead singer Jantina Noorman—Dutch by birth, American by training—seemed able to carry it off in a convincing fashion. Her inspired screeching, one suspects, is the way the performance of older music has to go.[18]

Why? For no other reason, it seems to me, than because it was weird. It was the sound of "someplace else," and right for its time, when history was taking an anthropological turn symbolized by the catchphrase "the past is a foreign

---

16. "Jantina Noorman, Pioneer of Dutch Folk Songs," interview with Eelco Schilder (2004), www.folkworld.de/31/e/dutch.html.
17. www.youtube.com/watch?v=DCsmgoQYXFY.
18. Joseph Kerman, *Contemplating Music* (Cambridge, MA: Harvard University Press, 1985), 207.

country."[19] Imaginary geographical exoticism could pass for temporal exoticism as well, and both exoticisms powerfully conveyed an aura of authenticity.

Far more influential than Noorman, and still repercussing today, is the Moorish style of performance for troubadour songs and other medieval monophonic repertories developed in the 1960s by another alumnus of George Hunter's seminal *collegium*, the lutenist Thomas Binkley (1931–95), who founded the Studio der frühen Musik in Munich around the same time that Beckett and Morrow were starting Musica Reservata. This style was founded not simply on intuition or imagination, but on real research: both historical research on Arab-European contacts at the time of the Crusades, and on ethnographic research on contemporary North African vocal and instrumental techniques (that is, contemporary with the researcher). That research has come under some hard scrutiny in recent years, and has been shown to have been heavily prejudiced by antiquated orientalist fantasies.[20] That did not impede its continued influence on performers who neither did the research nor read the critiques but were content to accept the hypothesis as settled fact.

Why? Because the hypothesis suited their predispositions, and because Binkley's alluring performances were accomplished and imaginative, and for that reason aesthetically persuasive. Still, lest we forget, Jantina Noorman's singing and Thomas Binkley's adaptation of troubadour songs to the format of Andalusian *nuba* performances were not widely admired and accepted just because they were imaginative or attractive, but also (and mainly) because they created for many listeners *l'effet de réel*, the "reality effect." They were taken as authentic. And so their acceptance was predicated on prior notions of the applicable reality. It was because we imagine the Middle Ages as a barbarous time that Michael Morrow sought "non-Western" models for his singers, and Joseph Kerman found the result convincing. As Kerman put it, the performances of Musica Reservata "provided a welcome note of vigour—even roughness—where daintiness, blandness, faintness, and wan melancholy had long held sway," and were therefore much to be preferred over such "suspiciously mellifluous groups" as Pro Cantione Antiqua, a now-forgotten all-male ensemble directed by Bruno Turner, which employed British cathedral countertenors to sing the parts in Jantina Noorman's range.[21]

There is no reason to suppose that Aquitainian castle culture was rough rather than mellifluous, or vigorous rather than dainty. On the contrary, there is every

---

19. From the first sentence of L. P. Hartley's novel *The Go-Between* (1953): "The past is a foreign country; they do things differently there." For the anthropological turn, see David Lowenthal, *The Past Is a Foreign Country* (Cambridge: Cambridge University Press, 1986).

20. See Shai Burstyn, "The 'Arabian Influence' Thesis Revisited," *Current Musicology* 46 (1990): 119–46; John Haines, "The Arabic Style of Performing Medieval Music," *Early Music* 29 (2001): 369–78.

21. Kerman, *Contemplating Music*, 207.

reason to suppose that (as Hendrik van der Werf, a notable musicological dissenter, has insisted) a high aristocratic culture like that of the troubadours would have prized the utmost refinement in performance (whatever that might have entailed in practical terms).[22] But refinement was familiar, and therefore subject to what familiarity breeds. It was the same when Serge Diaghilev brought the contemporary arts of Russia to Parisian and London audiences in the early twentieth century. He scored an enormous hit with a blood-and-thunder ballet about murder in the seraglio, set to Rimsky-Korsakov's *Sheherazade,* and nearly lost his shirt when he mounted Chaikovsky's *Sleeping Beauty.* It was the makeshift harem, not the actual *chef d'oeuvre* of the Mariyinsky Theater ballet, that evoked, in the minds of audiences, *du vrai russe,* as Prince Peter Lieven, a chronicler of Diaghilev's enterprise, noted with a twinkle.[23]

III. REALITY AS LETDOWN

And now for my favorite example of prejudice—in this case a specific "stupid suburban prejudice," to quote some famous words Ezra Pound supposedly confided to Allen Ginsberg—and its role in creating the reality effect in music.[24] When I was a college music major, one of the books we used in class to learn music history was the *Historical Anthology of Music,* or *HAM,* a two-volume collection of exemplary pieces put together at Harvard in the early 1940s by Archibald T. Davison (1883–1961) and Willi Apel (1893–1988), and published in 1946. For at least two decades *HAM* was the ubiquitous *vade mecum* for Anglophone music students, modeled on such German anthologies as Arnold Schering's *Geschichte der Musik in Beispielen* of 1931. By all odds its most amazing exhibit was "Der Juden Tantz" (The Jews' Dance) by the lutenist composer Hans Neusiedler (1508–63), published in 1544 (Ex. 19.1).

This little piece was long a favorite of Apel, a great connoisseur of musical oddities and puzzles. He had probably first encountered it while a student, in a transcription by Adolf Koczirz (1870–1941) that had appeared in 1911 in Guido Adler's venerable series *Denkmäler der Tonkunst in Oesterreich.*[25] He first edited it himself for an anthology titled *Musik aus früher Zeit* (Music from Early Times), published

---

22. See Hendrik van der Werf, *The Extant Troubadour Melodies: Transcriptions and Essays for Performers and Scholars* (Rochester, NY: Published by the author, 1984).
23. Kniaz Pyotr Alexandrovich Lieven, *The Birth of the Ballets Russes* (London: George Allen & Unwin, 1936), 106.
24. In full: "But the worst mistake I made was that stupid suburban prejudice of anti-Semitism. Spoiled everything." The phrase was first reported by Michael Reck in "A Conversation between Ezra Pound and Allen Ginsberg," *Evergreen Review* 55 (June 1968): 26–29, 84.
25. Vol. 18, no. 2 (1911): *Österreichische Lautenmusik im 16. Jahrhundert.*

EXAMPLE 19.1. "Der Juden Tantz" as it appears in *HAM*.

by Schott in 1934, two years before Apel fled Nazi Germany for America. In 1942, Apel printed a facsimile of the original publication as the culminating example of tablature in his famous notation textbook (the first in English), together with a partial transcription to serve students as a pony, and touted the piece as "remarkable for various reasons." It was, for one thing, "the earliest example of the so-called *scordatura*, that is, a deliberate deviation from the normal tuning" of the instrument.[26]

Neusiedler, the composer, had prefaced the piece with an elaborate, redundantly and somewhat confusingly written set of instructions that begins, "Here follows the Jews' Dance, and whoever wants to play it must tweak the lute differently."[27] It proceeds to list the six strings by their colloquial names, and to show how the pitch of each string must be matched to that of a stopped note on its neighbor (Fig. 19.1). The most remarkable aspect of the dance, according to Apel, was the result of this *scordatura*, which turned the piece into "one of the earliest examples, if not the

---

26. Willi Apel, *The Notation of Polyphonic Music 900–1600* (Cambridge, MA: Medieval Academy of America, 1942), 78.

27. "Hie volget der Juden Tantz / und wer in schlagen wil / der musz die Lautten anders ziehen." Neusiedler, *Das Ander Buch* [Second Book]: *Ein New künstlich Lautten Buch* (Nürnberg, 1544), 79–80 in http://vmirror.imslp.org/files/imglnks/usimg/3/3c/IMSLP272788-PMLP224574-neusiedler_das_ander_buch.pdf; rpt. in Apel, *Notation of Polyphonic Music*, 81 and 78 (translation amended).

German Lute Tablatures 81

FACSIMILE 22

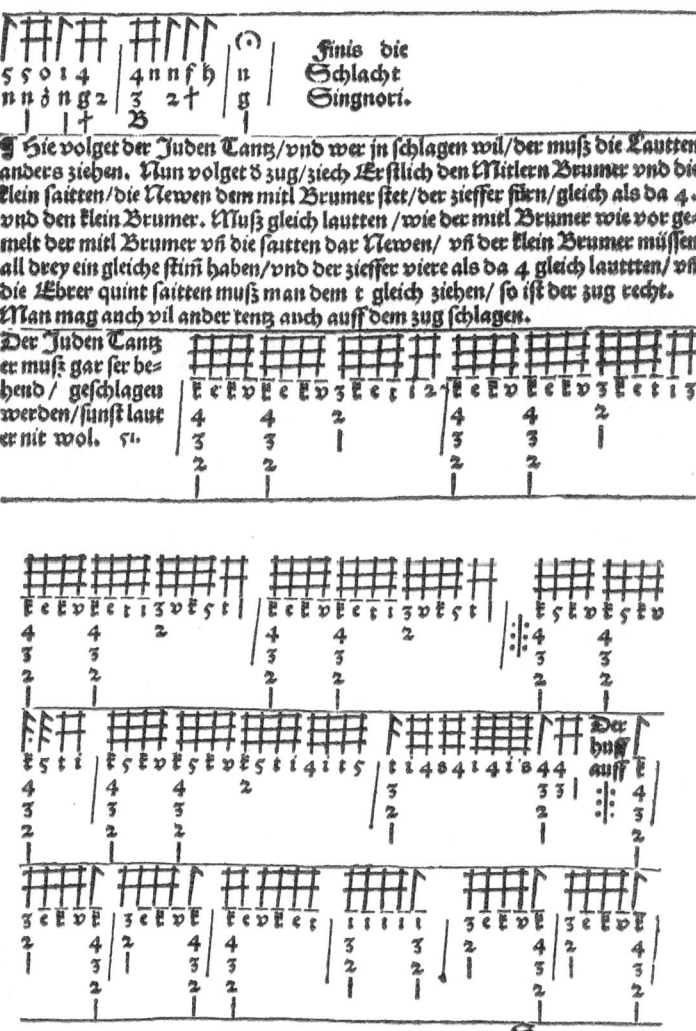

¶ Hie volget der Juden Tantz/vnd wer jn schlagen wil/der muß die Lautten anders ziehen. Nun volget 8 zug/ziech Erstlich den Mitlern Brumer vnd die klein saitten/die Newen dem mitl Brumer stet/der zieffer sthen/gleich als da 4. vnd den klein Brumer. Muß gleich lautten/wie der mitl Brumer wie vor ge= melt der mitl Brumer vñ die saitten dar Newen/ vñ der klein Brumer müssen all drey ein gleiche stiñ haben/vnd der zieffer viere als da 4 gleich lauttten/vñ die Ebrer quint saitten muß man dem t gleich ziehen/ so ist der zug recht. Man mag anch vil ander tentz anch auff dem zug schlagen.

Der Juden Tantz
er muß gar ser be=
hend/ geschlagen
werden/sunst laut
er nit wol.

Hans Newsidler, *Ein new künstlich Lautenbuch.* Nürnberg, 1544

FIGURE 19.1. Hans Neusiedler, "Der Juden Tantz" (*Ein New künstlich Lautten Buch*, [Nürnberg, 1544], f. 55).

earliest, of satire in music. As in almost all pieces of this genre, the satirical character is expressed by cacophonous dissonances. In fact, our dance is written in a strikingly modern idiom of bitonality such as rarely occurs before the advent of the twentieth century."[28]

When reprinting the piece in *HAM*, Apel called renewed attention to the "shrill dissonances, otherwise unheard of before the adventurous experiments of twentieth-century music, [which] result from the daring use of two conflicting tonal realms, D-sharp in the melody against E-natural in the harmony."[29] "Der Juden Tantz" has been recorded several times as Koczirz and Apel published it, both on the lute and as variously transcribed for other instruments.[30] In retrospect it seems incredible that Apel—or we students—could have accepted this transcription as correct; and sure enough, in 1963 the Belgian lutenist Michel Podolski published an article in which he showed that Apel, who had pointedly corrected some notes in Koczirz's transcription, had retained a beam in his own, having misread Neusiedler's tuning instructions.[31] Correctly transcribed, the piece is altogether conventional in harmony (Ex. 19.2), and, as Podolski goes on to show, it nearly concords with a similarly titled piece published two years later by Wolf Heckel, another German lutenist.[32]

With benefit of hindsight, it is easy enough to tell, even without consulting the original tablature or the corrected transcription, what the mistake must have been, because the "D-sharp" tonality is entirely confined to notes playable on the top string of the lute. Tune that string a semitone higher, as the *scordatura* prescribes when correctly interpreted, and everything is in E: harmonious, obviously correct, and of course disappointing to us who had loved—or at least been pleasantly titillated by—the "original." Years before I found Podolski's article I had found his recording of the piece, which he made as early as 1954; you can imagine my dissatisfaction when I put the disk on my turntable and heard his rather plodding performance of what was now a ploddingly conventional piece.[33]

28. Apel, *Notation of Polyphonic Music*, 78

29. Archibald T. Davison and Willi Apel, eds., *Historical Anthology of Music* (1946), vol. 1: *Oriental, Medieval, and Renaissance Music*, rev. ed. (Cambridge, MA: Harvard University Press, 1966), 108 (score), 227 (commentary).

30. E.g., by Konrad Ragossnig (Deutsche Grammophon, 1972): www.youtube.com/watch?v=MGHIbLuNYDA. For a recorded performance on the organetto: www.youtube.com/watch?v=fUkEy5p5WSU; for a performance by a Hungarian ensemble, accompanied (one regrets to say) by a Jew's harp: www.youtube.com/watch?v=Y4VcxYiOUSY.

31. Michel Podolski, "Le Juden Tantz: Analyse et transcription," *Revue belge de musicologie* 17 (1963): 29–38.

32. Ibid., 36.

33. *Sixteenth and Seventeenth Century Lute Music*, Period Records SPL 577 (ca. 1954). A more fluent performance than Podolski's of the corrected version, by Julian Bream (also recorded earlier than the uncorrected one by Ragossnig, referenced in n. 30), can be heard at www.youtube.com/watch?v=z55gwQLVqIc.

EXAMPLE 19.2. "Der Juden Tantz" as transcribed by Michel Podolski (*Revue belge de musicologie* 17 [1963]: 35).

Yet although as a college student I took Apel's transcription on faith, I was bemused even then at his remark in the commentary that the shrill dissonances "produce an extremely realistic picture, not lacking a touch of satire."[34] Realistic? Did he really think that Jewish music sounded like that in the sixteenth century? I can't believe that he really did, nor of course am I imputing an anti-Semitic prejudice to Apel, a Jewish refugee from Hitler, but it seems clear that the exoticism implied by the dance's title (and which turned out not to be reflected in its actual music) would have sanctioned any result at all no matter how absurd, and endowed it—for Apel, and for many others—with *l'effet de réel*. Endowed it quite unshakably, I might add: three years after Podolski's article appeared, a revised edition of *HAM*

34. Davison and Apel (eds.), *Historical Anthology of Music*, 1:227.

World's Oldest Song Reported Deciphered

Near-East Origin

By LACEY FOSBURGH
Special to The New York Times

BERKELEY, Calif., March 5—The soft sounds of what is now believed to be the oldest song in the world were played here today at the University of California.

"This has revolutionized the whole concept of the origin of Western music," Richard L. Crocker, professor of music history at Berkeley, said today.

The discovery proves that Western music is about 1,400 years older than previously known and dates back to the ancient Near-Eastern civilization of at least the second millenium B.C.

Scholars have always believed that Western music originated in Greece, but this indicates it came from the Near East.

"We always knew there was music in the earlier Assyro-Babylonian civilization, but until this, we did not know," Professor Crocker said, "that it had the same heptatonic diatonic scale that is characteristic of contemporary Western music and Greek music of the first millenium B.C."

The song, which sounds to contemporary Western ears like a lullaby, a hymn or a gentle folk song, was last heard, scholars said, about

Continued on Page 18, Column 1

Richard L. Crocker playing reproduction of a lyre
The New York Times/Teresa Zabala

Out of Prehistory

By HAROLD C. SCHONBERG

The startling discovery of the Hurrian cuneiform tablet containing a cult love song pushes back the frontier of notated music well over a thousand years.

An Appraisal

Up to now, the oldest piece of music in notated form has been a fragment of Greek papyrus containing a song in the "Orestes" of Euripides. That dates from the fourth century B.C. The new discovery is put at about 1800 B.C.

Listening to this music (heard in a two-minute excerpt on the telephone) puts a listener back into musical prehistory. The sound of the lyre, constructed by Prof. Robert R. Brown from 4,600-year-old instructions, has the primitive quality associated with crude plucked instruments. The music, proceding in double notes and short rhythmic phrases, usually in semitonal up-and-down shifts, sounds equally primitive as far as its actual texture goes.

But there is one surprise. Professor Brown, Prof. Anne D. Kilmer, who worked on the text, and Prof. Richard L. Crocker of the music department of the University of California in Berkeley, are confident that the piece of

Continued on Page 18, Column 3

FIGURE 19.2. *New York Times*, 6 March 1974.

was published, this time under the sole editorship of Apel, Davison having died in 1961. The transcription of "Der Juden Tantz" stands therein uncorrected (indeed, that is the edition shown in Ex. 19.1). I have always wondered whether Apel knew Podolski's article, and whether he preferred his exotic reality effect to the drab historical reality.

For familiarity, always a letdown, invariably militates against *l'effet de réel*. This point emerged rather dramatically in March 1974, when my now former (then future) colleague Richard L. Crocker became the first musicologist ever to get his picture on the front page of the *New York Times* (Fig. 19.2). He and an Assyriologist at Berkeley named Anne Draffkorn Kilmer announced the successful transcription of a Hurrian song that had been notated on a Babylonian cuneiform tablet around 1800 BCE, making it by considerably more than a millennium the oldest song in the world (Fig. 19.3a–b). The *Times* not only covered the announcement, replete with the photo of Prof. Crocker singing the melody to his own accompaniment on a reconstructed Sumerian lyre built by Robert R. Brown, a third Berkeley professor, but also commissioned an "appraisal" of the tune (based, as he put it, on a two-minute excerpt heard on the telephone) by its chief music critic, Harold C. Schonberg, which also appeared on the front page. What Schonberg heard can still be heard on YouTube.[35]

There was a marked contrast between the description of the song as given by the transcribers and the one given by the critic. Professors Kilmer and Crocker stressed that, although their findings needed to be corroborated by comparison with other, as yet undiscovered, cuneiform notations, "Assyriologists and musicologists both here [in America] and in Britain have voiced support for their findings." "The song sounds right to me the way it is now," Prof. Kilmer told the *Times* reporter, and Prof. Crocker waxed positively enthusiastic: "It sounds lovely, doesn't it? It isn't weird or strange, it's totally familiar to us because it is, after all, part of our own culture. The myth that so-called 'old music' has to sound nasal and whiney obviously isn't true.'"[36] But Mr. Schonberg was determined to find the melody exotic, and of course he managed to do so. "Listening to this music," he wrote,

> puts a listener back into musical prehistory. The sound of the lyre . . . has the primitive quality associated with crude plucked instruments. The music, proceeding in double notes and short rhythmic phrases, . . . sounds equally primitive as far as its actual texture goes. But there is one surprise. [Profs. Kilmer and Crocker] are confident that the piece of music was conceived in the equivalent of a modern diatonic scale. The three professors emphasize that the music is "a hypothetical transcription."
> . . . Many musical scholars believe that Babylonian music came from China. And, as the ancient melody is heard, there are a few passages that mildly suggest an Oriental flavor. But the Oriental scale is pentatonic, and there are no pentatonic elements in the Hurrian tune. Professor Kilmer and Professor Crocker can see no evidence that the music originated in China. . . . Tentative as the transcription is, there seems little doubt that the three professors in California have recaptured something of the feeling of the 4,000-year-old melody. Those who have heard early music—Japanese gagaku, for instance—will immediately recognize the ancient flavor of the melodic patterns. . . . It is a music that hits directly at the racial subconscious, and it takes the listener back through the ages nearly to the beginnings of mankind.[37]

35. www.youtube.com/watch?v=7ZatnTPhYWc.
36. Quotations from Lacey Fosburgh, "World's Oldest Song Reported Deciphered," *New York Times*, 6 March 1974.
37. Harold C. Schonberg, "Out of Prehistory: Song Puts the History of Music Back 1,000 Years," *New York Times*, 6 March 1974.

FIGURE 19.3A. Cuneiform tablet containing "a Hurrian cult song from ancient Ugarit."

FIGURE 19.3B. As transcribed by Anne Draffkorn Kilmer (Richard J. Dumbrill, *The Archaeomusicology of the Ancient Near East* [Victoria, BC: Trafford Publishing, 2005], 122).

The critic insisted on comparing the song not to "our own culture," as Prof. Crocker suggested we do, but to East Asian musics instead, including repertories, like the music of the Japanese royal court, that had no demonstrated or even speculated association with Babylon. Note, too, that Mr. Schonberg was as much at pains to emphasize the speculative nature of the transcription as the decipherers were to emphasize their belief in the accuracy of their findings. It is as if only the hope that, after more extensive study, the piece would turn out to be weird after all had allowed Mr. Schonberg tentatively to accept its authenticity.

It was the diatonic tuning that assured familiarity and therefore raised reflex doubts about authenticity; and therefore it became the main point of contention in commentaries and alternative solutions that appeared over the next two decades. The cuneiform notation had been based on the tuning of a nine-string lyre. Like Hans Neusiedler's notation, in other words, it was a tablature. Everything depended on the *accordatura*, the preliminary determination of the strings' pitches (which in the case of a lyre are only played open) and the intervals they formed with other strings. Beginning with the middle, or fifth, string, one is directed to proceed outward by fifths and fourths, until a full diatonic scale is achieved. There are seven ways of doing this, corresponding exactly to the seven diatonic modes that can be obtained on the white keys of a piano keyboard. As Richard Crocker observed, the relationship of these prescriptions to those of our own musical culture is obvious and straightforward—and therefore, for many, fishy.

The aspects of Kilmer's transcription that have remained speculative and therefore most immediately contestable were the melodic contour and the texture. There is no indication in the tuning directions as to whether one proceeds by rising fifths and falling fourths or the reverse; hence, a transcription of the Hurrian melody that inverted all of Kilmer's intervals, both melodic and harmonic, would have been theoretically just as compliant with the notation as the one that Crocker performed and Schonberg approved. As to texture: the most controversial aspect of Kilmer's reading was her decision to interpret the notation of intervals in the cuneiform tablet, which was done by naming pairs of strings, as literally entailing dyads (two-note chords). In an article that evaluated several interpretations of the cuneiform notation, the Oxford philologist Martin Litchfield West noted that "one's immediate reaction is skepticism at the notion of this kind of harmony existing in any ancient music," and "another objection is that it would be odd to have a notation capable of expressing only chords and not single notes."[38] (Other scholars have variously interpreted the designation of two-string intervals

---

38. M. L. West, "The Babylonian Musical Notation and the Hurrian Melodic Texts," *Music and Letters* 75 (1994): 161–79, at 173.

as implying melodic successions, acciaccaturas or grace notes, or even scale segments.)[39]

Despite these objections, Kilmer's version was the only one that West did not write off as wholly unconvincing, and he was obliged to admit that it did not contravene or unwarrantably supplement the information conveyed by the cuneiform tablet and what is known of the attendant theory (which is to say that it satisfied Occam's razor). West offered a solution of his own, no less speculative than Kilmer's, which avoided the constant two-part harmony and took the lower notes in Kilmer's dyads as the notes that constitute the melody. His solution also avoided arbitrary supplementation of the given information, or what William of Ockham himself called *pluralitas sine necessitatis*. What I particularly like about West's proposal is that it was by his own admission counterintuitive according to his own assumptions. He writes that "if one had had to make a guess at the nature of Near Eastern melody in the late second millennium BC, one might have speculated that it would be rather plain by comparison with later 'oriental' (Arabic-Persian) music, restricted in vocal compass, tonally stable, perhaps pentatonic in character, and proceeding predominantly by conjunct motion."[40] These were his confessed prejudices, based on his experience with Greek and Hebrew musical remains. Both Kilmer's solution and his own failed to meet them, since both solutions accepted the diatonic rather than pentatonic tuning of the lyre as basis for the melody. That he was nevertheless willing, however provisionally, to entertain them and even pronounce them superior to existing alternatives is to my mind a token of methodological scrupulousness worthy of emulation.

Failure of Kilmer's version to meet expectations nevertheless continued to bother those who considered their intuition to be something more than prejudice, and it especially bedeviled those who had trained their intuition to favor desirable political outcomes. Such investigators had new reasons to work at exoticizing the Hurrian song. One such scholar is Richard Dumbrill of the University of London (Royal Holloway), a self-styled archaeomusicologist who—in an effort to overcome the "supremacist" project of "acculturating Semitic musicology under the

---

39. The interpretations compared are: Hans Gustav Güterbock, "Musical Notation in Ugarit," *Revue d'Assyriologie et d'archéologie orientale* 64, no. 1 (1970): 45- 52; David Wulstan, "The Earliest Musical Notation," *Music and Letters* 52, no. 4 (1971): 365–82; Anne Draffkorn Kilmer, "The Cult Song with Music from Ancient Ugarit: Another Interpretation," *Revue d'Assyriologie et d'archéologie orientale* 68, no. 1 (1974): 69–82; Marcelle Duchesne-Guillemin, "Les Problèmes de la notation hourrite," *Revue d'Assyriologie et d'archéologie orientale* 69, no. 2 (1975): 159–73; and Raoul Gregory Vitale, "La Musique suméro-accadienne: Gamme et notation musicale," *Ugarit-Forschungen* 14 (1982): 241–63. (Of these, only Wulstan was a musicologist, the rest being Assyriologists.) West makes some further objections to specific features of Kilmer's transcription, but those noted above are the basic ones.

40. West, "Babylonian Musical Notation," 179.

Occidental yoke"—has posited a reading of the notation that replaces the diatonic intervals ostensibly prescribed by the cuneiform documents with the modes or *maqāmāt* of today's Arab musicians, on the assumption that these modes "were and are inscribed in the memory of the genetic unconscious" of all Middle Eastern musicians. As proof of the correctness of his hypothesis, Dumbrill offered this report:

> In Damascus, during the 2011 Oriental Landscapes Conference, I submitted my interpretation of H6 [the Hurrian song] to leading Maqam musicians at the Dar al-Assad Opera House. They hummed along [with] my interpretation as it was played. After my presentation, they corrected the melody which I was playing electronically, to its proper intonation, and suggested how to play it as it should [be played]. These musicians, after over 3000 years, recognized H6 as part of their heritage.[41]

It is worth noticing that Dumbrill made a claim similar to Crocker's about the viability of his version, except that Crocker, in the tradition of the Enlightenment, emphasized congruence with his own (that is, "our" own) heritage, and Dumbrill, following the Romantic tradition, emphasized congruence with the heritage of the other. A very atmospheric performance of the Dumbrill version, enhanced with sounds of rain and finger cymbals, may be found on YouTube.[42] It differs radically from Crocker and Kilmer's version in three distinct ways (actually reflecting two stages in Dumbrill's research). First, Dumbrill posited that the intervals notated on the cuneiform tablet descended rather than ascended from the pitch of reference, and accepted the theory, deemed implausible by both Kilmer and West, that the intervals called for by the notated pairs of strings represented not dyads but scale segments, so that Dumbrill's version of the melody amounted to a heavily embellished inversion of Kilmer's (Fig. 19.4).[43] But then, and more decisively exoticizing, came Dumbrill's eager adoption of the modifications his Arab listeners had counseled on the basis of their own contemporary practice, which at last allowed him to import into his version the augmented seconds that stereotypically signify the orient to occidental ears. As posted on YouTube, Dumbrill's revised transcription elicited from one listener the exclamation, "Holy shit it's like none of the other versions make any sense once you've heard this one"—impeccable testimony to *l'effet*

---

41. Richard Dumbrill, "The Truth about Babylonian Music," self-published paper available at www.academia.edu/32426527/THE_TRUTH_ABOUT_BABYLONIAN_MUSIC (the first quotation from p. 2, the remainder from p. 31).

42. www.youtube.com/watch?v=gynhfxQ1IO4; Dumbrill's earlier version without the augmented seconds can be found in another YouTube clip, in an arrangement that gives it the full Rimsky-Korsakov treatment: www.youtube.com/watch?v=NeP_ASoDqaU.

43. For a full report of Dumbrill's interpretation and its evolution, see Richard J. Dumbrill, *The Archaeomusicology of the Ancient Near East* (Victoria, BC: Trafford Publishing, 2005), 111–74; the transcription is on p. 130.

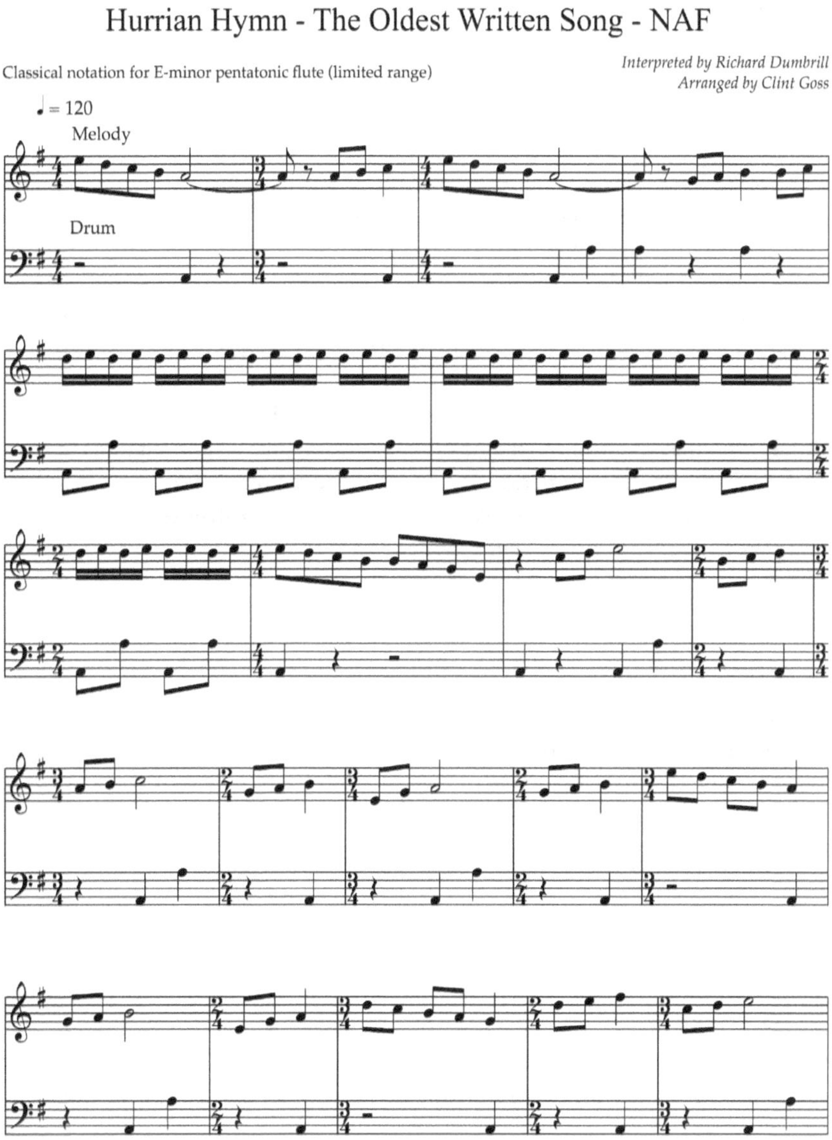
Hurrian Hymn - The Oldest Written Song - NAF
Classical notation for E-minor pentatonic flute (limited range)
Interpreted by Richard Dumbrill
Arranged by Clint Goss
♩ = 120
Melody
Drum

FIGURE 19.4. Hurrian song as transcribed by Richard J. Dumbrill.

de réel, and a triumph of what Robert Winter called "the search" for compelling strangeness.

IV. THE SOUND OF NOWHERE

One last instance related to performance will show what happens when the search is conducted in reverse, beginning not with evidence but with a zealously imagined or desired result. When record companies discovered, in the 1980s, that they could save a great deal of money by getting on the early-music bandwagon, a vogue for period performances of nineteenth-century music was launched well in front of the state of research on nineteenth-century performance practice, which only really got under way when Robert Philip and Clive Brown began issuing their books around the turn of the millennium.[44] The upshot, according to Michelle Dulak, a violinist and violist who took part in several such ad hoc attempts to reinvent a nineteenth-century period style, was a madcap quest in pursuit of truthiness. Recalling the San Francisco Bay Area's period-instrument premiere of Brahms's *Deutsches Requiem*, Dulak writes:

> The string players were in a particularly unfortunate position, as we knew hardly anything about Brahmsian performance practice but were highly conscious of the need to sound as different from modern strings as possible, so as to justify the outrageous cost of the orchestra (some of the winds ha[ving] been flown in from Europe). The solutions dictated to us (vibrato bulges on every long note, the careful avoidance of legato bow changes, the occasional deliberate slurpy portamento for which everyone was directed to use the same fingering, etc.) bore a suspicious resemblance to the kinds of things that unskilled players do unintentionally.[45]

This was a rather telling admission, given the once-frequent allegation that the claim of authenticity gave substandard performers and shoddy performances an alibi, or that interest in historical performance practice was motivated by time-travel fantasies rather than serious musicianship. Since I have made my share of such complaints, I readily acknowledge the dramatic improvement in the level of early-music performances in the four decades since I first wrote about them. But this improvement has been accompanied by an equally dramatic muting of the old authenticity claims. Those who still adhere to the claim are now in the minority,

---

44. Clive Brown, *Classical and Romantic Performing Practice, 1750–1900* (Oxford: Oxford University Press, 1999); Robert Philip, *Performing Music in the Age of Recording* (New Haven, CT: Yale University Press, 2004). See also Michael Musgrave and Bernard D. Sherman, *Performing Brahms: Early Evidence of Performance Style* (Cambridge: Cambridge University Press, 2003).

45. Michelle Dulak, "The Quiet Metamorphosis of 'Early Music,'" *repercussions* 2, no. 2 (Fall 1993): 45n.17.

and they still evince the sort of strange behavior that Michelle Dulak described, in pursuit not of reality but of the reality effect.

The most flagrant recent case, and one that is painful for me to relate, would seem to be that of Sir Roger Norrington, a conductor I once hailed as a great Beethoven performer, whose reputation today is more that of an eccentric or even a crank.[46] Sir Roger performs the orchestral music of the late nineteenth century *senza vibrato*, in a fashion that flatly contradicts the contemporary evidence available for that repertory in verbal testimony, in organ transcriptions that specify registration, and in early sound recordings, but he insists nevertheless that it is his performances, not the ear-witnesses or the old recordings, that reveal the historical reality. What his renditions reveal, of course, is the sort of reality effect that reality can never adequately provide, and for which reality can never compensate. The case for reality has been made once and for all by David Hurwitz in a crushing assemblage—directly provoked by Norrington's allegations—of contemporary reviews, extracts from conductors' manuals, and ear-witness testimony. He marshals recollections or prescriptions by Vincent D'Indy, Herbert Borodkin (who played violin in the New York Philharmonic under Mahler), Désiré-Émile Inghelbrecht, Hermann Scherchen, Eugene Goossens, Imogen Holst, Bruno Walter, and a host of others.[47] All to no avail: true believers in the reality effect can always find reasons to discount empirical evidence of a reality that contradicts their fantasies. In Sir Roger's case, the fantasy is that

> [v]ibrato did not become common in European or American orchestras until the 1930s. Yet, remarkably, players and listeners alike seem to have become entirely used to an orchestral sound that not one of the great composers before that time would have expected or imagined. When Berlioz and Schumann, Brahms and Wagner, Bruckner and Mahler, Schoenberg and Berg were composing their masterpieces, there was only one orchestral sound: a warm, expressive, pure tone, without glamorised vibrato. "Glamorous" describes the new sound well. The word was little used before the 1920s. It arrived with Hollywood, aerodynamic car design, radio, ocean liners and the early days of flight.[48]

Maestro Norrington fingers Fritz Kreisler (1875–1962) as the virtually single-handed culprit, who adulterated the "pure tone" that Berg and Berlioz knew by "drawing on the style of cafe musicians and Hungarian and Gypsy fiddlers." He invokes the style's disreputable racial origin with the zeal of a border guard—"exotic"

---

46. See R. Taruskin, "Beethoven: The New Antiquity," *Opus*, October 1987, 31–41, 42, 63; rpt. in Taruskin, *Text and Act*, 202–34.

47. David Hurwitz, "'So klingt Wien': Conductors, Orchestras, and Vibrato in the Nineteenth and Early Twentieth Centuries," *Music and Letters* 93 (2012): 29–60. For an even more compendious mobilization of evidence, see the same author's 117-page essay "Orchestral Vibrato, Historical Context, and the Evidence of the Printed Page," at www.classicstoday.com/features/ClassicsToday-Vibrato.pdf.

48. Roger Norrington, "Bad Vibrations," *Guardian*, 28 February 2003, 16.

here picking up some of its resonance from phrases like "exotic dancing," where the word is clearly a euphemism for "erotic." He emphasizes the point (or supposition) that the first orchestral players to jump on the vibrato bandwagon were "the more sensuous and entertainment-minded French players," rather than "the high-minded Germans," meanwhile wringing his hands at the thought of what Elgar might have felt "as his noble world slipped away."[49] And yet when Daniel Wakin, the very sharp music reporter of the *New York Times,* confronted Norrington with the evidence of Elgar's own recorded performances, the maestro had to concede that "early recordings of orchestras playing Elgar's music under the composer's own baton revealed a fair bit of vibrato." "But," Wakin continued, Norrington "contended that the practice was creeping into orchestras whether composers liked it or not, and that Elgar grew up as a musician listening to music without vibrato."[50]

It remains a mystery how he has determined this. Hurwitz, Wakin, and others have also noted the quaint contradiction between the history of vibrato, as Maestro Norrington recounts it, and that of *portamento,* the technique of sliding ("slurpily," as Michelle Dulak describes it) from pitch to pitch. Portamento can be found in profusion in virtually any recording of solo or orchestral strings made up until the 1920s, but it went decisively out of fashion exactly when Maestro Norrington claims that vibrato was coming in. The rejection of portamento comports tidily enough with the general "ban on pathos" that took hold in the arts after the Great War (the phenomenon to which chapter 20 in this book is devoted). That would be an unlikely moment to introduce continuous vibrato to warm up or "glamorize" the timbre of string instruments. The one putative change contradicts the other, lending further credence to the available aural evidence and oral testimony that vibrato had in fact continued unchanged, while portamento went out of fashion. But nothing daunted, Maestro Norrington, having it both ways, eschews both vibrato and portamento in his performances of Elgar, in the case of portamento discounting the copious evidence of Elgar's own preference—or at the very least, his tolerance—by pointing to Elgar's age at the time the recordings were made, as if to imply that he was too feeble, or possibly too deaf, to oppose the degenerate practices of younger musicians.

Elgar's "noble world" was neither an historical nor a geographical reality. It was a pure, unspecified "someplace else" (εξωτικός/*exotikos*), for which another name is Utopia. And that, finally, is the no-place where authenticity resides. As David Hurwitz has noted, "[E]liminating vibrato creates an instant 'differentness'" that gratifies the sense of discovery on which the early-music movement thrives and justifies itself, and also provides those who have assumed the movement's financial risk with an effective marketing ploy.[51]

49. Ibid.
50. Daniel J. Wakin, "Elgar without Vibrato? Fiddlesticks," *New York Times,* 12 August 2008.
51. Hurwitz, "'So klingt Wien,'" 55.

V. MORE FOLKY THAN THE FOLK

But let us turn now from temporal to geographical utopias. One of the signal tendencies in European and Euro-American music of the nineteenth century was the ongoing discovery by urban, professional musicians of the true lore of nations, the art and wisdom over which the unlettered denizens of the countryside stood guardian. If we take Johann Gottfried Herder's *Abhandlung über den Ursprung der Sprache* (Treatise on the Origin of Language) and his collections of what he was in point of fact the first to call *Volkslieder,* all published during the 1770s, as the fountainhead of this discovery, then the privileged territory, the cradle of European folklore—or, at least, of European folklorism—was the Baltic coast; for Herder was a Baltic German living in Riga, and the first peasant population whose folklore he studied consisted of Letts or Latvians, who inhabited the rural regions around the German-speaking provincial capital. Eastern and central Europe have since retained their focal position as repositories of folklore in the eyes of the more advanced and urbanized economies of western Europe and America—especially the folklore that was adapted to the forms and styles of professional art in the nineteenth and twentieth centuries.

So the question of its status—authentic or exotic?—is fraught with quandaries and ambiguities.[52] The matter is obviously in large part one of perspective. What was authentic to the Letts was exotic to the Germans; and from this we may draw a generalization based on the historical dynamic of ethnography: what is authentic at the moment of production or of culling is exotic by the time it reaches the consumer. This holds true even when producers and consumers belong to the same ethnic group. The role of mediator—that is, the agent who disseminates the cultural product of the folk among the literate—thus has, among its functions, that of exoticizing the authentic to the point where the exoticizing act becomes, if one may put it so, a fabricator of authenticity. In the case of music, this is the function performed by the artist-composer (who may also be the scholar-collector) when adapting folklore and giving it, to put it as Dvořák once did, "beautiful treatment in the higher forms of art."[53] The utopian versions of folklore thus purveyed to a literate public are often—even usually—altered for the sake of the reality effect, and I will end this survey with three examples of this seeming paradox, all drawn from the territories of central and eastern Europe, that appeared within a temporal span of fifteen years, from 1913 to 1928.

---

52. A whole book devoted to sorting them out is Joshua Walden, *Sounding Authentic: The Rural Miniature and Musical Modernism* (New York: Oxford University Press, 2014), which deals exclusively with folklore-based violin solos.

53. As paraphrased by Henry Krehbiel in the *New York Daily Tribune,* 17 December 1893, 7; quoted in Michael Beckerman, "Henry Krehbiel, Antonín Dvořák, and the Symphony 'From the New World,'" *MLA Notes* 49 (1992–93): 158.

EXAMPLE 19.3A–B. Opening bassoon melody of *Le Sacre du printemps* (b) and its source (a).

The earliest example comes from Stravinsky's *Sacre du printemps*. For a long time, it was believed on Stravinsky's say-so that the opening bassoon melody was the only adapted folk song in the ballet's score (Ex. 19.3). It was Lawrence Morton, one of Stravinsky's surviving Los Angeles friends, who first had the inspired idea of checking the ballet against the source of the one acknowledged original, a book of Lithuanian wedding songs assembled by a Polish priest named Anton Juszkiewicz (1819–80) and posthumously published in 1900.[54] Sure enough, Morton easily succeeded in identifying four more melodies from this book that had gone, unacknowledged, into *Le Sacre*.[55]

One of these was the tune played by the piccolo trumpet in D to initiate the frantic *Jeu de rapt*, or "Ritual of Abduction" (Ex. 19.4). Stravinsky altered many aspects of the notation in adapting this tune for his ballet: he transposed it, eliminated the third measure of the original, diminished its note values, increased the tempo, changed the meter, and so on. None of these changes affect the actual intervallic or rhythmic identity of the tune. But he also altered the fourth note from the end by lowering it a half step, so that it no longer has the sound, or suggests the function, of a leading tone. The removal of leading tones or their replacement by "lowered" or "modal" seventh degrees was a time-honored archaizing or otherwise exoticizing device by the time Stravinsky did it here. It was also a way of asserting some sort of nativism against the dominant or default ("unmarked") art-music style, as Max Bruch recognized when he teased his young English pupil Ralph Vaughan Williams: "Sie haben eine Leidenschaft für die kleine Septime!" (You have a weakness for the flat seventh).[56] More recently, yesterday's (or the day before yes-

---

54. Anton Juszkiewicz, *Melodje ludowe litewskie* (Cracow: Wydawnictwo Akademii Umiejętności, 1900).

55. Lawrence Morton, "Footnotes to Stravinsky Studies: 'Le Sacre du printemps,'" *Tempo*, n.s., no. 128 (March 1979): 9–16.

56. Quoted in Christopher Fifield, *Max Bruch: His Life and Works* (Woodbridge, UK: Boydell Press, 2005), 271.

EXAMPLE 19.4A-C. Trumpet melody in *Jeu de rapt* (c), its source (a), and its appearance in sketchbook (b).

terday's) early-music groups often refrained—as no fifteenth- or sixteenth-century musician would have ever done—from applying the *musica ficta* rule called *subsemitonium modi*, purging their performances of cadential leading tones so as to impress their listeners with the scrupulousness of their performance practice.[57] It is the equivalent of "antiquing" (or "distressing") a piece of furniture.

Whether invoked by Stravinsky, by Vaughan Williams, or by the Capella Antiqua of Munich, this sort of authenticity could seem to be counting cynically on the ignorance of consumers. But it may with equal justice be called naïve. The point, here as everywhere, now as always, is not literal truth but legibility; not reality but the reality effect as experienced by perpetrators as well as their ostensible marks. Vaughan Williams's *kleine Septime* served the same purpose, for him as much as for his eventual listeners, as Flaubert's barometer.

A somewhat later example comes from the work of Béla Bartók, the greatest of those who doubled in the twentieth century as scholar-collector and artist-arranger or -composer, and no one's idea of a cynic. His example shows us clearly how separate the two roles can be even when housed in a single psyche. They do

---

57. An example is a performance of Heinrich Isaac's motet *Rogamus te, piissima Virgo Maria* (a.k.a. *La mi la sol*) by a group calling itself Speculum Ensemble (www.youtube.com/watch?v=ariIYcSMS8s), possibly copying a once widely circulated recording by the Capella Antiqua München under its founder, Konrad Ruhland (1932–2010) (Isaac, *Missa super "O praeclara" La Mi La Sol: Motetten und Lieder um 1480–1517*, Telefunken SAWT 9544-A [1969]).

not coexist in time, the collector always preceding the arranger, and their equally legitimate objectives may diverge, even to the point of conflict.

No musical ethnographer was ever more fastidious than Bartók when it came to transcription. His descriptive notations of his field recordings are of a legendary finickiness, and so delayed the process of publication that some of his ethnographic works became posthumous. Likewise the detail with which he itemized the time and place of recording his cylinders, identifying the performers by ethnicity, age, gender, occupation, and so on. Similarly exigent were the prescriptions Bartók implied in his writings about the creative appropriation of folklore, emphasizing that the arranger's role is to be confined to that of supplying an artistic accompaniment to the transcribed material, "an ornamental setting for the precious stone: the peasant melody." The added material may ultimately be of greater prominence than the peasant melody itself: "the melody" in this case "serv[ing] as a 'motto' while that which is built around it is of real importance." Either way, the peasant melody is assumed to be inviolate, "unchanged or only slightly varied."[58] And yet, as David E. Schneider was among the first to point out, in actual practice Bartók the creative musician did not observe such stringent constraints. Far from confining himself to slight variations in his adaptations of peasant material, he often altered the melodies he collected in basic and sometimes very telling ways.

A vivid case in point is the opening melody in his Rhapsody for Violin no. 1. Example 19.5 reproduces an example from Schneider's monograph *Bartók, Hungary, and the Renewal of Tradition,* in which the source melody, collected by Bartók from a peasant fiddler in 1914 and transcribed with his usual fanatical precision in his collection *Rumanian Folk Music* (*RFM*), is placed above the tune as it appears in the finished score of 1928. Changed are the tempo, the rhythms, the ornamentation, the grace notes (both added and deleted), the use of multiple stops, bowing, and so forth.

Schneider emphasizes that some of Bartók's alterations, particularly the use of emphatic double-dotted short-long rhythms in m. 9 and m. 11, make the melody more typically (or stereotypically) Hungarian. And well they might, since the original melody was imparted to Bartók not by a Hungarian but by a Romanian fiddler. Bartók very uncharacteristically concealed this fact in the score, although his habit had previously been to include all the pertinent ethnographic information about adapted tunes in his original compositions. His reticence this time is not to be wondered at: Hungary and Romania had been enemies in World War I, and remained bitterly antagonistic afterward. Bartók had been denounced as unpatri-

---

58. Béla Bartók, "The Influence of Peasant Music on Modern Music," in *Béla Bartók Essays*, ed. Benjamin Suchoff (New York: St. Martin's Press, 1976); rpt. in Piero Weiss and Richard Taruskin, eds., *Music in the Western World: A History in Documents*, 2nd ed. (Belmont CA: Thomson/Schirmer, 2008), 379.

EXAMPLE 19.5. Comparison of "De ciuit" in *Rumanian Folk Music* (*RFM*), vol. 1 (melody no. 232), and in Bartók, Rhapsody for Violin no. 1 (from David E. Schneider, *Bartók, Hungary, and the Renewal of Tradition* 2006], Ex. 63 [pp. 210–11]).

otic for persisting in his study of Romanian music alongside Hungarian. So why, then, would he want to include a Romanian melody in his ostensibly Hungarian Rhapsody, and even disguise it as Hungarian?

The reason for the disguise is that it was in fact no disguise as far as Bartók was concerned, but rather a restoration. Bartók believed that this particular fiddle tune, though long since assimilated to the repertoire and performance practice of Romanian fiddlers, was actually a Hungarian *verbunkos*, or recruitment dance, and in adapting it he was in effect returning it to its Hungarian roots. "In the context of post-Trianon tensions," Schneider writes, alluding to the treaty that, among other things, awarded to Romania a large swath of Hungarian territory that included Bartók's birthplace,

[i]t is easy to see how Bartók, a Hungarian, could have been accused of musico-political aggression because of his reclamation of a tune preserved by generations of Romanian peasants, and thus how his arrangement of the tune could be interpreted as musical irredentism. This potential charge might well be one reason Bartók chose to withhold the concordance between the Rhapsodies' tunes and the regions of their origins from [potential performers as well as his correspondents]. Such reasoning is, however, dangerously incomplete, for it accepts the dialectical extremes of innocence and guilt imagined by Bartók's attackers, who reduced subtle theories of folk music to crude nationalistic extremes. Following a line of reasoning that directly translates Bartók's scientific or artistic endeavors into categories of political right and wrong means accepting notions of ethnic and musical purity that were antithetical to Bartók's own conception of folk music and its relationship to his original compositions.[59]

And what was "Bartók's own conception"? The First Rhapsody, writes Schneider, "is a perfect example of how Bartók, a believer in 'pure sources,' incorporated elements of Romanian and Hungarian folk styles, the peasant variant of the Gypsy *verbunkos*, and the cimbalom, an urbanized folk instrument, to create a virtuoso art-music of an intact, homogeneous peasant culture."[60] That intact, homogeneous culture was neither Romanian nor Hungarian, of course. It was Utopian, which is to say, no matter where you happen to be located in the terrestrial world, it was located "someplace else"—in some universally exotic and purified meta-ethnic hyperspace. As always, the reality effect trumps reality. Reality is never equal to the task of "true" representation.

VI. FOR THE GOYIM?

But I have saved for last my favorite Flaubertian barometer. It is found in the work of Leo (or Lev, or Leyb) Zeitlin (or Tseytlin) (1881–1930), a member of the St. Petersburg Society for Jewish Folk Music. This was an organization founded in 1908 by a group of former pupils of Nikolai Andreyevich Rimsky-Korsakov, and with his encouragement, although he had died shortly before the organization was incorporated. Its name was a misnomer: the Society's primary purpose was not to promote folk music but to promote art music composed by academically trained Jewish composers who sought to form a national school on the model of the Russian art music of the nineteenth century, including Rimsky-Korsakov's. The distorting name was dictated by General Daniyil Vasilievich Drachevsky (1858–1918),

---

59. David E. Schneider, *Bartók, Hungary, and the Renewal of Tradition: Case Studies in the Intersection of Modernity and Nationality* (Berkeley and Los Angeles: University of California Press, 2006), 208–9. The Treaty of Trianon (1920) was the legal instrument through which Hungary was dismembered and reduced, after World War I, to a third of the territory assigned to it within the former Hapsburg Empire.

60. Ibid., 201.

the chief of police and head of city administration in St. Petersburg, to whom the founders had applied for incorporation.[61]

According to an oft-repeated story from the memoirs of Solomon Rozovsky, one of the founders, Rimsky-Korsakov had declared that Jewish music "awaits its Glinka."[62] Just what this meant we may deduce from a comparison of Leo Zeitlin's best-known composition, a cello solo called *Eli Tsion,* and its eponymous source melody. Zeitlin composed the work in 1911 for cello and orchestra and published it in 1914 in piano reduction (Fig. 19.5). Its full title is *Eli Tsiyoyn: Fantazye iber a folksmelodye un trop fun "Shir hashirim"* (Lament, O Zion: Fantasia on a folk melody and the cantillation for "The Song of Songs").[63] The first of the two melodies on which Zeitlin drew (Ex. 19.6a, by kind courtesy of Paula Eisenstein Baker) had been published (as harmonized by the Rimsky-Korsakov pupil Alexander Matveyevich Zhitomirsky) by the ethnographer Zisman Kiselgof (1878–1939) in a collection issued in 1912 by the Society for Jewish Folk Music under the title *Lider-Zamelbuch far der yidisher shul un familie* (Songbook for the Jewish School and Family). Example 19.6b shows the beginning of the solo part as adapted by Zeitlin, in an edition by Eisenstein Baker and Robert Nelson published in 2009. And example 19.7 aligns the two versions for easy comparison.

As one can see, Zeitlin has treated the source melody as freely as Bartók would later do his, and in many of the same ways. To recall the list from that previous exhibit, they include tempo (slowed down from *andante* to *largo*), rhythms (from strict triple time to a recitative-like mutable meter), ornamentation and grace notes (all added by Zeitlin), and so forth. There is one discrepancy that goes further than anything in Bartók, however, but replicates—or rather, strangely complements—what Stravinsky did in fashioning the trumpet tune in his *Jeu de rapt:* in the fourth measure of Zeitlin's melody, the source's G has been raised to G-sharp, so that the interval that follows it becomes not a plain major second or whole step, as in the source melody, but a highly marked—or should I say fraught?—augmented second, an interval that is found in many exotic scales, including two that are often, but far from exclusively, employed in Jewish folk and religious music: (1) the Ahavoh

---

61. See Albert Weisser, *The Modern Renaissance of Jewish Music: Events and Figures, Eastern Europe and America* (New York: Bloch, 1954), 45.

62. For an account of this story's dissemination and consideration of its status as possibly apocryphal, see Paula Eisenstein Baker and Robert S. Nelson, Introduction to Leo Zeitlin, *Chamber Music,* ed. P. E. Baker and R. S. Nelson (Middleton, WI: A-R Editions, 2009), xlix–ln80.

63. It may be heard via YouTube in a performance by the cellist David Geringas, accompanied by Jascha Nemtsov: www.youtube.com/watch?v=1nh8_xPx4TQ; a more recent recording, by the cellist Aron Zelkowicz, accompanied by Luz Manriquez, in *Leo Zeitlin: Yiddish Songs, Chamber Music, and Declamations,* Russian Jewish Classics, vol. 1 (Toccata Classics, 2015), uses a revised edition of the score, corrected by the editor, Paula Eisenstein Baker. It too is available on YouTube, at www.youtube.com/watch?v=shZt2ufK6n4.

FIGURE 19.5. Leo Zeitlin, *Eli Zion* (St. Petersburg: Gesellschaft für jüdische Volksmusik, 1914).

EXAMPLE 19.6A. *Eli Zijojn, wejoreho,* arr. Alexander Zhitomirsky (*Lieder Sammelbuch für die jüdische Schule und Familie,* ed. Kisselgof, Zhitomirsky, and Lwow [St. Petersburg and Berlin: Gesellschaft für jüdische Volksmusik u. Leo Winz, 1912], 8).

EXAMPLE 19.6B. Leo Zeitlin, *Eli Tsion* (St. Petersburg: Gesellschaft für jüdische Volksmusik, 1914), mm. 1–16.

EXAMPLE 19.7. From second page of Paula Eisenstein Baker AMS handout "Art Music on Ashkenazi Jewish Themes: The Society for Jewish Folk Music (1908–1919)" (Baltimore, 1996).

Rabboh *shtayger* (or mode) of Ashkenazic synagogue cantillation, also known as the *frigish* by *klezmorim* or Yiddish-speaking folk musicians, possibly on a loose analogy with the Phrygian "church mode" in medieval European music theory; or (2) the scale that Avraham Zvi Idelsohn (1882–1938), following a nomenclature proposed by the Ukrainian musicologist Filaret Kolessa (1871–1947), called the "Ukrainian Doric." Given the D minor key signature of Zeitlin's composition (transposed from Kiselgof's A minor),[64] it would seem sufficient to follow the advice of the American ethnomusicologist Mark Slobin and simply call Zeitlin's G-sharp a "raised fourth."[65]

When I first observed this change, at a meeting of the American Musicological Society some thirty years ago, where Paula Eisenstein Baker first presented her research on Zeitlin's music, I was moved to comment that the G-sharp had been added "for the goyim"—that is, so that non-Jews would be able to recognize the melody as Jewish. It was obvious that Zeitlin had deliberately introduced an orientalizing or ghettoizing ingredient that made the tune inescapably legible. That was in keeping with the idea of "being a Glinka," for not only Glinka but all the Russian nationalist composers who had provided the model for the Society for Jewish Folk Music had, whenever they thought it necessary, improved upon the Russianness of their folklore sources so that their compositions would make a properly exotic (read: authentic) impression on modern urban audiences, both at home and

---

64. Kiselgof's original notation from his informant had been in G minor (information kindly provided by Paula Eisenstein Baker via email, 13 August 2016).

65. See Mark Slobin, "The Evolution of a Musical Symbol in Yiddish Culture," in *Studies in Jewish Folklore: Proceedings of a Regional Conference of the Association for Jewish Studies Held at the Spertus College of Judaica, Chicago, May 1–3, 1977*, ed. Frank Talmage (Cambridge, MA: Association for Jewish Studies, 1980), 314–15.

(especially) abroad. Like Glinka (and like Stravinsky), Zeitlin had, as we now say, performed an act of marking, or—if we disapprove—of "othering."

As the source melody reveals, actual Jews did not need augmented seconds in order to practice their Judaism musically; nor did a utilitarian arranger like Kiselgof see the need to enhance the melody's Jewishness. They dealt with music as part of their lived reality, not as a reality effect, and had no need for Barthes's "referential illusion." Kiselgof and his informants knew where they came from. If asked, they would have said, "Right here." Zeitlin's Jewish melody, precisely because it was intended as autonomous art and as representation, had to come from *someplace else* ("so you can't be here!")—a utopian space where Jews conformed to the unwritten rule that all ethnicities shall wear an identifying badge.

The self-evidence of the augmented second as a badge of Jewishness is actually something of a paradox. If we are to speak strictly of contemporary reality, as opposed to the reality effect, then we must acknowledge that the use of augmented seconds in eastern European folk music is a geographical rather than a specifically ethnic phenomenon, and one restricted to only a few locales. Slobin notes "considerable clustering among the Ukrainians and Rumanians, particularly in Moldavia, the Bukovina, somewhat less frequently in Maramures, and rarely if at all, in some other regions," and little or no occurrences in Slovak, Polish, Hungarian, Russian, or Belorussian folk song, except in areas bordering on Ukraine.[66] The incidence of modes or scales incorporating the augmented second is no greater in Yiddish folk song than in that of the majority populations in these territories. (Citing Moshe Beregovsky, Slobin gives a figure of 4.5 percent in folk song and 10–12 percent in instrumental tunes.) Moreover, the scale Jews call *frigish*, in which the augmented second comes between the second and third degrees, is congruent with the Hijaz mode of the "Arabo-Persian" classical music system that provided Richard Dumbrill with his "Hurrian" reality effect, and as such is widespread throughout the Middle East and the Mediterranean basin.

Ideas about its provenance are correspondingly numerous, and nebulous. Eric Werner (1901–88), a major authority on the history of Jewish music, proposed that the Ahavoh Rabboh *shtayger*, the synagogue cognate of the *frigish*, "was introduced to the West more than once and in different places," among them "Spain, Sicily, the Balkans, Ancient Greece, Armenia, Russia (almost certainly via the Black Sea) and North and East Africa."[67] Slobin drily comments that this is "certainly a generous spread for provenance." To compound the paradox, when a composer of Yiddish popular music for the stage like Avraham Goldfadn (1840–1908), the founder (at first in Romania) of the Yiddish secular theater, sought to portray

---

66. Ibid., 315–16.
67. Eric Werner, *A Voice Still Heard . . .: The Sacred Songs of the Ashkenazic Jews* (University Park: Pennsylvania State University Press, 1976), 57; quoted in Slobin, "Evolution," 316.

non-Jewish exotic types such as black servants or Turks, he resorted to the same augmented seconds that elsewhere signified Jews.[68] As we have already seen, it can perform the same signifying, exoticizing/authenticating role for a 3,500-year-old Hurrian melody from ancient Babylonia if it needs to.

So why, then, both the prevalence of augmented seconds in music meant to portray—or, more often, caricature—Jews in the work of gentile composers (and here I need only mention Musorgsky's famous "'Samuel' Goldenberg and 'Schmuÿle'" from his *Pictures at an Exhibition*),[69] and the proprietary attitude of Ashkenazic Jews themselves—Leyb Zeitlin, for one—toward a musical gesture that is far from exclusively theirs?

Or, to compound the paradox from the other end, consider another of Goldfadn's habits of appropriation. In a memoir, Goldfadn wrote that

> at times I smuggled in light melodies by Offenbach, Le Coq, Verdi, Meyerbeer, and even Wagner... because I wanted to raise the musical taste of the broad masses of my people. But, unfortunately, the tastes of the lower layers of the Jewish population were so contaminated that they simply couldn't bear European music.... I had to renounce these pointless attempts and take another path. I limited myself to preserving a particular Jewish folk music, characterized by a certain Phrygian mode.[70]

In practice, however, it seems that in his effort to make light classics palatable to his Jewish audiences, Goldfadn adulterated them with *frigish* strains. Idelsohn very plausibly identified one of Goldfadn's greatest hits, the "Oath" from his operetta *Shulamis*, as an adaptation of Violetta's aria "Ah forsè lui che l'anima" from *La Traviata* (Ex. 19.8).[71] Does Goldfadn's adaptation do anything more to Verdi's famous tune than give it a Yiddish accent?

An observation by Eric Werner would seem to imply that there was more to Goldfadn's appropriation than a mere inflection; and at the same time it offers a plausible additional motivation for Zeitlin's telltale G-sharp. The Ahavoh Rabboh liturgical mode, according to Werner, "was supposed to be the perfect expression of penitential contrition and deep lament—the theological ideal of a cantor's effect upon the worshippers" in eighteenth-century Poland, the birthplace of Hasidism. Moreover, Werner notes, "in spite of musicologists, the Eastern European hazanim (cantors) are still firmly (and wrongly) convinced that the Ahavah Rabah is principally theirs, and that all other appearances are borrowings from the world of

---

68. Slobin, "Evolution," 321–22.

69. On this particular usage, see R. Taruskin, "*Yevreyi* and *Zhidy*: A Memoir, a Survey, and a Plea," in *On Russian Music* (Berkeley and Los Angeles: University of California Press, 2009), 190–201, esp. 198–200.

70. Z. Zylbercwajg, *Leksikon fun yidishn teater*, vol. 1 (New York: Aetna Printers, 1931), 348; quoted in Slobin, "Evolution," 320.

71. Zylbercwajg, *Leksikon*, 349; cited in Slobin, "Evolution," 322.

EXAMPLE 19.8. Comparison of Goldfadn, "Oath," *Shulamis*, and Verdi, "Ah forsè lui che l'anima," *La Traviata* (from Mark Slobin, "The Evolution of a Musical Symbol in Yiddish Culture," in *Studies in Jewish Folklore*, ed. Frank Talmage [Cambridge, MA: Association for Jewish Studies, 1980], Ex. 6a–b, p. 323).

Eastern Jewish chant."[72] Accordingly, the frequency of the mode shoots up to 85 percent in the *nigunim*, or wordless devotional songs, of the Hasidim.[73] The mode has become conceptualized among Hasidism as a means of self-representation based on contrition or lament. As a symbol of Jewish piety and mourning, then, the mode, whittled down metonymically to a single augmented second, must have struck Zeitlin as indispensable for a composition titled "Lament, O Zion!" His representational (and self-representational) purpose as a Jewish composer of art music virtually demanded the appropriation in question. True, Zeitlin's augmented second, coming as it does between the third and fourth degrees of the D minor scale, is actually closer to the Ukrainian Doric than to the *frigish* or the Ahavoh Rabboh scales. The raised-fourth scale, however, is also used for "songs of lament, grief, and separation," although it has other contexts as well.[74]

So Zeitlin's appropriation of the augmented second was not for the goyim after all—or, at any rate, not just for them. It was also an aspect of affective representation, or what is loosely called expressive content. Either way, the overriding point is confirmed. The actual appropriated artifact, the song *Eli Tsiyoyn* as transcribed and published by Kiselgof, was in the eyes of the artist-composer an inadequate expression of the emotion the text ought to convey; and so, even in—or especially in—an adaptation of the song that divested it of its words, the augmented second was a necessary addition. Where reality proved deficient, the reality effect stood ready.

---

72. Werner, *A Voice*, 53, 57; quoted in Slobin, "Evolution," 319.
73. Werner, *A Voice*, 53; quoted in Slobin, "Evolution," 319.
74. Slobin, "Evolution," 319, citing Beregovsky, "Izmenennïy doriyskiy lad v yevreyskom muzïkal'nom fol'klore (k voprosu o semanticheskikh svoystvakh lada)" (The altered Dorian mode in Jewish musical folklore [on the question of the semantic properties of mode]), in *Problemï muzïkal'nogo fol'klora narodov SSSR*, ed. Izaly Zemtsovsky (Moscow: Muzïka, 1973).

In sum, the exoticizing move indicated more than Jewishness, even if Jewishness was ineluctably among the things it indicated (and possibly all it would have signified to goyim). As Slobin writes with reference to the varying intentions and interpretations the augmented second might serve, "For the in-group audience, the usages are appropriate and traditional, while for the mainstream viewer the melodies come across as packaged ethnic symbolism."[75] And even more to the point, the reference—for some traditional, for others exotic (for some self-defining, that is, and for others other-defining)—was among the professional, composerly traces that rendered Zeitlin's composition properly artistic: the work not of the folk, but of their Glinka.

Reality alone could not supply a Glinka with what he and his audience needed. It never does. Perhaps Quentin Crisp, the author of *The Naked Civil Servant*, did the best job saying why. Asked about the relationship between the filmed version of his famous memoir and his real life, he said, "Any film, even the worst, is at least better than real life."[76] Any one of the musicians named in this essay might have agreed—as long as the tape was not running.

---

75. Slobin, "Evolution," 327.
76. www.screenonline.org.uk/tv/id/499175/synopsis.html.

20

Pathos Is Banned

I. THE OTHER GUY

What, exactly, are we celebrating when we meet as musicologists to mark the centennial of World War I? Steven Shapin, an American historian and sociologist of science, recently offered a summary that might interest us as historians of the arts. "A hundred years or so ago," he writes,

> historians' predictions were driven by their conception of the laws of change—the rationally knowable principles that accounted for past events and made it possible to forecast the future. Providential history—invoking God's plan for human affairs—had lost its academic authority in the 18th century, displaced in the 19th and early 20th centuries by secular schemas: progressivist Whig interpretations of history; Auguste Comte's law of three successive stages in human history (the "theological" giving way to the "metaphysical" and then to the "positive" or "scientific" stage); the narratives of the march of civilization from myth to science . . .; the determining force of class conflict in Marxism; the environmental "challenge and response" theories of writers from Montesquieu and Malthus to Arnold Toynbee; the selection pressures identified by Social Darwinisms.[1]

Keynote address, international conference "The Great War 1914–1918 and Music: Compositional Strategies, Performing Practices, and Social Impacts," Golden Hall, Croatian Institute, Zagreb, 24 October 2017; published in Stanislav Tuksar and Monika Jurić Janjik, eds., *Prvi Svjetski Rat 1914–1918 i glazba/ The Great War 1914–1918 and Music* (Zagreb: Hrvatsko Muzikološko Društvo, 2019), 19–40.

1. Steven Shapin, "The Superhuman Upgrade" (a review of *Homo Deus: A Brief History of Tomorrow*, by Yuval Noah Harari), *London Review of Books*, 13 July 2017, 29.

It seems a feat of absentmindedness that Shapin left G. W. F. Hegel off his list—Hegel, the *Grossvater* of all nineteenth-century meliorists, the one who defined "the History of the World" as "nothing other than the progress of the consciousness of freedom [*der Fortschritt im Bewußtsein der Freiheit*]."[2] But Shapin does include Marx, who saw himself as Hegel's successor, and who succeeded, he thought, in turning Hegel's metaphysical theory into what Comte would have called a positive one, hence all the more reliable and uplifting. The centennial we are celebrating—if *celebrating* is the right word—is the centennial of the end of all that, the loss of all faith in *Fortschritt*, that assurance that everything is getting better all the time on a path to perfection.

My chief peculiarity among historians of twentieth-century music, if I may judge according to the reception my work has enjoyed—if *enjoyed* is the right word—is that I have regarded this loss of faith as a signal event in the century's musical history as well as its social and political history. I have cast my work explicitly as anti-Hegelian. In so doing I have charged the standard narrative of twentieth-century musical historiography with having perpetuated an outdated and discredited ideology. And while I am far from alone by now in this endeavor, resistance has been persistent, for Hegel lives on in the hearts of music historians and in musical discourse as he does nowhere else. This very year, 2017, has seen the publication of a book by Bálint András Varga titled *The Courage of Composers and the Tyranny of Taste*, consisting of interviews with thirty-eight *Weltgenies* describing their heroic struggles to uphold the autonomy of art. It is bursting with *Fortschritt*. On page 1 the author writes of James Joyce *progressing* from *Dubliners* to *Finnegans Wake* and Kazimir Malevich *progressing* from *Spring Garden in Bloom* to *Black Square on a White Field*.[3] Faith lives on despite everything, as indeed it must if practical musicians and composers are to go on in the face of its loss. But diminishing returns having so long ago set in, it seems incumbent at least on historians to give up, and expose, the pretense of aesthetic autonomy.

When my *Oxford History of Western Music* was reissued in a revised paperback edition in 2010, there had been four years in which to gauge its reception, and so I was able to state, in a preface to the new edition, that the fourth volume, which covered the first half of the twentieth century, "differ[ed] the most radically from previous accounts," not only by design but also by observed effect. The most conspicuous and easily designated difference consisted in

> a revised subperiodization whereby the early decades of the century, usually represented as marking a violent break with the technical and expressive traditions of the

---

2. G. W. F. Hegel, *Vorlesungen über die Philosophie der Geschichte*, ed. Eduard Gans, vol. 9 of *Hegel's Werke* (Berlin: Duncker & Homblot, 1837), 22.

3. Bálint András Varga, *The Courage of Composers and the Tyranny of Taste: Reflections on New Music* (Rochester, NY: University of Rochester Press, 2017), 1.

PATHOS IS BANNED   449

nineteenth century, are cast instead as an intensification—or maximalization, to use the word introduced [here]in—of those very traditions. The true break with tradition came in the 1920s with the movement, often identified as "neoclassicism," which the conventional narrative represents as a return, or regression, to traditional ways.[4]

The title of this talk, "Pathos Is Banned," is also the title of the eighth chapter of that fourth volume of the *Oxford History*, in which that "true break" is described, and in which the First World War is named as the watershed separating old from new. That war looms larger in my narrative than in most others, partly because I saw its effects not only as crucial but as lasting, and partly because other narratives have tended to minimize such effects, in keeping with their commitment to the relative autonomy of art. That commitment may be less widely shared among the self-selected cohort in this room today than it is in the musical and music-historical professions at large. I suspect that many of us seated here agree with the position advanced in the preface to my revised fourth volume, which "rejects the romantic viewpoint that asserts a fundamental divide between art history and world history," and in particular identifies the premise of autonomy as "impeding by design the investigation of the actual causes of aesthetic and stylistic evolution, which are to be sought within rather than outside the histories of social and political affairs."[5] I want to revisit that argument and demonstration today, in the first instance to add some more contemporary testimony to the evidence that justifies the claim, but also to show that the resistance the argument now elicits itself has a history—one that can be fruitfully investigated both as it pertains to artistic practice and as it pertains to commentary.

The first witness I shall call is Wyndham Lewis—or, as people tend to think of him now, "the other guy." Just as the Three Tenors consisted of Pavarotti, Domingo, and the other guy (named Carreras, in case you had forgotten), so the remarkable cohort of Anglo-modernists once known as the "Men of 1914" consisted of Joyce, Pound, Eliot, (sometimes) Yeats, or (as a token) Virginia Woolf—and the other guy, Lewis, who actually gave them their collective name. He was a far from negligible figure in his day. Canadian-born, and equally renowned as a writer and a painter, Lewis had a way of stating outright what has to be decoded in the work of the others. For example: "It is somewhat depressing to consider how as an artist one is always holding the mirror up to politics without knowing it."[6] That is just what I have been maintaining in the teeth of resistance, because it still depresses artists to consider such a possibility. But Lewis uncheerfully admitted it in 1937, in the intro-

---

4. R. Taruskin, *Music in the Early Twentieth Century*, vol. 4 of *The Oxford History of Western Music*, rev. ed. (New York: Oxford University Press, 2010), xx.
5. Ibid.
6. Wyndham Lewis, *Blasting and Bombardiering: An Autobiography (1914–1926)* (1937; London: John Calder; New York: Riverrun, 1982), 4.

duction to what he called his autobiography from 1914 to 1926, titled *Blasting and Bombardiering*. That book is all about the Great War and its horrendous effect on the arts. The blasting is what Lewis and the other men of 1914 were doing before the war, in Lewis's case as the editor of a noisy, very short-lived "little magazine" that was actually called *Blast*. It lasted only a year or so, from 1914 to 1915. Bombardiering is what Lewis actually did in the war, the first that involved aerial combat. And the autobiographical book, from which I will be quoting some more, is largely an account of how the war knocked the stuffing out of the proud, confident men of 1914, who by 1918 were the very ones whom Eliot would immortalize in 1925 as "The Hollow Men."

Another way in which Lewis made explicit what many left unsaid was in his openly confessed attraction, in the disillusioning aftermath of the war, to the right-wing politics that beguiled all the men of 1914 and many, many others, a politics now so blood-bespattered as to taint the group in ways that, in the case of the more canonized among them, has led to massive dispute and denial—but not in the case of Lewis. The fact that in 1931 he published a book called *Hitler*, which portrayed its subject as a "man of peace" unfairly targeted by Communist thugs, led of course, and despite his later recantation, to his being shunned as what W. H. Auden memorably called "that lonely old volcano of the Right."[7] That is obviously among the reasons why he is now just "the other guy." But he is also our best witness. The further you go into *Blasting and Bombardiering*, the more it becomes a lament at the destruction of the arts. One of the last chapters is called "Towards an Art-less Society," and it begins with the melancholy observation that

> [t]he Arts with their great capital A's are, considered as plants, decidedly unrobust. They are the sport, at the best, of political chance: parasitically dependent upon the good health of the social body.[8]

That may be as much an overstatement as the opposing dictum by Schopenhauer, against which I have so often inveighed, that "[a]longside world history there goes, guiltless and unstained by blood, the history of philosophy, science and the arts."[9] But overstated or not, Lewis's view epitomized the postwar pessimism that produced the ban on pathos. Intolerable suffering and buffeting had led to a massive loss of dedication. "The day was lost, for art, at Sarajevo," Lewis wrote in 1937. "World politics stepped in, and a war was started which has not ended yet: a 'war to end war.' But it merely ended art. It did not end war," and this because "by the time President Wilson had drawn up his famous Fourteen Points the will to

---

7. "Letter to Lord Byron," in W. H. Auden and Louis MacNeice, *Letters from Iceland* (London: Faber, 1937), 233.
8. Lewis, *Blasting and Bombardiering*, 257.
9. Arthur Schopenhauer, *Parerga und Paralipomena* (1851), in idem, *Sämtliche Werke in fünf Bänden* (Munich: Suhrkamp, 1986), 4:95.

play had been extinguished to all intents and purposes forever in our cowed and bankrupt democracies."[10] One by one Lewis surveys the damaged arts, cataloguing all the ways in which there had been "a backsliding of the intellect throughout the civilized world," as "glaringly demonstrated in the continued impoverishment of artistic expression, not in one art, but in every art."[11]

Skipping now to the paragraphs on music:

> If we turn to Opera, we are told that "Wagner is still the big box-office noise." (I quote from the *Star*, 6 May 1936.) No one supposes any longer that a "great" opera will ever be written again. As far as Opera is concerned, and for what that form of art is worth, the best Operas date from the last century. There will be no more Wagner, much less Mozart. And as to the supreme orchestral compositions, they all seem to have been written, too. There are no more Bachs or Beethovens just as there were no more Leonardos and Michelangelos after the Renaissance, only hasty reminders of what artists once excelled in doing, or despairing jokes, or jazzed-up echoes of perfection.
>
> These are not lost arts—much music is still written and very intelligent music, and the dying struggle of the visual arts is often impressive. But something has occurred in the world that has long ago caused the greatest creations to stop being born. No more will come.[12]

The most significant, and remarkable, thing about this jeremiad is something that can only be seen, not heard. The word "great" is placed in scare quotes on every occurrence, just as we so often see it done today in the name of "postmodernism" or whatever term we now apply to our current fallen state. That studied irony is the nub of the matter. There will be no more great art not because there will not be enough talent or skill among artists. There will be no more great art because we are no longer permitted to be great. And it was the recent political upheaval that banished greatness from the world. Lewis's explanation for this is another of his truly prophetic *aperçus*: "As far as it is possible to compute," he writes,

> it is unlikely the arts will again enjoy such a period of favourable calm as was experienced by those artists who came upon the scene between the French Revolution and the "Great War" (of 1914–18). That is the gist of the matter.[13]

I have not made a formal survey, but that is by a long way the earliest reference I know to what Eric Hobsbawm may have been the first actually to call "the long nineteenth century"—the century-plus of artistic, and especially of musical, greatness.[14] In the shattered twentieth century, that greatness was something to envy,

10. Lewis, *Bombing and Bombardiering*, 258.
11. Ibid., 260.
12. Ibid., 261.
13. Ibid., 264.
14. In the omnibus title of his trilogy, consisting of *The Age of Revolution: Europe 1789–1848* (1962), *The Age of Capital: 1848–1875* (1975), and *The Age of Empire: 1875–1914* (1987).

and therefore to mock. It was not for nothing, moreover, that two of the names Lewis cited in his musical elegy were Wagner and Beethoven—not only the two most admired composers of the nineteenth century, but also the most mocked.

Parodies of Wagner go back to Wagner's time, or almost. The classic Wagner spoof was by Emanuel Chabrier. You might remember his *Souvenirs de Munich* for piano four-hands, in which themes from *Tristan und Isolde* were embedded in the calculatedly clumsy strains of a quadrille. It is thought to date from 1887. And I'm sure you remember the ragtime Wagner of "Golliwog's Cakewalk" from Debussy's *Children's Corner Suite*, published in 1908. Keep in mind that both composers were deeply susceptible to Wagner's influence; that both of them were known to make efforts, in their serious work as well as in these, to shake that influence off; and that in both cases it was at *Tristan und Isolde,* the heaviest dose of Wagner toxin, that they aimed their darts.[15] The fact that they were French, of course, is relevant to our centennial theme; but it obviously reflects older Franco-Prussian animosities as well. We are well used to the truism that a Wagner hater lurks within every Wagner lover.

Overt Beethoven hatred had to await the coming of the Great War. It too had its serious proponents, such as Edward Dent.[16] But let's confine ourselves for the moment to the funnies, beginning with the moment in Prokofieff's *The Love for Three Oranges* (1919) when the melancholy Prince laughs at the sight of the old witch Fata Morgana's backside and provokes the curse to which the title refers. Or the moment in Manuel de Falla's *The Three-Cornered Hat* (also 1919) when the town bailiff comes knocking at the door. Both of them parody the world's most iconic symphony's most iconic moment, the opening unison of Beethoven's Fifth. But all parts of that symphony were fair game for derision. An actual wartime example was Stravinsky's *Souvenir d'un marche boche,* first published in Edith Wharton's charity book *Le Livre des sans-foyer* of 1915—an example that long went undetected since it does not cite the symphony's main handle, but instead the beginning of the coda in the finale.[17] That finale, of course, is one of the paramount musical laughingstocks. I am sure that Erik Satie was thinking of it when he wrote the absurd coda that ends the last piece in his *Embryons desséchés,* which actually predates the war by a year. But even before Beethoven became just another *boche,* as he was to Stravinsky, he was unassailably (which is to say irresistibly assailably) "great," and nowhere greater than in the Fifth—and that was enough for Satie, who soon had more company in derision, I'm sure, than he ever expected.

---

15. The best treatment of this love-hate relationship is Carolyn Abbate's, in "*Tristan* in the Composition of *Pelléas,*" *Nineteenth-Century Music* 5 (1980–81): 117–41.

16. In *Terpander* (New York: E. P. Dutton, 1927), his ironic Beethoven centennial meditation.

17. See R. Taruskin, *Stravinsky and the Russian Traditions* (Berkeley and Los Angeles: University of California Press, 1996), 1475.

I once heard an overly fastidious lecturer say that Satie was spoofing the finale in Beethoven's Eighth Symphony rather than the Fifth, evidently because the Eighth, like Satie's spoof, was in the key of F major, not the C major of the Fifth. But although the Eighth's coda is stout enough, the Fifth's is the icon that attracts iconoclasm. Mock the Fifth and you are mocking the whole idea of grand rhetoric, the thing the First World War is so widely credited with having killed off. But there is even more to it than that. *Musical* rhetoric was especially suspect in the war's aftermath. Philosophers going all the way back to Plato have acknowledged the danger of music, as I called it in the title of a book of essays that many have found provocative, because in the wake of so many totalitarian efforts at control that have offended twentieth-century liberal values, we no longer like to acknowledge that art can be dangerous.[18] But one hundred years ago and more, neither the danger nor the impulse to control it were thought strange.

Wagner's music was always its best exemplification—by design as well as by reputation. Wagner's music-dramatic theory and practice—and his mature musical style, which amounted to pretty much the same thing—were predicated on the assumption that music made a direct appeal to feeling that circumvented the intellect. It was to arouse and harness what he called the *Gefühlsverständis*—the intuitive emotional intelligence of listeners—that Wagner devised his Leitmotif technique, which depended so heavily on the device of allusion and the faculty of association.[19] And his harmonic innovations—vastly enlarging his music's range of tonal relations and dramatizing effects of harmonic departure and arrival (or what he called navigating the "sea of harmony")[20]—heightened the property to which Hanslick, his great opponent, alluded when he remarked that "the other arts persuade, but music invades us."[21] When these effects were synchronized in his mature dramas, the impact on listeners was (and is) overwhelming, to the point where Nietzsche could warn, in *The Birth of Tragedy*, that if its force were not delimited by the libretto's semantic specificity, Wagner's music would kill us, if we were truly musical. "To these genuine musicians," he wrote, "I direct the question whether

---

18. R. Taruskin, *The Danger of Music and Other Anti-Utopian Essays* (Berkeley and Los Angeles: University of California Press, 2009). Also see chapter 1 of this book.

19. See Richard Wagner, *Oper und Drama*, chap. 18 (in *Gesammelte Schriften und Dichtungen*, vol. 4 [Leipzig: Hesse & Becker, 1914], 82): "Dem dichtenden Verstande liegt nun, für den Eindruck seiner Mitteilung, gar nichts *am Glauben*, sondern nur am *Gefühlsverständnis*" (trans. William Ashton Ellis: "Now, for the operation of its message, the poetizing intellect has absolutely no concern with *Faith*, but only with an *understanding through the Feeling*" [*Richard Wagner's Prose Works*, vol. 2 (London: K. Paul, Trench, Trübner, 1900), 213]).

20. Wagner, *Oper und Drama*, chap. 22 (*Gesammelte Schriften*, 4:184): "Das bodenlose Meer der Harmonie."

21. Eduard Hanslick, *On the Musically Beautiful*, trans. Geoffrey Payzant (Indianapolis: Hackett, 1986), 50.

they can imagine a human being who would be able to perceive" a certain work of Wagner's "without any aid of word or image, purely as a tremendous symphonic movement, without expiring in a spasmodic unharnessing of all the wings of the soul."[22] Dangerous stuff!

The disillusioned mood at the end of the First World War did not so much disenchant Wagner's music as make its enchantment seem, while no less real than before, suddenly undesirable. Whereas during the long nineteenth century people sought out what in the *Oxford History* I called the "music trance," in the short twentieth they were exhorted to wake up. In place of "emotional hypnosis and sterile hedonism," wrote Boris Asafyev in his *Book about Stravinsky*, we want a music that responds to "the impetuous current of our lives with its resilient rhythms, its flying tempi and its subordination to the pulse of work."[23] Or as Kurt Weill put it, addressing a hypothetical roomful of schoolchildren: "I have just played you excerpts from the music of Wagner and his followers. . . . [T]his music made you feel sleepy or drunk, as alcohol or other drugs might have done. But you don't want to go to sleep."[24]

Stay awake, stay wary, don't be fooled again. That was as much the mood among artists in the war's aftermath as it was anyone's. "Art ought to be full clarity, high noon of the intellect," wrote José Ortega y Gasset, and it was one of the chief tenets of his aesthetic agenda, as set forth in his so notoriously titled tract *The Dehumanization of Art*. "Tears and laughter are aesthetically frauds," he warned.[25] *Gefühlsverständnis* is mere "psychic contagion, . . . an unconscious phenomenon." We need to keep our wits about us, and if art cannot help with that, if it keeps us wallowing instead in our gullible *Gefühle*, it is worse than useless. So from occupying the highest position among the arts, the way it did among the Romantics, music was demoted precipitously back to the debased estate to which Kant had assigned it in his *Critique of Judgment*, where he willingly allowed that music was "the highest among those arts that are valued for their pleasantness," but if "we estimate the worth of the beautiful arts by the culture they supply to the mind[,] . . . music will have the lowest place . . . because it merely plays with sensations."[26] Kant thought music just a pretty tinkling, or to use his own analogy, a sonic perfume, a purely sensuous phenomenon; and the only danger music could pose, accordingly, was the same as the danger posed by scent, that of unwelcome diffusion.

---

22. Friedrich Nietzsche, *The Birth of Tragedy*, in *The Basic Writings of Nietzsche*, trans. Walter Kaufmann (New York: The Modern Library, 2000), 126–27.

23. Boris Asaf'yev, *A Book about Stravinsky* (1926), trans. Richard F. French (Ann Arbor: UMI Research Press, 1982), 98–99.

24. "Der Musiker Weill," *Berliner Tagblatt*, 25 December 1928, as translated in *Musical Times* 70 (1 March 1929): 224.

25. José Ortega y Gasset, *The Dehumanization of Art* (1925), trans. Helene Weyl (Princeton, NJ: Princeton University Press, 1968), 27.

26. Immanuel Kant, *Critique of Judgment* (1795), trans. J. H. Bernard (New York: Hafner), 171.

But after the Great War music's pleasantness could no longer redeem it. It was not just an innocent tinkling or agreeable atmosphere. One couldn't go all the way back to Kant because Wagner had happened, and then the *boches,* and what was mindless now looked sinister. A new strain of anti-musical sentiment took hold alongside the anti-*boche,* and it affected musicians as much as it did other modern artists.

II. BOMBIC RESONANCE

Paul Fussell's famous cornucopia of spleen, *The Great War and Modern Memory,* pretty much avoids the subject of music, but it did point me in the direction of the linguist and literary critic I. A. Richards and his groundbreaking, once powerfully influential treatises on semantics, which provide the crispest examples I now know of musicophobia in the aftermath of the Great War. Fussell cites Richards in a chapter called "Adversary Proceedings," which concerns semantic oppositions. The point of the chapter was to show how a tendency toward radical dichotomies, casting ideas and topics in antagonistic binary pairs, was one of the mental habits that the war, with its ceaseless rhetoric of friend and foe, instilled in the thinkers and writers of the coming decades.

One of Fussell's exhibits is Richards's pamphlet *Science and Poetry,* in which the title words are cast as a pair of mutually exclusive and mutually inimical modes of thought. Fussell compares the original edition of the book, published in 1926, with its reissue nine years later, its paranoid rhetoric now muted as if to illustrate the point that the receding memory of the war and its attendant fears had attenuated what had seemed the clear warning of the original formulation.[27] Read almost a century later, Richards's screed will now remind those of us who know it of Milton Babbitt's renewed dichotomization of "humanistic" and "scientific" thinking,[28] which might well form an exhibit in some future Fussell's hypothetical compendium, *The Cold War and Modern [or Postmodern] Memory,* as if to show that the tendency to dichotomize waxes and wanes according to the political barometer. Although the valences have shifted—Richards sought salvation in a restored humanism, Babbitt in a ruthless scientism—their descriptions of the dichotomized terms are essentially the same.

Richards divides the scientific and the humanistic into two concurrent functions—he names them the "intellectual stream" and the "emotional stream"—

---

27. Paul Fussell, *The Great War and Modern Memory* (New York: Oxford University Press, 1975), 107–8.
28. As in his "Past and Present Concepts of the Nature and Limits of Music" (1961), reprinted in *The Collected Essays of Milton Babbitt,* ed. Stephen Peles et al. (Princeton, NJ: Princeton University Press, 2011), 78–85.

that carry the mind through the reading of a poem. These correspond to what, in a previous treatise, *The Meaning of Meaning* (jointly authored with C. K. Ogden), Richards had called "symbolic speech" and "evocative speech." "The difference between the two," he wrote,

> may be more exactly characterized as follows: In symbolic speech the essential considerations are the correctness of the symbolization and the truth of the references. In evocative speech the essential consideration is the character of the attitude aroused. Symbolic statements may indeed be used as a means of evoking attitudes, but when this use is occurring it will be noticed that the truth or falsity of the statements is of no consequence provided that they are accepted by the hearer.
>
> The means by which words may evoke feelings and attitudes are many and offer an alluring field of study to the literary psychologist. As sounds, and again as movements of articulation, and also through many subtle networks of association, the contexts of their occurrences in the past, they can play very directly upon the organized impulses of the affective-volitional systems. But above all these in importance, heightening and controlling and uniting these subordinate influences, are the rhythmic and metrical effects of word arrangements. If, as may reasonably be supposed, rhythms and especially metres have to a small degree an hypnotic effect, the very marked difference in evocative power between words as arranged and words without recurrent system is readily accounted for.... Emotionality, exaggeration of belief-feelings, the occulting of the critical faculties, the suppression of the questioning—"Is this so as a matter of fact?"—attitude, all these are characteristics of metrical experiences and fit in well with a hypnosis assumption.[29]

Ogden and Richards are speaking exactly about *Gefühlsverständnis*, as Wagner would say (indeed, did say), and about the hypnotic effects to which Asafyev, in his *Book about Stravinsky*, would also call attention. And while they emphasize rhythm and meter, they also make explicit reference to "subtle networks of association [between sounds], the contexts of their occurrences in the past," or precisely the mechanism through which Wagner's Leitmotif technique sought to "play very directly upon the organized impulses of the affective-volitional systems." This is no accidental echo. In an earlier part of the book, devoted to a history of "verbal magic" going all the way back to the Egyptians, Ogden and Richards describe the process whereby "verbal envelopes, void of all intelligible content," take the place of true bearers of semantic meaning, relying on "affective resonance" to divert the attention of listeners and "enable the manipulator of symbols" to escape detection.[30] Quoting Théodule-Armand Ribot, a French psychologist of language, they observe that when words exchange the symbolic function for the emotive, "they no

---

29. C[harles] K[ay] Ogden and I[vor] A[rmstrong] Richards, *The Meaning of Meaning: A Study of the Influence of Language upon Thought and of the Science of Symbolism* (New York: Harcourt, Brace & World, 1923), 239–40.

30. Ibid., 40, 42.

longer act as signs but as sounds; they are musical notations at the service of an emotional psychology." Switching to another authority, the Italian philosopher Eugenio Rignano, they add that when words are used this way they are "transformed into a kind of musical language stimulative of sentiments and emotions."[31]

And here, very cleverly, the authors demonstrate the power of verbal magic even in the act of exposing it. They quote a passage from Rignano that likens recourse to affective resonance—that is, the discarding of semantic precision in favor of emotional appeal—to "the shedding of the carapace by a crustacean," and add that this process has "a certain bombic capacity."[32]

Do you know what "bombic" means? I didn't. It was a commentary on this text by Vincent Sherry, in his excellent literary study *The Great War and the Language of Modernism*, that opened my eyes to what Ogden and Richards were up to:

"[A] certain *bombic* capacity": how does the restricted meaning of this highly specific word—of or pertaining to the silkworm [for that is what "bombic" means, deriving from their genus, christened *bombyx* by Linnaeus himself in 1758, and nothing more]—become relevant to the argument? If the silkworm's mutations are analogized to the carapace shedding [which in turn stands for the substitution of musical for rational discourse], there is surely a less curvaceously tropological way of saying so. But then, *bombic* is too good a sound, given the subject of "affective resonance," to be lost, even if it means that the loathed noises are creeping into the critics' speech, most audibly in the echo that bombic finds in the gorgeous, stuck-in-the-gorge coda of *cita barbara bombum*.[33]

That Latin phrase *cita barbara bombum* is a quote from Lucretius (*De rerum natura*, Book IV, l. 544): " . . . when barbaric Berecynthian pipe / Buzzes with raucous boomings . . . "[34] As Sherry's comments indicate, the word *bombic* serves to evoke what Ogden and Richards call "the harmonious series of emotional echoes with which the naïve mind responds";[35] and "similarly, across the broader scale of the passage, the interlingual weave of Latin and French phrases comprises its designed effect of rhetorical decoration yet clearly exceeds it, too, converting the logic of the case against music into its own language of en*chant*ment."[36]

---

31. Ibid., 42–43, relying on Ribot, *La Logique des sentiments* (Paris: Félix Alcan, 1905), 187 [recte 166–67], and Rignano, *The Psychology of Reasoning*, trans. Winifred A. Holl (New York: Harcourt, Brace & Co., 1923), chap. 11, on "Metaphysical Reasoning."
32. Ogden and Richards, *Meaning of Meaning*, 42.
33. Vincent Sherry, *The Great War and the Language of Modernism* (New York: Oxford University Press, 2003), 73.
34. T. Lucretius Carus, *Of the Nature of Things*, trans. William Ellery Leonard (New York: E. P. Dutton, 1916), 155.
35. Ogden and Richards, *Meaning of Meaning*, 43.
36. Sherry, *The Great War and the Language of Modernism*, 73.

The case against music. Ogden and Richards had mobilized the affective resonance of the word *bombic* with *booming* and *bomb* to conjure up the Great War as a testifying witness. By resorting to verbal magic themselves, they show the way that evocative or musical discourse had consorted "with the worst [that] history has had to offer." The "logical foolery" that had taken the world to a disastrous war in the name of liberal ideals amounted, as Sherry puts it, to

> far more than a set of simple tricks a poet might mimic, vindictively or not. Richards's critical concept puts poetry in touch with the disintegrating conditions of liberal rationalism.... In his [musical] model, poetry reenacts nothing less than the demise of the main myth of liberal modernity, as enacted in the public discourse of the Great War.[37]

By the time he wrote *Science and Poetry*, Richards's vocabulary had evolved further, from "evocative speech" to "emotional stream" to explicitly "musical discourse," finally to the term by which his theory is now remembered, and which, if we keep the theory of affective resonance in mind, had been calculated to bear a strong negative charge: *pseudo-statement*. Helen Vendler, a celebrated critic of poetry in her own right and a former pupil of Richards's at Harvard, insisted that Richards only "meant it scientifically, as in 'pseudopod,' but it was taken as contemptuous."[38] Not wrongly taken, I would insist, in the immediate environment of the postwar decade; for it applies to more than poetry. "The acceptance which a pseudo-statement receives," Richards wrote,

> is entirely governed by its effects upon our feelings and attitudes. Logic only comes in, if at all, in subordination, as a servant to our emotional response.... A pseudo-statement is "true" if it suits and serves some attitude or links together attitudes which on other grounds are desirable. A pseudo-statement is a form of words that is justified entirely by its effect in releasing or organising our impulses or attitudes.[39]

In the preface to a later edition of *Science and Poetry*, to which he appended a commentary, Richards was at pains to remind the reader that pseudo-statements are not merely false statements but rather statements "whose scientific truth or falsity is irrelevant to the purpose in hand."[40] It will not be lost on readers today, perhaps, that this definition comes near to the definition of *bullshit* given by the

---

37. Ibid., 74.
38. Helen Vendler, "I. A. Richards at Harvard," *Boston Review*, 1 April 1981, http://bostonreview.net/articles/helen-vendler-i-richards-harvard/.
39. I. A. Richards, *Science and Poetry* (New York: W. W. Norton, 1926), 67–68, 70.
40. I. A. Richards, *Poetries and Sciences: A Reissue with a Commentary of "Science and Poetry"* (New York: W. W. Norton, 1970), 7 (quoting in advance a clarifying statement added as a footnote on p. 60).

Princeton philosopher Harry Frankfurt in his eponymous treatise of 2005.[41] Richards's "pseudo-statement" corresponds, as well, with what decades later J. L. Austin would call speech acts.[42] Richards's concept entails the "performative" aspect of speech (which may of course be written as well as oral), the aspect that Austin counterposed to the "constative." This pair of terms closely parallels Richards's "symbolic" and "emotive" (that is, "musical") modes. In calling such forceful attention to the performative—that is, the power of language to impel action or affect belief—Richards was calling attention to what the artistic or "musical" use of language has in common with other uses, including sinister ones like rabble-rousing or propaganda. More frankly than any other writer at the time, he associated the efficacy of propaganda with that of music. His work amounted to one of the strongest and most explicit exposures of the danger of music in the disillusioned aftermath of the Great War.

As a critic of poetry rather than a scientist, Richards knew that there were babies in the bathwater. He took care to point out that he was not—repeat, *not*—valorizing the intellectual at the expense of the emotional or musical, or what he called the "active branch" of the poetic experience. "Some people who read verse," he wrote,

> ([and] they do not often read much of it), are so constituted that very little more happens than this intellectual stream of thoughts. It is perhaps superfluous to point out that they miss the real poem. To exaggerate this part of the experience, and give it too much importance on its own account, is a notable current tendency, and for many people explains why they do not read poetry.
>
> The active branch is what really matters; for from it all the energy of the whole agitation comes.[43]

But this attempt to clarify, written nine years after the original version had made its impact, is a weak retraction of a profoundly timely and pregnant claim, which accorded with many similar statements from artists in all media, who did indeed exaggerate the value of the intellectual stream, but only because they felt the other stream to have ruinously overflowed its banks. The relationship between Richards's original assertions and countless comparable statements by poets, composers, and performing musicians in the 1920s shows that Richards was only understating things when he called the emphasis of the constative over the performative a "notable current tendency." It was a tendency not only on the part of

---

41. Harry G. Frankfurt, *On Bullshit* (Princeton: Princeton University Press, 2005). The summary definition (61): "The liar cares about the truth and attempts to hide it; the bullshitter doesn't care if what they say is true or false, but rather only cares whether or not their listener is persuaded."

42. See J[ohn] L[angshaw] Austin, *How to Do Things with Words*, 2nd ed. (Cambridge, MA: Harvard University Press, 1962).

43. Richards, *Poetries and Sciences*, 25.

art-hating philistines, but also on the part of many of the leading artists of the immediate postwar era—from Ezra Pound's repudiation of "emotional" music as being like a drug (and his consequent endorsement of Arnold Dolmetsch's revival of the earlier music of "pattern and precision") to Igor Stravinsky's famous denial that music "can *express* anything at all."[44] The resonance is obvious, and the statements too well known to warrant requoting. The consequences of this repudiation, not only for the *composing* of postwar music but also for the *performance* of music ever since, are also well known and by now widely acknowledged. That is the ban on pathos to which my title, both here and in the *Oxford History*, refers.

III. NEVERTHELESS ...

As I say, I could easily multiply such expressions, and so, I'm sure, could you. I refrain from doing so not only because I believe the point has been jolly well made, but also because our tendency to keep looking for additional evidence of the ban on pathos can amount to a confirmation bias, and actually distort rather than clarify our view of the postwar decade as it affected the arts. I am very glad to have found Richards's discussion of musical discourse. It certainly amplifies my understanding of the sources of the ban, as I have identified it. But the ban was never enacted into law, and no one was ever under a compulsion to observe it, except insofar as trends may exert their power over those who worry about their reputations. Ezra Pound and Igor Stravinsky were two of the most prestigious artists of the 1920s and 30s. Their works were widely disseminated and widely emulated, and so were their ideas, all of which created a strong conformist pressure. But these ideas did not erase or negate preexisting ones, especially in their seniors. They took their place alongside those previously established in a spectrum of opinion and practice.

We all know that our descriptions of historical realities are schematic and simplistic. That is the only way we can make them intelligible. And revisionist history is especially susceptible to schematization and oversimplification, since in order to dislodge an existing opinion you have to summon maximum force. As one of my colleagues, a medievalist musicologist named Richard L. Crocker, put it more than fifty years ago at the end of a masterpiece of historical revisionism, "I have stated the case as forcefully as I know how, which probably means I overstated it; if so, the overstatement should be taken as, in all modesty, corrective in intent."[45] We can all always say that.

---

44. Ezra Pound, "Arnold Dolmetsch" (1915), in *Ezra Pound and Music: The Complete Criticism*. ed. R. Murray Schaefer (New York: New Directions, 1977), 38; Igor Stravinsky, *An Autobiography* (1935; New York: W. W. Norton, 1962), 53.

45. Richard L. Crocker, "The Troping Hypothesis," *Musical Quarterly* 52 (1966): 183–203, at 203.

PATHOS IS BANNED 461

Therefore, it is also always possible to counter or supplement revisionism with evidence of persistence. The editors of a recent volume of essays called *World War I and the Cultures of Modernity* have done that with respect to the issue I have been discussing, and the position with which my work has been associated. Strategically (and semiscornfully) identifying that view as the "traditionalist reading" of postwar culture (and I can understand their calling it that, since it is so much more the established view in literary studies than in musicology), they note that according to such

> readings of the issues, what had been Romanticist in aesthetics prior to 1914 did not emerge intact after 1918. On the contrary, just as the war had marked the arrival of mass culture, mass politics and mass society, so had its course and outcome eradicated for poets, painters and writers the right to follow a [Romanticist] muse. These scholarly polemics have recently found their challengers, among them works which show how Romanticist sensibilities persevered and even found invigoration after 1918 precisely because it was so urgent to reckon with death on a large scale and to render its ubiquity somehow special, sacred and of nature.[46]

It is indeed easy to show this, and worth doing from time to time. To put it the way Leonard B. Meyer did when theorizing the history of musical style, what innovators do is add items to the menu of what others may then choose to replicate[47]— which is only a paraphrase of what Debussy wrote to Stravinsky after receiving the score of *Le Sacre du printemps:* "It is a special satisfaction to tell you how much you have enlarged the boundaries of the permissible in the empire of sound."[48] In the early, medieval chapters of the *Oxford History*, when describing the invention of musical notation—that is, the revolutionary innovation that made possible the rest of the book—I took care to emphasize that notation never utterly supplanted oral practices or made them obsolete; that oral practices continued to coexist with literate practices from the beginning, and are still with us after a millennium of coexistence. By the time my narrative reached the twentieth century, I was no longer so insistently reminding readers that the new does not replace the old but joins it. So it may be appropriate to do that now, because the assumption that the so-called ban on pathos was universally observed is not only an instance of confirmation bias; it also exemplifies what I have sometimes called the poietic fallacy, the

---

46. Douglas Mackaman and Michael Mays, Introduction to *World War I and the Cultures of Modernity* (Jackson: University Press of Mississippi, 2000), xviii.

47. See L. B. Meyer, *Style and Music: Theory, History, and Ideology* (Chicago: University of Chicago Press, 1970).

48. Letter of 9 November 1913, in Igor Stravinsky and Robert Craft, *Conversations with Igor Stravinsky* (Garden City, NY: Doubleday, 1959), 55. Original French: "il y a une satisfaction spéciale à constater combien vous avez reculé les bornes permises de l'empire des sons" ([Robert Craft, ed.,] *Avec Stravinsky* [Monaco: Editions du Rocher, 1958], 201).

supposition that only what the most advanced or trendiest composers do constitutes the history of music.

Needless to say, but I'll say it anyway, "emotional" music kept right on being composed and performed after Ezra Pound pronounced it obsolete. In fact, far more of it was performed than of the newer music of pattern and precision, and that has obviously remained the case right up to the present. And it goes for emotional poetry as well, whatever its transgressions against (whose?) postwar taste. I myself can testify to this, and will. But first I summon to the witness box the critic Kenneth Burke.

Burke was a longer-lived contemporary of I. A. Richards who also wrote, at first disparagingly, about pseudo-statements. Here is how he described the way musical discourse works. "A man," he wrote,

> can extract courage from a poem by reading that he is captain of his soul; he can reënforce the same statement mimetically by walking down the street as vigorously as though he were the captain of his soul; or he can translate the mood into a more complex set of relationships by greeting an acquaintance as one captain-of-his-soul to another; and the two of them can embark on such a project as two captains-of-their-souls might embark upon.[49]

Burke did not identify the poem he was satirizing in this passage. He did not need to. Every child at school knew it at the time of his writing, and although I was in school about twenty years later, I know it too. It is "Invictus" (Latin for "unvanquished"), a poem first published in 1888 by the otherwise little-known Victorian poet William Ernest Henley (1849–1903). The part to which Burke alluded was its fourth and concluding quatrain:

> It matters not how strait the gate,
> How charged with punishments the scroll,
> I am the master of my fate:
> I am the captain of my soul.

I know it by heart, as do most Anglophones of my generation, and have quoted it from memory, not only because I was given it as an assignment to memorize, but because I heard it recited at elocution contests—something that my children have never known, but that was still commonly practiced at assemblies in elementary schools when I was going to one. Henley's sentiments, meant as the epitome of manliness and surely taken as such at the time of his poem's publication, will now strike many of us as childish. But that, obviously, is because we, unlike the author,

---

49. Kenneth Burke, "The Poetry of Action," in *Permanence and Change: An Anatomy of Purpose* (New York: New Republic, 1935), 255. The beginning of the quoted passage echoes Walt Whitman's *Song of Myself* (stanza 20, line 2): "How is it I extract strength from the beef I eat?" (*The Portable Walt Whitman*, ed. Mark van Doren [New York: Viking Press, 1945], 47).

are heirs to the ban on pathos, as was Kenneth Burke, who paints a fairly ridiculous figure of a reader swaggering down the street because he has allowed Henley's musical discourse to organize his impulses and attitudes.

And yet sixty or seventy years after the poem was printed, and a good thirty-five years after the Great War dealt what many thought a fatal blow to its fantasy of indomitable fortitude and perfect self-mastery, the poem was still being assigned in the belief that it provided schoolchildren with a good moral example. So, though arguably debased, things persist. And here is another poem that persisted, and that I also learned to recite as a child in the early 1950s:

> In Flanders fields the poppies grow
> Between the crosses, row on row,
> That mark our place; and in the sky
> The larks, still bravely singing, fly
> Scarce heard amid the guns below.
>
> We are the Dead. Short days ago
> We lived, felt dawn, saw sunset glow,
> Loved and were loved, and now we lie
> In Flanders fields.
>
> Take up our quarrel with the foe:
> To you from failing hands we throw
> The torch; be yours to hold it high.
> If ye break faith with us who die
> We shall not sleep, though poppies grow
> In Flanders fields.

This poem is an actual artifact of the Great War, and its author, like W.E. Henley, is known by this one effort alone. He was Major John McCrae (1872–1918), a Canadian military doctor, who in civilian life was a medical examiner for an insurance company, and who published these lines, anonymously and without a title, in the London magazine *Punch* on 8 December 1915, after officiating at the burial of a close friend and fellow officer killed in action in the second battle of Ypres. (McCrae's own death from pneumonia three years later was an indirect consequence of his service in the war.) "In Flanders Fields" became so popular that it led to the widespread custom of wearing poppies on memorial holidays throughout the English-speaking world—particularly, in America, on what was known when I was in grade school as Armistice Day (now called Veterans' Day), the yearly commemoration, on 11 November, of the Great War's end. Full of lofty thoughts and fiery rhetoric, the poem certainly shows "how Romanticist sensibilities persevered and even found invigoration" as a result of the war, and the postwar career of the poem only magnified it and amplified its music.

Naturally enough, Paul Fussell, in *The Great War and Modern Memory*, grand compendium that it is of postwar dyspepsia, has a great time excoriating this poem. After quoting the first two stanzas with faint (and feigned) approval ("so far, so pretty good"), he turns on it savagely:

> Things fall apart two-thirds of the way through as the vulgarities of "Stand Up! Stand Up and Play the Game!" [a recruitment slogan] begin to make inroads into the pastoral, and we suddenly have a recruiting-poster rhetoric apparently applicable to any war.... We finally see—and with a shock—what the last six lines really are: they are a propaganda argument—words like vicious and stupid would not seem to go too far—against a negotiated peace; and it could be said that for the purpose, the rhetoric of [militaristic preachers] is, alas, the appropriate one.[50]

This goes beyond literary critique all the way to political denunciation, accusing the poet of complicity in the deaths of soldiers who died because of the futile continuation of an unwinnable war. (This was of course a common argument made in Britain in the aftermath of a war that had cost the lives of a generation and ended not in a proclaimed victory but in just an armistice, i.e., precisely a negotiated peace.) We American schoolkids never heard any such interpretation of it, you may be sure. To us it was—or at least, was presented as being—uplifting and inspiring, full of old sentiments like *Dulce et decorum est pro patria mori* ("Sweet it is and proper to die for one's country"), the line from Horace that Wilfred Owen, a World War I poet whose verses we were never given to memorize, had placed sarcastically atop one of his bitterest laments at the waste of young lives. "Flanders Fields" sentiments could not be further removed from what we now call the modernist temper, or what, in the *Oxford History*, I identified as the true beginning of the twentieth century for music. Could a modernist composer set "In Flanders Fields" to music except sarcastically?

IV. MODERNISTS AND MAXIMALISTS

My question may appear to answer itself, self-evidently in the negative; but Americans reading this now are likely to know that a true answer will be complicated and equivocal, because one composer who is often thought of as a modernist—indeed, as the first and one of the greatest of American modernist composers—did set the poem, and did so without a trace of irony. I am talking about Charles Ives (1874–1954), who like John McCrae made his living in the insurance business, and who set the poem at the suggestion of his business partner, Julian Myrick, for performance at an insurance industry luncheon held at the Waldorf-Astoria hotel in

---

50. Fussell, *The Great War and Modern Memory*, 249–50. Fussell, like Burke as cited in note 49, begins with a parody, this time of Yeats, "The Second Coming" (1921), line 3: "Things fall apart; the centre cannot hold" (*The Collected Poetry of William Butler Yeats* [Overland Park, KS: Digireads, 2018], 145).

PATHOS IS BANNED   465

EXAMPLE 20.1. Ives, *In Flanders Fields* (1917), last stanza.

New York on 15 April 1917, only days after the United States had joined the hostilities, to raise money for the war effort.

Ives's music endorses the poem's patriotic appeal with a typically Ivesian mélange of patriotic allusions. The stanza that Paul Fussell so derided was especially germane to the civic purposes of the luncheon where the song was to be sung. Ives set it as a counterpoint of "La Marseillaise" against what could be construed either as "God Save the King" or as the hymn "America (My Country, 'tis of Thee)," so that you get three Allies for the price of two songs (Ex. 20.1). At the words "We throw the torch, be yours to hold it high," the voice part shifts to another American patriotic song, "Columbia, Gem of the Ocean" (at the words "The home

EXAMPLE 20.2. "Columbia, Gem of the Ocean" (1843, words and music by Thomas A'Becket).

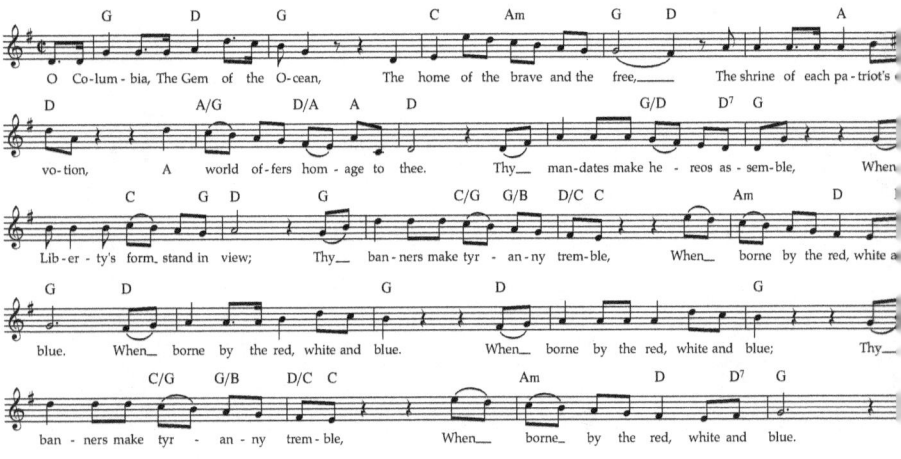

of the brave and the free"), thus giving each of the three Allies its own unambiguous referent in the music (Ex. 20.2). Elsewhere Ives's setting alludes to "Battle Cry of Freedom" and (rather oddly) to the wake-up bugle call "Reveille," at the words "We are the dead." That call would seem to leave no doubt that Ives's song is exactly what Fussell had disparagingly called McCrae's poem: a recruiting poster.

There has, consequently, been a fair amount of embarrassed commentary on the song from Ives scholars—discomfort seemingly directly proportional to the writers' level of investment in the image of Ives as a modernist—and some effort to mitigate discomfiture by reading the song against the grain.[51] In his comprehensive study of music and the Great War, Glenn Watkins has trouble maintaining, in the face of this song, that "Ives was essentially a pacifist" whose "ambivalence about the very idea of war was understood." He cites the song's quiet ending, in which the patriotic outburst is allowed "to fall away ... over the sound of fading march rhythms in the piano," as evidence of Ives's ambivalence.[52] Another writer who does so is the anonymous annotator to the text of the song as posted on the website of the Library of Congress, for whom it

---

51. For one especially strenuous attempt, see Alan Houtchens and Janis P. Stout, "'Scarce Heard amid the Guns Below': Intertextuality and Meaning in Charles Ives's War Songs," *Journal of Musicology* 15 (1997): 66–97, esp. 75–80.

52. Glenn Watkins, *Proof through the Night: Music and the Great War* (Berkeley and Los Angeles: University of California Press, 2003), 350.

PATHOS IS BANNED   467

EXAMPLE 20.3. End of Ives, "General William Booth Enters into Heaven" (1914).

depicts the conflicting emotions of patriotism and tragedy associated with armed struggle. The unrelieved sequence of dissonant intervals of the seventh as well as the octaves played in the low range of the piano with which the work begins establishes at once the work's ominous tone. While heroic elements are introduced which resemble the patterns and simple harmonies of hymn tunes—even fragmentary references to *America, La Marseillaise,* and *The Battle Cry of Freedom* may be heard—the persistent dark, percussive chords in the bass which permeate so much of the work are all that remain at its conclusion, reiterated more and more softly, like the solitary beat of a drum . . . steadily moving farther off into the distance, underscoring the tragic loss of so many lives as the price paid in war.[53]

But in April of 1917 that price was yet to be paid; and this interpretation is further undermined when the song is compared with other works by Ives. The trailing off at the end (as well as the pianistic evocation of drumbeats) are effects that occur and recur in so many Ives compositions as to preclude its being interpreted in this one case alone as an ironic commentary. Rather, it seems obvious that the eager recruits the poem has summoned are portrayed at the end as marching pluckily into battle, like the scruffy but fervent Salvation Army at the end of Ives's

53. www.loc.gov/item/ihas.200035609.

EXAMPLE 20.4. Debussy, end of "Feux d'artifice" (*Préludes*, Book II).

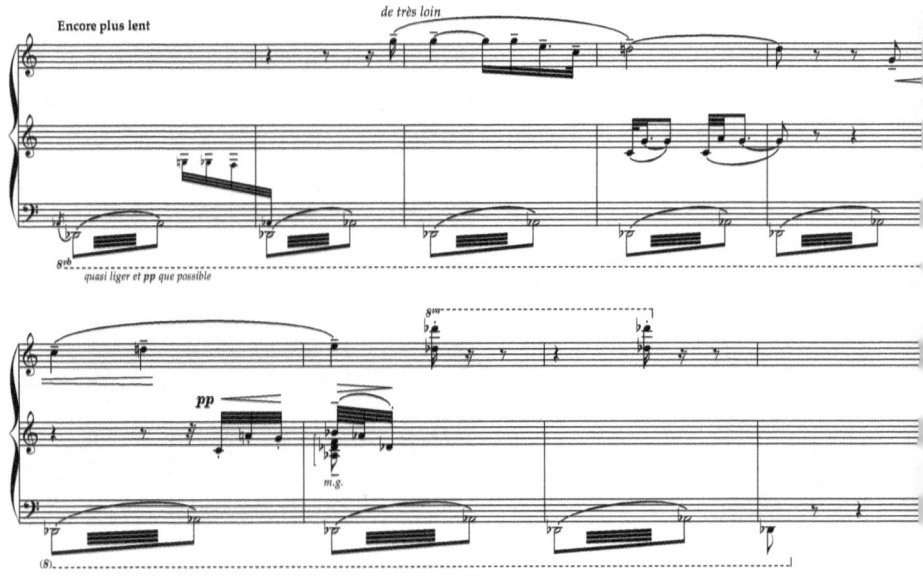

most famous song, his setting of Vachel Lindsay's "General William Booth Enters into Heaven" (Ex. 20.3).

Ives composed "General Booth" in 1914, the year the Great War began in Europe. "In Flanders Fields" was composed in 1917, when American participation in the war was still in prospect. Neither was a postwar composition, so that it may be wondered whether they can fairly be claimed as outliers or resisters to the postwar ban on pathos and the ensuing reign of irony. Ives's rhetorical use of national anthems, one might argue, is in line with Debussy's allusion to "La Marseillaise" in his *En Blanc et Noir* for two pianos (1915)—a subtle citation that comes at the end of a rather unsubtle battle piece in which the Germans are represented by a *marche boche* based on the Lutheran hymn "Ein feste Burg" (spoofed also by Stravinsky in *L'Histoire du soldat* in the last year of the war). One could also cite the ironic snatch of "Marseillaise" from afar (at "aux armes, citoyens!" the same snatch that Ives quotes) at the end of Debussy's prewar "Feux d'artifice" from the second book of *Préludes* (Ex. 20.4).

Against this objection one may adduce an Ives composition from 1924, when the ban on pathos was in full force among European and Euro-American modernists—a piece, moreover, that seems to show Ives at his most modernistic,

EXAMPLE 20.5. Ives, *Three Quarter-Tone Pieces*, III, mm. 48–57.

convincingly deploying the innovative technique of microtonal harmony. In the third of his *Three Quarter-Tone Pieces* for two pianos, "La Marseillaise" is once again placed in counterpoint with "America," the latter emerging gradually by a process of intervallic expansion from microtonal to chromatic to its familiar diatonic guise (Ex. 20.5).

Ives wrote his quarter-tone pieces for performance at a concert by the Franco-American Music Society, an outfit founded and run by his friend, the French-American pianist E(lie) Robert Schmitz (1889–1949). The juxtaposition of the two anthems fits nicely with the occasion, but the climactic arrival of the "Marseillaise" has the same effect (and—one feels fairly safe in assuming—the same intent) of uplift as did the same climactic juxtaposition in Ives's setting of "In Flanders Fields." It still sounds like an endorsement (by now nostalgic) of the old Franco-American alliance that had won the Great War.

That Ives still nurtured such allegiances and emotions is evident from other writings—political ones. Some of these are verbal only, but there is one that conveys Ives's unreconstructed political idealism in music as well as words: his song "An Election," subtitled "November 2, 1920," composed in disgust at the victory of Warren G. Harding, the Republican candidate and thus the candidate of the party to which Ives, like virtually all Yankees, had been devoted right up until the previous election (to the extent of having composed a campaign song for William McKinley in 1896).[54] Harding ran on a platform of repudiation against the internationalism of Woodrow Wilson and in particular against the League of Nations, which would have institutionalized the idealistic cause that President Wilson enunciated when demanding, in a speech delivered before Congress on 2 April 1917, that war be declared on Germany so that the world might be "made safe for democracy."[55] In the text, which he wrote himself, Ives complained that

> ... some men and women got tired of a big job;
> but, over there our men did not quit.
> They fought and died that better things might be!
> Perhaps some who stayed at home are beginning to forget and to quit.

I would propose reading that as Ives's dissent from the ban on pathos, indeed his dissent from postwar modernism. He was still holding on to the ideals that made the music of Sir Edward Elgar, for example, seem an anachronism in the ears of many after the Great War, but not to Ives. In *Essays before a Sonata,* the book Ives self-published in that same year, 1920, as "An Election," to accompany the self-publication of his Second Piano Sonata ("Concord, Mass.: 1840–1860") and explicate its literary program, you will find the following passage about Wagner and the music that followed in Wagner's wake, which may seem less than surprising in the context of the present essay. By the time of his middle age, Ives wrote—

> and long before the Hohenzollern hog-marched into Belgium—this music had become cloying, the melodies threadbare—a sense of something commonplace—yes—of make-believe came. These feelings were fought against for association's sake, and because of gratitude for bygone pleasures—but the former beauty and nobility were not there, and in their place stood irritating intervals of descending fourths and

---

54. C. E. Ives, "William Will: A Republican Campaign Song," published in 1896 in New York by Willis Woodward & Co.
55. Sixty-Fifth Congress, Session 1, Senate Document No. 5.

fifths. Those once transcendent progressions, luxuriant suggestions of Debussy chords of the 9th, 11th, etc., were becoming slimy. An unearned exultation—a sentimentality deadening something within hides around in the music. Wagner seems less and less to measure up to the substance and reality of César Franck, Brahms, d'Indy, or even Elgar (with all his tiresomeness), the wholesomeness, manliness, humility, and deep spiritual, possibly religious feeling of these men seem missing and not made up for by his (Wagner's) manner and eloquence, even if greater than theirs (which is very doubtful).[56]

Franck, Brahms, d'Indy, "even Elgar"—not Wagnerian decadence and what had followed from it—*that* was the music of Ives's Wilsonian idealism. The dehumanized ban-on-pathos crowd was Harding and his cynical inaugural appeal for a return to insouciance, or what the new president—proverbially—called "normalcy." To give the (to Ives) sickening passage in full, Harding's speech sonorously invoked "not heroics, but healing; not nostrums, but normalcy; not revolution, but restoration; not agitation, but adjustment; not surgery, but serenity; not the dramatic, but the dispassionate; not experiment, but equipoise; not submergence in internationality, but sustainment in triumphant nationality."[57] To Ives, this lovely bunch of alliteratively musical pseudo-statements merely amounted to isolationism, nor was it a return to anything. It was "breaking faith with us who die." In his music as well as in his rhetoric, Ives refused to dishonor that faith. In his continued commitment to the "Invictus" sentiment, he refused normalcy, the political counterpart to the ban on pathos.

And that is why, in the *Oxford History*, I used Ives, literally, as my textbook example to demonstrate the difference between maximalism and modernism. Modernism, as I have proposed, and will insist, is not a matter of style or genre. Modernism is an attitude toward modernity. Ives's attitude toward postwar modernity was rejection; his main mood was nostalgia. His was the old—downright Victorian—discourse against which the postwar modernists reacted. The fact that he used very advanced techniques that often paralleled and even anticipated those of the modernists who were his postwar contemporaries made him unique; but they did not make him a modernist. His work still exemplified my definition of maximalism as "a radical intensification of means toward accepted or traditional ends (or at least toward ends that could be so described)."[58] What finally put those means and ends asunder was the Great War, and that continues to be, in my view, its chief and enduring importance in the history of music.

56. Charles Ives, "Epilogue," in *Essays before a Sonata* (New York: Knickerbocker Press, 1920), 84–85.
57. Warren G. Harding, "Return to Normalcy," campaign speech of 14 May 1920, available at https://web.archive.org/web/20061003192206/https://teachingamericanhistory.org/library/index.asp?document=954.
58. R. Taruskin, *Music in the Early Twentieth Century*, 5.

21

Everybody Gotta Be Someplace
On Context

I. DOES IT REEK?

As you've probably guessed, my title is the punchline to an old, quite terrible joke. I found this version on a website simply called "Jokes":

> A man is making love to his best friend's wife when they hear the husband's car in the driveway. He dives into the closet.
> The husband comes in, goes to the closet to hang up his jacket, sees his friend standing there naked, and says, "Lenny, what are you doing here?" Lenny sheepishly shrugs and says, "Everybody gotta be someplace."[1]

And that, my friends, is context. Or at any rate, that is the way we think of context when we invoke it as an explanatory factor. Everything's gotta have one; that is, everything (and everyone) is situated. Situation tells you something you need to know (even if, like the husband in the joke, you might not want to know it), and so it needs willy-nilly to be taken into account. And what does it tell you? As usual, answers differ, as does their evaluation, and controversies arise.

One of the simplest, and therefore most controversial answers to the question *What is the function of context?* was given by the literary critic E. D. Hirsch, the

---

Keynote address, Fourteenth International Conference "Contextuality of Musicology—What, How, Why and Because," Belgrade, University of the Arts, 25 October 2018.

1. http://jo-kes.blogspot.com/2007/10/everybodys-gotta-be-somewhere.html (accessed 27 September 2018). The last word in the online version is *somewhere*. I have replaced it with the folksier *someplace* on the basis of my memory of hearing the comedian Myron Cohen tell the joke on television many decades ago.

472

dean of American "originalists," or "intentionalists," who was an embattled, deeply unfashionable figure during my formative years.

Hirsch took over from Gottlob Frege the distinction between the terms *Sinn* and *Bedeutung*. Translators of Frege usually render the title of the paper in which he proposed this distinction as "On Sense and Reference,"[2] but Hirsch preferred translating the terms as "meaning" and "significance," which he defined this way:

> "meaning" refers to the whole verbal meaning of a text, and "significance" to textual meaning in relation to a larger context, i.e. another mind, another era, a wider subject matter, an alien system of values, and so on. In other words, "significance" is textual meaning as related to some context, any context, beyond itself.[3]

Hirsch related these terms respectively to two phases of literary study: interpretation and criticism. The difference between them, he said, was that meaning was fixed at the time of utterance or creation, and recoverable, while significance, being relational, was mutable, and evolves. The paper in which these terms were first compared was an article Hirsch published in 1960, called "Objective Interpretation," so you can see why he had become an embattled figure—not to say a pariah—by the time I first quoted him, in an article I published in 1984. I was fully aware at the time that objectivity was by then hopelessly on the defensive, if not altogether in disrepute, and I fully accepted that any claim that the whole meaning of anything could be encompassed or even known by a scholar (or even by an author) was, in literal terms, untenable. And yet I found Hirsch's concepts useful and the use to which I put them fruitful. I still think the results I obtained by using them were valid, and so I still uphold the method that the terms implied—if not as an achievable goal, at least as a worthy asymptote.

My article was called "Musorgsky vs. Musorgsky: The Versions of *Boris*," and it was an attempt to address an old problem: that Musorgsky, who never finished another opera, finished *Boris Godunov* twice, and produced two versions that were not only different but actually incompatible, in many ways: formal, aesthetic, stylistic, even political. As I wrote, in preliminary justification of my method:

> [C]larification of the chronological, philological, and bibliographical record has not put an end to debate as to what the opera's optimum form should be, or what its composer's true intentions were.... [A]s long as the focus has been mainly on establishing the texts of the two authentic (i.e., authorial) versions of the opera and on describing their structures more or less independently—that is, on "meaning," as defined [by Hirsch]—no convincing rationale has ever been offered for the revision

---

2. See Gottlob Frege, "Über Sinn und Bedeutung," *Zeitschrift für Philosophie und philosophische Kritik* 100 (1892): 25–50; cf. "On Sense and Reference," trans. Max Black, in *Translations from the Philosophical Writings of Gottlob Frege*, ed. Peter Geach and M. Black (Oxford: Blackwell, 1980).

3. E. D. Hirsch, *The Aims of Interpretation* (Chicago: University of Chicago Press, 1976), 2–3.

in all its aspects, nor has any serious rationale for choosing [between] them ever been proposed.

It is here that considerations of "significance" can be of assistance. If Musorgsky's versions are not only described but compared, and not only compared but "inserted" into such vaster structures as the history of Russian opera, that of Russian historiography as embodied in Russian art and literature, and Musorgsky's own esthetic attitudes and their vicissitudes, we may . . . arrive at an account of the revision coherent enough to at last suggest motivation for all its aspects: the scenes added as well as the scenes removed and the scenes revised, the deletions in the remaining scenes as well as the interpolations.[4]

I borrowed the word *inserted* from an essay by the Marxist (and structuralist) philosopher Lucien Goldmann—admittedly a strange bedfellow for E. D. Hirsch, who was conspicuously conservative, but then I've always been a merry eclectic. Although he used a very different vocabulary, the French Marxist made a similar point to the American traditionalist, writing that "[t]he illumination of a meaningful structure constitutes a process of comprehending it; while insertion of it into a vaster structure is to explain it."[5]

As I say, I think my essay held water, and it has been absorbed into the standard historiography of its subject, so the application of the method seems to have borne fruit, and it is by its fruits that one should judge a method. At any rate, I have operated on that assumption, and stand by it to this day. Accordingly, my work has long been identified with contextualization. It is the feature of the *Oxford History of Western Music* that has been most consistently singled out for praise or blame.

Yes, blame: for there is still considerable opposition to contextualization among scholars in many fields. Opposition has actually been growing of late. And perhaps not altogether without reason. To call the process of contextualization one of "insertion," as I have done, is admittedly to oversimplify, which is a form of overstatement; and that oversimplifying metaphor has been among the factors contributing to a similarly hyperbolic backlash against contextualization, as you may have noticed, especially if you have run across this well-known and much-cited article (Fig. 21.1):

It came out a few years ago in the journal *New Literary History*. The author, a young critic named Rita Felski, teaches in the English department at the University of Virginia—strange to say, the very department where E. D. Hirsch held forth in days of yore. She may seem to be at the opposite end of the spectrum from Hirsch, but she has at least one thing in common with him: she has a sense of humor. As you have probably noticed, the title is in quotes, meaning that, as Felski points out

---

4. R. Taruskin, "Musorgsky vs. Musorgsky: The Versions of *Boris*," *Nineteenth-Century Music* 8 (1984–85): 91–118, 245–72, at 91–92; rpt. in Taruskin, *Musorgsky: Eight Essays and an Epilogue* (Princeton, NJ: Princeton University Press, 1993), 201–99.

5. Lucien Goldmann, "Genetic Structuralist Method in the History of Literature," in *Marxism and Art*, ed. Beryl Lang and Forrest Williams (New York: Longman, 1972), 249.

"Context Stinks!"

Rita Felski

MY TITLE IS A NONE-TOO-SUBTLE provocation, though not, I should point out, a self-authored one. What word could be more ubiquitous in literary and cultural studies: more earnestly invoked, more diligently defended, more devoutly kowtowed to? The once commonplace but now risible notion of "the work itself" has been endlessly dissected, dismembered, and dispatched into New Critical oblivion. Context is not optional. There are, to be sure, endless disputes between various subfields and splinter groups about what

FIGURE 21.1. Rita Felski, "'Context Stinks'" (*New Literary History* 42 [2011]: 573).

in her first sentence, it is not "self-authored." Indeed, it is a double, or perhaps I should say third-hand, quotation. Felski is quoting from Bruno Latour, the guru of Actor-Network Theory, which is enjoying a boom right now in the American academy; and Latour was quoting Rem Koolhaas, the Dutch architectural theorist, whose actual remark, the *locus classicus,* was a lot ruder than the version Felski put in her title.[6]

The successive appropriations have been quite typically opportunistic. Koolhaas's rejection of context was part of a neoliberal repudiation of the early "postmodernist" call for a more humane sensitivity to "the existing physical and political context" within which buildings were designed, "cultivating the existing circumstances, rather than projecting a utopian ideal." The Koolhaas battle cry signaled a renewed surge of "progressive" and "emancipatory" utopian rhetoric on behalf of libertarian modernism, reviving the autonomy paradigm against what was increasingly viewed as the "blinkered," confining if well-intentioned contextualist view.[7]

Latour appropriated the anticontextualist battle cry in protest against what he saw as a regressive tendency in systems analysis (since he is by training and expertise

---

6. It was, of course, "fuck context." Here is the full quote, properly *in context:* "[B]igness is no longer part of any urban tissue. It exists; at most, it coexists. Its subtext is fuck context" (Rem Koolhaas, Bruce Mau, and Hans Werlemann, *SMLXL* [New York: Monacelli Press, 1995], 502). See also Esin Komez Daglioglu, "The Context Debate: An Archaeology," *Architectural Theory Review* 20 (2015), available at www.tandfonline.com/doi/full/10.1080/13264826.2016.1170058.

7. Words and phrases in quotes are from Daglioglu, "The Context Debate."

a sociologist of business organizations), viewing contextualization as a failure of imagination that stood in the way of organizational innovation. For him, contextualism was code for resistance to change. Invoking context, he argued, was only a dodge to thwart the analysis of specifics and particulars by invoking categorical binary oppositions like human/nonhuman (which thwarts analysis of agency) or nature/culture (which thwarts analysis of behavior). Most purported contexts, he alleged, were only pseudo-explanatory clichés (he lists a few: "IBM corporate culture," "British isolationism," "market pressure," and "self-interest") which serve to hide from view, hence protect, the status quo. Received ideas "drown all the new interesting actors in a diluvium of older ones," he writes. One should study actual content rather than context. "Deploy the content with all its connections and you will have the context in addition." And that is why Latour regards the whole notion of context as "simply a way of stopping the description when you are tired or too lazy to go on."[8]

The influence of Actor-Network Theory on the study of art and its history, exemplified by Felski's article (which is basically an advertisement for Latour's ideas), is the next stage in this opportunistic appropriation. Like most manifestos, hers is wildly exaggerated, but that is how one gets one's ideas across. If she had called her article "Context Isn't Everything," it would have been a far more accurate title, just as it would have been more accurate if Susan Sontag had called her famous manifesto of 1964 "Against Overinterpretation" instead of "Against Interpretation." But in neither case would we be talking about them now. To argue, with Felski, that "the work of art is not *just* a historical document," or to oppose "a historicism that treats works of art *only* as cultural symptoms," is to rail against straw men, and she knows it.[9] Her aim when writing about artworks, she says, is to "do justice to both their singularity and their worldliness," to which I can only say, "Amen." So she is, like me, and like what I imagine any good scholar ought to be, a both/and person rather than an upholder of what I like to call The Great Either/Or. The danger of contexts, she warns (echoing Latour), is that, as usually conceptualized, contexts are static: "preformed beings" exercising "predetermined functions," "conveying predetermined meanings," and "project[ing] preexisting ideas and beliefs," which makes them places of confinement.[10] But this is a loaded critique, in which the practice of contextualization is equated with its abuse. What Felski is opposing are malpractices with which we who seriously contextualize artifacts, practices, and agents are well acquainted, and which we have learned to guard against in ways that I will describe.

As you no doubt already surmise, I regard all of the attitudes and practices I have been recounting, whether Koolhaas's, Latour's, or Felski's, as regressive. I will

---

8. Bruno Latour, *Reassembling the Social: An Introduction to Actor-Network-Theory* (Oxford: Oxford University Press, 2005), 147–48.

9. Rita Felski, "'Context Stinks!'" *New Literary History* 42 (2011): 573, 575; italics added.

10. Ibid., 576, 578, 583, 586. Further page references to this article will be made in the main text.

not presume to judge the validity or efficacy of Actor-Network Theory in its own domain of business administration, but its application to art studies has struck me, ironically enough, as a particularly objectionable oversimplification. What it simplifies away is responsible agency. It does this by inventing and admitting to its model of agency a new category, "nonhuman actors." I am on record as claiming (in italics, yet) that *Agents can only be people,* so of course I resist and reject that move.[11] Felski, whose whole argument is based on according agency to artworks, gives me a new opportunity to counter it.

She writes that "context is often wielded in punitive fashion to deprive the artwork of agency, to evacuate it of influence or impact, rendering it a puny, enfeebled, impoverished thing" (582). To invoke context is to inflate it, she writes; and, according to the rules of an imagined zero-sum game, to inflate context is to deflate text. (In fact, she contends, "we inflate content . . . *in order to* deflate text" [582; italics added].) We should treat artworks better than that, she says, because "if they are not to fade quickly from view, they must [be allowed to] persuade people to hang them on walls, watch them in movie theaters, purchase them on Amazon, dissect them in reviews, debate them with their friends" (584). But shouldn't we be identifying the actual persuaders alongside the hangers, watchers, purchasers, dissectors, debaters, and friends? To attribute their function to the artworks is to give them all an alibi, and that is the sort of idealization it should be our business to oppose.

Let me call Abraham Lincoln as my corroborating witness. According to a newspaper account of a meeting that took place in September 1862 between the president and some religious leaders who were pressing him to issue an immediate order of emancipation, they received this reply from the commander in chief:

> You remember the slave who asked his master, "If I should call a sheep's tail a leg, how many legs would it have?" "Five." "No, only four; for my calling the tail a leg would not make it so." Now, gentlemen, if I say to the slaves, "you are free," they will be no more free than at present.[12]

Never mind that a year later he did exactly that. What he said was correct, and it applies as well to artworks and other nonhuman, fictitious, or inanimate objects. There is no limit to what one may call an agent. Felski makes a list of potential agents just to show that there is no limit, and it includes "speed bumps, microbes, mugs, ships, baboons, newspapers, unreliable narrators, soap, silk dresses,

---

11. R. Taruskin, "The History of What?" (Introduction), in *The Oxford History of Western Music* (New York: Oxford University Press, 2005), 1:xxvi; rpt. in Taruskin, *Cursed Questions: On Music and Its Social Practices* (Oakland: University of California Press, 2020), 30–40. For a defense against Actor Network Theory, see Taruskin, "Agents and Causes and Ends, Oh My," *Journal of Musicology* 31 (2014): 272–93, at 289–93.

12. "What the President Said," *Daily Milwaukee News*, 23 September 1862, 1. See *The Quote Investigator* blog, https://quoteinvestigator.com/2015/11/15/legs/#return-note-12479-8.

strawberries, floor plans, telescopes, lists, paintings, cats, can openers"—literally anything. Every historian writes about such things, and so does every critic; but our normal habit is to regard them as components of the environment within which agents act. If we take the advice of the abolitionists in the story and say to them, "you are agents," will that make them so? Or is that only a nominalist conceit that threatens to divest the concept of agency of consciousness and responsibility? That is determinist thinking—not an aid to investigation but a substitute for it.

Felski anticipates this objection. "[L]et us steer well clear of technological or textual determinism," she instructs us, and assures us that "[t]o describe these radically disparate phenomena as actors is not at all to impute intentions, desires, or purposes to inanimate objects" (582).

Then why even bother calling the sheep's tail a leg? To say, as she does, that "[a]rtworks can only survive and thrive by making friends, creating allies, attracting disciples, inciting attachments, latching on to receptive hosts" is arbitrarily to reverse the current of agency: it is we and others of our own species who befriend, create, attract, incite, and latch. As Felski enumerates them in another hypothetical list, the agents that aid in the survival and subsistence of artworks include "fans, enthusiasts, fantasists, translators, dreamers, advertisers, entrepreneurs, and parodists." That is a list of humans, reminiscent of the ensemble of agents that for Howard Becker constituted an "art world."[13] But then she asks, "What was it about the James Bond novels in particular that attracted so many" fans, etc.? (587). You have to ask those attracted, not the novels that have attracted them. If you think the novels are telling you, you are only listening to yourself.

And where is the author in the list of agents? He does rate a mention a bit later on, but is weirdly deprived of his function: "The appeal of [Ian] Fleming's texts," Felski allows, "had much to do with their creation of a charismatic protagonist who moved easily into multiple media, times, and spaces, and proved adaptable to the interests and emotions of different audiences" (587–88). That is a list of contexts, I note in passing; but to recognize the success of the James Bond novels in adapting to so many contexts, I'd say, is tantamount to "imput[ing] intentions, desires, [and] purposes" to an author who gambled on a strategy and won. Is that not where the imputation belongs? To gamble on a strategy is an action, and one who gambles is an agent. To impute his achievement to his creations (which, we have already been assured, do not have intentions, desires, or purposes) just for the sake of the theory and its purity is merely to hide the creative (and, be it acknowledged, the commercial) gamble from view. That is the way of idealizers.

---

13. See Howard Becker, *Art Worlds* (Berkeley and Los Angeles: University of California Press, 1984).

All of this confusion can be avoided, it seems to me, if we remember that what we call contexts are in fact environments, and we who study them are ecologists at heart. Actual environments are neither singular nor static. They are not at all what Felski calls a box. They are more like what Heraclitus called a river. In warning us that "conventional models of historicizing and contextualizing prove deficient in accounting for the transtemporal movement and affective resonance of particular texts" (574), Felski makes an unwarranted and long-outdated assumption, imagining that the only context of interest to historians and critics is that of genesis and original intent. But most of us see historical context altogether differently by now. We see it as unbounded, extending potentially and often advantageously to the present. And to insert an artwork like *Boris Godunov* or an art-worker like Musorgsky into a historical context is less like putting them in a box than like throwing them into a vortex.

That is exactly what I had in mind when I wrote, in the introduction to the *Oxford History*, that "[t]he historian's trick is to shift the question from 'What does it mean?' to 'What has it meant?'"[14] Contextualization, in other words, is not confinement but enrichment. That is precisely why, although I am always interested in an artist's intention, I resist as loudly as anyone the attempt to turn our knowledge of it into a limit. "For us today," I wrote on the occasion of Mozart's bicentennial,

> *Don Giovanni* is not just the opera Mozart and da Ponte knew, bearing only the meanings it had for them and for the audience that greeted it in Prague two centuries ago. *Don Giovanni* is also something E. T. A. Hoffmann has known and construed, and Kierkegaard, and Charles Rosen, and Peter Sellars. Its meaning for us is mediated by all that has been thought and said about it since opening night, and is therefore incomparably richer than it was in 1787.[15]

So I regard as simply incorrect Felski's assumption that "[w]e are inculcated, in the name of history, into a remarkably static model of meaning, where texts are corralled amidst long-gone contexts and obsolete intertexts, incarcerated in the past, with no hope of parole" (578). A suitably open-ended notion of context is exactly what liberates texts from that prison. "The detachment of historical explanation," she writes, "is ruffled, even rattled, once we recognize that past texts have things to say on questions that matter to us, including the status of historical understanding itself" (580). Indeed, we ourselves are part of the context of whatever it is that we may study or investigate. And our objects of study are part of

---

14. R. Taruskin, *Oxford History*, 1:xvii.
15. R. Taruskin, *Text and Act: Essays on Music and Performance* (New York: Oxford University Press, 1995), 267. For some reason, this paragraph provoked the pianist Jeremy Denk into a rant: see "Taking on Taruskin," in *Think Denk: The Glamourous Life and Thoughts of a Concert Pianist*, 16 October 2011, available at http://jeremydenk.net/ in the archive.

our context. Many of us have recognized that by now, and also recognize that the questions that matter to Felski, and to us, only arise out of a context: *our* context, which (as T. S. Eliot once exquisitely observed) includes all the texts that we know.[16]

One of the most exquisite enunciations of the desirability of open-ended contextualism comes at the end of an article by Peter Schubert called "Authentic Analysis," in which he adjudicates the eternal dispute between those, on the one hand, who wish to limit the terms of present-day analysis of Renaissance music to the terms and concepts one can glean from theoretical writings contemporaneous with the composers, and those, on the other, who wish to limit the terms of all musical analysis to what are now considered to be transhistorically valid terms and concepts. (In the context of the North American academy, such transhistorical terms are prominently, and inevitably, Schenkerian terms.) Neither approach guarantees authentic results, Schubert writes. Nor is either to be excluded. Rather,

> Schenkerian analyses of fifteenth-century chansons fill a gap in documentation. That gap exists because we have questions we want answered about things we have found in the music, things we were able to find because of our experience (training, etc.) of tonal organization. Given the limits of Renaissance treatises, one way to "explain" large- and small-scale pitch organization [to our current satisfaction] is through analogy to tonal music. At worst such analyses are inconsistent, inefficient or unpersuasive, but never *a priori* wrong. Even if they contradict what historical evidence we have, they may be intellectually viable. We might find them irrelevant, but that just means that the author's purpose is different from ours. No analysis does more than open a narrow window on the piece, and different thinkers (or communities thereof) want different views.[17]

Sixteenth-century writers obviously could not predict the questions that twentieth-century historians would ask of them, but this does not prevent their answering those questions, because the context in which the questions are asked is drawn wide enough to include both the writers and the historians. And this will be true five hundred years from now, if twenty-sixth-century music historians are still interested in what we were thinking and doing back in the twenty-first.

This renders moot the eternal opposition of objective and subjective views. Understanding has to be of something, so there has to be an object; and somebody has to do the understanding, so there has to be a subject as well. The act of understanding is their meeting ground. That, of course, is what Hans-Georg Gadamer

---

16. "Some one said: 'The dead writers are remote from us because we know so much more than they did.' Precisely, and they are that which we know" ("Tradition and the Individual Talent" [1917], in T. S. Eliot, *Selected Essays 1917–1932* [New York: Harcourt Brace, 1932], 6).

17. Peter Schubert, "Authentic Analysis," *Journal of Musicology* 12 (1994): 3–18, at 17.

called *Horizontverschmelzung*, the "fusion of horizons," and contextualization (or what Gadamer called "situation") is what makes that possible.[18]

II. IMPOSITION AND AFFORDANCE

So context doesn't stink so badly after all. I think we are all in agreement about that, even Rita Felski in her less enthusiastic moods. So why the resistance, and whence the attraction of the alternative view that wants to eliminate environment as a factor by turning it into an agent or an ensemble of agents? I've made my case against "nonhuman actors" elsewhere.[19] Today I'd rather stay positive and try to give an idea of how I think environment, or context, is properly to be differentiated from agency. What is its conceptual function? What is its actual bearing on agency as we conceive the two when constructing historical narratives?

Let's start by considering its bearing on one important kind of action that historians must consider and philosophers assess, namely moral choices. How does one answer a question like this: Is it right or wrong, good or bad, to remove references to the Jews from the texts of Christian sacred music when publishing or performing it? In answering this question here, I will reduce to a minute or two the gist of a rather long paper that I used to give in the form of an illustrated lecture that has been posted on YouTube, so it is conceivable that you might know my answer already.[20] The full lecture contained about thirty music examples, but here I will only recall the first example and the last.

The first example is a famous one: Bach's *St. John Passion*, which is based on the one gospel of the four that names the Jews as culprits in the murder of Christ. There have been performances that have substituted euphemisms such as "die Leute" to replace the references, in the New Testament as translated by Martin Luther, to "die Juden," and such altered renditions have always drawn impassioned protests against desecrating a work of supreme aesthetic value. But then performances that retain the original text have also drawn protests for affronting the

---

18. See Hans-Georg Gadamer, *Truth and Method*, 2nd rev. ed., trans. Joel Weinsheimer and Donald G. Marshall (London and New York: Continuum, 2004), 301–2: "Every finite present has its limitations. We define the concept of 'situation' by saying that it represents a standpoint that limits the possibility of vision. Hence essential to the concept of situation is the concept of '*horizon*.' The horizon is the range of vision that includes everything that can be seen from a particular vantage point. . . . A person who has no horizon does not see far enough and hence over-values what is nearest to him. On the other hand, 'to have a horizon' means not being limited to what is nearby but being able to see beyond it. . . . Similarly, working out the hermeneutical situation means acquiring the right horizon of inquiry for the questions evoked by the encounter with tradition."

19. In Taruskin, "Agents and Causes and Ends, Oh My," 291–93, replying to Latour, *Reassembling the Social*, 71f.

20. See www.youtube.com/watch?v=v3rdqvJAoKU. A print version is available as "Did Somebody Say Censorship?" in Taruskin, *Cursed Questions*, 41–71.

sensibilities of today's Jews, who attend (and even participate in) performances of a work that in Bach's day was performed only before congregations of pious Lutherans. Does the fact that the original audience would not have been affronted, and that Bach could have had no intention of affronting Jews, whom he never expected to meet in church or perhaps anywhere, provide a sufficient basis for judging his work or for our decision?

The other example is a recording of Mozart's Requiem, produced in Germany in 1942, in which all references to the Jewish heritage of Christianity were purged from the liturgical text. The line *Te decet hymnus, Deus, in Sion; et tibi reddetur votum in Jerusalem* ("A hymn, O God, becometh Thee in Zion; and a vow shall be paid to Thee in Jerusalem") in the Introit was altered to remove the words *Zion* and *Jerusalem*, which became, respectively, *coelis* (heaven) and *terra* (earth). In the Offertory, the line *Quam olim Abrahae promisisti* ("As once Thou didst promise Abraham") became *Quam olim homini promisisti* ("As once Thou didst promise mankind").[21]

Here is how these textual emendations were justified in a contemporaneous review: "Mozart's Requiem is the most profound and deeply moving of all Masses for the Dead that are dedicated to the memory of the dear departed, and it should not be allowed to languish in obscurity simply because a handful of passages in the text are unsuited to our time."[22] "Our time," of course, was the Nazi time. But the justification is precisely the same as the one offered by those who alter the text of the *St. John Passion* to remove offensive references to "die Juden." One could with equal justice say of either act that the alteration has been done so that a "most profound and deeply moving" work of art "should not be allowed to languish in obscurity simply because a handful of passages in the text are unsuited to our time." In the case of the *St. John Passion* "our time" is the present, when public expressions of anti-Semitism have become unacceptable in many places. In either case the proposed modification can be interpreted either as a constraint on performance ("bad") or an enabler of performance ("good").

The act itself, as you see—whether we call it censorship or the exercise of discretion, bowdlerization or sanitation, expurgation or liberation—is morally and ethically neutral. Its evaluation depends entirely upon our reading of the context in which the modifying agents have acted—that is, on the values and purposes the act is seen to embody or serve. The motivating values are what count, and they cannot be inferred from the act itself, only from our knowledge of the context in which the

21. This recording, with its Nazified text, was reissued on CD in the Deutsche Grammophon Centenary Collection, vol. 1 (*The Early Years*): DG 459004 (1998), disc 5.

22. "Mozart's Requiem, die tiefste und erschütterndste aller dem Andenken teurer Toten gewidmeten Trauermessen, sollte nicht um einzelner unzeitgemässer Textstellen willen in den Schatten der Musikpflege zurücktreten" (Hermann Steffani in *Zeitschrift für Musik*, quoted in the notes accompanying the Deutsche Grammophon reissue referenced in note 21).

actors have acted, and our moral evaluation of it. For such knowledge and evaluation we are individually answerable. We cannot appeal to Bach or Mozart, to St. John or Abraham, to the Jews or to the Nazis, to validate our decision as to what to perform and how, if we are the performers, or to support our judgment if we are critics or reporters. It is entirely on us, and we must know the context in order to choose. That is why, where E. M. Forster said "only connect," I say "only contextualize!" And thus I wholeheartedly embrace situational ethics, also known as reflective morality. As defined by John Dewey, the guiding spirit of American pragmatist philosophy, reflective morality "demands observation of particular situations, rather than fixed adherence to a priori principles."[23] I calculated my presentation on censorship to demonstrate as crisply as possible the more general precept, enunciated by Joseph Fletcher, the most committed of American situational ethicists, that "in practice what in some times and places we call right is in other times and places wrong."[24]

And that is why I view context as being related dialectically to agency and creative production. A dialectic is a dynamic, a matter of pushing and pulling, of more or less powerful agents acting within and reacting to the contexts that enable and constrain their words and deeds, which those same words and deeds can affect and alter in their turn. To refine this definition I think it useful to relate historical contexts to two additional philosophical concepts.

One is *facticity*, which is just an English ersatz for *facticité*, a French ersatz for the German *Faktizität* as used in existentialist philosophy beginning with Heidegger, for whom it was interchangeable with a word of his own invention, *Geworfenheit*, from *werfen*, to throw, hence "thrown-ness."[25] We are thrown, he tells us, into a world not of our making. We are not responsible for the contingencies of our existence, but we are responsible for choosing our course of action within them. This context of contingency both limits our course and also provides us with our opportunities. Thus it both constrains and enables. That is the basic push and pull within which we act.

What conditions our choosing is best captured, I think, by the other concept I would introduce into the discussion: *affordance*, a term coined in 1966 by James Gibson, an animal psychologist.[26] It refers to environmental conditions or clues

---

23. John Dewey, *Ethics* (1932), in *The Collected Works of John Dewey*, vol. 7 (Carbondale: Southern Illinois University Press, 2008), 329.
24. Joseph Fletcher, "Naturalism, Situation Ethics, and Value Theory," in *Normative Ethics and Objective Reason*, ed. George F. McLean, Ethics at the Crossroads, vol. 1 (Washington, DC: Council for Research in Values and Philosophy, 1996), 28.
25. See Daniel O. Dahlstrom, *The Heidegger Dictionary* (London: Bloomsbury, 2013), 212 (s.v. *Thrownness*).
26. In James Gibson, *The Senses Considered as Perceptual Systems* (Boston: Houghton Mifflin, 1966).

that pose possibilities for action. Such actions are not necessarily the product of conscious thought: in Gibson's original model, affordances and their associated behaviors directly follow perception. Even when applied to humans, it remains for the analyst to determine the actual enabling and constraining conditions that underlie and engender the perceptual stimulus that impels what may have been an unreflective or subjectively unconnected response.

That assessment was the basis for the recent, widespread appropriation of affordance theory into the theory and history of the arts. Here is an example from— or rather, an application to—Haydn's creative biography. Toward the end of his life, Haydn told his biographer Griesinger that "instead of the many quartets, sonatas, and symphonies, he should have written more vocal music," and that he regretted that he did not become, as Mozart had done, "one of the foremost opera composers."[27] Haydn scholars have often expressed their surprise on reading this. "Curiously," wrote one, Haydn's "own comments about his works do not necessarily reflect what would appear to be his priorities in terms of actual composition."[28] Circling back to this curiosity after reviewing the statistics, the same scholar is left wondering at the discrepancy between what seems to have been Haydn's evaluation of his achievement, and the universal opinion of twentieth-century musicians "that his only serious achievements were his instrumental works.... How could he seriously argue that all his finest achievements are in the area of vocal music, and that he should not have expended so much time and energy on instrumental works?"[29]

This writer even asserts that "it seems more probable that he moved away from opera for his own artistic reasons rather than external circumstances or impositions."[30] But if we take into account the conditions that determined Haydn's activities, and particularly the conditions of his employment, there will no longer seem to be anything curious in his remarks, nor will we continue to entertain the vain assumption that we can deduce his or any eighteenth-century creator's aesthetic priorities merely by surveying their output.

That assumption is a misapprehension born of an anachronistic application of "Enlightenment" ideals—in this case the ideal of autonomous agency, which turns all external forces into "impositions." To wonder why Haydn did not write more operas or fewer symphonies is to forget, for example, that (in the words of Elaine Sisman) "the most intensively cultivated genre of Haydn's earlier career" was one he never would have dreamt of cultivating on his own—that is, the baryton trio, of which he composed 126 specimens (as against 107 symphonies, 68 string quartets,

---

27. Vernon Gotwals, ed. and trans., *Haydn: Two Contemporary Portraits* (Madison: University of Wisconsin Press, 1968), 63.

28. David P. Schroeder, *Haydn and the Enlightenment: The Late Symphonies and Their Audience* (Oxford: Clarendon Press, 1990), 66.

29. Ibid., 67.

30. Ibid., 5.

and 45 piano trios).[31] These reflected the priorities of Prince Nikolaus Eszterházy, the employer, not the employee; and those, in the eighteenth century, were the priorities that counted. Even in his ripest period, that of the London symphonies, Haydn was composing according to the terms of a contract, with J. P. Salomon, not according to the untrammeled dictates of his muse.

So that is why the proper model to apply, if one is looking to explain such choices as Haydn exercised in pursuance of his career, is neither impositions nor predilections, but rather affordances, or *environmental properties that offer action possibilities*, to boil it down to the smallest possible number of words. This defines the relationship between agents and their actions in a manner that allows a dynamic and dialectical account of what are too often presented as inert dichotomies.

Consider in this light the additional fact that after his return from London in 1795, Haydn stopped composing symphonies and, except for the opp. 76 and 77 quartets, turned his attention entirely to vocal genres: his two English oratorios (*The Creation*, 1798; *The Seasons*, 1801) and no fewer than six settings of the Roman Mass, composed between 1796 and 1802. In view of his stated apportionment of value, this might seem a reversion to predilection upon the cessation of impositions. But hold: some of the Masses were composed to mark the name day of Princess Maria Hermenegild, wife of Haydn's last patron, Prince Nikolaus II Eszterházy, the grandson of the baryton-playing Nikolaus I.[32] These Masses were thus the composer's last contracted labors, and what is a contract but an accepted (and in that sense self-imposed) obligation? One could argue either that the late Masses finally represented Haydn's predilections, or that they constituted the Eszterházy family's final imposition upon him.

Or one can argue, more realistically, that they were the final fruits of Haydn's unprecedentedly fertile response to his life's affordances. Those affordances—the possibilities for action tendered at various times by Count Morzin, the Princes Eszterházy, the publishing house of Artaria, the Loge Olympique de Paris, and J. P. Salomon—were what enabled a wheelwright's son to become the great musician of his age. And they were what constrained him from becoming the sort of opera composer that the (arguably) less well adapted Mozart became—Mozart, who never found a Haydnesque aristocratic niche until it was almost too late,[33] and therefore had to act more frequently, and riskily, on his own initiative, i.e., according to predilection.

---

31. Elaine R. Sisman, *Haydn and the Classical Variation* (Cambridge, MA: Harvard University Press, 1993), 128.
32. See Jeremiah McGrann, "Of Saints, Name Days, and Turks: Some Background on Haydn's Masses Written for Prince Nikolaus II Esterházy," *Journal of Musicological Research* 17 (1998): 195–210
33. See Christoph Wolff, *Mozart at the Gateway to His Fortune: Serving the Emperor, 1788–1791* (New York: W. W. Norton, 2012).

III. (CON)TE[X/N]T

So it is a combination of facticity, affordance, and dialectics that defines context in a way that promises the most fruitful application to music history and the interpretation of musical texts. That is what most of us, I would guess, now mean when we speak of "contextualism." We are indeed speaking of factors external—yet vitally connected—to the agent and the fruits of agency. We often widen our angle of observation to include aspects of the natural and social world, the worlds into which our historical agents are "thrown," which do not have an immediately apparent bearing on creative choices. We thus show ourselves to be aware of the nature of affordance even if we are not in the habit of using the word; for James Gibson's first premise was that an animal is not fully aware of the factors that condition its course of action. Neither was Haydn, and neither are we. That awareness that we are unaware—or, as we now commonly say, our known unknowns—are what impel us to bring to *our* consciousness what was not immediately present to the agents whose actions and products we study. That is certainly our business, though not necessarily theirs. And thus we insist, often in actual debate with our counterparts in the domain of music theory and analysis, that decontextualized approaches to the understanding of creative choices or the evaluation of their consequences afford only simulacra of understanding or explanation.

Such approaches are still widely practiced. Our theoretical and analytical colleagues gladly embrace them and often denounce us contextualizers with a zeal easily equal to ours in assailing them. They still rail against the "disenchantment of the world" (*Entzauberung der Welt*) that Max Weber rather ambivalently proclaimed just over a century ago, as the price one pays for science and technology and the power that comes with them.[34] Steven Rings, speaking on behalf of the American music theory profession in one of its official publications, in an article commissioned to mark the anniversary of the founding of the Society for Music Theory in America and defiantly titled "Music's Stubborn Enchantments (and Music Theory's)," has declared his (and their) unwillingness to pay that price. "Disenchantment," he writes,

> in various forms arguably pervades the postmodern humanities, as both diagnosis and method: the critical theorist disenchants, unmasks, demystifies. [He means Weber and/or Adorno. Us historians too?] Most music theorists, it need hardly be said, do something quite different. As the SMT celebrates its 40th year, music the-

---

34. Cf. Max Weber, *Wissenschaft als Beruf* (Science as a Vocation) (Munich: Duncker & Humblot, 1919), 9: "Die zunehmende Intellektualisierung und Rationalisierung bedeutet ... daß man, wenn man nur wollte, ... vielmehr alle Dinge—im Prinzip—durch Berechnen beherrschen könne. Das aber bedeutet: die Entzauberung der Welt" ("Increasing intellectualization and rationalization means ... that one could, if one wished, ... control all things—in principle—by calculation. But that means the disenchantment of the world").

ory—with its wide-eyed enthusiasms and unapologetic close readings, its loving attention to the sonic and the aesthetic, its frequent aloofness from the social and political—remains a discipline apart, a sort of blissed-out, sylvan glade within the Left-melancholic academy.[35]

But are things really so blissful within the sylvan glade? Rings's essay does not come off as unapologetic to my ear, but rather as a wrestling match with his own bad conscience, and it ends rather abruptly with what seems to be a desperate overreach for consolation, which he finds in the writings of a political theorist named Jane Bennett, who proposes that "to some small but irreducible extent, one must be enamored with existence and occasionally even enchanted [there it is!] in the face of it in order to be capable of donating some of one's scarce mortal resources to the care of others."[36] You must be happy, in other words, in order to be altruistic; and if music makes you happy, it is also making you good.

Thus, echoing Bennett, Rings writes that "enchantment can provide the somatic and affective fuel for interpersonal generosity and real-world political action"; and finally, quoting her again, "if enchantment can foster an intellectually laudable generosity of spirit, then the cultivation of an eye for the wonderful becomes something like an academic duty."[37]

I don't think we can content ourselves with this; nor ought we, for the sake of our discipline. Rings is preaching a false consciousness that has occasionally tempted me, too, when (for example) I have acted as adviser to students whose social conscience troubled them about the amount of good in the world they could accomplish as musicologists. Rather than offering them the Bennettian reassurances I suspected them of craving, but in which I did not fully believe, in a couple of cases I thought it only honest to counsel them to look elsewhere to satisfy their need for moral validation in what Rings calls "the real world," rather than the world for which their studies were preparing them. One of them has recently earned her MD and is now a practicing pediatrician; the other went to work for a progressive California politician. Both of them seem to be happy now, or at least happier than they were when I advised them, and so are the students who remained in the program to completion, who are doing good for the profession by practicing a more politically constructive kind of scholarship than one can achieve by indulging one's wide-eyed enthusiasms or performing unapologetic close (i.e., decontextualized) readings.

---

35. Steven Rings, "Music's Stubborn Enchantments (and Music Theory's)," *Music Theory Online* 24, no. 1 (March 2018), abstract: http://mtosmt.org/issues/mto.18.24.1/mto.18.24.1.rings.html.

36. Jane Bennett, *The Enchantment of Modern Life: Attachments, Crossings, and Ethics* (Princeton, NJ: Princeton University Press, 2001), 4; quoted in Rings, "Music's Stubborn Enchantments."

37. Bennett, *Enchantment*, 10; quoted in Rings, "Music's Stubborn Enchantments."

So we are all happy—my students who left, my students who stayed, and me. Although I try not to fool myself into thinking that my musicological work is a form of philanthropy, I do nevertheless think that contextualization serves as a moral validator of what we do, which puts me on a continuum with, rather than in opposition to, my most socially conscious pupils. I do believe we need to justify our acceptance of a salary by exercising skepticism as a defining attribute of our discipline. Without it, we lack a *raison d'être*. That probably identifies me in the eyes of many music theorists as a "Left puritan."[38] But those who would call me that are working within a tradition that has its own, perhaps equally questionable, political history.

And here I may have a surprise for you. I have been drawing the starkest and most ethically fraught contrast I know how between the contextualized brand of arts scholarship that is increasingly practiced in musicology as historical musicology and ethnomusicology converge, and the decontextualized brand that is still touted by the music theory establishment. It is a contrast not only of method but also of values and political implication.

What I am calling decontextualization has seven or eight decades of history behind it. An extreme was reached in what was known in America as New Criticism, a practice that arose in the 1940s when there was a lot to escape from in the surrounding reality. Building on the previous work of such British or British-American critics as T. E. Hulme, T. S. Eliot, and I. A. Richards, the New Critics were the ones who most passionately and seriously insisted, unlike Rita Felski, who did it only "in quotes" and with tongue in cheek, that Context Stank! The surprise, or paradox, that I fancy myself springing on you is that in its day, this most exigently decontextualized brand of criticism, which rigorously prohibited situating texts in time or place, which excluded all consideration of psychology or biography as factors that might help in explaining or interpreting texts, which fostered the critics to whom we owe the high and mighty "intentional fallacy" that detached texts from their authors (and also the "affective fallacy" that detached texts from their readers),[39] and which forms the acknowledged intellectual foundation of the sort of music analysis now practiced in the blissed-out wing of the Anglophone academy—this austerely purified and absolutist practice now synonymous with formalism was known in its day . . . (wait for it) . . . as *contextualism*.

---

38. See Henry Klumpenhouwer, "Commentary: Poststructuralism and Issues of Music Theory," In *Music/Ideology: Resisting the Aesthetic*, ed. Adam Krims (Amsterdam: G&B Arts, 1998), 289–310, at 299ff.

39. Cf. William K. Wimsatt and Monroe Beardsley, "The Intentional Fallacy," *Sewanee Review* 54 (1946): 468–88; idem, "The Affective Fallacy," *Sewanee Review* 57 (1949): 31–55. Both of these essays have been endlessly anthologized.

How is that possible? Let us hear from one of the purest and most representative New Critics, Cleanth Brooks, in his testamentary collection of essays, *The Well-Wrought Urn: Studies in the Structure of Poetry*, first published in 1947. Considering an apparent transgression by T. S. Eliot, who allowed criticism of Shelley's beliefs to creep into his assessment of Shelley's poetry, Brooks wrote that

> [c]ertain statements, explicit or implied, because they are not properly assimilated to a total context, wrench themselves free from the context, and demand to be judged on ethical or religious grounds. The fault may, of course, lie either with the poet or the reader: the poet may fail by not dramatizing the statement; the reader may fail by ignoring the context and considering the statement out of context.[40]

And here, for comparison, is a passage from the famous final chapter of the book, the title of which, "The Heresy of Paraphrase," long served as a shibboleth. The subject is the bad habit or sin of extracting propositions from poems, thus to encapsulate their meaning. To allow such a précis "to represent the essential poem," Brooks wrote, would be "to disregard the qualifications exerted by the total context as of no account, or else we have assumed that we can reproduce the effect of the total context in a condensed prose statement," which would, in effect, nullify, or at least obviate, whatever exceeded the condensation.[41]

What Brooks is calling the context, quite obviously, is what most of us would call the text. There is logic behind that seemingly paradoxical usage, beyond the mere love of paradox that their opponents accused New Critics of turning into a fetish. The exclusion of what *we* have been calling context for the sake of what *they* called context, if taken to an extreme, not only placed off-limits any and all consideration of social environment but even excluded the author and the reader from the interpretive function. This is the strongest version ever put forth of the principle of aesthetic autonomy—the absolute self-sufficiency and integrity of the text, in the case of literature, or of whatever artifact a particular medium produces, whether a painting, a sculpture, a musical score, or even a sound recording. Given its irreducible integrity, the autonomous artwork becomes the sole context within which any of the components that together define its identity can be considered. To abstract ideas from that autonomous entity and to evaluate them in terms that originate elsewhere than within the contemplated object itself, as T. S. Eliot admitted having done when reading Shelley's poetry, amounts to a violation of that irreducible integrity: a sin.

---

40. Cleanth Brooks, *The Well-Wrought Urn: Studies in the Structure of Poetry* (New York: Mariner Books, 1956), 253.
41. Ibid., 206.

Reducing the irreducible can be a result of error on the part of the critic, or of a flaw in the making of the object; but in any case it is an aesthetic failure. Art, to the extent that it *is* art, must be inviolate. It does not *have* a context; it *is* the context.

IV. ROOTS AND BRANCHES

The critic Murray Krieger, in one of the earliest retrospective evaluations of the Contextual Theory, his term for what we now know as New Criticism, recognized something its practitioners denied, namely its descent from earlier romantic and aestheticist theories, going back through Walter Pater and Arthur Schopenhauer (whom Krieger does not name) to the generations of Schelling and Kant, whom he does indeed name and credit, and quote at length. He warned against "the dangers, the tendencies toward reckless romanticism," which the Contextual Theory displayed despite its view of itself as a reaction against romanticism.[42]

There is poetic justice in this. What Krieger did, in effect, was to contextualize the Contextual Theory, and (as always happens when ideas are situated in the context of intellectual history) to relativize its claims. His critique pointed the way to the theory's eventual obsolescence. But uncovering its romantic legacy brings us back to music, because the position that New Critics advocated amounted to a gloss on the famous sentence that Walter Pater uttered in 1873, which Anglophone students of art and aesthetics can probably still recite by heart and in chorus: *All art constantly aspires towards the condition of music.*[43] For music was the art of arts: the one that most nearly eliminated the distinction between content and form and thus best exemplified aesthetic autonomy, or what later became known as contextualism, at its purest.

Cleanth Brooks makes it quite explicit. In defending his formalist injunction against paraphrase, which depends on the claim that nothing may be abstracted from a poem or put in any other form of words than that of the original context (that is, the poem as written), he echoed Walter Pater's identification of music as the prototype of aesthetic autonomy:

> The essential structure of a poem (as distinguished from the rational or logical structure of the "statement" which we abstract from it) resembles that of architecture or painting: *it is a pattern of resolved stresses.* Or, to move closer still to poetry by considering the temporal arts, the structure of a poem resembles that of a ballet or

---

42. Murray Krieger, *The New Apologists for Poetry* (Minneapolis: University of Minnesota Press, 1956), 140.

43. Walter Pater, "The School of Giorgione" (1873), in idem, *The Renaissance: Studies in Art and Poetry,* edited and with an introduction by Adam Philips (Oxford: Oxford University Press, 1986), 86.

musical composition. It is a pattern of resolutions and balances and harmonizations, developed through a temporal scheme.[44]

Music is thus the decontextualized art par excellence; or, to put it in new-critical terms—that is, in terms of our pseudo-paradox—music, because it is the most autonomous of the arts, is *the most contextual* of the arts.

Did any musician ever actually call it that? There is one. Let me quote him first and let you try to identify him before I do:

> [M]usical compositions of the kind under discussion possess a high degree of contextuality and autonomy. That is, the structural characteristics of a given work are less representative of a general class of characteristics than they are unique to the individual work itself. Particularly, principles of relatedness, upon which depends immediate coherence of continuity, are more likely to evolve in the course of the work than to be derived from generalized assumptions. Here again greater and new demands are made upon the perceptual and conceptual abilities of the listener.

That could have been written by any of the New Critics. Their peculiarly American tradition obviously informs it, and recognizing its traces will identify its author as American. Indeed, like most of the New Critics, he was a southern American, born (like the novelists William Faulkner and Stark Young) in the state of Mississippi. Yet even without these clues, anyone who has encountered them before will have no trouble in identifying the voice and ideas of Milton Babbitt.

The quoted passage comes from his emblematic defense of academic serial composition, a talk originally given at Tanglewood, the Boston Symphony Orchestra's summer music festival, in 1957, but known since its publication in 1958, for better or worse, by the mischievous title supplied by the editor of the magazine in which it first appeared: "Who Cares If You Listen?"[45]

This paragraph from the mother text has been endlessly glossed and explicated in the literature that has grown up around the "total serialism" of the mid-twentieth-century avant-garde. Fred Everett Maus captured well what I have been calling the pseudo-paradox involving the use within that literature of the word *contextual*. As used therein, Maus writes, the term "abbreviates the thought that local events should be interpreted with reference to the context provided by a unique individual composition, rather than a general theory—for instance a theory of tonal harmony," which, by situating it, would contradict its uniqueness, hence its autonomy. "It is a confusing term," Maus admits,

---

44. Brooks, *The Well-Wrought Urn*, 253.
45. Milton Babbitt, "Who Cares If You Listen?" *High Fidelity* 8, no. 2 (February 1958): 38–40, 126–27, at 39. The editor who gave it its notorious title was Roland Gelatt (1920–86). This essay, too, has been endlessly anthologized.

since musicologists also refer to "contextual interpretations"—that is, interpretations that move beyond the individual work to consider other musical and non-musical factors. So a "contextual" interpretation, in one usage, insists on [staying within] the boundary of the individual composition, while in the other usage, it insists on crossing that boundary.[46]

That confusion was actually quite familiar, and it created a familiar instability. Babbitt himself stressed that "[a]lthough in many fundamental respects this music is 'new,' it often also represents a vast extension of the methods of other musics, derived from a considered and extensive knowledge of their dynamic principles."[47] As we see, that applies not only to its sound and structure, but also to the discourse that surrounded it; for Babbitt shows himself to have been located, like all modernists and all formalists, on the same "late, late Romantic" continuum as the New Critics who took Walter Pater's explicit notion of autonomy and the implicit one of contextuality to their extremes.[48] Babbitt, you might say, rode it to the very end of the line, where extremes of rationalism and irrationalism, or (to put it another way) of perfect specificity and perfect opacity, ran up against one another and the process of deconstruction started on its inexorable way.

Mad magazine, the favorite humor magazine of American adolescent boys, gave an unwitting preview of that deconstruction of the concepts of autonomy and contextuality in 1957, the same year as Babbitt's famous talk. While not yet one of Babbitt's readers at the time, I was a devoted reader of *Mad* and still remember first reading the item I am about to display. It was a parody by the television comedian Ernie Kovacs of a newspaper feature called "Believe It or Not," consisting of strange or amazing facts (Fig. 21.2).

Utter one-of-a-kind contextuality is thus shown to be tantamount to utter meaninglessness. This was not exactly an unrecognized paradox: under a different name it was Wittgenstein's "Private Language Argument," which considered the (im)possibility of a language that only one person understood.[49] But recognition of *aporia*, or irresolvable contradiction, even though it came from the Greek for "without the possibility of passage," turned out to be no deterrent in practice. Quite the contrary: to invoke another eminent New Critic, Allen Tate, the ideals of autonomy and contextuality, which informed his critical practice, were both "perpetually necessary and . . . perpetually impossible," and their impossibility of realization "has its own glory."[50]

---

46. Fred Everett Maus, "Concepts of Musical Unity," in *Rethinking Music*, ed. Nicholas Cook and Mark Everist (Oxford: Oxford University Press, 1999), 191n52.

47. Babbitt, "Who Cares If You Listen?" 39.

48. For "late, late Romantic" see Leonard B. Meyer, "A Pride of Prejudices; or, Delight in Diversity," *Music Theory Spectrum* 13 (1991): 241–251, at 241.

49. Ludwig Wittgenstein, *Philosophical Investigations* (Oxford: Basil Blackwell, 1953), §243 et seq.

50. Allen Tate, "Is Literary Criticism Possible?" (1950), in idem, *The Man of Letters in the Modern World* (New York: Meridian Books, 1955), 174.

FIGURE 21.2. Ernie Kovacs, "Strangely Believe It!" *Mad*, no. 33 (June 1957) © E.C. Publications, Inc. Drawn by Wallace Wood.

But glory for whom? We musicologists know the answer better than anyone else, because we know better than anyone else the genealogy of the idea that art comes from nowhere and therefore exists in sublime decontextualization, unattached to any time or place. We remember what E. T. A. Hoffmann wrote in 1813, echoing the gospels:

> Our kingdom is not of this world, say the musicians, for where do we find in nature, like the painter or the sculptor, the prototype of our art? Sound dwells everywhere,

but the sounds—that is, the melodies—which speak the higher language of the spirit kingdom, reside in the human heart alone.[51]

Aesthetic autonomy is in essence a religious perception, and the whole history of the idea corroborates the diagnosis. I will quote one last *locus classicus*—my favorite (which is to say, my *bête noire*), which I've quoted countless times, so perfectly does it lay bare the *radix malorum*, the Root of All Evil, encapsulating the core of the notion and all its implications. In his *Parerga und Paralipomena* of 1851, the addendum to his magnum opus, *Die Welt als Wille und Vorstellung*, Schopenhauer wrote: "Intellectual life floats ethereally, like a fragrant cloud rising from fermentation, above the reality of the worldly activities that make up the lives of the peoples, governed by the will; alongside world history there goes, guiltless and unstained by blood, the history of philosophy, science, and the arts."[52] Long before I began bruiting this passage about, it was famous among musicians, because Hans Pfitzner had copied it out to stand as an epigraph atop the score of his opera *Palestrina*, which actually contains a scene of divine musical dictation.

In June 1917, when *Palestrina* was given its first performance in Munich, the First World War was in its third year and Germany was standing on the precipice of disaster. Pfitzner's opera about a divinely inspired composer who had written his immortal *Missa Papae Marcelli* almost four hundred years previously was in its actual context a timely consolation, and the epigraph from Schopenhauer was undoubtedly meant expressly to label it as such. It offered refuge in what a century later Steven Rings would call the "blissed-out, sylvan glade" of what we can either call *decontextualization* or *contextualism*, depending on the immediate heritage to which we profess our allegiance.

V. TIME AND TIDE

And this brings me, by way of conclusion, to a musically illustrated parable. A few months before writing this essay I researched and wrote a longer one to accompany an album of CDs the Berlin Philharmonic released in 2019, containing a

---

51. "Unser Reich ist nicht von dieser Welt, sagen die Musiker, denn wo finden wir in der Natur so wie der Maler und der Plastiker den Prototypus unserer Kunst?—Der Ton wohnt überall, die Töne, das heißt die Melodien, welche die höhere Sprache des Geisterreichs reden, ruhen nur in der Brust des Menschen" (E. T. A. Hoffmann, *Musikalische Novellen und Aufsatze*, vol. 1, ed. Edgar Istel [Regensburg, 1921], 162; trans. Stephen Rumph in "A Kingdom Not of This World: The Political Context of E. T. A. Hoffmann's Beethoven Criticism," *Nineteenth-Century Music* 19 [1995–96]: 50–67, at 50).

52. "Dieses intellektuelle Leben schwebt, wie eine ätherische Zugabe, ein sich aus der Gährung entwickelnder wohlriechender Duft über dem weltlichen Treiben, dem eigentlich realen, vom Willen geführten Leben der Völker, und neben der Weltgeschichte geht schuldlos und nicht blutbefleckt die Geschichte der Philosophie, der Wissenschaft und der Künste" (Arthur Schopenhauer, *Parerga und Paralipomena* [1851], in *Sämtliche Werke in fünf Bänden* [Munich: Suhrkamp, 1986], 4:95).

definitive collected edition of Wilhelm Furtwängler's recorded wartime performances with the orchestra, covering the period 1939–45.[53] These are famous recordings: the first musical performances ever preserved using the magnetophone, which was the name given to the earliest tape recorders. These devices were first developed in Nazi Germany and first used by radio stations in the German Reich and its occupied territories (as well as by the Gestapo, to record interrogations and confessions). The orchestra sent me a sheaf of documents along with the recordings as a source of factual information about the programs I was annotating. I actually found in them something much more valuable from my perspective than factual information, something that has an obvious and, as you will see, very poignant bearing on the substance of this essay.

The program of the first concert in the 1943–44 season carried a commentary by Karla Höcker, a popular writer on music, under the title "Zum Beginn" (At the Start). This season was the first to follow the German defeats in Stalingrad and Kursk. The army was in retreat on the eastern front and the German civilian population was subject to attack, especially by British bombers from the west. Along with Höcker's essay, the program carried on its first page a notice from the police that "at the first sounding of an air raid warning, without waiting for the actual alarm, the concert must be halted immediately; all doors will be opened and the audience must head for home or for an air raid shelter." This was no vain precaution. On 30 January 1944, only three months later, the Philharmonie, the orchestra's hall since 1882, would be destroyed by British bombers. To say that the atmosphere in the hall where the audience was perusing its programs in October 1943 was an unusual one would be an epic understatement. And here is what they read:

> We are gazing into the dark of a new winter, doubly dark for it is a winter of war, the course of which will be marked by hard necessities, by struggle, by renunciation and by tears. And in the midst of this darkness there rises, untouched by horrors of any kind, but gentle, enthralling, and consoling, the voice of everlasting German music! . . . We who are directly confronted with atrocities, we to whom the closeness of death has lent other, more anguished feelings along with a new and tougher consciousness—we recognize more clearly than any previous generation just what this music symbolizes. It is our world that sounds forth when the bows are set in motion, the world of a spirit that no enemy air raid can destroy, nor any bomb. It may be possible to destroy monuments that way, or rob churches and cathedrals of their venerable luster: but music is inviolable. . . . Anyone who is truly touched by this music, who allows his own life to glow within it as in a great flame, belongs to the world of this spirit. And that is what makes these long taken-for-granted Philharmonic concerts become, in the midst of war, not just a beautiful, more or less rewarding experience for individual music lovers, but a higher necessity. . . . That is why we gather together for the concerts of the Ber-

---

53. *Wilhelm Furtwängler: The Radio Recordings 1939–1945* (22 SACD, Berliner Philharmoniker Recordings, 2019).

liner Philharmoniker. That is why we need them more than ever before, at the beginning of this fifth year of the war.

I hope you will forgive the length of my quotation from this extraordinary document. Just how extraordinary a document it is will be palpable if you consider that it followed by half a year Joseph Goebbels's speech at the Berlin Sportpalast, proclaiming *totaler Krieg* (total war), which left the Berlin and Vienna Philharmonics the only functioning (that is, unconscripted) orchestras in Greater Germany, the *Grossdeutsches Reich*. Half a year later the sentiments to which Höcker gave expression (anguish, hard necessities, renunciation, tears) would have likely led to prosecution for *Wehrkraftzersetzung* (defeatism). Germany was again on a precipice, infinitely steeper than the one it had faced in Pfitzner's day, twenty-six years earlier. No wonder, then, that Höcker's words were a virtual paraphrase of Schopenhauer's. Where he had spoken of the arts and philosophy as being "guiltless and unstained by blood" (*schuldlos und nicht blutbefleckt*), she spoke of music, in the midst of war, as being "untouched by horrors of any kind" (*unangetastet durch jegliches Grauen*).

That safe space was an article of faith. To some of us, including some of our professional colleagues, it still is. Beethoven studies, in particular, remains a battlefield between contextualizers, who are nowadays more interested than ever in politics, including the politics of class and gender, and resolute idealizers, all the more *enragés* for having to make their professions explicit.[54]

54. If we take as the starting point "Getting Down off the Beanstalk," Susan McClary's shot-heard-round-the-world comparing a passage in Beethoven's Ninth Symphony to the "murderous rage of a rapist" in the January 1987 *Minnesota Composers Forum Newsletter* (even if we admit that the offending passage was in fact an analogy serving immanent description rather than a contextualization), its considerably softened reprinting in McClary's *Feminine Endings* (Minneapolis: University of Minnesota Press, 1991), and the reaction to it (e.g., Pieter van den Toorn, *Music, Politics, and the Academy* [Berkeley and Los Angeles: University of California Press, 1996], 23–34), then a survey of the frontline would include Tia DeNora, *Beethoven and the Construction of Genius: Musical Politics in Vienna 1792–1803* (Berkeley and Los Angeles: University of California Press, 1997), most emphatically a contextualization, and the reaction to *it* (e.g., Charles Rosen's furious review, "Did Beethoven Have All the Luck?" *New York Review of Books*, 14 November 1996, plus an ensuing exchange with the author ["Beethoven's Genius," *New York Review of Books*, 19 April 1997]; Rosen's review and his side of the exchange are reprinted in Charles Rosen, *Critical Entertainments* [Cambridge, MA: Harvard University Press, 2000]); Sanna Pederson's "Beethoven and Masculinity," in *Beethoven and His World*, ed. Scott Burnham and Michael P. Steinberg (Princeton, NJ: Princeton University Press, 2000), 313–31; and, post-millennium, a trio of contextual analyses—Stephen Rumph, *Beethoven after Napoleon: Political Romanticism in the Late Works* (Berkeley and Los Angeles: University of California Press, 2004); Nicholas Mathew and Benjamin Walton, eds., *The Invention of Beethoven and Rossini* (Cambridge: Cambridge University Press, 2013); and Nicholas Mathew, *Political Beethoven* (Cambridge: Cambridge University Press, 2016)—to which Lewis Lockwood's *Beethoven: The Music and the Life* (New York: W. W. Norton, 2005) offers the most substantial counterweight.

But this is a battle that is fought not only between scholars but also within scholars. A shrewd review in *Music Theory Online* of two strongly contextualized studies of Beethoven—one by Daniel Chua called *Beethoven and Freedom,* and the other, by Naomi Waltham-Smith, called *Music and Belonging between Revolution and Restoration*—began with what might have seemed a simple factual statement:

> Today, in light of a heightened ethical imperative ... with commitments to feminist musicology, critical race theory, and sound studies, any investigation of musical form on its own seems untenable. Responding to the shift in the disciplinary terrain, many scholars have turned away from the canonic exemplars of the music of Haydn, Mozart, and Beethoven and toward the sociopolitical significance of a broader range of works from the same period.

And yet, despite the promises their titles seemed to make, the reviewer noted in conclusion that

> both studies ... reinforce the severance of music from worldly life. As bold as they are at broaching the vital question of how the works of the Classical style might be assimilated into our contemporary disciplinary landscape, the books wind up shelving the question of politics in order to demonstrate that the works are amenable to the well-established analytical methods and stylistic typologies of eighteenth-century music scholarship.... Politics must continue to wait.[55]

But ward it off though we may, it doesn't wait. Resistance to politics, as one among many aspects of the worldly environment, is an act that should be read in the context of constant negotiation and contention that still surrounds the classical canon and constructs its significance, which is of course a political process. I hope that that swirl of contending views never dies down, for if it does, that will be the evidence that the classical canon no longer matters.

We may be getting close to that most undesirable resolution. But I call for continued contextualization and continued debate, and do my best to feed it, not out of what Craig Comen, the disappointed reviewer I've been quoting, dubbed "a heightened ethical imperative," but out of a wish to have our descriptions match our experience.

My own lived experience persuades me that aesthetic autonomy is not an attribute of art but rather a critical or philosophical posture that was from the beginning at utter variance with both musical ontology and musical engagement. My question to upholders of musical autonomy, authors and critics alike, is simple, and reopens the question of agency in terms that can be borrowed from Karla Höcker's text. Was "the voice of everlasting German music" (*die Stimme der ewigen*

---

55. Craig Comen, Review of *Beethoven and Freedom* by Daniel Chua and *Music and Belonging between Revolution and Restoration* by Naomi Waltham-Smith, *Music Theory Online* 24, no. 3 (September 2018), available at http://mtosmt.org/issues/mto.18.24.3/mto.18.24.3.comen.html.

deutschen Musik) always as "gentle and consoling" (*sanft . . . und trostreich*) as she maintained? Or was hers, not its, the consoling voice?

And what about Furtwängler, whose function it was to mediate between the hypothetical voice of German music, as conjured by Höcker, and its hearers? Having listened intently to five years' worth of performances by this artist who had been nurtured by the romantic faith, one for whom Pfitzner had been a key mentor, and one whose own writings on music overflowed with ruminations on the sanctity of art and its exemption from the cares of this world, I came away more convinced than ever that the notional acontextualism of perfect aesthetic autonomy has always given way under pressure to the realities of worldly contexts, the very thing the doctrine was devised to occlude.

If there is an ethical component to our task as historians, it is the imperative to report that inevitable and very moving devolution as a chapter in the history of ideas. From this point of view the tape-recorded wartime broadcasts of the Berlin Philharmonic under Wilhelm Furtwängler were a fabulous boon. They embody the most striking and moving collision I have ever witnessed between notional and actual contexts as applied to music.

The June 1943 broadcast taping of Beethoven's Fifth, at the tail end of the season before the one Höcker introduced with her palliative essay, can serve as vivid illustration. That symphony has always been a site of contradiction. In his epoch-making review of 1810, often cited as the foundational text of German romantic idealism as applied to music, E. T. A. Hoffmann fastened, as he always did, on what we might (with apologies to the media critic George Trow)[56] call the context of no-context, contending that the symphony "opens to mankind an unknown kingdom, a world which has nothing in common with the outer sensory world."[57]

Recent Beethoven scholarship has fastened on the dissonance between this Romantic description of Beethoven's sublimely autonomous music and the actual sounds it makes. Hoffmann's rapturous account of the Fifth is practically a new-critical reading *avant la lettre*. It is all about the resolution of tensions and the harmonious unity of form, but it never deigns to notice what is perhaps the most obvious thing about the work, especially if you are attending a live performance and see in front of you three trombones, a contrabassoon, and a piccolo, instruments endemic to military bands that had never previously been used by any composer of symphonies.

The very act of asserting the autonomy of art in the face of such a contradiction betrayed unease with that disjunction. So, at any rate, writes Stephen Rumph, who counters Hoffmann's claims by pointing beyond the fact of the symphony's instru-

---

56. Cf. George W. S. Trow, *Within the Context of No Context* (Boston: Little, Brown, 1981).

57. E. T. A. Hoffmann, *Schriften zur Musik: Nachlese*, ed. Friedrich Schapp (Munich, 1963), 34; trans. Rumph in "A Kingdom Not of This World," 51.

mentation to its musical imagery, which, he reminds us, "tell[s] of wars, nations, and political associations":

> Into the vacated space of Hoffmann's spirit realm rush a host of positive, material associations—France, Napoléon, glory, battlefields.... The sheer materiality of the Fifth Symphony—its insistent rhythms, its triumphal marches, its cathartic release into the major—threaten to expose Hoffmann's review as a critical *Phantasiestück*.[58]

And nowhere are the rhythms more insistent, the marches more triumphal, the release more cathartic than in Furtwängler's wartime performance. What sort of refuge was that?

To judge by the recorded evidence, the fraught context in which the Berlin Philharmonic performed the monuments of eternal German music over the course of the war had an ever-intensifying qualitative impact on the performances—or rather, on the conductor's performance practice, producing renditions that dramatically reflected the stresses of the social environment in which the concerts were taking place. Whatever their commitments to the autonomy principle, in short, artists ineluctably respond to their environments, affirming affordance theory in ways that, exactly in accordance with the theory, go beyond their conscious awareness or volition.

The very best evidence of that inexorable redoubling is the very last recording Furtwängler made in Berlin before the collapse of the Third Reich: a performance of Brahms's First Symphony, or rather of its finale, the tail end and sole survivor on tape from the concert of Tuesday, 23 January 1945, which took place in the Admiralspalast, the Philharmonic's temporary home after the bombing raid that had leveled the Philharmonie. By this time disaster loomed with certainty. On the very day of the concert, the US Army took St. Vith, the last German stronghold in the Ardennes, thus ending the so-called Battle of the Bulge and, with it, all effective German resistance. In the east, the Red Army crossed the Oder. According to his widow's recollection, moreover, the conductor was warned that day (by Albert Speer) that he had been declared *persona non grata* by Himmler and the SS, and was liable to arrest. After one last concert in Vienna with his other orchestra, he would flee to Switzerland and await catastrophe, certain that he would be tainted by the defeat and by accusations of collaboration. He would not conduct again in Berlin until May 1947.

And who was sitting in the audience that Tuesday afternoon? None other than Karla Höcker, whose account of that concert is the second entry in her now-celebrated diary (unpublished until 1984) of the cataclysmic year 1945:

> At noon we take the S-Bahn to the Admiralspalast, an operetta theater of faded red-velvet elegance. Now the Furtwängler concerts are given there—because it is the only

---

58. Rumph, "A Kingdom Not of This World," 65–66.

sizable hall that is still standing. On account of the current alarms in the evenings it starts early, around three o'clock. Packed house! In the second movement of the Mozart Symphony [no. 40 in G Minor] there is a scary moment: the lights go out. Only a few emergency bulbs cast their bluish glow over Furtwängler, who continues to direct those musicians who are still playing. Then the sound drains away, leaving only the first violins who know how it goes on for a while ... Furtwängler turns around, glances over the audience and the mute orchestra. Slowly he drops the baton. He leaves. The musicians follow.

But the audience stays put except for a few who go out into the courtyard for a smoke. And the orchestra members with their grey faces, between the grey hangings above the stage, huddle around Furtwängler like frightened animals. From this one can tell exactly what he is thinking, the same as everyone else. It's over.

After about an hour, though, the lights come back on. The bell rings. The audience return to their seats, the orchestra enters the stage. The oboe A. They tune up. Many listeners must be thinking, as I am, of the broken Mozart melody, which still seems to float in the room like an unanswered question. It is customary to repeat the last item after interruptions in a concert. But this time, no one is surprised that Furtwängler gives the downbeat for the Brahms symphony. It is as if Mozartean beauty, blissfulness itself, no longer has a place in this city.[59]

The performance Furtwängler and his orchestra gave in this unimaginable moment of mixed despair and defiance is certainly not beautiful, but, thanks to the recording of the finale that has miraculously survived, one can hear its astounding wildness. All concerned were performing, quite literally, as if there were no tomorrow. The music builds unbearable tension, abjures all "Brahmsian" restraint or relaxation, and in its raging subjectivity hits dumbfounding extravagances of tempo at both ends of the scale, vastly exceeding bounds of propriety that Furtwängler sternly upheld in less stressful times.

In the light of this wartime valedictory, one reads Furtwängler's earlier strictures against "distorted" performances with a rueful sense of irony. In one of his most famous essays, "Der Fall Wagner, frei nach Nietzsche" (The Wagner Case, Loosely after Nietzsche), Furtwängler had blamed such excesses on the ill effects of thoughtless "tradition," warning that

> [n]uances of emotion which were initially conveyed mutedly, gently, with sensitive restraint, become increasingly coarse and unrefined as time goes on. A slight easing of the tempo, for instance, becomes a massive ritardando, and gently dwelling on individual notes is turned into a succession of fermatas. It is a law of traditions that the longer they last, the more exaggerated their expression becomes.[60]

---

59. Karla Höcker, *Beschreibung eines Jahres: Berliner Notizen 1945* (Berlin: Arani, 1984), 13–14.
60. Wilhelm Furtwängler, "The Case of Wagner" (1941), in *Furtwängler on Music*, trans. and ed. Ronald Taylor (London: Routledge, 2016), 95.

But the stunning hyperboles in this Brahms finale amid the final throes of war were born not of tradition but of the moment. Afterward, Furtwängler regained his composure and his sobriety, as one can hear in the nine complete Brahms Firsts he recorded between 1947 and 1954. None conveys the extremes of anguish and excitement he achieved in his last wartime appearance in the doomed capital, or the extreme of what Tolstoy called "infectiousness" that envelops a listener even today, owing in part to the echoes in Brahms's finale of hymns and chorales, collective and participatory genres that embody with particular concreteness and urgency what Furtwängler regarded as the chief purpose of music. "With each performance," he wrote of Beethoven's Fifth, "there comes into existence a kind of ideal *Gemeinschaft*"—brotherhood or community.[61] That holds even truer of "Beethoven's Tenth" as played here, *in extremis*.

As they affirm the social value of music as a shared experience, these words belie that other notion beloved of Romantics, which asserts art's detachment from the social world and its sometimes bloody vicissitudes. The bloodiest of all wars brought the foremost classical musician in the country with the most distinguished tradition of classical music to a pinnacle that could be described from one standpoint as grotesque, but from another as setting a standard of heartrending communication neither he nor any other symphonic conductor was ever moved to duplicate.

Can we thank God for that gift without seeming to thank Him for the war? One has to feel somewhat guilty, as well as grateful, at being allowed to eavesdrop on this cataclysmic moment in the history of Germany and its music. It can only be adequately heard and described in its context, and I know nothing else that so ringingly confirms Carolyn Abbate's now famous call for a musicology that studies performances in addition, or even in preference, to texts.[62] What makes the call so compelling is that performances, in their uniqueness as acts, are even more specifically and concretely contextual than texts. Sounding documents like Furtwängler's wartime performances are a mine of meaning—or, more particularly, of significance. They do not let you forget that music, too, has always got to be someplace.

---

61. Furtwängler, "Beethoven and Us: On the First Movement of Beethoven's Fifth Symphony" (1951), in *Furtwängler on Music*, 57. For "infectiousness," see Lev Nikolayevich Tolstoy, *What Is Art?* (1898), chap. 15.

62. Carolyn Abbate, "Music—Drastic or Gnostic?" *Critical Inquiry* 30 (2004): 505–36.

22

Alluring Failure, Exhilarating Defeat

Music and Decadence in European Modernism: The Case of Central and Eastern Europe by Stephen Downes, Cambridge University Press, 2010, xiv + 371 pp., $95

Look up *decadent* on Google Images and what pops up on page one? Orgies? Degradation? Immoral acts? Yes, those; but also (and mainly) hairdos, poached lobster, pastries, chocolate, quilts—and, pleasing the Stravinskian in me, one of Hogarth's *Rake's Progress* etchings showing our hero being fitted for a suit. That, at any rate, is what I found when I performed the experiment. I had just finished Stephen Downes's exploration of sundry musical debaucheries and was feeling, you might say, stimulated.

But not surprised. The common denominator linking "serious" amoral decadence with frivolous indulgence is of course sensory gratification, carried to (somebody's idea of) excess. Think of Wagner composing world-transforming music all day and then retiring to his bath oils and satins. The (sometimes minimized or denied) association with hedonism is the one feature that all definitions of decadence seem to share. And so all through Downes's book one turns from the mind-boggling to the ear-tickling and back as one tests the musical examples at the keyboard. This is one book you really need to read near a piano. Without what Stravinsky called "le contact direct de la matière sonore," one misses everything.[1]

Look up *decadent* in the dictionary, the author reminds us, and one finds it is Latin for "fallen away." From what? From optimism and idealism and heroism, mainly; often from health and sanity as well. To anyone likely to be reading this, the word will conjure up the *fin de siècle*, roughly the period between the death of

---

Review of *Music and Decadence in European Modernism: The Case of Central and Eastern Europe* by Stephen Downes, *Music Library Association Notes* 67 (2010–11): 750–55.

1. Igor Stravinsky, *Chroniques de ma vie* (1936; Paris: Éditions Denoël, 1962), 14.

502

Wagner and the First World War. To every century there is an end, of course, but the term as such still refers, and will always refer, to the end of the nineteenth century, when not only artists but all culturally sensitive Europeans sensed and described a mood of moral dejection and retreat into the sensuous, using the D-word quite self-consciously about themselves, whether in self-censure (Croce, Spengler) or in self-congratulation (beginning with Walter Pater's *Marius the Epicurean* and culminating in Wilde and Whistler and Beardsley, to say nothing of the egregious Huysmans), so that applying it now is neither a judgment nor an anachronism. Thus Richard Gilman's famous fulmination, that the word was merely a turd slung at their betters by "monkey-minds," was at best half right.[2] The word was worn just as often as a badge of honor. The historian's task is to report and account for the full range of its uses and connotations, and while that is probably an unattainable aim, Stephen Downes makes an absorbing attempt.

Benedetto Croce, in *L'estetica* (1902), was one of the first to look at the phenomenon of decadence critically and historically. He thoroughly disapproved of it, sensing the return of an unwelcome cyclic phenomenon, the depression or cultural fatigue that follows historic disappointments or great strenuous achievements. As a remote predecessor he cited the poetry of Giambattista Marino ("not of the true, but the gaudy, the witty, the curious, the clever"), to modern scholars a famous letdown after the heights of the Renaissance and still the whipping-boy of the highminded. Among musicologists, recall Gary Tomlinson and the very Crocean strictures he levels at Marino's sensuality (his "poetics of *meraviglia*," his "overweening urge to dazzle his readers") in his study of late- and post-Renaissance vocal music.[3] For Croce, as for Spengler, decadence portended the decline of the West because it wantonly repudiated the sources of occidental moral and intellectual supremacy. No wonder investigating decadence has been a growth industry for cultural studies.

Except, until now, for the stuff we study. This book is the first full-length specialized musicological study of its kind. The general comparatist literature on the subject, meanwhile, has steered clear of music. David Weir's comprehensive *Decadence and the Making of Modernism* covers literature in detail and the visual arts both in prose and in a pictorial insert, but the only composer you will find in the index is Wagner, and the words on Wagner found within are those of uncomprehending *littérateurs* whom the author happens to quote, never the author's own.[4] Bram Dijkstra, in his marvelous *Idols of Perversity*—a book whose paperback

---

2. Richard Gilman, *Decadence: The Strange Life of an Epithet* (New York: Farrar, Straus & Giroux, 1979), 180.

3. Gary Tomlinson, *Monteverdi and the End of the Renaissance* (Berkeley and Los Angeles: University of California Press, 1980), 168.

4. Gary Weir, *Decadence and the Making of Modernism* (Amherst: University of Massachusetts Press, 1995).

edition has a painting of Salome on its cover—only mentions the most famous artistic embodiment of that figurehead of all decadent figureheads in a single bland paragraph, which states that "with reference to the works of Wagner and Strauss alone an encyclopedic register of the period's idols of perversity might be established without any difficulty."[5] Did I say bland? Smug would be more like it, since the author makes no attempt at compiling the list. Why? Obviously, I'd say, because the task would not have been for him without any difficulties. Nonmusicians tend to quail at the prospect of writing about music, and not without reason. You need a technical grasp of the subject to write illuminatingly about it even without using technical jargon, and most comparatists lack, or feel they lack, that competence. So this book is long overdue.

Downes's elegant working definition of his subject, more dispassionate than Croce's but clearly related to it, is worth quoting and remembering. Decadence, as he construes it on page 1, was

> a pessimistic critique of the bourgeois affirmation of subjective, psychological, physical and social progress and unity through the denigration of wholeness and wholesomeness and the celebration of the toxic and taboo. The energetics of the early riser were rejected in a turn to a protracted twilight of the idle. The work ethic and hopes of self-improvement were replaced by the provocative pose of the hedonist, the delights of ennui and lassitude, and the perverse pleasures of self-debasement.

That begins to suggest some of the historical conditions that gave rise to the extraordinary novelties in musical style the rest of the book will describe. Its geographical skew to the east stems from the author's long-standing interest in Polish music, and from an evident wish to even the score, most work on musical decadence, such as it is, being chiefly given over to the French music that more frankly embraced the sensual. In Germany, the land of philosophy, decadence was the negative twin of apocalypse and eschatology. Composers to the east of Germany, in Poland, Hungary, and Russia, shared these lofty preoccupations, and the pessimistic reaction to them as well. The book is in effect a study of musical responses against the grain to Schopenhauer and Nietzsche, and secondarily to other music that responded or reacted to the first-responders. Downes's central European decadence is a negative counterpart to Hermann Danuser's category (nominally borrowed from Rudolf Stephan) of *Weltanschauungsmusik*.

Stephan and Danuser's term, which might be translated as "philosophy music" (more clunkily as "music expressive of a worldview"), applies precisely to the sort of bourgeois affirmation that Downesian decadence pessimistically critiques. The uplifting inventory, following Wagner's precept, begins with Beethoven's Ninth;

---

5. Bram Dijkstra, *Idols of Perversity: Fantasies of Feminine Evil in Fin-de-Siècle Culture* (New York: Oxford University Press, 1988), 376.

continues, as per the teachings of the New German School, with *Tristan* and with the symphonic poems and program symphonies of Liszt; reaches its apogee in the Mahler of the *Titan* and *Resurrection* Symphonies (not to mention that of *A Thousand*), along with the pretentious Strauss of the more philosophical tone poems (*Tod und Verklärung, Also sprach Zarathustra*); and arrives at the end of its *Blütezeit* with Reger, Zemlinsky, and the early works of Schoenberg and Webern. (Kudos to Danuser, by the way, for recognizing Delius's *Mass of Life* as a supreme artifact of the genre.)[6] Downes's decadent counter-canon departs from the murky Wagner of the *Ring* and *Parsifal*, continues with the wanton Strauss of the early operas (*Salome* mugging and hogging the stage), and encompasses a host of composers whose rejection of bourgeois wholesomeness has kept them out of the still priggish academic canon even as they have often triumphed in the public sphere: Chaikovsky, Rachmaninoff, Scriabin, Wolf, Schreker, Szymanowski. A few more respectable figures hover in the margins: Bartók, Berg, and the inevitable Schoenberg; and there are a few up-to-now marginal figures such as Karłowicz and Lyadov, whom Downes is intent, at times quite persuasively, on making respectable. Mahler, for all his late excesses, is present only as a foil. Refreshing.

Decadents were a motley crew, and it is one of the virtues of this book that it makes no attempt to portray musical decadence as a movement or a program or a common cause. There is no intentional fallacy here; the author takes full responsibility for his construals; and if that means there are a great many interpretations of the soft "can-be-read-as" variety, it also means that readers are offered many suggestions and linkages that might never have otherwise occurred to them. Many of the figures treated here loathed and despised one another and recognized no mutual connection. Strange bedfellows abound, like Wagner and Rachmaninoff, who are discussed in a single chapter. (Rachmaninoff's own best-known comment about Wagner was made after his teacher, Sergey Taneyev, had finished reading through the first act of *Tristan* at a conservatory soirée and, as recorded by fellow pupil Leonid Sabaneyev, it consisted of four words: "1,500 pages to go.")[7]

What provides the link between Rachmaninoff and Wagner is "Pessimism and Nihilism," the title of the chapter they share. Downes organizes his commentary into five such topical chapters, preceded by a general introduction that outlines and justifies the breakdown and summarizes the skimpy existing scholarly literature on the subject: scattered pages by Lawrence Kramer, Simon Morrison, Boris Gasparov, William Kinderman, Anthony Barone, myself, "and even the profoundly skeptical Dahlhaus," as he lists those who have begun to establish beachheads on this "slippery terrain" (29). As you can already see from this preliminary roll call,

---

6. See Hermann Danuser, *Weltanschauungsmusik* (Schliengen: Edition Argus, 2009), chap. 6 ("Allnatur").

7. Leonid Sabaneyev, *Vospominaniya o Skryabine* (Moscow: Klassika—XXI, 2003), 16.

Downes reads widely. He has digested the work of historians (Richard Drake), literary critics (Gilman, Weir), Slavists (John Bowlt), philosophers (Martha Nussbaum, Lydia Goehr), music theorists (including those of hardest core, like David Lewin and Richard Cohn), and critical theorists (Deleuze, Lyotard, Žižek), as well as musicologists both traditional and "new." His method is one that I particularly value and strive to inculcate in my pupils—that of translating the contextual and conceptual and "culturological" into the technical analysis of scores—and his achievement, at its best, is exemplary. The book deserves to be read even by the wholesome for its repeated demonstrations of an integrated approach that adopts the widest possible interdisciplinary perspective, but in the end requires a fully equipped musicologist to achieve synthesis.

In the case of Rachmaninoff, for example, Downes investigates his trademark gloom by explicating his use of the flat submediant and the tritone root progression, principally in his two piano sonatas and *The Bells*. He is interested in these harmonic relations as syntactical devices (and here Rachmaninoff emerges as truly individual as befits his instantly recognizable style, the hackneyed critical consensus to the contrary notwithstanding), but also as semiotic markers. Downes compares Rachmaninoff in both regards to his one-time classmate Scriabin, using a distinction developed by Richard Drake (after the Italian literary historian Walter Binni) between "decadent romanticism" and "decadentism."[8] The former is what Mario Praz inventoried in his influential study *The Romantic Agony:* "an extreme, agonized last form in the development of ... morbid romanticism," as Downes defines it (97).[9] "Decadentism" is harder to define, but far more germane to Downes's project. Downes calls it "a radical transformation of romantic preoccupations into ... the elitist, esoteric and avant-garde." Drake himself is more pointed, specifying decadentism as "the beginning of the modern cultural idiom, stressing pure musicality as the supreme good in art as opposed to the more traditional didactic and entertaining functions of art."[10] "Pure musicality" here is a nod to Pater's famous dictum that all of the arts aspire to the condition of music, the art medium in which content, form, and style are mutually implicated to the greatest degree and ultimately, with any luck, indistinguishable.[11]

Artists who consider their styles to be an aspect of their content (and of their value) are the ones who will incline toward esoteric and elitist postures, and the

---

8. See Richard Drake, "Decadence, Decadentism, and Decadent Romanticism in Italy: Toward a Theory of Decadence," *Journal of Contemporary History* 17 (1982): 69–92.

9. See Mario Praz, *The Romantic Agony*, trans. Angus Davidson (London: Humphrey Milford, 1933); originally published in Italian (1930) with a far more suggestive title: *La carne, la morte e il diavolo nella letteratura romantica*, or Flesh, Death, and the Devil in Romantic Literature.

10. Drake, "Decadence, Decadentism, and Decadent Romanticism," 85.

11. For the famous dictum, see Walter Pater, *The Renaissance: Studies in Art and Poetry* (1873; London: Macmillan, 1922), 134.

source of those postures, Drake and Downes imply, is the Epicurean turn as exemplified by Marius, the title character of Pater's single novel, devoted to the pursuit of exquisite sensation.[12] It should already be evident that Drake's dualism will be an effective way of contrasting Rachmaninoff's decadent-romantic Byronism and Scriabin's decadentist Nietzscheanism, and Downes's technical analysis clinches the issue in a way that no other approach could manage, because it focuses, within their more obvious divergences, on very specific common features—indeed, ineffably specific features, to recall Mendelssohn's endorsement of music's advantage over language ("What a piece of music that I love tells me are thoughts not too *indefinite,* but too *definite* to be put into words").[13]

The longest discussion in the chapter on pessimism concerns Karłowicz, a composer whose music has never traveled very far beyond the borders of Poland. I speak figuratively, of course; there were no such borders (in the political sense) during Karłowicz's short lifetime (1876–1909), and Downes uses that fact to help account for the existential despair and defeatism—the anguish of the subjugated patriot—that suffuses Karłowicz's tone poems and symphonies even when their ostensible subject is personal, deflecting his symphonic structures from the euphoric Dionysian *Steigerungen* one finds in the untroubled (and apparently untroublable) Strauss toward "dissolution, liquidation or harmonic breakdown." In several long patches of technical commentary and one analytical graph, Downes details the delectable, voluptuous progressions (mainly half-step alterations) that record the debilitations and discouragements afflicting the composer's subject personae. The titillation thus afforded (here as well as in Rachmaninoff) is what identifies the decadent romantic as perverse hedonist. Where Scriabin the decadentist rallies toward ecstasy (as in his eponymous *Poem*), Karłowicz and Rachmaninoff wallow.

But here I must register a small complaint. Karłowicz is surely the least familiar of the protagonists in this study, and yet where Downes is generous almost to the point of profligacy with musical examples when discussing passages many of his readers will know by heart (the beginning and the end of *Tristan,* Brunnhilde's immolation, Salome's sickening kiss), there is not a single actual score excerpt to accompany the at times very intricate descriptions of Karłowicz's music. Downes is as good at blow-by-blows as any analyst, but even in his hands that sort of description has drastic limitations and makes heavy demands on a reader's patience. Unless it was the obduracy of an unenlightened publisher (in which case

---

12. Walter Pater, *Marius the Epicurean: His Sensations and Ideas* (1885, rev. 1892).
13. Felix Mendelssohn to Marc-André Souchay, 15 October 1842, in Mendelssohn, *Briefe aus den Jahren 1830 bis 1847,* ed. Paul and Carl Mendelssohn-Bartholdy, 7th ed. (Leipzig: Hermann Mendelssohn, 1899), pt. 2, 229; trans. Piero Weiss in Piero Weiss and Richard Taruskin, eds., *Music in the Western World: A History in Documents,* 2nd ed. (Belmont, CA: Thomson/Schirmer, 2008), 325.

he might have said so), I cannot guess the reason why the discussion of Karłowicz, whom the author seems quite bent on promoting, and who seems worthy of his efforts, should have been handicapped in this way.

The third chapter, "Degeneration and Regeneration," is all about Richards I and II. The main Wagnerian exhibit is of course *Götterdämmerung* (which Downes staunchly insists on calling *Twilight of the Gods*), with a sidelight on the passage where Freia's abduction in (all right) *The Rhinegold* makes the gods go grey. Following Carolyn Abbate and David Lewin, Downes shows how Wagner manipulates chromaticism to chart the fluctuations of Gibichung degeneracy and Brünnhildean resurgence, comparing the doubled ending of *Götterdämmerung* with similar twinned climaxes at the ends of Strauss's hopelessly (and lusciously) unregenerate *Salome* and *Elektra*. He gets into some fairly dicey tonality symbolism in this chapter (could it be, at this late date, after Alfred Lorenz?), insisting for example that the three tones in the augmented triad that accompanies Brünnhilde's heroic equestrian leap into oblivion "incorporates Grane's A, Siegfried's heroic F and the drama's final key of D flat" (why not say "the key of burning Valhalla," for Valhalla's grand opening in *Rheingold* had transpired in that very same key?), and that it thus "completes the 'counter-structures' which were left unresolved at Brünnhilde's giving of Grane to Siegfried in Act I scene i as a love token in exchange for the ring, when the tonality moved from E minor, through G minor to B flat, and then from F to a pause on the dominant of A, and closed with a long crescendo on an A triad as she asked that Siegfried often speak her name to the horse" (150–51).

Woof. This sort of thing can give casuistry a bad name. But if you like it, you'll love the identification of the "left-hand" component of the famous "bitonal" chord of necrophilia in *Salome* as the dominant of D minor, briefly associated earlier with the squabbling Jews, and the line of reasoning from there to the conclusion that the chord thus "degrades Salome's bodily ecstasy through its underpinning with the dominant of this dark, diseased, perverted Semitic key" (161). Otherwise, one is left to suppose, the girl radiates gentile good health.

Well, everyone is entitled to a lapse; and Downes recovers his reason in the next chapter, "Deformation and Dissolution," the subject of which is the prevalence of wave forms in music of the *fin de siècle*, as in Scriabin's *Poème de l'extase*, which Boris de Schloezer described as being "built on a series of upswings, with each successive wave rising higher and higher toward a final effort, liberation and ecstasy" (quoted on p. 177). Such a structure becomes "a primary feature of 'symphonic' process in the Wagnerian and post-Wagnerian style precisely because of its expressive and structural potential to generate development towards a long-postponed but long-anticipated 'end'" (181). Downes focuses on Wagner's song "Im Treibhaus," one of the Wesendonck lieder and the source of much of the Prelude to Act III of *Tristan*, to show how, "through its poetic content and musical continuation, this song presents an ... image of the final decadent fate of wave form as the waters vaporize in the debilitating heat and condense into precariously heavy drops about to meet their demise" (182). He traces echoes of Wagner's "microscopic musical drips" through the unavoidable *Salome*, arriving at Berg's Sonata, op. 1, as a last exhibit, which he associates, in an enviable sally, with "the emaciation of dissonance," comparing it with less-wasted counterparts in Mahler's Sixth Symphony (the theme of the Andante) and Brahms (the close of the Intermezzo, op. 119, no. 1).

It is in this chapter that Mahler is unexpectedly but satisfyingly cast (via the Sixth Symphony's diehard finale) as the great resister to the decadent surge; and, in a closing touch redolent of Harold Bloom—the very Bloom whom Downes goes so far out of his way (very curiously, in Bloomian terms!) to disavow in the next chapter—Schreker is cast as Wagner's epigone. The ballad in the second act of *Die ferne Klang* is cast as an "artificial wave," a sign of Schreker's "self-consciously ambiguous [or does he mean ambivalent?] position with regard to Wagner—seeking to break away from him, yet always overshadowed by him," but capable even in his failed resistance of creating "exquisitely colourful products" (223). There, one might say, lies the defining irony of decadence, alluring in its failures and exhilarating in defeat.

The following chapter, "Mannerism and Avant-Garde," is an exercise in ironic inversion. Recognizing that the first titular term has always carried a negative valence—would it have made a difference if Downes had instead called it "aestheticism," as I should have preferred?—and the second a positive one, he tries hard to show that within the terms of decadence the valences might easily be reversed. He does a very good job of showing how miniaturism, exemplified by Lyadov, can be fruitfully viewed as a variant of maximalism—a term he has borrowed from me, which makes me wonder why he wants to change its form and spelling to "maximilization" as if it were derived from Maximilian (Hapsburg? Steinberg?). By invoking Arnold Hauser's definition of mannerism, especially its emphasis on *Kunststücke* ("a piece of bravura, a triumphant conjuring trick, a firework display with flying sparks and colours," as quoted on p. 237), he is able to portray *Der Rosenkavalier* as a continuation along the path staked out by *Salome* and *Elektra*, rather than a backslide—and why not? Those earlier operas had never shown two girls in bed. On the obviously simulated orgasm—in the horns, of course—immediately before the curtain rises on the first scene, Downes observes, "It is all perhaps a bit kinky" (244). Ya think?

But my favorite move in this chapter is the concluding one. Having pointed to features in Strauss that, as it were, snatch the avant-garde from the jaws of kitsch, Downes turns about and performs the opposite maneuver on Schoenberg, a composer whom long-regnant academic shibboleths have insulated from the taint of decadence (attributed to him, in the standard narrative, only by the philistines of yore) and touted (though not without notorious divagations like Boulez's) as the *fons et origo* of an authentic avant-garde. What about *The Book of the Hanging*

Gardens, Downes asks. What about *Pierrot lunaire?* What about *Herzgewächse?* Tell it not in the seminar room, but these works have *texts.* Those texts abound in decadent (orientalist, voluptuous, putrescent, debauched) tropes, and those tropes correlate strongly with the "avant-garde" breakthroughs in the music.

Indeed, even without texts, Schoenberg's atonal music exhibits decadent traits as Downes defines them. They are precisely the mannerisms against which Boulez railed in *Schoenberg est mort:* "those constant anticipations, with expressive leaning on the key note, ... those false appoggiaturas ... which sound so terribly hollow."[14] They are on full display in Downes's Example 5.6, the opening bars of Schoenberg's Piano Piece op. 11, no. 1, usually cited as the great leap forward into atonality, and the piece the faithful Adorno was at such pains to dissociate from the Wagnerian *espressivo:* "no decoration or 'simulation' of passions, but instead only the undisguised rendering of 'shock' and 'trauma,'" as Downes partly quotes, partly paraphrases him on p. 267. Adorno cannot withstand Downes's exposure of "the ludic and nostalgic resemblances" in *Pierrot,* which belie the famous Frankfurter's claim that Schoenberg's "commitment to truth" at all times "negat[ed] decoration, semblance and play" (277).

The last chapter, "Convalescence and Primitivism," is devoted to recuperative moves. After an interesting discussion of Nietzsche's amateurish attempts to put his antidecadent polemics into musical practice by "correcting" Schumann (and, implicitly, Wagner) in his *Manfred-Meditation,* and a really fascinating demonstration of Wolf's attempts to heal Amfortas's wound by redirecting Wagner's frustrated leading-tone energy to resolution in two songs from the *Italienisches Liederbuch,* we arrive at the culminating exhibit. As if to balance the emphasis on Karłowicz at the beginning of the survey, the protagonist at the end is Szymanowski, to whom Downes has already devoted two whole books in addition to shorter studies. Where Nietzsche attempted a correction of Schumann, Szymanowski sought to correct Chopin—or rather, to correct what he perceived as a paralyzing misconstrual of Chopin's legacy. This he did, at the dawn of Polish independence, by replacing the faux folklore of Chopin's mazurkas with an infusion of the real thing, as observed in the Tatra Mountains in southwestern Poland. Downes finds evidence of his success in *King Roger,* Szymanowski's single opera, on a story adapted from Euripides's *Bacchae,* in which the new primitivism is allied to a Dionysian impulse pointedly educed not from Nietzsche but from Pater, a favorite of Szymanowski's, whose books provided the precedent for the title character's decision, again recalling Marius, to redirect his Dionysian energies not into cultish decadence but out into the world. The decisive moment is symbolized musically by the evocation of a Polish highland tune timed right before the dawn.

---

14. Pierre Boulez, "Schoenberg est mort" (1952), trans. Herbert Weinstock, in Weiss and Taruskin (eds.), *Music in the Western World,* 442.

One comes to the end of this study with a sense of repletion and high accomplishment. (The author's, not the publisher's: in a high-priced book like this there is no excuse for typos like "simulcrum," "somnalent," "they do represented," and many more, especially in the foreign-language texts.) As I have already suggested, there can be no definitive account of a tendency as variously motivated and exemplified—and as variously observed and imputed—as musical decadence. But despite its quirks and occasional totters, this account has shape and style, and impressive amplitude. Its analyses are surefooted and of high professional caliber, and it is written supply, with flashes of genuine wit. It offers a welcome alternative to the usual narrative of *fin-de-siècle* modernism. It will challenge many conventional assumptions and judgments about what is truly significant in the legacy of twentieth-century music. It is a breath of fresh fetid air.

23

Envoi

All Was Foreseen; Nothing Was Foreseen

Those of us lucky enough to reach our eighth decade of life are often aware of having crossed a line we were not aware of crossing at the time—the line between being a person with a future and becoming a person with a past. Not that we don't hope for a little more future, and look toward it in expectation of continued fulfilling work. But our past has become a resource for us, and if we are historians, our experiential memories have mingled with whatever we find in documents and books to create the thing the great German musicologist Carl Dahlhaus called "wissenschaftlich gefaßte Erinnerung," his definition of history—"systematized recollection," I guess you'd say in English.[1] Our lived experience helps us in the task of ordering our observations and inferences and making them meaningful; and thus, by informing our daily thinking, our past remains present to us.

So now that I have been asked to offer some reflections on my life and work, I have been thinking with greater concentration than ever about my personal past, and that is what has prompted my title with its bow toward a paradox I think many of us will find familiar.

In one sense the story of my life is so simple and straightforward that it could be summarized in one sentence: At the age of five I went to school and never left. In fact, if you had asked me when I was six what I wanted to be when I grew up, I would have said a professor. I visualized myself even then with a gray beard stand-

---

Commemorative lecture, Kyoto Prize award ceremony, Kyoto, Japan, 10 November 2017.

1. Carl Dahlhaus, *Grundlagen der Musikgeschichte* (Cologne: Musikverlag Hans Gerig, 1977), 12; in the standard English translation, *Foundations of Music History*, trans. J. B. Robinson (Cambridge: Cambridge University Press, 1983), the phrase is rendered misleadingly as "memory made scientific" (3).

ing in front of a class and lecturing—and as you see, I have it: the gray beard, that is. Until three years ago I lectured regularly before classes, and now I still do it quite frequently before audiences of various sizes and in many places. When I was six my stereotyped mental picture of myself as a professor included cap and gown, which American professors wear only once a year, and never in the classroom. But other than that you might say that my life and work were entirely foreseen by the age of six.

But you would be wrong. My path to what I foresaw for myself did not run smooth, and although I did end up in the classroom, for scholars that only describes the job, not the work. The job is what earns the money that supports the work—or as I used to joke, that supported my habit. The work is the activity that produces what the Russians call the *tvorchestvo*, the creative output. The job enters into it, but only as one strand in a skein. And when I think of the course my creative work has followed, I am always amazed at its contingency. Nothing about it was straightforward; nothing was predictable. So much was the result of happy accident—so much, indeed, that I half-believe in providence, even though I cannot profess any religious faith.

I used to remind my students that a significant career requires three things: aptitude, ambition, and luck—which is to say: we need the ability to do the work, and the capacity to formulate our own goals; we need the drive that motivates us to persevere in often arduous or tedious pursuit of our goals; and we need the opportunity that makes it possible to reach our goals. We are responsible for the first two, and we can prepare ourselves to seize the third, but only if opportunity knocks, and that is a matter of chance (as our language tells us by making one of the meanings of chance a synonym for opportunity).

It was chance that made a musicologist of me to begin with. Music was my consuming interest as early as I can remember, even as I nurtured the ambition to be a professor. My mother was a piano teacher and started me on piano lessons at the age of eight (with a friend of hers as my teacher: she knew better than to teach me herself). My father was an attorney and an enthusiastic amateur violinist; and very early in life I was informed that I would eventually play the cello so that we could have a family trio. I started those lessons at the age of eleven. At the age of thirteen I went to New York City's special high school for music and art, where I learned music theory and started to study composition. Even so, it was by no means a foregone conclusion that when I became a professor it would be of music, even though that is what I eventually did. There was family pressure, as so often there is, to choose a better-paying profession than an academic one; and there were other interests that unexpectedly impinged.

The most compelling of these was a result of a surprising event that befell my family. Both of my parents were American-born children of Jewish immigrants to the United States from what was then the Russian Empire. My father's family came from what is now Latvia, and my mother's from what is now Ukraine. Both of those territories were in what was known as the Pale of Settlement, the area on the western fringe of the empire where Jews were permitted to live. And those were precisely the territories that were occupied by the Germans during the Second World War. My grandparents were sure, and I grew up believing, that we had no relatives left in Eastern Europe; any who remained would have perished during the occupation.

And then in 1958, when I was thirteen, and after three of my four grandparents had died, we learned to our amazement that a whole family of cousins of my father had moved after the Russian revolution to Moscow and had grown up and flourished there. A delegation of rabbis from America had gone to the Soviet Union for a tour, and were met by an official guide whose surname was familiar to one of the rabbis, who had a man with the same name in his congregation at home. It turned out that the two men with similar names were half brothers, and that both of them were first cousins of my father's.

My father, who grew up speaking Yiddish, the language of the Eastern European Jews, began writing to his cousin, who sent us many gifts (including, for me, many recordings of Russian operas). I had to write thank-you notes in return. I did not know Yiddish, so writing to my Russian relatives became my first, and entirely unforeseen, incentive to study Russian when I got to college. It led to an overwhelming interest in that language and its literature, and I actually became a Russian major as a Columbia University undergraduate.

When I started graduate school at the same institution, I returned to music, my first love, but now I had a rather unusual bit of equipment for an American music student. I was not immediately moved to use it, however. As an undergraduate I continued to study composition, and was as strongly drawn to it as a field of professional study as I was to musicology. For two years I actually pursued a double program as a graduate student, studying musicology, so to speak, in the mornings and working on compositions in the afternoons. I was hopelessly torn between them. Whenever I was doing musicology I would think, "Ah, composition is so easy; all you have to do is make things up!"; and whenever I was working on a composition I would think, "Ah, musicology is so easy; all you have to do is look things up!"

What finally decided me in favor of musicology as a degree pursuit was an unexpected present. As a topic for a master's essay, then required of Columbia students, I wrote about Vladimir Stasov, the Russian arts journalist of the nineteenth century, who was so close to many of the Russian composers who were his contemporaries that in my thesis I called him "the sixth member of the Five." Hearing of this plan, my aunt in Moscow—the widow of the cousin of my father who had first made contact with us in America—persuaded a friend of hers to part with a huge three-volume edition of Stasov's writings and sent it to me to help with my research. Overwhelmed by her generosity, I determined that I had to find a way to go to Russia and meet her and my other relatives there, and the only way I saw to do this was to apply for a fellowship that would support a doctoral project there. And so I decided that I would pursue the doctorate in musicology, not composition, and that I would write about Russian music. I narrowed the subject down to Russian opera during the decade of the 1860s.

I was strongly advised not to do this. Neither Russian music nor nineteenth-century music were generally considered appropriate subjects for research in the American academy of those days. Until then I had been a most obedient student; indeed, there is an old edition of the so-called Hewitt catalogue of dissertations in musicology in which one can find my dissertation in progress as originally announced, on the Masses of Henricus Isaac, a fifteenth-century Flemish composer. But my life had taken some fateful turns and I now had compelling personal reasons to work in a field that did not promise success in America. What made my seemingly foolish choice of a dissertation topic ultimately profitable could not have been predicted at the time—and besides, another unforeseen turn brought me within a hair's breadth of leaving musicology—indeed, leaving the academy altogether.

The first research paper I wrote as a graduate student was on a topic assigned to me by the professor who taught the introductory proseminar which I attended in the fall of 1965. He was Paul Henry Lang, probably the most famous American musicologist of those days, and his manner of teaching was, by today's standards, impermissibly autocratic. Knowing that I played the cello, he assigned to me what surely seemed the most natural topic in the world, according to his lights and those of the discipline as it was then practiced: the transition, as he put it, from the viola da gamba to the cello in the eighteenth century. What I eventually found out in doing the assignment was that there never was such a transition. The early cellists were not former gambists, and the two instruments belonged to different families and had very different social uses. But that is not important. What was momentously important to me at the time was my discovery of the viola da gamba as an instrument that I could play. One of my classmates played it, and I asked her whether I could see her instrument and learn some rudiments of its playing technique. Sensing an opportunity to make a convert, she offered to get me an instrument that I could practice on, and she also put me in touch with her teacher. I became the most enthusiastic convert imaginable. You could say that I made the opposite transition to the one I was assigned to research. I went from being a cellist to being a gambist practically overnight. I practiced the gamba much more seriously than I ever practiced the cello, and much more seriously than I was then doing musicology. It really took over my life, and if I had had the chance I would have made it my profession.

And I almost got the chance. A few years after I had begun playing, the New York Pro Musica, the leading American performing ensemble for early music, and the only one in the country that could pay its members a living wage, advertised an opening for an unspecified string player. Both gambists and lutenists applied. After the auditions, the group let it be known that the choice would be between the top gambist and the top lutenist—that is, between me and one of my closest friends, who had auditioned on lute. They kept us waiting for more than a month before announcing that they had decided on the lutenist. I was dashed. It was perhaps the greatest disappointment of my life. If I had been offered the job I would have accepted it with joy, I would have withdrawn from the doctoral program at Columbia and become a full-time performing musician, and I would somehow have had to justify that decision to my grieving parents, who would have regarded the decision as a fatal mistake. But I never had to disappoint them like that; I don't think I even told them I had applied for the job.

I went back to Columbia, tail between my legs, and resolved on going through with the decision I have already described, to get a fellowship for a year's study in Moscow and write my dissertation on Russian opera. I did this very reluctantly and in a state of dejection. And now I will depart from strict chronology and fast-forward, as we say, a dozen years to the early 1980s, long after the New York Pro Musica had dissolved, after I had earned my doctorate and joined the faculty at Columbia, where I was by then the director of graduate studies, the person to whom applications for admission to the program were addressed. And who do you think addressed an application to me? None other than my old friend the lutenist who had beat me in our competition for a job with the now defunct Pro Musica. She was now out of work and belatedly seeking a degree in musicology that would enable her to find academic employment. I uttered a silent prayer of thanks for my narrow escape from her fate to the Providence in which (or in whom) I have half-believed ever since.

What I am calling Providence is of course contingency, or fortuity, or blind luck, which can come in all kinds of surprising disguises, including apparent failure in a performing career. Other manifestations of blind luck in my life have been undisguised, and so abundant as to destroy completely any idea I could ever have had that I owed the successes I have enjoyed solely to my own efforts and deserts. There is, for example, the matter I have already promised to explain, namely how my foolish decision to write a doctoral dissertation on a topic as unpromising as Russian opera eventually bore fruit. When I finished my dissertation, it certainly seemed like what we call a white elephant, "a possession," according to the dictionary, "that is useless or troublesome, especially one that is expensive to maintain or difficult to dispose of."[2] What one normally does to dispose of a dissertation, in addition to seeking publication of it as a book, is to get individual chapters published as articles in professional journals. I did not think there was any chance of doing that, considering the predilections of academic musicology and the editors

---

2. *Concise Oxford English Dictionary*, 12th ed. (Oxford: Oxford University Press, 2011), 1646.

of its publications. But then one day in 1976, the year I received my degree, I read an advertisement in one of the standard musicological journals that a new journal was being launched at the University of California, by the University of California Press, and with a trio of University of California professors as editors. The journal, unbelievably enough, was to be called *Nineteenth-Century Music*, and its stated purpose was to gain acceptance and currency for that repertoire within the American academy. The advertisement ended with a call for submissions.

It was a precisely crafted answer to my unstated prayers, and I feverishly produced a version of my dissertation's opening chapter, modified so as to be self-sufficient rather than a part of a longer narrative, and sent it off—this time with an actual uttered prayer. And several weeks later I heard back from the senior member of the editorial team, Prof. Joseph Kerman of Berkeley, who was (if Lang was the most famous) surely the second-most famous musicologist of those days, telling me that my article was accepted and would appear in the maiden issue of the new journal. In fact, it appeared in the second issue; but I was not counting or complaining. The new journal, with its straightforward focus, not only provided me with an outlet for a dissertation chapter; it became my scholarly home for the next several years. During that time I published four articles on Russian music, including a major study of Musorgsky's *Boris Godunov* that was serialized in two consecutive issues, so that my byline appeared in five issues out of the journal's first twelve—and I began to have a reputation. But this was not the only benefit I derived from this particular providential intervention, or even the major one. Becoming acquainted with Joseph Kerman was the real life-changer, culminating eventually in my moving, together with my growing family, to join the Berkeley faculty in 1987. Joe Kerman was on a mission to change musicology in fundamental ways, and luckily for me, he saw my work as useful to him in that endeavor. In return I had the benefit of his editorial hand, one of the most formative experiences in my life as a writer.

The *most* formative, however, was another that came to me just as fortuitously. One day in 1984 I was sitting in a restaurant near the Columbia campus, having breakfast and reading the newspaper, when an old friend showed up and told me some interesting news—that another of his friends, having bolted from the staff of a record collector's magazine called *High Fidelity*, was starting up his own more serious magazine called *Opus* and was looking for writers. Shortly afterwards, a Slavic scholar on the faculty of the University of California, whom I had met at a Stravinsky centennial conference in 1982, passed along to me a reviewing assignment from the *New Republic*, a journal of political opinion, which he was forced to decline so as to avoid the appearance of a conflict of interest. That is how I was put in contact with two editors, James Oestreich of *Opus* and Leon Wieseltier of the *New Republic*, with whom I collaborated regularly for almost thirty years, and through whom I became the one American musicologist to appear regularly—not as a critic but as a book and record reviewer and musical commentator—in the mass circulation press: "America's public musicologist," as I have often been called.

You can already see that it was pure happenstance that gave me my opportunity to become that, but it was even more fortuitous than that. I started writing for *Opus* in 1984, and the magazine folded in 1988—my second-biggest career setback, after being rejected by the New York Pro Musica. For two years I thought my little fling as a public musicologist had ended; but then Jim Oestreich got himself hired as the Sunday music editor at the *New York Times*. He began remustering his old troops, and that gave me access to the largest audience a writer on classical music in America could ever dream of having. Between 1990 and 2012 I published more than sixty pieces in the *New York Times*. I lasted there because I found it congenial to write about music in relation to what are always the primary concerns of any newspaper, that is, social and political issues—and I would be very surprised if that stint as a very public and often controversial commentator did not have a great deal to do with my ending up before you today. It was far from what anyone would call my most important work, and far from what I would hope to be my most lasting work; but however ephemeral, it was the work that brought my name to the attention of a readership that extended far beyond the walls of the academy.

But more important to me than that, the *New York Times* gave me my most rigorous and valuable training as a writer. Saying what I had to say within the confines of a newspaper column taught me a lesson few academic writers ever learn: it taught me to be concise. People often laugh when I say that, because I am known for writing outlandishly long books: my monograph on Stravinsky's so-called Russian period occupies two fat volumes and totals about 1,800 pages; *The Oxford History of Western Music* was originally published in six volumes, and ran to more than 4,000 pages. But I have striven, and exhorted my pupils as well, always to use the fewest possible words to say what you have to say, no matter how complex the argument and no matter how many parts it contains; and I firmly believe that it was only because I, as they say, "wrote short" that I could persuade my publishers to issue books that long. The *New York Times* taught me how to do it. And if I had not been sitting in the right restaurant on the right day in 1984, I never would have learned.

By now I suspect that you are convinced that, like everyone else, I stumbled blindly into what only in retrospect might look like a coherent career. How it happened may be an interesting story, and I hope it has been, but it is an ordinary tale. All careers look coherent in retrospect, but are likely to have been blind stumbles in prospect. And that observation contains an important lesson for historians, who are often tempted, by their knowledge of events and their outcomes, to construct deterministic narratives and even look for the laws that govern them. That is a folly that has led not only to a lot of bad historiography, but also to massive human suffering, because historical determinism is the natural ally of totalitarian politics.

But the fallacy of determinism is easily detected and described, and my little history of my own career shows how. It is only when we regard events in retrospect that their causes look like causes in the narrowest sense. What determinist historians do is construct their causal narratives backwards and then, forgetting that the past was once the unknown and unknowable future, recount them forwards with equal assurance that causes—which are in reality only anterior events and conditions—inevitably beget effects, which are in reality nothing more than outcomes. That fallacy of time reversal is what turns contingencies into apparent necessities. There was nothing inevitable about the collapse of the Soviet Union, for example, which no one foresaw until it was upon us, or of the tsarist empire before it; nothing inevitable about the so-called collapse of tonality (which never actually took place at all), and nothing inevitable about the shape of my career, or anyone else's. Nothing in any of these events could have been foreseen. As Alexei Yurchak put it in the title of his wonderful book on the Soviet demise, "Everything Was Forever, Until It Was No More."

So that is the end of my sermon, but not quite the end of my lecture; because I have not yet told you about the most astonishing contingencies that have enabled me to do the work I have been able to do. The first time any work of mine made waves within the profession was when I proposed that what was then called authentic performance practice—that is, the revival of old ways of performing old music—was not in fact the revival of historical performance styles but rather a newly invented style that took its bearings not from the aesthetics of the past, but from the aesthetics of modernity. It was indeed a modernist style, passing itself off (as modernist styles tend to do) as a historical revival. When I first advanced it, in 1981, the idea was regarded as counterintuitive, to say the least, but by the time I gave it its most extended exposition, in an essay published in 1988, it had won some currency, and by now it is the accepted view. What made it ultimately convincing was the evidence I was able to present in support.

I remember vividly the first time I encountered that evidence. I had just begun to do the research that led to my Stravinsky monograph. I came to Stravinsky from my previous study of Russian music, which began, as I have already mentioned, with my formal degree exercises, my Master's essay of 1968 on Stasov, and my doctoral dissertation of 1976, on Russian opera in the 1860s. At the same time, as I have also already mentioned, I was heavily engaged in the performance of early music as a viola da gamba player, and also, by then, as a choral conductor. These two aspects of my professional activity—Russian music research and early-music performance—were quite unrelated in their origins and quite remote from one another in their purview, and they had never touched, nor did I ever expect them to do so. They amounted, in Franz Liszt's expression, to a sort of *vie bifurquée*, a musical life divided—happily divided, I should say—in two.

But now that I had embarked on a study of Stravinsky, I needed to acquaint myself with the basic texts of aesthetic modernism. Since the best way of learning a new subject is to teach it, I announced a seminar on the theory of modernism, and began reading in preparation. One day, sitting in my office preparing for the first meeting of the class, I read two texts for the first time: *Speculations*, the collected essays of T. E. Hulme; and *La deshumanización del arte*, or *The Dehumanization of Art*, by José Ortega y Gasset, and it was one of my great Eureka! moments, because I immediately recognized in their words the discourse that reigned within the world of early music, and that had no counterpart at all in the actual historical texts on which the early-music movement professed to base its practice. Once I had realized this, it was easy to see that what we were calling authentic or historical performances of old music were no more like the performances the music would have had when it was new than a neoclassical concerto by Stravinsky resembled an actual concerto by Bach or Mozart. The assumption that the radical twentieth-century break from romantic, or nineteenth-century, performance practice was in fact a return to eighteenth-century and earlier ways was spurious. It was easy to show that the performances we were giving now did not have eighteenth-century counterparts. Now everyone can see this.

Why was I the first to see it? Only because, quite fortuitously, my musical life had been divided the way it was, into those two seemingly unrelated and unrelatable Russian-music and early-music halves. Only because I came to the reading of modernist texts having been trained in early music did I see the correspondences that are now almost universally acknowledged. If I with my idiosyncratic and fortuitous combination of interests had not made these discoveries, it is possible that no one would have made them. I was not uniquely gifted, certainly not clairvoyant; but I was uniquely equipped, and that was a matter of merest, sheerest chance.

And now for the most improbable, and therefore most amazing, set of contingencies of all. When I began my research on Stravinsky, I did not have in mind an ambitious plan comprehensively to study his early development in Russia and his early works against that background. I could not hope to write such a book, because there was a practical impediment: Stravinsky had kept most of his manuscripts in his personal possession, and after his death possession had passed to his heirs, who were divided into two hostile groups: his three surviving children, on the one hand, and his widow (not their mother but his second wife) and his assistant Robert Craft, on the other. From the moment of Stravinsky's death his estate was in litigation, and in consequence, inaccessible to scholars. My own early inquiries were answered, very discouragingly, by lawyers. Imagine, then, my elation when I received a phone call from a former graduate student at Columbia who was then employed as an assistant at the New York Public Library, to inform me that the New York Surrogate's Court had awarded the library temporary custodianship of the Stravinsky estate while its disposition was being adjudicated; that the library had made it a condition that, as long as it had custody, the contents of the estate would be made available to the public; and in consequence, that I now had free access to it, at a time when I lived a ten-minute subway ride from the library and—blessing of all blessings—I had just begun a full year's sabbatical from teaching that coincided almost exactly with the duration of the library's custodianship. For ten blessed months in 1983 and 1984 I virtually lived at the library, where I had a freedom of access to Stravinsky's manuscripts that no one has had since, for I was able to examine—and handle—the actual physical documents rather than microfilms or photocopies, which the Paul Sacher Foundation in Basel, Switzerland, the eventual purchaser of the estate, now only permits under exceptional circumstances.

This was a stroke of fortune such as I have never had before or since; nor has any other scholar that I know. But I have had many others, not as spectacular perhaps, but also crucial determinants on my life's course. I could go on regaling you with stories of my lucky life, but I am sure I have already told you more about it than you ever wanted to know, and you are already perhaps wondering whether I really deserve a prize for receiving so many blessings.

I wonder, too; and in my acceptance speech I have already said that no one can truly deserve such an award as the one you have seen fit to bestow on me. I also know, from rumblings that have reached my ear from afar, that my particular field of endeavor has made the award in certain quarters all the more a cause for wonder, and even a bit of annoyance. In announcing my selection, the Inamori Foundation seemed to anticipate this, taking note that a precedent had been broken in giving a prize that had formerly gone to composers and performers to a writer on music, and that perhaps explanations were in order. To honor my work, the Foundation stated in its citation, was to acknowledge "that, in music, creativity can be found not only in composition and performance, but also in meticulous discourse contextualizing the art." I will count it as the greatest of all my blessings if this generous assessment not only of my work but of my field of endeavor as well should set a precedent whereby it will not look so strange the next time a musicologist is taken as a worthy recipient of a prize in music.

That it was my work as a music historian that should have occasioned this broadening of the prize's purview is of course gratifying to me; but it too is attributable to newly propitious circumstances. It is widely acknowledged in the historical profession that the influence of economic and social globalization has brought about a "global turn" in historiography as well, whereby, in the words of Richard J. Evans, the eminent historian of twentieth-century Germany, "historical reputations are not made with narrowly empirical monographs, but with novel concepts and methodologies, new interpretations, and large-scale, ambitious works of synthesis."[3] For better or worse that's me with my six-volume *Oxford History of Western Music*, which owes its existence, as by now should go without

---

3. Richard J. Evans, "Unending History," *Times Literary Supplement*, 23 June 2017, 3.

saying, to another set, or rather a chain, of unforeseen and unforeseeable lucky breaks.

But from these fortuities has emerged, perhaps, a measure of poetic justice. Musicology, I seize my opportunity here to declare, deserves its recognition among musical pursuits. That it should be regarded as secondary to composition and performance—that Jean Sibelius, speaking on behalf of composers, should have been thought wise to observe that no statue was ever put up in honor of a critic—is only an historical happenstance, a prejudice. There have been other views. The philosopher Boethius ranked the three types of people who concern themselves with music in precisely the opposite order. At the bottom were performers, whose "efforts are devoted to the exhibition of their skills with instruments" and who "therefore act as slaves, without reasoning or thinking." In the middle came what we would call composers, but Boethius called poets, that is, "makers," who "compose more with their natural instinct than through the exercise of thought or reason." And on top were the people like me, whom Boethius exalts by calling us critics, that is, "judges," who, because they are "wholly devoted to reason and thought," are "able to judge modes, rhythms, the genera of songs and their mixtures," by virtue of their ability to use reason and thought in a manner "especially suited to the musical art."[4] So there.

I won't insist on that hierarchy, or any hierarchy. But I do think that we who tell the story get the last word, and deserve recognition for that. Those who presume to outrank us forget that we are the ones who have assigned them their place. One of my favorite stories—and, for reasons you will surely understand, one of the favorite stories of my pupils, to whom I loved to tell it—concerned the great Swedish economist Gunnar Myrdal, who, when warned by one of his teachers that he should be more respectful toward his elders, "because it is we who will determine your promotion," answered, "Yes, but it is we who will write your obituaries." (I read that, as it happens, in Myrdal's obituary.)[5] The quip has a particular relevance to the fantastic honor you have done me by recognizing my work as a musicologist alongside that of so many truly eminent composers and performers. With the exception of Cecil Taylor, who works within a tradition other than the one I have taken as my beat, I have written about all my predecessors, in some cases quite extensively.[6]

---

4. Boethius, *De institutione musica*, Book I, trans. Calvin Martin Bower, "Boethius's 'The Principles of Music': An Introduction, Translation, and Commentary" (PhD diss., George F. Peabody College, 1967), 103–4; adapted in Piero Weiss and Richard Taruskin, eds., *Music in the Western World: A History in Documents*, 2nd ed. (Belmont, CA: Thomson/Schirmer, 2008), 31–32.

5. "Gunnar Myrdal, Analyst of Race Crisis, Dies," *New York Times*, 18 May 1987, D14.

6. The quadrennial recipients in music have been Olivier Messiaen (1985), John Cage (1989), Witold Lutosławski (1993), Iannis Xenakis (1997), György Ligeti (2001), Nikolaus Harnoncourt (2005), Pierre Boulez (2009), and Cecil Taylor (2013).

And in all cases I have striven to do as the Kyoto Prize citation has noted: I have striven meticulously to contextualize their art.

I have not always been thanked for it. Contextualizing has meant describing their work seriously in the way I have described my own work today in a more ironic or parodistic vein—in terms of a dialectic, a push and pull between a more or less powerful agent and the enabling and constraining conditions within which the agent acts. In my own case I have spoken somewhat simplistically about luck. What I meant, of course, is that like all agents I could only exercise my abilities within a particular circumscribing environment. Like my predecessors, I strove to make the most of my opportunities, or what we now prefer to call "affordances," and in this I was aided by my ambition and the strategies I was able to contrive in order to realize it. To speak of enabling conditions, and particularly to speak of ambition and strategy, has often seemed, to those used to more idealizing or decorous accounts, to diminish the achievements of the great. But even those who have opposed my work—and I have been battered as well as flattered in its reception over the years—must be aware, if they are capable of introspection, that their own activity has been subject to constraints that they have had to negotiate through strategy.

The implicit endorsement the Kyoto Prize has given my efforts and methods, if it serves to encourage a more realistic and informative historiography of art, gives me an additional reason, and the most powerful one of all, to be grateful. Thank you.

ACKNOWLEDGMENTS

Richard Taruskin was diagnosed with stage four esophageal cancer on Wednesday, May 25, 2022, and was referred immediately for palliative care. He died thirty-eight days later, on July 1.

In the early days of such a diagnosis, there is an abundance of conflicting information, but in Richard's words, "When you are under palliative care the only kind of information you want to know concerns time." Although Richard accepted his prognosis, he had one last wish: to see this book (originally scheduled for release in Summer 2023) published.

On Day 15 his oncologist advised him that treatment with chemotherapy and/or radiation was the only option that might make this wish possible. From that point his course was set and he became fixated on achieving this goal. He was willing to endure months of discomfort on a liquid diet to reach this end. On Day 16 he notified his UC Press editor, Raina Polivka, of his condition and asked that she do what she could to expedite the process. She immediately assembled a team of colleagues to revise workflows and shorten schedules to get the project into production as quickly as possible. They found a path that would enable a copy of the book to get into Richard's hands by February, a substantial achievement.

Things moved quickly at UC Press while Richard underwent chemotherapy. On Day 22 Richard was able to see the cover design, to his immense delight. On June 17 (Day 24)—only eleven days after Raina had been notified of Richard's condition—the book was handed off to production.

Meanwhile, Richard's health took a turn for the worse. Throughout his hospitalization he thrived on visitors and affectionate emails from friends all over the world. Six colleagues flew from places across the country to spend full days visiting him, and this is what energized his resolve to keep going. Among these long-distance visitors was Peter Schmelz.

When the production schedule was released on June 27 (Day 34), it was clear to Richard that he would not be able to work on the first batch of copyedits only a week away, and he did not want to slow down production. For the first time in his career he had to acknowledge that he could not complete this massive project single-handedly. This enabled us to pose the question we knew had to be asked: "Who would you like to step in to do the work for you?" His answer was quick: Peter Schmelz. It was a relief to all of us that we could know Richard's wishes, and an even greater relief when Peter agreed without hesitation.

UC Press's rapid and steady progress toward publication encouraged Richard and took his mind off the looming reality of his situation. The momentum was palpable.

The Taruskin family wishes to convey our deepest thanks to Peter Schmelz, Raina Polivka, and all of the UC Press family who rose to this exceptional task in such a dramatic and visible way. It shaped Richard's last days in the way he would have chosen—focused on completing what he had long ago declared would be his final work, this examination of musical lives and times.

Cathy, Paul, and Tess Taruskin

INDEX

Photographs and illustrations are indicated by *italicized* page numbers.

Abbate, Carolyn, 33, 92, 202, 501, 508
Abert, Anna Amalie, 369
Abhandlung über den Ursprung der Sprache [Treatise on the Origin of Language] (Herder), 433
Abraham, Gerald, 368, 369, 370, 374
Abraham and Isaac (Stravinsky), 308
Acta Musicologica (journal), 145
Adams, John, 9, 10
"Adelaïde" (Beethoven), 60
Ader, Lidia, xix
Adler, Guido, 386, 417
Adorno, Theodor W., 62, 114, 139, 145, 203, 209, 296, 358, 387, 397, 404, 510
Africaine, L' (Meyerbeer), 77
Agoult, Marie d', 59
Aida (Verdi), 70, 71, 79, 83
Aleko (Rachmaninoff), 246
Alexander II, Tsar, 195, 211
Alexander Nevsky (Prokofieff), 270, 273, 354
Alexandrov, Anatoly, 15
Allanbrook, Wye J., 41, 376
Allen, Steve, 310
Alov, Alexander, 291
Also sprach Zarathustra (Strauss), 505
Alyabiev, Alexander Alexandrovich, 337
Amadeus (play and film), 348
Amazonas (Villa-Lobos), 399

"America (My Country, 'tis of Thee)," 465, 467, 469
American Musicological Society, xii, xiv, xxi, 4, 20, 152, 270
"Ancient Traditions—Today's Musical Life" (Kodály), 152–53
Anderson, Julian, 113
Andersson, Gerger, 369
Annals of Opera (Loewenberg), 69
Anthony, James R., 368
Antokoletz, Elliott, 101, 106
Apel, Willi, 417–18, 420, 421
"Apologiya nepriznaniya" ["In Defense of Non-recognition"] (Tarakanov), 277–79
Appia, Adolphe, 198–99
Applegate, Celia, xxv
"Approaching a History of Eighteenth-Century Music" (Heartz), 365
Arányi, Dezső (Desider), 89
Ariadne auf Naxos (Strauss), 87
Aristotle, 265–66
Arnold, Matthew, 24
"Arpád apánk" [Our Father Arpad] (Simonffy), 153–54, *153*
"Art Music on Ashkenazi Jewish Themes: The Society for Jewish Folk Music (1908–1919)" (Eisenstein Baker), *442*
Asafyev, Boris, 293, 390, 454, 456

527

Ashmole, Bernard, 37
Atovmyan, Levon, 273
Aubry, Pierre, xxvi
Auden, W. H., 27, 28, 302, 450
Augustine, St., 19, 59, 385
Austen, Jane, 271, 404
Austin, J. L., 459
Austin, William A., 270, 364
"Authentic Analysis" (P. Schubert), 480
Azanchevsky, Mikhail Pavlovich, 212, 227, 242

Babbitt, Milton, 6, 134–35, 136, 139, 455, 491, 492; *Composition for Four Instruments*, 33; *Three Compositions for Piano*, 134
Bacchae (Euripides), 510
Bach, Anna Magdalena (née Wülken), 170
Bach, C. P. E., 366, 373, 381
Bach, J. C., 375, 378
Bach, Johann Sebastian, 10, 61, 74, 103, 165, 166, 169–91, 346, 355, 366, 373, 483; Chromatic Fantasy, 175; *Die Kunst der Fuge (The Art of Fugue)*, 174; *Das Musikalisches Opfer (The Musical Offering)*, 174; *St. John Passion*, 16–18, 177, 184, 321, 481–82; *St. Matthew Passion*, 16–17, 180, 183, 185; *Wohltemperirte Clavier, Das (The Well-Tempered Clavier)*, 172, 175, 185
Bachianas Brasileiras (Villa-Lobos), 401
Bach's Cycle, Mozart's Arrow (Berger), 378
Bagazh (N. Nabokov), 301, 306
Baker, Paula Eisenstein, 439, 442
Bakhtin, Mikhail, 198, 202
Balakirev, Mily, 189, 195, 212–13, 221, 246
Balanchine, George, 300, 305, 306
Barish, Jonas, 53
Barnes, Julian, 303, 328–31, 332
Barone, Anthony, 505
Barthes, Roland, 409–13
Bartlett, Rosamund, 192, 200
Bartók, Béla, x–xii, xiv, 38, 98–109, 113, 143, 247, 269, 337, 339, 401, 435–36, 505; Concerto for Orchestra, 106, 107, 136, 145; *Contrasts*, 105, 122, 135; Divertimento for string orchestra, 122, 136; First Piano Concerto, 106, 117, 128; First String Quartet, 136; "The Folk Songs of Hungary," 149–50; Fourth String Quartet, 106, 107, 135; Hungarian Rhapsodies, 127–28; "Liszt Problems" (lecture, 1936), 125–31, 126, 142; *Mikrokosmos*, 144; *The Miraculous Mandarin*, 123; Orchestral Suite no. 1, 131, 132; "Racial Purity in Music," 119–20; Rhapsody for Violin no. 1, 436, 437, 438; *Rumanian Folk Music (RFM)*, 436–37, 437; Second Violin Concerto, 136; Sixth String Quartet, 117, 122, 136; Sonata for Two Pianos and Percussion, 105, 122, 135; Third Piano Concerto, 108, 136; Third String Quartet, 106, 107
Bartók, Hungary, and the Renewal of Tradition (Schneider), 131, 436
Bartók, Peter, xiii
Bartók Archívum, viii, ix
"Bartók Myth, The" (Palazzetti), 117–19
Bartoli, Cosimo, 387
Basil of Caesarea, St., 21, 157
Basner, Veniamin, 331
"Battle Cry of Freedom," 466, 467
Baudelaire, Charles, 63–64, 199–200, 201
Baumgarten, Alexander, 129
Bavarian State Opera, 11
Beach, Amy, 109
Beardsley, Aubrey, 503
Beatles, the, 402
Beck, Jean, xxvi
Becker, Gary S., 43
Becker, Howard S., 404, 478
Beckett, John, 414, 416
Beeson, Jack, 4
Beethoven, Ludwig van, viii–ix, 56, 61, 74, 165, 169, 176, 191, 194, 336–37, 373, 378, 452; "Adélaïde," 60; Eighth Symphony, 453; Emperor Concerto (No. 5 in E-flat Major), 58; *Eroica* (Symphony No. 3), 397; Fifth Symphony, 452, 453, 498, 501; *Heiliger Dankgesang* ("Solemn Song of Thanksgiving," String Quartet no. 15 in A Minor, op. 132), 108; *Missa solemnis*, 57, 413, 414; Ninth (Choral) Symphony, 12–13, 196, 504; Sonata no. 3 for Piano and Cello, op. 69, 184
Beethoven and Freedom (Chua), 497
Beethoven Quartet, 344, 345
Béla Bartók: Composition, Concepts, and Autograph Sources (Somfai), xi
Béla Bartók's Last Years: The Naked Face of Genius (Fassett), 123–24
Beleitungsmusik zu einer Lichtspielszene, op. 34 (Schoenberg), 294
Belïy, Andrey, 200
Bellermann, Johann Gottfried Heinrich, 214
Bellman, Jonathan, 411–12, 414
Bells, The [symphony] (Rachmaninoff), 506
Belyi, Viktor, 253
Bennett, Jane, 487
Beregovsky, Moshe, 443

INDEX   529

Berezowsky, Alice, 255, 258, 259, 260, 265, 269
Berezowsky, Nicolai Tikhonovich, 255, 261
Berg, Alban, 101, 102, 165, 277, 320, 431, 505; *Lyric Suite*, 294; Piano Sonata, op. 1, 509; Violin Concerto, 294
Berger, Karol, 378
Berio, Luciano, 283
Berlin, Isaiah, 302
Berlin Philharmonic, 494, 498, 499
Berlioz, Hector, 167, 168, 195, 431
Bernstein, Leonard, 161, 307, 317
Berry, Mark, 384, 387, 401–2
Beschreibung einer Reise durch Deutschland und die Schweiz (Nicolai), 376
Billroth, Theodor, 62, 63
Bilson, Malcolm, 381, 382
Binkley, Thomas, 416
Binni, Walter, 506
Birman, Serafima, 262
Birth of Tragedy, The (Nietzsche), 208, 453
Bizet, Georges, *Carmen*, 70, 71, 92
Blackmur, R. P., 387
Blake, Patricia, 302
Blasting and Bombardiering (Lewis), 450
Blok, Alexander, 200
Bloom, Harold, 509
Boethius, 19 20, 385, 522
Bohlman, Philip V., 25, 29
Bónis, Ferenc, 151
Book about Stravinsky (Asafyev), 454, 456
Book of the Hanging Gardens, The (Schoenberg), 509–10
Boris Godunov (Musorgsky), 218, 473–74, 479, 517
Borodin, Alexander, 109, 218, 245, 337; *Prince Igor*, xvi, 88, 92
Borodkin, Herbert, 431
Borthwick, Stuart, 404
Boston Symphony Orchestra, 10
Boulanger, Nadia, 358
Boulez, Pierre, 38, 99–100, 283, 293, 398, 509; *Schoenberg est mort*, 510; *Structures Ia*, 305
Bourdieu, Pierre, 22, 161, 394
Bourgeois gentilhomme, Le (Molière), 41
Bowen, José, 381
Bowlt, John, 506
Boyson, Frances, 404
Braden, Tom, 307
Brahms, Johannes, 61–62, 65, 71, 109, 112, 181, 205, 219, 311, 431, 471; Piano Concerto in D Minor, 180; *Deutsches Requiem*, 430; First Symphony, 62, 207, 499, 500, 501; Intermezzo, op. 119, no. 1, 509; Quintet in F Minor, 345
"Brahms the Progressive" (Schoenberg), 193
Brandt, Willy, 302
Brendel, Alfred, 38–39, 51, 62, 64, 65
Brendel, Franz, 128–29
Breve discorso sopra la musica moderna (Scacchi), 376
Brewer, Charles E., 369
Britten, Benjamin, xvii, 248, 340
Brodbeck, David, 71, 73, 74, 75, 77, 79, 80
Brooklyn Academy of Music, 10
Brooks, Cleanth, 489, 490
Brooks, Jeffrey, 323
Brown, Clive, 430
Brown, Irving, 302, 305
Brown, Malcolm H., 270
Brown, Robert R., 423
Browning, John, 309
Bruch, Max, 435
Bruckner, Anton, 109, 179, 203, 431
Bryusov, Valeriy, 200
Buckley, William F., 25
Budden, Julian, 154
Bukofzer, Manfred, 364, 371
Burden, Michael, 369
Burke, Edmund, 49, 50, 51, 56
Burke, Kenneth, 462, 463
Burkholder, J. Peter, 366
Burney, Charles, 45
Burnham, Scott, 13, 32
Busnoys, Antoine, xii, 386
Busoni, Feruccio, 98, 165, 189
Butcher, Samuel Henry, 266
Butler, Margaret R., 369

Cadmus et Hermione (Lully), 43
Cage, John, 186
Caldara, Antonio, 376
Callow, Simon, 379
Cambridge History of Eighteenth-Century Music, The (CH18), 367, 368, 370, 372, 373–78
Cambridge History of Music Criticism, The (CHMC), 383–88, 390, 392–93, 397, 398, 402, 405
Cambridge History of Nineteenth-Century Music, The (2001), 98
Cambridge History of Twentieth-Century Music, The (2004), 98, 99, 100, 101, 108
Canticum sacrum (Stravinsky), 308
Capella Antiqua, 435

530   INDEX

Carmen (Bizet), 70, 71, 92
Carmina burana (Orff), 33
Caron, Firminus, 386
Carpentier, Alejo, 398, 399
Carreras, José, 449
Carter, Elliott, 148–49, 302; First String Quartet, 306
Caruso, Enrico, 89
Casals, Pablo, 146
Casella, Alfredo, 336
Castiglione, Baldassare, 387
Castro, Paulo Ferreira de, 389, 391
Cello Sonata (Prokofieff), 270
Chabrier, Emanuel, 452
Chaikovsky, Pyotr Ilyich, 109, 145, 179, 180, 186, 194, 214, 218–19, 233, 246, 248, 249, 287, 314, 337, 505; *Eugene Onegin*, 209; Fifth Symphony, 206; Fourth Symphony, 206; *Sleeping Beauty*, 417; Suite for Orchestra, op. 43, 175; Symphony No. 6 (*Pathétique*), 189, 322; Third Piano Concerto, 189; *Variations on a Rococo Theme*, 63
Chausson, Ernest, 206
Chen, Jen-Yen, 368, 376, 377
Cherednichenko, Tatiana Vasil'yevna, 390
Cherubini, Luigi, 167; *Cours de contrepoint et de fugue*, 214
Chopin Frédéric, 61, 314, 378, 510; F-minor Fantasy, op. 49, 315
Chôros, nos. 8–14 (Villa-Lobos), 399
Chronicle of My Musical Life (Rimsky-Korsakov), 212, 213, 214, 217, 218, 222, 225, 238
Chrysander, Friedrich, 207
Chua, Daniel, 497
Churnside, Carrie, 387
Cinderella (Prokofieff), 270
Classical Style, The (Rosen), 63, 365–66
Classics for the Masses (Fairclough), 319
Clementi, Muzio, 378, 379, 381
Cliburn, Harvey L., Sr., 310
Cliburn, Van (Harvey Lavan Cliburn, Jr.), 309–18
Cliff, Nigel, 309, 310, 311, 313, 315, 316–18
Cohn, Richard, 231, 506
Colbert, Stephen, 68
Coleman, Peter, 300
Colonne, Édouard Juda, 189
"Columbia, Gem of the Ocean" (A'Becket), 465–66, 466
Comen, Craig, 497
Commanday, Robert, 404

Comparaison de la musique italienne et de la musique française (Lecerf de la Viéville), 43–44
Comte, Auguste, 446, 448
Concerto for Orchestra (Bartók), 106, 107, 136, 145
Concerto for Orchestra (Kodály), 147
Concerto for Piano and Winds (Stravinsky), 106
Concerto for Piano in C Major, K. 503 (Mozart), 314
Concerto for Piano in D Minor (Brahms), 180
Concerto for Piano no. 1 (Prokofieff), 245–46, 246
Concerto for Piano no. 1 (Rachmaninoff), 245–46
Concerto per due pianoforti soli (Stravinsky), 243
Concise History of Western Music, The (Hanning), 366
Confessions of Felix Krull, Confidence Man, The (Mann), 40–41
Congress for Cultural Freedom (CCF), 300, 302–4, 306, 307, 308, 330
Considerazioni sulla pittura (Mancini), 41
Contemplating Music: Challenges to Musicology (Kerman), 386, 415
Contrapunkt, Der [*Counterpoint*] (Bellermann), 214
Cook, Nicholas, 98, 99
Cooper, David, 131
Cooper, Kenneth, 4
Cooper, Michael, 2, 369
Copland, Aaron, 116, 248
Corelli, Arcangelo, 379, 380, 381
Corpus Musicae Popularis Hungaricae, 157, 158
Cortegiano, Il [*Book of the Courtier*] (Castiglione), 387
Couperin, François, 366
Courage of Composers and the Tyranny of Taste, The (Varga), 159, 448
Cours de contrepoint et de fugue (Cherubini), 214
Craft, Robert, 21, 104, 105, 108, 134, 250, 373, 520
Creation, The (Haydn), 367, 485
Creative Union (Tomoff), 320
Crisp, Quentin, 446
Critica musica (journal), 384
Critique of Judgment (Kant), 141, 454
Croce, Benedetto, 503, 504
Crocker, Richard L., xxi, xxii, xxiii, xxiv–xxv, xxvi, 422–23, 422, 426, 428, 460
Cui, César, 92, 218, 219
Current Musicology (journal), xxiii, xxiv, 3, 365

Cursed Questions (Taruskin), xxi
Czerny, Carl, 311

Dahlhaus, Carl, 101, 180, 205, 206, 312, 367, 505, 512
d'Alembert, Jean le Rond, 46, 47
Dalos, Anna, x, 146
Dance for Burgess (Varèse), 401
Daniél, Ernő, 160
Danuser, Hermann, 504, 505
D'Arcy Wood, Gillen, 53, 55
Dargomïzhsky, Alexander, 218; *Rusalka*, 195
David, Félicien, *Le Désert* (1844), 75
Davies, Sir Peter Maxwell, 112, 113
Davison, Archibald T., 417, 422
Death of Klinghoffer, The (Sellars/Adams/Goodman), 9–10, 404
Debussy, Claude, 101, 103, 143, 178, 401, 461, 471; *En Blanc et Noir*, 468; "Feux d'artifice," 468; "Golliwog's Cakewalk," 452; *Pelléas et Mélisande*, 193
Decadence and the Making of Modernism (Weir), 503
Degeyter, Pierre, 21
Dehumanization of Art, The (Ortega y Gasset), 454, 520
Deleuze, Gilles, 506
Delibes, Léo, *Lakmé*, 77
Delius, Frederick, *Mass of Life*, 505
Della Valle, Pietro, 390
Demon (A. Rubinstein), 88
Denisov, Edison Vasilievich, 276, 277, 279, 280
Denkmäler der Tonkunst in Oesterreich (Adler), 417
DeNora, Tia, 379
Dent, Edward, 452
Dentice, Luigi, 387
Désert, Le (David), 75
Deutsches Requiem, Ein (Brahms), 430
Dewey, John, 483
Diaghilev, Serge, 103, 193, 301, 304, 373, 417
Dickstein, Morris, 124
Diderot, Denis, 46
Dijkstra, Bram, 503–4
Dingle, Christopher, 383, 384, 402, 405
Dittmer, Luther, 20
Divas and Scholars (Gossett), 152
Divertimento for string orchestra (Bartók), 122, 136
Dmitrij (Dvořák), 207
Dmitry Shostakovich in Letters and Documents (2001), 15

Docta sanctorum (papal bull), 385–86
Dodekachordon (Glareanus), 386
Doktor Faustus (Mann), 266–67
Dolmetsch, Arnold, 460
Domingo, Placido, 449
Don Giovanni (Mozart), 479
Donington, Robert, 45
Don Quixote (N. Nabokov), 300
Dorfles, Gillo, 51
Downes, Olin, 24, 135, 137, 397–98
Downes, Stephen, 502, 504, 506, 507, 508, 509, 510
Drachevsky, General Daniyil Vasilievich, 438
Drake, Richard, 506, 507
Dramaticheskaya poèma [Dramatic Poem] (Karetnikov), 290–91, 292, 294
Dreyfus, Captain Alfred, 80
Druskin, Mikhail Semyonovich, xx
Dubinsky, Rostislav, xvii
Du chant (Hahn), 51
Duckles, Madeline, xiii
Duet with Nicky (Berezowsky), 256–59
Duke, Vernon, 256, 262–63, 271, 272
Dulak, Michelle, 430–31
Dumbrill, Rachel, 427, 428, 443
Duo dialoghi della musica (Dentici), 387
Dvořák, Antonin, 109, 180, 204–5, 206–7, 248, 249, 433; *Dmitrij*, 207; *Humoresque*, 205, 206; Symphony no. 9, "From the New World," 206, 207
Dwight, John Sullivan, 24
Dzerzhinsky, Ivan, *Quiet Flows the Don*, 349

Eagleton, Terry, 37
Eckhardt, Mária, xv
"Effet de réel, L'" ["The Reality Effect"] (Barthes), 409–10
Eggli, Eva, 312
Einstein, Alfred, 364
Eisen, Cliff, 370
Eisenhower, Dwight, 268, 269, 307, 309
Eisenstein, Sergei, 273, 354
Eisler, Hanns, 319
"Election, An" (Ives), 470
Elektra (Strauss), 508, 509
Elementary Training for Musicians (Hindemith, 1946), 158, *159*
Elena Pavlovna, Grand Duchess, 195, 211
Elgar, Sir Edward, 98, 109, 111, 115, 432, 470, 471
Eliot, T. S., 42, 46, 49, 124, 449, 450, 480, 488
Eli Zijojn, wejoreho (arr. Alexander Zhitomirsky), *441*

Eli Zion/Tsiyoyn (Zeitlin, 1914), 439, *440, 441,* 445
Embryons desséchés (Satie), 452, 453
Emery, Walter, 368
Emperor Concerto [No. 5 in E-flat Major] (Beethoven), 58
En Blanc et Noir (Debussy), 468
Encounter magazine, 302, 304, 306, 307
Encyclopédie (Diderot and d'Alembert), 46, 47, 49
Enesco, George, 103
Engel, Carl, 364
En Saga (Sibelius), 112
Entartete Musik [Degenerate Music] (Nazi exhibition, 1938), 105
"Entry of the Gladiators" (Fučik), 283
Erdődy, Countess Anna Maria von (née von Niczky), viii–ix
Erdődy von Monyorókerék und Monoszló, Count Joseph Georg, viii
Eroica [Symphony No. 3] (Beethoven), 397
Erwartung (Schoenberg), 305
Essays before a Sonata (Ives), 470
Esterházy, Prince Nikolaus, 274, 485
Estetica, L' (Croce), 503
Eugene Onegin (Chaikovsky), 209
Euler, Leonhard, 231, 243
Euripides, 510
Evans, Richard J., 521
Ewell, Philip, 404
Expositions and Developments (Stravinsky, 1962), 373
"Expression in Time of Objectivity" (Schneider), ix

Fairclough, Pauline, 319, 320, 321, 322, 327
Falla, Manuel de, *The Three-Cornered Hat*, 452
Fall of Berlin, The (film, 1950), 323, 332–33
Fall Wagner, Der (Nietzsche), 55, 202
"Fall Wagner, frei nach Nietzsche, Der" [The Wagner Case, Loosely after Nietzsche] (Furtwängler), 500
Famous Musicians of Jewish Origin (Saleski), 81
Fassett, Agatha, 123–24
"Fate of the Critic in the Clickbait Age, The" (A. Ross), 405
Faugues, Guillaume, 386
Faulkner, William, 491
Faust-Symphonie (Liszt), 38
Fay, Amy, 53–54
Fay, Laurel, xvii, xviii, 11
Felciano, Richard, xxii
Feldman, Morton, 113, 398
Felski, Rita, 474–75, 476–80, 481, 488

Fend, Michael, 369
Feramors (A. Rubinstein), 75, 79
Ferne Klang, Der (Schreker), 509
"Feux d'artifice" (Debussy), 468, *468*
Field, John, 54
Fiery Angel, The (Prokofieff), 263–64
Fifth Symphony (Shostakovich), 354
Film, színház, irodalom [Film, Theater, Literature] (magazine), 122
Finck, Henry T., 24
Finlandia (Sibelius), 114
Finscher, Ludwig, 165, 166
Firebird (Stravinsky), xvi, 147
Fiske, Roger, 369
Fitzenhagen, Wilhelm, 63, 64
Five Pieces for Orchestra, op. 16 (Schoenberg), 397
Flaubert, Gustave, 409, 435
Fleischer, Max, 65
Fletcher, Andrew, 160, 161
Fletcher, Joseph, 483
Fleurs du mal (Baudelaire), 199
Flood, The (Stravinsky), 308
F-minor Fantasy, op. 49 (Chopin), 315
"Folk Songs of Hungary, The" (Bartók), 149–50
Forte, Allen, 3, 32
Fosler-Lussier, Danielle, 107, 132, 137, 150
Franck, César, 109, 166, 208, 356, 471; Quintet in F Minor, 346; Symphony in D Minor, 206
Franco, Francisco, 303
Frankfurt, Harry, 459
Franz Liszt Academy (Hungary), x, xv
Frege, Gottlob, 473
Frescobaldi, Girolamo, 390
Freud, Sigmund, 83
Friedheim, Arthur, 310
Frisch, Walter, 180–81
Frith, Simon, 390, 402, 404
Frolova-Walker, Marina, 14, 15, 320, 323, 325, 326, 327, 335–36, 339, 348, 350
Fučik, Julius, "Entry of the Gladiators," 283
Furtwängler, Wilhelm, 354, 495, 498, 499–501
Fussell, Paul, 455, 464, 465
Fux, Johann Joseph, 179, 376

Gadamer, Hans-Georg, 480–81
Gagarin, Yuri, 309
Gaillard, Marius-François, 399
Galbraith, John Kenneth, 306
Galilei, Vincenzo, 19
García Caturla, Alejandro, 399
Gasparov, Boris, 505

Gass, William, 64
Gassmann, Florian, 98, 99
Gauk, Alexander, 293–94
Gautier, Théophile, 396
Geertz, Clifford, 371
Geiringer, Karl, 370
Geminiani, Francesco, 44–45, 46, 381
General History of Music, A (Burney), 45
"General William Booth Enters into Heaven" (Ives), 467–68, 467
Geologi [Geologists] (Karetnikov), 290
Gerber, Ernst Ludwig, 373
Gergiyev, Valeriy, 63, 280
Gerhard, Anselm, 379
Gershkovich, Philipp, 276
Gibson, James, 483–84, 486
Gilbert, W. S., xxvii, 410
Gilels, Emil, 311
Gillies, Malcolm, 118, 122
Gilman, Richard, 503, 506
Ginsberg, Allen, 417
Giroud, Vincent, 299, 300, 301, 304, 306, 308
Giudiccioni, Lelio, 390
Glareanus (Heinrich Glarean), 386
Glass, Philip, 9
Glazunov, Alexander, 246, 344, 346
Glière, Reinhold, 253
Glikman, Isaac, 331, 340, 344
Glinka, Mikhail, 60–61, 167, 195, 337, 443; *A Life for the Tsar*, 173; *Ruslan and Lyudmila*, 77, 78, 88, 89, 107, 238, 241, 242
Glinka Museum of Musical Art (Moscow), xvi, 15, 338
Gluck, Christoph Willibald, 194, 373
Goebbels, Joseph, 21, 133, 496
Goehr, Lydia, 25, 29, 57, 367, 506
Gogol, Nikolai, 173, 339
Goldenweiser, Alexander, 311
Goldfadn, Avraham, 443–44; *Shulamis*, 444, 445
Goldmann, Lucien, 474
Goldmark, Karl, 66–71, 77, 80, 94, 96; *Merlin*, 69, 79; *Rustic Wedding Symphony*, 69; *Sakuntala*, 77, 87; Violin Concerto, 69. See also *Königin von Saba, Die* [*The Queen of Sheba*] (Goldmark)
Golitsyn, Prince Nikolai Borisovich, 336–37
"Golliwog's Cakewalk" (Debussy), 452
Gombrowicz, Witold, 301
Goodman, Alice, 9
Goodwin, Doris Kearns, 5–6
Goodwin, Richard, 5–6

Gooley, Dana, 60
Goossens, Eugene, 431
Gorbachev, Mikhail, 317
Gorky, Maxim, 390
Gossett, Philip, 152
Götterdämmerung [Twilight of the Gods] (Wagner), 508
Gould, Glenn, 285, 288
Graça, Fernando Lopes, 392
Gradus ad Parnassum (Fux), 179
Graffman, Gary, 310
"Great Artists Serving Stalin Like a Dog" (Taruskin), 273
Great Friendship, The (Muradeli), 253
Great War and Modern Memory, The (Fussell), 455, 464
Great War and the Language of Modernism, The (Sherry), 457
Gregory I, Pope, 385
Grieg, Edvard, 109, 112, 115, 154, 191, 314
Griesinger, Georg August, 484
Griffiths, Paul, 148, 149
Grinberg, Moisei Abramovich, 348
Gromyko, Andrey, 315
Gruber, Roman Ilyich, 339, 342
Gubaidulina, Sofia, 277, 279
Guillaume Tell [*William Tell*] (Rossini), 154

Hahn, Reynaldo, 51
Hall, Cornelius A., 269, 270
Hamelin, Marc-André, 64–65
Hamer, Laura, 388, 402, 404
Hamilton, Kenneth, 59, 65
Handel, George Frideric, 16, 32, 73, 103, 205, 346, 357, 364, 365, 366, 381; *Israel in Egypt*, 18–19; *Solomon*, 68
Hanning, Barbara Russano, 366
Hanslick, Eduard, 26, 27, 28, 30, 31, 38, 77, 79, 201–2
Harbison, John, 9
Harding, Warren G., 470, 471
Harmonielehre (Schoenberg), 287
Harnoncourt, Nikolaus, 380
Harris, Roy, 112, 113, 326
Háry János Suite (Kodály), 144
Hauptmann, Moritz, 227–31, 227, 234, 236, 237–38, 242, 243
Hauser, Arnold, 509
Hausswald, Günter, 370
Haydn, Joseph, viii, xi, 40, 44, 47, 65, 143, 165, 191, 274, 365, 373, 382, 484; *The Creation*, 367, 485; *The Seasons*, 485

Haydn, Michael, 373
Hays, Ernie, 65
Heartz, Daniel, xiii, 365, 366, 367, 376
Hegel, Georg Wilhelm Friedrich, 448
Heidegger, Martin, 483
Heiliger Dankgesang ["Solemn Song of Thanksgiving"], from String Quartet in A Minor, op. 132 (Beethoven), 108
Heine, Heinrich, 58
Heinichen, Johann David, 44, 45, 46
Henderson, W. J., 24, 70, 463
Henley, William Ernest, 462
Hepburn, Katharine, 311
Herder, Johann Gottfried, 25–27, 28–30, 149, 433
Hero of Our Time, A (Lermontov), 15
Herzgewächse (Schoenberg), 510
Herzog, George, 121
Hicks, Anthony, 370
Hiley, David, xxvii
Hiller, Johann Adam, 377, 379
Himmler, Heinrich, 499
Hindemith, Paul, 120, 121, 122, 303, 339, 343, 356, 358, 401, 414; *Elementary Training for Musicians*, 158, 159; *Plöner Musiktag*, 159; *Wir bauen eine Stadt*, 159
Hirsch, E. D., 472–73, 474
Histoire du soldat, L' (Stravinsky), 468
Historical Anthology of Music (*HAM*), 417, 420, 421–22
Historisch-biographisches Lexicon der Tonkünstler (Gerber), 373
Hitler, Adolf, 123, 146, 421, 450
Hobsbawm, Eric, 451
Höcker, Karla, 495, 496, 497–98, 499–500
Hoffmann, E. T. A., 167–68, 174, 180, 194, 197, 199, 205, 479, 493–94, 498–99
Hogarth, William, 502
Holden, John, 393
Holmboe, Vagn, 112
Holoman, D. Kern, 4
Holst, Gustav, 98, 99
Holst, Imogen, 431
Hook, Sidney, 303
Hooker, Lynn, 131
Horowitz, Vladimir, 64–65, 311
"Horst Wessel Lied," 21
Hovhannes, Alan, 248, 401
Howard, Richard, 409
Hrabosky, Al, 65
Hughes, Rosemary, 370
Hulme, T. E., 4, 488, 520

Hume, David, 41, 46, 48
Hummel, Johann Nepomuk, 58, 172; Nocturne in F Major, op. 99, 172n20
Humoresque (Dvořák), 205, 206
Hungarian Rhapsodies (Liszt), 127–28
Hungarian Rhapsody, Second (Liszt), 38, 64–65
Hunke, Osip Karlovich, 225
Hunter, George, 414, 416
Hurrian song, 422–23, *422*, *424–25*, 426–28, *429*, 430
Hurwitz, David, 431, 432
Huysmans, Joris-Karl, 503

Idelsohn, Avraham Zvi, 442, 444
Ideology of the Aesthetic, The (Eagleton), 37
Idols of Perversity (Dijkstra), 503–4
Ikonnikov, Alexei, 391
Immortal Beloved (film, dir. Rose, 1994), ix
"Imperial School of Jurisprudence Some Forty Years Ago, The" (Stasov), 60–61
"Inclusive History for a Divided World? An" (Frolova-Walker), 335–36
Indy, Vincent d', 206, 431, 471
In Flanders Fields (Ives), 465, 468, 470
"In Flanders Fields" (McCrae), 463
Inghelbrecht, Désiré-Émile, 431
In Search of Wagner (Adorno), 209
Institute for Musicology (Hungarian Academy of Sciences), viii, ix
Intermezzo, op. 119, no. 1 (Brahms), 509
"Internationale, L'" (Degeyter), 21
International Musicological Society, xi, xx, 145, 364
International Review of the Aesthetics and Sociology of Music (journal), 117
"Invictus" (Henley, 1888), 462
Ioann Damaskin [John of Damascus] (Taneyev), 181, *182–83*, *184*, 189
Iofan, Boris Mikhailovich, 341
Iogansen, Yuliy Ivanovich (Julius Ernst Christian Johannsen), 225, 226–27, *226*, 228, 232, 234, 242, 243
Ionisation (Varèse), 399
Irving, John, 369, 379, 380, 381, 382
Isaac, Henricus, 515
Israel in Egypt (Handel), 18–19
Italienisches Liederbuch (Wolf), 510
Ivan Groznïy [*Ivan the Terrible*] (Prokofieff), 273–74
Ivanov, Vyacheslav, 200
Ivashkin, Alexander, xviii

INDEX   535

Ives, Charles: "An Election" (1920), 470; *Essays before a Sonata*, 470; *In Flanders Fields*, 464–66, 465, 468, 470; "General William Booth Enters into Heaven," 467–68, 467; Second Piano Sonata, 470; *Three Quarter-Tone Pieces*, 469, 469

Jackson, Larisa Petrushkevich, 228, 232, 234, 242
James, William, 410
Janáček, Leoš, 102, 139, 149, 154, 204, 209
Janis, Byron, 309
Jean Paul (J. P. Friedrich Richter), 197
Joachim, Joseph, 54, 61
Johannsen, Julius Ernst Christian. *See* Iogansen, Yuliy Ivanovich
John Chrysostom, St., 157
Johnson, Samuel, 409, 413
 hn XXII, Pope, 385–86
 us, Berta, 370
 Carys Wyn, 404
 vid Wyn, 363
 ʾul), 73
 ez, xxvi
 l, 302, 307
 449
 [The Jews' Dance] (Neusiedler,
  9, 421, 422
  –77, 76, 77, 194
 Jet, 134, 135, 137
  v), 283, 286
 Kab
  3
 Kael, P., 253, 269, 281, 284, 313,
 Kalevala
 Kalidasa,
 Kalligone (epic), 206
 Kant, Imman
  490
 Karetnikov, Nik 18, 55, 141, 454, 455,
  259, 280–98, 2
  (Dramatic Poe ikolayevich,
 Symphony, 281, heskaya poèma
 297; Geologi (Geo 92, 294; Fourth
 283, 286; Misteriya , 294, 295, 296,
 Mystery of the Apost ; Julius Fučik,
 Symphony, 293; Thema vla (The
 s variatsiami), 281, 282, 85; Second
 281; Vanina Vanini, 286, 2 riations (Temï
   rd Symphony,

Karetnikova, Olga, 282
Karlinsky, Simon, 8, 11
Karłowicz, Mieczysław, 505, 507–8, 510
Kasatkina, Natalia, 286, 290
Katz, Boris, xix
Kearns, Doris. *See* Goodwin, Doris Kearns
Keats, John, 247
Keefe, Simon P., 363, 370, 372, 373
Keiser, Reinhard, 377
Kennan, George, 306
Kenyon, Nicholas, 395
Kerman, Joseph, xiii, 386–87, 415, 517
Kernis, Aaron Jay, 9
Keynes, John Maynard, 307–8
Khachaturyan, Aram, 340, 352–53, 359; Violin Concerto, 349, 352
Khaikin, Boris, 254–55
Khomeini, Ayatollah, 8
Khomyakov, Alexey Stepanovich, 181
Khrennikov, Tikhon Nikolayevich, 253, 255, 284, 286
Khrushchev, Nikita, 309, 314, 315, 318, 323, 330
Kierkegaard, Søren, 479
Kilmer, Anne Draffkorn, 422–23, 426–28
Kinderman, William, 505
King, A. Hyatt, 370
King Roger (Szymanowski), 510
Kirnberger, Johann, 381
Kiselgof, Zisman, 439, 442, 443, 445
Kleinertz, Rainer, 369
Koch, Juan Martin, 14
Koczirz, Adolf, 417, 420
Kodály, Zoltán, 119, 125, 139, 143, 146–47, 149, 151, 158–62, 326, 401; "Ancient Traditions—Today's Musical Life," 152–53; Concerto for Orchestra, 147; *Háry János* Suite, 144; "Music in the Kindergarten," 155–56; Sonata for Solo Cello, op. 8, 144; Symphony in C Major, 147
Kohanovskaya, Romela, 279
Kolessa, Filaret, 442
Kolneder, Walter, 370
Komar, Vitaly, 323
Komlós, Katalin, x
Kondrashin, Kirill, 314
Königin von Saba, Die [*The Queen of Sheba*] (Goldmark), 67–74, 75, 77, 79–80; Anathema Scene, 88; Assad's Narrative, 94, 95; Astaroth's "Lockruf," 87, 88; Bacchanale, 80, 82; "Chor des Volkes," 86; Einzugmarsch sections, 84–85; "Der Freund ist dein," 90, 91; "Magische Töne," 89, 89; Prelude, 86, 93, 94

Konyok gorbunok [The Little Humpbacked Horse] (Shchedrin), 287
Koolhaas, Rem, 475, 476
Korabel'nikova, Lyudmila Zinov'yevna, 185
Korsakov, Sergei Ivanovich, 391
Kosygin, Alexey, 315
Koussevitzky, Serge, 181, 256, 257, 259, 260, 269, 271
Kovacs, Ernie, 492
Koval', Marian, *Yemel'yan Pugachov*, 254
Kovnatskaya, Lyudmila (Mila) Grigor'yevna, xvii, xix, xx, xxi
Kramer, Lawrence, 505
Krebs, Stanley Dale, 244–45, 248, 253
Krehbiel, Henry, 24, 69–70, 71, 73–74, 80
Kreisler, Fritz, 431
Kreisleriana (Hoffmann), 199, 200
Krenek, Ernst, 320, 336, 339, 340
Krieger, Murray, 490
Kruglikov, Semyon, 222
Krugozor (magazine), 284, 285
Krupskaya, Nadezhda, 322
Krutch, Joseph Wood, 51
Kunst der Fuge, Die [*The Art of Fugue*] (Bach), 174
Kunst und die Revolution, Die (Wagner), 196
Kunstwerk der Zukunft, Das (Wagner), 196, 197
Kupfer, Harry, 11, 14
Kurz, Selma, 87

Lady Macbeth of the Mtsensk District (Shostakovich), 5, 6–7, 8, 11, 14–15, 148, 305, 320, 330, 340, 341, 349, 354, 390
Laird, Paul R., 368
Lakmé (Delibes), 77
Lalla Rookh (Moore), 75, 79
Lalo, Édouard, *Rapsodie norvégienne*, 191
Lami, Emilio, 391
Landon, H. C. Robbins, 369
Lang, Paul Henry, 121, 314, 315, 364, 366, 376, 515, 517
Langer, Susanne, 26
Laokoön, or the Limitations of Poetry (Lessing), 26, 198–99
Laroche (Larosh), Hermann (German) Avgustovich, 79, 179, 414
LaRue, Jan, xii
Lasky, Melvin, 302, 306
Latour, Bruno, 475, 476
Launay, Denise, 368
Lawton, David, 151

Lazarev, Alexander, 280
Lecerf de la Viéville, Jean Laurent, 43–44
Lecocq, Charles, 444
Ledkovsky, Alexander, 299
Legend of the Invisible City of Kitezh, The (Rimsky-Korsakov), 204
Le Guin, Ursula K., 28
Leibowitz, René, 107, 114, 136, 139, 140, 145, 397
"Leiden und Größe Richard Wagners" [Sufferings and Greatness of Richard Wagner] (Mann), 249, 255, 268, 275
Leningrad Symphony (No. 7) (Shostakovich), 303
Lenz, Wilhelm von, 249
Lerdahl, Fred, xxvii
Lermontov, Mikhail, 15
Leschetitzky, Theodor, 311
Leskov, Nikolai, 6, 14
Lessing, Gotthold Ephraim, 26, 27, 30, 32, 198–99
Levinson, Jerrold, 29
Lewin, David, 32, 231, 506, 508
Lewis, Anthony, 369
Lewis, Wyndham, 449–51
Lexicon of Musical Invective (N. Slonimsky),
Lhévinne, Josef, 311
Lhévinne, Rosina, 310–11, 316
Liber de arte contrapuncti (Tinctoris), 386
Lider-Zamelbuch far der yidisher shul un [Songbook for the Jewish School an ily] (Kiselgof), 439
Liebestod ["Isoldens Verklärung"] (fro ner's *Tristan und Isolde*), 30, 33
Liebestraum (Liszt), 312
Lieutenant Kijé (Prokofieff), 270
Lieven, Prince Peter, 417
Life for the Tsar, A (Glinka), 173
Lina and Serge (Morrison), 255
Lindbergh, Charles, 328
Lindsay, Vachel, 468
Lippman, Edward, xxiv
Lisle, Rouget de, 21
Liszt, Franz, 37–38, 43, 45, 5 minor 102, 128–31, 176, 195, 2 e, 38; Baccalaureate Letter phony (*Ce* Piano Sonata, 38; F , 238; Second *Liebestraum*, 312; M —65; *Sonetto 123* qu'on entend sur l' Hungarian Rhap cture, 1936), 125– della Petrarca,
"Liszt Problems" (126, 142 son), 409
Lives of the Poet

INDEX   537

Livre des sans-foyer, Le (Wharton), 452
Locke, John, 49
Lockhart, Koraljka, 8
Lockhart, Kory, 12
Loewenberg, Alfred, 69
Lohengrin (Wagner), 74, 196, 200
Lolita (Nabokov), 299
London, Justin, 29
Longfellow, Henry Wadsworth, 206
Lorenz, Alfred, 508
Losev, Aleksey Fyodorovich, 200, 209
Louis XIV, 43, 274–75
Love for Three Oranges, The (Prokofieff), 270, 452
Lucretius, 457
Ludwig, king of Bavaria, 62, 63
Lully, Jean-Baptiste, 274; *Cadmus et Hermione*, 43
Luther, Martin, 481
Lutheranism, Anti-Judaism, and Bach's "St. John Passion" (Marissen), 17
Lvov, General Alexei Fyodorovich, 195
Lyadov, Anatoly, 225, 226, 228, 232, 234, 235, 242, 243, 505, 509
Lyndon Johnson and the American Dream (D. K. Goodwin), 5
Lynes, Russell, 51
Lyotard, Jean-François, 506
Lyric Suite (Berg), 294
Lysenko, Trofim, 323

Ma, Yo-Yo, 63
Maccabees (A. Rubinstein), 73
Macdonald, Dwight, 62
MacDowell, Edward, 109
Machaut, Guillaume de, 414
MacIntyre, Bruce, 376
MacLeish, Archibald, 301
Mad magazine, 492, 493
Mahler, Gustav, 87, 208, 293, 294, 296, 431; *Resurrection* Symphony (No. 2), 505; Sixth Symphony, 509; Symphony of a Thousand (No. 8), 505; *Titan* Symphony (No. 1), 505
Maksimenkov, Leonid, 320
Malevich, Kazimir, 448
Malthus, Thomas Robert, 446
Mancini, Giulio, 41
Mandelstam, Osip, 331
Manfred-Meditation (Nietzsche), 510
Mann, Thomas, 40, 49, 249, 255, 266–68, 275
Mann, William, 402
Mantagnier, Jean-Paul C., 368
Manulkina, Olga, xviii

Maria Nikolayevna, Grand Duchess, 195
Marino, Giambattista, 503
Marissen, Michael, 17, 184
Maritain, Jacques, 302
Marius the Epicurean (Pater), 503, 507
"Marseillaise, La" (Lisle), 21, 465, 467, 468, 469
Martinelli, Giovanni, 154
Marx, Hans Joachim, 370
Marx, Karl, 272, 448
Maryinsky Orchestra, 63
Maslow, Abraham, 20
Mass in E-flat Major (Schubert), 235
Mass of Life (Delius), 505
Masson, Paul-Marie, 369
Masur, Kurt, 273
Mattheson, Johann, 40–41, 384
Matuszewski, Ignacy, 196
Maus, Fred Everett, 384, 491–92
McClary, Susan, 12–13, 16
McCrae, Major John, 463, 464, 466
McGuinness, Rosamond, 370
McKinley, William, 470
McPherson, Aimee Semple, 66
McVeigh, Simon, 370
Meaning of Meaning, The (Richards and Ogden), 456
Meck, Nadezhda von, 175, 213, 217, 219
Medtner, Emiliy, 200
Medtner, Nikolai, 175, 311
Méhul, Étienne, 194; *Joseph*, 73
Meistersinger, Die (Wagner), 194, 195
Melamid, Alexander, 323
Melgunov, Nikolai, 196
Melovatskaya, Anna, 290
Men', Archpriest Alexander, 285
Menand, Louis, 51
Mendelson, Mira, 253–54
Mendelssohn, Felix, 75, 96, 165, 205, 209, 226, 507
Menell, Stephen, 41
Mengozzi, Stefano, 385
Meresyev, Alexey, 251, 252
Merezhensky, Dmitry, 200
Merlin (Goldmark), 69, 79
Messiaen, Olivier, 101
Metropolitan Opera (New York), 5, 10, 30, 70
Meyer, Leonard B., 127, 244, 403, 461
Meyerbeer, Giacomo, 96, 444; *L'africaine*, 77; *Ploërmel*, 168
Meyerhold, Vsevolod, 262
Michelet, Jules, 409–10
Mihály, Andras, 150

Mikado, The (Gilbert and Sullivan), 410
Mikhailov, Nikolai, 313
Mikoyan, Anastas, 315
Mikrokosmos (Bartók), 144
Mikusi, Balázs, x
Milardo, Judith, 415
Milhaud, Darius, 247–48, 302, 326, 401
Missa Papae Marcelli (Palestrina), 244, 494
Missa solemnis (Beethoven), 57, 413, 414
Mlada (Rimsky-Korsakov), 235
"Modulation and Tonal Space in the 'Practical Manual of Harmony'" (Jackson), 228
Molière, 41
Molino, Jean, 23–24, 385
Molldurtonart (minor/major key), 228, 230, 230, 231
Molotov, Vyacheslav, 353
Montesquieu, Baron de, 446
Monteux, Pierre, 398
Moore, Thomas, *Lalla Rookh*, 75, 79
Morgan, Robert P., 102–3
Móricz, Klára, ix
Morris, Tom, 10
Morrison, Simon, 245, 254, 255, 261, 262, 505
Morrow, Michael, 414–15, 416
Morton, Lawrence, 107, 296, 298, 434
Moscheles, Ignaz, 226
Moscow Conservatory, xvi, xvii, xix, 276, 281, 283, 285, 310, 321, 344
"Moscow Nights" (Solovyov-Sedoy), 254
Mosenthal, Salomon Hermann, 75, 87
Moser, Hans-Joachim, xxv
Mosolov, Alexander, *Zavod* (*The Iron Foundry*), 321, 327
Mountain Symphony [*Ce qu'on entend sur la montagne*] (Liszt), 238
Movements for Piano and Orchestra (Stravinsky), 308
Moy, Ron, 404
Mozart, Leopold, 40
Mozart, Wolfgang Amadeus, 44, 47, 65, 143, 165, 191, 194, 245, 248–49, 274, 365, 373, 381, 483; Piano Concerto in C Major, K. 503, 314; *Don Giovanni*, 479; Requiem, 482; Symphony No. 40 in G Minor, 500; *Die Zauberflöte* (*The Magic Flute*), 90
"Muddle Instead of Music" (Zaslavsky article in *Pravda*), 330, 331–32, 338, 341, 353, 390
Mukhina, Vera, 325, 342, 347
Murray, Christopher Brent, 388, 401
Musica Divina (Proske), 179

Musical Quarterly, xxvi, 134, 364
Music and Aesthetic Reality (Zangwill), 31
Music and Belonging between Revolution and Restoration (Waltham-Smith), 497
Musica nel XX secolo, La (N. Nabokov, 1954), 304
Musica Reservata, 414, 416
Music Divided (Fosler-Lussier), 150
"Music—Drastic or Gnostic?" (Abbate), 33
"Music in American Society" symposium (1967), 20
Music in America's Cold War Diplomacy (Fosler-Lussier), 316
Music in European Capitals (Heartz), 366
Music in Our Time (Salazar), 364
Music in the Baroque Era (Bukofzer), 371
"Music in the Kindergarten" (Kodály), 155, 155–56
Music in Western Civilization (Lang), 364
Music on the Frontline (Wellens), 300
"Music's Stubborn Enchantments (and Music Theory's)" (Rings), 486
Music Study in Germany (A. Fay), 53–54
Music Theory Online, 497
Musikalisches Opfer, Das [*The Musical Offering*] (Bach), 174
Musik als Klangrede (Harnoncourt), 380
Musik aus früher Zeit [Music from Early Times] (Apel, ed.), 417
Musique et la mise en scène, La (Appia), 198
Musorgsky, Modest, 178, 245, 322; *Boris Godunov*, 218, 473–74, 479, 517; *Pictures at an Exhibition*, 444; *Rayok* (The Peepshow), 179
Mussolini, Benito, 123, 146
Muti, Riccardo, 151
Muzïka iz bïvshego SSSR [Music from the Former USSR] (Tsenova, ed.), 277
Muzïkal'naya akademiya (journal), xvi
Muzsika (journal), x
Myaskovsky, Nikolai, 141, 253, 271, 327, 340, 359; Eighteenth Symphony, 391; Twenty-First Symphony, 326, 358
Myrdal, Gunnar, 522
Myrick, Julian, 464
Mysterium (Scriabin), 206, 208
Mysteriya apostola Pavla [The Mystery of the Apostle Paul] (Karetnikov), 285

Nabokov, Dominique Cibiel, 300
Nabokov, Nicolas, 256, 299–308, 330; *Bagazh*, 301, 306; *La musica nel XX secolo*, 304; *Ode*, 301; *L'Oeuvre du XXème siècle*, 304, 305; Old

Friends and New Music, 256, 301; *Symboli chrestiani*, 299; *Union Pacific*, 301
Nabokov, Vladimir, 25
Nabokova, Sofia Dmitrievna, 299
Nagasaki (Schnittke), 286
Naked Civil Servant, The (Crisp), 446
Na strazhe mira [Guarding the Peace] (Prokofieff), 271
Nattiez, Jean-Jacques, 23
Natur der Harmonik und der Metrik, Die [*The Nature of Harmony and Meter*] (Hauptmann), 229, 230, 234
Naumov, Vladimir, 291
Nejedlý, Zdeněk, 209
Nelson, Robert, 439
Németh, Mária, 90
Neue Musikzeitung, 13
Neue Zeitschrift für Musik (journal), 128
Neuhaus, Heinrich (Genrikh Neygauz), 311
Neusiedler, Hans, 17, 418, 420, 426
New Grove 2 [New Grove Dictionary of Music and Musicians], 384
Newman, Joel, xxii
New Oxford History of Music (NOHM), xxvii, 368–70, 372, 374
New Republic, 1, 5, 8, 11, 517
New World Symphony (No. 9) (Dvořák), 206, 207
New York Philharmonic, 5, 207, 431
New York Pro Musica, 515–16, 518
New York Times, 1, 4, 5, 8, 63, 70, 135, 137, 273, 322, 354–55, 404, 518; "Electronic Prying Grows," 306; "It's Official: Many Orchestras Are Now Charities," 2; "World's Oldest Song Reported Deciphered," 422–23, 422
Nicholas I (Nikolai), Tsar, 195, 211
Nicolai, Friedrich, 376
Nicolas Nabokov: A Life in Freedom and Music (Giroud), 299
Nielsen, Carl, 112
Nietzsche, Friedrich, 19, 55, 192, 193, 196, 200, 208, 453, 504; *Manfred-Meditation*, 510
Nilsson, Birgit, 30
Nineteenth-Century Music (journal), 98, 517
Ninth Symphony (Beethoven), 12–13
Nocturne for the Left Hand, op. 9, no. 2 (Scriabin), 311
Noise of Time, The (Barnes), 303, 328–29, 331
Noneto (Villa-Lobos), 399
Noorman, Jantina, 414–16
Noose Hangs High, The (film, 1948), 405–7
Norrington, Sir Roger, 431

North, Roger, 379
Nose, The (Shostakovich), 15, 339, 340
Nussbaum, Martha, 506

"Objective Interpretation" (Hirsch), 473
O'Bryan, Rildia Bee, 310
Ockham, William of, 427
Ode (N. Nabokov), 301
Odoyevsky, Prince Vladimir Fyodorovich, 167–74, 194
Oedipus Rex (Stravinsky), 305
Oestreich, James, 1, 4, 63, 517, 518
Oeuvre du XXème siècle, L' (N. Nabokov, 1952), 304, 305
Offenbach, Jacques, 166, 444
Ogden, Charles Kay, 456–58
Old Friends and New Music (N. Nabokov), 256, 301
Olleson, Edward, 368
O nata lux de lumine (Tallis), 244
On Russian Music (Taruskin), xix*n*21
On the Aesthetic Education of Man (Schiller), 41
On the Field of Kulikovo (Shaporin), 326
"Opera and the Periodization of 18th-Century Music" (Heartz), 365
Oper und Drama (Wagner), 197
Oppenheimer, Robert, 306, 307
Opus (magazine), 4–5, 517, 518
Oramo, Ilkka, 109, 111, 112, 113–15, 117, 120
Oresteia (Taneyev), 180, 204
Orff, Carl, 336; *Carmina burana*, 33
Origins, The [Rozhdeniye Sotsrealizma] (Komar and Melamid), 323, 324
Ortega y Gasset, José, 4, 454, 520
Ostrovsky, Alexander, 6
Otten, Georg Dietrich, 62
Owen, Wilfrid, 464
Oxford History of Western Music, The, vii, x, xvi, xxi, xxvii, 16, 17, 99, 109, 110–11, 115, 116–17, 139, 149, 160, 363, 399, 448, 461, 471, 474, 518, 521–22; "Music and Totalitarian Society," 336; *Music in the Early Twentieth Century*, 112; *Music in the Late Twentieth Century*, 112; "Pathos Is Banned," 449

Paganini, Niccolò, 56
Page, Christopher, 384, 385
Palazzetti, Nicolò, 117–19, 120, 122, 123
Palestrina (Pfitzner), 494
Palestrina, Giovanni Pierluigi da, 179; *Missa Papae Marcelli*, 244, 494

540 INDEX

Panteleeva, Olga, xix–xx
Paralèle des Italiens et des Français (Raguenet), 43
Paraphrases on an Unchanging Theme (Rimsky-Korsakov), 176, 177
Parerga und paralipomena (Schopenhauer), 141, 494
Parsifal (Wagner), 198, 505
Passport to Paris (Duke), 256
Pasternak, Boris, 331
Pásztory-Bartók, Ditta, 106, 120, 123
Pater, Walter, 22–24, 25, 490–91, 492, 502, 506, 507, 510
Pavarotti, Luciano, 449
Péchés de vieillesse ["Sins of Old Age"] (Rossini), 186
Peraino, Judith, xxi
Perle, George, xiv, 101
Persichetti, Vincent, 401
Pesni nashikh dney [Songs of Our Time] (Prokofieff), 271
Pesnya o rodine [Song of the Fatherland] (Prokofieff), 251
Peter and the Wolf (Prokofieff), 258, 268–69, 270, 271
Peter the Great, 275
Petrenko, Kirill, 11
Petrushka (Stravinsky), 130
Pettersson, Allan, 112
Pfitzner, Hans, 496, 498; *Palestrina*, 494
Philip, Robert, 430
Philosophical Inquiry into the Origin of Our Ideas of the Sublime and Beautiful (Burke), 49
Philosophie der Kunst (Schelling), 197–98
Piano Concerto, First (Bartók), 106, 117, 128
Piano Concerto, First (Prokofieff), 270
Piano Concerto, Second (Saint-Saëns), 166
Piano Concerto, Third (Bartók), 108, 136
Piano Concerto, Third (Chaikovsky), 189
Piano Piece op. 11, no. 1 (Schoenberg), 510
Piano Quintet (Shostakovich), 325, 326, 340, 344, 346–60
Piano Quintet in G Minor, op. 30 (Taneyev), 345, 346
Piano Sonata, Fifth (Prokofieff), 247
Piano Sonata, Second (Ives), 470
Piano Sonata, Seventh (Prokofieff), 270
Piccinni, Niccolò, 375
Pictures at an Exhibition (Musorgsky), 444
Pierrot lunaire (Schoenberg), 510
Plato, 19, 26, 160, 453

Pleyel, Ignaz, 173, 373
Pliny, 41
Plisetskaya, Maya, 287
Ploërmel (Meyerbeer), 168
Plöner Musiktag (Hindemith), 159
Plot against America, The (Roth), 328
Podolski, Michel, 420, 421
Podvizhnoy kontrapunkt strogogo pis'ma [Invertible Counterpoint in the Strict Style] (Taneyev), 186
Poème de l'extase [The Poem of Ecstasy] (Scriabin), 205, 507, 508
Poetics (Aristotle), 265, 266
Poétique musicale [Poetics of Music] (Stravinsky), 27, 42, 193, 321
Polevoy, Boris, 251
Polnoye sobraniye sochineniy (Rimsky-Korsakov), 223
Ponte, Lorenzo da, 479
Po prochtenii psalma [Upon the Reading of the Psalm] (Taneyev), 181
Popular Music Genres (Moy), 404
Porcupine, The (Barnes), 329, 334
Porter, Andrew, 301
Poskryobyshev, Alexander Nikolayevich, 303, 323, 332
Potter, Pamela, xxv
Poulenc, Francis, 248; *Rapsodie nègre*, 398–99
Pound, Ezra, 124, 417, 449, 460, 462
Pozzi, Raffaele, 387, 405
Practical Manual of Harmony (Rimsky-Korsakov), 222
Praz, Mario, 506
Prelude and Fugue for Piano in G-sharp Minor, op. 29 (Taneyev), 186
Presley, Elvis, 203, 309, 317
Pribaoutki (Stravinsky), 103
Prince Igor (Borodin), xvi, 88, 92
Probleme der musikalischen Wertästhetik im 19. Jahrhundert (Eggli), 312
Pro Cantione Antiqua, 416
Professiya kompozitor [My Profession Is Composer] (documentary film, 1992), 285–86, 296
Prokofieff, Sergei, 105, 141, 245, 245–49, 265–75, 302, 327, 340, 354–57, 359; *Alexander Nevsky*, 270, 273; *Cello Sonata*, 270; *Cinderella*, 270; *The Fiery Angel*, 263–64; Fifth Symphony, 270; *Lieutenant Kijé*, 270; *The Love for Three Oranges*, 270, 452; *Na strazhe mira* (Guarding the Peace), 271; *Pesnya o rodine* (Song of the Fatherland), 251; *Peter and the Wolf*, 258, 268–

INDEX   541

69, 270, 271; Piano Concerto no. 1, 245–46, 246, 270; Piano Sonata no. 5, 247; *Rassvetai, moguchiy krai* (Flourish, Mighty Land), 271; *Romeo and Juliet*, 263, 270; Second Violin Sonata, 270; *Semyon Kotko*, 262; Seventh Piano Sonata, 270; *The Story of a Real Man (Povest' o nastoyashchem cheloveke)*, 250–51, 252–54; Symphony-Concerto, 270; *Velikan (The Giant)*, 245; *War and Peace*, 248, 270; *Zdravitsa*, 32, 138–39, 271–72, 274, 275, 321
Prokofiev, Oleg, 274
Prokofieva, Lina Ivanovna, 256, 258–62, 265, 271
Proske, Carl, 179
Proust, Marcel, 51
Pskovityanka [The Maid of Pskov] (Rimsky-Korsakov), 92, 213, 217
Pulcinella (Stravinsky), 398
Pushkin, Alexander, 322, 337
Pyatnitsky Choir, 333
Pythagoras, 19

Queen of Sheba, The. See *Königin von Saba, Die [The Queen of Sheba]* (Goldmark)
"Questions about Music" (Sessions), 27
Quiet Flows the Don (Sholokhov novel; Dzerzhinsky opera), 349, 352

Rabinovich, David Abramovich, 343, 345, 355, 357
Rachmaninoff, Sergei, 64–65, 104, 175, 183, 186, 189, 195, 310, 311, 314, 321–22, 505, 507; *Aleko*, 246; *The Bells* (symphony), 506; First Piano Concerto, 245–46
"Racial Purity in Music" (Bartók), 119–20
Rácz, Aladár, xiii
Radcliffe, Philip, 369
Rae, Caroline, 398, 399
Ragionamenti accademici sopra alcuni luoghi difficili di Dante (Bartoli), 387
Raguenet, Abbé François, 43, 44
Rake's Progress, The (Hogarth), 502
Rake's Progress, The (Stravinsky), 308
Rakhmanova, Marina Pavlovna, xvi
Rákosi, Mátyás, 133, 151
Rameau, Jean-Philippe, 81, 366
Rapsodie nègre (Poulenc), 398–99
Rapsodie norvégienne (Lalo), 191
Rasputin, Grigory, 300
Rassvetai, moguchiy krai [Flourish, Mighty Land] (Prokofieff), 271
Rathbone, Basil, 269
Ravel, Maurice, 101, 103, 143, 401

Ray, Robert B., 396
Rayok [The Peepshow] (Musorgsky), 179
Razumovsky, Count Andrey Kirillovich, 336
Redfern, Sophie, 405
Redlich, Hans, 381
Reese, Gustave, 364
Reger, Max, 165, 176, 180, 189, 505
Reich, Steve, 283
Reicha, Anton, 167
Reinecke, Carl, 59
Republic, The (Plato), 19, 26
Requiem (Mozart), 482
Respighi, Ottorino, 336
Resurrection Symphony (No. 2) (Mahler), 505
Revai, József, 132
"Reveille," 466
Rhapsody for Violin no. 1 (Bartók), 436, 437, 438
Ribbentrop, Joachim von, 353
Ribot, Théodule-Armand, 456
Richards, I(vor) A(rmstrong), 455–59, 462, 488
Richard Wagner in Bayreuth (Nietzsche), 192, 208
Richter, Ernst Friedrich, 226–27
Richter, Pál, x
Richter, Sviatoslav, 186, 245, 311, 313
Riemann, Hugo, 231
Rignano, Eugenio, 457
Riley, Matthew, 228
Rimsky-Korsakov, Nikolai, 101, 175–76, 177–78, 183, 203, 228–30, 235, 438; *Chronicle of My Musical Life*, 212, 213, 214, 217, 218, 222, 225, 238; *The Legend of the Invisible City of Kitezh*, 204; *Mlada*, 235; *Paraphrases on an Unchanging Theme*, 176, 177; *Polnoye sobraniye sochineniy*, 223; *Practical Manual of Harmony*, 222; *Pskovityanka* [The Maid of Pskov], 92, 213, 217; *Sadko*, 187, 191, 212, 235; *Sheherazade*, 417; *Snegurochka*, 242; String Quartet in F Major, op. 12, 213, 214–15, 215–16, 235; Symphony no. 2 (*Antar*), 220–21, 238; Symphony no. 3 in C Major, op. 32, 217–18, 220, 235, 236, 237, 239–41, 242
Ring des Nibelugen, Der (Wagner), 195, 196, 202, 505; *Götterdämmerung* (Twilight of the Gods), 508; *The Rhinegold*, 508; *Die Walküre* (The Valkyrie), 194, 353
Rings, Steven, 486–87, 494
Ritchie, Margaret, 414
Rite of Spring, The [*Le sacre du printemps*] (Stravinsky), 3, 32, 103, 305, 307, 397, 398, 434, 434, 461; *Jeu de rapt* ("Ritual of Abduction"), 435, 439
Ritmicas V and VI (Roldán), 399

Robbins, Jerome, 306
Robinson, Harlow, 268, 274
Rockefeller, John D., 51
Rodzinski, Artur, 7
Roldán, Amadeo, *Ritmicas* V and VI, 399
Romantic Agony, The (Praz), 506
Romeo and Juliet (Prokofieff), 263, 270
Ropartz, Guy, 206
Rorem, Ned, 24, 301
Rose, Bernard, ix
Rose, Stephen, 368
Rosen, Charles, 17–18, 37–39, 51, 62–63, 65, 246, 365–66, 367, 371, 378, 479
Rosenberg, Donald, 396
Rosenfeld, Paul, 397
Rosenkavalier, Der (Strauss), 509
Rosenthal, Bernice Glatzer, 200, 205
Rosow, Lois, 369
Ross, Alex, 405
Ross, King, 65
Rossellini, Isabella, ix
Rossini, Gioachino: *Guillaume Tell* (*William Tell*), 154; *Péchés de vieillesse* ("Sins of Old Age"), 186
Rostropovich, Mstislav, 248, 302
Roth, Philip, 328
Rouget, Gilbert, 20
Rozhdestvensky, Gennady, 284
Rozovsky, Solomon, 439
Rubinstein, Anton, 175, 194, 211, 212, 310–11; *Demon*, 88; *Feramors*, 75, 79; *Maccabees*, 73; *Sulamith*, 73. See also *Thurm zu Babel, Der* [*Tower of Babel*]
Rubinstein, Arthur, 399
Rubinstein, Nikolai, 181, 218
Rudepoema (Villa-Lobos), 399
Rue, Pierre de la, 98
Rules for Playing in a True Taste on the Violin, German Flute, Violoncello, and Harpsichord (Geminiani), 44–45
Rumanian Folk Music [*RFM*] (Bartók), 436–37, 437
Rumph, Stephen, 498–99
Rusalka (Dargomïzhsky), 195
Rushdie, Salman, 8
Ruslan and Lyudmila (Glinka), 77, 78, 88, 89, 107, 238, 241, 242
Russell, Anna, 193
Russkiye nochi [*Russian Nights*] (Odoyevsky), 167, 168, 169, 172
Rustic Wedding Symphony (Goldmark), 69
Ryle, Gilbert, 371

Sabaneyev, Leonid, 505
Sachs, Hans, 267
Sackville-West, Vita, 27
Sadko (Rimsky-Korsakov), 187, 191, 212, 235
Saeverud, Harald, 112
Safonoff, Vasiliy, 311
Saint-Saëns, Camille, 81, 109, 180, 248, 249; *Samson et Dalila*, 80, *81*; Second Piano Concerto, 166
St. John Passion (Bach), 16–18, 177, 184, 321, 481–82
St. Matthew Passion (Bach), 16–17, 180, 183, *185*
St. Petersburg Conservatory, xvii, 175, 212, 222
St. Pierre, Kelly, 386
Sakuntala (Goldmark), 77, 87
Salazar, Adolfo, 364
Saleski, Gdal, 81, 83
Salome (Strauss), 87, 508, 509
Salomon, J. P., 485
Samson et Dalila (Saint-Saëns), 80, *81*
Sand, George, 58
San Francisco Opera, 6, 8
San Francisco Symphony, 6
Sartre, Jean-Paul, 107, 136
Satanic Verses, The (Rushdie), 8
Satie, Erik, *Embryons desséchés*, 452, 453
Saunders, Frances Stonor, 300, 301, 303, 308
Savenko, Svetlana Il'yinichna, xvi
Scacchi, Marco, 376
Scarlatti, Domenico, 389
Schaffer, Peter, 348
Schama, Simon, 379
Schelling, Friedrich Wilhelm Joseph, 197, 205, 490
Scherchen, Hermann, 431
Scherzo à la russe (Stravinsky), 107
Schiller, Friedrich, 41, 42
Schlesinger, Arthur, Jr., 306
Schloezer, Boris, 206, 508
Schmelz, Peter, 282, 286, 287, 390, 391
Schmitz, E(lie) Robert, 499
Schnabel, Artur, 56–57, 59
Schneider, David E., ix, 105–6, 119, 131, 436, 437, 438
Schnittke, Alfred, 276, 277, 279, 280, 296; *Nagasaki*, 286
Schoenberg, Arnold, 24, 62, 102, 103, 108, 111, 114, 116, 120, 132, 139, 145, 150, 165, 176, 243, 303, 308, 319, 336, 339, 431, 505; *Beleitungsmusik zu einer Lichtspielszene*, op. 34, 294; *The Book*

INDEX   543

of the Hanging Gardens, 509–10; "Brahms the Progressive," 193; *Erwartung*, 305; Five Pieces for Orchestra, 397; *Harmonielehre*, 287; *Herzgewächse*, 510; Piano Piece op. 11, no. 1, 510; *Pierrot lunaire*, 510; Variations for Orchestra, op, 31, 174, 320
Schoenberg est mort (Boulez), 510
Schonberg, Harold C., xxvi, 423, 426
Schönzeler, Hans-Hubert, 203
Schopenhauer, Arthur, xxv, xxvi, 26, 108, 141, 490, 494, 496, 504; *Parerga und paralipomena*, 141, 494; *Welt als Wille und Vorstellung, Die* [The World as Will and Representation], 494
Schreker, Franz, 505; *Der ferne Klang*, 509
Schroeder, David, 369
Schubart, Mark, 316
Schubert, Franz, 24, 60, 93, 101, 205, 220; Mass in E-flat Major, 235; Quartet in G Major, 235; String Quintet in C Major, 221; Symphony in C Major, 219
Schubert, Peter, 480
Schumann, Clara, 54, 61–62, 311
Schumann, Robert, 165, 176, 197, 205, 219, 246, 314, 346, 431, 510; Quintet in E-flat Major, 345; "Widmung" (Dedication), op. 24, no. 1, 311, 315, 316
Schwantner, Joseph, 9
Schwarz, Boris, 270
Science and Poetry (Richards), 455, 458
Scriabin, Alexander, 175, 181, 505, 506; *Mysterium*, 206, 208; Nocturne for the Left Hand, op, 9, no. 2, 311; *Poème de l'extase* (The Poem of Ecstasy), 205, 507, 508
Scruton, Roger, 412, 413
Seaman, Gerald, 369
Seasons, The (Haydn), 485
Secular Commedia, The (Allanbrook), 376
Seidl, Anton, 207
Selected Writings of Zoltán Kodály, The, 151
Selitsky, Alexander Yakovlevich, 280, 290
Sellars, Peter, 9, 479
Semyon Kotko (Prokofieff), 262
Serapionsbrüder, Die (Hoffmann), 167–68, 169
Serkin, Rudolf, 310
Serov, Alexander, 79, 225n20; *Judith*, 75, 76–77, 76, 77, 194
Sessions, Roger, 26, 27, 28
Shapin, Steven, 446–47
Shaporin, Yury, 253, 327; *On the Field of Kulikovo*, 326
Shchedrin, Rodion, 286

Sheherazade (Rimsky-Korsakov), 417
Shelley, Percy Bysshe, 489
Sherman, Bernard, 381
Sherry, Vincent, 457, 458
Sholokhov, Mikhail, 349
Shostakovich, Dmitry, xv, xvii, xviii, 104, 116, 137, 138, 139, 161, 288, 294, 327, 328–60; Eighth String Quartet, 330, 331; Eighth Symphony, 333; Fifteenth Symphony, 147; Fifth Symphony, 148, 149, 252, 255, 307, 338, 341, 342, 351, 354; First String Quartet, 342–43; First Symphony, 339; Fourth Symphony, 342, 343; *Lady Macbeth of the Mtsensk District*, 5, 6–7, 8, 11, 14–15, 148, 305, 320, 330, 340, 341, 349, 354, 390; *Leningrad* Symphony (No. 7), 148, 327, 303; *The Nose*, 15, 339, 340; Piano Quintet, 325, 326, 340, 344, 346–60; Second Symphony ("To October"), 321, 338; *Song of the Forests*, 327, 332; Third Symphony, 338
Shostakovich, Irina Antonovna, xviii
Shostakovich: A Life Remembered (Wilson), 330
Shostakovich and Stalin (Volkov), 325, 348
"Shostakovich and Us" (Taruskin), xvii
Shreffler, Anne C., 308
Shulamis (Goldfadn), 444, 445
Sibelius, Jan, 98, 99, 103, 109, 111, 112–17, 397, 522; *En Saga*, 112; *Finlandia*, 114; *Tapiola*, 112; *The Tempest*, 113–14
Siegfried (Wagner), 194
Simonffy, Kálmán, "Árpád apánk," 153–54, 153
Sinyavsky, Andrey (Abram Tertz), 264, 265
Sisman, Elaine, 484
Slatkin, Leonard, 314
Sleeping Beauty (Chaikovsky), 417
Slezak, Leo, 89, 93
Slobin, Mark, 442, 443, 446
Slonimsky, Nicolas, 397
Smart, Mary Ann, 376
Smirnov, Dima, 276–77
Smith, Peter, 368
Smrž, Jiří, 251
Snegurochka (Rimsky-Korsakov), 242
Society for Music Theory, The, 13
Socrates, vii, xxiii
Sofronitsky, Vladimir, 311
Soler, Antonio, 375
Solomon (Handel), 68
Solovyov-Sedoy, Vasiliy, 254, 316
Solzhenitsyn, Alexander, 293
Somfai, László (Laci), viii–x, xii, xiii–xv, xvii, xx, 97, 106

Sonata for Piano, op. 1 (Berg), 509
Sonata for Solo Cello, op. 8 (Kodály), 144
Sonata for Two Pianos (Stravinsky), 107
Sonata for Two Pianos and Percussion (Bartók), 105, 122, 135
Sonata no. 3 for Piano and Cello, op. 69 (Beethoven), 184
Sonate for piano (Stravinsky), 243
Sonetto 123 della Petrarca (Liszt), 311
Song of Hiawatha (Longfellow), 206
Song of Love (film, 1947), 311
Song of the Forests (Shostakovich), 327, 332
Sound Effects (Frith), 403
Souvenir d'un marche boche (Stravinsky), 452
Souvenirs de Munich (Chabrier), 452
Sovetskaya muzïka (journal), xvi, 132, 137, 253, 277, 351, 353
Specht, Richard, 87
Speculations (Hulme), 520
Speer, Albert, 499
Spencer, Peter, 394
Spender, Stephen, 302, 306
Spengler, Oswald, 503
Spink, Ian, 370
Spohr, Louis, 234
Stalin, Joseph, 7, 8, 14, 21, 104, 152, 268, 269, 272, 275, 286, 303, 315, 319, 323–26, 324, 329, 331, 332, 349–50, 358
Stalin's Music Prize (Frolova-Walker), 320, 323, 348
Standard Operas, The (1899), 69
Stasevich, Abram, 273
Stasov, Vladimir Vasilievich, 60, 169, 177–78, 186, 514
Steinberg, Maximilian, 250, 339
Steinberg, Michael, 395
Steiner, George, 24
Steinitz, Paul, 368
Stendahl, 286
Sternfeld, Frederick William, 370
Stevens, Halsey, 122
Stewart-MacDonald, Rohan, 369, 378, 379
Stiedry, Fritz, 319, 320
Stigler, George J., 43
Stockhausen, Karlheinz, 283
Stokowski, Leopold, 269
Storm, The (Ostrovsky), 6–7
Story of a Real Man, The [*Povest' o nastoyashchem cheloveke*] (Prokofieff), 250–51, 252–54
Strauss, Richard, 101, 102, 294, 507; *Also sprach Zarathustra*, 505; *Ariadne auf Naxos*, 87;

Elektra, 508, 509; *Der Rosenkavalier*, 509; *Salome*, 87, 508, 509; *Tod und Verklärung*, 505
Stravinsky, Igor, xii, xiii, xvii, 4, 21–22, 50, 56, 97, 99, 101, 104–8, 120, 122, 132, 134, 139, 145, 150, 235, 269, 286, 296, 298, 302, 303, 354, 358, 443, 460, 502, 519–20; *Abraham and Isaac*, 308; *Canticum sacrum*, 308; Concerto for Piano and Winds, 106; *Concerto per due pianoforti soli*, 243; *Expositions and Developments*, 373; *Firebird*, xvi, 147; *The Flood*, 308; *L'Histoire du soldat*, 468; *Movements* for Piano and Orchestra, 308; *Oedipus Rex*, 305; *Petrushka*, 130; *Poétique musicale* (Poetics of Music), 27, 42, 193, 321; *Pribaoutki*, 103; *Pulcinella*, 398; *The Rake's Progress*, 308; *The Rite of Spring* (*Le sacre du printemps*), 3, 32, 103, 305, 307, 397, 398, 434, 434, 461; *Scherzo à la russe*, 107; Sonata for Two Pianos, 107; *Sonate* for piano, 243; *Souvenir d'un marche boche*, 452; *Svadebka* (*Les Noces*), 103; Symphony in C, 326, 359; Symphony in Three Movements, 107; *Threni*, 308; *Variations*, 146
Structure of Atonal Music, The (Forte), 3
Structures Ia (Boulez), 305
Strunk, Oliver, 26–27
Stuckenschmidt, Hans Heinz, 320
Suite for Orchestra, op. 43 (Chaikovsky), 175
Sulamith (A. Rubinstein), 73
Sullivan, Arthur, xxvii
Sullivan, Jack, 63
Sutcliffe, Tom, 405
Svadebka [*Les Noces*] (Stravinsky), 103
Sylvester I, Pope, 157
Symboli chrestiani (N. Nabokov), 299
Szabo, Ferenc, 132–33, 136–37, 139
Szell, George, 310
Szymanowski, Karol, 505; *King Roger*, 510

Tagore, Rabindranath, 322
Tallián, Tibor, x, 97
Tallis, Thomas, *O nata lux de lumine*, 244
Tamberlick, Enrico, 154
Tan, Shzr Ee, 393, 395, 396, 397, 402–3, 404, 404–5
Taneyev, Sergey Ivanovich, 167, 175–78, 195, 346, 356, 505; *Ioann Damaskin* (John of Damascus), 181, 182–83, 184, 189; *Oresteia*, 180, 204; Piano Quintet in G Minor, op. 30, 345, 346; *Po prochtenii psalma* (Upon the Reading of the Psalm), 181; Prelude and Fugue for Piano in G-sharp Minor, op. 29, 186; String Quartet in G Major, op. 14, 186–87, 187–88, 190

Tanner, Michael, 268
Tannhäuser (Wagner), 74, 168, 195, 207
Tapiola (Sibelius), 112
Tappert, Wilhelm, 397
Tarakanov, Mikhail Yevgen'yevich, 277–79
Tarnopolsky, Vladimir, xix
Tartini, Giuseppe, 380
Tate, Alan, 492
Taylor, Cecil, 522
Taylor, Timothy D., 393–94, 395
Tchaikovsky, Pyotr Ilyich. *See* Chaikovsky, Pyotr Ilyich
Tcharos, Stefanie, 370
Tempest, The (Sibelius), 113–14
Testimony (Volkov), xv, xviii, 8, 303, 325, 330, 347, 348
Thalberg, Sigismund, 59
Thank You, Comrade Stalin! Soviet Public Culture from Revolution to Cold War (Brooks), 324
Themes and Variations [*Temï s variatsiami*] (Karetnikov), 281, 282, 287
Theses on Feuerbach (Marx), 272
Thomson, Virgil, 302, 364, 397
Thousand Clowns, A (film, 1965), 67
Threat to the Cosmic Order (Ostwald and Zegans, eds.), 202–3
Three Compositions for Piano (Babbitt), 134
Three-Cornered Hat, The (Falla), 452
Three Quarter-Tone Pieces (Ives), 469, 469
Threni (Stravinsky), 308
Thurm zu Babel, Der [*Tower of Babel*] (A. Rubinstein), 75, 76–77, 76, 77, 78, 83
Tieck, Ludwig, 180
Tinctoris, Johannes, xxvi, 386
Titan Symphony (No. 1) (Mahler), 505
Todd, R. Larry, 22, 23
Tod und Verklärung (Strauss), 505
Toffler, Alvin, 25n49
Tolstoy, Alexey, 252, 311
Tolstoy, Lev, 19, 21, 22, 161, 181, 193, 328, 329
Tolstoya, Sophia Andreyevna, 181
Tomlinson, Gary, 371, 503
Tomoff, Kiril, 316, 320
Tonality and Atonality in Sixteenth-Century Music (Lowinsky), xxvi
Tonsprachen des Abendlandes, Die (Moser), xxv
Toscanini, Arturo, 118, 152, 161
Tovey, Donald Francis, 13
Toynbee, Arnold, 446
Traviata, La (Verdi), 444, 445

Treatise of Good Taste in the Art of Musick, A (Geminiani), 44–45
Trial Begins, The (Tertz), 264
Tristan und Isolde (Wagner), 30, 32, 74, 194, 195, 199, 201, 205, 208, 452, 505, 507, 508–9
Trois Contes (Flaubert), 409
"Troping Hypothesis, The" (Crocker), xxiii
Trovatore, Il (Verdi), 151–52
Trow, George, 498
Tsenova, Valeria, 277, 279
Tunley, David, 370
Turner, Bruno, 416
Twentieth-Century Music (Morgan), 102
Tsyganov, Dmitry, 344
Tyulin, Yuriy Nikolaevich, 225

Union of Soviet Composers, xvi, 132, 252, 253, 277, 330, 353, 354
Union Pacific (N. Nabokov), 301
Urban VIII, Pope, 41
Ustvolskaya, Galina, 277, 291

Vallotti, Francesco Antonio, 381
Van Cliburn: Concert Pianist (documentary film, 1994), 314
Vanina Vanini (Karetnikov), 286, 287, 294
Van Vechten, Carl, 397
Vaqueras, Raimbaut de, 415
Varèse, Edgar, 399, 400; *Dance for Burgess*, 401; *Ionisation*, 399
Varga, Bálint András, 159, 160, 448
Variations (Stravinsky), 146
Variations for Orchestra, op. 31 (Schoenberg), 174, 320
Variations for Piano, op. 27 (Webern), 285
Variations on a Rococo Theme (Chaikovsky), 63
Vasilyov, Vladimir, 286, 290
Vaughan Williams, Ralph, 98, 109, 154, 435
Velikan [*The Giant*] (Prokofieff), 245
Velimirović, Miloš, 270
Vendler, Helen, 458
Venosta, Marquis de (fictional character), 39, 40, 46, 49, 55
Verdi, Giuseppe, 154; *Aida*, 70, 71, 79, 83; *La Traviata*, 444; *Il Trovatore*, 151–52
Veress, Sándor, 121
Veter' [*The Wind*] (film, 1958), 290, 291
Vienna Opera, 73, 87
Vietinghoff-Scheel, Baron Boris, 195
Vikár, Béla, 119

Vikárius, László, x, 122
Villa-Lobos, Heitor, 400; *Amazonas*, 399; *Bachianas Brasileiras*, 401; *Chôros*, nos. 8–14, 399; *Noneto*, 399; *Rudepoema*, 399
Violin Concerto (Khachaturyan), 349
Violin Concerto, Second (Bartók), 136
Violin Sonata, Second (Prokofieff), 270
Virtuosi Abroad: Soviet Music and Imperial Competition during the Cold War, 1945–1958 (Tomoff), 316
Visszatekintés (Bónis, ed.), 151
Vivaldi, Antonio, 366
Vlasova, Yekaterina, 320
Volkov, Solomon, xv, xviii, 8, 11, 14, 15, 303, 325, 326, 330, 331, 348, 349–50
Voltaire, 46, 47, 49, 81
Vozvrashcheniye Pushkina [Pushkin's Return] (N. Nabokov), 299
Vyshinsky, Andrey, 331

Wackenroder, Wilhelm Heinrich, 180
Wagner, Richard, 15, 19, 55, 71, 93, 95–96, 129, 165, 192–210, 249, 267, 397, 431, 451, 453–54, 456, 470, 471; *Götterdämmerung* [Twilight of the Gods], 508; *Die Kunst und die Revolution*, 196; *Das Kunstwerk der Zukunft*, 196, 197; *Lohengrin*, 74, 196, 200; *Die Meistersinger*, 194, 195; *Oper und Drama*, 197; *Parsifal*, 198, 505; *Der Ring des Nibelungen*, 194, 195, 196, 202, 353, 505; *Siegfried*, 194; *Tannhäuser*, 74, 168, 195, 207; *Tristan und Isolde*, 30, 32, 74, 194, 195, 199, 201, 205, 208, 452, 505, 507, 508–9
Wagner and Russia (Bartlett), 192
Wagner in Russia, Poland, and the Czech Lands (Muir and Belina-Johnson, eds.), 192
Wagner lexicon, A (Tappert), 397
Wakin, Daniel, 432
Walker, Alan, 38
Walküre, Die. See *Ring des Nibelungen, Der* (Wagner)
Walter, Bruno, 339, 431
Waltham-Smith, Naomi, 497
Walton, William, 112, 113, 326
Wangermée, Roger, 145
War and Peace (Prokofieff), 248, 270
War and Peace (Tolstoy), 328, 329
Waters, John, 37
Watkins, Glenn, 466
Wave in the Mind, The (Le Guin), 28
Weber, Carl Maria von, 58, 61
Weber, Max, 486

Webern, Anton, 165, 176, 194, 276, 294, 336, 505; String Quartet, op. 28, 174; Variations for Piano, op. 27, 285
"Web of Culture, The" (Tomlinson), 371
Webster, James, 367
Weir, David, 503, 506
Weiss, Piero, 21
Wellens, Ian, 300
Wellesz, Egon, 370
Well-Wrought Urn, The (Brooks), 489
Welt als Wille und Vorstellung, Die [The World as Will and Representation] (Schopenhauer), 494
Werckmeister, Andreas, 381
Werf, Hendrik van der, 417
Werner, Eric, 443, 444
West, Martin Litchfield, 426, 427
Westrup, Sir Jack Allan, 369
Wharton, Edith, 452
What Is Art? (Tolstoy), 193
Whistler, James, 503
Whittall, Arnold, 32
Who Paid the Piper? The CIA and the Cultural Cold War (Saunders), 300
"Why Is Wagner Worth Saving?" (Žižek), 209–10
"Widmung" (Dedication), op. 24, no. 1 (Schumann), 311, 315, 316
Wielhorsky, Count Matvey, 168–69, 195
Wielhorsky, Count Mikhail, 168–69
Wieseltier, Leon, 1, 517
Wilde, Oscar, 503
Will, George, 317
Will, Richard, 370, 373
Wilson, Elizabeth, 330, 331
Wilson, Woodrow, 450, 470
Winckelmann, Johann Joachim, 388
Winter, Peter, 377
Winter, Robert, 413, 414, 430
Wir bauen eine Stadt (Hindemith), 159
Wittgenstein, Ludwig, 492
Wohltemperirte Clavier, Das (*The Well-Tempered Clavier*) (Bach), 172, 175, 185
Wolf, Hugo, 505; *Italienisches Liederbuch*, 510
Wolff, Hellmuth Christian, 368, 369
Wood, Hugh, 115
Woolf, Virginia, 27, 449
Worker and Collective Farm Woman [*Rabochiy i kolkhoznitsa*] (Mukhina), 325–26, 342, 347
World War I and the Cultures of Modernity (anthology, 2000), 461

Yeats, William Butler, 449
Yeltsin, Boris, 287

Yemel'yan Pugachov (Koval'), 254
Young, Percy, 147, 381
Young, Stark, 491
Yurchak, Alexei, 519

Zakharov, Vladimir, 333
Zangwill, Nick, 31
Zaremba, Nikolai, 179
Zaslavsky, David Iosifovich, 331–32, 332, 390–91; "Muddle Instead of Music," 330, 331–32, 338, 341, 353, 390
Zaslaw, Neal, 365
Zauberflöte, Die [*The Magic Flute*] (Mozart), 90
Zavod [*The Iron Foundry*] (Mosolov), 321, 327
Zdravitsa (Prokofieff), 32, 138–39, 271–72, 274, 275, 321

Zeitlin (Tseytlin), Leo/Lev/Leyb, 438–39, 442, 443, 446; *Eli Zion* (1914), 439, *440, 441,* 445
Zemlinsky, Alexander von, 505
Zenck, Claudia Maurer, 369, 377
Zhdanov, Andrey, 21, 22, 151, 161, 303, 330, 332, 341
Zhitomirsky, Alexander Matveyevich, 439
Zhitomirsky, Daniel Vladimirovich, 351–52, 353, 354, 355
Zhivkov, Todor, 329
Žiūraitis, Algis, 288
Žižek, Slavoj, 209–10, 506
Zohn, Steven, 370
Zöllner, Eva, 370
"Zum Beginn" [At the start] (Höcker), 495
Zwillich, Ellen Taaffe, 9

Founded in 1893,
UNIVERSITY OF CALIFORNIA PRESS
publishes bold, progressive books and journals
on topics in the arts, humanities, social sciences,
and natural sciences—with a focus on social
justice issues—that inspire thought and action
among readers worldwide.

The UC PRESS FOUNDATION
raises funds to uphold the press's vital role
as an independent, nonprofit publisher, and
receives philanthropic support from a wide
range of individuals and institutions—and from
committed readers like you. To learn more, visit
ucpress.edu/supportus.

www.ingramcontent.com/pod-product-compliance
Lightning Source LLC
Chambersburg PA
CBHW021413300426
44114CB00010B/477